From Humanism to Hobbes

Studies in Rhetoric and Politics

C000145745

The aim of this collection is to illustrate the pervasive influence of humanist rhetoric on early-modern literature and philosophy. The first half of the book focuses on the classical rules of judicial rhetoric. One chapter considers the place of these rules in Shakespeare's *The Merchant of Venice*, while two others concentrate on the technique of rhetorical redescription, pointing to its use in Machiavelli's *The Prince* as well as in several of Shakespeare's plays, notably *Coriolanus*. The second half of the book examines the humanist background to the philosophy of Thomas Hobbes. A major new essay discusses his typically humanist preoccupation with the visual presentation of his political ideas, while other chapters explore the rhetorical sources of his theory of persons and personation, thereby offering new insights into his views about citizenship, political representation, rights and obligations and the concept of the state.

Quentin Skinner is Professor of the Humanities at Queen Mary University of London. He is a Fellow of the British Academy and the Academia Europaea, and a foreign member of the American Academy, the Academia Nazionale dei Lincei and many other learned societies. He has been awarded honorary degrees by numerous major universities, including Chicago, Harvard and Oxford. His scholarship, which is available in more than two dozen languages, has won him many awards, including the Wolfson Prize for History and a Balzan Prize. His two-volume study, *The Foundations of Modern Political Thought* (1978), was listed by *The Times Literary Supplement* in 1996 as one of the hundred most influential books since World War II. His other books include *Reason and Rhetoric in the Philosophy of Hobbes* (1996), *Liberty Before Liberalism* (1998), *Machiavelli* (2000), *Hobbes and Republican Liberty* (2008), *Forensic Shakespeare* (2014) and a three-volume collection of essays, *Visions of Politics* (2002).

From Humanism to Hobbes

Studies in Rhetoric and Politics

Quentin Skinner

Queen Mary University of London

CAMBRIDGE
UNIVERSITY PRESS

CAMBRIDGE
UNIVERSITY PRESS

University Printing House, Cambridge CB2 8BS, United Kingdom

One Liberty Plaza, 20th Floor, New York, NY 10006, USA

477 Williamstown Road, Port Melbourne, VIC 3207, Australia

314–321, 3rd Floor, Plot 3, Splendor Forum, Jasola District Centre, New Delhi – 110025, India

79 Anson Road, #06–04/06, Singapore 079906

Cambridge University Press is part of the University of Cambridge.

It furthers the University's mission by disseminating knowledge in the pursuit of education, learning, and research at the highest international levels of excellence.

www.cambridge.org
Information on this title: www.cambridge.org/9781107128859
DOI: 10.1017/9781316415559

First published 2018
Reprinted 2019

Printed in the United Kingdom by TJ International Ltd. Padstow Cornwall

A catalogue record for this publication is available from the British Library.

ISBN 978-1-107-12885-9 Hardback
ISBN 978-1-107-56936-2 Paperback

Contents

Illustrations

Acknowledgements

My first thanks must go to Richard Fisher. It was he who, as Managing Director of the Cambridge University Press, encouraged me to think of putting together the essays I have produced since the appearance of my previous collection, *Visions of Politics*, in 2002. Two volumes were originally envisaged, but on rereading my work I came to see that none of it warranted republication in its original form, and that much of it did not warrant republication at all. I eventually decided, with the help of the Press's referees, to concentrate on reshaping one group of interconnected studies, and the present volume is the result. Some new chapters have been added, while my earlier essays have been revised to remove overlaps and repetitions, to make clear the links between them, and to bring them up to date with the latest scholarship. They have also been enlarged, in some instances extensively, and in these cases I have retitled them. They were all read in their original form by a number of experts, whose assistance is gratefully acknowledged in notes at the beginning of each chapter. The same notes extend my thanks to the editors and publishers who have allowed me to reuse this earlier work. I need to add a special word of appreciation to Rachel Platt, who negotiated permission for me to include three pieces originally published by Oxford University Press.

I owe an immense debt to Queen Mary University of London, where I have been teaching since 2008. My colleagues in the School of History remain warmly welcoming, and I feel especially grateful to Miri Rubin, Colin Jones and Julian Jackson for doing so much, as successive Chairs of the School, to make it a civilised and distinguished place in which to work. To the School's Director of Administration, Emma Yates, I am obliged for many kindnesses, and I particularly want to thank her for securing a grant from the University to pay for the illustrations in this book. I have learned a great deal from my colleagues in intellectual history, especially Warren Boutcher, David Colclough, Mira Siegelberg, Gareth Stedman Jones, Georgios Varouxakis and above all Richard Bourke. I also want to acknowledge how much I owe to the outstanding group of PhD students I have supervised at Queen Mary on topics closely related to the themes of this book: Alexandra Chadwick, Signy Gutnick-Allen, Elliott Karstadt, Vanessa Lim, Joanne Paul, Lorenzo Sabbadini and Clare Whitehead.

Many friends have discussed my research with me throughout the years when I have been writing the essays in this book. I name them with the deepest gratitude: David Armitage, Annabel Brett, Hannah Dawson, John Dunn, Marco Geuna, Raymond Geuss, Paul Ginsborg, Angus Gowland, Kinch Hoekstra, Fred Inglis, Melissa Lane, Jonathan Lear, Noel Malcolm, Eric Nelson, Markku Peltonen, Philip Pettit, John Pocock, Pete Stacey, Tim Stanton, Keith Thomas, John Thompson, Richard Tuck and last but by no means least James Tully. I am also most grateful for the advice of the Cambridge University Press's two highly perceptive referees. To Noel Malcolm I owe special thanks – as does every student of Hobbes – for the pleasure of being able to work with his definitive edition of Hobbes's *Leviathan*, one of the great editorial achievements of our time.

My research has mainly been conducted in the British Library and the Library of the Warburg Institute, University of London, and I am extremely grateful for the courtesy and efficiency of their staff. For creating the images I have used as illustrations, and for granting me permission to reproduce them, my thanks are due to the British Library, the Cambridge University Library, the Cambridge University Press, the Houghton Library of Harvard University and the Huntington Library. I am much indebted to all these institutions for their helpfulness as well as their technical expertise.

I reserve my most heartfelt thanks for Susan James. She has read all the chapters that follow, often in several different versions, continually bringing to bear her exceptional knowledge and understanding of early-modern philosophy. As a result she has improved my book beyond recognition, in addition to showing a seemingly inexhaustible patience and enthusiasm for my project. The value of her support, and of our children Olivia and Marcus, is beyond words.

I cannot speak with sufficient admiration of my friends at the Cambridge University Press. This year marks the fortieth anniversary of the publication of my first book with the Press, and throughout these years I have been privileged to work with a succession of outstanding editors: first Jeremy Mynott, then Richard Fisher, now Elizabeth Friend-Smith. Jeremy Mynott has once again given me meticulous and invaluable advice. Richard Fisher, after setting my project in motion, has generously kept in touch about its progress. Elizabeth Friend-Smith is part of the same great tradition, and I have benefited at every stage from her complete professionalism as well as her warm encouragement.

As this book goes to press I am pleased to be able to add some words of appreciation to the production team. To Sarah Lambert I am much indebted for reformatting two of my chapters, and to Auriol Griffith-Jones for last-minute help with formatting my index. To Jeremy Langworthy I am deeply grateful for his wonderfully attentive copy-editing, as well as for an enjoyable correspondence. To Emma Collison I owe particular thanks for technical assistance with the illustrations, and for overseeing the process of production not merely with unfailing efficiency but with great patience and thoughtfulness.

I corrected the proofs of this book while serving as Visiting Professor at the University of Chicago. I should like to add my warmest thanks to my hosts in Chicago, Jonathan Lear and Robert Pippin, and special thanks to Richard Strier, and to the staff of the University Library, for help with checking references.

Conventions

Abbreviations. The following abbreviations are used in the footnotes:

BL: British Library
BN: Bibliothèque Nationale
DBI: Dizionario Biografico degli Italiani
DNB: Dictionary of National Biography
ODNB: Oxford Dictionary of National Biography
OED: Oxford English Dictionary
OLD: Oxford Latin Dictionary
TLN: Through line number

Bibliographies. These are simply checklists of the primary and secondary sources quoted in the text. They make no pretence of being systematic guides to the critical literature on the themes I discuss. Readers in need of such a guide in the case of Shakespeare should consult the *World Shakespeare Bibliography*, and in the case of Hobbes should consult the 'Bulletin Hobbes' issued annually online by the Hobbes International Association. My bibliography of printed primary sources lists anonymous works by title. Where a work was published anonymously but its author's name is known I place the name in square brackets.

Classical names and titles. I refer to ancient writers in their most familiar single-name style, both in the text and bibliographies. I transliterate Greek titles, but all others are given in their original form.

Dates. Generally I follow my sources, except that I date by the common era, and treat the year as beginning on 1 January rather than 25 March.

Gender. I try to use gender neutral language so far as possible. But sometimes it is clear that, when the writers I discuss say 'he' they emphatically do not mean 'he or she' and in those cases I have felt obliged to follow their usage to avoid altering their sense.

References. I use the author-date system when quoting from primary as well as secondary sources, but I make one modification to it. When quoting from primary sources unattributable to any one author (for example, collections of documents, Parliamentary debates, etc.) I refer to them by the names of their editors, but I list them in the bibliography of printed primary sources. When quoting from Shakespeare's plays I give the TLN and page numbers from Shakespeare 1986, but I add Act-scene-line references from the relevant New Cambridge edition in each case. All references to journals in the bibliography of secondary sources are given in Arabic numerals. But when I refer in the footnotes to chapters and sections of books I sometimes use Roman and sometimes Arabic numbering, depending on the preference shown by the author or editor of the work concerned. When referring to the Bible I simply cite the relevant Book, chapter and verse; when quoting from the Bible I use the Authorised (King James) version of 1611.

Transcriptions. My general rule is to preserve original spelling, capitalisation and punctuation. But I expand contractions, remove diphthongs, ligatures and diacritical marks, correct some obvious typographical errors and change 'u' to 'v' and 'i' to 'j' in accordance with modern orthography. When quoting from Shakespeare I follow Shakespeare 1986 (the original spelling version) although with the modifications just mentioned. My use of Shakespeare 1986 extends to the spelling of names (so that I speak, for example, of Shylocke and Anthonio). When quoting from Latin texts I use 'v' as well as 'u', change 'j' to 'i', expand contractions and omit diacritical marks. I thin out the extensive italicisation found in some early-modern pamphlets, and I allow myself to change lower-case initial letters to upper, and vice versa, when fitting quotations around my own prose.

Translations. When quoting from classical sources, and from early-modern sources in languages other than English, all translations are my own unless specifically noted. I make extensive use of the editions published in the Loeb Classical Library, which contain facing-page versions in English, but here too I have preferred to translate for myself. My main reason is that some Loeb translations are very free, and tend to obscure some of the technical terminology – especially rhetorical terminology – that I need to highlight. I must emphasise, however, that I am grateful for the availability of the Loeb editions, and have generally been guided by them, often to the extent of adopting turns of phrase. I am no less grateful for the *Oxford Latin Dictionary*, to which I have invariably deferred in giving definitions of terms.

1   Introduction

Thomas Hobbes warns us in *The Elements of Law* that, although 'words be the signs we have of one another's opinions and intentions', these signs are never easy to read. Because of 'the diversity of contexture' in which our words occur, and because of the company they keep, it is difficult to rescue them from equivocation and ambiguity. Ruminating on the implications of this difficulty, Hobbes concludes that 'it must be extreme hard to find out the opinions and meanings of those men that are gone from us long ago, and have left us no other signification thereof but their books'. The problem we face is that their writings 'cannot possibly be understood without history enough to discover those aforementioned circumstances, and also without great prudence to observe them.'[1]

My aim in the chapters that follow is to take Hobbes's warning to heart and try to follow his advice. My aspiration – to express it in Hobbes's words – is to supply enough history to understand the meanings and intentions of the writers I discuss by recovering the circumstances in which they wrote. As a first step in this direction, I need to clarify my use of the word 'humanism' in the title and body of this book. Some commentators have objected that the term lacks any precise meaning, and in particular that its use in connection with Hobbes's civil science 'confuses rather than illuminates' Hobbes's thought.[2] But I have done my best to employ the term with a consistent meaning that was at the same time well-known to Hobbes and his contemporaries. When I speak of 'humanism' and 'the humanities', I am simply referring to a specific academic curriculum widely followed in the grammar schools and universities of early-modern England.

When early-modern pedagogues spoke of what Erasmus in his *Apophthegmes* calls 'the liberall studies of humanitiee',[3] and what James Cleland in his treatise on education describes as 'Humanities',[4] they were

---

[1] Hobbes 1969, 13. 8, p. 68.   [2] Evrigenis 2014, p. 25.   [3] Erasmus 1542, fo. 63r.
[4] See Cleland 1607, p. 79 on the teaching of 'Grammar, and Humanities'.

recommending a course of instruction comprising five elements: grammar, rhetoric, poetry, history and moral philosophy.[5] The emphasis in the grammar schools was overwhelmingly on the first two components in this syllabus. William Kempe in his *Education of Children* of 1588 proposes that at least five years of schooling should be devoted to grammar, that is, the learning of the Latin language.[6] Progressing to the sixth form, pupils should then be introduced to logic and rhetoric, but with a continuing focus on the use of Latin to write 'themes' in correct rhetorical style.[7] The principles of rhetoric were generally inculcated by studying one of the classical handbooks. Quintilian was sometimes rather ambitiously recommended, but the most popular manuals were the pseudo-Ciceronian *Rhetorica ad Herennium* and several of Cicero's works. When Juan Luis Vives lays out his ideal curriculum in his *De tradendis disciplinis* of 1531 he refers to the *Ad Herennium* as one of the most useful introductions,[8] and this judgment was strongly endorsed by Johannes Sturm in his *De literarum ludis* of 1538. Sturm suggests that a child's education should begin at the age of five or six and thereafter continue for nine years.[9] The study of rhetoric should begin in the fifth year, and the most suitable textbook to use is again said to be the *Ad Herennium*.[10]

This was the syllabus that William Shakespeare would have followed as a pupil at the King's New School at Stratford-upon-Avon in the 1570s, and one of my aims in the first part of this book is to uncover the traces left by Shakespeare's rhetorical education on the construction of several of his plays.[11] Although the Elizabethan statutes of the King's New School have not survived, a number of records from comparable institutions suggest that the recommendations of the humanist pedagogues were widely taken up, and that Shakespeare would have been well-drilled in Roman rhetorical thought.[12] The statutes of 1550 for the Grammar School at Bury St Edmunds state that, in the most senior form, 'the master should read Quintilian's *Institutio oratoria*, or else the precepts of Rhetoric contained in the *Ad Herennium*.'[13] The ordinances of 1556 for Norwich Grammar School likewise specify that Quintilian should be read

---

[5] Kristeller 1961, pp. 92–119; Skinner 1996, pp. 19–40. The information in this and the next paragraph is drawn from Skinner 2014, pp. 27–9.

[6] On Kempe see Baldwin 1944, vol. 1, pp. 437–49; Howell 1956, pp. 258–61.

[7] Kempe 1588, sig. G, 2v to sig. H, 1r. For a full analysis of these stages see Green 2009, pp. 129–90. On grammar see Percival 1983 and Crane 1993, pp. 79–86; on rhetoric see Curtis 2002.

[8] Vives 1913, p. 183.   [9] Sturm 1538, fo. 14r.   [10] Sturm 1538, fos. 19v, 20r, 23v.

[11] On Shakespeare and rhetorical 'themes' see Skinner 2009c.

[12] On the probable curriculum see Whitaker 1953, pp. 14–44. On grammar school curricula in this period see Cressy 1975, pp. 70–94.

[13] BL Lansdowne MS 119, fo. 14r, item 25: 'Institutiones Oratorias Quintilliani, aut praeceptiones Rhetoricae eas quae sunt apud Herennium a ludimagistro audiunto'.

'in the highest fourme',[14] while the 1574 statutes of Leicester Grammar School call for the *Ad Herennium* to be read at least twice a week.[15]

Those students who proceeded from grammar school to university were required to immerse themselves in the full five-part syllabus of the *studia humanitatis*. Chapter 6 outlines the resulting course of reading that undergraduates were expected to follow at the University of Cambridge in the early decades of the seventeenth century. One highly gifted student who received this form of education was Thomas Hobbes. He studied not at Cambridge but at Oxford, where he was an undergraduate at Magdalen Hall between 1604 and 1608. But it is evident from the University statutes that the syllabus there was very similar to the one at Cambridge.[16] Hobbes complains in his verse autobiography, composed in 1672, that he was made to waste his time at Oxford on scholastic absurdities.[17] But this criticism appears to stem more from his later political animus against the Universities than from an accurate recollection of what he was taught.[18] As one expert has put it, the curriculum in force at Oxford in Hobbes's time was 'quintessentially humanistic in nature'.[19] Hobbes would have been required to devote four terms to ancient rhetoric, with Cicero's *Orations* and Aristotle's *Art of Rhetoric* among the set texts.[20] He would then have spent at least two terms on Latin poetry, specialising in Horace and Virgil, and would also have been expected to attend university lectures on moral philosophy and Roman rhetorical thought. The set texts for the former course would have included Plato's *Republic* and Aristotle's *Ethics*, while the latter course centred on Quintilian's *Institutio oratoria*.[21]

One of my aims in the second half of this book is to reveal the extent to which this educational background left its mark on Hobbes's civil science. A number of commentators have already investigated Hobbes's debt to some of the leading thinkers and scholarly movements of the Renaissance.[22] My objective is to supplement this strand in the recent historiography by showing that the cultural shift 'from humanism to Hobbes' was by no means so long a march as has sometimes been supposed.

The principal aspiration of the Renaissance educationalists who revived the *studia humanitatis* was to inculcate an ideal of persuasive

---

[14] Saunders 1932, pp. 136, 147.   [15] Cross 1953, p. 16.
[16] On the 'essential harmony' between the curricula at Oxford and at Cambridge see Feingold 1997, p. 212.
[17] Hobbes 1839a, pp. lxxxvi–lxxxvii.
[18] For these criticisms see Hobbes 2012, vol. 2, ch. 30, pp. 532–4.
[19] Feingold 1997, p. 213.   [20] Gibson (ed.) 1931, p. 378.
[21] Gibson (ed.) 1931, pp. 344, 390.
[22] See, for example, Schuhmann, 1983, 1988, 1990; Kahn 1985; Skinner 1996; Malcolm 2007; Borrelli 2009; Paganini 2010a, 2010b and 2016; Santi 2012; Iori 2015.

writing and speech.[23] This in turn explains why they assigned the study of rhetoric a pivotal place. The classical rhetoricians were chiefly valued for their advice about how to present an argument in a 'winning' style. The same aspiration explains why the classical poets and even the historians were accorded so much prominence. One of the grounds for studying them, it was widely agreed, is that they offer the most inspiring models for writing and speaking with compelling rhetorical effect. As George Puttenham explains in his *Arte of English Poesie* of 1589, poetry in particular is so 'eloquent and rethoricall' that it 'invegleth the judgement of man', thereby helping to ensure that 'the heart by impression of the eare shalbe most affectionatly bent and directed.'[24]

The basic reason for insisting on the value of this kind of education was an eminently practical one. We shall see in chapter 6 that, among students graduating from Oxford and Cambridge in Hobbes's youth, some would have been preparing for a career in law, others would have been aiming to enter public life, while the great majority would have been seeking preferment in the Church. As John Milton observes in his tract *On Education* of 1644 – not without some contempt – the Universities consequently served as training grounds for divinity, law and state affairs.[25] These were all professions in which an ability to speak effectively in public was arguably the most relevant skill of all.[26] The rhetoricians of the English Renaissance, especially those writing after the Reformation had taken root, particularly underline the need for preachers to master the rules of eloquence. As Thomas Wilson warns in his *Arte of Rhetorique* of 1553, any clergyman who lacks the requisite oratorical skills is 'like some tymes to preache to the bare walles'.[27] By contrast, anyone who knows how to speak 'winningly' is 'not onelye to be taken for a singuler manne, but rather to be counted for halfe a God'.[28]

The rhetoricians are chiefly interested in the rules of forensic speech, and here they focus on two essential points in explaining how to present an oration in a winning style. You need to know how many sections your speech ought ideally to contain; and you also need to reflect, before you begin to speak, on the moral character of your cause and the nature of the legal 'issues' to which it gives rise. I consider these topics at the start of chapter 4, after which I focus on the trial of Shylocke in *The Merchant of*

---

[23] Connolly 2007; Cox 2010, pp. 173–8.   [24] [Puttenham] 1589, p. 5.
[25] [Milton] 1644, p. 3. On the politics of rhetorical education see Connolly 2009.
[26] On rhetoric and citizenship see Peltonen 2007 and Peltonen 2013, pp. 13–97.
[27] Wilson 1553, sig. A, 2v. On Wilson see Mack 2002, pp. 76–8, 83–4, 96–9; Shrank 2004, pp. 182–219.
[28] Wilson 1553, sig. A, 3r.

Venice, revealing the extent to which the classical rules of judicial rhetoric provide the organising structure of the scene.

I am also much concerned with a further general rule laid down by the classical rhetoricians about how to present a case with the fullest persuasive force. Besides knowing how to organise your speech, you must learn how to arouse the emotions of your audience. To understand the importance of this commitment, we need to take note of a basic distinction marked by the rhetoricians between those disciplines in which proof is possible and those in which we can never hope to do more than induce people to accept our beliefs.[29] Cicero and Quintilian agree that, while it may be possible to reason conclusively in subjects like grammar and mathematics, the sorts of issues typically debated in the law-courts and public assemblies are such that, in Quintilian's words, 'two wise men may with just cause take up one or the other side, since it is possible in such cases for reason to lead even the wise to dispute among themselves.'[30] These are instances, in other words, in which 'the weapons of powerful speech can always be wielded *in utramque partem*, on either side of the case.'[31]

If there are always two sides to the question in legal and political disputes, what you need to learn is how to inveigle your auditors (in Puttenham's phrase) to come round to your side. The rhetoricians agree that you can never perform this feat if you are lacking in wisdom and the associated capacity for rational argument. Without these intellectual talents, Cicero cautions, your discourse will be garrulous and inane.[32] But you can never rely on reason alone to carry you to victory in the war of words, simply because it will always be possible to adduce good reasons *in utramque partem*. This is the moment at which the rhetoricians conclude that, if you wish to speak winningly, you will need to learn how to arouse the emotions of your auditors in such a way as to impel them towards your side. As Antonius puts it with characteristic frankness in *De oratore*, 'you must try to move them so that they become ruled not by deliberation and judgment but rather by sheer impetus and perturbation of mind.'[33]

One of the most potent methods of moving and perturbing an audience, the rhetoricians agree, is to speak with what Quintilian describes as

---

[29] See, for example, Cicero 1942, I. X. 44, vol. 1, pp. 32–4.
[30] Quintilian 2001, 2. 17. 32, vol. 1, p. 390: 'duos sapientes aliquando iustae causae in diversum trahant, quando etiam pugnaturos eos inter se, si ratio ita duxerit, credunt'.
[31] Quintilian 2001, 2. 16. 10, vol. 1, p. 374: 'in utramque partem valet arma facundiae.'
[32] Cicero 1942, I. V. 17, vol. 1, pp. 12–14 and I. VI. 20, vol. 1, p. 16.
[33] Cicero 1942, II. XLII. 178, vol. 1, p. 324: 'ipse sic moveatur, ut impetu quodam animi et perturbatione, magis quam iudicio aut consilio regatur.' For a fuller discussion see Skinner 1996, pp. 120–7.

enargeia, exceptional vividness.[34] You must find the means, as he likes
to put it, to convert your auditors into spectators, presenting them with
an *imago* or picture 'that will lead them to feel they were present at the
scene.'[35] The effect of such verbal painting is that 'our passions are
aroused just as much as if we were actually witnessing the events
themselves'.[36] You must therefore learn to appeal, in Quintilian's phrase,
'to the eyes of the mind',[37] a technique that always 'strikes the emotions'
with particular force.[38]

If we ask how the art of words can be deployed to produce such
mesmeric effects, Quintilian answers that the painting of verbal images
is one of the most characteristic and valuable functions of the figures and
tropes of speech. A number of the *figurae* have the distinctive power 'to
give such a form to things by means of the words employed as to leave the
impression that they have been seen rather than heard'.[39] But above all
you must cultivate the *tropi*, and especially the master tropes of simile and
metaphor, 'by means of which the feelings are especially aroused'.[40]

As we shall see in chapter 10, a number of early-modern writers on
rhetoric and the visual arts went on to develop a further argument about
the capacity of images to arouse. If it is true, they suggest, that the use of
verbal imagery enables us to speak more memorably and persuasively,
this implies that a yet more potent means of winning an audience round to
our point of view will be to supply them with *actual* images to accompany
the statement of our case. These writers accordingly begin to treat the
insertion of such illustrations as akin to the use of similes and metaphors,
and hence as a means of communicating with irresistible *enargeia*.[41]

A classic formulation of this argument can be found in Franciscus
Junius's treatise on aesthetics, *The Painting of the Ancients*, first published
in English in 1638. Junius mounts a comparison between 'Eloquent
Writers and Painters', noting that 'the one studieth to set forth in lively
colours, what the other goeth about to adorn with eloquence'.[42] He
acknowledges that both 'have a hidden force to move and compell our

---

[34] Quintilian 2001, 4. 2. 64, vol. 2, p. 250; 6. 2. 32, vol. 3, p. 60; 8. 3. 61–2, vol. 3,
pp. 374–6. Cf. Cicero 1942, III. LIII. 202, vol. 2, p. 160. For a discussion see Plett 2012.
[35] Quintilian 2001, 4. 2. 123, vol. 2, p. 278: 'imago, quae velut in rem praesentem
perducere audientes videtur'. For a discussion see Skinner 1996, pp. 182–8.
[36] Quintilian 2001, 6. 2. 32, vol. 3, p. 60: 'adfectus non aliter quam si rebus ipsis intersimus
sequentur.'
[37] See Quintilian 2001, 8. 3. 62, vol. 3, p. 376 on the appeal 'oculis mentis'.
[38] Quintilian 2001, 8. 3. 67, vol. 3, p. 378: 'in adfectus … penetrat'.
[39] Quintilian 2001, 9. 2. 40, vol. 4, p. 56: 'quaedam forma rerum ita expressa verbis ut cerni
potius videatur quam audiri.'
[40] Quintilian 2001, 8. 6. 19, vol. 3, p. 434: 'Nam tralatio [*sic*] permovendis animis
plerumque'.
[41] See Bath 1994, pp. 48–56.   [42] Junius 1638, p. 55.

minds to severall Passions', offering as an example that 'he is the best Historian that can adorne his Narration with such forcible figures and lively colours of Rhetorike, as to make it like unto a Picture.'[43] But actual pictures 'doe it more effectually; seeing things that sinke into our hearts by the means of our eares, ... doe more faintly stirre our minde, then such things as are drunke in by the eyes.'[44] Even Quintilian is willing to acknowledge that a painting can 'so insinuate it selfe into our most inward affections, that it seemeth now and then to be of greater force then Eloquence it selfe.'[45]

Hobbes was committed throughout his intellectual career to a similar view about the place of images in our cognitive life, and in chapter 10 I examine the most obvious reflection of this commitment. This I take to lie in his enduring concern with the visual representation of his political ideas, and his consequent inclusion of emblematic frontispieces in his works of civil science as well as his translations of classical texts. My principal aim in chapter 10 is to provide an interpretation of the various frontispieces Hobbes himself commissioned. But I attempt at the same time to outline the more general development of the English humanist frontispiece, seeking to pinpoint Hobbes's place within the longer history of this characteristically Renaissance genre.

A further suggestion about the arousing of the passions that the classical rhetoricians consider at remarkable length relates to the phenomenon of laughter. They all agree that laughter is the sign of an overpowering emotion, and that the emotion usually being expressed is one of contempt. As Quintilian points out, to laugh (*ridere*) is virtually the same as to deride (*deridere*).[46] But this is to say that, if you succeed in making your auditors laugh, this will be because you have succeeded in making them view your adversaries with scorn. A talent for exciting laughter is consequently taken to be one of the most effective means of winning an audience round to your point of view.

In chapter 8 I seek to uncover the moral and social significance of these assumptions about the psychology of laughter. I begin by focusing on some widespread humanist beliefs about the disciplining impact of ridicule, and the associated project of encouraging derisive laughter as a means of enforcing the rules of civility. I end by considering Hobbes's increasingly stern rejection of laughter as a tool of argument, and his wish to foster a different form of civil education designed to encourage the 'constant Civil Amity' that peace and security require.[47]

---

[43] Junius 1638, pp. 54, 55.   [44] Junius 1638, pp. 55–6.   [45] Junius 1638, p. 56.
[46] Quintilian 2001, 6. 3. 8, vol. 3, p. 66: 'a derisu non procul abest risus'.
[47] Hobbes 2012, vol. 3, A Review, and Conclusion, p. 1132.

As I have noted, the classical rhetoricians place much emphasis on the persuasive powers inherent in the figures and tropes of speech. These powers can be so extensive, they argue, that some *figurae* should be recognised as having a moral and even an epistemological importance. They offer a number of instances, and one of my objectives in this book is to bring out the significance of two of the most complex examples they discuss: paradiastole and prosopopoeia.

The figure of paradiastole, which provides me with my theme in chapter 5, is the name given by the rhetoricians to the technique of rhetorical redescription, the technique of manipulating the application of evaluative terms. Among the earliest Roman rhetoricians, it is held to be an instance of paradiastole when we expose and denounce our adversaries for attempting to redescribe their vices as virtues. This is the view taken by the author of the *Ad Herennium*, who audaciously advises us, in his section on deliberative speech, to try to demonstrate that what our adversaries call prudence is indiscreet cleverness, what they call courage is inconsiderate recklessness, and so on.[48] According to Quintilian, however, it is not when we try to expose such alleged virtues as vices, but rather when we try to excuse our own vices as virtues, that the technique of rhetorical redescription comes into play. It is thus an instance of paradiastole 'when you call *yourself* wise rather than crafty, or courageous rather than reckless'.[49]

I examine the first of these understandings of paradiastole in chapter 3, in which I illustrate the role it plays in Machiavelli's argument in *The Prince*. Machiavelli is celebrated for insisting that rulers ought not to bind themselves to follow the requirements of the virtues if they wish to maintain their states. But his argument has I think been partly misunderstood. In the case of the so-called princely virtues – liberality and clemency – what Machiavelli contends is that rulers ought not to follow what are generally *held* to be their requirements. According to Machiavelli, the corruption of the modern age is so pervasive that what is regarded as liberality is in fact extravagance, and what is regarded as clemency is in fact laxity and over-indulgence. To an extent that has not I think been recognised, an anxiety about the potentially ruinous impact of rhetorical redescription lies at the heart of Machiavelli's argument.

I turn in chapter 5 to examine Quintilian's alternative way of thinking about paradiastole as the technique of excusing one's own vices by redescribing them as virtues. First I chart the evolution of this more dominant

[48] *Rhetorica ad Herennium* 1954, III. III. 6, pp. 166–8. For the passage in full see below, chapter 5, note 11.
[49] Quintilian 2001, 9. 3. 63, vol. 4, p. 138: 'Cum te pro astuto sapientem appelles, pro confidente fortem'. Italics added.

tradition, and then I point to its presence in several of Shakespeare's plays. A number of morally ambiguous characters – Falstaff, Shylocke, Alcibiades – invoke the technique in attempting to excuse their conduct, but in each case they are immediately exposed for trying to play a well-known rhetorical trick. But I also consider one instance – that of Coriolanus – in which Shakespeare explores a more complex and disquieting possibility. Coriolanus is condemned throughout the play for his pride and haughtiness, but he is also commended for nobleness and magnanimity. Is his alleged nobility merely pride? Or his seeming pride true nobility? These questions hover over much of the action of the play, but they are never unambiguously answered, and we are left with the unsettling sense that they may not be capable of being resolved.

Of even greater importance for my general argument is the second of the *figurae* on which I concentrate, that of prosopopoeia. According to Quintilian, this is the figure we deploy whenever we invent fictitious speeches and attribute them to persons other than ourselves, thereby adopting their *prosopon* or mask.[50] 'By means of this way of speaking', Quintilian adds, 'even cities and peoples can acquire a voice.'[51] I show in chapter 2 how this rhetorical figure supplies Hobbes with his analysis of personhood in *Leviathan*, and consequently underlies his view of political representation as the authorised personation of what Hobbes describes as the person 'by Fiction' of the state[52] – an apparent translation of Quintilian's phrase *personae fictione*, 'persons by fiction'.[53] In chapter 9 I explore Hobbes's resulting theory of political representation, and in chapter 12 I focus on his central assumption that the seat of sovereignty is occupied not by the natural person of the sovereign but rather by the represented person of the state. It is a surprisingly short step from the rhetoricians and their stage-play world of fictional persons to Hobbes's epoch-making contention that the sovereign is the person authorised to wear the *persona* or mask of the state.

Although Hobbes is a theorist of state sovereignty, he always takes care to allow that, because the state is nothing more than a *persona fictione*, it is incapable of acting except through the agency of the sovereign who represents it. This is not to say that Hobbes is a royalist. By the time he came to write *Leviathan* he had reached the unequivocal conclusion that 'the end of Obedience is Protection'.[54] Whenever we find ourselves

---

[50] Quintilian 2001, 3. 8. 52–4, vol. 2, p. 140–2 and especially 6. 1. 25. vol. 3, p. 30 on 'fictae alienarum personarum orationes'. On prosopopoeia see Alexander 2007.
[51] Quintilian 2001, 9. 2. 31, vol. 4, p. 50: 'in hoc genere dicendi . . . Urbes etiam populique vocem accipiunt.'
[52] Hobbes 2012, vol. 2, ch. 16, p. 246.   [53] Quintilian 2001, 9. 3. 89, vol. 4, p. 154.
[54] Hobbes 2012, vol. 2, ch. 21, p. 344.

successfully protected – under whatever form of regime – we should make it our watchword that 'the present ought alwaies to be preferred'.[55] But Hobbes certainly reveals a preference for monarchy over all other forms of government. He can admittedly be read against the grain as a proponent of democracy,[56] and he undoubtedly argues in *De cive* that democracy must be the original form of government.[57] As I argue in chapter 11, however, he always presents himself in the mature formulation of his civil science as a strong defender of absolute monarchy.[58]

I pave the way for this argument in chapter 7, in which I focus on what I call the neo-Roman doctrine that the antonym of political liberty is slavery. As I show, this view rose to prominence in English public debate during the generation preceding the outbreak of the civil war in 1642. It was first applied to denounce the royal prerogative as a form of arbitrary and hence enslaving power, and subsequently to support the claim that a self-governing republic is the only form of rule under which political liberty can be sustained. Hobbes steps forward in *Leviathan* as a vehement enemy of this way of thinking about the freedom of subjects, and in *Behemoth* he assails the 'Democraticall Gentlemen' in the House of Commons who had espoused these arguments as destroyers of the English state.[59]

Hobbes's response to the democratical gentlemen is to argue that complete and undivided political authority must always be placed in the hands of a single person or assembly. No sovereign can ever be subject to law, and no subject can ever have a right to depose his sovereign or set him aside. Hobbes even repudiates any suggestion that the nearest heir of a ruling monarch has a natural or God-given right to succeed. To endorse such a right would be to limit the powers of reigning sovereigns, and for Hobbes the idea of limited sovereignty is a contradiction in terms. He accordingly concludes that 'there is no perfect forme of Government, where the disposing of the Succession is not in the present Soveraign.'[60] Hobbes never wavers from this commitment, and as we shall see in chapter 11 it was still at the forefront of his mind when he wrote his final observations on the nature of sovereign power in the year of his death.

My chief aim in this Introduction has been to bring to the surface my main preoccupations in the chapters that follow. I should like to end by noting two theoretical commitments that likewise underpin my approach throughout this book. The first can best be expressed in negative terms by saying that I am sceptical about the project of writing histories of

[55] Hobbes 2012, vol. 3, ch. 42, p. 868.   [56] As in Martel 2007.
[57] As emphasised in Tuck 2015. But for Hobbes's doubts about democracy see Hoekstra 2006.
[58] On Hobbes's absolutism see Goldie 2011, Sommerville 2016.
[59] Hobbes 2010, pp. 141, 158.   [60] Hobbes 2012, vol. 2, ch. 19, p. 298.

concepts. One of the problems we face in trying to make sense of our social world is that complex conceptual disputes are often disguised by shared vocabularies. I illustrate this phenomenon most extensively in chapters 9 and 10, in which I show that there has never been any agreed concept to which the terms *representation* and *the state* may be said to refer. I consequently focus not on the history of concepts but rather on their verbal expression and their uses in argument. The other and related commitment underlying the following chapters is that, even in the case of the most canonical texts, it seems to me most illuminating to treat them essentially as interventions in pre-existing debates, and to concentrate on trying to recover the problems they were originally designed to solve. There is much we can learn from the texts I consider, but only if we begin by letting them speak so far as possible in their own terms.

2   Classical Rhetoric and the Personation of the State

I

Among the humanist allegiances that Hobbes continues to display in the later stages of his intellectual career, one of the most striking appears in his analysis in chapters 16 and 17 of *Leviathan* of the concept of the *persona civitatis*, the person of the state. Although Hobbes's vocabulary in these passages reflects his close acquaintance with the theory of represented persons as elaborated by the Commentators on Roman Law, the authority on whom he principally relies is Cicero, the writer most deeply venerated by the humanist pedagogues of the English Renaissance.[1] As early as 1531 Sir Thomas Elyot in his *Boke named the Governour* had singled out 'the warke of Cicero, called in latin *De officiis*' for its incomparable combination of 'gravitie with dilectation: excellent wysedome with divine eloquence', and had recommended it as a text that everyone must be sure to read.[2] Hobbes appears to have taken this advice to heart, for it is to the *De officiis* that he owes almost the entire analysis of personhood that underpins his theory about the sovereignty of the *civitas* or state.

The most influential claim that Cicero makes about the *persona civitatis* can be found in his discussion of *personae* in Book I of *De officiis*. There he begins by presenting two general arguments about personhood. One is that, 'while there are great differences between us in our bodily powers', part of what it means to be a person is to be embodied.[3] His other and connected claim is that everyone possesses a rational nature, and that 'from this source the rational method of finding out our duty is ascertained'.[4] From these contentions it proved a short step to the

This chapter is largely a new piece of work, although it incorporates some material from Skinner 2002a (with permission from the Cambridge University Press) and Skinner 2005b (with permission from John Wiley and Sons). For many helpful discussions, and for commenting on drafts, I am deeply grateful to David Ciepley, Susan James, Philip Pettit and Pete Stacey.

[1] See Foisneau 2010, pp. 79–82. On the legal background see McLean 1999, esp. pp. 12–14. For Cicero on personhood see Reiss 2003, pp. 120–38.
[2] Elyot 1531, fos. 41r–v. On Cicero in Tudor England see Jones 1998.
[3] Cicero 1913, I. XXX. 107, p. 108: 'enim in corporibus magnae dissimilitudines sunt'.
[4] Cicero 1913, I. XXX. 107, p. 108: 'ex qua ratio inveniendi officii exquiritur'.

articulation of the view later given classic expression by Boethius in *De personis*. To speak of a person, Boethius maintains, is to refer to 'an individual substance of rational nature'.[5] Aquinas in his *Summa theologiae* raises some possible objections to Boethius's definition, but eventually he ratifies it in full, a move that had the effect of turning it into a long-standing orthodoxy.[6] As we shall see in chapter 12, Boethius's definition was to survive unchanged to form the basis of Pufendorf's attack on the analysis of personhood put forward by Hobbes in *Leviathan*.

Cicero adds two observations that partly contrast with Boethius's account and undoubtedly carry him far beyond it. He first proposes that to be a person of a determinate character is to some degree a matter not of endowment but of choice. Like actors in the theatre, who take on a variety of roles, we discharge a number of different functions in our public and personal lives. Cicero describes these as *personae*, an allusion to the masks or *personae* worn by actors on the Greek and Roman stage.[7] As substantial and rational agents, everyone plays many parts, all of which have their own *officia* or duties attached to them. To cite Cicero's own examples, one man may choose the life of a soldier, another that of an advocate, another that of a judge.[8]

Cicero's further observation is that, again like actors in the theatre, we can in addition take on the parts of others, assuming their *personae* and, as it were, speaking their lines. Cicero elaborates this thought in a number of different works. He notes in *De legibus* how it is possible to adopt the *persona* of someone who may not be in a position to act on their own account, as in the case of heirs who take the place of the dead in the performance of rites.[9] He speaks in similar vein in Book II of *De oratore*, in which he makes the figure of Antonius disclose some of the secrets that made him such a successful advocate. When he appears in court, Antonius explains, 'I am not acting the part of another person, but am author of my own actions'.[10] He behaves very differently, however, when preparing a case. At this stage he first interviews his client, and then tries to work out not only what he ought to say himself, but also how his opponent is likely to riposte and how the judge may in turn react. He summarises his account of this exercise by saying that 'I sustain as one

[5] Boethius 1571, III. fo. 12r: 'Est enim persona, (ut dictum est) naturae rationabilis individua subsistentia'.
[6] Aquinas 1950, Ia. 29. 1, vol. 1, pp. 155–6: 'Persona est rationalis naturae individua substantia'.
[7] Cicero 1913, I. XXXI. 114, p. 116. See Brito Vieira 2009, pp. 75–144.
[8] Cicero 1913, I. XXXII. 116, p. 118 and III. X. 43, p. 310.
[9] Cicero 1928, II. XIX. 48, pp. 430–2.
[10] Cicero 1942, II. XLVII, 194, vol. 1, p. 338: 'neque actor essem alienae personae, sed auctor meae'.

man, with as much impartiality as possible, the role of three persons, my own, that of my adversary and that of the judge.'[11]

These are precisely the passages that Hobbes singles out in chapter 16 of *Leviathan* when he explains what it means to personate or represent someone else:

> The Word Person is latine: instead whereof the Greeks have πρόσωπον, which signifies the *Face*, as *Persona* in latine signifies the *disguise*, or *outward appearance* of a man, counterfeited on the Stage; and somtimes more particularly that part of it, which disguiseth the face, as a Mask or Visard: And from the Stage, hath been translated to any Representer of speech and action, as well in Tribunalls, as Theaters. So that a *Person*, is the same that an *Actor* is, both on the Stage and in common Conversation; and to *Personate*, is to *Act*, or *Represent* himselfe, or an other; and he that acteth another, is said to beare his Person, or act in his name; (in which sence *Cicero* useth it where he saies, *Unus sustineo tres Personas; Mei, Adversarii, & Iudicis*, I beare three Persons; my own, my Adversaries, and the Judges;)[12]

The insight here taken by Hobbes from Cicero's theatrical understanding of representation is that it must be a sufficient condition of validly representing someone else that I should be capable of speaking and acting effectively in their name. For Cicero, as for Hobbes, representation is a matter of personating other people, not impersonating them.

Cicero offers one ancillary thought that later proved of no less significance. Once we conceive of legal and political representation as nothing more than speaking and acting in the name of others, we can think not merely of representing other persons, but also of representing *res* or things and even purely legal or fictional entities.[13] Cicero gives several examples in his *De inventione* in the course of discussing how best to sum up a case in court. You can introduce an element of variety by speaking not in your own person but in the person of the city, or in the person of the laws themselves.[14] He returns to the argument when he speaks in *De officiis* about the representation of the *civitas* or state. There he describes it as 'the distinctive duty of the magistrate to understand that he bears the person of the *civitas*' and must perform the functions of the state.[15] This is the formula Hobbes likewise invokes in the Latin version of *Leviathan* to

---

[11] Cicero 1942, II. XXIV. 102, vol. 1, p. 274: 'tres personas unus sustineo summa animi aequitate, meam, adversarii, iudicis'. Cf. Quintilian 2001, 3. 8. 49–54, vol. 2, pp. 138–42.

[12] Hobbes 2012, vol. 2, ch. 16, p. 244.   [13] Cicero 1949, I. LII. 99, p. 148.

[14] Cicero 1949, I. LII. 99, p. 150.

[15] Cicero 1913, I. XXXIV. 124, p. 126: 'proprium munus magistratus intellegere se gerere personam civitatis'. For *gerere* as 'to bear, carry' and also 'to perform the functions of' see OLD.

describe the obligation of sovereigns,[16] while in the English version he translates Cicero's phrase by saying that the sovereign 'carryeth this Person' of the *civitas* or state, thereby speaking and acting in its name.[17]

Cicero's analysis was later elaborated by Quintilian in his *Institutio oratoria*, a discussion to which Hobbes is no less clearly indebted.[18] Quintilian picks up the term *prosopon* (πρόσωπον), which had originally been used – as we have seen Hobbes noting – to refer to 'the *disguise*, or *outward appearance* of a man, counterfeited on the Stage'. This leads Quintilian to speak of prosopopoeia, which he defines as the rhetorical technique of inventing fictitious speeches and ascribing them to *personae* other than ourselves.[19] Quintilian contemplates with evident relish the range of persons and things to which words and actions can be attributed once we allow that it is possible to speak and act through being personified or represented. 'By means of this way of speaking the dead are raised, and cities and even peoples acquire a voice.'[20] Quintilian accordingly takes himself to be describing a whole world not merely of *fictae orationes*, 'fictitious speeches',[21] but also of *personae fictione*, 'persons by fiction'.[22] Hobbes repeats the latter phrase in chapter 16 of *Leviathan*, observing that 'There are few things, that are uncapable of being represented by Fiction', including even 'Inanimate things'.[23]

Quintilian summarises by saying that he has been speaking of how 'we are able to counterfeit bodies and speech'.[24] This way of explicating the figure of prosopopoeia was subsequently much developed by the rhetorical writers of the English Renaissance. Richard Sherry in his pioneering *Treatise of the Figures* of 1550 already refers to 'prosopopey' as the technique we deploy 'when we fayne persons'.[25] Abraham Fraunce in his *Arcadian Rhetorike* of 1588 similarly defines prosopopoeia as 'a fayning of any person, when in our speach we represent the person of anie, and make it speake as though he were there present'.[26] Hobbes adopts the same usage in *Leviathan*, arguing that whenever our words or actions are considered '*as representing the words or actions of an other man, or of any*

---

[16] Hobbes 2012, vol. 2, ch. 17, p. 263: 'Is autem qui Civitatis Personam gerit'.

[17] Hobbes 2012, vol. 2, ch. 16, p. 262.

[18] The catalogue of the Hardwick library drawn up by Hobbes includes a folio copy of Quintilian. See Hobbes MSS (Chatsworth), MS E. 1. A, p. 107.

[19] Quintilian 2001, 3. 8. 52–4, vol. 2, p. 140–2 and especially 6. 1. 25. vol. 3, p. 30 on 'fictae alienarum personarum orationes'.

[20] Quintilian 2001, 9. 2. 31, vol. 4, p. 50: 'in hoc genere dicendi et inferos excitare . . . Urbes etiam populique vocem accipiunt.'

[21] See Quintilian 2001, 6.1. 25, vol. 3, p. 30 on 'fictae . . . orationes'.

[22] Quintilian 2001, 9. 3. 89, vol. 4, p. 154.   [23] Hobbes 2012, vol. 2, ch. 16, p. 246.

[24] Quintilian 2001, 9. 2. 31, vol. 4, p. 50: 'corpora et verba fingimus'.

[25] Sherry 1550, sig. E, 2r.   [26] Fraunce 1588, sig. G, 2r.

other thing to whom they are attributed', we are speaking of 'a Feigned or *Artificiall person*'.[27]

Henry Peacham in his *Garden of Eloquence* of 1593 provides a more extended analysis of prosopopoeia. He likewise defines it as 'the faining of a person', adding by way of illustration that by these means it is possible to 'attribute a person to a commonwealth', so that 'this figure maketh the commonwealth to speake'.[28] Hobbes repeats the formula when speaking of the commonwealth in *Leviathan*. He similarly describes how, by a process of authorisation, the members of a multitude are able to institute a sovereign representative whose words and actions are then attributed to the person 'by Fiction' of the commonwealth or state, so that 'the name of the person Commanding' is *Persona Civitatis*, the Person of the Common-wealth.'[29]

We can sum up this rhetorical analysis of personhood by noting that it involves two claims which subsequently proved of cardinal importance in helping to crystallise the concept of the sovereign state. When Cicero refers to the capacity of magistrates *gerere personam civitatis*, he treats the *civitas* as a distinct legal entity, and at the same time identifies the chief magistrate as the name of the agent with an obligation to pursue the goals of the *civitas* by way of acting in its name. It turns out, in other words, that when Cicero at the outset of his discussion characterises persons as rational substances, he is referring only to one class of persons. To count as a person, both he and Quintilian end by suggesting, it is not necessary to have a bodily substance; it may be sufficient that some natural person has been accredited to play your part.

As this analysis became embedded in early Christian culture, Cicero's employment of the phrase *gerere personam* to express the idea of speaking and acting in the name of someone else began to be supplemented by the use of the verb *repraesentare* to convey the same thought. This latter usage is foreign to classical Latin, in which the noun *repraesentatio* and the related verb *repraesentare* had been exclusively employed to express the very different – although not unrelated – idea of bringing something absent back into the present. One context in which we encounter this usage is in legal discourse, and especially in arguments about the payment of legacies and the repayment of debts. Both acts are viewed in Roman law as instances in which a sum of money promised by one party to another is brought forward for immediate payment. Cicero already employs the terms *repraesentare* and *repraesentatio* when speaking of

---

[27] Hobbes 2012, vol. 2, ch. 16, p. 244.   [28] Peacham 1593, p. 134.
[29] Hobbes 2012, vol. 2, ch. 16, p. 244; ch. 26, p. 414.

handing over money without delay,[30] and these are likewise among the standard uses of the terms in Justinian's *Digest*, in which *repraesentatio* is treated as the special benefit of receiving a legacy in the form of cash.[31]

The other context in which we encounter the same vocabulary is of much greater significance for my present argument. The verb *repraesentare* was widely used in classical Latin to refer to the act of bringing something back to the present by way of producing an image or likeness – a *repraesentatio* – of its external bodily appearance. The implication in this instance is that something absent is being re-presented to the gaze. The most transfixing means of achieving this effect was agreed to be through the arts of painting and sculpture. Pliny offers what became a celebrated example in his chapters on the evolution of painting in his *Historia Naturalis*. The artist Parrhasius is reported to have produced a picture of some curtains so realistically represented (*repraesentata*) that his rival Zeuxis, not realising that he was looking at a painting, asked for the curtains to be drawn aside so that he could look at the picture he expected to see behind them.[32] According to the rhetoricians, however, we can sometimes achieve an equally spellbinding effect entirely through the force of eloquence. This contention sometimes prompts Quintilian to treat the skill of speaking with *enargeia* – with exceptional vividness – as equivalent to *repraesentatio*, the technique of 'holding out' a person or event to be inspected.[33] Like Horace, who had maintained in a celebrated dictum that 'a poem is like a picture',[34] Quintilian thinks of *repraesentatio* as the ability to produce descriptions so telling that the scene 'appears to be visible'.[35]

If we turn to the discussion of legal and political representation in early Christian culture we find a strong continuity with these classical usages. The terms *repraesentatio* and *repraesentare* are still employed to refer to situations in which one person or group may be said to stand for another by way of supplying an image or epitome of their external appearance. We find Tertullian speaking, for example, of the general council of the Church as 'a *repraesentatio* of the whole of Christianity'.[36] But we also begin to encounter the same terminology in circumstances in which the writers of classical Latin would instead have used the phrase *gerere personam*, to bear someone's person or act in their name. An early

---

[30] Cicero 1999, XII. 29, vol. 3, p. 320 and XII. 31, vol. 3, p. 326.
[31] *The Digest* 1985, 33. 4. 1. 2, vol. 3, p. 115; 35. 1. 36. 1, vol. 3, p. 187.
[32] Pliny 1952, XXXVI, 65, pp. 308–10.
[33] Quintilian 2001, 8. 3. 61, vol. 3, p. 374: 'quodam modo ostendit'.
[34] Horace 1926, p. 480, l. 361: 'ut pictura poesis'.
[35] Quintilian 2001, 8. 3. 62, vol. 3, p. 374: 'ut cerni videantur'.
[36] See Hofmann 1974, pp. 49–50 on Tertullian's view of the General Council as a 'repraesentatio totius nominis Christiani'.

instance can be found in the letters of St Ambrose. He writes to the people of Thessalonica to commiserate with them on the death of their bishop, who had successfully protected the province by way of negotiating with the barbarian tribes. Ambrose is concerned that it may not be possible to find a successor to speak for them so powerfully, and he expresses his anxiety by asking 'who will now be able to represent us?'[37] An even clearer example can be found in the letters of Gregory the Great. Nominating a bishop to serve in Sicily, Gregory writes to reassure the local congregation that they will continue to be no less effectively looked after. The bishop will act as a deputy, whom Gregory will advise, thereby ensuring that the bishop will be able to act with full authority in his name. As Gregory puts it, 'our authority will be represented (*repraesentetur*) by someone to whom we give instructions when we ourselves are unable to be present.'[38]

It is not difficult to see how this semantic shift took place, with the eventual result that *gerere personam* and *repraesentare* came to be used interchangeably – as they are by Hobbes – to designate the act of speaking and acting in the name of someone else. Gregory might be thought to have it in mind that, if the person substituting for him as bishop is to discharge his role effectively, it will be important that he should not only have authority to act in Gregory's name, but should also appear as a worthy substitute and 'look the part'. This is by no means to say, however, that it is essential to the Ciceronian idea of legal and political representation that representatives should resemble or replicate the outward demeanour of the persons they represent. Some scholars have admittedly argued that, when Cicero uses the verb *gerere*, he must be understood to mean that the representative should aim 'to assume the appearance' of the person being represented.[39] But this is to repeat the mistake allegedly made by Lord Cornbury when colonial governor of New York and New Jersey in the early eighteenth century. Because he was acting as a representative of Queen Anne, he is said to have considered it his duty to open State Assemblies wearing female dress. If this was indeed how he presented himself,[40] his error was not to recognise that what is required to 'look the part' of a reigning monarch is simply to behave in a suitably regal style, that is, a style of dignity and stateliness. Representation, in other words, is a matter of personating other people, not impersonating them.

---

[37] Ambrose 1845, col. 958: 'hunc nobis quis poterit repraesentare?'
[38] Gregory 1887–99, vol. 1, p. 1: 'ubi nos praesentes esse non possumus, nostra per eum, cui praecipimus, repraesentetur auctoritas.'
[39] See Crignon 2012, p. 236 and n., where he translates 'gerere' as 'endosser', thereby making both Cicero and Hobbes speak of 'putting on' someone's appearance.
[40] Bonomi 1998, p. 15 shows that the story is almost certainly false.

Before leaving Gregory the Great's account of representation, we need to note that his use of the verb *repraesentare* raises two of the most basic and unresolved questions that arise about all representatives, whether individuals or assemblies. One is whether they should be regarded as nothing more than delegates of those whom they represent. Gregory emphatically endorses this view in the case of individual deputies, assuming that they will at all times remain under the orders of those who appoint them. This has remained the standard understanding of legal representation: lawyers speaking for clients in court are expected to act at their behest, and specifically to do their best to win a favourable verdict. But in the case of political representation the status of elected representatives has never ceased to be a subject of debate. As we shall see in chapter 12, the Levellers in the English revolution maintained that the duty of Members of Parliament is to find out the views of their constituents and then attempt to have those views enacted into law. More usually, however, such assemblies have been taken to acquire the status of trustees with discretion to act according to their own judgment. This was the response of the English parliamentarians to the Levellers, and remains the standard understanding of political representation in modern democracies, although here again no stable agreement has ever been reached.

The other question is whether there is ever a case for saying that representatives need to constitute an image or likeness of those whom they represent. As we have found, this suggestion is apt to look absurd when one individual is representing another. But as I show in chapter 12, the exponents of 'virtual' representation have always insisted that, in the case of representative assemblies, some such act of mimesis is indispensable, just as Hobbes's followers have continued to insist that this is no less a misunderstanding than in the case of an advocate representing a client in court, where no effort to produce a resemblance is required. Here again no stable agreement on the issue has ever been reached.

II

Cicero wrote *De officiis* at a moment of optimism for protagonists of what he describes as the *civitas vera* of republican Rome. Julius Caesar had just been assassinated and his dictatorship brought to a sudden end, a development implicitly but warmly welcomed by Cicero in his discussion of tyranny in Book III.[41] Before long, however, the concept of the *civitas* ceased to play a role of much significance in Western European political thought. Cicero's ideal of the free state in which citizens play an active

---

[41] Cicero 1913, III. VI. 32, p. 298.

part in government was initially replaced by a system in which they were turned into subjects of divine emperors who alone wielded *imperium* or *summa potestas*, supreme political power. This trend was further accelerated with the creation of the Holy Roman Empire and the gradual establishment of national monarchies in Christian Europe. The rule of kings came to be widely regarded as a God-given form of lordship, and not merely as the best but the only legitimate form of government. John of Salisbury was recapitulating a great deal of conventional wisdom when he affirmed in his *Policraticus* of 1159 that all rulers constitute 'a kind of image on earth of the divine majesty', and that they not only stand above the laws but 'can be said to partake in a large measure of divine virtue themselves'.[42]

This is not to say, however, that Cicero's vision of rulers as nothing more than authorised representatives of the *civitas* was lost to sight. A Ciceronian analysis of representation was revived at an early stage as a means of explicating the organisation of the Christian Church. St Augustine alludes in his *De agone christiano* to Cicero's claim that magistrates bear the person of the *civitas*, and argues that it can similarly be said that 'not without cause did Peter among all the Apostles uphold the *persona* of the Catholic Church'.[43] Peter was able to discharge this role because 'the keys of the kingdom of heaven were given to the Church when they were given to him' as its representative.[44] When Anselm composed his *Enarrationes* on St Matthew's Gospel at the end of the twelfth century, he likewise asserted that 'Peter bears the person of the Church'.[45] This is said to explain why he was able to say that 'if my brother has sinned against me, that is, the Church, it is obvious that he is sinning against the Church'.[46] Aquinas later speaks in similar terms of the *persona Ecclesiae* in the course of considering the relative fruitfulness of a Mass when conducted by a good or a bad priest. When a bad priest offers private orations they are not fruitful, but when he conducts the Mass he is speaking 'in the person of the entire Church, of which a priest is a minister'.[47] As a result, his speech is fruitful not only in the Mass, 'but in

---

[42] Salisbury 1909, vol. 1, p. 236: 'in terris quaedam divinae maiestatis imago ... magnum quid divinae virtutis declaratur inesse principibus'.

[43] Augustine 1791, ch. 30, p. 141: 'Non enim sine caussa [*sic*] inter omnes Apostolicos huic Ecclesiae Catholicae personam sustinet Petrus'.

[44] Augustine 1791, ch. 30, p. 141: 'huic enim Ecclesiae claves regni caelorum datae sunt, cum Petro datae sunt'.

[45] Anselm 1854, ch. 18, pp. 1405 and 1409: 'Petrus gerit hic personam Ecclesiae'.

[46] Anselm 1854, ch. 18, p. 1409: 'Si frater meus peccaverit in me, id est Ecclesiam, scilicet ... peccat in Ecclesiam'.

[47] Aquinas 1950, III. 82. 6, vol. 3, p. 556: 'in persona totius Ecclesiae, cuius sacerdos est minister'.

every other oration delivered in discharging his ecclesiastical duties, in which *gerit personam Ecclesiae*, he represents or bears the person of the Church'.[48]

Around the beginning of the twelfth century there arose a development of even greater significance for the revival of the Ciceronian vision of magistrates as representatives of the *civitas*. A growing number of cities in the so-called *Regnum Italicum* began to take it upon themselves, in defiance of the papacy as well as the Holy Roman Empire, to appoint their own 'consuls' and invest them with supreme judicial authority. This happened at Pisa in 1085, at Milan, Genoa, and Arezzo before 1100 and at Bologna, Padua, Florence, Lucca, Siena and elsewhere by the 1140s.[49] During the second half of the century a further development took place. The consular system was gradually replaced by a form of government centred on ruling councils chaired by officials known as *podestà*, so called because they were granted *potestas* or ruling power in executive as well as judicial affairs. Such a system was in operation at Padua by the 1170s, at Milan by the 1180s, and at Florence, Pisa, Siena and Arezzo by the end of the century.[50] The outcome was that, by the beginning of the thirteenth century, many of the richest cities of Lombardy and Tuscany had acquired the status of independent city-republics with written constitutions guaranteeing their elective and self-governing arrangements.[51]

As these *civitates* proliferated, they were accommodated into the legal theory of the period as instances of *universitates personarum*, forms of association in which someone holds authority to act in the name of the institution as a whole.[52] The communes of Florence, Pisa and Siena are described in legal documents as *universitates* from the start of the thirteenth century,[53] thereby joining a rich array of *universitates personarum* already recognised in civil and canon law, including hospitals, cathedral chapters, monastic foundations and universities.[54] A less familiar example that acquired some fame during this period was the French association known as the *fratres pontis*, who established corporations to raise alms for travellers, using the money to construct and maintain the three great medieval bridges over the Rhône.[55] The *fratres* built hospitals in conjunction with their bridges to help travellers who fell sick, and at

---

[48] Aquinas 1950, III. 82. 6, vol. 3, p. 556: 'sed omnes aliae eius orationes quas facit in ecclesiasticis officiis, in quibus gerit personam Ecclesiae'.
[49] Waley 1988, pp. 32, 35; Jones 1997, pp. 130–51; Ferente 2013, pp. 158–64.
[50] Artifoni 1986, pp. 688–93; Waley 1988, pp. 32–68.
[51] For a survey see Costa 1999, pp. 3–50.   [52] Gillet 1927, pp. 68, 75.
[53] Banchi (ed.) 1866, p. 6 (Siena), p. 9 (Pisa), p. 37 (Florence).
[54] See Michaud-Quantin 1970, pp. 82–90 on *capituli* and pp. 111–17 on *civitates*.
[55] See Boyer 1964 on the bridges at Avignon, Lyon and Pont Saint Esprit.

Avignon they built a chapel on the bridge itself.[56] These corporations began to decline in the fourteenth century, but their fame endured into the Renaissance. Hobbes clearly knew about them, perhaps from the time he spent with his friend Thomas de Martel in Montaubon in 1646.[57] When in chapter 16 of *Leviathan* Hobbes introduces his fundamental assumption that 'There are few things, that are uncapable of being represented by Fiction', he offers three examples of legal entities capable of acting through the agency of a representative. By a fiction of law, even 'a Church, an Hospital, a Bridge, may be personated by a Rector, Master, or Overseer', who 'may have Authority to procure their maintenance, given them by those that are Owners, or Governours of those things.'[58] To the modern eye this list is apt to look eccentric and miscellaneous, but to early-modern readers the church, the hospital and the bridge would have belonged together, and it would not have seemed strange for Hobbes to have given them pride of place.

The opening decades of the thirteenth century saw the emergence of a distinctive political literature in which leading officials of the new *civitates* of the *Regnum Italicum* were instructed in the proper discharge of their duties.[59] The earliest of these works to have survived is the anonymous *Oculus pastoralis*, which has usually been dated to the 1220s.[60] This was followed by Orfino da Lodi's *De regimine et sapientia potestatis*, an encomium on justice composed in leonine verse in the 1240s.[61] The next of these advice-books – by far the fullest and most important – was the *Liber de regimine civitatum* by Giovanni da Viterbo (*c*.1200–*c*.1260), probably completed in the 1250s.[62] This was followed – and to some degree plagiarised[63] – by Brunetto Latini (1220–1294) in his *Livres dou trésor* of 1266, a widely used encyclopedia that ends with a section entitled 'On the government of cities'.[64] These writers were in turn dependent on a number of earlier treatises in which the virtues required of political leaders had already been anatomised in more broadly based terms. Originally emanating from the French cathedral schools, these texts first began to circulate in the middle decades of the twelfth century. Hildebert of Tours'

---

[56] Boyer 1964, p. 642. On hospitals and bridges see Michaud-Quantin 1970, pp. 94–102.
[57] For this visit see Hobbes 1994, letter 40, vol. 1, pp. 126–7.
[58] Hobbes 2012, vol. 2, ch. 16, p. 246.
[59] On this literature see Geuna 2006; Artifoni 2012.
[60] For this dating see Franceschi 1966, p. 3; on the *Oculus* see Pennington 1993, pp. 39–44.
[61] For this dating see Sorbelli 1944, p. 61.
[62] For this dating see Folena 1959, p. 97. But Sorbelli 1944, pp. 94–6 suggests the 1260s, while Zorzi in DBI (2001) suggests the 1230s.
[63] As noted in Najemy 1994.
[64] For this dating see Sorbelli 1944, pp. 99–104; Carmody 1948, pp. xiii–xx, xxii–xxxii.

Moralis philosophia was written in the 1120s;[65] the *Moralium dogma philo-sophorum* attributed to Guillaume de Conches followed a decade or two later;[66] Alain de Lille's *De virtutibus et vitiis* can be dated to the 1160s;[67] and the tradition may be said to have culminated in Guillaume Perault's massive *Summae virtutum ac vitiorum* of *c*.1240.[68]

The most striking feature of these advice-books is that they are not directed at kings or emperors; they are exclusively addressed to the elected leaders and ruling councils of the Italian *civitates*. Latini begins by mounting an invidious comparison between 'France and other countries, which are subject to the rule of kings and other perpetual princes'[69] and the situation in Italy, in which 'the communities of the cities elect those whom they judge will be most profitable to the common good of the city and all its subjects.'[70] These *officiaus*, as Latini calls them,[71] are usually designated as *rectores*[72] or *potestates*,[73] although sometimes as *prelati*[74] or *praeses*.[75] The extent of their authority is described by Giovanni da Viterbo in two chapters devoted to the question of how the concept of *potestas* should be understood. As Justinian's *Digest* had laid down, the main criterion is the possession of the *ius gladii*, the right to wield the sword of justice, which the *Digest* had in turn equated with *merum imperium*,[76] and which the majority of Glossators consequently took to be the exclusive right of the Holy Roman Emperor. Giovanni agrees that emperors possess *imperium*,[77] but nevertheless insists that the powers of *rectores* in independent *civitates* include the *ius gladii*, which is given to them directly by God.[78] This power is not personal, but is granted on condition that they exercise it *nomine universitatis*, in the name of the community and for the good of the

---

[65] For this dating see Migne 1854, p. 1007.
[66] Williams 1957 pp. 737–8 suggests a date between 1145 and 1170. He doubts the attribution to Conches (pp. 742–6), but Holmberg in Conches 1929 and Boutry 2004 both accept it.
[67] For this dating see Evans 1983, pp. 15, 17.
[68] For this dating see Dondaine 1948, pp. 186–7.
[69] Latini 1948, p. 392: 'France et les autres païs, ki sont sozmis a la signorie des rois et des autres princes perpetueus'.
[70] Latini 1948, p. 392: 'li communité des viles eslisent . . . tel comme il quident qu'il soit plus proufitables au commun preu de la vile et de tous lor subtés'.
[71] Latini 1948, p. 392.
[72] *Oculus* 1966, pp. 23, 63; Giovanni da Viterbo 1901, pp. 217–18 *et passim*.
[73] *Oculus* 1966, p. 23; Giovanni da Viterbo 1901, p. 217 *et passim*; cf. Latini 1948, p. 392 on 'poestés'.
[74] Orfino da Lodi 1869, pp. 50, 51; Giovanni da Viterbo 1901, p. 268.
[75] Giovanni da Viterbo 1901, pp. 218, 244.
[76] *The Digest* 1985, 2. 1. 3, vol. 1, p. 40: 'merum [imperium] est imperium habere gladii potestatem'.
[77] Giovanni da Viterbo 1901, ch. 128, p. 266.
[78] Giovanni da Viterbo 1901, ch. 129, p. 267.

city as a whole.[79] As Giovanni lays down, as soon as a *rector* is elected to office he must acknowledge that he is merely the minister of those who have elected him, his status being that of a public servant.[80]

The nature of the service that *rectores* must provide is repeatedly underlined. They must never act, as the *Oculus* puts it, 'merely according to their own will and judgment'.[81] They must recognise that, in Orfino da Lodi's words, 'a *rector* is always bound by the law'.[82] Giovanni da Viterbo similarly argues that a *rector* 'ought to be, and ought to regard himself as being, tied by the laws'.[83] The Sienese Constitution of 1309–10 likewise states, in virtually every rubric concerning the ruling council of the *Nove Signori*, that 'they ought and are bound' to act as the laws and the constitution of the city prescribe.[84]

The aim in following the laws must be to ensure that justice is unwaveringly upheld. 'Love justice, you who judge the earth.' This injunction, the opening of the apocryphal Book of Wisdom, resounds throughout these texts.[85] The *rector* is enjoined to pursue the dictates of justice unswervingly, 'not in the least falling away', as the *Oculus* puts it, 'either to right or to left'.[86] He must act 'so that justice is served and everyone is given their due, without making exceptions for anyone'.[87] Giovanni da Viterbo in his chapter on 'what kind of a *rector* should be sought out by a *civitas* and elected to power'[88] confirms that the *civitas* must aim to find someone who will ensure that 'everyone receives their due, and the city is ruled in justice and equity'.[89] The final goal, as Latini summarises, is to ensure 'that the city is governed according to right and according to truth'.[90]

It cannot be said, however, that any of these writers view the *civitas* in Ciceronian terms as a distinct legal *persona* whose purposes the *rector* has a

---

[79] See Banchi (ed.) 1866, p. 9 on acting 'vice et nomine universitatis' (of Pisa, 1228) and p. 22 on acting 'vice et nomine Comunis et universitatis' (of Siena, 1228).

[80] Giovanni da Viterbo 1901, p. 259: 'publice servit'.

[81] *Oculus* 1966, p. 33: 'Nichil ex arbitrio suo'.

[82] Orfino da Lodi 1869, p. 55: 'Rector ... lege tenetur'.

[83] Giovanni da Viterbo 1901, p. 235: 'debet esse et se existimare legibus alligatum'.

[84] Lisini (ed.) 1903, vol. 2, p. 498: the Nove 'sieno tenuti et debiano'; cf. vol. 2, pp. 499, 500, 501 *et passim*.

[85] See *Oculus* 1966, pp. 36, 66; Giovanni da Viterbo 1901, pp. 246, 257; Latini 1948, pp. 273, 414. For a discussion see Artifoni 1997.

[86] *Oculus* 1966, p. 36: 'non declinantes omnino ad dexteram vel sinistram'. Cf. Latini 1948, p. 392: 'ne a diestre ne a senestre'.

[87] *Oculus* 1966, p. 25: 'servando iustitiam, cuique sine personarum acceptione tribuendo ius suum'.

[88] Giovanni da Viterbo 1901, p. 220: 'Qualis rector querendus sit civitati et eligendus in potestatem'.

[89] Giovanni da Viterbo 1901, p. 220: 'ius suum cuilibet reddatur, et regatur civitas in iustitia et equitate.'

[90] Latini 1948, p. 403: 'que la cités ki est governee selonc droit et selonc verité'.

duty to serve. They invariably refer to the *civitas* not as an agent but rather as a passive object of attention and care. Giovanni da Viterbo twice quotes the passage from the *De officiis* in which Cicero speaks about the duty of magistrates *gerere personam civitatis*, to fulfil the purposes of the city by way of acting in its name. But Giovanni alters the passage to make it say that the fundamental obligation is *gerere curam civitatis*, to take care of the city and look after it.[91] Civic leaders should of course promote the glory and greatness of their communities, and Giovanni explicitly counsels them to call on God to help them bring 'greatness, peace, concord, exaltation and prosperity' to the *civitas* given into their charge.[92] But when Giovanni suggests the wording of the oath to be sworn by incoming *rectores*, his main concern is that they should 'administer, maintain and preserve the safety of the *civitas*' and at the same time 'maintain and look after each individual citizen, the small as well as the great'.[93] Latini has much less to say about exaltation and greatness, and underlines even more strongly that the city needs above all to be guarded, cared for, kept in safety and preserved in peace.[94]

If we turn, however, to the earlier treatises on the virtues required of civic leaders, we find them articulating a recognisably Ciceronian vision of the duty of chief magistrates to represent the person of the *civitas* in such a way as to exercise its powers for the good of all. The author of the *Moralium dogma philosophorum* speaks of the *civitas* as a distinct *persona*,[95] while Hildebert in his *Moralis philosophia* refers by name to Cicero as the originator of this line of thought.[96] These writers also endorse Cicero's contention that the duty of magistrates is *gerere personam civitatis*, to act in the name of the city or state. As Hildebert explains, 'the duties of magistrates are diverse', and 'the specific duty of *praelati*, as Cicero says, is to recognise that they represent or bear the person of the *civitas*.'[97] Conches follows Hildebert word for word,[98] while Perault reaches the same conclusion in considering the distinctive contributions of young and old to civic life. 'Among the old, the labours of the body are seen to

---

[91] Giovanni da Viterbo 1901, p. 225: 'est enim proprium munus magistratus intelligere se gerere curam civitatis'.
[92] Giovanni da Viterbo 1901, p. 231: 'granneça, pax, concordia, exaltatio et bonus status'.
[93] Giovanni da Viterbo 1901, p. 228: 'gubernare, manutenere et salvare hanc civitatem ... et omnes et singulos tam parvos quam magnos ... manutenere et tueri'.
[94] Latini 1948, pp. 396, 398, 401, 403.   [95] Conches 1929, p. 47.
[96] Hildebert of Tours 1854, p. 1038.
[97] Hildebert of Tours 1854, p. 1038: 'Magistratuum quoque diversa sunt officia. Praelati quidem officium est, ut ait TULLIUS, aestimare se gerere personam civitatis'.
[98] Conches 1929, pp. 47: 'Prelati quidem officium est estimare se gerere personam civitatis'.

diminish, but the labour of the mind ought to be exercised'.[99] If they are private persons, their duty 'is simply to live justly with their fellow citizens'.[100] But if they are *praelati* 'they should recognise that they bear the person of the *civitas*', and thus have a duty to speak and act in its name.[101]

III

If we now shift our attention from the political to the legal writers of the same period, we find these views about representation far more self-consciously articulated. The seminal contribution was made by the Bolognese canon lawyer Sinibaldo dei Fieschi (*c.*1195–1254), who became Pope Innocent IV in 1243. One of Innocent's concerns as a canonist was that *universitates* were proving excessively vulnerable to excommunication. In 1246 he promulgated a series of decretals in which he declared the practice illegal, and subsequently commented on his own law in his *Apparatus Decretalium*, giving a highly influential explanation for his judgment.[102] Glossing the rubric *On the sentence of excommunication*,[103] he argued that 'only individual persons can be excommunicated, and for an offence they themselves have committed'.[104] He then contended that *universitates* 'are not the names of persons but are *nomina iuris*', the names of purely legal entities,[105] adding that any *universitas* must consequently be acknowledged to exist in a separate realm as 'a mental name and a disembodied thing'.[106] From this argument his desired conclusion readily followed. If only individuals can be excommunicated, and if *universitates* exist in a realm distinct from such embodied persons, 'then a *universitas* cannot be excommunicated'.[107]

The great significance of Innocent's argument lies in the account it offers of purely legal entities. If all *universitates* exist in a separate realm of

---

[99] Perault 1587, fo. 118r: 'Senibus vero labores corporis videntur esse minuendi. Animis vero his exercendus est.'

[100] Perault 1587, fo. 118r: 'iure cum civibus vivere'.

[101] Perault 1587, fo. 118r: 'praelati vero est estimare se gerere personam civitatis'.

[102] Eschmann 1946, p. 8; Todescan 1979, pp. 92–9.

[103] Innocent IV 1481, V. 39, rubric *De sententia excommunicationis*, sig. 2E, 8v to sig. 2G, 3r.

[104] Innocent IV 1481, commentary on V. 39. 52 (gloss *Consiliarios*), sig. 2F, 8v: 'Istae speciales personae excommunicantur pro proprio delicto'.

[105] Innocent IV 1481, commentary on V. 39. 52 (gloss *Consiliarios*), sig. 2F, 8v: 'haec nomina sunt iuris et non personarum.'

[106] See Innocent IV 1481, commentary on V. 39. 64 (gloss *Culpabiles*), sig. 2G, 2v. Innocent takes the example of a Cathedral chapter, arguing that any such capitulum is a 'nomen intellectuale et res incorporalis'.

[107] Innocent IV 1481, commentary on V. 39. 52 (gloss *Consiliarios*), sig. 2F, 8v: 'Universitas autem non potest excommunicari'.

incorporeal beings, they must have an existence wholly distinct from that of the individual persons who constitute the *universitas* as a whole. Here Innocent not only introduces a metaphysical argument in favour of the existence of purely legal entities,[108] but his insertion of *universitates* into the suggested class had the effect of turning it into a large and important one, including not merely such corporations as cathedral chapters and universities but also the *civitas* or state. But Innocent also emphasises that, notwithstanding their purely legal existence, *universitates* are not only capable of acting in the real world but of wielding ecclesiastical and political power. These further conclusions are emphatically underlined in the gloss *Culpabiles*. When it is said 'that a cathedral chapter does something, it is to be understood that the canons and other members of the chapter perform the action, because the chapter itself is unable to do anything except through the agency of those who are members of it'.[109] If, however, such a *universitas* appoints a procurator with authority to act in its name, then it can properly be said that 'through the agency of its procurator' the *universitas* is able 'to take decisions and act'.[110] As the gloss *Consiliaros* had already explained, it is always possible for the *rectores* of a *universitas* to be mandated by the *universitas* itself, and hence to be able validly to speak and act in its name.[111]

From these arguments it proved a short step to the conclusion Cicero had originally adumbrated. The jurists next proceed to define a wide class of *personae* who are said to exist in a purely legal realm, but are nevertheless capable of acting in the real world by virtue of being – as they now begin to say – *personae repraesentata*, persons represented by others who have been granted authority to play their roles and speak their lines. By the early fourteenth century we find a number of Italian jurists writing in these terms about a broad range of corporations or *universitates*.[112] Cino da Pistoia (1270–1336), a civil lawyer and a friend of Dante's,[113]

---

[108] As Eschmann 1946, pp. 33–6 emphasises, this constitutes Innocent's major contribution to the debate about *universitates*. An earlier generation of scholars, influenced by Otto von Gierke, had argued that Innocent should be regarded as the inventor of the doctrine that corporations are fictive persons, and some still appear to uphold this view. See, for example, Maiolo 2007, pp. 244–5; Crignon 2012, pp. 269–70. But Innocent nowhere invokes the concept of a *persona ficta* in discussing the rubric on excommunication. For criticisms of Gierke's interpretation see Gillet 1927; Tierney 1955.

[109] Innocent IV 1481, commentary on V. 39. 64 (gloss *Culpabiles*), sig. 2G, 2v: 'quod capitulum aliquid faciat, intelligendum est, quod canonici et alia membra capituli illud faciant: quia capitulum . . . nihil facere potest nisi per membra sua.'

[110] See Innocent IV 1481, commentary on V. 39. 64 (gloss *Culpabiles*), sig. 2G, 2v: on how a universitas is able 'agere . . . per procuratorem suum'.

[111] See Innocent IV 1481, commentary on V. 39. 52 (gloss *Consiliarios*), sig. 2F, 8v on rectores acting 'de mandato universitatis' and hence 'suo nomine'.

[112] See Todescan 1979, pp. 102–28.   [113] See Ferente 2016, pp. 100–1.

considers in his *Lectura super Codicis* the case of hospitals and their concern for the destitute. He is interested in what should be said about the costs incurred by hospital governors in looking after orphans left in their care. The expense, he rules, 'is not to be charged against these people, and is not to be recovered from them, but rather from the hospital itself, which is a *persona representata*', and is thus capable of meeting the costs through the agency of those who represent it and have charge of its resources.[114]

Soon afterward we find Bartolus of Sassoferrato (1313–1357) invoking the same vocabulary in commenting on the standing of corporations of masters and scholars – universities in the modern sense. He first does so when glossing the rubric *De collegiis illicitis* in the *Digest*. Like Innocent IV, he begins by examining the belief – common among early Glossators such as Accursius – that a *universitas* amounts to nothing more than the individuals who compose it.[115] Bartolus briskly responds that 'this opinion is not true', because 'what is due to a *universitas* is not due to its individual members, the reason being that a *universitas* is a *persona representata* in itself', a distinct person endowed with characteristic obligations and privileges.[116] Later he reverts to the issue at greater length when glossing the rubric *De poenis*.[117] Here he is interested – again like Innocent IV – in whether a *universitas* may be capable of committing crimes and hence being liable to punishment, and as a preliminary to offering his own judgment he explicitly refers to Innocent and his claim that a *universitas* is a *nomen iuris*, a distinct legal entity.[118]

Explaining the nature of this entity, Bartolus begins by considering the position of those who ask 'whether a *universitas* is anything other than its members, and who say that it is not'.[119] He concedes that, 'if we are speaking truly, properly and according to what really exists, then what these people say is true, for a university of scholars is nothing other than the scholars themselves'.[120] However, he goes on, 'according to a fiction of the law, what these people say is not true, because a university

---

[114] Cino da Pistoia 1493, rubric *De episcopis et cleris*, gloss *Orphanotrophos*, sig. B, 3r: 'non imputat eis, & tunc non repetet ab eis sed repetet ab ipso hospitali, quod est persona representata'.

[115] On this early orthodoxy see Canning 1982, p. 23.

[116] Bartolus 1588c, rubric *De collegiis illicitis*, gloss *Non licet*, p. 407: 'ista opinio non est vera. Nam quod est universitatis, non est singulorum: quoniam universitas est persona representata per se'.

[117] Bartolus 1588c, pp. 549–69. On this passage see Maiolo 2007, pp. 246–8.

[118] Bartolus 1588c, rubric *De poenis*, gloss *Nonnunquam*, p. 560.

[119] Bartolus 1588c, rubric *De poenis*, gloss *Nonnunquam*, p. 560: 'an universitas sit aliud quam homines universitatis [et] dicunt, quod non'.

[120] Bartolus 1588c, rubric *De poenis*, gloss *Nonnunquam*, p. 560: 'si quidem loquamur realiter vere & proprie, ipsi dicunt verum. Nam nil aliud universitas scholarium, quam scholares'.

represents a single person, and this person is something other than the scholars or men of the university'.[121] We can see why this must be so as soon as we reflect that 'even if all the scholars leave and are replaced by others, the university remains the same, just as when all those who make up a people die and are substituted by others, it remains the same people'.[122] Bartolus concludes that 'in the same way, according to a fiction of law, any *universitas* or corporation is something other than the persons who make up the corporation, because it is a type of *persona repraesentata*, a person represented by others'.[123]

Most significantly, we find the jurists speaking in the same terms about the independent *civitates* of Italy. Alberto de Gandino (1245–1310) already treats the *civitas* as a *persona repraesentata* in his *Quaestiones Statutorum*. He begins by declaring that 'the first point to be established is who can make statutes', and he responds by saying that 'it is the *civitas* itself that makes statutes'.[124] His next question is 'by what means should a *civitas* make statutes',[125] and here he replies that 'public officials are able to make statutes in the name of the *universitas* as a whole'.[126] Alberico de Rosate (*c.*1290–*c.*1355)[127] in his *Commentarii* on the *Digest* is even more explicit in declaring that 'in those who act as administrators of a municipality, the municipality itself is represented'.[128] He also maintains that, because 'the *rectores* of *civitates* are able to act, to convene meetings and to pass judgments in the cause of their *civitates*',[129] we may say that a magistrate 'who governs and administers a *civitas* acts as the representative of the *civitas*', so that his judgments as well as his powers are those of the *civitas* itself.[130]

---

[121] Bartolus 1588c, rubric *De poenis*, gloss *Nonnunquam*, p. 560: 'secundum fictionem iuris ipsi non dicunt verum. Nam universitas repraesentat unam personam, quae est aliud a scholaribus, seu ab hominibus universitatis'.

[122] Bartolus 1588c, rubric *De poenis*, gloss *Nonnunquam*, p. 560: 'recedentibus omnibus istis scholaribus, & aliis redeuntibus, eadem tamen universitas est. Item mortuis omnibus de populo, & aliis subrogatis, idem est populus'.

[123] Bartolus 1588c, rubric *De poenis*, gloss *Nonnunquam*, p. 560: 'sic aliud est universitas quam personae quae faciunt universitatem secundum iuris fictione: quia est quaedam persona repraesentata'.

[124] Alberto de Gandino 1891, p. 157: 'Primo qui statuta facere possunt videndum est, et dic quod civitas'.

[125] Alberto de Gandino 1891, p. 157: 'qualiter statutum debet facere civitas'.

[126] Alberto de Gandino 1891, p. 157: 'decuriones statuta facere possunt ... universitatis nomine'.

[127] On Alberico see Schaede 2004, pp. 197–8.

[128] Alberico de Rosate 1586, Lex XCVI, gloss *Municipibus*, para. 1: 'in administratoribus municipii representatur ipsum municipium.'

[129] Alberico de Rosate 1586, Lex XCVI, gloss *Municipibus*, para. 2: 'rectores civitatum possunt agere, & conveniri, & iurare in causa civitatum'.

[130] Alberico de Rosate 1586, Lex XCVI, gloss *Municipibus*, para. 3: 'magistratus repraesentat civitatem quam regit, & administrat'.

Bartolus takes up the same argument much more systematically in his commentaries on the *Digest* and his *Tractatus de regimine civitatis*.[131] A *civitas*, he lays down, is a species of *universitas*,[132] so that 'a *civitas* as a whole is *una persona*', a single legal person.[133] This *persona representata* is the name of the authority that makes statutes,[134] inflicts penalties[135] and serves as judge of appeals,[136] and is consequently the name of the holder of *merum imperium*, supreme political power.[137] For Bartolus the most important examples of such sovereign *civitates* are the Italian city-republics. As he observes in his gloss on the rubric *De publicis iudiciis* in the *Digest*, 'today every *civitas* in Italy, and especially in Tuscany, refuses to recognise any holder of dominion over it, and each city possesses *merum imperium* in itself'.[138] More generally, it may be said 'of all *civitates* that recognise no superior power over them in temporal affairs that they possess *imperium* in themselves', and consequently count as independent sovereign states.[139]

As we have seen, Bartolus concedes that, as a species of *universitas*, a *civitas* is nothing more than a *nomen iuris*, a purely legal entity.[140] If a *civitas* is to exercise political power, some person or group must be assigned authority to act in its name, and in the case of the Italian city-republics this right is possessed either by the people as a whole, or else by those whom they have elected as *rectores* to represent them. Bartolus underlines the point when glossing the rubric *Ne quid in loco sacro* in the *Digest*. Any instance in which the people of a *civitas* 'is a free people, subject to no one, there the people is the ruler of that city', and may legislate according to its own will.[141] Later he confirms in his gloss on the

---

[131] On the *Tractatus* see Blythe 1992, pp. 171–7; Maiolo 2007, pp. 267–84.

[132] See, for example, Bartolus 1588b, rubric *De damno infecto*, gloss *Cum res*, p. 69 on the type of universitas 'quae consistit civitatem'.

[133] Bartolus 1588d, p. 418: 'tota civitas est una persona'.

[134] See Bartolus 1588a, rubric *De minoribus*, gloss *Denique*, p. 430 on the right of *civitates* to make statutes.

[135] See, for example, Bartolus 1588c, rubric *De poenis*, gloss *Relegati*, pp. 551–2 on the right of *civitates* to inflict the penalty of exile.

[136] See Bartolus 1588c, rubric *De appellationibus*, gloss *Si quis*, p. 580 on the right of a *civitas* to be *iudex appellationis*.

[137] See Bartolus 1588c, rubric *De publicis iudiciis*, gloss *si publico*, p. 423: 'quaelibet civitas . . . habet merum Imperium in seipsa'. See also Bartolus 1588c, rubric *De decretis*, gloss *Ambitiosa*, p. 669: '[civitates] . . . in se habent imperium'.

[138] Bartolus 1588c, rubric *De publicis iudiciis*, gloss *si publico*, p. 423: 'quaelibet civitas Italiae hodie, & praecipue in Tuscia, dominum non recognoscat, . . . & habet merum imperium in seipsa'.

[139] Bartolus 1588c, rubric *De decretis*, gloss *Ambitiosa*, p. 669: 'in illis civitatibus, quae de facto in temporalibus non recognoscunt superiorem, . . . in se habent imperium'.

[140] Bartolus 1588c, rubric *De poenis*, gloss *Nonnunquam*, p. 560.

[141] Bartolus 1588b, rubric *Ne quid in loco sacro*, gloss *In muris*, p. 431: 'est populus liber, nemini subditus: ideo hoc populus est princeps in hac civitate'.

rubric *De damno infecto* that 'all *rectores* in Italy nowadays exercise *merum imperium*' in temporal affairs.[142]

What is vital to Bartolus, however, is that when the people or their *rectores* enact and impose laws, they do so in the name of the *civitas* itself.[143] It is the *civitas* that must be regarded as *sibi princeps*, as its own ruler, and hence as the site of sovereign power.[144] This is Bartolus's final response to those who say of judges in the cities of the *Regnum Italicum* that there are some issues on which they are not competent to deliver verdicts, because 'a mere judge cannot do so, but only a *Princeps* and no one else'.[145] The making of such judgments, Bartolus retorts, is certainly possible 'in the case of the cities of Italy, because these cities are *Principes* unto themselves'.[146] As he later confirms in his *Tractatus*, what needs to be understood in the case of the *rectores* of independent cities is that 'regalian' rights – the most important being the right to legislate[147] – 'do not belong to them, but rather to the *civitates* over which they rule'.[148]

By this stage these assumptions were beginning to be reflected in the political art and architecture in which the Italian city-republics liked to celebrate the values of their public life.[149] When Filippo Calendario ornamented the Piazzetta façade of the Venetian Palazzo Ducale in the mid-fourteenth century, one of the medallions he carved showed the *persona civitatis* as the bearer of supreme power.[150] We see a crowned woman in classical robes, behind whose head is incised the word VENECIA (Figure 2.1). She sits on a throne of judgment, flanked by the lions of St Mark, and dominates the waves beneath her feet. She brandishes a sword in her right hand, thereby conveying that the *civitas* itself is the possessor of the *ius gladii* and is consequently the wielder of

---

[142] See Bartolus 1588b, rubric *De damno infecto*, gloss *Cum res*, p. 69 on *merum imperium* and on how 'omnes rectores ... hodie per Italiam exercent'.

[143] As Ryan 2000, p. 83 puts it, 'the city taken as an abstraction' is held to be 'its own superior'.

[144] Bartolus 1588a, rubric *De minoribus*, gloss *Denique*, p. 430: 'civitas sibi princeps est'; Bartolus 1588c, rubric *De appellationibus*, gloss *Si quis*, p. 580: 'civitas, quae non recognoscit superiorem ... sibi Princeps est'.

[145] Bartolus 1588c, rubric *De poenis*, gloss *Relegati*, p. 552: 'non potest dare iudex ... sed solus Princeps potest, & non alius.'

[146] Bartolus 1588c, rubric *De poenis*, gloss *Relegati*, p. 552: 'in istis civitatibus Italiae, quia ipsae sunt principes sibi ipsis'.

[147] On 'regalian' rights see Woolf 1913, pp. 132–4. These were originally itemised in the *Constitutio de Regalibus* promulgated by the Emperor Frederick I at the Diet of Roncaglia in 1158.

[148] See Bartolus 1588d, p. 418 on 'rectores civitatum', of whom it is said that 'nec ad eos competunt regalia, sed ad civitates quas regunt.'

[149] On 'art as politics' in Siena see Smith and Steinhoff 2012.

[150] For this date and ascription see Wolters 1976, vol. 1, pp. 46, 178–9. Wolters also claims (vol. 1, p. 47) that this is the earliest surviving personification of the city of Venice. He identified the two figures subdued by the lions as Anger and Pride.

Figure 2.1 Calendario, Filippo (*c*.1350). 'Venecia', Palazzo Ducale, Venice.

imperium or *summa potestas* over Venice. The cartouche above her left arm confirms her sovereignty as well as her power, proclaiming that 'just and courageous on my throne, I keep the furious sea beneath my foot'.[151] The ruler of the *civitas* is shown to be the *civitas* itself.

The same period saw the creation of a more complex image of the *civitas* as a *persona repraesentata* in Ambrogio Lorenzetti's fresco-cycle in the Sala dei Nove of the Palazzo Pubblico in Siena. The room was

[151] 'Fortis iusta trono furias mare sub pede pono.'

Figure 2.2 Lorenzetti, Ambrogio (1337–9). Fresco on northern wall, Sala dei Nove, Palazzo Pubblico, Siena.

designed as the Council chamber for the *Nove Signori*, the merchant oligarchy who governed Siena between 1287 and 1355.[152] The northern wall presents a tableau of virtuous government in which two enthroned figures occupy a dominant place (Figure 2.2). The one on the left is recognisable as Justice. She holds a pair of scales, and the *titulus* around her head quotes the opening words of the Book of Wisdom in which rulers are enjoined to love justice[153] – a passage frequently cited, as we have seen, by the writers of advice-books for magistrates. The larger enthroned male figure on the right is more enigmatic, and his identity has been the subject of much debate, but he appears to carry a dual significance (Figure 2.3).[154] On the one hand he is associated with the symbols of magistracy. He is seated on a throne of judgment, and he wears a jewel-encrusted robe of an almost imperial kind. He is holding a sceptre in his right hand, an insignium of supreme authority, while in his left he carries a shield with which to defend his people. But in spite of his regal appearance he is not a holder of absolute power. His authority is not kingly – he does not wear a crown – and he is shown to have no discretion in the execution of justice. He looks directly ahead, inclining (as Latini had demanded) 'neither to right nor to left', a sign of his incapacity to bend the rule of law.[155] He is also shown (as Giovanni da Viterbo had required) to be

---

[152] On the Nove Signori see Bowsky 1981.

[153] The titulus reads 'DILIGITE (IUSTITIA)M Q(UI) IUDICATIS TE(RR)AM'.

[154] For the fullest recent discussions see Skinner 2002a, pp. 39–117 and Boucheron 2013.

[155] Latini 1948, p. 392: 'ne a diestre ne a senestre'.

Figure 2.3 Lorenzetti, Ambrogio (1337–9). Right-hand section of fresco on northern wall, Sala dei Nove, Palazzo Pubblico, Siena.

'tied' by the dictates of justice.[156] The double rope of concord originating in the hands of Justice is knotted around his right wrist, preventing him from wielding his sceptre with an untied hand. Above his head float the three 'theological' virtues of faith, hope and charity, and he is surrounded by five political virtues in the company of peace. Accompanied as he is by a total of nine virtuous qualities, he appears to offer a symbolic representation of the *Nove Signori*, the body of nine elected *rectores* of Siena.

At the same time, however, the regal figure offers a symbolic representation of the *civitas* itself. Around his shoulders are displayed the letters C.S.C.V.[157] The initials are those of the *Commune Senarum, Civitas Virginis*, the commune of Siena, the *civitas* whose patron was and is the Virgin Mary.[158] He is dressed in black and white, then as now the heraldic colours of the Sienese commune. At his feet a she-wolf suckles a pair of twins, a reminder of the ancient Roman republic whose insignia the Sienese had adopted in 1297.[159] On his shield can still be faintly discerned an image of the Virgin Mary, originally chosen by the Sienese as their special patron in 1260.[160] Perhaps most significantly, the regal figure is portrayed as grey-bearded, white-haired and thus as *persona*

[156] See Giovanni da Viterbo 1901, p. 235 on rectores as 'legibus alligatum'.
[157] The inscription now reads C.S.C.C.V. But the second 'C' is a later interpolation. See Skinner 2002a, pp. 78–9 and n.
[158] On Siena as the city of the Virgin see Bowsky 1981, pp. 160, 288.
[159] Larner 1971, p. 113; cf. Southard 1978, pp. 47, 66.
[160] Southard 1978, p. 48; Bowsky 1981, pp. 274–5.

sena – as an old person, but at the same time as Sena, the Latin name for Siena.[161]

Putting these two iconographical schemes together, we arrive at the main political message of the tableau as a whole. We are being invited to acknowledge that justice will be enthroned, and peace will be established at the heart of civic life, if and only if the *civitas* is governed by *rectores* or *signori* of whom it may be said that they represent or bear the person of the *civitas* itself. Whereas Calendario's statue of Venecia offers an icon of the *persona civitatis* as the holder of supreme power, Lorenzetti provides an even more explicitly Ciceronian image. He illustrates the type of virtuous magistracy that may be said to represent the *civitas*, exercising its powers for the good of all by acting in its name.

IV

By the middle of the fourteenth century, the legal and political writers I have been considering had arrived at a distinctive view about the location of *imperium* or *summa potestas*. They take as their starting-point the postulate that there exists a separate realm of legal entities which includes all forms of *universitates* and hence encompasses *civitates* or states. They concede that the incorporeal persons of *civitates* are incapable of acting on their own behalf, but they nevertheless insist that they are capable of speech and action, and of such a kind as to mark them out as the owners of sovereign power. This is because, like any other type of *universitas*, a *civitas* or state may be regarded as a *persona repraesentata*, a person susceptible of being represented by an appointed rector or magistracy. Provided that such representatives have authority to bear the *persona* of the state, their actions will count as those of the state itself. The state is consequently able to act through the medium of its representatives, and can thus be identified as the 'subject' or owner of the powers exercised in its name.

While this analysis eventually became fundamental to the modern theory of state sovereignty, it was never the dominant mode of thinking about *imperium* and *potestas* in medieval Italian legal and political thought. The basic aspiration of the writers I have been discussing was to vindicate the standing of the Italian city-republics as independent communities governing themselves through elected magistracies. But technically these *civitates* were fiefs of the Holy Roman Empire, which at first attempted in a series of military campaigns to bring the cities back under control. These attempts were largely abandoned by the beginning

---

[161] Southard 1978, p. 60.

of the thirteenth century, but for a long time afterwards it remained one of the ideological projects of the Italian Law Schools to defend the over-arching legal right of the Empire to exercise *imperium* and *potestas* over the *Regnum Italicum* as a whole.[162]

The way in which this project was realised was chiefly through glossing the so-called *Lex regia* or 'regal law' cited by Ulpian in Book I of the *Digest*.[163] This alleged enactment was an invention of later Roman jurists designed to explain how the emperors originally acquired *imperium* from the Roman people. According to Ulpian's formulation 'what pleases the emperor has the force of law: this is because, by the *lex regia*, which has been enacted about his *imperium*, the people confer upon him, and to him, all their *imperium* and *potestas*.'[164]

The question raised by the Glossators was how this act of conferment should be understood. Irnerius was the first to put forward what became the orthodox answer, and his interpretation was subsequently taken up by Rogerius, Placentinus and most influentially by Lothair of Cremona in his debate with Azo Portius in the presence of the emperor Henry VI at the end of the twelfth century.[165] Azo (*c.*1150–1230) provides an account of the debate in his *Lectura super codicem* in which he begins with Lothair's statement of the case. According to Lothair 'the Roman people no longer possess the *potestas* to make laws they originally possessed',[166] the reason being that 'by the *lex regia* the *populus* trans-ferred to the emperor every right they possessed.'[167] Not surprisingly, this was the verdict favoured by Henry VI himself, and it was subse-quently reaffirmed by many Glossators and Commentators, most weigh-tily by Bartolus's pupil Baldus de Ubaldis at the end of the fourteenth century.[168] But Azo denies it outright. He never asserts, however, that *potestas* in the case of the *civitates* of the *Regnum Italicum* may be said to be the property of the *civitates* themselves. Rather he assigns perpetual

---

[162] Pennington 1993, pp. 8–37; Ryan 2000, pp. 66–71.

[163] On the *Lex regia* see Lee 2016, pp. 25–39.

[164] *The Digest* 1985, I. 4. 1, vol. 1, p. 14: 'Quod principi placuit, legis habet vigorem: utpote cum lege regia, quae de imperio eius lata est, populus ei et in eum omne suum imperium et potestatem conferat.'

[165] On their encounter see Lee 2016, pp. 86–90. For the views of Irnerius, Placentinus and Rogerius on the *Lex regia* see Carlyle 1932, pp. 59–63.

[166] Azo 1966b, I. XIV. 11, p. 44: 'populus Romanus non habet potestatem legis condendae, quod olim habebat'. This echoes the judgment of Placentinus, who had claimed that the populus 'reserved no power to itself' – 'nullam [potestatem] sibi reservavit'. See Carlyle 1932, p. 61n.

[167] Azo 1966b, I. XIV. 11, p. 44: 'lege regia in eum transtulit populus omne ius quod habebat'. This repeats the judgment of Rogerius, who had claimed that the populus transferred (transtulit) their power. See Carlyle 1932, p. 61n.

[168] Canning 1987, pp. 55–64.

potestas to legislate and wield the sword of justice to the *totus populus*, the body of the people as a whole.

Azo arrives at this conclusion by way of reinterpreting the act of conferment described in the *Lex regia*. 'My own view', he writes in his *Lectura*, 'is that the people never transferred this power except in such a way that they were at the same time able to retain it.'[169] He explains his reasoning in the course of glossing the rubric *De legibus* at the start of his *Summa super codicem*. 'When it is said that the *potestas* of the people was transferred, this means that it was conceded, not that the *populus* entirely abdicated it.'[170] This interpretation is confirmed by the fact that, at more than one juncture in Roman history, 'even after they had transferred their *potestas*, the people were nevertheless able to revoke the transfer at a subsequent stage'.[171] Later in the *Lectura*, glossing the rubric *Longa consuetudo*, Azo adds a corollary destined to be endlessly discussed. 'From this it follows that, although the emperor possesses greater *potestas* than any individual member of the people, he does not possess greater *potestas* than the *totus populus*, the people as a whole'.[172]

We later encounter a no less emphatic commitment to the ideal of popular sovereignty among those who defended the autonomy of the Italian city-republics in Aristotelian rather than in strictly legal terms.[173] By far the most important of these writers was Marsilius of Padua (1275–1342) in his *Defensor pacis* of 1324.[174] Analysing the concept of the Legislator in Book I chapter 12, Marsilius lays it down that the authority to make laws can only be held by those who possess the power to enforce obedience. He then affirms that 'this *potestas* to compel the observation of the laws, which takes the form of a coercive force over transgressors, can only be that of the universal body of the people',[175] although the same power can equally well (and perhaps more effectively) be exercised 'by the prevailing part of the people acting as representatives of the whole'.[176] From these premises Marsilius deduces a theory of popular sovereignty. 'It follows', he concludes, 'that the authority to

---

[169] Azo 1966b, I. XIV. 11, p. 44: 'dic quod non transtulit ita quin sibi retineret.'

[170] Azo 1966a, I. 14, p. 9: 'potestas ... dicitur enim translata id est concessa, non quod populus omnino a se abdicaverit.'

[171] Azo 1966a, I. 14, p. 9: 'nam et olim transtulerat, sed tamen postea revocavit.'

[172] Azo 1966b, VIII. LIII. 2, p. 671: 'unde non est maior potestatis imperator quam totus populus, sed quam quilibet de populo'.

[173] On this theme see Ferente 2016.

[174] I translate from Marsilius 1928, but I am indebted to Brett's translation in Marsilius 2005.

[175] Marsilius 1928, I. XII. 6, p. 52: 'potestas observationis legum, cuius tantummodo est potentia transgressorum coactiva; hoc autem est universitas.'

[176] Marsilius 1928, I. XII. 5, p. 50: 'aut eius valentior pars, quae totam universitatem repraesentat'.

make laws can only be that of the universal body of the people or its prevailing part.'[177]

This sovereign body is described in two different ways, although Marsilius treats them as interchangeable. When he ascribes *potestas* to the people, he sometimes equates the *populus* with the *universa multitudo*, the entire multitude.[178] Generally, however, he prefers to equate the *populus* with the *universitas civium*, the corporate body of the citizens.[179] The rival contention that *potestas* ought instead to be seen as a property of the *persona civitatis* – the contention that Bartolus, Alberico de Rosate and other Commentators were putting forward at the same time – is entertained by Marsilius at no point. Although he once refers – quoting Aristotle – to the concept of the *civitas*, which he defines as a community of free people, he never ascribes any powers to such *civitates* themselves.[180] And although he speaks of the representation of the *populus* by its *valentior pars*, he has no conception of the *civitas* as a *persona repraesentata* that might be capable of exercising *potestas* by way of being represented by *rectores* authorised to speak and act in its name.

While Marsilius speaks in a neo-Aristotelian idiom, it is remarkable how far the debate between the exponents of monarchical absolutism and popular sovereignty continued to be mounted throughout the early-modern period in the terms originally set by Azo and Lothair. The violent arguments between the monarchists and their Huguenot adversaries in the French religious wars were largely conducted in the same vocabulary, with the Huguenots restating Azo's claims about the inalienability of the people's power. The most influential of these treatises, the *Vindiciae, contra tyrannos* of 1579, argues that *legitima potestas* is naturally and originally possessed by the *populus universus*, who hold it in the form of *dominium*, and are thus the lords and proprietors of sovereign power.[181] The concept of the *civitas* is never invoked at any point; as the title of the book makes clear, the question is entirely about the relative powers of the *princeps* and the *populus*.[182] When the *populus* consents to be governed, the covenant they make with their ruler is conditional on his performance of the fundamental duty of kingship, that of ruling justly and for the benefit of all.[183] The agreement consequently takes the form – and

---

[177] Marsilius 1928, I. XII. 6, p. 52: 'Ergo ipsius [sc. 'universitas aut ipsius valentior pars'] solius est legum lationis auctoritas'.
[178] Marsilius 1928, I. XII. 5, pp. 50–1; I. XII. 6, p. 52.
[179] Marsilius 1928, I. XII. 3, p. 49; I. XII. 5, pp. 50–1; I. XII. 6–8, pp. 52–3.
[180] Marsilius 1928, I. XII. 6, p. 52: 'civitas est communitas liberorum'.
[181] *Vindiciae* 1579, pp. 85–6, 89; cf. *Vindiciae* 1994, pp. 74–5, 77–8.
[182] *Vindiciae* 1579, title-page; cf. *Vindiciae* 1994, p. 3.
[183] *Vindiciae* 1579, pp. 108, 113; cf. *Vindiciae* 1994, pp. 93, 95.

here the *Lex regia* is cited[184] – of a *concessio*, and specifically an act of entrustment of the people's *dominium*, which they can revoke at any time.[185] The people are inferior in power to the king as individuals (*singuli inferiores*) but as a *universitas* or corporate body they are superior (*universi superiores*), so that the king is a mere *minister* or servant of the commonwealth.[186]

The protagonists of absolute monarchy retorted by reviving the argument to which Azo had originally replied. The most systematic of these responses was produced by William Barclay (1546–1608), who coined the term 'monarchomachs' or 'king-wounders' in his *De regno et regali potestate* of 1600, in which Books III and IV directly target the *Vindiciae*.[187] Barclay begins by conceding that, while 'Monarchy is the best form of *imperium*', kings 'are not given immediately by God',[188] so that 'the people are able to constitute their King'.[189] But 'once a king has been accepted and inaugurated, no element of right is left to the people'.[190] Here Barclay rests his case almost entirely on the *Lex regia* as formulated by Ulpian ('most estimable of men').[191] He quotes Ulpian's contention that the *populus* 'transferred all their *imperium* and *potestas*' to the emperor,[192] arguing that they must be understood to have committed, granted and made tribute of it[193] so as to make God alone the superior of the king.[194] Although kings may initially have been constituted by the people, 'any King is superior to the *universus populus*, the whole corporate body of the people, and not merely superior to each one of his individual subjects'.[195]

The same distinctions continue to underpin much of the debate between the protagonists of Crown and Parliament at the outbreak of the English civil wars. Henry Parker, the leading theorist of the parliamentarian cause, yet again restates Azo's case, closely following the formulation given to it by the author of the *Vindiciae, contra tyrannos*.

---

[184] *Vindiciae* 1579, pp. 161–2; cf. *Vindiciae* 1994, pp. 131–2. Lee 2016, p. 149 is thus mistaken in saying that 'the Monarchomachs remarkably avoided using the Roman *Lex regia* in their analysis of popular sovereignty'.

[185] *Vindiciae* 1579, pp. 162, 197, 206–7; cf. *Vindiciae* 1994, pp. 132, 159, 167.

[186] *Vindiciae* 1579, pp. 48, 89, 107; cf. *Vindiciae* 1994, pp. 47, 78, 92.

[187] Barclay 1600, pp. 105–338.

[188] Barclay 1600, 2. 2, p. 110: 'Monarchia optimum imperii genus . . . [sed] Reges non dari a Deo immediate'.

[189] Barclay 1600, 2. 2, pp. 114: 'populus constituere Regem potest'.

[190] Barclay 1600, 2. 2, p. 114: 'post acceptum & inauguratum Regem, populo . . . iuris nihil est reliqui'.

[191] See Barclay 1600, 2. 4, p. 125 on Ulpian as 'vir optimus'.

[192] Barclay 1600, 2. 4, p. 127: 'populus . . . omne suum imperium & potestatem conferat'.

[193] Barclay 1600, 2. 4, pp. 124–5: 'populus . . . commisit . . . dedidit . . . Regi tributum fuit'.

[194] Barclay 1600, 2. 4, p. 131: 'Rex ergo, cum Deum solum superiorem habet'.

[195] Barclay 1600, 2. 4, p. 127: 'Regem universo populo superiorem esse . . . & non solum singulos'.

Parker opens his *Observations* of 1642 by declaring that political power 'is originally inherent in the people' as a 'politique corporation', who hold it in the form of dominion and are thus the owners of everything. The people agree to 'derive' this power into the hands of their rulers, authorising them to act for the good of all. But the contract between king and people is such that the people never donate but merely entrust the use of their dominion, and in doing so 'may ordaine what conditions, and prefix what bounds' they choose. As a result, 'we see that power is but secondary and derivative in Princes'. Although any king is *singulis maior*, greater in power than his individual subjects, he is always *universis minor*, lesser in power than the body of the people as a whole.[196]

Among the many royalists who responded to Parker, the most tenacious was Hobbes's future antagonist John Bramhall in his *Serpent Salve* of 1643, in which Bramhall recycles yet again the substance of Lothair's case against Azo.[197] Suppose we admit 'that Power is originally inherent in the People', who voluntarily submit to the rule of kings. They may nevertheless resolve to 'divest' themselves of their power and set up an absolute and perpetual form of sovereignty.[198] This is what happened in the case of the English monarchy, with the result that the king is 'a true Possessor of Soveraigne Power'.[199] He was granted not 'a conditionall donation from the People' but absolute sovereignty in the form of 'a trust irrecoverable'.[200] As for Parker's conclusion that the king is of lesser standing than the body of the people, Bramhall retorts that the alienation of right involved in the political covenant means that 'not onely individuall Persons, but the whole compacted Body Politicke of the Kingdome, are not onely lesse then His Majesty, but doe owe unto him a naturall and humble obedience'.[201]

Like the Commentators who spoke of the *civitas* as a *persona*, a number of these writers refer to the concept of legal personality. Baldus explains how 'a corporate person can be understood as a single person, although it may consist of many bodies',[202] while the author of the *Vindiciae* observes that 'a *universitas* of men may be said to play the role of one person'.[203] The same usage recurs in the leading monarchomach writer of the next generation, Johannes Althusius,[204] as well as in the works of his immediate successors, notably Johann Werdenhagen in his *Politica Generalis* of

---

[196] [Parker] 1642, pp. 1–2.   [197] On Bramhall see Daly 1971; Smith 1994, pp. 220–3.
[198] Bramhall 1643, p. 14.   [199] Bramhall 1643, p. 21.   [200] Bramhall 1643, pp. 43–4.
[201] Bramhall 1643, p. 21.
[202] See Canning 1987, p. 265: 'persona universalis que unius persona intellectum habet, tamen ex multis corporibus constat'.
[203] *Vindiciae* 1579, p. 37: 'universitas enim hominum unius personae vicem sustinet'. Cf. *Vindiciae* 1994, p. 38.
[204] See, for example, Althusius 1932, ch. 18, p. 140.

1632.[205] But the legal person to whom these theorists refer is never the *persona civitatis*, the person of the state; it is always the *persona populi*, the person constituted by the body of the people.[206] Baldus's example of 'a corporate person that can be understood to be a single person' is the *populus*;[207] Althusius speaks of how *rectores* can bear the *persona* of the *populus universus*;[208] and Werdenhagen notes 'that the term *persona* can be applied not merely to a single man but to the whole *populus*'.[209] None of these writers, in other words, is a theorist of state sovereignty. The question they address is never about the powers of the *civitas*, but always about the disposition of power between *populus* and *princeps*, the people and the prince.

V

It was into this long-standing debate that Thomas Hobbes stepped with his first work of political theory, *The Elements of Law*, which he circulated in manuscript in the spring of 1640. Hobbes's epoch-making contribution takes the form of the claim that the entire terms of the debate need to be reconsidered. He feels beset, as he later tells us in *Leviathan*, by two rival but equally unsatisfactory arguments about the location of sovereign power, one of which is calling for 'too great Liberty' while the other is calling for 'too much Authority'.[210] His aim is to pass between the swords of the two sides unwounded, and his means of doing so is to ground his political theory on the Ciceronian and jurisprudential strands of thinking about the *persona civitatis* I have sketched. He already makes this aspiration clear in *The Elements*, in which he observes that 'though in the charters of subordinate corporations, a corporation be declared to be one person in law, yet the same hath not been taken notice of in the body of a commonwealth or city, nor have any of those innumerable writers of politics observed any such union'.[211] As this crucial passage indicates, it is the person of the *civitas* that Hobbes wishes us to recognise not merely as 'one person in law' but as the seat of power.

[205] Werdenhagen 1632, II. 6.
[206] It is thus misleading to associate these discussions of legal personality with Hobbes, as I did in Skinner 2002a, pp. 389–92. Cf. also Santi 2012, pp. 33–6.
[207] See Canning 1987, p. 265: 'persona universalis que unius persona intellectum habet . . . ut populus'.
[208] Althusius 1932, ch. 18, p. 140: 'rectores . . . universum populum . . . personam gerunt'. Althusius speaks of the representation of the *populus universus*, not of the *universitas* of the *civitas*. But for a different interpretation see Hoekstra 2013b, pp. 1086–7.
[209] Werdenhagen 1632, II. VI. 23, p. 131: 'Non tantum uni homini, sed etiam toti populi applicatur'.
[210] Hobbes 2012, vol. 2, Epistle, p. [4].   [211] Hobbes 1969, 27. 7, p. 174.

Hobbes's claims about the originality of his approach are admittedly somewhat exaggerated. As I have shown, the contention that sovereign power should be regarded as the defining attribute of the state had already been articulated by a number of Commentators on Roman law. Hobbes is clearly aware of this tradition of thought, and he may even have been directly indebted to Bartolus's formulation of the case in his *Tractatus de regimine civitatis*. There Bartolus had argued that 'Art or artifice is better to the extent that nature is imitated',[212] and that the *civitas* imitates the nature of man, so that the state can be described as 'a single artificial man', *homo artificialis*.[213] Hobbes likewise speaks in the Introduction to *Leviathan* of art 'imitating that Rationall and most excellent worke of Nature, *Man*' by way of creating the STATE or CIVITAS, of which he too says that it is 'but an Artificiall Man', *Homo artificialis*.[214] Bartolus's fundamental assertion about the character of this artificial man had been that 'the whole state is one person', *una persona*,[215] and more specifically that the state takes the form of a *persona repraesentata* capable of acting through the agency of those who represent it. Hobbes too speaks in *Leviathan* of the commonwealth or state as '*One Person*' – '*Civitas Persona una est*',[216] and in the Latin version of his text he classifies the sovereign as a *Persona Representativa*, a representative who acts in the name of a *persona repraesentata*, someone who is thereby represented.[217]

Nor was Hobbes the first political theorist to revert to this earlier strand of legal thinking about the *civitas* as the basic 'subject' of supreme power. A similar move had already been made by a number of writers who, like Hobbes, felt the need to reappraise the terms of the increasingly bloodstained quarrel between the protagonists of monarchical absolutism and popular sovereignty. Among these writers, by far the most influential was Hugo Grotius, who fell victim to the quarrel in his native Netherlands and went into exile in France – like Hobbes a generation later – to escape the threat of death at home. When Grotius turns in Book I of his *De iure belli ac pacis* of 1625 to explicate the concept of *imperium* or *summa potestas*,[218] he dismisses out of hand any suggestion that sovereignty is an inalienable

---

[212] Bartolus 1588d, p. 418: 'Ars seu artificium tanto est melius, quanto magis imitatur naturam'.

[213] Bartolus 1588d, p. 418: 'tota civitas est ... unus homo artificialis'.

[214] Hobbes 2012, vol. 2, The Introduction, p. 16; for 'Homo artificialis' see p. 17.

[215] Bartolus 1588d, p. 418: 'tota civitas est una persona'.

[216] Hobbes 2012, vol. 2, ch. 17, p. 260; for '*Civitas Persona una est*' see p. 261.

[217] Hobbes 2012, vol. 2, ch. 16, p. 245.

[218] Grotius 1625, I. III, p. 53 is headed *Summi imperii explicatio*, which is translated in Grotius 2005, I. III, p. 240 as 'An Explication of the supreme power'. Grotius occasionally speaks in his ensuing discussion of *imperium*. See, for example, Grotius 1625, I. III, p. 67. But he usually speaks of *summa potestas*. See, for example, Grotius 1625, I. III, pp. 65, 67, 74.

property of the body of the people. He notes the damage already inflicted by this mistaken belief, which involves a failure to recognise that any free people can always decide 'to deliver up themselves to any one or more Persons, and transfer the Right of governing them upon him or them, without reserving any Share of that right to themselves'.[219] He is scarcely any more satisfied, however, with the rival contention that we ought instead to regard our rulers as absolute owners of *summa potestas*. What these absolutists fail to acknowledge, he argues, is that 'the Generality of Sovereigns are not Masters of their States with a full Right of Property', but are often the holders of a mere right of use.[220]

Who, then, is the true possessor of *summa potestas* in a *civitas* or state? Grotius presents his answer in the form of an introduction to his critique of the two warring ideologies of his age. He distinguishes between the proper and common 'subjects' of sovereignty, concluding that 'the proper Subject is one or more Persons, according to the Laws and Customs' of the nation concerned.[221] But just as the body is the common subject of sight, while the eye is its proper subject,[222] so the common subject of sovereignty – in subordination to which the proper subject operates – is the *civitas* itself.[223] The outcome of Grotius's argument is thus that 'the common Subject of Supreme Power is the State'.[224]

Grotius's argument has sometimes been treated as the founding moment in the emergence of the modern theory of state personality.[225] There is no doubt that Hobbes was aware of Grotius's analysis,[226] and sometimes he closely echoes it.[227] Nevertheless, Hobbes remains largely justified in his assertion that, at least within the Anglophone tradition, he is the first political theorist to articulate a systematic theory of the sovereign state. This is the theory he presents most fully in chapters 16 and 17 of *Leviathan*, in which he lays out two principal arguments. First he offers an essentially Ciceronian analysis of political representation in response

---

[219] Grotius 2005, I. III, p. 261.

[220] Grotius 2005, I. III, p. 296; cf. p. 280 on the possession of merely usufructuary rights.

[221] Grotius 2005, I. III, p. 260.   [222] Grotius 2005, I. III, p. 259.

[223] See Brett 2002, pp. 45–51 on how Hobbes shares with Grotius the view that the *civitas* is the site of supreme power.

[224] Grotius 2005, I. III, p. 259. Cf. Grotius 1625, I. III, p. 67: 'summae potestati subiectum commune est civitas'.

[225] See, for example, Hofmann 1974, pp. 116–285; Friedeburg 2016, pp. 333–6. But these accounts seem to me to underestimate Grotius's debt to the earlier legal traditions I have discussed.

[226] The catalogue of the Hardwick library drawn up by Hobbes includes 'Grotius de Iure Belli ac Pacis'. See Hobbes MSS (Chatsworth), MS E. 1. A, p. 84.

[227] For a particularly striking echo, compare Hobbes 2012, vol. 2, ch. 18, p. 282 on how life is never 'without some incommodity' with Grotius 1625, I. III, p. 68 on 'nunquam incommodis'.

to the parliamentarian assertion that what must be 'virtually' represented is the sovereign body of the people. How Hobbes counters this argument provides me with my main theme in chapter 9. Then he applies his rival theory of representation to explain how it is possible for the person of the state to possess and exercise sovereignty. How he developed this case – thereby responding to the protagonists of monarchical as well as popular sovereignty – provides the theme of my concluding chapter, in which I seek to establish Hobbes's pivotal place in the evolution of the modern theory of the sovereign state.

3   Machiavelli on Misunderstanding Princely *Virtù*

I

There is a moment in George Eliot's fictional portrayal of Machiavelli in *Romola* when she imagines him responding to a criticism of his seemingly wicked beliefs. 'My doctrine', he is made to reply, 'is the doctrine of all men who seek an end a little farther off than their own noses.'[1] As Eliot implies, the question of how far the realisation of our purposes may require us to behave immorally is never far from Machiavelli's mind. This is particularly true in *The Prince*, in which he repeatedly scrutinises the relationship between the moral virtues and the powers by which – by virtue of which – political leaders can attain their highest goals.

To understand how Machiavelli thinks about this question, and hence about the concept of *virtù* in *The Prince*, we need to begin by considering his views about the goals that rulers should set themselves. The highest end to which they should aspire is that of doing great things that will bring them honour and praise, and eventually lead to glory and fame.[2] Chapter XXI of *The Prince* is devoted to considering 'What a prince should do in order to be thought outstanding'.[3] Machiavelli lays it down that 'above all else a prince should strive in all his actions to give himself the reputation of being a great man'.[4] By way of illustration he singles out Ferdinand of Aragon, who is said 'to have become, for fame and glory, the first king in Christendom'[5] in consequence of 'having always done and ordered great

This chapter is a revised version of Skinner 2017a. For permission to make use of this earlier work I am indebted to John Tryneski and the Chicago University Press. For commenting on drafts I am deeply grateful to Jérémie Barthas, Susan James, William Klein, Pete Stacey and James Tully.
[1] Eliot 1996, p. 495.
[2] On doing great things (*gran cose*) see Machiavelli 1995, XVI. 7, p. 106; XVI. 14, p. 107; XVIII. 1, p. 115. On glory in *The Prince* see Owen 2017.
[3] Machiavelli 1995, XXI. 1, p. 146: 'Quod principem deceat ut egregius habeatur'.
[4] Machiavelli 1995, XXI. 10, p. 149: 'soprattutto uno principe si debbe ingegnare dare di sé in ogni sua azione fama di uomo grande'.
[5] Machiavelli 1995, XXI. 2, p. 147: 'è diventato per fama e per gloria el primo re de' cristiani'. Machiavelli appears to be recording what was generally believed, but Benner 2014, p. 76 detects irony.

things'.[6] Machiavelli returns to the topic in the closing *Exhortatio* of *The Prince*, in which he optimistically concludes that there has never been a more propitious time in Italy 'for a prudent and *virtuoso* prince to introduce a new form of government that will bring honour to himself and good to the body of his subjects'.[7]

No ruler, however, can hope to tread the paths of glory unless he has first succeeded in achieving a more prosaic goal. To cite the formula that echoes through the central chapters of *The Prince*, he must manage *mantenere lo stato*, to maintain his status and standing as a prince, and at the same time to preserve the stability of the *stato* or state.[8] Machiavelli informs us in chapter IV that his chief concern is with 'the difficulties that princes have in managing to maintain a state when they have newly occupied it',[9] and he boasts in chapter XXIV that, if his advice is followed, 'this will enable a new prince to appear a well-established one', more firm and secure in his state.[10] As he explains in chapter XV, he is writing for anyone 'who wishes to maintain himself as a prince'.[11] The fundamental question is always what rulers should do 'in order to conquer and maintain the state'.[12]

The general precepts that Machiavelli goes on to offer are couched in negative terms. Rulers must first of all ensure that they do nothing to incur the hatred of the people.[13] Here he warns us that 'what above all makes a prince hated is being rapacious and a usurper of the property or womenfolk of his subjects'.[14] His other general rule is that rulers must avoid doing anything that may cause them to become despised.[15] Here he tells us that 'what makes a prince contemptible is if he is held to be changeable, light, effeminate, pusillanimous, irresolute'.[16] He adds in his most

---

[6] Machiavelli 1995, XXI. 7, p. 148: 'sempre ha fatte et ordite cose grandi'.

[7] Machiavelli 1995, XXVI. 1, p. 168: 'a uno prudente e virtuoso d'introdurvi forma che facessi onore a lui e bene alla università delli uomini di quella'.

[8] That Machiavelli speaks not merely about how to maintain one's status as a prince, but also about the apparatus of the state, is emphasised in Stacey 2013. Note that, although Machiavelli 1995, XX. 30, p. 145 numbers Caterina Sforza as a *principe* of his time, he normally uses the male pronoun when referring to *principi*, and in this I follow him.

[9] Machiavelli 1995, IV. 1, p. 24: 'le difficultà le quali s'hanno a tenere uno stato occupato di nuovo'.

[10] Machiavelli 1995, XXIV. 1, p. 159: 'fanno parere antico uno principe nuovo'.

[11] Machiavelli 1995, XV. 6, p. 103: 'volendosi uno principe mantenere'.

[12] See Machiavelli 1995, XVIII. 18, p. 119: 'per ... vincere e mantenere lo stato'. See also Machiavelli 1995, XIX. 37, p. 129 on how to act 'mantenere lo stato'.

[13] On the importance of avoiding *odio* see Machiavelli 1995, VII. 45, p. 53; XIX. 18, p. 124; XIX. 24, p. 126.

[14] Machiavelli 1995, XIX. 2, p. 120: 'Odioso soprattutto lo fa, ... essere rapace et usurpatore della roba e delle donne de' sudditi'.

[15] On the dangers of being *contennendo* see Machiavelli 1995, XIV. 4, p. 98; XVI. 11, p. 107; XXIII. 3, p. 156.

[16] Machiavelli 1995, XIX. 4, p. 120: 'Contennendo lo fa essere tenuto vario, leggeri, effeminato, pusillanime, irresoluto'.

minatory tone that 'a prince must guard himself against such conduct as from a reef, and ensure that all his actions exhibit greatness, spiritedness, weightiness and strength'.[17]

The danger that Machiavelli underlines is that, if you become either hated or despised, you will very soon lose your state and probably your life as well. He draws the moral at considerable length in chapter XIX, in which he surveys the fortunes of the Roman emperors between the time of Marcus Aurelius and Maximinus. Maximinus's predecessor Alexander was a good man, but he was held to be effeminate, became an object of contempt and was assassinated.[18] Alexander's predecessor Caracalla was a man of great talent, but his cruelty made him hateful to everyone and he was murdered by his own bodyguard.[19] Worst of all, Commodus and Maximinus were hated as well as despised, and both fell victim to successful conspiracies.[20]

Besides outlining the goals that rulers must set themselves, Machiavelli has much to say about the means by which these goals can be realised. He concedes that no one can establish and maintain a state without enjoying a considerable measure of luck. Some rulers rise to power entirely by *fortuna*, although in this case Machiavelli believes that, 'while they become princes with little labour, it is only with great labour that they are able to maintain themselves'.[21] The surest means to acquire and successfully hold on to a state is to rely not on *fortuna* but entirely on your own *virtù* as a prince.[22] Machiavelli first formulates this thesis in chapter VI, in which he discusses – in the words of his chapter-heading – 'New principalities acquired by means of one's own arms and one's own *virtus*'.[23] 'What I say', he explains, 'is that in wholly new principalities, where there is a new prince, one finds greater or lesser difficulty in maintaining them according to how great or small is the *virtù* of the person by whom they are acquired.'[24]

Machiavelli mentions two rulers whose conduct is said to bear witness to this truth. One is Hiero of Syracuse, about whom he speaks in a tone of unequivocal admiration voiced nowhere else in *The Prince*.[25] 'From being

---

[17] Machiavelli 1995, XIX. 4, pp. 120–1: 'da che uno principe si debbe guardare come da uno scoglio, e ingegnarsi che nelle azioni sua si riconosca grandezza, animosità, gravità, fortezza'.

[18] Machiavelli 1995, XIX. 39, p. 129.   [19] Machiavelli 1995, XIX. 50–3, pp. 132–3.

[20] Machiavelli 1995, XIX. 54–60, pp. 134–5.

[21] Machiavelli 1995, VII. 1, p. 38: 'con poca fatica diventono, ma con assai si mantengono'.

[22] Although in modern Italian the word is usually spelled thus, it appears in Machiavelli 1995 as *virtù*, and in quoting I accordingly follow this usage.

[23] Machiavelli 1995, VI. p. 32: 'De principatibus novis qui armis propriis et virtute acquiruntur'.

[24] Machiavelli 1995, VI. 4, pp. 32–3: 'Dico adunque che ne' principati tutti nuovi, dove sia uno nuovo principe, si truova a mantenergli piú o meno difficultà secondo che piú o meno è virtuoso colui che gli acquista.'

[25] Benner 2014, pp. 79–83 detects irony.

a private citizen, Hiero rose to become prince of Syracuse, and although he endured much labour in acquiring his state he found little difficulty in maintaining it.'[26] This was because 'he was a man of exceptional *virtú*' who owed nothing to *fortuna* except the opportunity to display his great military and political capacities.[27] The other ruler whom Machiavelli singles out is the emperor Septimius Severus, who was always able to govern happily in spite of the burdens he placed on the people.[28] As with Hiero, this was because 'in Severus there was so much *virtú*' that his armies remained admiring and satisfied, while the people 'were to a large degree stupefied and astonished'.[29] Machiavelli corroborates his analysis when he asks in chapter XXIV why so many Italian rulers of his own time have lost their states. They claim to have suffered bad luck, but 'they ought not to blame *fortuna*, but rather their own indolence and ineffectiveness.'[30] The truth is 'that those defences alone are good, certain and durable which depend on yourself and your own *virtú*.'[31]

Speaking of the specific attributes that constitute the general quality of *virtus*, the Roman moralists had pointed to four elements that later came to be known as the 'cardinal' virtues: wisdom, justice, courage and temperance. Of all the classical discussions of these qualities, the most widely cited in Renaissance Italy was Cicero's in *De officiis*, a book that Machiavelli had probably known ever since his father repeatedly borrowed a copy in the 1470s.[32] Cicero begins with wisdom, the virtue 'that most closely relates to human nature'.[33] Although he speaks of *sapientia*, it is not the Greek ideal of *sophia* or contemplative wisdom that he values, but rather that of *phronesis* or practical wisdom, a term he translates as *prudentia*.[34] He goes so far as to state that 'it is contrary to moral duty to withdraw from public life into our studies',[35] urging us to see that 'the whole praise of virtue lies in action', and hence in contributing to the prudent conduct of civil affairs.[36]

---

[26] Machiavelli 1995, VI. 27 and 29, p. 38: 'Costui di privato diventò principe di Siracusa ... lui durò assai fatica in acquistare e poca in mantenere.'

[27] Machiavelli 1995, VI. 28, p. 38: 'E fu di tanta virtú'.

[28] Machiavelli 1995, XIX. 41, p. 130.

[29] Machiavelli 1995, XIX. 41, p. 130: 'in Severo fu tanta virtú che ... questi [populi] rimanevano quodammodo stupidi e attoniti'.

[30] Machiavelli 1995, XXIV. 8, p. 160: 'non accusino la fortuna, ma la ignavia loro'.

[31] Machiavelli 1995, XXIV. 10, p. 161: 'quelle difese solamente sono buone, sono certe, sono durabili, che dependono da te proprio e da la virtú tua'.

[32] On Machiavelli's father's classical reading see Machiavelli 1954, pp. 11, 31, 35, 58, 88, 123, 138.

[33] Cicero 1913, I. VI. 18, p. 18: 'maxime naturam attingit humanam'.

[34] Cicero 1913, I. V. 15, p. 16.

[35] Cicero 1913, I. VI. 19, p. 20: 'studio a rebus gerendis abduci contra officium est.'

[36] Cicero 1913, I. VI. 19, p. 20: 'Virtutis enim laus omnis in actione consistit'.

Next Cicero considers the closely associated virtue of justice. He begins by arguing that the basic requirement of just dealing is that we should render to each his due while making sure that we do no harm to anyone.[37] He then explores two specific implications of his argument. The first is that 'the foundation of justice is *fides*, that is, constancy and truth in relation to promises and agreements'.[38] This commitment is summarised in the maxim *fides conservanda*, that good faith must always be observed.[39] Cicero's other specific concern is with the character of injustice, whether it arises from doing injury or from failing to prevent it. This part of his discussion culminates in the claim that 'there are two ways in which injustice may be done, either by force or by fraud'.[40] Both are said to be 'entirely alien to man, fraud because it seems to be acting in the manner of a fox, and force in the manner of a lion'.[41] Such behaviour is wholly unworthy of the *vir*, the truly manly man who is at the same time the eponymous possessor of *virtus*.

As well as focusing on justice and injustice, the Roman moralists consider a further range of qualities that later came to be classified as distinctively 'princely' virtues. One of these is said to be liberality. Cicero includes a section 'on kindness and liberality' immediately after his discussion of justice in Book I of *De officiis*,[42] but the fullest and most influential handling of the topic can be found in Seneca's *De beneficiis*, a work endlessly cited by the early Italian writers of handbooks for princes and magistrates.[43] The other leading princely virtue is said to be mercy or compassion, the subject of Seneca's *De clementia*.[44] This quality was agreed to be peculiarly an attribute of rulers, since its exercise presupposes the prerogative of setting aside justice in the name of a higher good. As Seneca declares, 'there is no one in whom clemency is more appropriate than kings and princes.'[45]

---

[37] Cicero 1913, I. V. 15, p. 16; I. VII. 20, p. 22.

[38] Cicero 1913, I. VII. 23, p. 24: 'Fundamentum autem est iustitiae fides, id est dictorum conventorumque constantia et veritas'. On *fides publica* see De Wilde 2011.

[39] Cicero 1913, I. XIII. 39, p. 42. The only exception is when the keeping of a promise would do more harm than good. See Cicero 1913, I. X. 31, pp. 30–4. But if this exception were to be given sufficient latitude, Cicero's doctrine might seem close to Machiavelli's.

[40] Cicero 1913, I. XIII. 41, p. 44: 'Cum autem duobus modis, id est vi aut fraude, fiat iniuria'.

[41] Cicero 1913, I. XIII. 41, p. 44: 'fraus quasi vulpeculae, vis leonis videtur; utrumque homine alienissimum'.

[42] See the section 'De beneficentia ac de liberalitate' in Cicero 1913, I. XIV. 42 to I. XVIII. 60, pp. 46–62.

[43] See Seneca 1935, especially the opening encomium to *liberalitas*, I. IV. 2–3, p. 18. For the use of Seneca's text in Italy from as early as the thirteenth century see Stacey 2007, pp. 100–4.

[44] Seneca 1928. For Seneca on clemency and cruelty see Stacey 2007, pp. 54–5, 61–5.

[45] Seneca 1928, I. 3. 3, p. 364: 'Nullum tamen clementia ex omnibus magis quam regem aut principem decet.' On Seneca's treatise see Stacey 2007, pp. 30–72.

Nothing more strongly reflects Machiavelli's preoccupation with classical humanism than the fact that, when he turns in the central chapters of *The Prince* to examine the qualities that rulers should cultivate, he concentrates on precisely the same list of princely virtues.[46] When he asks at the start of chapter XV 'what should be the methods and conduct of a prince in relation to his subjects or allies',[47] he begins by mentioning the attributes of liberality, clemency and the keeping of good faith.[48] When he proceeds to interrogate the conduct of rulers in greater detail in his next three chapters, he focuses once again on the princely virtues. Chapter XVI is entitled 'On liberality and parsimony';[49] chapter XVII is entitled 'On cruelty and clemency';[50] and chapter XVIII opens with a consideration of the Ciceronian ideal of *fides*.[51]

Despite this close engagement with the humanist tradition, commentators have usually seen in these chapters a complete repudiation of the classical ideal of *virtus*. The Roman moralists, seconded by the Christian humanists of the Renaissance, had argued that *virtus* is the all-embracing name of those qualities which enable rulers to govern honourably and successfully. Machiavelli responds, we are told, by asserting that the mark of a truly *virtuoso* prince is to recognise that a ruler's 'first duty' is to 'avoid those virtues that endanger the state' and to recognise that 'the necessity of preserving the state' requires 'that a prince depart from the customary virtues'.[52]

This is not how Machiavelli argues, however, in the case of the princely virtues. Here his chief contention is that rulers must stand ready to depart from what these virtues are normally *held* or *taken* to prescribe. He speaks in chapter XV about how some rulers are *tenuto* or held to be liberal and others miserly, and how some are held to be cruel and others compassionate.[53] He speaks again in chapter XVI about what are held to be the requirements of liberality,[54] and in chapter XVII about what are similarly held to be the requirements of mercy.[55] These remarks are coupled with the observation that, in the corrupt world in which we

---

[46] On Machiavelli's vocabulary in these chapters see Najemy 1995, pp. 95–103.

[47] Machiavelli 1995, XV. 1, p. 102: 'quali debbino essere e' modi e governi di uno principe o co' sudditi o con li amici.' For a commentary see Benner 2013, pp. 179–224. Benner refers to Machiavelli's rhetorical strategies, but without mentioning the figure of paradiastole, on which I concentrate in what follows.

[48] See Machiavelli 1995, XV, 8–9, p. 103 on being *liberale* and *donatore; piatoso*; and *fedele*.

[49] Machiavelli 1995, XVI, p. 104: 'De liberalitate et parsimonia'.

[50] See Machiavelli 1995, XVII, p. 108, which reads 'De crudelitate et pietate'. But cf. Machiavelli 1532a (the *editio princeps*), in which the chapter-headings are translated into Italian, which reads (fo. 22r) 'Della Crudeltà, et Clemenza'.

[51] Machiavelli 1995, XVIII, 1–11, pp. 115–17.   [52] Bobbitt 2013, pp. 35, 41.

[53] Machiavelli 1995, XV. 8, p. 103.   [54] Machiavelli 1995, XVI. 1, p. 104.

[55] Machiavelli 1995, XVII. 1, p. 108.

live, the language of virtue and vice has become subject to so much manipulation that many courses of action nowadays regarded as virtuous are in fact instances of vice, while many others condemned as vicious are instances of virtue. The outcome, as he complains in chapter XV, is that many traits appear to be virtuous when they are not, and many other traits only appear to be vices.[56]

The first of these contentions about the virtues – that they will sometimes have to be avoided in the name of maintaining the state – has been extensively discussed. But the second contention – that some apparent virtues are instances of vice – has rarely been examined, and it seems to me that the relationship between the two arguments has never been properly clarified. My strategy in what follows will accordingly be to focus on Machiavelli's second line of thought. I shall first consider its provenance, and then its specific contribution to his broader analysis of the virtues and their place in public life.

II

When Machiavelli complains that some virtues are being made to appear as vices, and some vices as virtues, he is referring to the technique of rhetorical redescription that came to be known as paradiastole. About this technique I shall have much to say in chapter 5. For the moment I need only indicate the line of descent by which Machiavelli would have come to know about it. Aristotle in his *Art of Rhetoric* had provided the earliest extant analysis in a work of rhetorical theory of how the terms we use to describe and appraise moral and immoral behaviour can be successfully manipulated. Because virtue is always a mean between two opposed vices, as he lays down in the *Nicomachean Ethics*, such commendable qualities as courage and generosity can sometimes appear more like rashness and extravagance.[57] Enlarging on this observation in Book I of his *Rhetoric*, he suggests that this makes it possible to denigrate virtuous actions by assigning them the names of neighbouring vices, and to excuse immoral actions by assigning them the names of neighbouring virtues.[58]

Machiavelli would not have been able to read this discussion in Greek, but he may nevertheless have had some knowledge of Aristotle's text. George of Trebizond, who lived in Florence in the early 1440s, completed at around that time a Latin translation of the *Rhetoric*,[59] which was printed in Venice in 1478[60] and included in an Aldine collection of rhetorical

---

[56] Machiavelli 1995, XV. 12, p. 104.   [57] Aristotle 1985, p. 50.
[58] Aristotle 1926, I. IX. 28–9, pp. 96–8.   [59] Monfasani 1976, pp. 43–5, 55.
[60] Green and Murphy 2006, p. 34.

texts in 1523.[61] If we turn to the discussion of rhetorical redescription in Book I, we find that one of Aristotle's examples is designed to show how virtue can be denigrated. As George of Trebizond translates, we can redescribe and thereby condemn someone 'who is moderate and exhibits calmness of soul' by claiming 'that he is merely cowardly and a deceiver'.[62] Aristotle is more interested, however, in showing how it is possible for vices to be excused. As George of Trebizond translates, we can redescribe and thereby commend someone who is arrogant as magnificent and honourable,[63] and we can similarly redescribe someone who is violent as courageous, and someone who is extravagant as a person of liberality.[64]

This analysis was subsequently elaborated by the Roman rhetoricians, and especially by Quintilian in his *Institutio oratoria*. It is striking, however, that Quintilian has nothing to say about denigrating the virtues. He treats rhetorical redescription entirely as a means of excusing reprehensible behaviour, especially our own behaviour, and he labels the technique paradiastole.[65] When he illustrates the use of the device, he repeats two of the examples already given by Aristotle: violence or recklessness can be redescribed and thereby praised as courage, while extravagance can be redescribed and commended as liberality.[66] To these he adds three other examples already mentioned in earlier rhetorical handbooks: the slanderous can be excused as frank, the deceitful as worldly-wise, the avaricious as thrifty and scrupulous.[67]

Quintilian's way of thinking about rhetorical redescription was the one that broadly prevailed. His analysis was repeated word for word by Isidore of Seville in his *Etymologies*, perhaps the most widely read encyclopedia of late antiquity, and repeated yet again by Antonio Mancinelli in his *Carmen de figuris*, one of the earliest Renaissance treatises on *elocutio*.[68] Both writers speak of paradiastole,[69] and both describe it specifically as a

---

[61] George of Trebizond 1523, the edition from which I quote.

[62] George of Trebizond 1523, fo. 114v: 'ut si moderatum, ac mitioris animi timidum & insidiatorem'.

[63] George of Trebizond 1523, fo. 114v: 'arrogantem, magnificum atque honestum'.

[64] George of Trebizond 1523, fo. 114v: 'ferocem fortem esse, prodigum liberalem'.

[65] Quintilian 2001, 9. 3. 65, vol. 4, p. 138.

[66] Quintilian 2001, 3. 7. 25, vol. 2, p. 114: 'pro temerario fortem, prodigo liberalem'. See also Quintilian 2001, 8. 6. 36, vol. 3, p. 444: 'pro temeritate virtus aut pro luxuria liberalitas'.

[67] These examples can already be found in the *De figuris* of Rutilius Lupus (*c.*20 CE). See Rutilius Lupus 1970, p. 8. Quintilian repeats Rutilius's first example at 5. 13. 26, vol. 2, p. 480 (maledicus/liberus); his second at 9. 3. 65, vol. 4, p. 138 (astutus/sapiens); his third at 4. 2. 77, vol. 2, p. 256 (avaritia/parsimonia), again at 5. 13. 26, vol. 2, p. 480 (sordidus/parcus) and again at 9. 3. 65, vol. 4, p. 138 (inliberalis/diligens).

[68] On Mancinelli see Skinner 1996, pp. 151–2; Stacey 2007, pp. 216–17.

[69] Isidore 1983, p. 81; Mancinelli 1493, sig. H, 1r.

device for excusing the vices, especially our own vices. They also reiterate most of Quintilian's examples: the avaricious can be redescribed as thrifty,[70] the reckless as courageous,[71] the extravagant as liberal,[72] the deceitful as worldly-wise.[73]

Within the Roman tradition, however, there was a strongly contrasting way of thinking about the manipulation of evaluative terms. Some rhetoricians argued that, instead of redescribing the vices as virtues, our primary aim should be that of exposing and denouncing any adversary who attempts to play this rhetorical trick.[74] This is the strategy recommended by the author of the *Rhetorica ad Herennium*, the earliest surviving Roman manual on the fivefold art of eloquence.[75] The *Ad Herennium* was widely used as a textbook in the schools of *quattrocento* Italy,[76] and it has been shown that Machiavelli not only knew the work well, but explicitly drew on its account of political deliberation in *The Prince*.[77] The discussion of rhetorical redescription can be found in the main section on deliberative eloquence in Book III.[78] There we are audaciously told to argue that what our adversary calls justice is in fact weakness; what he calls prudence is offensive cleverness; what he thinks of as temperance is dissolute negligence; and what he regards as courage is inconsiderate recklessness.[79]

A similar discussion can be found in the handbook of *c.*20 CE attributed to P. Rutilius Lupus and entitled *De figuris*.[80] I discuss this text more fully in chapter 5; here it will suffice to note that Rutilius already gives the name paradiastole to the technique of rhetorical redescription, and appears to be the earliest Roman rhetorician to use the term.[81] But by contrast with later writers (such as Quintilian) who contend that the device is in play whenever we redescribe our vices as virtues, Rutilius agrees with the *Ad Herennium* that the technique in question is that of exposing and denouncing this rhetorical trick. Unlike the author of the *Ad Herennium*,

---

[70] See Isidore 1983, p. 81 on inliberalis/diligens.

[71] See Isidore 1983, p. 81 on inconsideratus/fortis and Mancinelli 1493, sig. H, 1r on confidens/fortis.

[72] See Mancinelli 1493, sig. H, 1r on prodigus/liberalis.

[73] See Isidore 1983, p. 81 and Mancinelli 1493, sig. H, 1r on astutus/sapiens.

[74] For this distinction I am indebted to Tuck 1996, pp. 203–4, although he seems to me to place Quintilian and his followers on the wrong side of it.

[75] Caplan 1954, p. vii dates it to *c.*80 BCE.

[76] On its influence see Grendler 1989, pp. 212–15. On its use in the schools of *quattrocento* Florence see Black 2001, pp. 428–34.

[77] See Cox 1997. On deliberative rhetoric in *The Prince* see Cox 2010, pp. 178–81. On the *Rhetorica ad Herennium* and the organisation of *The Prince* see Viroli 1998, pp. 75–97.

[78] For a discussion see Cox 1997, pp. 1131–2.

[79] *Rhetorica ad Herennium* 1954, III. III. 6, pp. 166–8. For the passage in full see below, chapter 5, note 11.

[80] See Tuck 1996, pp. 203–4; Skinner 2007, pp. 150–1.   [81] Rutilius Lupus, 1970, p. 8.

however, Rutilius lays no claim to originality in making the point. He simply refers us to Hyperides, an Attic orator of the fourth century BCE, who had made a speech in denunciation of Aristophon in which he had declared that (as Rutilius translates) 'there is no vice in which you are able to glory by praising it as a virtue'.[82] As Rutilius's translation continues, 'you have no hope of proving that you should be understood as wise rather than crafty, or courageous rather than reckless, or careful in family matters rather than niggardly, or severe rather than ill-willed.'[83]

By drawing on this tradition of rhetorical argument, Rutilius associates himself at the same time with a number of philosophers and historians who had similarly denounced the manipulation of moral terms. The earliest to excoriate the abuse had been Thucydides in the passage from Book III of his history in which he had explained how *stasis* or civil strife arose in Corcyra.[84] Machiavelli could well have known about this famous passage from Lorenzo Valla's Latin translation, which he completed in 1452 and circulated in manuscript before its publication in 1483.[85] Thucydides's discussion centres on the moment when the pro-Athenian *demos* in Corcyra first rose in revolt against the oligarchy. He relates how the factions sought to excuse their vicious behaviour by redescribing it in commendatory terms.[86] As Valla translates, 'recklessness came to be called courage, while aggression was ascribed to manliness'.[87] By contrast with the rhetoricians, however, Thucydides is no less interested in denouncing the denigration of virtue. One example he gives is that (in Valla's translation) 'honourable hesitation came to be regarded as cowardice'.[88] He also describes how 'modesty of demeanour was considered a method of

---

[82] Rutilius Lupus, 1970, p. 8, quoting Hyperides 1944, p. 575: 'Nullum est enim vitium, quo ut virtutis laude gloriari possis.'

[83] Rutilius Lupus 1970, p. 8: 'Non enim probas te pro astute sapientem intelligenti, pro confidente fortem, pro inliberali diligentem rei familiaris, pro malivolo severum.'

[84] Thucydides 2013, III. 70–83, pp. 206–14.

[85] See Chambers 2008, pp. XI–XIV, who notes that the work was reprinted in 1513, the year in which Machiavelli drafted *The Prince*. For this draft, and for Machiavelli's final revisions in 1515, see Connell 2015, pp. 94–111. Chambers 2008 also notes that Valla's translation was reprinted again in 1528, and that Stephanus produced an edition of the Greek text accompanied by Valla's translation in 1564. It is from this version that I quote. On Machiavelli's possible access to Valla's translation see Canfora 1997, pp. 31–2. As an indication of its possible influence on Machiavelli, see his account in the *Discorsi* of a later massacre in Corcyra discussed by Thucydides in Book IV. See Thucydides 2013, IV. 46–8, pp. 263–4 and cf. Machiavelli 2000, II. 2, pp. 140–1.

[86] Canfora 1997, Simonetta 1997 and Benner 2009, pp. 88–97 all examine Machiavelli's apparent debt to Thucydides, but without considering this passage. But for a discussion see Klein 2007, pp. 396–400.

[87] Thucydides 1564, III. 110, p. 77: 'Temeritas enim fortitudo ... vocabatur ... indignatio virilitati adscribebatur'.

[88] Thucydides 1564, III. 110, p. 77: 'considerata cunctatio honesta formido'.

concealing weakness',[89] while 'a willingness to deliberate and calculate was seen as deceitfulness and an evasion of responsibility'.[90]

Thucydides's account appears to have been in Plato's mind when, in Book VIII of *The Republic*, he speaks of the Lotus-eaters and their success in corrupting the mind of the young oligarch.[91] Machiavelli could also have known of this discussion, for Marsilio Ficino's Latin translation of *The Republic* had been printed in Florence as early as 1484 and in Venice in 1491.[92] Plato explains that one way in which the Lotus-eaters managed to spread corruption was by denigrating the virtues. Repeating an example given by Thucydides, he speaks (in Ficino's translation) of how they sought to ridicule moderation by calling it weakness,[93] adding that they spoke with detestation of modesty and condemned it as a failure of generosity.[94] Plato is more concerned, however, with the Lotus-eaters' efforts to excuse the vices. Taking another of Thucydides's illustrations, he speaks of how they redescribed recklessness as courage,[95] and at the same time commended insolence as a sign of good breeding,[96] licence as freedom[97] and extravagance as splendid liberality.[98]

A similar disgust was later expressed by several of the Roman historians, notably Sallust, Livy and Tacitus, with all of whose works Machiavelli was closely acquainted. Sometimes they too speak of the damage that can be done by denigrating the virtues. Livy, for example, again echoing one of Thucydides's examples, tells the story of Fabius Maximus's cavalry commander at the time when Fabius was employing delaying tactics in the face of Hannibal's march on Rome. Livy records that 'Hannibal himself was not more enraged by these prudent measures than was the master of horse',[99] who assailed Fabius 'as half-hearted, not deliberate, and as a coward, not a man of caution'.[100] Like Plato, however, the Roman historians are more concerned with the dangers that arise when vices are

---

[89] Thucydides 1564, III. 110, p. 77: 'considerata ... modestia, ignaviae velamentum'. As we have seen, this example was subsequently echoed by Aristotle. But Aristotle's advice (later repeated by Quintilian) is not that we should expose the trick but make use of it.

[90] Thucydides 1564, III. 110, p. 77: 'tuto consultare ... tergiversatio erat'. See Fryde 1983, pp. 97–8 and n. on how Valla calls attention to the significance of these examples for his own times. On the use of Thucydides in the Renaissance see Pade 2006.

[91] Plato 1935, 560c to 561a, pp. 296–300.

[92] I quote from Plato 1484, the Florence edition.

[93] Plato 1484, fo. 355v, col. 1: 'Temperantiam vero ignaviam nominantes'.

[94] Plato 1484, fo. 355v, col. 1: 'Modestiam ... illiberalitatem penitus detestantur'.

[95] Plato 1484, fo. 355v, col. 2: 'nominant ... impudentiam/fortitudinem'.

[96] Plato 1484, fo. 355v, col. 2: 'petulantiam ingenuam educationem nominant.'

[97] Plato 1484, fo. 355v, col. 2: 'nominant ... licentiam/libertatem'.

[98] Plato 1484, fo. 355v, col. 2: 'nominant ... prodigalitatem/magnificentiam'.

[99] Livy 1929, XXII. XIII. 12, p. 240: 'non Hannibalem magis infestum tam sanis consiliis habebat quam magistrum equitum'.

[100] Livy 1929, XXII. XIII. 12, pp. 240–2: 'pro cunctatore segnem, pro cauto timidus'.

excused. Sallust in his *Bellum Catilinae* records a speech of Marcus Cato lamenting that 'the squandering of the goods of others is nowadays called liberality, while recklessness in wrongdoing is called courage'.[101] In similar vein Tacitus records a speech of Piso's reviling the emperor Otho. Not only did he deceive the people 'by imposing his extravagance under the guise of liberality'[102] but 'with false names he called severity what was in fact savagery, and parsimony what was in fact avarice'.[103]

III

When Machiavelli discusses the princely virtues in the central chapters of *The Prince*, he pursues two distinct but complementary lines of argument. He first contends that a ruler who wishes to maintain his state will sometimes need to act in defiance of the virtues. He explains in chapter XV that 'there is so much distance between how one lives and how one ought to live that anyone who gives up doing what is done for what ought to be done will learn the more quickly how to destroy rather than how to preserve himself.'[104] Summarising in chapter XVIII, he concludes that a truly *virtuoso* ruler must therefore 'know how to enter upon bad behaviour when this is required.'[105] To Cicero's objection that this will lower us to the level of the beasts he unrepentantly responds that he is guilty as charged. 'For a prince it is necessary to know how to make good use of the beast as well as the man',[106] and 'from among the beasts the prince should choose the fox and the lion', thereby acknowledging that guile and violence are among the qualities that rulers must cultivate.[107] They need to recognise that one of their duties is 'to learn how not to be good'.[108]

One way of paraphrasing this aspect of Machiavelli's thinking would be to say that, in effect, he redefines the concept of *virtù*.[109] He agrees that it

---

[101] Sallust 1921, LII. 11, p. 102: 'bona aliena largiri liberalitas, malarum rerum audacia fortitudo vocatur'. For a discussion see Skinner 1996, p. 162. Also cited in Benner 2013, p. 194. On Sallust's presence in Machiavelli's texts see Fontano 2003.

[102] Tacitus 1925, I. XXX, p. 52: 'luxuria specie liberalitatis imponit'.

[103] Tacitus 1925, I. XXXVII, p. 64: 'falsis nominibus severitatem pro saevitia, parsimoniam pro avaritia . . . appellat'. For a discussion see Skinner 1996, p. 163. Also cited in Benner 2013, p. 188.

[104] Machiavelli 1995, XV. 5, pp. 102–3: 'gli è tanto discosto da come si vive a come si doverrebbe vivere, che colui che lascia quello che si fa, per quello che si doverrebbe fare, impara piú presto la ruina che la perservazione sua'.

[105] Machiavelli 1995, XVIII. 15, p. 118: 'sapere entrare nel male, necessitato'.

[106] Machiavelli 1995, XVIII. 4, p. 115: 'pertanto a uno principe è necessario sapere bene usare la bestia e lo uomo'.

[107] Machiavelli 1995, XVIII. 7, p. 116: 'uno principe . . . debbe di quelle pigliare la golpe e il lione'.

[108] Machiavelli 1995, XV. 6, p. 103: 'imparare a potere essere non buono'.

[109] See Skinner 2000, p. 44.

is only by exercising the qualities of a truly *virtuoso* ruler that a prince can maintain his state. But he no longer equates princely virtuosity with the practice of the moral virtues. A *virtuoso* ruler will follow the dictates of the virtues whenever possible, but he will chiefly be distinguished by his skill at judging when it may be more appropriate to ignore them. The term *virtù* thus comes to be used by Machiavelli to denote whatever range of attributes – moral or otherwise – actually enable a prince to maintain his state.

While this argument is undoubtedly of great importance to Machiavelli, I am more concerned with the supplementary claim he puts forward when he turns to scrutinise the princely virtues of liberality, clemency and good faith. Here his contention is not that, if you wish to maintain your state, you may need to act in defiance of what these virtues prescribe. As we have seen, what he argues is that you must stand ready to act in defiance of what, in our corrupt and degenerate world, these virtues are *held* or *taken* to prescribe. But this advice is coupled with the suggestion that, if you cultivate a proper understanding of these virtues, and if you follow what they genuinely require, you will find that they can help you to maintain your state.

Admittedly this line of thought is not pursued with complete consistency. Sometimes Machiavelli classifies the observance of good faith as one of the virtues that a ruler must be willing to set aside,[110] and when he discusses the virtue of liberality in chapter XVI he appears at one moment to repudiate not merely what is generally held to count as liberality but the virtue itself. He seems, that is, to counsel any ruler who wishes *mantenere lo stato* to avoid all forms of generosity and to cultivate meanness in their place. To follow this alternative course, he admits, will be to embrace a vice. But meanness 'is one of the vices that enable a prince to rule'.[111]

This is not, however, the argument that Machiavelli chiefly elaborates in chapter XVI. Rather he mounts an attack on seeming liberality. He begins by considering the type of conduct best suited to winning a prince 'the name of being a liberal man'.[112] The kind of ruler who is nowadays *tenuto* or held to be liberal[113] is someone 'who will consume all his resources in generous works in order to uphold his reputation for liberality'.[114] But to act in this way, Machiavelli insists, is not in the least to exhibit the virtue of

---

[110] See, for example, Machiavelli 1995, XVIII. 14, p. 118.

[111] See Machiavelli 1995, XVI. 11, p. 107, where he suggests that to be 'misero' is 'uno di quelli vizi che lo fanno regnare.'

[112] Machiavelli 1995, XVI. 3, p. 105: 'el nome di liberale'.

[113] Barthas 2013, p. 89 suggests that, in the first of its two occurrences here, *tenuto* should be understood as *obbligato*, and only in the second as *riputato*.

[114] Machiavelli 1995, XVI. 2–3, p. 105: 'consumerà in simili opere tutte le sua facultà [per] mantenere el nome del liberale'.

liberality; rather it is to show yourself unwilling 'to give up any quality of extravagance'.[115] Like Plato, and like Sallust and Tacitus, Machiavelli is pointing out and condemning the corruption of those who seek to excuse extravagance by redescribing it as liberality.[116]

Next Machiavelli undertakes to demonstrate that those who are normally held to be liberal are far from displaying that quality. To follow his somewhat elusive argument, we first need to recall his two general claims about princely *virtù* and the preservation of the state: that the term *virtù* refers to whatever attributes enable a prince *mantenere lo stato*; and that the quickest way to lose your state is to become hated or despised. Machiavelli now observes that any ruler who consumes his resources in order to uphold a reputation for liberality will soon fall into poverty, at which point he will become despised and 'little esteemed by everyone'.[117] To avoid this danger 'he will find it necessary, if he wishes to preserve the name of being a liberal man, to tax his people excessively'.[118] But this policy will cause him to appear rapacious, 'which will start to make him hated by his subjects'.[119] If, in short, a prince consistently behaves so as to be regarded as liberal, he will soon become hated and despised, and will consequently lose his state. As Machiavelli has laid down, however, the kind of liberality that forms part of the *virtù* of a prince must by definition be a quality that helps him maintain his state. It follows that rulers who act to gain a reputation for being liberal cannot be exhibiting the genuine virtue of liberality. The moral is that, as Machiavelli has already argued in chapter XV, rulers must be careful not to confuse the princely virtues 'with other attributes that may appear to be virtues, but will bring you ruin if you embrace them.'[120] One such attribute is liberality as it is commonly but corruptly understood.[121]

Machiavelli next turns in chapter XVII to examine the princely virtue of clemency, again focusing on the type of behaviour nowadays *tenuto* or held to be compassionate. He contrasts the conduct of Cesare Borgia, whose settlement of the Romagna gave him a reputation for cruelty, with

---

[115] Machiavelli 1995, XVI. 2, p. 105: 'lasciare indreto alcuna qualità di suntuosità'.

[116] Machiavelli was not the first Renaissance Italian writer to pick up this classical point. Barthas 2013, p. 87 notes that Cristoforo Landino in his commentary on Dante (printed in Florence in 1481) had already referred to it.

[117] See Machiavelli 1995, XVI. 3, p. 105 on how such a prince will be 'poco stimare da ciascuno divenendo povero.'

[118] Machiavelli 1995, XVI. 3, p. 105: 'sarà necessitato . . . se si vorrà mantenere el nome del liberale, gravare e' populi estraordinariamente'.

[119] Machiavelli 1995, XVI. 3, p. 105: 'comincerà a farlo odioso a' sudditi'.

[120] Machiavelli 1995, XV. 12, p. 104: 'qualche cosa che parrà virtú, e seguendola sarebbe la ruina sua'.

[121] Stacey 2014, pp. 205–6 notes that Machiavelli in his tract of 1503 on how to deal with the rebels in the Valdichiana had already argued in similar terms.

that of the Florentines when civil strife broke out in Pistoia in 1499. Rather than executing the leaders of the uprising with a view to ending the violence, the Florentines decided 'in order to avoid the name of cruelty' that they would not intervene, in consequence of which 'they allowed Pistoia to be destroyed'.[122] Later Machiavelli reflects in similar vein on Scipio Africanus, who was celebrated for his clemency, and offers two instances of Scipio's allegedly compassionate behaviour. One was that, when leading Rome's armies in Spain, 'he gave his soldiers more licence than was suited to military discipline'.[123] The other was that, when one of Scipio's legates destroyed the city of Locri, 'the citizens were never avenged, and nor was the insolence of his legate ever punished'.[124]

Machiavelli protests that these are not examples of clemency at all.[125] 'If we consider aright',[126] we shall see that the response of the Florentines to the uprising in Pistoia was an instance of *troppa pietà*, mere over-indulgence.[127] It would have been 'much more compassionate'[128] if they had executed the ringleaders 'rather than allowing the entire population to be harmed'.[129] Likewise with Scipio, whose supposed clemency was again a sign of *troppa pietà* stemming in his case from a *natura facile*, a lax character.[130] The compassion for which he has so often been praised was in fact a *qualità dannosa*, a harmful quality.[131]

As in his discussion of liberality, Machiavelli next offers to demonstrate that those who are commonly held to be merciful and compassionate are not in fact displaying those qualities. His argument is once again grounded on his contention that *virtù* is the name of the attributes that enable a ruler to maintain his state. If this is so, then the behaviour of the Florentines in Pistoia cannot have been an instance of genuine clemency, because the effect was to destroy a community instead of saving it.[132] Nor

---

[122] Machiavelli 1995, XVII. 3, pp. 108–9: 'per fuggire il nome di crudele, lasciò distruggere Pistoia'.

[123] Machiavelli 1995, XVII. 19, p. 114: 'aveva data alli suoi soldati piú licenza che alla disciplina militare non si conveniva.'

[124] Machiavelli 1995, XVII. 21, p. 114: 'non furno vendicati né fu da lui la insolenzia di quello legato corretta'.

[125] Kapust 2007, pp. 444, 447 draws a parallel between Machiavelli's view of clemency and Sallust's account of how Cato condemned the *misericordia* of Julius Caesar as merely an apparent virtue.

[126] Machiavelli 1995, XVII. 3, p. 108: 'si considera bene'.

[127] Machiavelli 1995, XVII. 4, p. 109.

[128] Machiavelli 1995, XVII. 4, p. 109: 'piú pietoso'.

[129] See Machiavelli 1995, XVII. 4, p. 109 on how the Florentines managed 'offendere una universalità intera'.

[130] On Scipio, his *natura facile* and his exercise of *troppa pietà*, see Machiavelli 1995, XVII. 19, p. 113 and XVII. 21, p. 114.

[131] See Machiavelli 1995, XVII. 22, p. 114 on 'questa sua qualità dannosa'.

[132] Machiavelli 1995, XVII. 4, p. 109.

was Scipio's conduct in Spain genuinely clement, because it had the effect of prompting a mutiny and thereby weakening Rome.[133]

One of Machiavelli's aims in both these chapters is to expose the habit of excusing bad and incompetent behaviour by redescribing it with the name of a neighbouring virtue. If we turn to chapter XVIII, we find him no less interested in the disposition to denigrate good behaviour by stigmatising it with the name of a vice. His chapter-heading promises a discussion of 'How princes should keep their word' – *Quomodo fides a principibus sit servanda*.[134] Here he alludes to Cicero's maxim *fides conservanda*, that good faith must always be upheld, a commitment so important in Italian Renaissance thought that *fides* was sometimes treated as a fifth cardinal virtue. A notable *cinquecento* example can be seen in the portrayal of the cardinal virtues in the church of Madonna dell' Orto in Venice. Courage, prudence, justice and temperance are duly pictured, but they are shown in the company of *Fides*, which is placed at the centre of the iconographical scheme. Machiavelli recalls this way of thinking when he notes that 'everyone understands how laudable it is for a prince to maintain faith and live with integrity rather than deceit'.[135] The princes we are invited to admire are 'those who base their conduct on loyalty and trustworthiness'.[136]

To these pieties Machiavelli responds that they embody a dangerous misunderstanding of *fides*. To insist on honouring one's word while living in a world in which men rarely keep their promises is the merest imprudence. 'No prudent ruler can observe good faith, and nor ought he to do so, when such observance will turn against him'.[137] The quality of *fides*, understood as a willingness to keep faith under all circumstances, can only be the name of a seeming virtue. It cannot form part of the *virtù* of a prudent prince, since it will often lead him to lose rather than maintain his state. With this analysis of what the Ciceronian virtue of *prudentia* dictates, Machiavelli reiterates a warning already issued by Livy and

---

[133] Machiavelli 1995, XVII. 20, p. 114.

[134] Machiavelli 1995, XVIII, p. 115: 'Quomodo fides a principibus sit servanda'.

[135] Machiavelli 1995, XVIII. 1, p. 115: 'Quanto sia laudabile in uno principe il mantenere la fede e vivere con integrità e non con astuzia, ciascuno lo intende'.

[136] Machiavelli 1995, XVIII. 1, p. 115: 'quelli che si sono fondati in sua realtà'. But here my translation follows the two earliest printings of Machiavelli's text, in which the phrase 'fondati in sua realtà' appears as 'fondati insù la lealtà'. See Machiavelli 1532a, fo. 23r and Machiavelli 1532b, fo. 26v. For the printer of Machiavelli 1532a (Antonio Blado of Rome) see Machiavelli 1532a, fo. 49v. For the printer of Machiavelli 1532b (Bernardo Giunto of Florence) see Machiavelli 1532b, fo. 69v.

[137] Machiavelli 1995, XVIII. 8, p. 116: 'Non può pertanto uno signore prudente, né debbe, osservare la fede quando tale osservanzia gli torni contro'. On prudence in Machiavelli see Garver 2003, esp. pp. 81–6.

much earlier by Thucydides: we must never allow prudent calculations to be redescribed and condemned as cowardice or deceitfulness.

IV

Machiavelli is not unaware that his argument leaves him with a difficulty. It may be true that most people are mistaken about the character of the princely virtues. But they remain strongly attached to their corrupt beliefs, in consequence of which they regularly criticise prudence as deceitfulness, while praising laxity as compassion and extravagance as liberality. So if, like Louis XII of France, you refuse to spend lavishly and ostentatiously, you will not only find yourself accused of failing in liberality, but will gain for yourself 'the infamy of a miser'.[138] Likewise, if you refuse, like Cesare Borgia, to spare those who threaten your rule, you will not only be denounced for lack of clemency but will face the greater infamy of being thought cruel and inhumane.[139]

Machiavelli responds by waving these anxieties aside. There is every reason to hope that in time your subjects will come to recognise that they have been mistaken about the character of the princely virtues, and will give up their destructive beliefs. This is certainly what happened in the face of 'the long-standing parsimony'[140] that enabled Louis XII 'to wage so many wars without ever having to impose an extraordinary tax on his subjects'.[141] The people were eventually able to see that the king had in fact been behaving 'with liberality towards everyone from whom he took nothing, who were infinite, and with miserliness only towards those to whom he gave nothing, who were few'.[142] Machiavelli accordingly feels able to conclude that 'if he is prudent, a prince ought not to worry about being given the name of a miser, because in course of time he will be regarded more and more as a man of liberality'.[143]

A similar paradox is defended in chapter XVII in relation to the alleged cruelties perpetrated by Cesare Borgia at the outset of his rule in the Romagna. By eliminating factions and punishing the excesses of his subordinates 'he was able to restore the Romagna, to unite it and return

---

[138] See Machiavelli 1995, XVI. 4, p. 105 on the 'infamia del misero'.

[139] See Machiavelli 1995, XVII. 2, p. 108 on how Borgia was 'tenuto . . . crudele'.

[140] See Machiavelli 1995, XVI. 9, p. 106 on Louis XII and on 'la lunga parsimonia sua'.

[141] See Machiavelli 1995, XVI. 9, p. 106 on how 'El re di Francia presente ha fatto tante guerre sanza porre uno dazio estraordinario a' sua'.

[142] Machiavelli 1995, XVI. 6, p. 106: 'viene a usare liberalità a tutti quelli a chi e' non toglie, che sono infiniti, e miseria a tutti coloro a chi e' non dà, che sono pochi.'

[143] Machiavelli 1995, XVI. 5, pp. 105–6: 'Uno principe . . . debbe, s'egli è prudente, non si curare del nome del misero; perché col tempo sarà tenuto sempre piú liberale'.

it to peace and good faith'.[144] As before, the moral is said to be that 'a prince ought not to worry about incurring the infamy of being called a cruel man' if his behaviour is such that harsh methods soon cease to be necessary instead of having to be constantly employed.[145] He will in time be seen to have acted 'with far greater compassion' than if he had failed to crush his rivals and thereby allowed disorders to proliferate.[146]

The conclusion at which Machiavelli arrives may thus be said to stand in strong contrast with his views about the other moral virtues. As he always makes clear, he considers such attributes as charity, humanity and religiousness to be wholly good and virtuous qualities.[147] But he makes it equally clear that, if a ruler wishes *mantenere lo stato*, he will often be obliged to set them aside. He evidently wishes to reassure us, however, that in the case of the princely virtues this dilemma does not arise. Here it is not the observance of these virtues that may cause you to lose your state, but only the observance of what they are corruptly and mistakenly taken to prescribe. Properly understood, the princely virtues are among the qualities that go to make up the *virtù* of a prince, thereby helping him to fulfil his primary duty of maintaining the state in a condition of security and peace.

---

[144] Machiavelli 1995, XVII. 2, p. 108: 'aveva racconcia la Romagna, unitola, ridottola in pace e in fede'. Najemy 2013 concentrates on chapter VII, thereby implying that Machiavelli was more critical of Borgia's policies.

[145] Machiavelli 1995, XVII. 4, p. 109: 'Debbe pertanto uno principe non si curare della infamia del crudele'.

[146] See Machiavelli 1995, XVII. 3, p. 108 on how Borgia acted in a manner 'molto più piatoso' than if he had spared those who initially threatened his rule.

[147] See Machiavelli 1995, XVIII. 14, p.118 on carità, umanità and religione.

4   Judicial Rhetoric in *The Merchant of Venice*

I

My aim is to explore a new approach to some familiar questions about the trial scene in *The Merchant of Venice*. What are the intellectual materials out of which the scene is constructed? Can we hope to identify the sources of Shakespeare's technical vocabulary and legal arguments?[1] Until recently, two related answers dominated the critical literature. One claimed that the trial scene 'symbolises the confrontation of Judaism and Christianity as theological systems' and 'develops the sharpest opposition of Old Law and New in terms of their respective theological principles, Justice and Mercy'.[2] Among the many commentators who adopted this perspective, some took the main allegorical contrast to be between Shylocke and Anthonio,[3] with Anthonio standing for charity and love by contrast with Shylocke's demand for strict justice.[4] But most preferred to see in Portia the emblematic figure who calls for 'the reconciliation of Justice and Mercy'[5] and represents the view that 'the New Law takes precedence over the Old'.[6]

The other and more specific claim I wish to reconsider was frequently allied with this approach. The trial was also taken to reflect the belief,

---

This chapter is a revised and extended version of Skinner 2017b. For permission to draw on this earlier work I am indebted to the Oxford University Press. For commenting on drafts I am deeply grateful to Daniel Blank, Kathy Eden, Lorna Hutson, Susan James, Claire Landis, Katharine Maus, Rhodri Lewis and Richard Strier. Many thanks also to Alan Cromartie and B. J. Sokol for additional references.

[1] On the significance of these questions see Zurcher 2010, p. 270.

[2] For the pioneering discussion (here quoted) see Lewalski, 1962, pp. 331, 338. But Barber 2012 (originally published in 1959) had already gestured at a similar reading, speaking (p. 212) of the contrast 'between Old Testament legalism and New Testament reliance on grace'. For similar claims see Danson 1978, p. 70; Colley 1980, p. 184; Tovey 1981, p. 229; Willson 1995, p. 713; Carpi 2005, p. 2322; Hirschfield 2006, p. 61; Flood 2008, p. 177, and for further references see Sokol and Sokol 1999.

[3] Lewalski 1962, p. 331; Colley 1980, p. 184; Tovey 1981, p. 232; Flood 2008, p. 177.

[4] Tovey 1981, p. 232; Flood 2008, p. 177; Carpi 2005, p. 2322.

[5] Willson 1995, p. 711. See also Danson 1978, p. 63; Cunningham and Slimp 2002, p. 244; Gay 2008, p. 55.

[6] Colley 1980, p. 185.

increasingly widespread in Elizabethan England, that the most effective means of arriving at a merciful rather than an unduly rigorous verdict is to apply the principles of equitable jurisdiction in place of the stricter demand for justice embodied in common law.[7] Seen from this perspective, the trial came to be viewed as a dramatisation of 'the conflict between the two systems of law',[8] with Portia 'adopting precisely the attitude of the Court of Chancery of the period'.[9]

These arguments undoubtedly capture something of importance about the structure of the trial scene. As a number of critics have recently pointed out, however, they both run into difficulties. One problem arises in connection with the alleged symbolic contrast between Shylocke and Anthonio. If the former is a representative of the Old Law, he must be presumed to have some acquaintance with the relevant books of the Old Testament. But these contain repeated calls for justice to be tempered with mercy, and in the book of Micah we are even rhetorically asked 'what doth the Lord require of thee, but to do justly, and to love mercy, and to walk humbly with thy God?'[10] A further problem is that it is hard to see in Anthonio a proponent of love and charity by contrast with Shylocke. Just as Shylocke expresses hatred for Anthonio,[11] so Anthonio compares Shylocke with the devil and warns that he will continue to spurn and spit on him.[12] Both characters lead sober lives, but both are troubled by violent feelings of loathing and perhaps self-loathing too.[13]

It is likewise difficult to see in Portia someone devoted to the further-ance of equity in its legal meaning, or even in its broader sense as a principle of impartiality. Her celebrated paean to the quality of mercy can hardly be construed as an appeal to equitable jurisdiction in place of strict justice. She calls for mercy, not equity, a concept to which she makes no reference.[14] But mercy is not the same as equity, even if the aim of applying equitable jurisdiction is usually to bring about a more merciful outcome.[15] As William West explains in his section on Chancery in his

---

[7] Here the pioneering article is MacKay 1964. See also Keeton 1967, pp. 144–5; Knight 1974; Danson 1978, pp. 83–6; Mahood 2003a, p. 17; Platt 2009, pp. 112–15.

[8] Carpi 2005, p. 2320.   [9] Keeton 1967, p. 145.

[10] See Micah 6: 8, as noted in Halio 1993, p. 60. See also Yaffe 1997, pp. 159–60; Sokol and Sokol 1999, p. 422; Stritmatter 2000, p. 71.

[11] Shakespeare 1986, *The Merchant of Venice* (hereafter *MofV*), TLN 357, p. 484 (1. 3. 34) and TLN 1868, p. 500 (4. 1. 60).

[12] Shakespeare 1986, *MofV*, TLN 414, p. 485 (1. 3. 91) and TLN 445–6, p. 485 (1. 3. 122–3).

[13] On their similarities see Moisan 1987, p. 105; Lyon 1988, p. 109; Kornstein 1994, p. 64; Ryan 2009, pp. 116–18.

[14] As noted in Billelo 2007, p. 112; Watt 2009, p. 217.

[15] On this point see Tucker 1976; Holmer 1995, pp. 212–13; Sokol and Sokol 1999, p. 426; Billelo 2007, p. 114.

Symboleography of 1601, 'there is a difference betweene Equitie, and Clemencie: for Equitie is alwaies most firmly knit to the wil of the Law'.[16] Portia is unable in consequence to ask for equity to be applied, because everyone in the court accepts the legality of Shylocke's bond.[17] She is left appealing not from one jurisdiction to another, but rather to a higher realm above the reach of law.[18]

Once Shylocke rejects her appeal, moreover, Portia abandons any concern for compassion and love. It is she who most explicitly invokes the Old Law when she tells Shylocke that, 'as thou urgest justice, be assurd / Thou shalt have justice more then thou desirst.'[19] Nor is her conduct of the trial equitable in the more general sense. She arrives as an imposter in borrowed robes, fraudulently allowing the duke of Venice to welcome her as a Doctor of Laws from Rome.[20] She fails to inform the duke of several disabling objections to her taking part in the trial, including the consideration that she is sheltering Shylocke's daughter, that Shylocke's loan to Anthonio was taken out in favour of her husband, and that any payment made in lieu of the bond will need to be drawn from her own resources. When she proceeds to conduct the trial she acts both as prosecutor and judge, and she concludes by demanding a criminal conviction in a civil suit.[21]

The problem with these objections, however, is that if we accept them – as I think we must – we need to find some new answers to the questions I posed at the outset. The suggestion I wish to explore is that we ought not to attempt to relate the trial scene directly to the legal ideas or practices of late Elizabethan England. We ought instead to focus on Shakespeare's reliance on the advice contained in a number of rhetorical handbooks about how to conduct a persuasive case in court. Although the scene fashioned by Shakespeare out of these sources is one of deep ambivalence and complexity, there is a clear organising structure underlying its convoluted surface. This structure, I shall argue, is provided by the classical rules of judicial rhetoric.

II

The handbooks on which I chiefly wish to concentrate are Cicero's *De inventione*, the anonymous *Rhetorica ad Herennium*, and Quintilian's *Institutio oratoria*. As I argued in chapter 1, Shakespeare was undoubtedly

---

[16] See 'Of the Chauncerie' in West 1601, fos. 173v–304v, at fo. 175v.
[17] As noted in Billelo 2007.
[18] See Sokol and Sokol 1999, p. 426; Posner, 2009, pp. 148–9.
[19] Shakespeare 1986, *MofV*, TLN 2122–3, p. 503 (4. 1. 311–12).
[20] Shakespeare 1986, *MofV*, TLN 1961 and 1974, p. 501 (4. 1. 152 and 164).
[21] Hood Phillips 1972 notes numerous objections raised by lawyers to the conduct of the trial; Posner 2009, pp. 142–9 reviews what he describes as its legal absurdities.

acquainted with all these works, and this would equally have been true of every member of his original audience who had been a beneficiary, like Shakespeare himself, of an education at an Elizabethan grammar school. It is worth adding that if Shakespeare decided – as seems certain – to renew acquaintance with these texts in the early 1590s, they would have been readily available to him.[22] One of his schoolfellows had been Richard Field, who became an apprentice to the London printer Thomas Vautrollier in 1579.[23] Two years after Vautrollier's death in 1587 Field married Vautrollier's widow and took over the running of his business.[24] Among the items of stock he inherited would have been Vautrollier's edition of the *Ad Herennium* and Cicero's *De inventione*, which he had published as a single volume in 1579.[25] The likelihood that Field supplied Shakespeare with a copy is much increased by the closeness of their connections during the early 1590s. It was Field who issued – as publisher as well as printer – the first work of Shakespeare's to appear, his *Venus and Adonis* of 1593,[26] and a year later he printed Shakespeare's *Lucrece*.[27] Most suggestive of all, *Lucrece* addresses an issue extensively examined in the *De inventione* as well as the *Ad Herennium*, that of how to handle a so-called 'assumptive' plea in court.[28] This is also the question that Portia confronts at the outset of the trial in *The Merchant of Venice*, a play that Shakespeare completed less than two years after the publication of *Lucrece*.[29] As we shall see, not only is Portia's initial plea assumptive, but in mounting it she follows to the letter the advice contained in the rhetorical manuals about how to approach this most unpromising type of legal case.

Although it is evident that Shakespeare was closely acquainted with the *Ad Herennium* and Quintilian's *Institutio oratoria*,[30] I shall mainly take my quotations from Cicero's *De inventione*, since several references in the text of *The Merchant of Venice* indicate that this was the handbook at the front of Shakespeare's mind while he was writing the trial scene. Cicero begins by listing the three forms of rhetorical utterance and the five components of a judicial speech, after which he turns to examine what he describes as the *constitutio* of a legal cause.[31] Thomas Wilson in his *Arte of Rhetorique* had proposed that *constitutio* should be translated as 'issue',[32] a suggestion quickly adopted by English legal as well as

---

[22] For the following details I draw on Skinner 2014, pp. 31–3.
[23] Arber 1875–94, vol. 2, p. 30.   [24] LeFanu 1959–64, p. 14; Nicholl 2007, p. 175.
[25] Cicero 1579.   [26] Shakespeare 1593.   [27] Shakespeare 1594.
[28] Skinner 2014, pp. 124–9, 205–9.
[29] Wiggins with Richardson 2013, p. 341 gives 1596 as the 'best guess' for the completion of the work.
[30] For evidence see Skinner 2014, p. 9n.   [31] Cicero 1949, I. VIII. 10, p. 20.
[32] Wilson 1553, sig. M, 4v.

rhetorical writers.[33] To ask about the *constitutio* of a legal cause was thus taken to be equivalent to enquiring into the specific question at issue, the question to be answered in court. As Cicero summarises, 'the *constitutio* is the name we give to the *quaestio* out of which the *causa* is born'.[34] Given that there will always be two sides to any such question, we can also say that we are speaking of the specific *controversia* or dispute in need of being resolved.[35] To speak of a judicial *causa*, the *Ad Herennium* agrees, is thus to refer to a controversy between two declared adversaries.[36]

During the trial scene in *The Merchant of Venice*, all parties reveal a precise knowledge of this legal vocabulary. The scene opens with the duke addressing Anthonio the merchant:

> DUKE What, is *Anthonio* heere?
> ANTHONIO   Ready, so please your grace.
> DUKE I am sorry for thee, thou art come to aunswere
> A stonie adversarie,   TLN 1810–12, p. 499 (4. 1. 1–4)

As the duke points out, Anthonio is confronting an adversary who has raised a legal question, and Anthonio must now answer it. Shylocke had earlier spoken in similar terms when Anthonio was being carried off to gaol:

> Thou call'dst me dogge before thou hadst a cause,
> But since I am a dog, beware my phanges,
>
> TLN 1610–11, p. 497 (3. 3. 6–7)

Shylocke is complaining that Anthonio has previously insulted him without having any reason or cause. But as he indicates, Anthonio now has a definite cause: he is party to a legal suit which Shylocke is about to bring to court.

Formally opening the proceedings, the duke observes that the question before the court arises because Shylocke 'now exacts the penalty' of his bond with Anthonio, which is 'a pound of this poore Merchants flesh'.[37] The duke subsequently announces the appointment of Bellario, a learned doctor from Padua, to determine the case. But Bellario explains in a letter to the court that he is sick, and has sent a young doctor from Rome named Balthazer (Portia in disguise) to act in his place. Meanwhile, Bellario

---

[33] Among legal writers, see, for example, Smith 1982, p. 96.

[34] Cicero 1949, I. VIII. 10, p. 20: 'quaestionem ex qua causa nascitur constitutionem appellamus.'

[35] Cicero 1949, I. VIII. 10, p. 20.

[36] *Rhetorica ad Herennium* 1954, I. II. 2, p. 4: 'Iudiciale est quod positum est in controversia'.

[37] Shakespeare 1986, *MofV*, TLN 1830–1, p. 500 (4. 1. 22–3). Anthonio has entered into a penal bond with conditional defeasance, a type of agreement still enforceable in Shakespeare's time. See Posner 2009, p. 143.

adds, he has 'acquainted him with the cause in controversie between the Jew and Anthonio the Merchant'.[38] Portia now enters, and the duke greets her in correct judicial style:

> Are you acquainted with the difference
> That holds this present question in the Court.
>
> TLN 1977–8, p. 501 (4. 1. 167–8)

As we have seen, to ask about a *quaestio* before a court is to enquire into the *constitutio* of the cause. Portia duly responds that 'I am enformed throughly of the cause'.[39] She is ready for the trial to begin.

If we return to Cicero's analysis of the specific questions liable to arise at this juncture, we find that (after some prevarication) he isolates three main possibilities. The *quaestio* may prove to be about a matter of fact; that is, about whether or not some particular action or event took place. When this is the issue to be decided, we are said to be dealing with a *constitutio coniecturalis*, and here the correct procedure is to put forward a conjecture about what may have happened and set about testing it.[40]

A second possibility is that, as Cicero and the *Ad Herennium* agree, the problem may arise *in scripto*.[41] The controversy, in other words, may be about the interpretation of 'something in writing', and hence about the meaning of a text. When this is the question at issue, we are said to be dealing with a *constitutio negotialis*, or what the *Ad Herennium* prefers to call a *constitutio legitima*.[42] As both writers warn, these causes give rise to a number of distinctive hermeneutic difficulties. Some of these will be about matters of detail such as ambiguities and the definition of terms, but two more general problems will also need to be addressed, and both writers begin by singling them out.

First you will need to make a decision about whether to focus on the *verba ipsa* of the text, or whether to ask for the *sententia scriptoris* to be investigated.[43] You must decide, in Cicero's words, whether to call on those judging your case 'to pay attention to nothing except what exactly is written',[44] or else to concentrate on 'the intention of your adversaries'.[45] You must also take care to ensure that your plea is not challenged or

---

[38] Shakespeare 1986, *MofV*, TLN 1962–3, p. 501 (4. 1. 153–4).
[39] Shakespeare 1986, *MofV*, TLN 1979, p. 501 (4. 1. 169).
[40] Cicero 1949, I. VIII. 10, p. 20; *Rhetorica ad Herennium* 1954, I. XI. 18, p. 34.
[41] Cicero 1949, I. XII. 17, p. 34; *Rhetorica ad Herennium* 1954, I. XI. 19, p. 34.
[42] Cicero 1949, I. XI. 14, p. 30; *Rhetorica ad Herennium* 1954, I. XI. 19, p. 34.
[43] Cicero 1949, I. XIII. 17, p. 34 and II. XLII. 121–2, p. 290; *Rhetorica ad Herennium* 1954, I. XI. 19, p. 34.
[44] Cicero 1949, II. XLIII. 125, p. 292: 'nihil eos qui iudicent nisi id quod scriptum spectare oportere'.
[45] See Cicero 1949, II. XLIII. 125, p. 292 on the 'intentio adversarium' and II. XLVII. 138, p. 306 on speaking 'contra scriptum'.

nullified by the existence of a *lex contraria*, a contrary law.[46] The danger here arises 'when one law permits or orders something to be done, while another forbids it'.[47] This kind of contradiction can all too readily undermine your case, because it may be open to your adversary to argue that the law supporting his side 'is concerned with matters of greater importance', and ought therefore to be upheld by the court.[48]

The third and final possibility is that you may be involved in a *constitutio iuridicalis* or 'juridical' cause, in which the question at issue is whether some particular action has or has not been performed *recte* and *iure*.[49] To recover how these terms were understood in Shakespeare's time, we need to turn for a moment to the Latin-English dictionaries of the period.[50] They agree that, when we speak of having acted *recte*, we are claiming to have behaved rightfully as opposed to wrongfully, and hence without blame.[51] They likewise agree that, when we speak of acting *iure*, we are either laying claim to something we own 'of good ryght', or else to something allowed to us by 'Lawe, right [and] good dealing' in civil affairs.[52]

Reflecting on such juridical causes, Cicero distinguishes two different possibilities. You may be able to argue that your case is *absoluta*. 'Here the question as to what is *ius* and contrary to *ius* will be contained in your plea itself', as will 'the question of what is *rectus* and what is not *rectus*'.[53] You will be able to affirm, in short, that the plea you are laying before the court is wholly in accordance with justice and right. The alternative is that your case may be *adsumptiva*. You may be obliged to admit to acting in

---

[46] Cicero 1949, II. XLIX. 144, p. 312; *Rhetorica ad Herennium* 1954, I. XI. 20, p. 36.

[47] *Rhetorica ad Herennium* 1954, I. XI. 20, p. 36: 'cum alia lex iubet aut permittit, alia vetat quippiam fieri'.

[48] See Cicero 1949, II. XLIX. 145, p. 312 on which of the contrary laws 'ad maiores … pertineat'.

[49] On acting *recte* see Cicero 1949, I. XI. 14, p. 30 and II. XXIII. 69, p. 232; *Rhetorica ad Herennium* 1954, I. XIV. 24, p. 44. On acting *iure* see Cicero 1949, I. XI. 15, p. 30; *Rhetorica ad Herennium* 1954, I. XIV. 24, p. 42.

[50] The pioneering work is Elyot 1559. See Starnes 1954, pp. 48–67. The major Elizabethan Latin-English dictionary is Cooper 1565. See Starnes 1954, pp. 85–110. Thomas 1592, a revision of the first edition of 1587, eventually superseded Cooper. See Starnes 1954, pp. 114–38. Elyot's text, originally published in 1538, was revised by Cooper, and Cooper 1565 draws heavily on it, while Thomas in turn draws heavily on Cooper. See Starnes 1954, pp. 68, 86, 95, 114–15. Veron 1575, originally published in 1552, is independent of the Elyot-Cooper-Thomas line of descent. First published in 1552, the text was revised and enlarged by Rudolph Waddington for the 1575 edition, which was reissued in 1584. See Starnes 1954, pp. 139–46.

[51] Elyot 1559, sig. 3P, 2v and 3r; Cooper 1565, sig. 5O, 3v; Thomas 1592, sig. 2S, 1v.

[52] Elyot 1559, sig. 2R, 8v; Cooper 1565, sig. 3Y, 2v; Thomas 1592, sig. 2D, 1v.

[53] See Cicero 1949, I. XI. 15, p. 30: 'Absoluta est quae ipsa in se continet iuris et iniuria quaestionem'. Cf. Cicero 1949, II. XXIII. 69, p. 232: 'Absoluta est quae ipsa in se … recti et non recti quaestionem continet.'

such a way that 'it is not possible to offer any firm response' to your adversary in court.[54] If you find yourself in this predicament, your only recourse will be to produce a *confessio*, an admission of your adversary's case combined with a plea for mercy or a request to be pardoned.[55] This type of plea can in turn take one of two forms. You may be able to attempt a *purgatio*, an excuse based on admitting the facts while denying responsibility. But you may find that you can only submit a *deprecatio*, admitting that you acted *cum consulto*, with full intention and foresight, while nevertheless asking to be acquitted.[56]

Cicero warns that it is extremely rare for such assumptive cases to succeed. But when he turns at the end of Book I of *De inventione* to discuss the most persuasive means of rounding off a speech, he nonetheless offers some advice about how to win forgiveness from a court. You will need to present what he calls a *conquestio*, 'a type of oration specifically designed to capture the pity of your hearers' and thus to induce a merciful response.[57] As to how this can be done, he places his entire faith in the use of *loci communes*, resonant and widely accepted maxims which you can invoke and apply to your case. He ends by listing a number of specific *loci* that can be deployed to arouse compassion, ending with the suggestion that we should speak 'so as to show that our own soul is filled with mercy towards others', and that we hope for mercy ourselves.[58]

As soon as Shylocke is summoned into court, he makes it clear that he considers his cause to be a *constitutio iuridicalis*, and at the same time *absoluta* in character. As we have seen, to assert that your cause is absolute is in part to claim that you have acted *recte*, without doing any wrong, and are thus free of blame. This is the contention with which Shylocke answers the duke's outraged question: 'How shalt thou hope for mercy rendring none?' Shylocke responds: 'What judgment shall I dread doing no wrong?'[59] You must also seek to establish that your cause is just, and thus that you are simply laying claim to what is yours by right. This is how Shylocke opens his case, alluding to the traditional definition of justice as *ius suum tribuere*, the act of rendering to each his due:

---

[54] Cicero 1949, I. XI. 15, p. 30: 'assumptiva [est] quae ipsa ex se nihil dat firmi ad recusationem'.
[55] Cicero 1949, I. XI. 15, p. 30.
[56] Cicero 1949, I. XI. 15, p. 30; *Rhetorica ad Herennium* 1954, I. XIV. 24, pp. 42–6.
[57] Cicero 1949, I. LV. 106, p. 156: 'Conquestio est oratio auditorum misericordiam captans'.
[58] Cicero 1949, I. LVI. 109, p. 160: 'animum nostrum in alios misericordem esse ostendimus'.
[59] Shakespeare 1986, *MofV*, TLN 1896–7, p. 500 (4. 1. 88–9).

> I have possest your grace of what I purpose,
> And by our holy Sabaoth have I sworne
> To have the due and forfet of my bond,   TLN 1843–5, p. 500 (4. 1. 35–7)

Shylocke reiterates his argument when putting his final request to the duke:

> The pound of flesh which I demaund of him
> Is deerely bought, tis mine and I will have it:
> If you deny me, fie upon your Law,
> There is no force in the decrees of Venice:
> I stand for judgement, aunswer, shall I have it?
>
> > TLN 1907–11, p. 500 (4. 1. 99–103)

With this demand for *ius* in the sense of right and good dealing, Shylocke brings the statement of his plea to a close.

Many critics have treated these calls for justice as a clear indication that allegorically Shylocke 'stands for Judaism with its emphasis upon obedience to the law' and must therefore be seen as 'the embodiment of the Old Law'.[60] But this reading arguably fails to identify the specific sources on which Shakespeare draws, which are classical rather than Judaic or Christian in provenance. According to the Roman rhetorical tradition, anyone whose cause is at once juridical and absolute must be expected to pursue their rights with complete fixity of purpose. As Cicero says, 'these are cases in which either a reward or a penalty is being sought according to what is equitable and right', and we must assume that all plaintiffs will equally want to achieve these results.[61] Shylocke's race and religion are not relevant, or at least not at this moment in the trial.

III

After anatomising the different *genera* of *constitutiones*, Cicero devotes the rest of Book I of his *De inventione* to his other major concern, the correct way of organising the components of a judicial speech.[62] Before offering his analysis, however, he pauses to consider the moral standing of the various types of cause that typically come before the courts. If you are planning to enter a plea, 'it is essential to think beforehand about the type of cause in which you are involved', and again there are said to be three main possibilities.[63]

---

[60] Tovey 1981, p. 232; Lewalski 1962, p. 339. See also Colley 1980, p. 184; Willson 1995, p. 713.
[61] Cicero 1949, I. XI. 14, p. 30: 'Iuridicalis est in qua aequi et recti natura aut praemi aut poenae ratio quaeritur'. See also *Rhetorica ad Herennium* 1954, I. XIV. 24, p. 42.
[62] The transition occurs at Cicero 1949, I. XIV. 19, p. 38.
[63] Cicero 1949, I. XV. 20, p. 40: 'necesse est genus suae causae diligenter ante cognoscere'.

If you are fortunate, you may be engaged in a *causa honesta*. An 'honest' cause 'is one that can be expected immediately to win goodwill in the mind of your audience without your even having to make a speech about it'.[64] The reason, the *Ad Herennium* explains, is that in such a cause 'you will be defending something that seems to everyone worthy of defending, or attacking something that seems to everyone deserving of attack'.[65] A second and associated possibility is that your cause may be partly honest and partly *turpis* in character. If we return to the Latin-English dictionaries of the period, we find that *turpis* is held to mean 'foule: filthie: Dishonest: unhonorable'.[66] Cicero duly notes that any cause liable to this kind of assessment is sure to give rise to some offence.[67]

While the *causa honesta* and the *causa turpis* are taken to be the principal types of plea,[68] Cicero and Quintilian both consider the further possibility that your cause may be *admirabilis*.[69] According to the Latin-English dictionaries, to classify an utterance as *admirabilis* is to view it as 'mervaylous, to be wondred at', and hence as 'strange'.[70] For example, when we speak paradoxically, we say something 'straunge and contrary to the opinion of the most parte', thereby making it 'a marvelous, wonderfull, and strange thing to heare'.[71] To speak of a strange cause is thus to refer to a plea that will seem to most people an astonishing one to put forward in court.

Cicero warns that it is difficult to defend strange causes with any expectation of success, because 'the minds of those who are about to hear you will be alienated' from your side of the case.[72] He concedes that it may be possible to enter such a plea with what he calls a 'straightforward' exordium instead of speaking in an 'insinuating' style.[73] But he advises that, if you follow this somewhat hazardous course – more appropriate to an honest cause – you must take particular care when you introduce your plea. You must be sure to begin either with a narrative of the salient facts, or else by offering 'an extremely strong reason in support of your case'.[74]

---

[64] Cicero 1949, I. XV. 20, p. 40: 'Honestum causae genus est cui statim sine oratione nostra favet auditoris animus'.

[65] *Rhetorica ad Herennium* 1954, I. III. 5, p. 10: 'cum aut id defendimus quod ab omnibus defendendum videtur, aut oppugnabimus quod ad omnibus videtur oppugnari debere'.

[66] Cooper 1565, sig. 6K, 5v, repeated in Thomas 1592, sig. 3C, 5v.

[67] Cicero 1949, I. XV. 20, p. 40: 'et benivolentiam pariat et offensionem'.

[68] For example, in *Rhetorica ad Herennium* 1954, I. III. 5, p. 10.

[69] They also consider further *genera*, while agreeing that they are of little significance. See Cicero 1949, I. XV. 20, p. 40; Quintilian 2001, 4. 1. 41, vol. 2, p. 198.

[70] Elyot 1559, sig. B, 6r; Cooper 1565, sig. D, 1r; Thomas 1592, sig. B, 4r.

[71] Cooper 1565, sig. 4T, 1r; Thomas 1592, sig. 2L, 4r.

[72] Cicero 1949, I. XV. 20, p. 40: 'a quo est alienatus animus eorum qui audituri sunt'.

[73] Cicero 1949, I. XV. 21, p. 42.

[74] Cicero 1949, I. XV. 21, p. 42: 'ab aliqua firmissima ratione nostrae dictionis'.

No one ever suggests that Shylocke's cause is inherently *turpis* or foul, and thus can simply be dismissed. Anthonio opens by conceding that Shylocke's plea is valid, so that 'no lawfull meanes can carry me / Out of his envies reach'.[75] When Portia makes her appearance, she likewise begins by assuring Shylocke that 'the Venetian law / Cannot impugne you as you doe proceed'.[76] The duke, however, is far from willing to conclude that Shylocke's cause must therefore be regarded as *honesta* or honest.[77] On the contrary, he excoriates Shylocke in his opening address for his unnatural cruelty, condemns him for his malice and urges him to withdraw his plea.[78]

How then should Shylocke's cause be classified? We already find the answer in one of Shakespeare's sources, Alexander Silvayn's story in *The Orator* (translated by Lazarus Piot in 1596) of 'a Jew, who would for his debt have a pound of the flesh of a Christian'.[79] There the Jew's cause is described as 'admirable' and 'strange'.[80] Quintilian in his discussion of strange causes characterises them as 'those which are out of line with the opinion of all men', and in his opening speech the duke appears to echo this thought.[81] He not only refers to Shylocke's 'strange apparant cruelty', but ends by declaring that such inhumanity is so strange that anyone in the world, including even Turks and Tartars, would be bound to reject it.[82] This way of thinking about Shylocke's cause is subsequently confirmed when Portia first addresses him:

> PORTIA Is your name *Shylocke*?
> SHYLOCKE   *Shylocke* is my name.
> PORTIA Of a strange nature is the sute you follow,
>
> TLN 1982–3, p. 501 (4. 1. 172–3)

Portia agrees with the duke that Shylocke's cause can only be classified as a *causa admirabilis*, a strange suit.[83]

Despite this characterisation, it would be an easy matter according to the duke for Shylocke to change direction and pursue his cause in an honest style. This call to Shylocke to convert his *causa admirabilis* into a *causa honesta* is the main burden of the duke's opening speech.[84]

---

[75] Shakespeare 1986, *MofV*, TLN 1817–18, p. 499 (4. 1. 9–10).
[76] Shakespeare 1986, *MofV*, TLN 1984–5, p. 501 (4. 1. 174–5).
[77] That is, as a cause obviously worthy of defence. See *Rhetorica ad Herennium* 1954, I. III. 5, p. 10.
[78] Shakespeare 1986, *MofV*, TLN 1826–34, p. 500 (4. 1. 18–26).
[79] Silvayn 1596, p. 400.   [80] Silvayn 1596, p. 401.
[81] Quintilian 2001, 4. 1. 21, vol. 2, p. 198: 'admirabile . . . est praeter opinionem hominum'.
[82] Shakespeare 1986, *MofV*, TLN 1829, 1838–40, p. 500 (4. 1. 21, 30–2).
[83] For different readings see Holderness 1993, p. 46; Kornstein 1994, p. 67.
[84] Although it is often treated as nothing more than an exordium designed to secure goodwill. See, for example, Leimberg 2011, p. 162.

According to the Latin-English dictionaries of the period, to display the quality of being *honestus* is to be good, laudable and virtuous;[85] more specifically, it is to exhibit kindness and gentleness;[86] even more specifically, it is to show dignity and good manners.[87] These are precisely the virtues that the duke urges Shylocke to display. He first asks Shylocke to show that he is 'toucht with humaine gentlenes and love'.[88] If he possesses this element of honesty, he will be moved to 'Forgive a moytie of the principall' that Anthonio is due to pay.[89] He also calls on Shylocke to recognise that he owes Anthonio a duty of 'tender curtesie'.[90] If he possesses this further element of honesty, he cannot fail when thinking of Anthonio to feel 'comiseration of his state'.[91]

The duke draws to a close by announcing that 'We all expect a gentle aunswere Jewe'.[92] Acting in a gentle manner is part of being honest, but the apposition gentle/Jew suggests that the duke is also asking Shylocke to give an allegedly Gentile instead of a Jewish response.[93] According to a number of late sixteenth-century writers, to speak of 'Jewish dealings' – as François de la Noue asserts – is to refer to 'a subvertion of the lawe of common charitie'.[94] More specifically, as Matteo Bandello counsels in his *Tragicall Discourses*, you need to reckon with 'the extreame pointe' of 'Jewishe creweltie'.[95] With his racist wordplay, the duke is in effect making a similar demand that Shylocke should avoid acting cruelly and with lack of charity.

Faced with the command to present his case in an honest style, Shylocke responds not merely with a vehement refusal, but with something akin to a satire on the duke's self-righteousness. First he rejects the call to pursue his suit with love and gentleness. He concludes his opening speech by confessing that he bears 'a lodgd hate, and a certain loathing' for Anthonio, which is why he is willing to follow 'A loosing sute against him.'[96] When Bassanio objects that 'This is no aunswer thou unfeeling man', Shylocke dismisses him with the scathing reminder that, given the absolute nature of his plea, 'I am not bound to please thee with my answers.'[97]

[85] Cooper 1565, sig. 3L, 3v; Veron 1575, sig. V, 4v.
[86] Veron 1575, sig. V, 4v; Thomas 1592, sig. Z, 1r.
[87] Elyot 1559, sig. 2M, 7r; Veron 1575, sig. V, 4v; Thomas 1592, sig. Z, 1r.
[88] Shakespeare 1986, *MofV*, TLN 1833, p. 500 (4. 1. 25).
[89] Shakespeare 1986, *MofV*, TLN 1834, p. 500 (4. 1. 26).
[90] Shakespeare 1986, *MofV*, TLN 1841, p. 500 (4. 1. 33).
[91] Shakespeare 1986, *MofV*, TLN 1838, p. 500 (4. 1. 30).
[92] Shakespeare 1986, *MofV*, TLN 1842, p. 500 (4. 1. 34).
[93] As noted in Holderness 1993, p. 48; Yaffe 1997, p. 16.   [94] De la Noue 1587, p. 50.
[95] Bandello 1567, fos. 77v–78r.
[96] Shakespeare 1986, *MofV*, TLN 1870, p. 500 (4. 1. 62).
[97] Shakespeare 1986, *MofV*, TLN 1871 and 1873, p. 500 (4. 1. 63, 65).

Still more vehement is Shylocke's refusal to act with dignity and tender courtesy. Cicero had advised that, if you choose to develop a strange cause in a 'straightforward' style, you must begin by offering 'an extremely strong reason in support of your case'.[98] Shylocke appears to acknowledge that this is what is expected of him:

> Youle ask me why I rather choose to have
> A weight of carrion flesh, then to receave
> Three thousand ducats: TLN 1848–50, p. 500 (4. 1. 40–2)

His response, however, is that there is no particular reason for his preference, and that he is under no obligation to supply one.[99] He presses home his point with a series of comparisons:

> Some men there are love not a gaping pigge.
> Some that are mad if they behold a Cat.
> And others when the bagpipe sings ith nose,
> Cannot containe their urine.   TLN 1855–8, p. 500 (4. 1. 47–50)

The duke had called for tender courtesy, but Shylocke reacts by talking about pigs, cats, bagpipes and an irrepressible urge to urinate. It is as if he is trying to list the most undignified examples he can think of, the examples most calculated to exhibit contempt for the customary pieties.

As we have seen, Cicero warns that, if you are bent on pursuing a strange cause, 'the minds of those who are about to hear you will be alienated' from your side of the case, so that you will be liable to be treated as *alienus*.[100] If we return to the Latin-English dictionaries we find that to describe someone in these terms was to suggest that they are 'of an other sorte' and 'none of ours'; that they are foreign or alien to humankind.[101] This is how the duke responds to Shylocke at the outset of the trial, describing him to Anthonio as 'an inhumaine wretch, / Uncapable of pitty'.[102] When Bassanio attempts to reason with Shylocke, Anthonio reiterates the duke's view that Shylocke is nothing more than a natural or at best a brutish force:

> I pray you think you question with the Jewe,
> You may as well goe stand upon the Beach
> And bid the maine flood bate his usuall height,

---

[98] Cicero 1949, I. XV. 21, p. 42: 'ab aliqua firmissima ratione nostrae dictionis'.
[99] On Shylocke's refusal (or perhaps incapacity) to account for his own motives see Strier 2010.
[100] Cicero 1949, I. XV. 20, p. 40: 'a quo est alienatus animus eorum qui audituri sunt'.
[101] Cooper 1565, sig. G, 1v.
[102] Shakespeare 1986, *MofV*, TLN 1812–13, p. 499 (4. 1. 4–5).

> You may as well use question with the Woolfe,
> Why he hath made the Ewe bleate for the Lambe:
>
> TLN 1878–82, p. 500 (4. 1. 70–4)

As Anthonio observes, there is undoubtedly a *quaestio* to be raised with Shylocke, but it makes no sense to discuss it with someone of such pitiless violence. Gratiano later repeats the image of Shylocke as a lethally hostile animal:

> Thy currish spirit
> Governd a Woolfe, who hangd for humaine slaughter
> Even from the gallowes did his fell soule fleete,
> And whilest thou layest in thy unhallowed dam;
> Infusd it selfe in thee: for thy desires
> Are wolvish, bloody, starv'd, and ravenous.
>
> TLN 1941–6, p. 501 (4. 1. 133–8)

Shylocke's immediate penalty for demanding that his strange cause be heard is that everyone regards him as 'none of ours'.

Cicero implies that anyone pursuing such a cause will be liable to be viewed with this kind of antipathy. There can be no doubt, however, that at this juncture Shylocke is the victim of a specifically racist hostility, and that he has been similarly stereotyped in a number of earlier scenes. When Launcelot Gobbo decides to leave Shylocke and become Bassanio's servant, the reason he gives is that 'my Maister's a very Jewe … I am famisht in his service.'[103] When Jessica elopes with Lorenzo, Solario mocks Shylocke for being so obsessed with the money stolen from him that he cannot distinguish between the loss of his ducats and the loss of his daughter.[104] Whenever anyone addresses Shylocke, his name cannot fail to remind us of his anxiety to lock up his house and lock away his goods,[105] especially in contrast with Anthonio's pledge to Bassanio that 'my extreamest meanes / Lie all unlockt to your occasions.'[106] The reaction of the Venetians to Shylocke not only reflects a racist prejudice, but arguably encourages a similar racism beyond the world of the play.

IV

When Portia enters the court, she begins by apparently conceding the whole of Shylocke's case:

---

[103] Shakespeare 1986, *MofV*, TLN 643–5, p. 487 (2. 2. 85–7).
[104] Shakespeare 1986, *MofV*, TLN 1019–21, p. 491 (2. 8. 15–17).
[105] As noted in Tiffany 2002, pp. 358–60.
[106] Shakespeare 1986, *MofV*, TLN 831, 854–5, p. 489 (2. 5. 28, 51–2); cf. TLN 138–9, p. 482 (1. 1. 137–8).

> PORTIA Of a strange nature is the sute you follow,
> Yet in such rule, that the Venetian law
> Cannot impugne you as you doe proceed.
> *(To Anthonio)* You stand within his danger, doe you not.
> ANTHONIO I, so he sayes.
> PORTIA   Doe you confesse the bond?
> ANTHONIO I doe.   TLN 1983–8, p. 501 (4. 1. 173–8)

Portia acknowledges that Shylocke's cause is juridical: the facts about the bond are not in dispute; the only question is what law and justice prescribe. She also accepts that Shylocke's plea is absolute: he is simply claiming a right, and cannot be legally impugned. The only plea she can enter on Anthonio's behalf will therefore have to be correspondingly assumptive. She can do no more, in other words, than enter a *confessio* in his name. Nor can she hope to do so in the form of a *purgatio*, admitting that Anthonio signed his agreement while denying that he did so *cum consulto*. As Anthonio has just acknowledged, he freely consented to the terms of Shylocke's bond. Portia is thus left with no option but to offer a *deprecatio* – a straightforward plea for mercy – and she wastes no time in making this move:

> PORTIA   Doe you confesse the bond?
> ANTHONIO I doe.
> PORTIA   Then must the Jew be mercifull.
> TLN 1987–8, p. 501(4. 1. 77–8)

As Portia recognises, Anthonio is in the desperate position of a defendant who lacks a legal case.

Faced with the insistence that he must be merciful, Shylocke retorts 'On what compulsion must I, tell me that.'[107] Without further preamble, Portia responds by delivering her celebrated speech on the quality of mercy as a heavenly gift. Critics have sometimes described the sudden introduction of this intensely sententious oration as a magnificent irrelevance.[108] But Portia is reacting in exactly the manner recommended by the classical theorists of judicial rhetoric. As we have seen, they advise that, if you have no option but to issue a *deprecatio*, you must ground it as much as possible on familiar and resonant *loci communes*, concentrating on such topics as the value of mercy and the infirmity of mankind, and culminating in the affirmation that your own heart is filled with compassion towards others.[109]

---

[107] Shakespeare 1986, *MofV*, TLN 1989, p. 501 (4. 1. 179).

[108] See, for example, Danson 1978, p. 63, who also quotes D. J. Palmer describing the speech as 'a piece of superfluous rhetoric'.

[109] Cicero 1949, I. LVI. 109, p. 160. On 'gathering' and 'framing' commonplaces see Crane 1993.

Portia begins by telling Shylocke that, in asking what should compel him to be merciful, he has misapprehended the nature of the virtue:

> The qualitie of mercie is not straind,
> It droppeth as the gentle raine from heaven
> Upon the place beneath: TLN 1990–2, p. 501 (4. 1. 180–2)

Because mercy stands in contrast with the demands of law, it can only be exercised without straining or constraint, and we should therefore think of it as similar to other gifts of God. Here Shakespeare alludes to a prayer found in several of the collections of meditations popular in Elizabethan England. They counsel that, in times of 'raging tempests, and unseasonable weather' we should appeal to God 'of thy mercie' to 'convert the thunder into gentle raine'.[110] Shakespeare transforms the prayer into an image likening mercy itself to gentle rain dropping from heaven upon the place beneath.

Next Portia offers Shylocke a number of reasons for exhibiting mercy towards Anthonio instead of calling for strict justice. One consideration frequently emphasised by the Tudor writers of commonplace books was that, as John Larke puts it in *The boke of wysdome*, 'he whiche shall have mercye of another, he shall fynde mercy for him selfe'.[111] Thomas Cogan in *The Well of Wisedome* agrees that 'he that is mercifull doth himselfe a benefite'.[112] Portia begins by speaking of mercy in the same terms:

> it is twise blest,
> It blesseth him that gives, and him that takes,
>
> TLN 1992–3, p. 501 (4. 1. 182–3)

She then proceeds to invoke a further set of popular maxims and principles. Seneca in his *De clementia* had assured Nero that 'the man who holds a place closest to the gods is the one who is kind and generous',[113] a sentiment that gained wide currency after Domenicus Mirabellius included it in his book of *sententiae* in the form of the claim that 'nothing is more befitting than mercy in a prince'.[114] Robert Hitchcock in his translation of Francisco Sansovino, which appeared as *The Quintesence*

---

[110] See, for example, Habermann 1579, pp. 326, 331; Bentley 1582, p. 479. For a later example see [Bodenham] 1600, p. 2, *sub* 'Of God': 'If God dart lightning, soon he dewes down raine.' I have not seen any edition of the play in which Shakespeare's allusion has been recognised.

[111] Larke 1532, sig. P, 1r; cf. Larke 1575, sig. J, 8r.

[112] Cogan 1577, p. 67. Cf. Proverbs 11. 17: 'The merciful man doeth good to his own soul'.

[113] Seneca 1928, I. XIX. 9, p. 414: 'proximum illis [deis] locum tenet is, qui . . . beneficus ac largus [est]'.

[114] Mirabellius 1600, p. 164, col. 2, citing 'Seneca, De Clementia': 'Nullum magis decet clementia, quam principem'. Seneca's text became widely available after several Venetian printings in the late fifteenth century, followed by editions in Basel, Lyon,

of wit in 1590, similarly describes 'using of clemencie' as 'a thing proper and perticular to great and woorthy minds'.[115] Octavianus Mirandula goes still further in his collection of *loci communes* when he adds, quoting Claudian, that 'mercy alone makes us equal to the gods'.[116] Portia draws heavily on this received wisdom in developing her case:[117]

> Tis mightiest in the mightiest, it becomes
> The throned Monarch better then his crowne. ....
> It is an attribut to God himselfe;
> And earthly power doth then show likest gods
> When mercie seasons justice:
>
>   TLN 1994–5, 2001–3, pp. 501–2 (4. 1. 184–5, 191–3)

With these familiar sentiments Portia rounds off her paean to mercy as a godlike quality.

Portia's *laudatio* is by no means at an end, however, for she concludes by adding a specifically Christian argument no less frequently encountered in Elizabethan compilations of *loci communes*. If we call for justice instead of mercy, the argument runs, we can never hope to be saved. Cogan speaks of him 'that sheweth no mercy' and asks 'how dare he aske forgivenes of his sinnes';[118] Larke reminds us that 'Our lorde Jhesu sayth, pardon other gladly if thou wylt have pardon';[119] John Marbeck in his *Booke Of Notes and Common places* adds that 'There shall be no judgment without mercie, for because ther can no man living, be found cleane'.[120] Portia ends by closely echoing these admonitions:

> Though justice be thy plea, consider this,
> That in the course of justice, none of us
> Should see salvation: we doe pray for mercy,
> And that same prayer, doth teach us all to render
> The deedes of mercie.   TLN 2004–8, p. 502 (4. 1. 194–8)

Paris and elsewhere. Mirabellius's work was first published in 1503 and thereafter frequently reprinted. On Mirabellius see Moss 1996, pp. 206–7; Skinner 2014, p. 296.

[115] Hitchcock 1590, fo. 40v.

[116] Mirandula 1598, p. 174: 'sola deos aequat clementia nobis'. While Mirandula 1598 was the first London printing, the text had been circulating widely since its first publication in 1507. See Moss 1996, pp. 95, 189; Skinner 2014, pp. 296–7.

[117] It is usually said that Portia is drawing directly from the Bible. See, for example, Noble 1935, p. 167; Stritmatter 2000, pp. 70–2; Flood 2008, pp. 176–7. I am arguing that, by the time Shakespeare was writing, the 'wisdom' books of the Old Testament had been so extensively mined in collections of commonplaces that many of their maxims had passed into general currency. See also Mahood 2003b, pp. 199–200.

[118] Cogan 1577, p. 67, referring to Ecclesiasticus 28. 4.

[119] Larke 1532, sig. P, 1r; cf. Larke 1575, sig. J, 8r.

[120] Marbeck 1581, p. 783: *sub* 'Originall sinne'. Marbeck refers us to Basil's commentary on Psalm 32. For the entry on 'Mercie' see Marbeck 1581, p. 709.

Finally she acknowledges that she is offering nothing more than a *depreca-tio*, and admits that the only reason why she has spoken at such length is 'To mittigate the justice of thy plea'.[121]

Portia's speech offers a magnificent example of Shakespeare's capacity (much celebrated by T. S. Eliot) to conjure great poetry out of conventional materials, but it is perhaps not surprising that her argument makes no impression on Shylocke, especially as her commonplaces are entirely classical and Christian in provenance. This is doubtless what Shakespeare's original audience would have expected, but it is not clear why such exhortations should carry weight with someone not of the Christian faith. Certainly Shylocke at once makes it clear that he remains unmoved. He reverts to his earlier insistence that he is simply asking for his undoubted legal rights:

> My deeds upon my head, I crave the law,
> The penalty and forfaite of my bond.   TLN 2012–13, p. 502 (4. 1. 202–3)

With this final rejection of mercy in favour of law the trial appears to be at an end. Portia accepts the justice of Shylocke's plea, 'Which if thou follow, this strict Court of Venice / Must needes give sentence gainst the Merchant there.'[122] Bassanio calls on her to wrest the law in Anthonio's favour, but she explains that 'It must not be, there is no power in Venice / Can altar a decree established'.[123] Portia's concession has sometimes been construed as an 'intrusion of equity' upon the legal order.[124] But as Shylocke recognises, it constitutes an acknowledgement of the legal order, an admission that Shylocke's contract is a valid one and grants him legal rights. He duly reacts with a cry of congratulation: 'A Daniell come to judgement: yea a Daniell'.[125] As far as he is concerned, the claim that his plea is absolute has finally been vindicated.

V

Turning to Portia at what he takes to be his moment of triumph, Shylocke exclaims 'O wise young Judge how I doe honour thee'.[126] With her next words, however, Portia suddenly opens up a new vista, possibly reminding us (some critics have suggested) that *porta* in Latin means a door.[127]

---

[121] Shakespeare 1986, *MofV*, TLN 2009, p. 502 (4. 1. 199).
[122] Shakespeare 1986, *MofV*, TLN 2010–11, p. 502 (4. 1. 200–1).
[123] Shakespeare 1986, *MofV*, TLN 2024–5, p. 502 (4. 1. 214–15).
[124] See, for example, Fortier 2005, p. 125.
[125] Shakespeare 1986, *MofV*, TLN 2029, p. 502 (4. 1. 219).
[126] Shakespeare 1986, *MofV*, TLN 2030, p. 502 (4. 1. 220).
[127] See, for example, Tiffany 2002, p. 360.

She now asks Shylocke 'I pray you let me looke upon the bond'.[128] She is giving notice that the question at issue is not exclusively *iuridicalis*, a matter of determining whether Shylocke's plea is in line with law and right; it is also *negotialis*, a matter of how to interpret a specific written document, in this case the text of his bond.

At first this shift of perspective appears to make no difference. As soon as Portia studies the contract, she declares:

> Why this bond is forfeit
> And lawfully by this the Jew may claime
> A pound of flesh, to be by him cut off
> Neerest the Merchants hart: TLN 2036–9, p. 502 (4. 1. 226–9)

She therefore makes one final appeal: 'be mercifull, / Take thrice thy money, bid me teare the bond.'[129] But Shylocke answers as before by demanding justice according to the terms of his agreement:

> I charge you by the law,
> Whereof you are a well deserving piller,
> Proceede to judgement: by my soule I sweare,
> There is no power in the tongue of man
> To alter me, I stay here on my Bond.   TLN 2044–8, p. 502 (4. 1. 234–8)

Anthonio now echoes Shylocke's demand for judgment, and Portia responds by delivering her verdict:

> Why than thus it is
> You must prepare your bosome for his knife.
>   TLN 2050–1, p. 502 (4. 1. 240–1)

Shylocke cannot resist another triumphant cry: 'O noble Judge, o excellent young man.'[130]

By this time, however, many members of Shakespeare's original audience would undoubtedly have been shaking their heads. To anyone schooled in the classical *ars rhetorica*, Shylocke's exclamation would have sounded unguardedly premature. He appears oblivious of the consideration that, if the question now before the court arises out of a *constitutio negotialis*, and is thus about how the text of his bond should be interpreted, he will need to move with considerable care as he approaches the two hermeneutic questions that cannot fail to arise.

The first is whether he should take his stand exclusively on the *verba ipsa*, 'the very words' of his bond, or whether he should make some appeal

---

128 Shakespeare 1986, *MofV*, TLN 2031, p. 502 (4. 1. 221).
129 Shakespeare 1986, *MofV*, TLN 2039–40 (4. 1. 229–30).
130 Shakespeare 1986, *MofV*, TLN 2052, p. 502 (4. 1. 242).

to the *sententia scriptoris*, the intentions and purposes underlying the text. Portia is always careful to maintain a balance between the two. When she initially concedes the lawfulness of Shylocke's bond, she does so in part because the precise wording requires it, but also because the intention underlying the relevant law makes it applicable to the case in hand:

> For the intent and purpose of the law
> Hath full relation to the penaltie,
> Which heere appeareth due upon the bond.
>
> TLN 2053–5, p. 502 (4. 1. 243–5)

Later she reaffirms the importance of such underlying purposes when she instructs Shylocke to 'Have by some Surgion *Shylocke* on your charge, / To stop his wounds, least he doe bleed to death.'[131] Conceding that this requirement is not explicitly mentioned in the bond, she argues that this is not the only matter to be taken into account. 'It is not so exprest, but what of that? / Twere good you doe so much for charitie.'[132] Although the bond says nothing explicit about the need for this degree of humanity, it is too obvious to need spelling out.

By contrast, Shylocke always insists on the exact wording of his agreement and nothing more. 'I stay here on my Bond'.[133] When Portia pronounces that this allows him to cut a pound of flesh 'Neerest the Merchants hart',[134] he relishes the exactitude of her phrasing, even quoting Cicero's formula about 'the very words':

> I, his breast,
> So sayes the bond, doth it not noble Judge?
> Neerest his hart, those are the very words.
>
> TLN 2058–60, p. 502 (4. 1. 248–50)

When Portia calls for a surgeon to stand by, Shylocke responds by insisting once more on the exact wording of his agreement. His reason for ignoring her request is that no such requirement appears in the text. 'I cannot finde it, tis not in the bond.'[135]

To Shakespeare's original audience, Shylocke's preference would have been likely to appear a characteristically Jewish one. We encounter this assumption, for example, in Juan Huarte's *Examination of men's Wits* of 1594, in which we are cautioned that 'the words of the law are not to be taken after the Jewish manner, that is, to construe onely the letter'. We not only need 'to beare in minde the formall words', but also 'to take away or

---

[131] Shakespeare 1986, *MofV*, TLN 2063–4, p. 502 (4. 1. 253–4).
[132] Shakespeare 1986, *MofV*, TLN 2066–7, p. 502 (4. 1. 256–7).
[133] Shakespeare 1986, *MofV*, TLN 2048, p. 502 (4. 1. 238).
[134] Shakespeare 1986, *MofV*, TLN 2039, p. 502 (4. 1. 229).
[135] Shakespeare 1986, *MofV*, TLN 2068, p. 502 (4. 1. 258).

adjoine that which the law [it]selfe doth not expresse'.[136] As with Portia's earlier remarks about the strangeness of Shylocke's cause, the categories of judicial rhetoric are here used to call attention to Shylocke's alien and specifically Jewish identity.

To 'adjoin' something not expressed in his bond is far from being Shylocke's instinct, but he next finds that he would have done well to heed this advice. As soon as he says to Portia 'I pray thee pursue sentence', he is made to see that in asking solely for the words of his bond to be considered he has made a disastrous choice.[137] Portia reiterates her judgment, presenting it in two parts. First she allows Shylocke his pound of flesh:

> The Court awards it, and the law doth give it. . . .
> And you must cut this flesh from off his breast,
> The law alowes it, and the court awards it.
>
> TLN 2106, 2108–9, p. 503 (4. 1. 295–6, 298–9)

Portia's complex rhetorical construction[138] – court/awards/law/law/court/ awards – accentuates the seeming finality of her verdict, and Shylocke turns at once to Anthonio: 'come prepare'.[139] But Portia interrupts him to deliver the second part of her judgment:

> Tarry a little, there is some thing else,
> This bond doth give thee heere no jote of blood,
> The words expresly are a pound of flesh:
>
> TLN 2111–13, p. 503 (4. 1. 301–3)

Shylocke has asked for nothing but the words of his bond to be considered, and what they expressly state is that he is allowed flesh but nothing more.

The disastrousness of Shylocke's choice is suddenly revealed. He ought to have followed Portia's lead and asked in addition for the *sententia scriptoris* to be assessed. As Cicero had explained, if you address the underlying purpose of any legal arrangement, you can always argue that 'something which seems inherently obvious does not need to be expressly stated'.[140] Shylocke could have claimed that, since it is inherently obvious that no one can cut off a pound of flesh without spilling blood, his bond must be understood to permit him blood as well as flesh, because it would otherwise be impossible for him to be granted any flesh.[141] Rather remarkably, Portia appears to hint at this solution when she refers to the relevance of intentions and purposes. But she evidently feels safe in

---

[136] Huarte 1594, p. 158.   [137] Shakespeare 1986, *MofV*, TLN 2104, p. 503 (4. 1. 294).
[138] Portia is using the figure of epanodos, on which see Skinner 2014, pp. 111, 150–1.
[139] Shakespeare 1986, *MofV*, TLN 2110, p. 503 (4. 1. 300).
[140] Cicero 1949, II. XLVII. 139, p. 306: 'eum quae perspicua videret esse non ascripsisse'.
[141] As noted in Kornstein 1994, p. 70; Posner 2009, p. 144.

assuming that Shylocke will continue to view his bond, in Huarte's words, 'after the Jewish manner', and this assumption proves correct. Shylocke is thus left facing the dilemma that the words of his bond allow him flesh but no blood.

The overwhelming majority of critics have taken this to be the crux of the case. They begin by quoting the line 'This bond doth give thee heere no jote of blood'.[142] They then announce – in a much repeated metaphor – that this is the moment at which the tables are turned.[143] The reason, we are told, is that Shylocke 'cannot have the flesh' after all; it has been 'made impossible' for his bond to be executed, so that the penalty becomes 'unenforceable' and 'cannot be exacted'.[144] Portia is thus able to win by nothing more than a verbal quibble and a trick.[145]

It is arguable, however, that to treat this moment as pivotal is to overlook the most essential element in the construction of Portia's case. Here Shakespeare departs markedly from his two principal sources. One of these is the story in Alexander Silvayn's *Orator* about the Jew 'who would for his debt have a pound of the flesh of a Christian'. The Jew brings his case before 'the ordinarie Judge of that place', who pronounces that the Jew may 'cut a just pound of the Christians flesh', but that 'if he cut either more or lesse, then his owne head should be smitten off'.[146] This summary adjudication is presented as the issue to be debated, and the rest of the Declamation is taken up with the Jew's appeal against the sentence and the Christian's response. Shakespeare's other source is Ser Giovanni Fiorentino's *Il pecorone*, and in this telling of the story the judge likewise begins by announcing on his own authority that 'if you take more or less than a pound, I shall have your head struck off'. The judge adds that the bond 'makes no mention of the shedding of blood', and thereupon sends for the executioner 'to bring the block and axe', proclaiming that 'if I see one drop of blood spilt, off goes your head.'[147]

---

[142] Keeton 1967, p. 144; Danson 1978, p. 119; Benston 1991, p. 174; Halio 1993, p. 61; Gross 2006, p. 100; Adelman 2008, p. 125; Ryan 2009, p. 119; Watt 2009, p. 216; Drakakis 2010, p. 103; Margolies 2012, p. 101.

[143] For this image see Benston 1991, p. 174; Halio 1993, p. 62; Mahood 2003a, pp. 16, 22; Ryan 2009, p. 119; Barber 2012, p. 210; Margolies 2012, p. 101. Fortier 2005, p. 129 prefers to say that 'Shylock's downfall comes when Portia applies a legalistic interpretation to the words of the bond', while Strier 2013, p. 191 says that 'the "no jot of blood" proviso brings the proceedings to a halt.'

[144] For these claims see, respectively, Brown 1955, p. lii; Tiffany 2010, p. 180; Gross 2006, p. 100; Billelo 2007, p. 109; Zurcher 2010, p. 274.

[145] On Portia's quibbling see Brown 1955, p. xlix; Keeton 1967, p. 140; Margolies 2012, p. 101. On her alleged trick see Colley 1980, p. 185; Harmon 2004, p. 103; Watt 2009, p. 214; Margolies 2012, p. 103.

[146] Silvayn 1596, p. 401.   [147] Bullough 1957–75, vol. 1, p. 473.

Shakespeare offers something very different from these arbitrary judgments. He continues to follow the classical rhetoricians and their analysis of the two questions that any plaintiff must consider before bringing forward a *constitutio negotialis*. The first is whether to ask for the *sententia scriptoris* to be considered. If Shylocke had followed this option, he would undoubtedly have been able to answer Portia's initial objection that his bond allows him flesh but no blood. But he would still have been left confronting the second question: is it possible that there may be a *lex contraria* challenging the legal standing of the bond as a whole? It is evident from Shylocke's way of presenting his case – as Portia has clearly noticed – that this is not a question he has asked himself. But as she next goes on to disclose, there is in fact a *lex contraria* – or rather, two distinct *leges contrariae* – that stand in Shylocke's way.

The first is intended to deter acts of violence against Christians in Venice. Portia quotes the relevant provisions:

> Take then thy bond, take thou thy pound of flesh,
> But in the cutting it, if thou doost shed
> One drop of Christian blood, thy lands and goods
> Are by the lawes of Venice confiscate
> Unto the state of Venice.   TLN 2114–18, p. 503 (4. 1. 304–8)

Shylocke is stunned. 'Is that the law?'[148] It seems extraordinary that he should not have known about a piece of legislation expressly designed to shield Christian citizens of Venice from violence.[149] But Portia is able to assure him that there is indeed such a law, and that 'Thy selfe shalt see the Act' in which it is promulgated.[150]

Cicero had particularly admonished plaintiffs to ensure that their cause is not subject to being overturned by a contrary law 'dealing with more important matters', since 'this is the law that will be taken to have the greater claim to be upheld'.[151] It is Shylocke's failure to heed this advice that enables Portia to triumph over him. As she admits throughout the trial, the law in Venice extends to the protection of aliens, so that Shylocke has private rights that the court must respect.[152] But such rights are subject to public law, and hence to the provisions of such Acts of state as the one designed to protect

---

[148] Shakespeare 1986, *MofV*, TLN 2120, p. 503 (4. 1. 310).

[149] As noted in Posner 2009, p. 145 and in Julius 2010, p. 192.

[150] Shakespeare 1986, *MofV*, TLN 2121, p. 503 (4. 1. 310). The only commentary I have read in which the importance of contrary laws is discussed is Donawerth 1984, pp. 208–9. Leimberg 2011, p. 93 mentions contrary laws, but misleadingly claims that 'two laws contradict each other in the written text' of Shylocke's bond.

[151] See Cicero 1949, II. XLVIII. 145, p. 312 on the need to consider 'utra lex ad maiores . . . pertineat', since 'ea maxime conservanda putetur'. See also Quintilian 2001, 7. 7. 7–8, vol. 3, p. 274.

[152] As noted in Ward 1999, p. 132.

Christians from harm. One might wonder if, in a commercial city such as Venice, the granting of such protection is manifestly of greater importance than the upholding of freedom of contract.[153] But no one questions Portia's contention that, if Shylocke insists on the terms of his bond, the penalty annexed to his violation of the contrary law will come into effect.

It is misleading, therefore, to treat Portia's observation that Shylocke's bond allows him flesh but not blood as the turning-point in the trial on the grounds that this makes his bond impossible to execute.[154] He can still insist on its terms, and Portia urges him to do so. 'Take then thy bond, take thou thy pound of flesh'.[155] But if he does so, he will be obliged to pay the penalty for infringing the relevant contrary law, and will forfeit his estate. The reason why this moment marks the true turning-point is that Portia has correctly guessed that, as soon as Shylocke is made aware of the penalty, he will find it too severe to contemplate. His bond is not unenforceable; rather the effect of the contrary law is to make him decide not to enforce it. He instantly recalls Portia's initial offer to pay him three times what he is owed, and he now accepts. 'I take this offer then, pay the bond thrice / And let the Christian goe.'[156]

Shylocke appears confident that his proposal will be well received. But he is next made to see how crucial it was that Portia's earlier offer prompted him to refuse in open court anything except the terms of his agreement. 'I stay here on my Bond.'[157] She is now able to point out that, because he has already rejected any alternative, the penalty due to him under the law is the only settlement the court can make. First she reiterates her judgment:

> Soft, the Jew shal have all justice, soft no hast,
> He shall have nothing but the penalty. TLN 2127–8, p. 503 (4. 1. 317–18)

Then she spells out the implications:

> Therefore prepare thee to cut of the flesh,
> Shed thou no blood, nor cut thou lesse nor more
> But just a pound of flesh: if thou tak'st more
> Or lesse then a just pound, be it but so much
> As makes it light or heavy in the substance,
> Or the devision of the twentith part
> Of one poore scruple, nay if the scale doe turne
> But in the estimation of a hayre,
> Thou dyest, and all thy goods are confiscate.
> TLN 2130–8, p. 503 (4. 1. 320–8)

---

[153] As noted in Strier 2013, pp. 190–2.   [154] As noted in Holmer 1995, pp. 199, 207.
[155] Shakespeare 1986, *MofV*, TLN 2114, p. 503 (4. 1. 304).
[156] Shakespeare 1986, *MofV*, TLN 2125–6, p. 503 (4. 1. 314–15).
[157] Shakespeare 1986, *MofV*, TLN 2048, p. 502 (4. 1. 238)

Portia speaks with triumphant *amplificatio*, but it might be thought that here she overreaches and even contradicts herself. She seems to have forgotten that, although the contrary law specifies a confiscation of goods, it makes no mention of a sentence of death. She also speaks in outright violation of her earlier plea for everyone to render deeds of mercy instead of calling for the imposition of merciless justice.

Portia remains adamant, however, that Shylocke 'shall have meerely justice and his bond.'[158] It is now Shylocke's turn to ask for mercy, and when Portia rejects his plea he has no alternative but to give up:

> SHYLOCKE Shall I not have barely my principall?
> PORTIA Thou shalt have nothing but the forfaiture
> To be so taken at thy perrill Jew.
> SHYLOCKE Why then the devill give him good of it:
> Ile stay no longer question.   TLN 2148–52, p. 503 (4. 1. 338–42)

The question to which Shylocke here refers, the *quaestio* he had brought before the court, was whether he should be permitted to impose his penal bond. With his own decision not to impose it, the *quaestio* is resolved. There is nothing more to be said, as he duly acknowledges with his declaration that 'Ile stay no longer question'.

According to Portia, however, there is a great deal more to be said. She now informs Shylocke that there is a second *lex contraria* standing in his way. As she explains, this further enactment is specifically designed to prevent aliens such as Shylocke from plotting, even indirectly, against the life of any Venetian citizen:

> Tarry Jew,
> The law hath yet another hold on you.
> It is enacted in the lawes of Venice,
> If it be prov'd against an alien,
> That by direct, or indirect attempts
> He seeke the life of any Cittizen,
> The party gainst the which he doth contrive,
> Shall seaze one halfe his goods, the other halfe
> Comes to the privie coffer of the State,
> And the offenders life lies in the mercy
> Of the Duke onely, gainst all other voyce.
> In which predicament I say thou standst:
>   TLN 2152–63, p. 503 (4. 1. 342–53)

The first contrary law had left Shylocke's right to his pound of flesh unquestioned; it had merely triggered a penalty so severe as to make him decide not to enforce it. But this further contrary law calls into

---

[158] Shakespeare 1986, *MofV*, TLN 2145, p. 503 (4. 1. 335).

question the legality of the bond itself, involving as it does an indirect attempt by an alien on the life of a Venetian citizen. Whereas the effect of the first law had simply been to leave Shylocke empty-handed, the effect of the second is to convict him of a capital crime.

It seems even more extraordinary that Shylocke should not have known about a law expressly designed to protect Venetian citizens from the machinations of aliens such as himself.[159] But in the face of this further onslaught he has no defence and is shocked into silence. The duke spares his life, and Anthonio announces that he will be content if Shylocke retains the half of his goods forfeited to the state, on condition that three demands be met: that Shylocke should eventually will this half to Lorenzo and Jessica; that the half coming to Anthonio should eventually go to Lorenzo; and that Shylocke should immediately become a Christian. If these arrangements are agreed, he says, he will be content. Portia now asks: 'Art thou contented Jew?'[160] Shylocke has lost half his estate as well as his place in his community, but he has no choice but to echo Anthonio. 'I am content'.[161] There is no escaping the force of the contrary laws.

---

[159] Smith 2013 stresses that Shylocke's alien status is what is chiefly significant. On the position of aliens (including Jews) in Shakespeare's London see Shapiro 1996, pp. 187–9.
[160] Shakespeare 1986, *MofV*, TLN 2199, p. 504 (4. 1. 389).
[161] Shakespeare 1986, *MofV*, TLN 2199, p. 504 (4. 1. 390).

5   Rhetorical Redescription and its Uses in Shakespeare

I

I begin with the two earliest English handbooks in which the technique of rhetorical redescription is named as *paradiastole* and defined. The first is Henry Peacham's *Garden of Eloquence* of 1577; the second is George Puttenham's *Arte of English Poesie* of 1589.[1] Peacham lists the technique among the figures of amplification used to 'garnish matters and causes'.[2] He considers it immediately after discussing meiosis – to which it is said to be 'nye kin' – and he defines it as follows:

> Paradiastole ... is when by a mannerly interpretation, we doe excuse our own vices, or other mens whom we doe defend, by calling them vertues.[3]

Puttenham pursues the comparison between meiosis and paradiastole at greater length. When you 'diminish and abbase a thing by way of spight or mallice, as it were to deprave it', this is an instance of meiosis. The contrast with paradiastole is then spelled out:

> But if such moderation of words tend to flattery, or soothing, or excusing, it is by the figure *Paradiastole*, which therfore nothing improperly we call the *Curry-favell*, as when we make the best of a bad thing, or turne a signification to the more plausible sence: ... moderating and abating the force of the matter by craft, and for a pleasing purpose.[4]

Puttenham later reiterates that, whereas meiosis – which he labels 'the *disabler*'[5] – has the effect of denigrating what is described, paradiastole is used to exculpate. When we employ rhetorical redescription 'to make an

This chapter is a revised and much extended version of Skinner 2007. For permission to draw on this earlier work I am indebted to the Cambridge University Press. For commenting on drafts I am deeply grateful to Sylvia Adamson, Gavin Alexander, Katrin Ettenhuber, Stephen Greenblatt, Susan James and Jason Scott-Warren.
[1] There is also a definition (but an unilluminating one) in Sherry 1550, fo. 39v. For discussions of paradiastole see Javitch 1972; Whigham 1984, pp. 40–2, 204–5; Cox 1989, pp. 53–5; Condren 1994, 78–84; Skinner 1996, pp. 142–80; Tuck 1996, pp. 195–9; Skinner 2002a, pp. 264–85; Moriarty 2011, pp. 2–3, 149, 232–5, 241–4.
[2] Peacham 1577, sig. N, 2r.   [3] Peacham 1577, sig. N, 4v.
[4] [Puttenham] 1589, p. 154.   [5] [Puttenham] 1589, p. 154.

offence seeme lesse then it is, by giving a terme more favorable and of lesse vehemencie then the troth requires', then such 'phrases of extenuation' are not instances of meiosis but 'fall more aptly to the office of the figure *Curry favell*'.[6]

Both Peacham and Puttenham are self-conscious about the need to rework the conventions of classical rhetoric for their Elizabethan audience, an aspiration most clearly reflected in Puttenham's efforts to domesticate the outlandish names for the figures of speech inherited by the Roman rhetoricians from their Greek authorities. But at the same time they remain heavily dependent on the body of ancient treatises in which these figures had first been anatomised. As I noted in chapter 3, the earliest surviving work in which paradiastole had been isolated and defined had been the *De figuris sententiarum et elocutionis* attributed to P. Rutilius Lupus and dated to *c.*20CE. Rutilius's handbook was printed in Venice in 1519 and republished in the Aldine collection of rhetorical texts in 1523, as well as in several editions later in the century.[7] As originally printed, it took the form of forty-one sections arranged in two Books, with each section devoted to one of the figures, the names of which are given in transliteration from the Greek together with definitions and illustrations in each case. Book I, Section 4 is headed 'Paradiastole', and the full entry reads as follows:

This *schema* distinguishes between two or more things that seem to have the same force, and teaches us how far they are distinct from one another by assigning the right meaning to each of them. Hyperides: For when you attempt to deceive the opinion of others, you frustrate yourself. You are not able to show that you should be understood as wise rather than crafty, or courageous rather than reckless, or careful in family matters rather than niggardly, or severe rather than ill-willed. There is no vice in which you are able to glory by praising it as a virtue. The same *schema* can readily be used yet more impressively when a reason is added to the judgment. This can be done in the following way: Hence do not so often call yourself frugal when you are avaricious. For someone who is frugal makes use of what is sufficient; you on the contrary, because of your avarice, want more than you have. So what will follow will not be the fruits of thrift but rather the miseries of destitution.[8]

---

[6] [Puttenham] 1589, p. 184.
[7] The BN catalogue records editions in 1530 (Paris), 1540 (Lyon) and 1541 (Paris).
[8] Rutilius Lupus 1970, p. 8: 'Hoc schema duas aut plures res, quae videntur unam vim habere, disiungit et quantum distent docet, suam cuique propriam sententiam subiungendo. Hyperidis: Nam cum ceterorum opinionem fallere conaris, tu tete frustraris. Non enim probas te pro astuto sapientem intelligenti, pro confidente fortem, pro inliberali diligentem rei familiaris, pro malivolo severum. Nullum est enim vitium, quo ut virtutis laude gloriari possis. Hoc idem schema solet illustrius fieri, cum ratio proposito subiungitur. Id est huius modi. Quapropter noli te saepius parcum appellare, cum sis avarus. Nam qui parcus est, utitur eo quod satis est; tu contra propter avaritiam, quo plus habes, magis eges. Ita non tam diligentiae fructus quam inopiae miseria sequitur.'

The figure of Hyperides to whom Rutilius here refers was an Attic orator of the fourth century BCE. Hyperides had made a celebrated speech, a fragment of which survives, in which he had denounced Aristophon for attempting to commend his vices as virtues, and it is the technique of exposing this self-praising trick that Rutilius labels paradiastole.[9]

Rutilius's discussion may have been indebted to the popular Roman handbook known as the *Rhetorica ad Herennium*. As I noted in chapter 3, this had been produced by a contemporary of Cicero's, and until the ascription was disproved by Raphael Regius in the 1490s it was frequently attributed to Cicero himself.[10] The author of the *Ad Herennium* never uses the term paradiastole, but in the course of Book III he treats us to some hyperbolical advice about how to employ the technique in a court of law:

What our adversary calls justice we shall demonstrate to be weakness, and a lazy and corrupt form of liberality; what he names prudence we shall say is inept, indiscreet and offensive cleverness; what he speaks of as temperance we shall speak of as lazy and dissolute negligence; what he names courage we shall call the inconsiderate recklessness of a gladiator.[11]

It may even be possible, we are being told, to redescribe the four cardinal virtues as instances of vice.

Like the Elizabethan rhetoricians, Rutilius and the author of the *Ad Herennium* think of paradiastole as a technique for manipulating the language of virtue and vice. As will be obvious from my quotations, however, the Elizabethan writers strongly disagree with them about the point or purpose of using the technique. The Roman writers speak of paradiastole as the figure in play when we unmask someone for deceitfully laying claim to a virtue and show that they deserve to be condemned. The ultimate aim is to denigrate our rivals and adversaries. By contrast, the Elizabethan writers speak of paradiastole as the figure we employ when we defend someone against an accusation of vice and show that they deserve to be praised. The ultimate aim is to excuse, and normally to excuse ourselves.

It seems to have been Quintilian in his *Institutio oratoria* who reversed the direction of paradiastole in this way. He picks up Rutilius's discussion in Book VIII, but his revision – or perhaps misunderstanding – becomes clear as soon as he lists his examples. For Rutilius it had been an instance of paradiastole when we criticise someone for trying to claim that he is wise when he is merely crafty, or courageous when he is

---

[9] Hyperides 1944, p. 575.   [10] See Skinner 1996, pp. 32–3.
[11] *Rhetorica ad Herennium* 1954, III. III. 6, pp. 166–8: 'is qui contra dicet iustitiam vocabit, nos demonstrabimus ignaviam esse et inertiam ac pravam liberalitatem; quam prudentiam appellarit, ineptam et garrulam et odiosam scientiam esse dicemus; quam ille modestiam dicet esse, eam nos inertiam et dissolutam neglegentiam esse dicemus; quam ille fortitudinem nominarit, eam nos gladiatoriam et inconsideratam appellabimus temeritatem.'

merely reckless, and so on. But according to Quintilian the figure is in play 'whenever you call *yourself* wise rather than crafty, or courageous rather than reckless'.[12] Although Quintilian takes over Rutilius's illustrations, he thinks of paradiastole not as a means of unmasking but of excusing vice.

Among the rhetorical theorists of later antiquity, it was Quintilian's understanding that largely prevailed. If we turn to the anonymous fifth-century handbook entitled *De figuris*, the first example we encounter under the heading paradiastole is that of someone 'who calls himself courageous when he is merely frenzied'.[13] Still more revealing is the treatment of paradiastole in Book II of Isidore of Seville's *Libri etymologiarum*. When Isidore discusses the figure, he appears to take his illustrations directly from Rutilius Lupus. The framework into which he fits them, however, is the one supplied by Quintilian. 'It is a case of *Paradiastole*', Isidore explains, 'whenever we distinguish what we say by means of interpretation: "When you call yourself wise rather than crafty, or courageous rather than heedless, or careful rather than niggardly."'[14]

With the revival of the *Ars rhetorica* in the Renaissance, it was Quintilian's view that principally gained currency once more. The earliest Renaissance text in which paradiastole is defined and illustrated is Antonio Mancinelli's *Carmen de Figuris*, which was printed in Venice in 1493 and frequently republished.[15] As Mancinelli admits, he is wholly reliant on Quintilian,[16] and simply quotes him to the effect that 'it is an instance of paradiastole when you call yourself wise rather than crafty, or courageous rather than reckless'.[17] His analysis served in turn as a major source for Johann Susenbrotus in his *Epitome Troporum ac Schematum*, perhaps the most widely used treatise on *elocutio* of the later sixteenth century. First printed in Germany, the *Epitome* was republished in London as early as 1562 and went through at least four further English editions in the next generation.[18] Susenbrotus specifically refers us to Mancinelli, and his own list of examples begins by repeating Quintilian word for word.[19]

---

[12] Quintilian 2001, 9. 3. 63, vol. 4, p. 138: 'Cum te pro astuto sapientem appelles, pro confidente fortem'. Italics added.

[13] *De figuris* 1993, p. 86: 'Dum fortem, quae sit vaecors ... vocat se'.

[14] Isidore 1983, p. 81: '*Paradiastole* est, quotiens id, quod dicimus, interpretatione discernimus: "Cum te pro astuto sapientem appellas, pro inconsiderato fortem, pro inliberali diligentem."'

[15] The BL catalogue records four editions published between 1493 and 1503.

[16] Mancinelli 1493, sig. H, 1r explicitly states that he is writing 'teste Fabio libro nono', that is, according to the authority of Quintilian in Book IX of his *Institutio oratoria*.

[17] Mancinelli 1493, sig. H, 1r: 'Paradiastole sit ... quum te pro astuto sapientem appellas, pro confidente fortem'.

[18] The BL catalogue lists London printings (all Latin) in 1562, 1570, 1572, 1608 and 1621.

[19] Susenbrotus 1562, p. 46: 'cum pro astuto sapientem appelles: pro confidente, fortem: pro illiberali, diligentem'.

It is true that some Renaissance rhetoricians revert to Rutilius's original suggestion that paradiastole names the technique not of practising but of unmasking the art of rhetorical redescription.[20] This is the view of Jean Despautère in his *De figuris* of 1520,[21] and of Gerard Vossius in his *Oratorum Institutionum* of 1606, for whom paradiastole is a form of definition in which 'a false name for something is set aside and the true name applied to it'.[22] If we return, however, to the English rhetoricians of the sixteenth century, we find that without exception they prefer to endorse and develop Quintilian's contrasting account. The first to follow this path was Thomas Wilson in his *Arte of Rhetorique* of 1553.[23] Wilson never uses the term paradiastole, but in anatomising 'the firste kinde of Amplification', which occurs 'when by changing a woorde, in augmentynge we use a greater, but in diminishynge we use a lesse', he notes that this is the technique we deploy whenever 'we give vices, the names of vertue'.[24] As we have seen, Henry Peacham explicitly refers to this technique as paradiastole, characterising it as 'a fit instrument of excuse'.[25] Angel Day in his *Declaration* of 1592 similarly takes this to be the figure in play whenever 'with a milde interpretation' we palliate our own or other people's faults.[26]

The principal way in which the Tudor rhetoricians reveal their dependence on the Roman tradition is in their choice of examples. The first case mentioned by most of the Roman rhetoricians had been that of trying to characterise yourself not as crafty but as wise.[27] Mancinelli and Susenbrotus repeat the example,[28] and Peacham likewise pronounces it an instance of paradiastole when we seek to justify 'deepe dissimulation' by calling it 'singuler wisdome'.[29] A second Roman example had been that of claiming to be careful rather than niggardly.[30] Again Susenbrotus repeats it,[31] and again the Tudor rhetoricians follow suit. Wilson refers to those who call 'a snudge, or pynche penye, a good husbande',[32] while Puttenham writes of those who call 'the niggard, thriftie'[33] and Peacham

---

[20] As noted in Tuck 1996.

[21] Despauterius 1555, sig. D, 1r, quoting Rutilius Lupus. I use the Antwerp edition (1555) rather than the first edition (Paris, 1520).

[22] Vossius 1609, p. 791: 'rei falsum nomen adimitur, verumque imponitur'.

[23] On Wilson see Shrank 2004, pp. 182–219.   [24] Wilson 1553, fos. 66v, 67r.

[25] Peacham 1593, p. 168.   [26] Day 1592, p. 90.

[27] See Rutilius Lupus 1970, p. 8, Quintilian 2001, 9. 3. 63, vol. 4, p. 138 and Isidore 1983, p. 81 on astutus/sapiens.

[28] See Mancinelli 1493, sig. H, 1r and Susenbrotus 1562, p. 46 on astutus/sapiens.

[29] Peacham 1577, sig. N, 4v. See also Day 1592, p. 90; Peacham 1593, p. 168.

[30] See Quintilian 2001, 9. 3. 63, vol. 4, p. 138 and Isidore 1983, p. 81 on inliberalis/diligens.

[31] See Susenbrotus 1562, p. 46 on illiberalis/diligens.   [32] Wilson 1553, fo. 67r.

[33] [Puttenham] 1589, p. 154.

adds that some people justify 'insatiable avarice' by redescribing it as 'good husbandrie'.[34]

Rutilius had introduced the further example of someone who describes himself as merely severe when he is in fact ill-willed, and Quintilian mentions the possibility of excusing cruelty as sternness.[35] Susenbrotus draws on both these discussions[36] and Wilson similarly observes that 'a cruell or mercilesse man' can be redescribed as nothing more than 'somewhat soore in judgement'.[37] Rutilius's final instance had been that of someone who praises himself as courageous when he is merely reckless.[38] Quintilian and Isidore both adapt the example, as do Mancinelli and Susenbrotus,[39] and once again the Tudor rhetoricians follow suit. Puttenham writes of excusing 'the foolish-hardy' as 'valiant or couragious',[40] and Day similarly notes that one can call 'a man furious or rash, valiant'.[41] Peacham even suggests that it may be possible to justify a murder by calling it a manly deed.[42]

II

Among the standard examples of paradiastole I have been listing, the case of attempting to excuse a reckless action by redescribing it as courageous is of particular significance. By contrast with the other cases I have cited, which survive only in Roman and later sources, this example can already be found in a number of ancient Greek texts. Among these the most influential was Aristotle's *Art of Rhetoric*. As I showed in chapter 3, Aristotle's treatise became widely known after George of Trebizond's Latin translation was printed in Venice in 1478 and reissued in the Aldine collection of rhetorical texts in 1523. Over the course of the century three further Latin translations appeared: Ermolao Barbaro's in 1544, Carolo Sigonio's in 1565 and Antonio Maioraggio's in 1591.[43] By the end of the Elizabethan era Aristotle's text had become part of the general currency of Latin rhetorical thought.

---

[34] Peacham 1593, p. 168.
[35] See Rutilius Lupus 1970, p. 8 on malivolens/severus and Quintilian 2001, 11. 1. 90, vol. 5, p. 56 on asperus/severus.
[36] Susenbrotus 1562, p. 78: 'cum crudelem appellamus paulo severiorem'. But he offers this example under the heading of meiosis rather than paradiastole.
[37] Wilson 1553, fo. 67r.   [38] See Rutilius Lupus 1970, p. 8 on fortis/confidens.
[39] See Quintilian 2001, 9. 3. 63, vol. 4, p. 138; Isidore 1983, p. 81; Mancinelli 1493, sig. H, 1r; and Susenbrotus 1562, p. 46 on confidens (or inconsideratus)/fortis.
[40] [Puttenham] 1589, p. 154.   [41] Day 1592, pp. 62–3.   [42] Peacham 1577, sig. N, 4v.
[43] I quote Sigonio's and Maioraggio's translations from their original editions and Barbaro's from the Paris edition of 1559.

George of Trebizond introduces Aristotle's discussion of rhetorical redescription by making him say that, if we aspire to speak persuasively, we must ensure that, 'when it comes to praise and blame, those things which are close to being morally worthy are accepted as having the quality itself'.[44] One of Aristotle's examples is that of trying to defend a savage man as brave.[45] Barbaro and Maioraggio offer similar translations, speaking of those who try to praise temerity as courage,[46] while Sigonio refers to those who deliberately confuse courage with mere audacity.[47]

As I suggested in chapter 3, Aristotle's analysis appears to have been influenced by two earlier accounts. One was Thucydides's discussion in Book III of his *History* of how civil strife arose in Corcyra, and how this led to the deliberate manipulation of evaluative terms.[48] Thucydides's observations became widely known after Lorenzo Valla's Latin translation of the *History* was published in 1483, and was subsequently reprinted several times in the first half of the sixteenth century.[49] Valla's text was also translated into French in 1534, and this version formed the basis for the English translation by Thomas Nicolls published in 1550.[50] Nicolls renders the celebrated passage in Book III by saying that, as soon as conflict broke out among the citizens of Corcyra, 'all the evylles whiche they committed, they disguised and named by newe and unaccustomed names'.[51] His first illustration is that 'temeritie and rashnes, they named magnanymytie and noblenes of courage, so that the rashe were named vertuous defendors of theyr frendes'.[52]

A further important conduit for the transmission of Thucydides's account was Plutarch's essay 'How a man may discerne a flatterer from a friend', which gained wide currency in English after its publication by Philemon Holland in his translation of Plutarch's *Moralia* in 1603. Plutarch notes that '*Thucydides* in his storie writeth: That during civill seditions and warres, men transferred the accustomed significations of words unto other things for to justifie their deeds'. The first instance he offers is that 'for desparate rashnesse, without all reason, was reputed

---

[44] George of Trebizond 1523, fo. 114v: 'Ea quoque accipienda sunt, quae honestis propinqua sunt, tanquam ad laudem, vel vituperationem conferentia'.

[45] See George of Trebizond 1523, fo. 114v on ferox/fortis.

[46] See Barbaro 1559 p. 32 on temeritas/fortitudo and Maioraggio 1591, fo. 70r, col. 1 on temerarius/fortis.

[47] See Sigonio 1565, p. 49 on audax/fortis.

[48] Thucydides 2013, III. 70–83, pp. 206–14.

[49] There were printings in Venice in 1513, 1528 and 1555; Paris in 1527, 1555 and 1564; Cologne in 1550; Basel in 1564. Details from BL and BN catalogues.

[50] See Thucydides 1534; Thucydides 1550.   [51] Thucydides 1550, fo. ccr.

[52] Thucydides 1550, fo. ccr.

valour, and called Love-friend'.[53] He uses the example to introduce his denunciation of flatterers for perverting the 'inward natures and dispositions' of men by 'giving to vices the names of vertues'.[54]

The other account of rhetorical redescription on which Aristotle seems to have drawn is Plato's in Book VIII of *The Republic*. This discussion does not appear to have been familiar to the rhetorical theorists of the early Renaissance, although some of Plato's examples may have been known through their inclusion in Plutarch's essay on the flatterer. Plato's own analysis only became widely available after the appearance of Marsilio Ficino's *Platonis Opera*, first printed in Florence in 1484 and repeatedly reissued throughout the sixteenth century.[55] As I noted in chapter 3, Plato speaks of how the Lotus-eaters managed to corrupt the young oligarch.[56] One of their methods was to criticise worthy actions while exonerating behaviour that had usually been condemned. For instance, as Ficino's translation puts it, 'they called insolence the behaviour of those who had been nobly brought up'.[57] Aristotle adapts the example in his *Art of Rhetoric*, in which he argues – in the vocabulary developed by his sixteenth-century translators – that an arrogant, proud or contumacious person can always represent himself as magnificent, honourable, splendid and great.[58] Among the Renaissance rhetoricians, Susenbrotus was the first to reiterate that haughtiness can be redescribed as nobility,[59] and Angel Day similarly notes that it is an instance of paradiastole to call 'him that is proud magnanimous'.[60] The example gained wider currency with the publication in 1603 of Holland's translation of Plutarch, in which he had warned that flatterers like to excuse pride as magnanimity.[61]

A second instance examined by Plato had been that – in the words of Ficino's translation – 'prodigality came to be redescribed as magnificence'.[62] Here again Aristotle takes up the example, although his Renaissance

[53] Plutarch 1603, p. 93. This example had already been made known to English readers by William Jones in his translation of Justus Lipsius's *Politicorum libri sex* in 1594. See Lipsius 1594, p. 69, where Jones translates Lipsius as saying that 'whatsoever is rash and headie, that is deemed by them to be couragiously and valiauntly enterprised'.
[54] Plutarch 1603, p. 93.
[55] There were printings in Venice in 1491, 1517 and 1581; Basel in 1546, 1551 and 1561; Lyon in 1550 and 1588; and Geneva in 1592. Details from BL and BN catalogues.
[56] Plato 1935, 560c to 561a, pp. 296–300.
[57] Plato 1484, fo. 355v, col. 2: 'petulentiam ingenuam educationem nominant'.
[58] See George of Trebizond 1523, fo. 114v on arrogans/magnificus atque honestus; Barbaro 1559, p. 32 on superbus/magnificus & splendidus; Sigonio 1565, p. 49 on contumax/magnificus ac grandis; Maioraggio 1591, fo. 70r, col. 1 on contumax/magnificus & gravis.
[59] See Susenbrotus 1562, p. 46 on fastidiosus/magnanimus.   [60] Day 1592, p. 63.
[61] Plutarch 1603, p. 93.
[62] Plato 1484, fo. 355v, col. 2: 'nominant ... prodigalitatem/magnificentiam'.

translators alter its force, speaking instead of excusing prodigality by calling it liberality.[63] From these sources the discussion passed to the Tudor rhetoricians. Wilson and Puttenham both speak of calling 'a spende all, a liberall gentilman',[64] and Day agrees that it is a case of paradiastole when we call 'a prodigall man, *liberall*'.[65] Once again the example gained wider currency with the publication of Holland's translation of Plutarch, in which he invites his readers 'to consider and observe in flatterers, how they terme prodigalitie by the name of liberalitie'.[66]

A further example stemming from the Greek tradition was that of excusing an enraged or indignant man by redescribing his behaviour as manly and straightforward. We already find Thucydides observing that (in Nicolls's translation) as soon as the cities of Greece fell into civil war, 'a headlonge indignation' was praised as 'manhode and hardyness', while 'he that shewed hymselfe always furious, was reputed a faythfull frende, and he that spake againste hym, was holden for suspect'.[67] Plato writes in similar vein, arguing that one of the signs of the corruption attendant on the shift from oligarchy to democracy is that 'unbridled behaviour comes to be described as an expression of liberty'.[68] Aristotle in his *Art of Rhetoric* generalises Thucydides's observation, noting that – in the vocabulary of his Renaissance translators – an enraged or truculent person can hope to excuse his conduct as that of someone who is merely open and simple of heart.[69]

There are signs that some Renaissance writers may have known about this last example at first hand. Thomas Wyatt in his *c.*1536 version of Luigi Alammani's satire on the life of courtiers protests against the same mistaken ideal of manliness:[70]

> And he that suffereth offence without blame
> Call him pitiful, and him true and plain
> That raileth reckless to every man's shame.[71]

[63] See George of Trebizond 1523, fo. 114v on prodigus/liberalis; Barbaro 1559, p. 32 on prodigalitas/liberalitas; Sigonio 1565, p. 49 on asotus/liberalis; Maioraggio 1591, fo. 70r, col. 1 on prodigus/liberalis. For the same contrast see also Mancinelli 1493, sig. H, 1r; Susenbrotus 1562, p. 46.

[64] Wilson 1553, fo. 67r; [Puttenham] 1589, p. 154.   [65] Day 1592, p. 90.

[66] Plutarch 1603, p. 93.   [67] Thucydides 1550, fo. ccr.

[68] Plato 1484, fo. 355v, col. 2: 'nominant: licentiam libertatem'.

[69] See George of Trebizond 1523, fo. 114v and Sigonio 1565, p. 49 on iracundus ac furiosus/simplex; Barbaro 1559, p. 32 on iracundus & furiosus/apertus & simplex; Maioraggio 1591, fo. 70r, col. 1 on iracundus & truculentus/ingenii simplex.

[70] For Alammani, and for a reprinting of the poem used by Wyatt, see Mason 1986, pp. 260–3. On Wyatt's rejection of courtly cynicism see Greenblatt 1980, pp. 127–56.

[71] Wyatt 1978, p. 188, lines 70–2. But Wyatt is at this point closely following his Italian source, on which see Wyatt 1978, pp. 439, 444.

These sentiments likewise gained wider currency after the publication of Holland's translation of Plutarch, in which another of his complaints about flatterers is that they like to denigrate modesty as 'effeminate unmanlinesse', and to praise those who are hasty and wrathful as hardy and valiant.[72]

We need finally to take note of one instance that may have passed directly from Plato's discussion in the *Republic* to the rhetoricians of the English Renaissance, although Plutarch may once again have served as an intermediary source.[73] According to Plato, a further consequence arising from the corruption of the soul under democracy is that brazen and shameless persons begin to be praised for high spirits and manliness.[74] Aristotle omits the example, but several Tudor rhetoricians treat it as a standard case of paradiastole. Peacham complains of whoredom being tolerated as 'youthful delight',[75] and Puttenham speaks of those who dismiss 'a great riot, or outrage' as nothing more than 'an youthful pranke'.[76]

Besides providing a broader range of illustrations, one other contrast between the Greek and Roman discussions of paradiastole needs to be noted. According to the understanding that came to predominate in Roman rhetorical thought, the point of using the technique is to excuse the vices. Among the Greek writers, however, it is always assumed that the same device can equally well be employed to denigrate the virtues. Although Rutilius adopts something like this perspective when treating paradiastole as a means to unmask hypocrisies, he is chiefly interested, like the author of the *Ad Herennium*, in the complex possibility of countering one's adversaries by undermining their efforts to commend themselves. By contrast, the Greek writers focus on the simpler strategy of casting doubt on forms of behaviour normally regarded as worthy of praise. Thucydides offers the example of impugning 'prudent consultation' by calling it 'cloked deceate'.[77] He also speaks of the possibility – later mentioned by Plato[78] – of ridiculing modesty by describing it as 'covered pusillanimytie or cowardenes'.[79] The English Renaissance rhetoricians rarely mention this form of rhetorical redescription, but a considerable number of later sixteenth-century moralists take it up, usually with explicit reference to Thucydides's account.[80]

---

[72] Plutarch 1603, p. 93.   [73] See Plutarch 1603, p. 93.
[74] Plato 1484, fo. 355v, col. 2: 'nominant impudentiam/fortitudinem'.
[75] Peacham 1577, sig. N, 4v.   [76] [Puttenham] 1589, p. 154.
[77] Thucydides 1550, fo. ccr.   [78] See Plato 1484, fo. 355v, col. 1 on pudor/fatuitas.
[79] Thucydides 1550, fo. ccr.
[80] See, for example, Guazzo 1581, pp. 13–14; Lipsius 1594, p. 69; Silvayn 1596, pp. 106, 146; Barckley 1598, pp. 314–15.

One might finally ask what the Tudor rhetoricians managed to add to these earlier taxonomies. The answer is that they contribute almost nothing of their own at all. Wilson proposes one new example, which Peacham repeats, that of excusing gluttony and drunkenness as good fellowship.[81] Peacham adds two more, both of which gesture at his puritan sympathies. One is that of excusing idolatry as 'pure religion', the other that of excusing pride as 'cleanlynesse'.[82] Apart from this, however, the Tudor rhetoricians are little more than mouthpieces for their classical authorities.

III

Although the writers I have been examining undoubtedly isolate a distinct rhetorical technique, it remains to show how it can be practised with success. The numerous treatises on the good life circulating in early Tudor England point to the obvious difficulty: the virtues and vices appear to be the names of diametrically opposed qualities. As John Larke argues in *The boke of wysdome*, moral conflict is always between 'contraries':[83] between prudence and folly, chastity and lechery, liberality and covetousness,[84] and even more antithetically between temperance and intemperance, constancy and inconstancy, justice and injustice.[85] But if the virtues and vices are such clearly opposed principles, how can we ever hope to redescribe the one as the other without being instantly accused of playing an obvious rhetorical trick?

By way of answer, the rhetoricians like to appeal to one of the governing assumptions of Aristotelian moral philosophy: that every virtue consists in a mean between two opposed vices. Among the moral treatises of the early Elizabethan period, Sir Thomas Hoby's translation of Baldassare Castiglione's *Book of the Courtier* includes perhaps the most influential discussion of the claim. As Lord Octavian explains in Book IV, virtue is always 'placed in the middle beetwene two extreme vyces, the one for the overmuch, and the other for the overlitle'.[86] Soon afterwards Cornelius Valerius, whose treatise on the virtues appeared as *The Casket of Jewels* in 1571, added an explicit reference to the source of the argument. Agreeing that 'vertue is a meane in middes degree', he informs us that this insight is

---

[81] The example already occurs in Wyatt 1978, p. 188, line 64: 'As drunkenness good fellowship to call'. See also Fulbecke 1587, sig. E, 2r, who complains that nowadays 'a confederate in venereous practises' will be 'accounted immediatly a good fellow'.
[82] Peacham 1577, sig. N, 4v.   [83] Larke 1532, fos. 7v, 9v, 27v, 45r, 50r, 56r.
[84] Larke 1532, fos. 9v, 27v, 56r.   [85] Larke 1532, fos. 7v, 46v, 50r.
[86] Castiglione 1994, p. 329.

owed to Aristotle, by whom virtue is defined as 'a custome of the minde enterprised through reason situated in mediocritie'.[87]

If virtue is a mean, it follows that many of the vices, far from being 'contraries' of the virtues, are likely to appear disconcertingly similar to them. Castiglione goes so far as to argue that for every virtue there will always be a 'nexte vice'.[88] Some good and bad qualities, Valerius suggests, may even be members of the same family, with a number of vices being 'cousin germain to Vertue'.[89] Both add that, if these implications are recognised, it becomes easy to see how vices can be redescribed as virtues. As Aristotle had noted in the *Art of Rhetoric*, it will only be necessary to propose that (in the words of Sigonio's translation) 'those qualities which are in the neighbourhood of those actually present have an identical force'.[90] Castiglione and Valerius both invoke stock examples of paradiastole by way of making the point. As the count observes in *The Book of the Courtier*, we can always call 'him that is sawcye, bolde: hym that is sober, drie: hym that is seelye, good: hym that is unhappye, wittie: and lykewyse in the reste.'[91] Valerius agrees that often the vices are 'not so easely espied, as when craftinesse or subtiltie is gaiged agaynst wisedome, cruelty against Justice, lewdhardinesse agaynst manlinesse'.[92]

The power of paradiastole to disorder the virtues came to be incapsulated in two favourite metaphors. One speaks of cloaking vices to lend them a spurious appearance of goodness. The count in *The Book of the Courtier* observes that we can always hope to 'cover' a vice 'with the name of the nexte vertue'.[93] Plutarch complains in his *Moralia* that 'fine words and affected speeches' are 'oftentimes framed to cloke dishonest and villanous deeds.'[94] Henry Peacham turns the image into the definition of paradiastole, describing it as the figure we use 'to cover vices with the mantles of vertues'.[95]

The other metaphor speaks of colouring vices to make them look acceptable. Here it might be thought that an even graver doubt is being expressed. To speak of cloaking a vice implies that a genuine virtue is being covered up, but to refer to the act of colouring might seem to imply that we can alter the appearance of virtue and vice at will. This certainly appears to be Wyatt's anxiety in his satire on court life, in which he denounces those who apply 'colours of device' to 'join the mean with each

[87] Valerius 1571, sig. D, 1r–v.   [88] Castiglione 1994, p. 37.
[89] Valerius 1571, sig. F, 2v.
[90] Sigonio 1565, p. 49: 'vero sunt etiam quae vicina sunt iis, quae adsunt, tanquam idem valentia'.
[91] Castiglione 1994, p. 37.   [92] Valerius 1571, sig. F, 2v.   [93] Castiglione 1994, p. 37.
[94] Plutarch 1603, p. 36.   [95] Peacham 1593, p. 169.

extremity'.[96] Plutarch in his essay on flatterers similarly speaks of how they like to 'colour' the vices, as in excusing 'tyrannie and crueltie' with 'the goodly names of Justice and Hatred of wickednesse'.[97] Angel Day goes so far as to define paradiastole as the figure we employ when 'wee color others or our owne faultes'.[98]

It remains to consider what attitude the rhetoricians adopt towards paradiastole and its power to cloak or colour the vices. Classical writers on the *Ars rhetorica* had always taken pride in the ability of powerful orators to make us change our minds about the right way of 'seeing' particular actions and events. Cicero had even put into the mouth of Crassus in the *De oratore* the view that this may be the highest rhetorical skill of all. There will always be two sides to any question, and the aim of the orator should be to show that plausible arguments can always be constructed *in utramque partem*, on either side of the case. 'We ought', as Crassus says, 'to have enough intelligence, power and art to speak *in utramque partem*' on all the leading issues in the moral sciences: 'on virtue, on duty, on equity and goodness, on dignity, benefit, honour, ignominy, reward, punishment and all similar things'.[99]

If one of the aims of eloquence is that of prompting us to examine the same question from contrasting perspectives, then a skilful use of paradiastole will obviously be a valuable art to cultivate. Once the *Ars rhetorica* became incorporated into Christian culture, however, the possibility began to be viewed with greater nervousness, even by the rhetoricians themselves. They are anxious to insist that the question as to whether any given action should properly be described as virtuous can always be settled with finality. But they are obliged to recognise that paradiastole acts to undermine any such certainty. Susenbrotus concludes that this is one of the moments at which the art of rhetoric overreaches itself:

Paradiastole is used whenever, by means of an excessively polite interpretation, we speak ingratiatingly so as to express approval of our own vices or those of others, as the ridiculous and reprobate are accustomed to do, who scratch each other's backs in exactly this way, as the proverb has it.[100]

Thomas Wilson and Henry Peacham strongly confirm these doubts.[101] Although Peacham offers a neutral analysis of paradiastole in the 1577

---

[96] Wyatt 1978, p. 187, lines 59–60.   [97] Plutarch 1603, p. 93.   [98] Day 1592, p. 90.
[99] Cicero 1942, III. XXVII. 107, vol. 2, pp. 84–6: 'de virtute, de officio, de aequo et bono, de dignitate, utilitate, honore, ignominia, praemio, poena similibusque de rebus in utramque partem dicendi animos et vim et artem habere debemus.'
[100] Susenbrotus 1562, p. 46: 'Paradiastole ... est cum civili interpretatione nostris aut aliorum vitiis assentando blandimur, ut praeposteri ... solent, qui sese haud secus ac muli mutuum scabant, ut est in proverbio'.
[101] Wilson 1553, fo. 69r.

edition of his *Garden of Eloquence*, his expanded edition of 1593 treats it as a 'vice of speech'.[102] Peacham is anxious to assure us that misleading redescriptions can undoubtedly be corrected, but he leaves us with the ironic spectacle of a rhetorician criticising the art of rhetoric for possessing the very power that its exponents normally liked to praise.

IV

Although the technique of rhetorical redescription was increasingly assailed by moralists and rhetoricians alike, those with a professional interest in demonstrating that it is always possible to argue *in utramque partem* found the lure of paradiastole irresistible. So it is hardly surprising to find that, in the years following the publication of the rhetorical handbooks I have been considering, there was a growing awareness of its literary as well as forensic possibilities. John Lyly employs the figure in several of his orations in *Euphues*, and even alludes to Nicolls's translation of Thucydides when lamenting that the modest and shamefast are nowadays likely to be reviled for cowardice.[103] Marlowe was aware of this example, and puts it to dramatic use in Part II of *Tamburlaine*, in which the tyrant kills his son for excusing his refusal to fight as 'manly wise' when Tamburlaine regards it as pusillanimous.[104] Shakespeare likewise displays an interest in such redescriptions from an early stage, and it is especially striking to find him making use of both the metaphors favoured by the rhetoricians to explain how it is possible for vices to be excused.

As we have seen, one of these had spoken of 'colouring' the vices to make them look like virtues. Polonius invokes the image in Act III of *Hamlet* when arranging for Ophelia to confront Hamlet, although as usual his thinking is somewhat confused:

> reade on this booke,
> That show of such an exercise may cullour
> Your lonelines; we are oft too blame in this,
> Tis too much proov'd, that with devotions visage
> And pious action we do sugar ore
> The devill himselfe.   TLN 1582–7, p. 753 (3. 1. 44–9)

Polonius orders his daughter to colour her behaviour in such a way as to make Hamlet feel guilty, but at the same time he condemns such acts of colouring as devilish tricks.

---

[102] Peacham 1593, pp. 168–9.   [103] Lyly 1868, p. 115.
[104] Marlowe 1998, IV. 1. 17 and IV. 1 91, pp. 125, 128.

No such hesitation afflicts the politic Cardinal Beauford in *2 Henry VI*. When Queen Margaret proposes that Gloster be summarily killed, he responds by warning her about the importance of rhetorical colouring:

> That he should dye, is worthie pollicie,
> But yet we want a Colour for his death:
> 'Tis meet he be condemn'd by course of Law.
>
> TLN 1416–18, p. 81 (III. 1. 235–7)

It is ironic that Gloster should later complain – as he does when Catesby presents him with the head of the murdered Hastings – that he himself has been deceived by the same rhetorical trick:

> I tooke him for the plainest harmlesse Creature,
> That breathed upon the earth, a christian,
> Made him my booke, wherein my soule recorded,
> The history of all her secret thoughts:
> So smoothe he daubd his vice with shew of vertue,
>
> TLN 1896–1900, p. 231 (III. 5. 24–28)

As the use of 'daubd' implies, the colouring may not even have to be skilfully applied to be rhetorically effective.

Shakespeare also likes to invoke the image of cloaking our vices. When Lucrece fears that she might be thought to have consented to Tarquin's rape, she laments that 'my true eyes have never practiz'd how / To cloake offences with a cunning brow'.[105] By contrast, Luciana in *The Comedie of Errors* enthusiastically recommends just such a stratagem at the moment when, supposing the bewildered Antipholus to be her sister's husband, she upbraids him for his seeming coldness:

> Muffle your false love with some shew of blindnesse:
> Let not my sister read it in your eye:
> Be not thy tongue thy owne shames Orator:
> Looke sweet, speake faire, become disloyaltie:
> Apparell vice like vertues harbenger:
> Beare a faire presence, though your heart be tainted,
> Teach sinne the carriage of a holy Saint,
> Be secret false: what need she be acquainted?
>
> TLN 732–9, p. 301 (3. 2. 8–15)

The ability of sin and evil to deceive us by lying hidden is likewise what preoccupies Bassanio in *The Merchant of Venice* when he is trying to

---

[105] Shakespeare 1986, *Lucrece*, TLN 748–9, p. 278.

choose between the three caskets.[106] Turning to the golden one, he sets it aside:

> So may the outward showes be least themselves,
> The world is still deceav'd with ornament.
> In Law, what plea so tainted and corrupt,
> But being season'd with a gracious voyce,
> Obscures the show of evill. In religion
> What damned error but some sober brow
> Will blesse it, and approve it with a text,
> Hiding the grosnes with faire ornament:

>   TLN 1353–60, p. 495 (3. 2. 73–80)

Speaking of verbal ornaments that deceive, Bassanio is partly referring in a general way to the *ornamenta*, the figures and tropes of speech. But when he speaks of hiding grossness with fair ornament, he appears to be referring more specifically to the power of paradiastole to cover and obscure the vices by giving them an outward show of goodness.

As well as being acutely aware of what the rhetoricians tell us about paradiastole, Shakespeare is much interested in the use of the technique as (in Peacham's phrase) an instrument of excuse.[107] As we have seen, the most widely discussed example of the technique was that of redescribing an action as bold when it was merely reckless. With this in mind, it is worth recalling the scene from *The second part of Henry the fourth* in which Mistress Quickly informs the Lord Chief Justice that Falstaff has broken his promise to marry her. The Chief Justice rounds on Falstaff in a manner remarkably reminiscent of Castiglione's count, reproving him for his 'confident brow' and 'impudent sawcines.'[108] But Falstaff directly quotes Castiglione back at him: what you call 'impudent sawcinesse' is really 'honorable boldnes'.[109] It is part of the comedy, however, that Falstaff avails himself with such effrontery of one of the stock examples of paradiastole, and the Chief Justice knows too much about the art of rhetoric to let him to get away with it. He even appears to know the specific objection that Henry Peacham had raised against the use of paradiastole, that it 'opposeth the truth by false tearmes'.[110] As the Chief Justice likewise

---

[106] Whitney 1586, p. 226 had already referred to the deceiving quality of 'outward showes' in his emblem on 'sugred speache'.
[107] Peacham 1593, p. 168.
[108] Shakespeare 1986, *2 Henry IV*, TLN 722–3, p. 582 (2. 1. 86–8).
[109] Castiglione 1994, p. 37 speaks of 'calling him that is sawcye, bolde'. Falstaff says 'You cal honorable boldnes impudent sawcinesse'. Shakespeare 1986, *2 Henry IV*, TLN 734, p. 582 (II. 1. 96–7). I have not seen any edition of the play in which the source of Falstaff's remark has been identified.
[110] Peacham 1593, p. 167.

objects, Falstaff is simply 'wrenching the true cause, the false way'.[111] He is
instantly exposed for trying to play a well-known rhetorical trick.

A further stock example was that of attempting (in Peacham's words) to
justify 'insatiable avarice' by redescribing it as 'good husbandrie'.[112] This
being so, it is similarly worth reconsidering the scene at the beginning of
The Merchant of Venice in which Anthonio and Bassanio meet Shylocke
to agree the terms of their penal bond. As soon as Shylocke enters, he
declares his hatred of Anthonio for lending out money gratis, for assailing
his own taking of interest, and for accusing him, he later adds, of cut-
throat practices.[113] Reacting to Anthonio's rebukes, Shylocke offers precisely the account of himself that the rhetoricians had recommended.
First he redescribes his alleged avarice as thrift:

> He hates our sacred Nation, and he rayles
> Even there where Merchants most doe congregate
> On me, my bargaines, and my well-wone thrift,
> Which hee calls interrest.   TLN 363–6, p. 484 (1. 3. 40–3)

Next he tells the story of Jacob's good husbandry in grazing his uncle
Laban's sheep. Jacob was told he would be given all the lambs that were
born parti-coloured, and he found a way of increasing their number:

> The skilful sheepheard pyld me certaine wands,
> And in the dooing of the deede of kind
> He stuck them up before the fulsome Ewes,
> Who then conceaving, did in eaning time
> Fall party-colour'd lambs, and those were *Jacobs*.
> This was a way to thrive, and he was blest:
> And thrift is blessing if men steale it not.
>   TLN 400–6, pp. 484–5 (1. 3. 76–82)

Shylocke not only excuses Jacob's conduct; he redescribes it as positively
virtuous. He found a way to thrive without stealing, a form of increase
sanctified by the Bible itself.

Shylocke's use of paradiastole may at first sight seem a world away from
Falstaff's effronteries. He not only pleads his case in passionate verse, but
his sincerity is much harder to doubt. Like Falstaff, however, he is playing
a familiar rhetorical trick, and Anthonio immediately denounces it:

> Marke you this *Bassanio*,
> The devill can cite Scripture for his purpose,
> An evill soule producing holy witnes

---

[111] Shakespeare 1986, *2 Henry IV*, TLN 721, p. 582 (2. 1. 86).
[112] Peacham 1593, p. 168.
[113] Shakespeare 1986, *MofV*, TLN 359, 365–6, 427, pp. 484–5 (1. 3. 36, 42–3, 104).

> Is like a villaine with a smiling cheeke,
> A goodly apple rotten at the hart.
> O what a goodly out-side falshood hath.
>
> TLN 413–18, p. 485 (1. 3. 89–94)

Anthonio's vehemence echoes Susenbrotus, who had warned that 'when vices are displayed under the guise of virtue, the Devil himself can be transfigured into an Angel of light'.[114]

Yet another stock example of paradiastole was that of excusing an act of murder by redescribing the killer not as furious but as valiant[115] and the murder itself as a manly deed.[116] Lady Macbeth speaks in these terms at the moment when Macbeth is meditating the murder of Banquo. 'When you durst do it, then you were a man'.[117] Yet more strikingly, there are two other Shakespearean tragedies in which the possibility of redescribing a murder in such a way as to excuse it is examined at length. The issue is first raised at the beginning of Act II of *Julius Caesar*. Brutus meditates in soliloquy on his intention to assassinate Caesar, and then shares with the other conspirators his sense of how the action might be justified. He reflects that Caesar 'would be crown'd' and thus that, if Rome is to avoid this possible abuse of greatness, 'it must be by his death'.[118] As he is obliged to admit, however, Caesar has done nothing to make him deserving of such a violent end. This in turn means that, as Brutus later warns the conspirators, they are liable to appear basely envious if they kill Caesar, and will also be open to an accusation of sheer butchery.[119] But if there is no possibility of justifying Caesar's assassination by considering – as Brutus puts it – 'the thing he is', how can it be justified? Brutus recognises that his own behaviour and that of his fellow conspirators will need to be rhetorically redescribed:

> since the Quarrell
> Will beare no colour, for the thing he is,
> Fashion it thus;   TLN 590–2, p. 681 (2. 1. 28–30)

He will need to 'fashion' his act to give it a pleasing rhetorical shape; more specifically, he will need to 'colour' it to yield a more attractive appearance.

Considering how this can be done, Brutus begins by gesturing at the suggestion that murder can sometimes be excused as a manly deed. One

---

[114] Susenbrotus 1562, p. 46. 'cum vitia sub virtutis specie sese ostendant ... Satanas transfiguratur in Angelum lucis'.
[115] Day 1592, pp. 62–3.   [116] Peacham 1577, sig. N, 4v.
[117] Shakespeare 1986, *Macbeth*, TLN 445, p. 1108 (1. 7. 49).
[118] Shakespeare 1986, *Julius Caesar* (hereafter *J.C.*) TLN 572, 574, p. 681 (2. 1. 10, 12, 18).
[119] Shakespeare 1986, *J.C.*, TLN 726, 728, 740, pp. 682–3 (2. 1. 164, 166, 178).

way to avoid looking merely envious of Caesar will be to 'kill him Boldly, but not Wrathfully'.[120] Brutus's main suggestion, however, comes from a more elevated source, the justification of tyrannicide in Book III of Cicero's *De officiis*. Cicero had appealed to the familiar image of the body politic, treating tyrants as poison in need of being expelled if the body is to survive.[121] William Baldwin elaborates the image in his *Treatice of Morall Philosophy*, one of the most popular collections of *loci communes* in late Tudor England.[122] A good ruler is 'lyke a common fountaine or springe'; if he becomes impure and poisonous, the people will be left without remedy 'untill the fountaine be purged'.[123]

The image of purgation is the one Brutus eventually adopts to justify his killing of Caesar. In his soliloquy he compares Caesar with a serpent's egg, a source of venom that needs to be crushed in the shell if the body of Rome is to avoid being poisoned.[124] In his later speech to the conspirators he places the same image at the heart of the rhetorical redescription on which he finally takes his stand:

> This shall make
> Our purpose Necessary, and not Envious.
> Which so appearing to the common eyes,
> We shall be call'd Purgers, not Murderers.
>
> TLN 739–42, p. 683 (1. 1. 177–80)

Purgers, not murderers. So convinced is Brutus by his redescription that he not only commends it to his fellow conspirators but predicts it will be accepted without demur by the people at large.

By contrast with Falstaff and Shylocke, Brutus's use of paradiastole owes little to the rhetoricians and their stock examples. He takes his redescription from one of the most widely respected works of moral philosophy of his own as well as Shakespeare's age. Nor is he instantly challenged, as happens with Falstaff and Shylocke. The conspirators silently accept his justification, and after the assassination it is shown to have exactly the power Brutus had promised. Addressing the plebeians, Brutus explains that Caesar was ambitious, which is why he slew him.[125] He does not repeat his earlier reference to purging the body politic,

---

[120] Shakespeare 1986, *J.C.*, TLN 734, p. 683 (2. 1. 172).
[121] Cicero 1913, III. VI. 32, p. 298. On tyrants as 'poysonfull' see Cicero 1534, sig. Q, 8r.
[122] Baldwin's treatise, first published in 1547, was reprinted at least three times in the 1550s. The text was enlarged by Thomas Palfreyman in 1567, and in this version, further enlarged in 1579, it went through at least ten further printings before the end of the century. The edition here used is that of 1579.
[123] Baldwin 1579, fo. 72v.
[124] Shakespeare 1986, *J.C.*, TLN 576, 578, 594–6, p. 681 (2. 1. 14, 16, 32–4).
[125] Shakespeare 1986, *J.C.*, TLN 1413–14, p. 690 (3. 2. 23).

but this is how the plebeians spontaneously construct his act. 'This *Caesar* was a Tyrant' declares the First Plebeian; to which the Third Plebeian adds 'we are blest that Rome is rid of him'.[126] They agree that the conspirators have rid the city of something noxious; they are purgers, not murderers.

Brutus's victory, however, is a rhetorical one, open to the danger that an orator adept at arguing *in utramque partem* may be capable of undermining his version of events. This is what Cassius dreads,[127] and this is what Antony achieves in his response to Brutus's address to the people. Antony persuades them that Caesar was *not* ambitious: 'Ambition should be made of sterner stuffe'.[128] He is consequently able to insist that the conspirators *were* merely envious: 'See what a rent the envious *Caska* made'.[129] By this stage they have already repudiated Brutus's justification for his act. As soon as Antony refers to 'the Honourable men, / Whose Daggers have stabb'd *Caesar*',[130] the Fourth Plebeian suddenly shouts: 'They were Villaines, Murderers'.[131] Murderers, not purgers. Brutus's redescription is fatally inverted, and the next we hear of him is that he and Cassius 'Are rid like Madmen through the Gates of Rome'.[132] We are left with a final, ironic play on the idea of purgation: they have rid through the gates, and Rome is rid of them.

The other tragedy in which an attempt is made to excuse a murder is *Timon of Athens*,[133] a play Shakespeare seems to have completed as late as 1608.[134] Towards the end of Act III Alcibiades appears before the senators of Athens to plead for the life of a friend condemned to death for killing a man in a duel.[135] Describing how his friend conducted himself, Alcibiades recurs to one of the stock examples of paradiastole:

> He is a Man (setting his Fate aside)
> Of comely Vertues,
> Nor did he soyle the fact with Cowardice.
> (An Honour in him, which buyes out his fault)

---

[126] Shakespeare 1986, *J.C.*, TLN 1456–7, p. 690 (3. 2. 61–2).
[127] Shakespeare 1986, *J.C.*, TLN 1322–5, p. 688 (3. 1. 232–5).
[128] Shakespeare 1986, *J.C.*, TLN 1479, p. 691 (3. 2. 84).
[129] Shakespeare 1986, *J.C.*, TLN 1559, p. 692 (3. 2. 166).
[130] Shakespeare 1986, *J.C.*, TLN 1538–9, p. 692 (3. 2. 143–4).
[131] Shakespeare 1986, *J.C.*, TLN 1542, p. 692 (3. 2. 147).
[132] Shakespeare 1986, *J.C.*, TLN 1648, p. 693 (3. 2. 259).
[133] My analysis of this scene draws on Skinner 2014, pp. 155–60.
[134] Klein 2001, p. 1 tentatively dates the play to 1607–8; Jowett 2004, p. 4 suggests early 1606; Dawson and Minton 2008, p. 12 suggest 1607 or earlier.
[135] It is now regarded as certain that Shakespeare wrote *Timon of Athens* in collaboration with Thomas Middleton. See Wells and Taylor 1987, pp. 127–8; Vickers 2002, pp. 244–90; Jowett 2004, title-page. So it cannot be certain that Shakespeare wrote the scene with which I am concerned. However, the latest editors of the play believe that most probably he did. See Dawson and Minton 2008, p. 405.

> But with a Noble Fury, and faire spirit,
> Seeing his Reputation touch'd to death,
> He did oppose his Foe:
> And with such sober and unnoted passion
> He did behave his anger ere 'twas spent,
> As if he had but prov'd an Argument.
>
> TLN 1121–30, p. 1013 (3. 5. 14–23)

Like Angel Day, Alcibiades redescribes fury as valiance and lack of cowardice;[136] and like Henry Peacham he adds that murder can sometimes be regarded as a manly act of honour and virtue.[137]

More quickly than Brutus, however, Alcibiades is made to recognise that his attempted redescription has failed. The First Senator is all too familiar with such rhetorical tricks:

> You undergo too strict a Paradox,
> Striving to make an ugly deed looke faire:
> Your words have tooke such paines, as if they labour'd
> To bring Man-slaughter into forme, and set Quarrelling
> Upon the head of Valour; which indeede
> Is Valour mis-begot, and came into the world,
> When Sects, and Factions were newly borne.
>
> TLN 1131–7, pp. 1013–14 (3. 5. 24–30)

The laboured character of Alcibiades's oratory conveys to the First Senator the thought that his words themselves are in labour, painfully bringing to birth a misbegotten and paradoxical conception of valour, a quality not to be found among those who duel to the death.

Having uncovered Alcibiades's attempted deception, the First Senator proceeds to explain the true concept of valour, which resides not in injurious action but in magnanimous endurance:

> Hee's truly Valiant, that can wisely suffer
> The worst that man can breath, and make his Wrongs, his Out-sides,
> To weare them like his Rayment, carelessely,
> And ne're preferre his injuries to his heart,
> To bring it into danger.   TLN 1138–42, p. 1014 (3. 5. 31–6)

When Alcibiades tries to protest, the First Senator tells him once again that he is merely trying 'to make an ugly deed looke faire':

> You cannot make grosse sinnes looke cleare,
> To revenge is no Valour, but to beare. TLN 1145–6, p. 1014 (3. 5. 39–40)

---

[136] Day 1592, pp. 62–3.   [137] Peacham 1577, sig. N, 4v.

With his rhyming couplet the senator signals an end to the argument. Alcibiades's plea is refused, and he ends by abandoning all thought of persuasion and vows a terrible revenge.

V

Despite the anxieties expressed by the rhetoricians about the dangers of paradiastole, they typically assume that its power to unsettle the virtues can be exposed and controlled. Because the technique (as Henry Peacham puts it) 'opposeth the truth by false termes, and wrong names', it ought to be possible to reimpose the right names without great difficulty.[138] As we have seen, Shakespeare is usually content to endorse this view of things. Falstaff is instantly contradicted when he claims that breaking a promise can be honourable boldness; so is Shylocke when he argues that usury is a form of thrift; so are Brutus and Alcibiades when they suggest that murder can be an act of purgation or manliness. There is one play, however, in which Shakespeare puts the case that, even when someone may appear to be excusing an obvious and serious vice, it may not be possible to settle with any assurance how their behaviour should be appraised. The play in question is *The Tragedy of Coriolanus*, in which Shakespeare's recurrent use of paradiastole gives rise to some profoundly enigmatic effects.

There are numerous moments in the play when it becomes evident that the technique of rhetorical redescription is very much on Shakespeare's mind.[139] When Coriolanus denounces the Senate's decision to give corn to the people free of charge, he couples his protest with a warning to the Senators:

> Thus we debase
> The Nature of our Seats, and make the Rabble
> Call our Cares, Feares;   TLN 1583–5, p. 1243 (3. 1. 136–8)

Coriolanus echoes one of the anxieties that, as we have seen, Thucydides had originally expressed: that it is all too easy in times of civil strife for modesty and prudence to be denigrated as cowardliness and deceit.[140] Later in the same scene, when the Tribunes incite the people to lay hands on Coriolanus and he vows to withstand them, he is dissuaded by Cominius from behaving with such dangerous recklessness:

---

[138] Peacham 1593, p. 168.
[139] For a full analysis of the rhetoric of the play see Peltonen 2009.
[140] Thucydides 1550, fo. ccr.

But now 'tis oddes beyond Arithmetick,
And Manhood is call'd Foolerie, when it stands
Against a falling Fabrick.   TLN 1689–91, p. 1244 (3. 1. 247–9)

Cominius likewise echoes Thucydides, who had spoken of how headlong behaviour can be falsely praised as manhood,[141] and at the same time he alludes to George Puttenham's observation that sometimes the merely 'foolish-hardy' may be commended as 'valiant or couragious'.[142]

It is in the assessment of Coriolanus's character, however, that Shakespeare makes his most extended use of paradiastole. For his knowledge of Coriolanus he is chiefly indebted to Plutarch's *Lives of the Noble Grecians and Romanes*, a work he knew intimately from Thomas North's translation of 1579. Plutarch opens his biography by stressing Coriolanus's commendable qualities. 'This *Martius* naturall wit and great harte dyd marvelously sturre up his corage, to doe and attempt notable actes'. He was 'never overcome with pleasure, nor money', and he 'would endure easely all manner of paynes and travailles', so that everyone 'well liked and commended his stowtnes and temperancie.'[143] Above all Plutarch emphasises Coriolanus's 'wonderfull corage & valliantnes',[144] which led the Consul Cominius, after the conquest of the city of Corioles, to order that henceforth he should be called Coriolanus, declaring that 'his vallaint acts have wonne him that name before our nomination'.[145]

It has been suggested that 'Shakespeare follows Plutarch in depicting Coriolanus as the supreme exemplification of *virtus*'.[146] But Plutarch is far from depicting Coriolanus as a man of unambiguously admirable qualities. He tells us that, in spite of his great qualities, his fellow-citizens found him 'altogether unfit for any mans conversation'. They came to feel that they 'could not be acquainted with him', because 'his behaviour was so unpleasaunt'.[147] The reason, Plutarch explains, is that Coriolanus's manner was habitually lordly and insolent.[148] He 'never yelded in any respect', and sought 'to overcome allwayes, and to have the upper hande in all matters'.[149] He was incapable of tolerating the least opposition, and prone to be 'caried awaye with the vehemencie of anger, and desire of revenge'.[150]

Plutarch notes that Coriolanus sought to redescribe these vices in order to vindicate himself in his own and other men's eyes. He gave it out that his seemingly lordly behaviour was 'a token of magnanimitie' which

---

[141] Thucydides 1550, fo. ccr.   [142] [Puttenham] 1589, p. 154.
[143] Plutarch 1579, p. 237.   [144] Plutarch 1579, p. 241.   [145] Plutarch 1579, p. 242.
[146] Rackin 1983, p. 69.   [147] Plutarch 1579, p. 237.   [148] Plutarch 1579, p. 237.
[149] Plutarch 1579, p. 245.
[150] Plutarch 1579, p. 248. Miles 1996, pp. 117–22 places more weight on Plutarch's references to Coriolanus's obstinacy.

revealed him to be a man 'nobly bent' and 'of no base and fainte corage'.[151] Plutarch, however, does not for a moment allow this estimation to stand. While conceding that Coriolanus accomplished many valiant deeds, he insists that even his 'noble actes and vertues' were performed in a manner 'hatefull even to those that received benefit by them'.[152] Summarising his accusations in the course of comparing Coriolanus with Alcibiades, Plutarch concludes that Coriolanus was far from being noble and magnanimous; rather he was 'arrogant, prowde, and tyrannicall', a man with a 'hawty stomake' and a 'hawtie obstinate minde'.[153]

As we have seen, the question as to whether someone should be commended as noble or condemned as proud was one of the stock examples of paradiastole. We already find it in Aristotle, and it was taken up by a number of Renaissance rhetoricians, notably Johann Susenbrotus and Angel Day. As I shall seek to show, it was also taken up by Shakespeare, who uses it almost as a structuring device throughout *The Tragedy of Coriolanus*, as well as a means of dramatising some of the deepest ambiguities in the character of Coriolanus himself.

The play opens with a seeming corroboration of Plutarch's hostile verdict. A group of mutinous citizens bewail the famine in Rome, and the First Citizen proposes that they kill Coriolanus, 'chiefe enemy to the people', to draw attention to their plight.[154] The Second Citizen demurs, calling on them to 'consider you what Services he ha's done for his Country'.[155] But the First Citizen responds: 'Very well, and could bee content to give him good report for't, but that hee payes himselfe with beeing proud.' When the Second Citizen begs him to 'speak not maliciously', the First Citizen contemptuously repeats that 'though soft conscienc'd men can be content to say' that Coriolanus acted for the good of his country, the truth is that 'he did it to please his Mother, and to be partly proud, which he is, even to the altitude of his vertue.'[156]

When Coriolanus enters, he at once gives plentiful evidence for the First Citizen's judgment, addressing the assembled citizens in tones of withering haughtiness. He begins by denouncing them as 'dissentious rogues' and accuses them of cowardice. 'What would you have, you Curres, / That like not Peace, nor Warre?' Next he condemns their brutish untrustworthiness. 'He that trusts to you, / Where he should finde you Lyons, findes you Hares: / Where Foxes, Geese.' He ends by dismissing them as hopelessly

---

[151] Plutarch 1579, p. 245.   [152] Plutarch 1579, p. 261.
[153] Plutarch 1579, pp. 260, 262.
[154] Shakespeare 1986, *The Tragedy of Coriolanus* (hereafter *T.C.*), TLN 5, p. 1225 (1. 1. 5).
[155] Shakespeare 1986, *T.C.*, TLN 27–8, p. 1225 (1. 1. 22–3).
[156] Shakespeare 1986, *T.C.*, TLN 29–31, 32, 34–7, p. 1225 (1. 1. 26, 28–30).

fickle. 'With every Minute you do change a Minde, / And call him Noble, that was now your Hate: / Him vilde, that was your Garland.'[157]

When Coriolanus next appears, the Volscians have renewed their attack on Rome. Coriolanus carries the fight to the gates of Corioles, but his forces are beaten back. He reacts by cursing his soldiers with still greater violence and contempt, reviling them as 'Shames of Rome' and berating them for running away 'from Slaves, that Apes would beate'.[158] By contrast with these incorrigibly base and cowardly plebeians, Coriolanus at all times makes it clear that he regards himself as a man of true nobility. He boasts of 'my Noble Heart';[159] he vows that he will never behave with any 'inherent Basenesse';[160] and he associates himself with those who 'preferre / A Noble life, before a Long'.[161]

As the tragedy unfolds, Coriolanus's overbearing manner is increasingly condemned. When the Senate appoints Tribunes to look after the interests of the people, their first words are about Coriolanus's intolerable pride:

> SCICINIUS Was ever man so proud as is this *Martius*?
> BRUTUS He has no equall. ....
> The present Warres devoure him, he is growne
> Too proud to be so valiant.
> TLN 250–1, 257–8, p. 1227 (1. 1. 236–7, 242–3)

Later the Tribunes complain in similar style to the patrician Menenius when he invites them to say 'In what enormity is *Martius* poore in, that you two have not in abundance?' Ignoring the sarcasm, the Tribunes respond as before:

> BRUTUS He's poore in no one fault, but stor'd with all.
> SCICINIUS Especially in Pride.   TLN 770–3, p. 1234 (2. 1. 14–17)

After Coriolanus has been banished, one of the Tribunes offers a summary of his character:

> *Caius Martius* was
> A worthy Officer i'th' Warre, but Insolent,
> O'recome with Pride,   TLN 2531–3, p. 1254 (4. 6. 31–3)

The Tribunes congratulate themselves that, with his insolence removed, 'Rome / Sits safe and still, without him.'[162]

[157] Shakespeare 1986, *T.C.*, TLN 160, 164–8, 178–80, p. 1226 (1. 1. 147, 151–5, 165–7).
[158] Shakespeare 1986, *T.C.*, TLN 459, 462, 464, p. 1230 (1. 4. 32, 35, 37).
[159] Shakespeare 1986, *T.C.*, TLN 1883, p. 1246 (3. 2 100).
[160] Shakespeare 1986, *T.C.*, TLN 1906, p. 1247 (3. 2. 124).
[161] Shakespeare 1986, *T.C.*, TLN 1600–1, p. 1243 (3. 1. 153–4).
[162] Shakespeare 1986, *T.C.*, TLN 2539, p. 1254 (4. 6. 38–9).

114 From Humanism to Hobbes

The Tribunes are of course Coriolanus's enemies, but similar doubts are voiced even by his mother Volumnia, especially at the moment when Coriolanus baulks at making a direct appeal to the plebeians in his bid to be elected Consul.[163] Coriolanus views his own reaction as a sure indication of his true nobility, but Volumnia criticises his 'dangerous Stoutnesse', his incapacity to see the need for compromise. She praises his courage, although she takes credit for it herself, but at the same time she disowns his pride:

> Do thou as thou list,
> Thy Valiantnesse was mine, thou suck'st it from me:
> But owe thy Pride thy selfe.   TLN 1910–13, p. 1247 (3. 2. 128–31)

Coriolanus feels obliged to yield, but when he confronts the plebeians he cannot manage to hide his contempt. He immediately wishes them in the fires of lowest hell, and the Tribunes summarily banish him.[164]

Among those who denounce Coriolanus's pride, none does so with greater bitterness than his adversary Auffidius, the leader of the Volscians. Exiled by his fellow citizens, Coriolanus deserts to Auffidius's cause and offers to join him in a renewed attack on Rome. Auffidius at first welcomes Coriolanus, hailing him as 'all-Noble *Martius*' and praising him as 'Thou Noble thing'.[165] But soon he too finds himself reflecting on Coriolanus's overweening pride:

> He beares himselfe more proudlier,
> Even to my person, then I thought he would
> When first I did embrace him.   TLN 2676–8, p. 1255 (4. 7. 8–10)

Auffidius goes on to ask himself how it came about that Coriolanus, at first 'a Noble servant' to Rome, proved unable to 'Carry his Honors eeven'. Was it due to pride, which 'ever taints / The happy man'? Or was it the result of a 'defect of judgement'? Or was it simply that he could not manage 'to be other then one thing'? At first Auffidius decides that 'he hath spices of them all' and concludes that 'our Vertues / Lie in th' interpretation of the time'.[166] But when Coriolanus betrays him and returns to Rome, Auffidius comes to see in him nothing but the pride of an 'Insolent Villaine', and these are the words with which he and the conspirators fall on Coriolanus and kill him.[167]

---

[163] For readings of this scene see Kahn 1997, pp. 147–59; Chernaik 2011, pp. 183–95.

[164] Shakespeare 1986, *T.C.*, TLN 2000, 2034, p. 1248 (3. 3. 73, 108).

[165] Shakespeare 1986, *T.C.*, TLN 2369, 2379, p. 1252 (4. 5. 103, 113).

[166] Shakespeare 1986, *T.C.*, TLN 2704–7, 2710, 2714, 2717–18, p. 1256 (4. 7. 35–6, 38–9, 42, 46, 49–50).

[167] Shakespeare 1986, *T.C.*, TLN 3308, 3319, p. 1262 (5. 6. 121, 131). Miles 1996, p. 152 takes Auffidius to be saying that Coriolanus's constancy 'may be the key to his tragedy'.

While Coriolanus's insolence is widely condemned, Shakespeare is far from endorsing Plutarch's verdict that he was a man who simply attempted to redescribe his pride as nobility. Shakespeare introduces into the story a number of characters who speak vehemently on the other side of the case.[168] These include, most obviously, the leaders of the army, inhabitants of a simple moral world. They not only revere Coriolanus as a hero of outstanding valour, but think of him as a man of unquestionable nobility. Cominius, the commander-in-chief, salutes him at the outset as 'Noble *Martius*',[169] while the general Titus Lartius likewise hails him as 'Noble Fellow' and 'Thou worthiest *Martius*'.[170]

More significant is the admiration expressed by the politic figure of Menenius Agrippa. Menenius is mentioned only once in Plutarch's narrative, but he is fashioned into a leading character by Shakespeare, who presents him as a good-natured patrician trusted by nobles and people alike. He commends Coriolanus to the hostile Tribunes as 'the Noble *Martius*', while mocking them for saying that '*Martius* is proud' when they themselves are such 'proud, violent, testie Magistrates'.[171] He speaks of Coriolanus's 'Noble service' and agrees with Cominius that 'Hee's right Noble'.[172] When one of the patricians laments that Coriolanus 'ha's marr'd his fortune' by behaving arrogantly towards the plebeians,[173] Menenius not only excuses him but praises his noble lack of political wiliness:

> His nature is too noble for the World:
> He would not flatter *Neptune* for his Trident,
> Or *Jove*, for's power to Thunder.   TLN 1700–2, p. 1244 (3. 1. 257–9)

To Menenius, Coriolanus remains 'noble *Martius*' from the moment when he first greets him in the opening scene of the play.[174]

Of still greater significance is the fact that even the plebeians do not speak with one voice in condemning Coriolanus's pride. It is true that most of them eventually display the fickleness for which he begins by denouncing them. But at the outset of his bid for the Consulship one citizen proposes that 'if he tel us his Noble deeds, we must also tell him

---

But Auffidius only once mentions Coriolanus's constancy, and at the end speaks only of his boastfulness and insolence.

[168] As a result, Goldman 1981 notes, the word 'noble' appears more frequently than in any other Shakespearean text.

[169] Shakespeare 1986, *T.C.*, TLN 245, p. 1227 (1. 1. 231).

[170] Shakespeare 1986, *T.C.*, TLN 480, p. 1230 (1. 4. 56) and TLN 515, p. 1231 (1. 5. 25).

[171] Shakespeare 1986, *T.C.*, TLN 764, 797, 844–5, pp. 1234–5 (2. 1. 8, 36, 72–4).

[172] Shakespeare 1986, *T.C.*, TLN 1063, 1152, pp. 1237–8 (2. 2. 34, 123).

[173] Shakespeare 1986, *T.C.*, TLN 1699, p. 1244 (3. 1. 256).

[174] Shakespeare 1986, *T.C.*, TLN 159, p. 1226 (1. 1. 146).

our Noble acceptance of them', partly because 'Ingratitude is monstrous' but also because 'there was never a worthier man'.[175] Yet more strikingly, this passage is preceded by a scene in which two officials who are engaged in preparing the Capitol for the consular election converse almost in the manner of a chorus about Coriolanus's character. The first declares 'That's a brave fellow: but hee's vengeance prowd.' The second sees Coriolanus not as proud but as noble, arguing that he appears 'neyther to care whether they love, or hate him' and 'out of his Noble carelesnesse lets them plainely see't.' The first begins by replying that 'hee seekes their hate with greater devotion, then they can render it him', but on reflection he begins to change his mind. When the second suggests that it would be 'a kinde of ingratefull Injurie' not to choose him as Consul, the first suddenly announces his agreement and brings the argument to a close. 'No more of him, hee's a worthy man'.[176]

The debate about pride *versus* nobility is brought to a sudden and tragic climax in the final scene of the play. Auffidius justifies his decision to assassinate Coriolanus by recalling how he eventually felt despised and overborne by Coriolanus's pride:

> Till at the last
> I seem'd his Follower, not Partner; and
> He wadg'd me with his Countenance, as if
> I had bin Mercenary.[177]   TLN 3226–9, p. 1261 (5. 6. 37–40)

He goes so far as to confess that, having been humiliated by Coriolanus, he now hopes that 'Ile renew me in his fall'.[178] Condemning Coriolanus at the last for his boastfulness and insolence, he joins the conspirators in killing him, after which he stands in triumph on his corpse.[179] As soon as Coriolanus is dead, however, one of the Volscian lords cries out: 'Thou hast done a deed, whereat / Valour will weepe'.[180] A second lord commands: 'Let him be regarded / As the most Noble Coarse, that ever Herald / Did follow to his Urne.'[181] Auffidius now declares that 'My Rage

---

[175] Shakespeare 1986, *T.C.*, TLN 1191–3, 1222–3, p. 1238 (2. 3. 7–8, 34).

[176] Shakespeare 1986, *T.C.*, TLN 1028–9, 1035–8, 1041–2, 1054–5, 1058, pp. 1236–7 (2. 2. 5, 11–13, 16, 25–6, 29).

[177] Here Shakespeare closely follows Plutarch 1579, p. 253, where he says of Auffidius that 'it grieved him to see his owne reputation bleamished, through *Martius* great fame and honour', adding that 'this fell out the more, because every man honoured *Martius*, and thought he only could doe all, and that all other governours and captaines must be content with suche credit and authoritie, as he would please to countenaunce them with.'

[178] Shakespeare 1986, *T.C.*, TLN 3237, p. 1261 (5. 6. 48).

[179] Shakespeare 1986, *T.C.*, TLN 3308, 3319, p. 1262 (5. 6. 121, 131–2).

[180] Shakespeare 1986, *T.C.*, TLN 3321–2, p. 1262 (5. 6. 135).

[181] Shakespeare 1986, *T.C.*, TLN 3332–4, p. 1263 (5. 6. 145–7).

is gone, / And I am strucke with sorrow', and ends by promising that Coriolanus 'shall have a Noble Memory.'[182] But should Coriolanus be remembered as noble? Or as proud and insolent? The question remains hanging in the air as his body is borne away.

Shakespeare makes frequent use of paradiastole, but usually with the aim of showing that rhetorical redescriptions can readily be identified and set aside. The great exception is *Coriolanus*, in which the ambiguities are never stabilised. We can of course insist on pronouncing a verdict on Coriolanus's character if we wish, and this is what many recent commentators have done. Coriolanus is taken to be a man of high virtues, even the embodiment of an heroic ideal of magnanimity.[183] But his great qualities, especially of courage, manliness and steadfastness, are said to be appropriate only to the battlefield; when transferred to the political arena they prove not merely irrelevant but catastrophic in effect.[184] I have been suggesting, however, that this vision of the play imposes a solution on a puzzle that Shakespeare leaves unresolved. Coriolanus is clear about his own nobleness and magnanimity, but Shakespeare makes it hard for us to be clear about Coriolanus. Using the figure of paradiastole to set the terms of the debate, Shakespeare stands back from the resulting exchanges, which are conducted *in utramque partem* throughout the play. It is part of his argument, I am suggesting, that disputes of this nature can never be finally resolved.

[182] Shakespeare 1986, *T.C.*, TLN 3336–7, 3343, p. 1263 (5. 6. 149, 156).
[183] See, for example, Miles 1996, p. 157.
[184] For aspects of this interpretation see Rackin 1983; Miles 1996, esp. pp. 150–7; Holloway 2007.

6 The Generation of John Milton at Cambridge

I

The most vivid glimpse of John Milton as an undergraduate at Christ's College Cambridge is provided by John Aubrey in his *Brief Lives*. According to Aubrey, Milton 'was a very hard student in the University, and performed all his exercises there with very good applause'.[1] But he also seems to have cut a dashing figure among his contemporaries. 'His harmonicall and ingeniose soul', Aubrey goes on, 'did lodge in a beautifull and well-proportioned body', the most notable features of which were his 'exceeding faire' complexion and his 'abroun hayre'. Aubrey adds in a much-quoted aside that Milton's complexion 'was so faire that they called him *the lady of Christ's College.*'[2]

John Milton was admitted as a member of Christ's College on 12 February 1625 and studied there for the next seven years, taking his BA degree in 1628 and graduating as Master of Arts in 1632.[3] What was the University like at that time? What sort of life would Milton have led as a student? What were the academic exercises he performed to such good applause? These are not easy questions to answer with any precision, but the task is greatly eased by the existence of two exceptionally illuminating sets of documents. First there is the *Biographical Register* of Christ's College compiled by the philologist John Peile, who served as Master of the College between 1887 and 1910. This source has been little exploited for the period I am discussing, but it is possible to glean from it a mass of information about the changing size and social composition of the College in its formative years. Still more enlightening is the series of account books kept by Joseph Mede, a Fellow of the College who must have been well-known to the young John Milton, given that Mede served as one of the

This chapter is a revised and extended version of Skinner 2005a. For permission to make use of this earlier work I am indebted to David Reynolds and to Christ's College Cambridge. I am deeply grateful to Susan James and David Reynolds for commenting on drafts, and to Lucy Brown for invaluable research assistance.

[1] Aubrey 1898, vol. 2, p. 63. [2] Aubrey 1898, vol. 2, p. 67.
[3] Peile 1910–13, vol. 1, p. 363. Cf. Lewalski 2000, pp. 17, 551.

College tutors from 1613 until his death in 1638.[4] Mede itemised virtually every expense his pupils incurred, making it possible not merely to piece together a detailed portrait of their daily lives, but also to determine exactly what was being taught at Christ's while Milton was studying there.

II

John Milton first arrived at Christ's shortly after his sixteenth birthday.[5] His biographers have sometimes wondered why he made the transition from school to university at such a relatively late age, and have tried to explain what held him back.[6] But it is a myth to suppose that undergraduates in Milton's time were typically much younger than nowadays. There are no reliable statistics for the year of Milton's admission, but in his second year at Christ's the average age of those entering the College was seventeen. The figure then hovered between sixteen and seventeen for the next three years, stabilising at seventeen in the early 1630s before rising

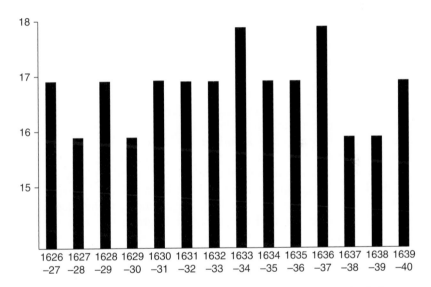

Figure 6.1 Average age of undergraduates entering Christ's College Cambridge 1626–40.

[4] On Mede see Peile 1900, pp. 133–6; Jue 2006, pp. 7–16. Rumrich 1986 alleges a direct influence of Mede on Milton. I speak of 'Mede' – although his account books at Christ's College are catalogued under 'Mead' – because the former spelling is the one that appears in his published work.
[5] Aubrey 1898, vol. 2, p. 62.   [6] Clark 1948, pp. 29–30; Fletcher 1956–61, vol. 2, p. 44.

to eighteen in the academic year 1633–4. If we look at the whole period between 1626 and 1640 (Figure 6.1), we find that Milton was in fact slightly below the average age of those admitted to the College at that time.

All students at the University of Cambridge in this period would have come from schools in which they had already received an extensive grounding in grammar, that is, the Latin language. (Hence the name grammar schools.) The University Injunctions required candidates for matriculation to be tested before their arrival to ensure that they knew Latin 'sufficiently'.[7] The need for this examination arose not merely because some university teaching was still conducted in Latin, but also because the statutes rather optimistically called for students to speak Latin at all times when within the College bounds.[8]

The town within which the colleges first began to arise in the closing decades of the thirteenth century was by Milton's time largely dominated by the University. The population of Cambridge in the early seventeenth century probably amounted to little more than 5,000,[9] but according to a near-contemporary estimate the presence of the University added 3,000 more.[10] Christ's was one of sixteen colleges, the sizes of which varied considerably. The largest, Trinity College, had a total of 440 people living in it in the 1620s, while the smallest, Trinity Hall, contained only 60.[11] Christ's at the time of Milton's arrival was of middling size. There were thirteen Fellows, together with 156 undergraduates and an unknown number of post-graduates studying for their Master's degree. With the coming of the civil war in 1642 these figures suddenly declined, after which they recovered only very slowly and uncertainly. The number of students graduating from Cambridge in Milton's time was probably higher than at any period until the beginning of the twentieth century.[12]

The academic year commenced in mid-October and ran until the start of July, but undergraduates seem to have been allowed to begin their studies at almost any time. If we look, for example, at the *Biographical Register* for 1624–5, we find that seven undergraduates were admitted between October and December, and nine more – including John Milton – between January and March. But the usual time for coming into residence was even later, and in that academic year twenty-nine new undergraduates arrived at Christ's between April and early July.

Milton and his contemporaries were entering a College that had remained in many ways unaltered since its foundation in 1505. The buildings would have looked much the same; the size of the Fellowship

[7] *Collections of Statutes* 1840, p. 319.   [8] Rackham (ed.) 1927, pp. 24, 48–50.
[9] Clark and Gray 1921, pp. 137–8; Fletcher 1956–61, vol. 2, p. 13.
[10] [Langbaine] 1651, p. 17.   [11] [Langbaine] 1651, pp. 7, 15.
[12] Venn 1897–1901, vol. 1, p. xxi.

had barely increased; and the College's basic purpose remained that of preparing young men for ecclesiastical careers. However, these surface similarities masked deep processes of change. Although most students were still training for the Church, the Church itself had suffered a violent transformation as a result of the anti-papal reforms of the 1530s and the Protestant settlement of 1559. Cambridge had subsequently become a centre of Puritanism, and Christ's had emerged as perhaps the most radical College of all. One of its Fellows, William Perkins, had been summoned before the Vice Chancellor's court in 1587 for preaching in the College chapel against the superstitious practice of kneeling to receive the sacrament.[13] Another Fellow, Francis Johnson, had been imprisoned two years later for pointing out that the rule of bishops was not sanctioned by the Scriptures, and demanding that the Church should instead be governed by elders.[14] These scandals were a thing of the past by the 1620s, but the College's puritan reputation lingered on, and may have been one reason why Milton's parents chose to send him there.[15]

A further important change lay in the social composition of the College. Christ's had been founded to cater for poor scholars, and it was still taking a considerable number of these so-called sizars in Milton's time. Besides receiving a subsidy from the College, sizars often paid their way through university by waiting on other students and acting as servants to the Fellows. Early in the seventeenth century, however, we find them beginning to be outnumbered for the first time in several generations by so-called pensioners.[16] The term 'pensioner' was the name given to an undergraduate who (as Aubrey says of Milton) lived 'at his owne chardge only', paying his fees in the form of a regular 'pension' to the College.[17] These students were invariably the sons of well-to-do parents, as in the case of Milton, whose father was a successful money-lender and scrivener who had amassed (in Aubrey's words) 'a plentifull estate'.[18] After 1610 there was scarcely a year in which pensioners were not in a large majority. If we look, for example, at the academic year 1627–8 – the year in which Milton took his BA – we find that thirty-four undergraduates were admitted as pensioners compared with only nine as sizars. The College

---

[13] Porter 1958, pp. 180–2.   [14] Porter 1958, pp. 141–2, 157–63.
[15] Lewalski 2000, p. 18.
[16] Stone 1964, p. 67 sees a change of this kind in early-modern Oxford as well as Cambridge, but dates it to the mid-sixteenth century. This generalisation is not supported by the evidence from Christ's. There are signs that the College admitted more pensioners than sizars from an early stage. It was during the period when Stone sees an increase in more prosperous students that, especially between c.1570 and c.1610, the poorer students at Christ's regularly outnumbered the better-off. At Christ's it was only after this time that the change associated by Stone with the mid-sixteenth century became marked.
[17] Aubrey 1898, vol. 2, p. 63.   [18] Aubrey 1898, vol. 2, p. 62.

was well on its way to entrenching, in defiance of its Foundress's wishes, a social trend that has never been fully reversed.

Still more striking was the appearance during this period of the sons of the gentry and nobility among the ranks of the undergraduates. These students were admitted as Fellow-commoners, so-called because they had the privilege of taking their meals or 'commons' with the Fellows rather than with the other undergraduates. They often came into residence with their own servants, and some of them lived in sumptuous style. There are no records of any such students at Christ's in the first generation of its existence, and even in the second half of the sixteenth century they appear only sporadically, with an average of around one per year. After 1610, however, they suddenly became far more numerous. From then until the outbreak of the civil war in 1642 the average number of Fellow-commoners rose to over four each year, and in some years there were as many as nine. Among Milton's contemporaries, perhaps the most conspicuous was William Halford, who must have caused a considerable stir when he arrived from Oundle in May 1632. He began by tipping the College butler two shillings and sixpence for saving him the trouble of signing his name in the College register, and went on to buy himself a gown costing £8, more than sixty times the normal price.[19] Halford stayed for less than two years, effortlessly maintaining the same level of expense, and left the College without taking a degree.

Most striking of all was the growth in size of the student body at this time. (See Figure 6.2.) Here it is instructive to compare the statistics for Christ's with the general growth of undergraduate numbers at Oxford and Cambridge recorded by Lawrence Stone in his classic study of what he called 'the educational revolution' in England between 1560 and 1640. According to Stone 'the first wave of expansion began in the 1560s'.[20] As Figure 6.2 shows, however, the fastest rate of early expansion at Christ's occurred in the mid-1540s, and it was only in the mid-1560s that the same level was again attained. Stone goes on to claim that expansion then 'reached a peak in about 1583, to be followed by a lull which lasted until the accession of James' in 1603.[21] But at Christ's the peak was reached only after many oscillations, and what happened between 1583 and 1603 was not a lull but a catastrophic decline, followed by an equally sudden rise and a further drop. Stone ends by stating that 'after 1604 there began a second great movement which lasted until the outbreak of the Civil War'.[22] But at Christ's we find that, although there was undoubtedly a rise in numbers, it was at first checked for a time, and then peaked in the late 1620s, after which it fell away sharply and recovered only slightly at the end of the 1630s.

[19] Peile 1910–13, vol. 1, p. 419; cf. Christ's College MS T. 11. 3, fo. 179r.
[20] Stone 1964, p. 50.   [21] Stone 1964, p. 50.   [22] Stone 1964, p. 51.

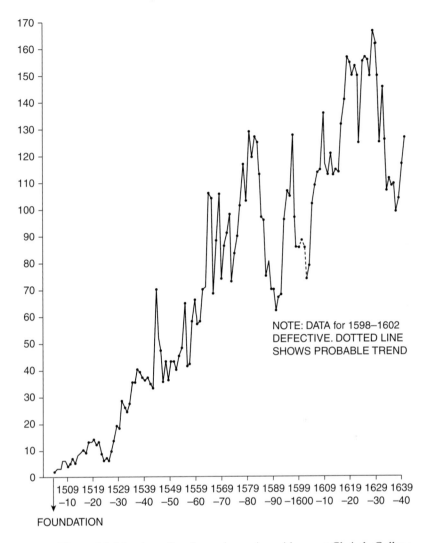

NOTE: DATA for 1598–1602 DEFECTIVE. DOTTED LINE SHOWS PROBABLE TREND

Figure 6.2 Number of undergraduates in residence at Christ's College Cambridge 1505–1640.

The early history of Christ's conspicuously fails to fit the contours of Lawrence Stone's triumphalist narrative. Nevertheless, the story is one of impressive development. The College in its first generation was a very modest foundation, with the number of undergraduates exceeding a total of forty on a regular basis only after about thirty-five years. By contrast, between 1603 and the outbreak of the civil war in 1642 there was only one year in which the number fell below a hundred, and during the period when Milton was a student the size of the undergraduate body averaged 159 per year.

Given that the original buildings had been designed to house only twelve Fellows and forty-seven scholars,[23] one consequence was that the College became intolerably overcrowded. The original statutes had called for each chamber to be shared by two students, but in Milton's time it was usual for at least four undergraduates to be sleeping in the same room.[24] The problem was exacerbated by the right of Fellow-commoners to occupy rooms of their own. When, for example, the son of Sir John Isham came into residence in April 1627, he was not only given a large chamber but space for his servant as well. He immediately 'dressed' his suite, as Joseph Mede records, with carpets, hangings and 'a Canopie and Curtaines', all for his exclusive use.[25]

Faced with an urgent need to provide additional accommodation, the College initially responded in 1613 by erecting a wooden structure behind the main buildings, which became known by the revealing but discouraging name of Rats' Hall.[26] Rats' Hall was three storeys high and evidently contained twelve chambers, but it was still not enough, and in the 1630s the College launched an appeal to finance further development. Milton did not contribute, but the initiative raised over £2,500, and enabled a magnificent new building with sixteen large chambers to be opened just before the outbreak of the civil war in 1642.[27]

With so much overcrowding, it is perhaps not surprising that the College did not feel able to charge very high rents. As Joseph Mede's account books show, the usual price for occupying a space in a sleeping chamber was one shilling and threepence per term. To this, however, you needed to add at least as much again for the cost of candles, together with two shillings a term for the use of a college servant and up to three shillings a quarter in the winter months for coal. If, moreover, you felt the need for a study of your own in addition to a sleeping chamber, your costs began to rise steeply. Mede's pupil Zachary Wildbore slept in a room in Rats' Hall for which he paid the standard rent of one shilling and threepence, but he also had a study there for which he had to pay over twelve times that amount.[28]

---

[23] Rackham (ed.) 1927, pp. 78, 100.   [24] Rackham (ed.) 1927, pp. vii, 52, 110.

[25] Peile 1910–13, vol. 1, p. 382; Christ's College MS T. 11. 3, fo. 89r.

[26] Peile 1900, p. 36.

[27] Christ's College MSS, Shelf 85: *A catalogue of the names of ye Benefactors for the new Building, 1639,* fo. 12r.

[28] Christ's College MS T. 11. 3, fo. 24v.

The daily routine of student life was strictly regulated by the University and College statutes, and the resulting timetable was a demanding one. The day began soon after 5 a.m. with prayers in Chapel, followed by the reading of a homily by one of the Fellows.[29] After morning service breakfast was served by the sizars at around 6 a.m., and then there were university lectures in the schools from 7 a.m. to 9 a.m. on Mondays to Thursdays.[30] After lectures it was time for dinner, which must have been served at around 11 a.m., given that the College statutes called for the hour between noon and one to be devoted, at least on Mondays and Thursdays, to scholarly exercises.[31] The afternoons were free, although in Christ's the statutes prescribed some supplementary teaching between 3 p.m. and 5 p.m. on four days of the week.[32] There was then a service in Chapel at 6 p.m. followed by supper in hall.[33] The University statutes required the College gate to be locked by 8 p.m., with an extension to 9 p.m. in summer. The key was thereupon handed over to the Master, and no one – including the Fellows – was subsequently allowed to go out.[34]

The aim appears to have been to create a way of life virtually bounded by the College walls. The College even employed its own barber and laundry-women so that students would have no need to leave the College precincts for these services.[35] If an undergraduate required for any reason to go out of College, he was enjoined by the University statutes to be soberly dressed, to be accompanied by at least one friend and to have gained permission beforehand. It was forbidden to loiter in the streets, to go to the market or to enter any tavern, although the statutes did permit undergraduates, when their parents were visiting, to accompany them to respectable hotels.[36]

This was not perhaps a very healthy way of life, and there is a distressing amount of evidence in Joseph Mede's account books about student illnesses. During Milton's second year, eight of Mede's pupils had to be permitted additional food during Lent because they were too weak to endure the fast. The saddest case was that of Joseph Browne, who suddenly fell ill in March 1632 after less than a year in College. Mede took him to a physician 'for Counsell & judgment' in the middle of the month, after which we read of copious blood-letting at the neck and a special payment to a butcher for sheep's entrails 'to lay to his head'. Despite these ministrations, and the services of a nurse who was paid eleven shillings

[29] Rackham (ed.) 1927, p. 106.   [30] *The Statutes*, 1838, p. 4.
[31] Rackham (ed.) 1927, p. 98.   [32] Rackham (ed.) 1927, p. 98.
[33] Masson 1881–94, vol. 1, p. 136.
[34] *The Statutes* 1838, p. 41; cf. Rackham (ed.) 1927, p. 90.
[35] Rackham (ed.) 1927, pp. 92, 112.   [36] *The Statutes* 1838, pp. 31–2.

for 'careful and laborious tending', Joseph Browne died before the end of the month at the age of only eighteen.[37]

As well as suffering from numerous ailments, everyone stood in constant terror of the plague. No sooner had Milton arrived in Cambridge than a devastating outbreak in London claimed some 35,000 lives.[38] Cambridge was largely spared, but the University had to close in early summer and did not fully reopen until December. Far worse was the outbreak of 1630, in which Cambridge lost nearly 10 per cent of its population. The disease arrived in April, eventually killing over a hundred people in the parish of St Andrew's alone, and thus in the immediate vicinity of Christ's.[39] The University had to shut down for the remainder of the year and everyone was sent home.

John Milton spent these months at his parents' house in Hammersmith, where he occupied himself in writing a number of his earliest poems. It was probably at this time that he completed his ode *On The Morning of Christ's Nativity*, the first draft of which, he tells us, he wrote on Christmas morning 1629.[40] To this period also belong his earliest English sonnets and his first published poem, his sixteen-line epitaph on Shakespeare, which initially appeared in the second folio of Shakespeare's plays in 1632.[41] It is worth quoting in full:

> What needs my Shakespeare for his honoured bones,
> The labour of an age in pilèd stones,
> Or that his hallowed relics should be hid
> Under a star-ypointing pyramid?
> Dear son of Memory, great heir of fame,
> What need'st thou such weak witness of thy name?
> Thou in our wonder and astonishment
> Hast built thyself a live-long monument.
> For whilst to th' shame of slow-endeavouring art,
> Thy easy numbers flow, and that each heart
> Hath from the leaves of thy unvalued book,
> Those Delphic lines with deep impression took,
> Then thou, our fancy of itself bereaving,
> Dost make us marble with too much conceiving;
> And so sepúlchred in such pomp dost lie,
> That kings for such a tomb would wish to die.[42]

The confidence with which the young Milton here claims 'my Shakespeare' as his model is arresting, to say the least.[43] So too is the originality with

[37] See *Christ's College Magazine* 1888, pp. 1–7.   [38] Parker 1968, vol. 1, p. 29.
[39] Heywood and Wright 1854, vol. 2, p. 390.
[40] For Milton's account see Lewalski 2000, pp. 37–8.   [41] Lewalski, 2000, pp. 39, 41.
[42] Milton 1998, p. 19.   [43] As noted in Lewalski 2000, p. 41.

which he reworks Horace's dictum that poets create their own most lasting memorials in the form of their works.[44] With Shakespeare, Milton suggests, it is the continuing wonder experienced by his readers that provides him with a yet more enduring monument.

After this interlude Milton returned to Cambridge towards the end of 1630. As we have seen, he was a serious student, and the academic syllabus was a daunting one. It would be a mistake, however, to suppose that the reality of undergraduate life closely mirrored the requirements of the statutes. To judge from the constant stream of remonstrations issued by the University, many of the more stringent rules and regulations were simply ignored.[45] One repeated complaint was that undergraduates were failing to dress with appropriate frugality and soberness. This development was blamed as early as 1578 on 'children of gentlemen and men of welth' who were entering the University and bringing with them 'very costly and disguised manner of apparrell and other attires unseemly for students'.[46] We hear of undergraduates growing their hair (as Milton did) to unsuitable lengths, sporting extravagant hats adorned with feathers and swaggering about with rapiers and swords. Still more frequently we hear of expensive silks and velvets being worn in riotously inappropriate colours and ostentatiously adorned with tassels and lace.[47]

The undergraduates also showed little willingness to remain confined to their colleges as the statutes required. They went to cock-fights and bear-baitings; they attended plays performed at visiting fairs; and they travelled to neighbouring villages to take part in football matches, where they got into serious fights.[48] They paid high fees to learn dancing and fencing, although both activities were punishable under the statutes by large fines.[49] They roamed the town and frequented the three leading taverns – the Dolphin, the Rose and the Mitre – which came to be known as 'the best tutors in the University'.[50] There they gambled and smoked as well as drank, while many of them 'resorted' (in the words of the 1630 Injunctions) to the daughters of the innkeepers and other women with

---

[44] With his reference to the pyramids, and to building a lasting monument, Milton echoes Horace 1914, III. XXX, p. 278.

[45] See *The Statutes* 1838, pp. 5–6 for the fines levied for non-attendance at university lectures.

[46] Heywood and Wright 1854, vol. 1, p. 217.

[47] Heywood and Wright 1854, vol. 1, p. 219, 397–405. There are frequent references to the purchase of silk, lace and velvet in Mede's accounts.

[48] Heywood and Wright 1854, vol. 1, pp. 305–6; vol. 2, pp. 33–8, 212–14. Cf. Venn 1913, pp. 118–20.

[49] *The Statutes* 1838, p. 31.   [50] Fletcher 1956–61, vol. 2, p. 59.

whom they contrived 'to mispend their time' and 'otherwise misbehave themselves'.[51]

The cloistered life envisaged by the statutes was further undermined by the fact that the rules about residence do not seem to have been strictly enforced. Milton provides a good example, for he tells us that he spent the spring of 1626, at the end of his second year, living in London rather than Cambridge.[52] By this time, moreover, the ease with which students could move in and out of the town had been greatly improved by one of Cambridge's notable figures, the University carrier Thomas Hobson. It was he who had the idea of hiring out horses to students, and who added the proviso – to ensure that no horse was over-exercised – that customers had to take whichever one had been longest in the stable. This arrangement came to be known as 'Hobson's choice', which *The Oxford English Dictionary* defines as 'the option of taking the one thing offered or nothing'. There is evidence in Joseph Mede's account books that the undergraduates at Christ's made extensive use of Hobson's facility, even though his services did not come cheap. Mede's pupil Charles Taysbrough had to pay four shillings in 1626 to travel to Suffolk, while John Roffey had to pay seven shillings in 1632 to hire a horse to take him to London.[53]

For those going to London, however, Hobson offered a less costly means of transport. He travelled to the city by wagon every week, and he accepted passengers for a fare of three shillings and fourpence.[54] Although he was over eighty years old by the time Milton became an undergraduate, Hobson was still making his weekly journey, which he gave up only when the outbreak of plague in 1630 led to a prohibition on such movements. The enforced leisure seems to have broken his spirit, and he died shortly afterwards.[55] Milton composed two verse epitaphs in his memory in 1631,[56] both of which are among the most high-spirited of his early poems.

> Here lieth one who did most truly prove,
> That he could never die while he could move;
> So hung his destiny never to rot
> While he might still jog on and keep his trot; ...
> Rest that gives all men life, gave him his death,
> And too much breathing put him out of breath;
> Nor were it contradiction to affirm
> Too long vacation hastened on his term.

[51] Heywood and Wright 1854, vol. 2, p. 377.   [52] Masson 1881–94, vol. 1, pp. 163–7.
[53] Christ's College MS T. 11. 3, fos. 65v, 161v.
[54] Christ's College MS T. 11. 1, fo. 5v.   [55] Masson 1881–94, vol. 1, pp. 134–5, 240.
[56] For this dating see Lewalski 2000, pp. 41–2.

Merely to drive away the time he sickened,
Fainted, and died, nor would with ale be quickened;
Nay, quoth he, on his swooning bed outstretched,
If I may not carry, sure I'll ne'er be fetched ...[57]

III

Among the questions that Joseph Mede's account-books enable us to answer, the most significant relate to the syllabus followed by Milton and his contemporaries at Christ's. Some undergraduates admittedly arrived at the College with no intention of taking a degree, and most of them probably studied rather little. Among Milton's contemporaries there was one Fellow-commoner, Henry Kendall, who lived in the College but was never even formally admitted as a student. A still larger number left the University without a degree because they had arrived with the ambition of moving after a couple of years to train as lawyers at the Inns of Court. There were four such undergraduates at Christ's in Milton's year, two of whom went on to Lincoln's Inn, one to Gray's Inn and one to the Middle Temple. Soon afterwards Milton's brother Christopher followed the same trajectory, leaving Christ's for the Middle Temple after only five terms and setting himself up in legal practice in the mid-1630s.[58]

Among Milton's contemporaries, virtually everyone else took the four-year course leading to the Bachelor's degree, while over half remained for an extra three years and proceeded to the degree of Master of Arts. The outline of the BA course was broadly laid down in the University statutes, the most recent version of which had come into force in 1570. The first year was devoted to rhetoric, with the regulations specifying that the main texts to be studied were Quintilian's *Institutio oratoria* and one of the oratorical works of Cicero.[59] Then came two years of logic, for which the recommended text was either Cicero's *Topica* or Aristotle's *Elenchi*,[60] after which the final year was devoted to natural and moral philosophy. The latter subject was chiefly taught out of Aristotle, the two set texts being the *Politics* and the *Nicomachean Ethics*.[61] Natural Philosophy was taken to include physics and cosmology, and in this case the recommended texts were Pliny's *Historia Naturalis* and Aristotle's *Problemata*,

---

[57] Milton 1998, pp. 20–1.   [58] Lewalski 2000, p. 55.
[59] *The Statutes* 1838, pp. 5, 6. For the comparable place of rhetoric in the Oxford curriculum see Feingold 1997, pp. 247–56.
[60] *The Statutes* 1838, p. 5.
[61] For the comparable place of moral philosophy in the Oxford curriculum see Feingold 1997, pp. 306–27.

an apocryphal work mainly concerned with medical questions and assorted physical phenomena.[62]

When Milton published his tract *Of Education* in 1644, he expressed deep dissatisfaction with this syllabus. He criticises the teaching of rhetoric, arguing that a subject of such importance ought to be placed last in order rather than first, and ought to be taught out of Plato, Aristotle and Cicero rather than Quintilian.[63] He objects even more strongly to the teaching of logic, complaining that it confronts 'young unmatriculated novices at first comming with the most intellective abstractions', so that they quickly find themselves lost 'in fadomles and unquiet deeps of controversie'. The effect is that most students 'grow into hatred and contempt of learning, mockt and deluded all this while with ragged notions and babblements, while they expected worthy and delightfull knowledge'.[64]

Milton was far from alone in finding the official curriculum unsatisfactory. There are frequent complaints from the University about non-attendance at lectures, and there are several signs that the colleges were finding it desirable to take over the teaching of undergraduates themselves. Christ's had its own Lecturers in Rhetoric and Logic by the 1620s, and most instruction seems to have taken place within the College.[65] The new system was undoubtedly preferable, making it easier for students to read the set texts for themselves and discuss them with their Tutors at their own pace, rather than trying to take notes (often by candlelight) while listening to lecturers expounding the same texts in the schools.

The rise of college-based teaching also allowed for more variety in the syllabus, and in the case of Christ's it is possible to work out exactly what was taught. Joseph Mede's account-books include complete lists of the books he asked his pupils to buy, and at what stage in their academic careers.[66] With this information it is possible to work out the order in which Mede introduced the different parts of the curriculum, and the extent to which he accepted, supplemented or ignored the teaching regulations laid down by the University. We can also determine (by some simple arithmetic) how much Mede charged for his services. The cost of tuition to a Fellow-commoner turns out to have been one pound five shillings per term, while to a pensioner like Milton the normal charge was fifteen shillings.

Mede paid little heed to the University regulations in the case of the Fellow-commoners, concentrating instead on trying to ensure that they

[62] *The Statutes* 1838, p. 5.   [63] [Milton] 1644, pp. 5–6.   [64] [Milton] 1644, p. 2.
[65] Masson 1881–94, vol. 1, p. 130; Peile 1910–13, vol. 1, p. 267.
[66] For a catalogue of the purchases recorded in Mede's account-books see Fletcher 1956–61, vol. 2, Appendix I, pp. 353–622.

acquired some elegant and gentlemanly accomplishments. Some took French lessons, for which special teachers had to be found, while others spent much of their time learning to read and play music.[67] With his more academic students, by contrast, Mede liked to make a number of substantial additions to the official curriculum. Sometimes he taught some mathematics, using as a textbook either Thomas Blundeville's *Exercises* in arithmetic and geometry or Bartholomew Keckermann's *Systema Totius Mathematices*.[68] But above all he offered far more in the way of religious instruction than the regulations required. Sixteen of his students in the period between 1625 and 1632 bought the so-called Heidelberg Catechism, the most popular statement of the Protestant faith to emerge from Reformation Germany. Ten more bought the complete Bible, presumably in the Authorised version of 1611, although this was an expensive book to acquire, usually costing at least seven or eight shillings. A considerable number bought lexicons to help them understand the Greek New Testament, including four copies of Johann Scapula's enormous Greek-Latin dictionary, while seven bought the Greek New Testament itself. Yet more impressively, six students bought Hebrew lexicons for use with the Old Testament, while seven bought the Hebrew version of the Psalms and three more the Hebrew version of the Book of Samuel. With his habitual modesty, however, Mede appears never to have drawn the attention of his students to his own important work of biblical criticism, the *Clavis Apocalyptica*, first published in 1627 and translated into English in 1643.[69]

Apart from these additions, Mede seems to have been content to follow the University curriculum, concentrating as required on rhetoric, logic and philosophy. But whereas the statutes called for the first year to be spent on rhetoric, Mede had a strong preference for starting his students off on logic, whether or not they were reading for a degree. The textbook he liked to use was some version of the *Systema Logicae* of the ubiquitous Bartholomew Keckermann. Keckermann had been a schoolmaster in the Gymnasium at Danzig, and had managed in the course of a brief lifetime (1573–1609) to produce a series of exceptionally successful textbooks on logic, rhetoric, theology, philosophy and mathematics, each unerringly aimed at the burgeoning undergraduate market.[70] Mede usually asked his pupils to buy the 'lesser' version of Keckermann's *Systema*,[71] but many of

---

[67] Christ's College MS T. 11. 3, fos. 81v–85v, 97v–98r.
[68] First published 1617. See Freedman 1997, p. 347.   [69] Mede 1643.
[70] Fletcher 1956–61, vol. 2, p. 150. On Keckermann see Costello 1958, pp. 85–6, 90–100; Schmitt 1988, pp. 822–3.
[71] On the *minus* version, first published in 1606, see Freedman 1997, p. 343.

them acquired the 'greater' version as well,[72] and Mede seems to have lost no time in telling them to make these essential purchases. In at least a dozen cases, the first item that appears on an undergraduate's account – often before the fee for matriculating as a member of the University – is a charge for one or another version of Keckermann's logical works.

Mede's attitude to the University regulations about the teaching of logic seems to have been ambivalent. As we have seen, the recommended texts were Cicero's *Topica* and Aristotle's *Elenchi*, his study of fallacious reasoning. Mede ignores the *Topica*, a book he never once asked his students to buy, but he seems to have carried the study of Aristotle's logic much further than the statutes required. It is particularly impressive to find him requiring a considerable number of his pupils to buy the complete edition of Aristotle's *Organon*, the system of which the *Elenchi* forms the final part. If Mede really guided his students through the whole of that complex work, he equipped them with a training in syllogistic reasoning of the most comprehensive kind.

After this grounding in logic, Mede's pupils were introduced to the study of rhetoric. To judge from the pattern of their book buying, they usually turned to this subject early in their second year. Mede occasionally seems to have taught the subject out of a textbook, but it is striking that he never required his pupils to buy Quintilian's *Institutio oratoria*, the text recommended by the University. He preferred Cicero's *De oratore*, and among contemporary authorities he sometimes added Gerard Vossius's *Rhetorices Contractae*, an Oxford edition of which was published in 1631,[73] or Bartholomew Keckermann's *Systema Rhetoricae*, which had first appeared in 1608.[74]

Generally, however, Mede seems to have agreed with Erasmus that the best means of teaching students to speak and write effectively is to introduce them to the finest literature. It was chiefly with this end in mind that undergraduates in Milton's day were asked to study poetry and history, and a large number of literary and historical works duly appear in the lists of books purchased by Mede's students for this part of the course. Among the poets Mede seems to have had a special fondness for Juvenal, and several of his pupils also bought a popular anthology of ancient Greek verse. But Mede's overwhelming preference was for Homer, whose *Odyssey* was regularly acquired by his students, sometimes as early as their second term. Among the historians Mede largely concentrated on the leading Latin writers, including Sallust, Caesar, Livy and Tacitus. But here too he had a favourite, although in this case a markedly

[72] On the *maius* version, first published in 1600, see Freedman 1997, p. 340.
[73] See Vossius 1631.   [74] Freedman 1997, p. 344.

eccentric one. He constantly recommended Johann Sleiden's *De Quatuor Summis Imperiis*, a brief survey, originally published in 1556, of the histories of Babylon, Persia, Greece and Rome.[75] It is not clear why Mede so much admired this rather elementary work, but it was one of the books he most frequently told his pupils to buy.

With students in their third and fourth years Mede continued to follow the official curriculum, focusing as required on natural and moral philosophy. But when teaching natural philosophy he ignored the statute enjoining the study of Aristotle's *Problemata*, and only occasionally recommended any of Aristotle's texts at all. He chose to teach the subject almost entirely from modern textbooks containing a synthesis of current views about cosmology, psychology and physics. He tried out a number of these works at different times, including Franco Burgersdijck's survey of natural and moral philosophy, of which an Oxford edition was published in 1631,[76] as well as Bartholomew Keckermann's *Systema Physicum* of 1610.[77] But his preferred compendium was Johannes Magirus's *Physiologiae Peripateticae*, originally published in Frankfurt in 1597, with a London edition in 1619, a text bought by at least a dozen of his pupils during these years.[78]

To judge from the pattern of book purchases, the final subject that Mede's students were asked to tackle was moral philosophy. By contrast with his method of teaching the physical sciences, Mede made little use of textbooks for this part of the course and appears to have concentrated on a small number of well-known primary works. As we have seen, the two texts officially recommended were Aristotle's *Politics* and *Ethics*. Mede never studied the *Politics* with his students, but he regularly taught the *Nicomachean Ethics*, and a considerable number of his pupils bought the book. However, his own view of ethics seems to have been out of line with Aristotle's emphasis on the virtues and the nature of the good life. Mede was evidently more interested in inculcating an essentially practical ideal of good manners and 'civil conversation'. He appears, in other words, to have shared the characteristically humanist approach to moral theory I shall discuss in chapter 8. Of the two works he recommends most frequently, one was Henry Peacham's *The Compleat Gentleman*, which had appeared as recently as 1622.[79] This was chiefly concerned with the proper 'carriage' of a gentleman and the sort of studies that promote a civilised and sociable life. The other was Giovanni della Casa's *Galateus*

---

[75] See Sleiden 1556.
[76] See Burgersdicius 1631. On Burgersdijck see Schmitt 1988, p. 811.
[77] Freedman 1997, p. 346.
[78] See Magirus 1619. On Magirus see Schmitt 1988, p. 825.   [79] See Peacham 1622.

seu de Morum Honestate, first published in Italian in 1558.[80] As we shall see in chapter 8, this was even more straightforwardly a book about civil conversation, with detailed instructions about how to eat, dress, speak and comport oneself in a noble yet affable style. The *Galateus* was by far Mede's favourite work on moral theory, and he never ceased to urge it on his pupils throughout his teaching career.

IV

After four years of study, students were required to take a series of examinations leading to the conferment of the BA degree.[81] These took the form of public disputations, and the University statutes required undergraduates to prepare for these occasions by performing at least two similar exercises in their colleges.[82] Candidates for the BA were required to appear twice in the schools as Opponents and three times as Respondents.[83] The task of a Respondent was to defend a given proposition put forward for debate, while that of an Opponent was to raise objections to it. Of these two 'Acts', the more challenging was that of the Respondent, and in playing this role the student became the centre of a highly ritualised event.

As soon as a student felt ready to undertake his Responsions, he was required to suggest three subjects for discussion and affix his proposals to the door of the schools three days before the disputation was due to take place.[84] The statutes laid down that the questions for debate needed to be approved beforehand by the Vice Chancellor, and that the whole occasion should be 'fit and decorous'.[85] The requirement of decorum was evidently introduced to counter undergraduate levity, while the requirement of fitness alluded to the understanding that some questions were beyond argument. For example, in theological disputations one often encounters questions about such matters as the applicability of the Mosaic Law, but never about such matters as the existence of God or the divinity of Christ.

Once the questions had been agreed, the Respondent presented himself in the schools at one o'clock in the afternoon to wrangle for two hours with his Opponents.[86] The proceedings were opened by a Moderator, who announced the specific topic to be discussed. The surviving evidence

---

[80] See Casa 1619. Fletcher 1961, vol. 2, pp. 577–9 shows this Latin edition to have been the one used by Mede's students.
[81] Masson 1881–94, vol. 1, pp. 140–2; Parker 1968, vol. 1, pp. 52–3.
[82] *The Statutes* 1838, p. 6; cf. Rackham (ed.) 1927, pp. 74, 88.
[83] *The Statutes* 1838, p. 7.   [84] *The Statutes* 1838, p. 13.   [85] *The Statutes* 1838, p. 27.
[86] *The Statutes* 1838, p. 13.

about the range of topics debated is unfortunately somewhat fragmentary. But among the disputations in moral philosophy around this time we find such propositions as 'Equality in a state is dangerous' and 'The middle way is the safest means of conserving a state', while among disputations in natural philosophy we find 'Our senses never deceive us' and 'Gold can be produced by chemical art'.[87]

After the specific topic had been disclosed, the so-called Father of the Respondent stepped forward. He would normally be a Fellow of the candidate's college, and it was his duty to introduce his pupil and offer a preliminary outline of his argument. Then came a licensed interruption – which often caused trouble – from a figure known as the Prevaricator. He sat on a three legged-stool known as the Tripos, and was given the task of satirising the proceedings. When the proposition 'Gold can be produced by chemical art' was debated in 1631, James Duport as Prevaricator proved syllogistically that this must undoubtedly be the case. If gold can be produced, he reasoned, it can only be by science or by art. But it can easily be produced without science, because doctors often produce a great deal of gold for themselves without having any science at all. Therefore they must produce it by art.[88]

Following this interruption, the Respondent rose to present his case. If he was a candidate for a higher degree, this was the moment at which the University ushers handed out copies of the printed Latin verses in which he was expected to have summarised his argument in correct rhetorical style. One of the Fellows of Christ's had to act as a Respondent for such a degree in 1628, and had the ingenious idea of persuading Milton to write the requisite verses for him.[89] The proposition under debate was that Nature is liable to old age, and Milton argued the contrary case, producing in the process one of his most spectacular Latin poems.[90]

Once the Respondent had spoken, the Father rose to restate his pupil's position and counter some possible objections to it. Then the Moderator called on the Opponents to refute the Respondent's arguments. Usually there would be three Opponents, also candidates for the BA degree, but still at the stage of putting forward criticisms rather than having to resolve them. After they had stated their objections, it was up to the Respondent, mustering as much extempore Latin as possible, to reiterate their arguments and dispose of them one by one in proper syllogistic style. This could be a nerve-racking exercise even for senior members of the

---

[87] Heywood and Wright 1854, vol. 2, p. 155.   [88] Wordsworth 1968, p. 282.
[89] Parker 1968, vol. 1, pp. 43–4.
[90] Masson 1881–94, vol. 1, pp. 199–203; for the poem see Milton 1998, pp. 567–9. But Lewalski 2000, pp. 29–30 thinks Milton's contribution may have been his briefer and more lighthearted *De Idea Platonica*, for which see Milton 1998, pp. 571–2.

University, as is clear from a report of the disputation staged for the visit of King James I to the University in 1615. On this occasion the Respondent was William Roberts of Queens' College, later bishop of Bangor, and one of his Opponents was William Chappell of Christ's, John Milton's first tutor. Roberts was so overwhelmed by Chappell's objections that he fainted. King James, a great admirer of his own skills in disputation, thereupon took up the case on Roberts's behalf, but Chappell proceeded to refute his sovereign no less unmercifully, and appears to have basked for years in the glory of that day.[91]

After the Respondent had done his best to reply to his Opponents, the Moderator brought the proceedings to a close by offering the right measure of praise to everyone involved. With this ordeal over, the chief requirements for the BA degree had been satisfied. It only remained for candidates to become 'Quaestionists', that is, to submit to a final examination in which they were asked about the nature of syllogistic reasoning.[92] If their answers were satisfactory they were said to be 'Determiners', after which they were declared by the Proctors to have attained the standing of full Bachelors of Arts.

V

One might finally ask what became of John Milton's contemporaries after they had taken their degrees. Of the fifteen other students admitted in the same half-year, four have left no mark on the historical record. Two more departed without degrees to go to Inns of Court, and one of these, Richard Earle, went on to enjoy a prominent public career, becoming a baronet in 1629 and sheriff of Lincoln in 1647. All the others became clergymen, and all but one eventually sank into decent obscurity in country parsonages. Only Robert Pory, a friend of Milton's at St Paul's School as well as at Christ's, carved out a more imposing place for himself in the Church. Although he suffered in the civil wars as an alleged Arminian, he later flourished mightily as a notorious pluralist under the restored monarchy after 1660.[93]

Milton likewise sank into obscurity for some years after graduating, returning to live with his parents in Hammersmith and moving with them three years later to their country retreat at Horton. He was by no means vegetating, however, but was systematically working his way through a self-imposed course of reading in history, theology and philosophy, and at the same time trying out his vocation as a poet. One outcome was the

[91] Masson 1881–94, vol. 1, p. 128.   [92] *The Statutes* 1838, p. 6.
[93] For details see the article by Stephen Wright in ODNB.

composition of his masque *Comus*, first performed at Ludlow Castle in September 1634 and published in 1637. But by far the most important product of these years was *Lycidas*, the greatest of his early poems.

Although nothing is known about the circumstances in which *Lycidas* was composed, it is possible that Milton was commissioned to write it by some of the Fellows of Christ's. The poem was occasioned by the death of Edward King, a junior contemporary of Milton's who had become a Fellow of the College. King was shipwrecked and drowned in 1637 at the age of twenty-five while crossing to visit his family in Ireland, and his colleagues decided to issue a volume of poems in his memory. The resulting collection was published in two sections, with separate title-pages, in 1638. The first part, entitled *Justa Edouardo King naufrago*,[94] consisted of encomia in Greek and Latin verse;[94] the second, entitled *Obsequies to the memorie of Mr Edward King*, contained thirteen poems in English, among which *Lycidas* appeared over the initials 'J. M.'[95]

While most contributors limited themselves to conventional expressions of admiration and grief, Milton took the opportunity to produce a meditation not merely on the death of his friend but on lost youth, unfulfilled gifts and the futility of ambition in the face of the fates.

> Alas! What boots it with uncessant care
> To tend the homely slighted shepherd's trade,
> And strictly meditate the thankless Muse?
> Were it not better done as other do,
> To sport with Amaryllis in the shade,
> Hid in the tangles of Neaera's hair?
> Fame is the spur that the clear spirit doth raise
> (That last infirmity of noble mind)
> To scorn delights, and live laborious days;
> But the fair guerdon where we hope to find,
> And think to burst out into sudden blaze,
> Comes the blind Fury with th'abhorrèd shears,
> And slits the thin-spun life.[96]

Milton's long poem – nearly 200 lines – brings the volume to a close, as if in acknowledgement of its unsurpassable qualities.

After the 1630s Milton maintained no further links with Cambridge, and in later life he always spoke disparagingly of the training he had received there. In his *Reasons of Church Government* of 1641 he bitterly complains that 'honest and ingenuous natures coming to the Universities

---

[94] *Justa Edouardo King naufrago* 1638.
[95] *Obsequies* 1638. 'Lycidas' appears at pp. 20–5.
[96] I quote from Milton 1998, p. 43. However, the original version of this passage printed in *Obsequies* 1638, p. 22 contains some important variants, and these I have adopted.

to store themselves with good and solid learning' encounter nothing but 'thorny lectures of monkish and miserable sophistry',[97] and in his tract *Of Education* of 1644 he dismisses the University curriculum as an 'asinine feast of sowthistles and brambles'.[98] Nevertheless, he seems to have retained some affection for his College, as he makes clear in his *Apology* of 1642. He is glad, he writes, to have the opportunity 'to acknowledge publickly with all gratefull minde, that more then ordinary favour and respect which I found above any of my equals at the hands of those curteous and learned men, the Fellowes of that Colledge wherein I spent some yeares'.[99] Describing them as 'ingenuous and friendly men who were ever the countnancers of vertuous and hopefull wits', he feels able to bid them a fond farewell.[100]

---

[97] [Milton] 1641, p. 62.   [98] [Milton] 1644, p. 3.   [99] [Milton] 1642, p. 12.
[100] [Milton] 1642, p. 12.

7   Rethinking Liberty in the English Revolution

I

If we wish to improve our understanding of the English revolution, one of the topics we shall need to reconsider is the debate between Crown and Parliament over the issue of political liberty. Admittedly this may appear a woefully hackneyed claim to make. Surely the traditional whig interpretation always took the Crown's attacks on the freedom of subjects to be among the leading causes of the civil war? And surely it was one of the main aspirations of what Alan Cromartie has described as the hyper-whig interpretation popularised by Conrad Russell and his disciples to cast doubt on precisely that article of faith?[1] Has not the theme of liberty already been done to death?

My answer is that I am interested in a view of liberty different from the one examined by the whig historians and their hyper-whig adversaries. These schools of thought were alike concerned with whether or not there was an assault on freedom in the sense of an increased campaign of interference with the legal rights and liberties of subjects in the decades before 1642.[2] According to the whigs, the Crown was engaged on just such a campaign of lawless oppression, which in turn explains why the presentation of the Petition of Right in 1628 was always treated as a pivotal moment in the whig grand narrative. The Petition specifically charges that, although the people of England possess 'divers Rights and Liberties' under the law, they are being prevented from exercising them, subjected to vexatious compulsion and otherwise 'molested and disquieted' in a manner 'wholly and directly contrary' to the customs and statutes of the realm.[3] Further objections about Crown interference were

This chapter is a revised and extended version of Skinner 2006. For permission to make use of this earlier work I am indebted to *History Workshop Journal*, and for negotiating the permission I owe special thanks to Tessa Chynoweth. For commenting on drafts I am deeply grateful to Ben Braddick, Rachel Foxley, Laura Gowing, Kinch Hoekstra, Susan James, Philip Pettit and Lyndal Roper.
[1] See Cromartie 1999.   [2] See, for example, the discussions in Hexter (ed.) 1992.
[3] Gardiner (ed.) 1906, pp. 66–70.

raised as soon as Parliament reconvened in 1640. This was the moment when Henry Parker emerged as the most resourceful protagonist of the parliamentarian cause. Parker's *Case of Shipmony*, first published in November 1640, begins by complaining in the same vein that the use of the royal prerogative to impose levies and forced loans 'is incompatible with popular liberty.'[4] The tract ends by expressing the fear that England may soon be reduced to the level of France, where the king's absolute powers have oppressed the people and ruined the state.[5]

According to the hyper-whigs, the whig historians habitually over-estimated these dangers. How could there have been any serious constitutional threat when the people's liberties had already been legally secured in the course of the sixteenth century?[6] The whigs may indeed have exaggerated the threat, although it seems to me that their critics have in turn underestimated it. But whatever the rights and wrongs of this well-worn dispute, I have no desire to rehearse them here. As I have said, I want to focus on a contrasting sense in which the Crown's critics spoke about a loss of liberty. During the same period, they began to put forward the separate and seemingly hyperbolical claim that the people of England no longer enjoyed the status of free men. The very existence of the king's prerogatives, they alleged, reduces the entire nation to a state of bondage and servitude.

Among the parliamentarian writers who pursued this line of thought, there was broad agreement about two elements in the idea of liberty. They accept that all men are by nature free from subjection to positive law. But they also agree that, even under the rule of law, it remains possible to live as a free man. To retain this status, two conditions must be satisfied. One is that you should be able to exercise your rights and liberties without undue interference. While this is a necessary condition, however, it is not sufficient, for it is possible to enjoy your liberties to the fullest degree without being a free man. If the continuation of your liberties depends on the arbitrary will of anyone else, then you are not a free man but a slave, even though you may have complete *de facto* enjoyment of your liberties, and may therefore be able to act entirely as you choose. Being free to act solely because there is someone who has chosen not to hinder you is what reduces you from the standing of a free man to a state of servitude. The second necessary condition of living as a free man under a system of positive law is therefore that your capacity to exercise your rights and liberties must never be subject to anyone else's will, must never be a matter of grace as opposed to right.[7]

---

[4] [Parker] 1640, p. 2.   [5] [Parker], 1640, pp. 44–6.
[6] See Cromartie 1999, pp. 76–120. For further critiques of the hyper-whigs see Sommerville 1996 and Sommerville 1999, pp. 224–65.
[7] For expositions and defences of this view of freedom see Pettit 1997; Pettit 2012; Skinner 1998; Skinner 2002c; Skinner 2008b. For a related discussion see Tully 1999.

As a number of royalist writers promptly demanded, what freedom can I be said to lack if I have complete enjoyment of my rights and liberties? John Bramhall vehemently presses the point in his *Serpent's Salve* of 1643. 'If the Libertie of the Subject be from Grace, not from pactions or agreements, is it therefore the lesse? or the lesse to be regarded? what is freer then gift?'[8] The answer given by the writers I am considering is that your awareness of your dependence will act as a bridle and a spur. If you are condemned to living in dependence on the goodwill of a master, there will be many things you cannot manage to say or do, and many other things you cannot forbear from saying or doing. You will find, in other words, that you are obliged to censor yourself for fear of what might happen if you were to speak or act in defiance of the master on whom you depend.

The parliamentarian writers liked to illustrate this argument by reference to the bishops in the House of Lords. The right of the bishops to sit in the Upper House was withdrawn in February 1642. The justification for this decision stemmed from the contention that they had never acted as anything other than slavish and servile hirelings of the Crown. As Richard Ward explains in *The Vindication of the Parliament*, 'having their dependance upon the *King*', they felt constrained to 'side with him, in any thing, though it were adjudged by the *Parliament* to be destructive and hurtfull to the Kingdome.'[9] The author of *An Honest Broker* agrees that, due to their 'total dependances' on the king, the bishops were inevitably committed to 'advancing the Court by enslaving the Countrey.'[10] Both writers conclude that there can be no place for such dangerous servility in a free Parliament.

Bracton had opened his *De Legibus et Consuetudinibus Angliae* by drawing exactly this contrast between the free man and the slave, in consequence of which the distinction became firmly embedded in English common law from an early stage.[11] For the origins of the contrast, however, we need to go back to the law of Rome, and in particular to the rubric *De statu hominis* at the outset of Justinian's *Digest*, from which Bracton's analysis was derived.[12] There we are told that slavery can be defined as 'an institution of the *ius gentium* by which someone is, contrary to nature, made subject to the dominion of someone else'.[13] This in turn is said to furnish a definition of civil liberty. If everyone in a civil association is either bond or free, then a *civis* or free subject must be someone who is not under the dominion of anyone else, but is *sui iuris*, capable of acting in their own right. It likewise follows that what it means for someone to

[8] Bramhall 1643, p. 12.   [9] [Ward], 1642, p. 19.   [10] *A Miracle* 1643, sig. D, 4r.
[11] Bracton 1640, I. VI, fo. 5.   [12] For a discussion see Skinner 1998, pp. 36–57.
[13] *The Digest* 1985, I. V. 4. 35, vol 1, p. 15: 'Servitus est constitutio iuris gentium, qua quis dominio alieno contra naturam subicitur.'

lack the status of a free subject must be to live *in potestate*, subservient to the will of a master who wields dominating power.[14]

This classical contrast between the *liber homo* and the *servus*, the free man and the slave, underpinned much of the vocabulary in which the concept of individual liberty was discussed in the debates between Crown and Parliament in the opening decades of the seventeenth century. When I first attempted to analyse these disputes, I accordingly characterised the views of those who contrasted freedom with servitude as 'neo-Roman' in character. But I now see that something more needs to be said about what I had supposed to be a harmless label if confusion is to be avoided. I am not suggesting, as some of my critics have assumed, that the early-modern parliamentarians whose understanding of personal liberty I label neo-Roman were necessarily drawing on a wide knowledge of Roman legal and political thought.[15] When I used 'neo-Roman' as a shorthand, I was simply referring to the belief that the antonym of liberty is servitude. I spoke of this as a neo-Roman commitment simply because it embodies the classic distinction between free and unfree persons enunciated at the outset of Justinian's *Digest*.

When this distinction was taken up by Bracton in his *De Legibus*, the forms of servitude said to contrast with the status of the free man were extended. Rather than deploying the straightforward distinction in the *Digest* between the *liber homo* and the *servus*, Bracton and his successors count bondsmen and villeins among the unfree, on the grounds that they too are in some respects subject to masters who possess arbitrary powers. The sense in which Bracton's analysis is neo-Roman simply arises from his agreement with the *Digest* that the fundamental distinction in the law of persons is between the free and the unfree, and that what it means to be unfree is to live *in potestate*, in subjection to the arbitrary will of someone else.

During the debates between Crown and Parliament in the early seventeenth century, we already encounter this distinction in Sir Thomas Hedley's great speech to the House of Commons in 1610, in which he questioned the prerogative right of the Crown to impose levies without parliamentary consent.[16] Hedley's central contention was that 'in point of profit or property of lands and goods, there is a great difference betwixt the king's free subjects and his bondmen; for the king may by commission at his pleasure seize the lands and goods of his *villani*', whereas if he seizes

---

[14] *The Digest* 1985, I. VI. 1. 36, vol. 1, p. 17.

[15] This misunderstanding, no doubt my own fault, has given rise to some irrelevant criticisms of my argument. See, for example, Walker 2006 and Sommerville 2007, pp. 211–16.

[16] For a full analysis see Peltonen 1995, pp. 220–8.

the property of free subjects by a similar exercise of arbitrary power the effect will be to introduce 'a promiscuous confusion of a freeman and a bound slave'.[17]

The same argument resurfaced in the Parliament of 1628, particularly in the protests over Charles I's exaction of the Forced Loan two years earlier.[18] Sir Dudley Digges opened the debate by denouncing those who say that 'he is no great monarch' who cannot take 'whatsoever he will'. Any king who 'is not tied to the laws' and who rules merely according to his will is no better than 'a king of slaves'.[19] Sir John Eliot echoed the argument, stressing that the very fact of being 'liable to the command of a higher power' is what takes away our liberty.[20] Speaking soon afterwards in the debate about the Petition of Right, Sir John Strangeways reaffirmed that such prerogatives undoubtedly serve to enslave, roundly concluding that 'the great work of this day, you know, is to free the subject'.[21]

After these bruising attacks in 1628, and after a brief and chaotic parliamentary session in 1629, Charles I and his advisers resolved to abandon Parliament and impose a system of personal rule. They were able to sustain this policy for nearly eleven years, but by the Autumn of 1639 the Crown's financial embarrassments had become so acute that a new Parliament had to be called. Meanwhile the government's efforts to manage without parliamentary subsidies had given rise to even more controversial uses of the royal prerogative, the most unpopular of which was the extension of the 'ship money' paid by the kingdom's seaports into a general levy in the later 1630s. As a result, the so-called Short Parliament that finally met in April 1640 reverted with even greater urgency to discussing the subversion of liberty. Speaker after speaker denounced the use of the prerogative to 'make void the lawes of the kingdome' and 'impeach the Liberty of the Subject', while accusing the king's advisers of assuring him that 'his prerogative is above all Lawes and that his Subjects are but slaves.'[22]

Charles I initially resolved on an immediate dissolution, but his financial difficulties proved so intractable that he found himself unable to avoid summoning a new Parliament, which duly met in November 1640. Refusing the Crown's pleas for a subsidy, the House of Commons fell yet again to denouncing what Sir John Holland described as 'the late inundations of the prerogative royal, which have broken out and almost overturned our liberties.'[23] Sir John Culpepper warned that if the king can

---

[17] Foster (ed.) 1966, vol. 2, p. 192.
[18] On opposition rhetoric in Charles I's early parliaments see Peltonen 2013, pp. 186–217.
[19] Johnson *et al.* (eds.) 1977a, p. 66.   [20] Johnson *et al.* (eds.) 1977a, p. 72.
[21] Johnson *et al.* (eds.) 1977b, p. 214.
[22] Cope and Coates (eds.) 1977, pp. 136, 137, 140, 142.
[23] Cobbett and Hansard (eds.) 1807a, col. 648.

'impose what and when he pleases, we owe all that is left to the goodness of the king, not to the law'.[24] Lord Digby concluded that 'our Liberties, the very spirit and essence of our weal, which should differ us from slaves, and speak us Englishmen, are torn away'.[25]

This was the moment when Henry Parker stepped forward with his *Case of Shipmony*, which he issued to coincide with the opening of the Long Parliament.[26] As we have seen, his tract begins and ends with a plea to prevent rights and liberties from being tyrannically undermined. But Parker's central contention is that the very existence of the king's power to impose levies without consent has the effect of reducing the people to servitude. Like Culpepper, Parker objects that the imposition of ship-money presupposes that 'the meere will of the Prince is law', and that 'he may charge the Kingdome thereupon at his discretion, though they assent not'.[27] But if the king is able to claim such discretionary powers, then we depend as subjects not upon the law, to which we have given our consent, but merely upon the will of the king. As Parker insists, however, to depend upon the will of anyone else is what it means to live in servitude. He concludes that, if it is left to the king's 'sole indisputable judgement' to 'lay charges as often and as great as he pleases', the effect will be to transform us into 'the most despicable slaves in the whole world.'[28]

This distinction between liberty and dependence, and hence between free men and slaves, was taken up by most of the leading parliamentarian spokesmen at the beginning of the civil war.[29] We encounter it in Henry Parker's *Observations* of July 1642,[30] in John Marsh's *Debate in Law* of September 1642,[31] in Richard Ward's *Vindication of the Parliament* of October 1642,[32] and in such anonymous tracts of early 1643 as *A Soveraigne Salve*,[33] *An Honest Broker*[34] and *Touching the Fundamentall Lawes*.[35] Perhaps the clearest summary can be found in John Goodwin's *Anti-Cavalierisme*, first published in October 1642. According to Goodwin, what it means to be 'free men and women' is to have 'the disposall of your selves and of all your wayes' according to your will, rather than being subject to the will of anyone else. If your rulers are in possession of discretionary powers, you will be obliged to live 'by the lawes of their lusts and

[24] Cobbett and Hansard (eds.) 1807a, col. 655.
[25] Cobbett and Hansard (eds.) 1807a, col. 664.
[26] For a full analysis see Mendle 1995, pp. 32–50.   [27] [Parker] 1640, pp. 5, 17.
[28] [Parker] 1640, p. 21.
[29] The dates of all tracts cited in this paragraph are taken from the BL (Thomason) copies.
[30] [Parker] 1642, pp. 9–10, 17, 43–4. See also [Parker] 1643, pp. 6–7.
[31] Marsh 1642, pp. 13, 24.   [32] [Ward] 1642, pp. 12, 28.
[33] *A Soveraigne Salve* 1643, pp. 16–17, 36–8.
[34] *A Miracle* 1643, sig. C, 2v–3r, sig. E, 3v–4v.
[35] *Touching the Fundamentall Lawes* 1643, pp. 10, 12 (*recte* 14).

pleasures' and 'to be at their arbitterments and wills in all things.' But if they are able to 'make themselves Lords over you' in this fashion, then your birthright of 'civill or politick libertie' will be cancelled, and you will be reduced to 'a miserable slavery and bondage.'[36]

Although most of the spokesmen I have been quoting refer only to free men, Goodwin not only speaks explicitly of 'free men and women', but argues that the defence of liberty against enslavement 'is a service wherein women also may quit themselves like men, whose prayers commonly are as masculine, and doe as great and severe execution, as the prayers of men.'[37] Does Goodwin think that a woman can act in the style of a free man? The question looks paradoxical, and among humanist writers on citizenship the paradox had always been emphasised. Discussing the place of women in civil associations, they had generally drawn on classical assumptions about the figure of the *vir*, the eponymous possessor of *virtus* or civic virtue. One consequence was that the rights and duties of citizenship came to be seen in strictly gendered terms. When the humanists speak of the *vir*, what they have in mind is a virile character by contrast with a woman. But if the distinctive quality of the *vir* is the possession of *virtus* or civic virtue, then it follows that the attributes needed for effective citizenship must be specifically male. Among humanist pedagogues, this distinction was frequently used to explain why no useful purpose can be served by granting women the kind of education recommended for young men. As I emphasised in chapter 6, the education in question was based on the cultivation of the rhetorical arts. But as Leonardo Bruni asks in discussing the teaching of women, why should an effort to master the art of rhetoric 'consume the powers of a woman, who never sees the forum?' 'The contests of the forum', he goes on, 'are the sphere of men'; the ability to speak 'winningly' is a talent required only in the public sphere, in which women have no place.[38]

If we return, however, to the texts of Roman and common law, the position begins to look less clear.[39] The rubric *De statu hominis* in the *Digest* defines citizenship as the distinctive attribute not of the *vir* but of the *liber homo*. But it is crucial that, whereas the word *vir* denotes a man by contrast with a woman, the word *homo* simply means 'human being' and hence 'man or woman'. The effect is to raise the question of gender in relation to citizenship in a different way. To be a citizen it is necessary to be a *liber homo*; but to be a *liber homo* it is only necessary to be *sui iuris*, capable of acting independently of anyone else's will. But if this is so, then there seems no reason why at least some women – those with

---

[36] Goodwin [John] 1642, pp. 38–9.   [37] Goodwin [John] 1642, p. 4.
[38] Bruni 1987, p. 244.   [39] On these complexities see Hughes 2012, esp. pp. 14–22.

sufficient financial means – should not be capable of acting in a spirit of full independence. What, then, is to prevent them (other than the gender of the Latin words involved) from being counted as *liberi homines*, and hence from taking charge of households and businesses? This possibility was admittedly circumscribed in English law by the rule that a woman's property as well as her person became subject upon marriage to the will of her husband. But a number of anomalies remained. What about unmarried women who possess their own inheritances? And what about widows whose property may have come to them in the form of outright bequests?

These questions were never squarely faced, but they remained to haunt the protagonists of Parliament throughout the 1640s. Ironically but unsurprisingly, it was the royalists who spoke up for greater inclusiveness, especially in the course of ridiculing the parliamentarian theory of representative government. Dudley Digges's critique of Henry Parker in his *Answer to a Printed Book*, first published in November 1642, provides the earliest example.[40] Parker had argued in his *Observations* that, when Parliament makes a resolution, it is exactly as if the decision has been taken *ab omnibus*, because the whole 'generality' elects its representatives in Parliament.[41] Digges retorts that this conclusion cannot possibly be justified so long as 'women generally by reason of their Sexe are excluded' from having a vote.[42] Soon afterwards Sir John Spelman in *A View of a Printed Book* responded to Parker yet more pointedly. If we are to speak of representing the whole generality, Spelman observes, the right to vote will need to be massively extended. Among those who will have to be enfranchised are inheritrixes – that is, heiresses who hold their own property by inheritance. So too with jointresses – that is, widows with property settled on them for life. Why, as Spelman asks, should they be 'over mastered' by 'the Votes of those that are deputed by a minor number of the people?' He concludes that, as these and other examples show, it is blatantly false to say that members of Parliament are 'sent with equallity from all parts' and are 'sent by all'. So 'how doe they then represent all?'[43] How indeed? But it took several centuries for Spelman's objection to be met.

Johann Sommerville has recently argued that 'it is difficult to sustain the claim that there was any developed tradition of republican or neo-Roman thought before the Civil War' in England.[44] He is certainly right in saying that it was possible to defend a neo-Roman view of individual liberty without being a republican, and that neo-Roman ideas had been

---

[40] Date (20 November 1642) from BL (Thomason) copy.   [41] [Parker] 1642, pp. 5–6, 8.
[42] [Digges] 1642, p. 15. The BL (Thomason) copy ascribes this tract to 'Falk. Chily^{w:} Digges & ye rest of ye University'.
[43] [Spelman] 1643, sig. D, 2r.   [44] Sommerville 2007, p. 216.

filtered through the common law from at least the middle of the thirteenth century. But it seems unhelpfully contrarian to ignore the extent to which the distinctively Roman contrast between freedom and dependence underpinned discussions about individual liberty in the opening decades of the seventeenth century. As I have been labouring to illustrate, when critics of the Crown in the early 1640s stressed the need to uphold the freedom of their fellow subjects, they were not speaking merely or even mainly in common law terms about the need to prevent their rights and liberties from being oppressed and curtailed. They were speaking in neo-Roman terms about the need to rescue the free-born people of England from the loss of their standing as free men, and sometimes as free women too. They were speaking, as they liked to proclaim, about the need to free the entire nation from its unjust condition of bondage and servitude.

II

If we were to give due prominence to the theory of freedom I have been anatomising, we might I think be led to appraise at least three episodes in the revolutionary decade of the 1640s rather differently. First of all, we would be able to improve our understanding of why Crown and Parliament arrived at an unbridgeable impasse in the first half of 1642, and consequently why civil war broke out in the summer of that year. Next I want to suggest that, if we were to foreground the neo-Roman theory, we would be able to supplement existing accounts of what was at stake in the constitutional debates held at Putney in October and November 1647. Finally, I want to draw attention to the role played by the neo-Roman theory in helping to legitimise the abolition of the monarchy and the establishment of the Commonwealth in 1649.

I turn first to reconsider why the war of words between Crown and Parliament escalated into a military confrontation in the summer of 1642. The story that needs retelling – if only because recent anti-whig historians have barely mentioned it[45] – begins on 26 January 1642. This was the day when the House of Commons petitioned the king that 'the whole *Militia* of the Kingdome may be put into the hands of such persons as shall be recommended unto your Majestie' by Parliament.[46] By the middle of February the two Houses had agreed on a draft Ordinance granting them control of the militia, and this was duly presented to the king. Professing himself amazed, Charles at first sought to temporise, but on 28 February

---

[45] Scarcely mentioned in Worden 2009; not at all in Cust 2015. But see Vallance 2015, esp. pp. 436–8.
[46] Husbands (ed.) 1643, p. 59.

he eventually made it clear that he would veto any such proposal if it were put to him. His tone was adamant: 'he cannot consent', he replied; 'he can by no meanes doe it.'[47]

Confronted by this promise to impose the veto – the so-called prerogative of the Negative Voice – Parliament reacted by making a series of genuinely revolutionary moves. On 1 March the two Houses announced that, if the king continued to withhold his consent, they would pass the Militia Ordinance on their own authority. Four days later they did so, and on 15 March they went on to declare that the Ordinance 'doth oblige the people, and ought to be obeyed by the Fundamentall Laws of this Kingdome' notwithstanding its failure to secure the royal assent.[48]

This declaration changed the entire terms of the debate. Parliament was no longer merely demanding control of the militia; it was claiming the right to bypass the king's prerogative of the Negative Voice. It is hardly surprising, therefore, that Charles I should have taken this moment to be a sticking-point, as he was to recall in his speech on the scaffold seven years later.[49] He immediately countered that the Negative Voice is a fundamental and unquestionable feature of the constitution. No subject can be 'Obliged to Obey any Act, Order, or Injunction to which His Majesty hath not given His consent.'[50] Two months later, in his reply to Parliament's *Remonstrance* of 19 May, he prophetically added that he was prepared to uphold this doctrine 'with the sacrifice of Our life.'[51]

It is easy to understand why the king reacted so vehemently. As he was to explain in his *Answer to the XIX Propositions* in June 1642, to refuse him 'the freedom of Our Answer' was to deny him any distinctive part in the legislative process and was consequently 'destructive to all Our Rights.'[52] What proved fatal, however, was that Charles's insistence on his prerogative turned out to be no less a sticking-point for Parliament. They responded that, in matters of national importance, the king does not possess a Negative Voice. Sometimes they concede that the royal assent needs to be solicited, although they frequently add that the king has no right to withhold it.[53] But at other times they urge the stronger claim that, once the two Houses have promulgated a law, it becomes 'a high breach of the privilege of Parliament' for such a proposal to be 'controverted' or 'contradicted'. The royal assent, in other words, does not even have to be sought, and no attempt to impose a veto can have any binding force.[54]

During the spring of 1642, the argument over the Negative Voice began to put the Crown and Parliament on a collision course. But what made

[47] Husbands (ed.) 1643, pp. 90–1.   [48] Husbands (ed.) 1643, p. 112.
[49] [Charles I] 1649, p. 4.   [50] Husbands (ed.) 1643, pp. 113–14.
[51] Husbands (ed.) 1643, p. 254.   [52] [Charles I] 1642, pp. 3, 13.
[53] Husbands (ed.) 1643, p. 268.   [54] Husbands (ed.) 1643, p. 114.

Parliament dig in its heels at this particular point? Charles I had never threatened to use his veto at any previous stage in his negotiations with Parliament, and until this moment it had barely seemed a matter for concern even to his leading adversaries. As recently as December 1641, even John Pym had spoken of the king's undoubted prerogative 'in making and enacting laws by parliament', and had acknowledged that it rests 'only in his power, to pass or refuse the votes of Parliament.'[55]

The answer depends on recognising the importance of the neo-Roman theory of liberty in the minds of Charles's opponents. As soon as Charles made it clear that he would impose his veto, they became fully alerted to the hitherto latent fact that every decision of the two Houses of Parliament was subject to the mere will of the king. But to live in subjection to the mere will of someone else, they had laid down, is to live in slavery. The inference they drew was that, since Parliament turns out to be wholly dependent on the will of the king, and since it is at the same time the representative assembly of the nation, the whole of the English people must be living in a condition of national servitude.

The first leading publicist to deploy this argument was Henry Parker in his *Observations* of July 1642. If we allow the king to act in the last resort as 'the sole, supream competent Judge', then 'we resign all into his hands, we give lifes, liberties, Laws, Parliaments, all to be held at meer discretion.'[56] But this will open up 'a gap to as vast and arbitrary a prerogative as the Grand Seignior has' in Constantinople.[57] Charles I had already complained in his *Answer to the XIX Propositions* that without his Negative Voice he would be reduced from the status of a king of England to a duke of Venice.[58] Parker daringly picks up the objection as a way of clinching his argument about national servitude. 'Let us look upon the Venetians, and such other free Nations' and ask ourselves why they are 'so extreamly jealous over their Princes.' They fear 'that their Princes will dote upon their owne wills' and thereby reduce their subjects to slavery. It is 'meerely for fear of this bondage' that they prefer to avoid the rule of hereditary kings.[59]

These claims were quickly taken up by other writers on behalf of Parliament.[60] The author of *Reasons Why this Kingdome ought to adhere to the Parliament* blamed the king for arrogating 'an unlimited declarative power of Law', so that 'the last Appeale must be to his discretion and understanding, and consequently, the Legislative power His alone.' He warned that, if this is allowed, 'this whole Kingdome shall consist only of a

---

[55] Cobbett and Hansard (eds.) 1807a, col. 1003.   [56] [Parker] 1642, pp. 43–4.
[57] [Parker] 1642, p. 17.   [58] [Charles I] 1642, p. 17.   [59] [Parker] 1642, p. 26.
[60] For a fuller survey see Skinner 2002a, pp. 338–42.

King, a Parliament, and Slaves.'[61] A *Remonstrance* published a few days later reiterated that, if the kingdom is to be governed merely 'by the will of the Prince and his Favourites', they will soon be able to 'become masters of our Religion and liberties to make us slaves.'[62] Soon afterwards, the writer of *Considerations for the Commons* appealed to the nation to recognise that, if the king 'may at pleasure take away the very essence of Parliaments meerely by his owne dissent', there can be no doubt that the people of England are living 'like slaves.'[63]

Against these contentions the Crown's supporters reacted with high indignation. They treat the claim that England is an enslaved nation as an absurd hyperbole, and allow themselves to wonder if the parliamentarians can possibly believe their own rhetoric. They insist that 'his Majestie abhorres the thought of chaining us to such a slavery', and that Parker 'doth plainly abuse his Majestie in this Argument, & doth desperately corrupt his present cause.'[64] Dudley Digges in his *Answer to a Printed Book* treats it as the merest 'impudence of malice' on Parker's part to suggest that the king and his councillors would ever attempt to 'pull upon their posterity and Countrey perpetuall slavery'. It should be obvious to everyone that the king would 'hazard His Crown in defence of the subjects Liberty, and desires nothing more, than the utter abolition of all Arbitrary rule'. Digges darkly hints at parliamentarian hypocrisy, concluding that some of the king's opponents 'may ayme at getting greater fortunes, by pretending they are in danger to loose what they have' when in fact they are in no danger at all.[65]

It is true that the parliamentarians' claims about national servitude often sound hyperbolical, and it is possible that some of them may have been rationalising a political campaign they were pursuing for reasons of a different and less avowable kind. However, the question of whether they believed their own rhetoric is historically of less significance than the fact that their emphasis on national servitude proved a successful means of legitimising their attacks on the Crown. The king's policies undoubtedly lent some plausibility to their claims about the undermining of liberty, and these claims were soon echoed by Parliament itself. The *Declaration* issued by the two Houses on 14 July described 'the free-born English Nation' as facing a stark choice between Parliament and 'the King seduced by Jesuiticall Counsell and Cavaliers, who have designed all to slavery and confusion.'[66] The *Declaration* of 4 August, in which Parliament finally announced its decision to take up defensive arms, reiterated that the

---

[61] *Reasons* 1642, pp. 11, 14. Date (1 August 1642) from BL (Thomason) copy.
[62] *A Remonstrance* 1642, p. 5.   [63] *Considerations* 1642, sig. A, 3v.
[64] *Animadversions* 1642, p. 7. Date (9 July 1642) from BL (Thomason) copy.
[65] [Digges] 1642, p. 54.   [66] Husbands (ed.) 1643, p. 464.

king's intentions have always been the same. Not only is he aiming to keep control of the militia, but to govern 'by the will of the Prince', and in this way 'to destroy the Parliament, and be masters of our religion and liberties, to make us slaves.'[67]

The question raised by this final *Declaration* is what the free-born people of England should do to save themselves, confronted as they are by a misled king and a Malignant Party whose ambition is 'to cut up the freedom of Parliament by the root' and 'make them the instruments of slavery.'[68] The resounding answer is that they must be prepared to fight. The members of the two Houses state that they themselves are now resolved 'to expose our lives and fortunes' to uphold 'the power and priviledge of Parliament.' Together with the securing of 'true Religion', this is 'the true cause for which we raise an Army' and for which 'we will live and dye.'[69]

III

The next juncture at which the neo-Roman theory of liberty came to the fore was when the spokesmen for the new model army, including a number of Leveller leaders, met to debate with the military grandees, Henry Ireton and Oliver Cromwell.[70] These discussions took place at the army's encampment in Putney between 28 October and 11 November 1647, and one of the topics extensively considered was the franchise.[71] The question of how best to explain the attitudes of the two sides towards the right to vote was extensively canvassed in the heyday of Marxist interpretations of the English revolution, but as Philip Baker has recently observed 'the issue has been discussed rarely, if at all, in recent decades'.[72] My reason for returning to the question is to suggest that, if we bring to bear the distinction I have been highlighting between freedom and slavery, we may be able to explain this aspect of the Putney debates in a new and more satisfying way.[73]

The Marxist assessment of the debates, as classically outlined by C. B. Macpherson, was that the Leveller spokesmen were in basic agreement about the suffrage. They thought of it as a civil and not a natural right, as a result of which they 'consistently excluded from their franchise proposals two substantial categories of men, namely servants or wage-earners, and

[67] Husbands (ed.) 1643, p. 497.   [68] Husbands (ed.) 1643, p. 494.
[69] Husbands (ed.) 1643, p. 498.
[70] On relations between the army spokesmen and civilian Levellers see Foxley 2013, pp. 153–60.
[71] Foxley 2013, pp. 151–2.   [72] Baker 2013, p. 104.
[73] See also Mendle 2001, esp. pp. 139–40, and for a related discussion see Glover 1999.

those in receipt of alms.'[74] Among the Levellers who spoke at Putney, Macpherson's prize exhibits were accordingly Thomas Reade and Maximilian Petty, both of whom undoubtedly insisted that, in Petty's words, 'we would exclude apprentices, or servants, or those that take alms' from having any right to vote.[75] One irony of this commitment, as Macpherson acknowledged, was that in this part of the argument Reade and Petty had no quarrel with Oliver Cromwell and Henry Ireton, both of whom likewise assumed that, in Cromwell's words, 'servants, while servants, are not included.'[76]

No sooner, however, had Macpherson proclaimed this 'underlying consistency' to be one of the cardinal 'facts' about Leveller political theory[77] than Keith Thomas showed that it failed to represent even the majority view of those who supported the Leveller cause at Putney.[78] As Thomas rightly emphasised, most of the Levellers expressed the strongly contrasting opinion that the right to vote was a natural right of 'every man', of 'every person in England', of 'every individual person in the kingdom.'[79] The reason why this must be so, as Colonel Thomas Rainborough asserted in a celebrated intervention, is that 'every man that is to live under a government ought first by his own consent to put himself under that government.' Even 'the poorest man in England' must therefore have the right to vote, since no one is 'bound in a strict sense to that government that he hath not had a voice to put himself under.'[80] Captain Lewis Audley later reiterated the point more briskly. 'The right of every free-born man to elect' simply follows from the rule that anything 'which concerns all ought to be debated by all.'[81]

Keith Thomas was undoubtedly justified in claiming that most Levellers at Putney accepted this argument, and consequently treated the right to vote as a right of every adult male. But C. B. Macpherson was equally justified in claiming that Petty and Reade, no less than Cromwell and Ireton, always insisted that servants, apprentices and alms-takers should be excluded. The question that accordingly remains is why these spokesmen rejected the idea of universal male enfranchisement.

Here again Macpherson and Thomas answered in strongly contrasting terms. According to Macpherson, the Levellers believed that servants and

[74] Macpherson 1962, p. 107.
[75] For Petty's formula, quoted in Macpherson 1962, p. 123, see Woodhouse (ed.) 1938, p. 83. Foxley 2013, pp. 111–12 notes that John Lilburne never commented on these proposed exclusions.
[76] Woodhouse (ed.) 1938, p. 82.   [77] Macpherson 1962, pp. 110, 136.
[78] Thomas 1972, pp. 57–78. See also Hampsher-Monk 1976, esp. pp. 398–406.
[79] For these phrases see Woodhouse (ed.) 1938, pp. 53, 59, 66, 75, 80.
[80] Woodhouse (ed.) 1938, pp. 53, 61. John Wildman speaks in similar terms at p. 66.
[81] Woodhouse (ed.) 1938, p. 81.

alms-takers as well as apprentices had 'lost a crucial part of their native freedom or property, namely the property in their own capacities or labour.'[82] By accepting wages or alms, they had alienated their right in their labour, and it was this act of alienation that lost them the 'full freedom' they needed in order to qualify for the vote.[83] Thomas, by contrast, doubted whether any general theory underpinned the various exclusions demanded by Petty and Reade. He conceded that most of the Levellers seem to have treated apprenticeship as a self-evident reason for disenfranchisement, and he noted that this was likewise true in the case of criminal delinquency. But he concluded that 'there is little indication in the Leveller writings of other circumstances under which birth-right could be forfeited.'[84]

Thomas was surely right to be sceptical about Macpherson's explanation. It would be difficult to show that any of the Levellers embraced the Marxist conception of labour-power that Macpherson imputed to them. But was Thomas justified in his further claim that there is no general explanation to be given of why some Levellers wished to limit the franchise? His conclusion has certainly had a profound impact on the literature. It has never to my knowledge been challenged, and this part of the story remains where his classic study left it. It is symptomatic that, when Christopher Thompson later singled out Petty's contribution to the dispute, he went so far as to assert that Petty's exclusion of servants and alms-takers was not based on any identifiable theoretical principle, but was merely a change of position adopted 'for tactical reasons' in the course of the debate.[85]

If we revert, however, to the view of liberty I have been highlighting, we find that there was in fact a general theory underpinning Ireton and Cromwell's agreement with Petty and Reade. They all assume a distinction between being free-born and being a free man, and they all believe – by contrast with Rainborough – that the right to vote depends on being a free man, not simply on the universal condition of being free-born. Ireton explicitly calls for the franchise to be confined to 'free men', explaining that by 'free men' he means those who are 'not given up to the wills of others' and are thus 'freed from dependence.'[86] Petty repeats that 'an equal voice in elections' should be granted only to those who 'have not lost their birthright' of liberty, and endorses Ireton's account of how this birthright is lost.[87] 'The reason why we would exclude apprentices, or servants, or those that take alms, is because they depend upon the will of

[82] Macpherson 1962, p. 144.   [83] Macpherson 1962, p. 146.   [84] Thomas 1972, p. 76.
[85] Thompson 1980, p. 69.   [86] Woodhouse (ed.) 1938, pp. 78, 82.
[87] Woodhouse (ed.) 1938, p. 53.

other men.' They are not independent agents, but are 'bound to the will of other men.'[88] They are excluded because they are living, as Reade puts it, in a state of 'voluntary servitude.'[89]

We still find it assumed, even in recent studies of the Putney debates, that the issue dividing Ireton and Cromwell from the main body of Leveller opinion was whether 'the basis of political rights', including the right to vote, should be grounded on 'property ownership or birthright'.[90] It is misleading, however, to suggest that, in rejecting birthright as the criterion, Ireton and Cromwell simply plumped for property ownership as the alternative. Like Reade and Petty, Ireton maintains that what qualifies you to vote is having an independent will. The reason why he equates this condition with property ownership is that he believes that only those with sufficient property to give them independence from the will of others will be capable of casting a genuinely free vote. As he expresses the point, only someone with property may be said to have 'a permanent interest' in the kingdom, an interest 'upon which he may live, and live a freeman without dependence.' It is not the mere fact of owning property, but the distinctive ability of those with property to 'live upon it as freemen', and consequently act without servility, that gives them the entitlement to vote.[91] This was to remain the view of the leading defenders of the English 'free state' in the 1650s. As James Harrington was to express it in his *System of Politics*, 'the man that cannot live upon his own must be a servant; but he that can live upon his own may be a freeman.'[92]

The corollary of Cromwell and Ireton's view is that those without property should be excluded from the franchise on the grounds that they do not have a genuinely independent voice. Petty explicitly supports this conclusion, echoing the parliamentarian writers who had similarly rejected the right of bishops to vote in the House of Lords. He contends that, where we are dealing with servants who have masters, we know that, because 'they depend upon the will of other men', they will 'be afraid to displease them'. The right decision must therefore be to deny them any separate voice, because their voice will never be genuinely separate. We ought instead to regard them as 'included in their masters', because it will certainly be their master's will that they express.[93]

It is true that these claims gave rise to a highly restricted view of the right to vote. But it is not true, as Macpherson affirmed, that those Levellers who argued in these terms were repudiating the idea of universal manhood suffrage.[94] The idea of universal *manhood* suffrage, as opposed

---

[88] Woodhouse (ed.) 1938, p. 83.   [89] Woodhouse (ed.) 1938, p. 83.
[90] Crawford 2001, p. 200.   [91] Woodhouse (ed.) 1938, p. 62.
[92] Harrington 1992, p. 269.   [93] Woodhouse (ed.) 1938, p. 83.
[94] Macpherson 1962, pp. 107, 109.

to universal *male* suffrage, is precisely what Reade and Petty (no less than Cromwell and Ireton) appear to embrace. The reason why this commitment nevertheless gives rise to a limited franchise is that a large percentage of men, according to their view of things, lack the necessary attribute of manhood. Servants undoubtedly lack it, and so do bishops. To be 'your own man', rather than someone else's creature, and hence to be in possession of true manhood, requires you to be capable of acting *sui iuris*, of making up your mind independently of the will and desires of anyone else. This is the test failed by servants, alms-takers, bishops and many other seemingly elevated persons, and this is why they all deserve to be excluded.

It is not clear what the other Leveller spokesmen felt about this line of argument. One might have expected them to respond that we cannot voluntarily relinquish our birthright of liberty, and thus that any social arrangements under which liberty is forfeited must be illegitimate. But in fact they seem to have allowed that it is possible to enter into a state of voluntary servitude, while denying that this is enough to justify disenfranchisement. They believed that, in order to qualify for the right to vote, it is sufficient to be able to give your consent to government. But they also believed that, in order to give your consent, it is sufficient to be able to reason about your predicament. 'This gift of reason without other property', as Rainborough called it, is taken to be enough to endow all adult males with the right to vote, even if they may be living as servants or in receipt of alms.[95]

Before leaving the Levellers, it is worth adding a footnote about the underlying social ideal of 'being your own man'. One issue much discussed in recent political theory has been the concept of self-ownership.[96] What does it mean, as John Locke is famous for having argued, to say that everyone has an entitlement to the proprietership of their own person? One way of improving our understanding of this peculiar and elusive concept might be to reflect on parliamentarian and Leveller discussions about what it means 'to be your own man' and thus 'to live like a man' instead of living in servitude.

Consider, for example, the intensely rhetorical opening of Richard Overton's Leveller tract, *An Arrow Against All Tyrants*, first published in October 1646.[97] The natural condition of mankind, Overton begins, is a condition of liberty enjoyed 'equally and alike' by everyone. This liberty consists in part of a right to act freely, a right to enjoy your natural rights without being 'invaded or usurped' by anyone else. But this pristine

[95] Woodhouse (ed.) 1938, pp. 55–6.   [96] See for example Cohen 1995.
[97] For Overton on manhood and self-propriety see McDowell 2003, pp. 66–70.

liberty also consists in a right of self-ownership, 'for every one, as he is himselfe, so he hath a selfe-propriety, else could he not be himselfe.' I may therefore be said to have a natural right to 'enjoy *my selfe* and my selfe propriety.'[98]

One of the questions Overton asks is how this natural right of self-ownership can be lost or taken away. We are said to forfeit it when anyone else acquires 'power over us' to do 'as they list', without there being any means of controlling their arbitrary will and its potential exorbitancies. It makes no difference if those who 'have power over us, to save us or destroy us' prefer to save us, so that they act 'for our weale' rather than 'for our woe'. Although they may leave us with the enjoyment of our freedom and rights, we remain at their mercy and in consequence lose the essence of our liberty. If we depend upon their mere goodwill for the maintenance of our rights, we shall be living not as 'free people' but in a state of bondage, thraldom and servitude.[99]

The loss of liberty we suffer when we acquire a master is thus equated with a loss of self-ownership, a loss of our 'naturall propriety, right and freedome' to 'live like men' as opposed to living like slaves.[100] By contrast, the condition of self-ownership is equated with the ability to act according to our own will, and hence with the ability to 'own' (that is, take responsibility for) the consequences of our actions. So long as we are not beholden to anyone else, our actions – just like our goods – may be said to be fully our own. We may be said, in other words, to be our own person, not a mere creature of anyone else.[101] This appears to have been the universal understanding of the phrase. Even Hobbes, who did so much to undermine the idea of freedom as a matter of being *sui iuris*, feels obliged to admit that, when we describe someone as being 'his own person', what we mean is that he 'acteth by his own authority' as opposed to acting 'by the authority of another.'[102] Given that there has been so much discussion of late about the meaning of self-ownership, it is striking to find that those who first introduced the concept into Anglophone political discourse meant something so precise and straightforward by it. To have full property in yourself, they are telling us, is simply to be able to act independently of the arbitrary will of anyone else.

---

[98] Overton 1646, p. 3.   [99] Overton 1646, pp. 4, 5, 6.   [100] Overton 1646, pp. 5, 6.

[101] Macpherson 1962, pp. 140–1 quotes the opening of Overton 1646 and recognises (pp. 148, 153) that the Levellers define unfreedom in terms of dependence. But he then insists (pp. 148, 150) that they define freedom in terms of the capacity freely to dispose of one's own labour, thereby missing the point, as I see it, about 'being your own man'.

[102] Hobbes 1840a, p. 311.

IV

I turn finally to consider the role played by the neo-Roman theory of liberty in helping to legitimise the English Commonwealth.[103] On 17 March 1649 the House of Commons passed an Act announcing 'the abolition of the kingly office'.[104] The nation was said to be reaffirming 'its just and ancient right, of being governed by its own representatives or national meetings in council, from time to time chosen and entrusted for that purpose by the people'.[105] Five days later the Commons printed a *Declaration* explaining that they were now in the process 'of Setling the present Government in the way of A Free State'.[106] By a 'free state', they explained, they meant a republican form of rule. 'The *Representatives* of the *People* now Assembled in *Parliament*, have judged it *necessary* to change the *Government* of this *Nation* from the former *Monarchy*, (unto which by many injurious incroachments it had arrived) into a *Republique*'.[107] As the Act of 17 March had already explained, in resoundingly neo-Roman terms, the reason for this decision was that 'the office of a king' had been found to be 'dangerous to the liberty, safety, and public interest of the people', and the royal prerogative had been used 'to oppress and impoverish and enslave the subject'.[108]

This version of events was instantly challenged by most of the political nation, including many spokesmen who had hitherto been enemies of the royalist cause. The most vociferous of these critics deployed the same neo-Roman vocabulary to argue that the only change currently taking place was the replacement of one form of enslaving tyranny by another. This was the reaction of the Presbyterians who had been excluded from the House of Commons by the army in December 1648 in order to secure a majority for putting the king on trial. Among their spokesmen was the indefatigable William Prynne, whose *Arraignment* of February 1649 charged the army and Parliament with an attempt to bring the people 'into perpetuall slavery and bondage to their Vast, Unlimited, Lawlesse, Arbitrary' form of rule. According to Prynne, these acts of treason and tyranny had not only been facilitated by the army, but 'their Armies were raised purposely to effect all these Designes', which 'wee now finde effected, and fully accomplished'.[109]

---

[103] For the debate about the legitimacy of the new regime, and Hobbes's place in that debate, see Wallace 1964; Burgess 1986 and 1990; Barber 1998, pp. 174–201; Skinner 2002b, pp. 264–307; Hoekstra 2003. For 'republican' liberty in the 1650s see Scott 2004, pp. 151–69.
[104] Gardiner (ed.) 1906, p. 386.   [105] Gardiner (ed.) 1906, p. 386.
[106] *A Declaration* 1649, title-page. Date (22 March 1649) from BL (Thomason) copy.
[107] *A Declaration* 1649, p. 20.   [108] Gardiner (ed.) 1906, p. 385.
[109] Prynne 1649, p. 6.

Still more vociferous were the Levellers, and none more so than John Lilburne, who published *Englands New Chains Discovered* in March 1649, directing his fire against the Council of State established in the previous month.[110] Lilburne protests that, in spite of 'all those specious pretenses, and high Notions of Liberty, with those extraordinary courses that have of late bin taken', we can now see that the underlying aim was 'the more securely and unsuspectedly to attain to an absolute domination over the Common-wealth'.[111] The council of state is usurping the power of Parliament, so that 'after these fair blossoms of hopefull liberty, breaks forth this bitter fruit, of the vilest and basest bondage that ever English men groan'd under'. The aim of the military junto is to make themselves 'Lords and Masters, both of Parliament and People'.[112]

It is true that a far larger number of commentators immediately professed themselves willing to accept the new regime. But it cannot be said that their reasons for doing so generally echoed with much enthusiasm the claims of Parliament about the ending of enslavement and the inauguration of a new era of liberty. Many preferred to argue in pragmatic terms that, if the new regime brings protection and peace, this may be said to grant it a sufficient title to be obeyed.[113] A still larger number insisted that the new government is undoubtedly a usurping one, and should only be accepted on the grounds that, like all established powers, it must be recognised as an ordinance of God.[114]

This is not to say that the Rump and Council of State wholly lacked for supporters willing to vindicate their cause. During the months after the execution of Charles I, two celebratory lines of argument emerged. One took the form of reverting to the 'monarchomach' theory of popular sovereignty I discussed in chapter 2. It is symptomatic that the most influential of the monarchomach texts, the *Vindiciae, contra tyrannos*, was published for the first time in an English translation in 1648. By far the most eloquent work to argue in these terms was John Milton's *Tenure of Kings and Magistrates*, largely written at the time of Charles I's trial and first published on 13 February 1649.[115] Milton begins by acknowledging that, although all men are naturally born free, they usually submit to forms of government capable of restraining violations of 'peace and common right.'[116] When they do so, however, they merely entrust their

---

[110] Lilburne 1649a. Date (1 March 1649) from BL (Thomason) copy.
[111] Lilburne 1649a, sig. A, 3v.   [112] Lilburne 1649a, sig. B, 1r–v.
[113] For these pamphleteers see Skinner 2002b, pp. 296–302.
[114] The most prolific of these writers was John Dury, who published at least nine pamphlets arguing this case between 1649 and 1651. On Dury see Wallace 1964, pp. 393–403 and Mandelbrote 2007.
[115] Date from BL (Thomason) copy.   [116] Milton 1991, pp. 8–9.

powers to their rulers 'to doe impartial justice by Law', with the result that 'the power of Kings and Magistrates is nothing else, but what is only derivative, transferr'd and committed them in trust from the People, to the Common good of them all'.[117] The power itself always 'remaines fundamentally' with the people, who retain the right, when instituting a king or chief magistrate, to 'choose him or reject him, retaine him or despose him though no Tyrant, meerly by the liberty and right of free born Men, to be govern'd as seems to them best.'[118]

Milton regards it as unquestionable that Charles I (whom he never deigns to mention by name) ruled as a tyrant. He acted with 'contempt of all Laws' and spent seven years 'warring and destroying of his best Subjects' while his people suffered enslavement from his 'boasted prerogative unaccountable'.[119] Milton accordingly defends in emphatic terms the right of the English people to remove him from office and look forward instead to 'the flourishing deeds of a reformed Commonwealth'.[120] Without this right, the people 'may please thir fancy with a ridiculous and painted freedom, fit to coz'n babies; but are indeed under tyranny and servitude', since they will be living 'in the tenure and occupation of another inheriting Lord' whose government 'hangs over them as a Lordly scourge'.[121] But in spite of this revolutionary commitment, Milton continues to structure his argument around the monarchomach contrast between monarchy and tyranny. He never denies that monarchy suitably constrained by law is a legitimate form of government, and he repeatedly contrasts the rule of tyrants with good and just kings.[122] History teaches us 'how great a good and happiness a just King is', just as it teaches that 'so great a mischeife is a Tyrant'.[123]

By contrast with this line of thought, a fully fledged neo-Roman defence of the English Commonwealth began to emerge in which no distinction was drawn between lawful monarchies and illegal tyrannies. This was the principal argument mounted by the Rump Parliament itself. The Act of 17 March 1649 abolishing the office of king not only condemned the enslaving rule of Charles I; it also argued in broader terms that, 'usually and naturally any one person in such power' can be expected to reduce his people to servitude. This is because any king 'makes it his interest to incroach upon the just freedom and liberty of the people, and to promote the setting up of their own will and power above the laws, so that they might enslave these kingdoms to their own lust'.[124]

---

[117] Milton 1991, pp. 9–10.   [118] Milton 1991, pp. 10, 13.   [119] Milton 1991, pp. 4, 18.
[120] Milton 1991, p. 32.   [121] Milton 1991, p. 32.   [122] Milton 1991, pp. 14, 16.
[123] Milton 1991, pp. 16–17.   [124] Gardiner (ed.) 1906, p. 385.

The same equation between monarchy and tyranny was proclaimed by a number of the Rump's supporters over the next two years. We already find the author of *The Armies Vindication* arguing in these terms as early as January 1649. If we ask 'what form of Government is best', we cannot fail to answer that 'Monarchie is worst'. The truth is that 'Monarchy is Tyranny' and reduces its subjects to 'meer slavery'.[125] Later in the year, Henry Robinson in his *Short Discourse* similarly claimed that 'Monarchy and Tyranny' are 'very neer of kin', so that 'Royalty and Liberty have never heartily embraced each other'.[126] Marchamont Nedham went on to develop the argument in his *Case of the Commonwealth* in May 1650, declaring that 'there is no difference between king and tyrant', and calling on the people of England to 'become as zealous as the ancient Romans were in defense of their freedom'.[127] Writing nearly two years later, with the Commonwealth well-established, Francis Osborne felt able to dismiss all princes as 'Monsters in power'.[128] He praises the English Parliament for granting the people 'redemption out of Monarchical thraldom' after a long period in which they had been 'willing to sell themselves for Slaves',[129] and he maintains that those nations which have 'never at all admitted any Kings' are the ones 'celebrated for most wisdome, felicity, and continuance'.[130]

The reason why these writers refuse to see any difference between monarchy and tyranny is a wholly neo-Roman one. Kings invariably possess discretionary and prerogative powers, leaving the rights and liberties of their subjects dependent on their arbitrary will. But to live in dependence on the will of others, they all agree, is what it means to live in servitude. This is the argument already put forward in *The Armies Vindication* of January 1649. As soon as we reflect on the 'marks of Sovereignty' that are taken to be 'the Rights and prerogatives proper to Monarchs', we cannot fail to see that 'there is nothing left the people but meer slavery'.[131] Henry Robinson in his *Short Discourse* similarly speaks of 'Prerogative Tyranny'. He argues that prerogative powers 'have little cognisance of justice, or reason' with the result that their exercise leads to 'bondage and misery' among the people.[132] Francis Osborne concludes that kings intend 'nothing more than the augmentation of their

---

[125] Philodemius 1649, pp. 6, 63–4. Date (11 January 1649) from BL (Thomason) copy.
[126] [Robinson] 1649, p. 11. Date (24 October 1649) from BL (Thomason) copy; attribution from Wallace 1964, p. 392.
[127] Nedham 1969, pp. 127–8. Date (8 May 1650) from BL (Thomason) copy.
[128] [Osborne] 1652, p. 12. Date (18 February 1652) from BL (Thomason) copy; attribution from Wallace 1964, p. 405.
[129] [Osborne] 1652, pp. 34–5.   [130] [Osborne] 1652, p. 23.
[131] Philodemius 1649, pp. 63–4.   [132] [Robinson] 1649, pp. 14, 16.

owne Arbitrary power', and that their prerogatives are 'destructive to the very essence of Liberty'.[133]

Perhaps the most striking of these tracts, composed in rhymed penta-meter verse, appeared early in 1651 under the title *Radius Heliconicus: Or, The Resolution of a Free State*. We are warned that, although kingly powers are habitually described in 'a mild construction' as prerogatives, they cannot fail to bring 'the cruelty of Domination' and vassalage. If we wish to live as free men, we must rescue our 'free born Common-weale' from 'the base yoke of bondage' and 'all the dependencies of tyranny'. This was the act of rescue performed when the Roman republic was founded, and the poem ends with a call to the people of England to emulate Rome's resulting greatness:

> Why should we
> Be lesse couragious? Though not Roman bands,
> Yet we have Roman hearts, and Roman hands.[134]

To have a Roman heart is to recognise that man has 'a free / tenure and birthright of his libertie', and consequently ought never 'to stoop / To that thing Monarchy'.[135]

Except for Marchamont Nedham, who became editor of the government newspaper *Mercurius Politicus*,[136] it cannot be said that any of these writers were prominent spokesmen for the commonwealth cause. Nevertheless, these were the propagandists who put the neo-Roman theory of liberty to the most radical use in the constitutional debates of the English revolution, deploying it not merely to condemn the government of Charles I but to equate monarchy with tyranny. With this intervention, the political outlook that has come to be known as 'republican exclusivism' entered the main-stream of English political thought.[137]

---

[133] [Osborne] 1652, p. 17.

[134] Fletcher 1651, single-sheet pamphlet. Date (28 February 1651) from BL (Thomason) copy.

[135] Fletcher 1651.

[136] On Nedham as editor of *Mercurius Politicus* see Norbrook 1999, pp. 221–5; Worden 2007, pp. 19–25, 252–4.

[137] On republican exclusivism see Nelson 2007, Hankins 2010.

8   Hobbes on Civil Conversation

I

Hobbes warns us in chapter 13 of *Leviathan* about three elements in our nature that cannot fail to engender quarrels and war. The first is our competitiveness, which makes us try to master the persons and property of others. The next is our associated lack of trust, which prompts us to anticipate and react to any threatened assaults. The third is our thirst for glory, which leads us to regard with hostility any apparent signs of being undervalued. These propensities render us 'dissociate' from one another, as a result of which 'men have no pleasure, (but on the contrary a great deale of griefe) in keeping company'.[1] Still worse, we are 'apt to invade, and destroy one another', whether in the name of making gains or protecting ourselves or upholding our elevated sense of our worth.[2] Cumulatively these invasions give rise to a war 'of every man, against every man' in which everyone is equally condemned to live 'without other security, than what their own strength, and their own invention shall furnish them withall'.[3]

If any form of social life is to be possible, these destructive tendencies will need to be curbed and controlled. Hobbes concludes that the only means of winning security will be for everyone to agree on a 'visible Power to keep them in awe, and tye them by feare of punishment' from engaging in acts of violence.[4] More specifically, the one and only route to security is said to lie in covenanting, every man with every man, to 'conferre all their power and strength upon one Man, or upon one Assembly of men',

This chapter is a revised and much extended version of Skinner 2016. For permission to draw on this earlier work I am indebted to the Oxford University Press. For commenting on drafts I am deeply grateful to Laurens van Apeldoorn, Robin Celikates, Kinch Hoekstra, Susan James, Noel Malcolm, A. L. Martinich, Nicola Panichi, Tim Raylor, Richard Strier, Keith Thomas and Phil Withington. To Raffaella Santi I owe particular thanks for extensive correspondence and help.

[1] Hobbes 2012, vol. 2, ch. 13, p. 190.   [2] Hobbes 2012, vol. 2, ch. 13, pp. 190, 194.
[3] Hobbes 2012, vol. 2, ch. 13, p. 192.   [4] Hobbes 2012, vol. 2, ch. 17, p. 254.

thereby agreeing to 'submit their Wills, every one to his Will, and their Judgements, to his Judgment'.[5] By this means the sovereign will have 'the use of so much Power and Strength conferred on him, that by terror thereof, he is inabled to conforme the wills of them all, to Peace at home, and mutuall ayd against their enemies abroad.'[6]

Hobbes's analysis in chapter 13 of the unsociable qualities that dictate this drastic solution appears at first sight to be complete. If we turn to chapter 15, however, we find that he has more to say. While competitiveness, lack of trust and the desire for glory are said to be 'in the nature of man', and consequently attributes of all mankind,[7] he now adds that some people suffer in addition from a range of more specific social vices that are scarcely less liable to produce conflict and war. One is vaingloriousness, which he had already contrasted with the pursuit of glory in analysing the passions in chapter 6. He takes 'that exultation of the mind which is called GLORYING' to consist in the joy arising from the recognition of one's power and ability, so that glorying is 'the same with Confidence'.[8] By contrast, vainglory 'consisteth in the feigning or supposing of abilities in our selves, which we know are not', and takes the form of 'a foolish over-rating' of our worth.[9] This lack of confidence leads vainglorious people to be vengeful, reluctant to offer pardon and prone to 'glorying in the hurt of another'. But this 'glorying to no end' is not only 'contrary to reason' but 'tendeth to the introduction of Warre'.[10]

Four additional vices are said to be equally inimical to what Hobbes calls 'peaceable, sociable, and comfortable living', and these are anatomised in the latter part of chapter 15.[11] Some people are deficient in gratitude; they are reluctant to act trustfully or benevolently, and consequently 'remain still in the condition of *War*'.[12] Others are incapable of sociability; they are '*Stubborn, Insociable, Froward, Intractable*', and prone to act 'contrary to the fundamentall Law of Nature, which commandeth *to seek Peace*'.[13] Still others lack a sense of equality; they are prideful, consider themselves better than other people and refuse to 'enter into conditions of Peace'.[14] Finally, some are wholly lacking in modesty; they suffer from arrogance, and 'require for themselves, that which they would

---

[5] Hobbes 2012, vol. 2, ch. 17, p. 260.   [6] Hobbes 2012, vol. 2, ch. 17, p. 260.
[7] Hobbes 2012, vol. 2, ch. 13, p. 192. Here I differ from Slomp 2007, pp. 184–5, who argues that, while glory is treated in *The Elements of Law* and *De cive* as 'the ultimate mover of mankind', in *Leviathan* Hobbes 'conveys the impression that only some people are glory-seekers.'
[8] Hobbes 2012, vol. 2, ch. 6, p. 88.
[9] Hobbes 2012, vol. 2, ch. 6, p. 88 and ch. 27, p. 460.
[10] Hobbes 2012, vol. 2, ch. 15, p. 232.   [11] Hobbes 2012, vol. 2, ch. 15, p. 242.
[12] Hobbes 2012, vol. 2, ch. 15, p. 230.   [13] Hobbes 2012, vol. 2, ch. 15, p. 232.
[14] Hobbes 2012, vol. 2, ch. 15, p. 234.

not have to be granted to others', once again undermining the possibility of a peaceable life.[15]

At the beginning of chapter 17 Hobbes argues that these additional threats to human security will similarly have to be controlled by coercive force. He even suggests, rather strangely, that the requirement of modesty will have to be enforced by 'the terrour of some Power'.[16] But he never enlarges on this suggestion, nor does he ever explain how the use of legal means to compel men to follow the social virtues would be practicable. Perhaps this is not surprising, for it obviously makes little sense to suppose that such traits of character as sociability, forbearance and modesty are susceptible of being created and enforced by law. Even if we cannot hope, however, to use terror to impose sociability on the froward, or forbearance on the vainglorious, or modesty on the arrogant, it remains obvious that these contentious forms of behaviour will somehow have to be resisted and controlled – or at least managed and coped with – if any tolerable social life is to be sustained. How, then, can this be done?

II

The question of how to cope with those who lack civility had been widely canvassed in Renaissance moral theory, and especially in the genre of Italian writings on *la civil conversazione*.[17] Among numerous treatises on the subject, those which enjoyed the widest circulation in England were Baldessare Castiglione's *Libro del cortegiano* of 1528, Giovanni della Casa's *Galateo* of 1558 and Stefano Guazzo's *Civil conversazione* of 1574.[18] All these texts were soon translated into English,[19] and Castiglione's *Courtier* was reprinted at least six times in London before the end of the sixteenth century.[20] A number of imitations soon appeared, including Simon Robson's *Courte of civill courtesie* of 1577, which purported to be a translation of an Italian text,[21] and Lodowick Bryskett's dialogue of 1606 entitled *A discourse of civill life*, the avowed aim of which

---

[15] Hobbes 2012, vol. 2, ch. 15, p. 234. For Hobbes on modesty see Cooper 2010. But for Hobbes the antonym of modesty is not vainglory (as argued in Cooper 2010, p. 242) but arrogance.

[16] Hobbes 2012, vol. 2, ch. 17, p. 254.

[17] On the shift from Medieval *courtoisie* to Renaissance *civilité* see Elias 1994, pp. 56–65.

[18] These writers are considered together in Whigham 1984, Panichi 1994 and Borrelli 2000, pp. 67–92. See also Burke 1993, pp. 98–102; Ménager 1995, pp. 149–85. On Guazzo see Santi 2013; on della Casa see Farneti 2000. For the reception of the genre in Tudor England see Peltonen 2003, pp. 17–35; Richards 2003, pp. 29–33, 44–7, 63–4.

[19] See Castiglione 1561; Casa 1576; Guazzo 1581.

[20] The BL catalogue records two printings in English (1561, 1588) and four in Latin (1571, 1577, 1585, 1593).

[21] Richards 2003, p. 13.

was 'to frame a gentleman fit for civill conversation'.[22] The final section of James Cleland's *Institution of a young noble man* of 1607 likewise considers 'young Noble mens Dutie in their Civil conversation',[23] while Henry Peacham's *Compleat Gentleman* of 1622 includes an outline of the education suited to the gentry and nobility 'to bring them up in science and civilitie'.[24]

When these writers discuss what Castiglione (in Thomas Hoby's translation of 1561) describes as 'manerlye conversation',[25] they are not referring merely or even principally to the conventions of civilised speech. As Guazzo makes clear when criticising those who refuse to take part in conversation, he does not mean that they are unwilling to talk; he means that they are unwilling to consort with others or come together in social life. The contrast he draws throughout *The Civile Conversation*, as George Pettie expresses it in his translation of 1581, is always between 'solitarinesse and Conversation'.[26] Guazzo's aspiration is to show that 'solitarinesse ought to be taken altogether out of the world, & company & conversation to be chosen.'[27] 'Too be shorte', he concludes, 'my meaning is, that civile conversation is an honest commendable and vertuous kinde of living in the world.'[28]

Castiglione similarly speaks in *The Courtier* about how a man should conduct himself 'in hys lyving and conversation.'[29] When the respected figure of Federico Fregoso raises the question in Book II, he expresses himself largely in negative terms. A courtier must never be 'stubborne and full of contencion', thereby stirring men to argument, and he must be 'no lyer, no boaster, nor fonde flatterer'.[30] Later Federico adds that, besides taking care never to show 'a proude and haughtye stomake',[31] courtiers must never 'bragg and boast of them selves', nor imitate the kind of vainglorious braggart who leads a life of ignoble violence while supposing 'that he hath wonne great glorye'.[32] A good courtier will always behave with reverence and respect, and will never stray beyond the recognised boundaries of social life.[33]

The underlying suggestion that the ideal of civil conversation can best be grasped by reflecting on what it means to fail in civility was taken up at greater length by Guazzo in the opening book of *The Civile Conversation*.

---

[22] Bryskett 1606, p. 5.   [23] Cleland 1607, p. 163.   [24] Peacham 1622, p. 27.
[25] Castiglione 1994, p. 102.   [26] Guazzo 1581, Bk 1, fo. 18r.
[27] Guazzo 1581, Bk 1, fo. 17v.
[28] Guazzo 1581, Bk 1, fos. 22r–v. For a similar understanding of conversation see Peacham 1622, pp. 7–8. On the modern understanding of conversation in this period see Thomas 2009, pp. 222–3.
[29] Castiglione 1994, p. 149.   [30] Castiglione 1994, p. 121.
[31] Castiglione 1994, p. 155.   [32] Castiglione 1994, pp. 143–4, 155.
[33] Castiglione 1994, p. 121.

The figure of Annibale in the dialogue begins by distinguishing between those whose lack of sociability debars them from civil conversation and those who cannot easily be excluded even when their conduct leaves much to be desired.[34] Focusing on the latter group, Annibale proceeds to enumerate the vices that undermine the conditions of civilised life. First he speaks of the slanderous, who 'with the falsenesse of their tongues, seeke to blemishe the brightnesse of others names.'[35] Then he turns to the contentious and the obstinate,[36] who are ready 'even for very trifles' to engage in 'dyre debate and strife'.[37] These are the people whom della Casa had already described (in Robert Peterson's translation of 1576) as the 'froward', whose conversation 'consisteth in overtwharting other mens desiers', and whose testiness converts friends into foes.[38] Annibale agrees that we are speaking of 'cavillers and Sophists, who at every woorde wil overthwart us, and as they say, seeke knottes in Bulrushes'.[39] Next Annibale criticises the 'boasters, & vaine glorious',[40] the sort of people whom Guazzo had condemned at the outset of the dialogue when assuring Annibale that he is not 'any of those vainglorious persons, which contende earnestly to the intent to be counted more brave fellowes then other'.[41] Here too Guazzo echoes della Casa, who had spoken with similar distaste of those who 'make a vaine glorious boasting of them selves: vaunting and telling in a bravery, what wonderfull exploits they have doone'.[42] Finally Annibale rounds on those who suffer from 'arrogancie', and are consequently so 'full of presumption, and blinded with the love of themselves', that they 'see not their owne imperfections, and never care to knowe what opinion the worlde hath of them'.[43]

Given that all these vices are inimical to social life, they will somehow have to be managed and controlled. But this brings us back to our original question: how can this be done? Here the writers on civil conversation may be said to draw an implicit distinction between those forms of behaviour which are likely to strike us as merely embarrassing or irritating, and those which are seriously insulting or offensive. They agree that, in the latter case, where a gentleman's standing or reputation may be in question, there is only one proper response, which is to issue a challenge to a duel.[44] When the count in Book I of Castiglione's *Courtier* lists the attributes of the ideal courtier, he simply assumes that one reason why

---

[34] For this distinction see Guazzo 1581, Bk 1, fo. 27r.   [35] Guazzo 1581, Bk 1, fo. 27r.
[36] Guazzo 1581, Bk 1, fo. 39v.   [37] Guazzo 1581, Bk 1, fo. 40v.   [38] Casa 1576, p. 25.
[39] Guazzo 1581, Bk 1, fo. 34r.   [40] Guazzo 1581, Bk 1, fo. 41v.
[41] Guazzo 1581, Bk 1, fo. 6r.   [42] Casa 1576, p. 36.   [43] Guazzo 1581, Bk 2, fo 2v.
[44] The attempt in Elias 1994, pp. 443–56 to chart a movement from a medieval 'warrior society' to 'the pacified social space' of the Renaissance underestimates the significance of the duel. On the duel and civil conversation see Peltonen 2003, pp. 44–58; on the code of honour see Thomas 2009, pp. 156–9.

courtiers need 'to be skilfull on those weapons that are used ordinarily emong gentlemen' is that 'there happen often times variaunces betwene one gentleman and an other, wherepon ensueth a combat.'[45] He counsels us to 'have a foresight in the quarelles and controversies that may happen', and never to 'runne rashely to these combattes'.[46] But he insists that a courtier must stand ready to fight whenever 'he muste needs to save his estimation withall', and that 'whan a man perceiveth that he is entred so farre that hee can not drawe backe', he must 'be utterly resolved with hymselfe, and always shewe a readinesse and a stomake'.[47] Guazzo like-wise observes that duelling is not merely a frequent occurrence, but that men of honour can hardly avoid such combats if they are to maintain their reputations intact. As Annibale remarks, he has known many occasions on which 'certaine Gentlemen have convayed themselves into some close place, where because the one would not live with the name of an evil speaker, & the other of a false accuser, they have made an ende of their lives and their quarrels both together.'[48]

Simon Robson in his *Courte of civill courtesie* of 1577 speaks yet more strongly about the need to stand ready to exact revenge. If someone impugns your honour with 'reprochefull names', there can be no question of allowing such an insult to pass. You must 'either offer the first blowe (if the place serve for it) or els chalenge him into the feild'.[49] Robson is even willing to provide advice on how such challenges should be phrased. You must declare that, 'if any body have any quarell to mee, I have businesse into sutche a place, sutche a day, at sutche an hower: I wil have but my selfe and my man, or but my selfe and my freinde, there hee may finde mee if hee dare'.[50] By these means the civilities will be upheld, but your lethal purpose will nevertheless be made clear.[51]

If, however, you are confronted not with insults but merely with ill-mannered and contemptuous behaviour, then the advice given by the writers on civil conversation – although not without some misgivings – is that you should be ready to repay like with like and speak contemptuously in turn. Bernardo declares in *The Courtier* that 'it is not amysse to scoff and mocke at vices',[52] while Annibale in Guazzo's *Civile Conversation* agrees that sometimes it is right 'to return one scoffe with another'.[53] More specifically, you should seek to shame uncivil persons, bringing them into line by means of satirising and ridiculing them 'in manner of mockerie, or of scorn' until

---

[45] Castiglione 1994, p. 47.   [46] Castiglione 1994, p. 47.   [47] Castiglione 1994, p. 47.
[48] Guazzo, 1581, Bk 1, fo. 29v.   [49] Robson 1577, p. 24.   [50] Robson 1577, p. 21.
[51] Robson's acceptance of duelling was not endorsed by later English writers on civil conversation. Cleland 1607, p. 236 regards it as a last extremity, while Bryskett 1606, p. 66 denounces 'this foolish custome and wicked act'.
[52] Castiglione 1994, p. 156.   [53] Guazzo 1581, Bk 1, fo. 30v.

they 'are driven to amende their manners and life.'[54] Castiglione and Guazzo are proposing, in other words, that 'laughing to scorn' may be one of the most effective means of curbing incivility. Robson in his *Courte of Civill courtesie* adds that the danger of being mocked and ridiculed is never far away. A young gentleman in particular needs to be aware that 'it is unpossible for him to bee so compleat in all perfections of beehaviour, but that some thynge remaynes in him worthy the laughyng at'.[55]

These suggestions about the disciplining power of ridicule derive from a number of more general beliefs shared by the writers on civil conversation about the nature of laughter and the range of emotions it may be said to express. The accounts they offer owe an obvious debt to Aristotle in his *Rhetoric* and the Roman rhetoricians influenced by his analysis, especially Cicero and Quintilian.[56] Hobbes is no less indebted to the same authorities, and it is important in this connection to remember that he was not only a warm admirer of Aristotle's *Rhetoric* – which he characterised to John Aubrey as 'rare'[57] – but was also the author of the earliest English translation of Aristotle's text, which he published anonymously as *A Briefe of the Art of Rhetorique* in 1637.[58]

Aristotle examines the phenomenon of laughter in the passage from Book II of the *Rhetoric* in which he reflects on the manners of youth. One characteristic of young people is said to be that (in the words of Hobbes's translation) they are 'Lovers of Mirth, and by consequence love to jest at others'.[59] Enquiring into the feelings expressed by their mirth, Aristotle argues that '*Jesting* is witty Contumely', having previously explained that contumely 'is the disgracing of another for his own pastime'.[60] Aristotle's basic idea is thus that the laughter induced by jesting is usually an expression of scorn, a suggestion already present in his earlier observation that among the sources of pleasure are 'ridiculous Actions, Sayings and Persons'.[61] As he points out,[62] he had already pursued these implications in his *Poetics*, especially in his brief section on comedy.[63] Comedy deals in the risible, and the risible is an aspect of the shameful, the ugly or the base.

---

[54] Guazzo 1581, Bk 2, fo. 4v.   [55] Robson 1577, p. 10.

[56] My discussion of the classical sources closely follows some earlier attempts I have made to understand them, but at the same time corrects and extends my previous accounts. Cf. Skinner 1996, pp. 198–211 and Skinner 2004. For Cicero and Quintilian on laughter see Beard 2014, pp. 100–27.

[57] Aubrey 1898, vol. 1, p. 357.

[58] Hobbes began by making a Latin paraphrase of Aristotle's text, which he seems to have produced in the early 1630s; his translation of 1637 is based on it. For the Latin paraphrase see Hobbes MSS (Chatsworth), Hobbes MS D. 1.

[59] [Hobbes] 1986, p. 86.   [60] [Hobbes] 1986, pp. 70, 86.   [61] [Hobbes] 1986, p. 57.

[62] Aristotle 1926, I. 11. 28, p. 128, and III. 18. 7, p. 466.

[63] It may be, however, that Aristotle is referring to a fuller discussion in the now lost Bk II of his *Poetics*.

If we find ourselves laughing at others, it will be because they exhibit some fault or mark of shame which, while not painful, makes them appropriate objects of contempt.[64]

These assumptions are more fully explored by the Roman rhetoricians, and most fully by Cicero in Book II of his *De oratore*, in which the figure of Caesar is persuaded to discourse about the concept of the laughable. He begins by offering a restatement of Aristotle's argument. 'The place or region in which laughable matters may be said to be found is occupied by *turpitudo* and *deformitas*'.[65] Caesar speaks of *deformitas* only at the end of his introductory remarks, where he brutally observes that 'in physical deformity and weaknesses of the body there is a lot of good material for making jokes'.[66] He mainly concentrates on the potential for derisive laughter to be found in those whose conduct is *turpis*, base or foul, shameful or ignoble. As he summarises, 'the things that chiefly and even solely provoke laughter are the sorts of remarks that note and call attention to something shameful, although without doing so in a shameful way'.[67] We do not laugh at serious improbity, for this deserves punishment as opposed to mockery; nor should we laugh at people's misery, for no one likes to see the wretched taunted. We should recognise that 'the materials for producing ridicule are to be found in the vices of those who neither enjoy esteem nor have suffered calamity'.[68] It is here that we come upon the base and the shameful, whose vices are deserving of mockery and whose manners 'if elegantly touched on, give rise to laughter.'[69]

The other leading rhetorician to examine the connections between laughter and scorn is Quintilian in Book 6 of his *Institutio oratoria*. He quotes Cicero's contention that laughter 'has its source in a certain kind of *deformitas* or *turpitudo*',[70] and adds that 'those sayings which excite laughter are often false (which is always ignoble), often cleverly distorted, always base and never honourable'.[71] He concludes that 'laughter is

---

[64] Aristotle 1995, 1449a, p. 44.

[65] Cicero 1942, II. LVIII. 236, vol. 1, p. 372: 'Locus autem, et regio quasi ridiculi … turpitudine et deformitate quadam continetur'.

[66] Cicero 1942, II. LIX. 238, vol. 1, p. 374: 'Est etiam deformitatis et corporis vitiorum satis bella materies ad iocandum'.

[67] Cicero 1942, II. LVIII. 236, vol. 1, p. 372: 'haec enim ridentur vel sola, vel maxime, quae notant et designant turpitudinem aliquam non turpiter.' On Cicero and laughter as ridicule see O'Callaghan 2007, pp. 38–41.

[68] Cicero 1942, II. LIX 238, vol. 1, p. 374: 'materies omnis ridiculorum est in istis vitiis quae sunt in vita hominum neque carorum neque calamitosorum'.

[69] Cicero 1942, II. LIX. 238, vol. 1, p. 374: 'eaque belle agitate ridentur'.

[70] Quintilian 2001, 6. 3. 8, vol. 3, p. 66, referring to Cicero 1942 II. LVIII. 236, vol. 1, p. 372: '[Risus habet] sedem in deformitate aliqua et turpitudine.'

[71] Quintilian 2001, 6. 3. 6, vol. 3, p. 66: 'ridiculum dictum plerumque falsum est [hoc semper humile], saepe ex industria depravatum, praeterea <semper humile,> nunquam honorificum'.

never far removed from derision', and thus that the overriding emotion expressed by it will normally be one of disdainful superiority.[72] As he later summarises, 'the most ambitious way of glorying over others is to speak derisively'.[73]

It was essentially this view of laughter that the Renaissance writers on civil conversation inherited.[74] We find it most fully restated by Castiglione in Book II of *The Courtier*, in which Bernardo Bibbiena responds at length to Lady Emilia's request to explain the value of jests and 'howe we should use them'.[75] What passion of the soul, Bernardo begins by asking, can be so powerful as to make us burst out in an almost uncontrollable way, as we do when we laugh? One of the feelings involved must always be some form of joy or happiness. As Bernardo puts it, laughing 'alwaies is a token of a certein jocundenesse and merrie moode that he feeleth inwardlie in his minde'.[76] But this joy is of a peculiar kind, appearing as it does to be connected with feelings of contempt. Whenever we laugh we are 'mockinge and scorninge', seeking 'to scoff and mocke at vices'.[77] Later in the discussion he repeats that most jesting is 'grounded upon scofffing', and involves 'deceit, or dissimulacion, or mockinge, or rebukinge' of others.[78]

This analysis is strongly endorsed by the English writers on civil conversation. Simon Robson in his *Courte of civill courtesie* treats it as obvious that to laugh is to mock or deride.[79] To say that someone's behaviour is 'worthy the laughyng at' is to claim that it deserves 'disprayse, or mockyng' by those who have a better sense of how to comport themselves.[80] Lodowick Bryskett writes in similar terms in his *Discourse of civill life*. He acknowledges that urbanity requires our jesting to be 'sharpe and wittie, and yet not bitter or overbiting', but he adds that 'a discreet or wittie jest cannot be much worth, or move men to laugh, unles it have a certaine deceit or offence intended'.[81]

We encounter a comparable line of argument among the neo-Ciceronian rhetoricians of the same period, who are no less interested in the power of words to affect people's behaviour, and hence to regulate social life. Thomas Wilson in his pioneering *Arte of Rhetorique* of 1553 includes an extensive section entitled 'Of delityng the hearers, and stirryng them to laughter.' 'We laugh alwaies', he writes, 'at those thynges,

[72] Quintilian 2001, 6. 3. 8, vol. 3, p. 66: 'A derisu non procul abest risus.'
[73] Quintilian 2001, 11. 1. 22, vol. 5, p. 20: 'Ambitiosissimum gloriandi genus est etiam deridere.'
[74] Herrick 1964, pp. 36–57.   [75] Castiglione 1994, p. 153.
[76] Castiglione 1994, p. 154.   [77] Castiglione 1994, pp. 155–6.
[78] Castiglione 1994, pp. 179, 188.   [79] Robson 1577, pp. 10–11.
[80] Robson 1577, p. 10.   [81] Bryskett 1606, p. 246.

whiche either onely or chiefly touche handsomely, and wittely some especiall fault, or fonde behavior in some one body, or some one thing', and our aim in provoking laughter will generally be to elicit 'scorne out right'.[82]

The writers on civil conversation next consider what specific actions or attributes particularly deserve to be laughed to scorn. First they reiterate that physical deformity affords an excellent subject for jokes. Castiglione goes so far as to suggest that 'the hedspring that laughing matters arise of, consisteth in a certain deformitie or ill favourednesse'.[83] If we shift, however, from physical to moral deformity, we come upon a marked contrast between these writers and their classical authorities. Cicero had argued that neither tragic miseries nor grave improbities are fit subjects for laughter; our mockery should be reserved for those who are *turpis*, foul or base in some way. The Renaissance writers agree that, as Bernardo puts it in *The Courtier*, we ought not to 'scoff and mocke' at serious wickedness, nor at persons 'of such miserye that it should move compassion'.[84] But when they turn to those who deserve to be laughed at, they prefer to speak of using ridicule not against those who are foul and base, but rather against those who display the specific vices of incivility.

They agree, in consequence, that among those who particularly deserve to be laughed to scorn are those who suffer from the sin of pride. Bernardo insists in *The Courtier* that we rightly scoff at those who are 'proude and haughtye', especially if they flaunt 'their auntientrye and noblenesse of birth'.[85] Guazzo adds that, the more a man speaks pridefully about his ancestors, 'the more vile and contemptible hee sheweth himselfe'.[86] Peacham reiterates that those who insist on 'vaunting of their long pedigrees' display a pitiful pride deserving of nothing but contempt.[87]

The other vices of incivility that particularly deserve to be laughed to scorn are said to be vainglory and boastfulness. Bernardo in *The Courtier* denounces those who 'bragg and boast of themselves',[88] while Guazzo complains about those who suffer from 'vaineglorie', roundly concluding that 'they are to bee laughed at'.[89] Peacham likewise dismisses the 'miserable ambition' of those who magnify their importance, observing that their behaviour would have been enough to give Democritus 'laughing matter for his life'.[90] Cleland in his treatise of 1607 on the education of the nobility issues a stern warning 'to behave

---

[82] Wilson 1553, sig. T, 2v–3r.   [83] Castiglione 1994, p. 155.
[84] Castiglione 1994, p. 156.   [85] Castiglione 1994, p. 163.
[86] Guazzo 1581, Bk 2, fos. 37r–v.   [87] Peacham 1622, pp. 16–17.
[88] Castiglione 1994, p. 155.   [89] Guazzo 1581, Bk 2, fos. 39r–v.
[90] Peacham 1622, p. 15.

your selves so modestlie, that nether your advancement maie be envied, nor your debasing laught at.'[91]

III

We can now see how the writers on civil conversation arrive at the conclusion that laughter can serve as a potent means of social control. They have laid it down that to laugh is generally to express scorn and contempt. If, then, we can manage to direct our laughter against the froward, the vainglorious and the prideful – in a word, against the uncivil – we can perhaps cure them of their incivility. Since they will not wish to be viewed with scorn, we can expect them to take considerable pains to alter their behaviour, if only to avoid further ridicule. Laughter can thus be used as a means of discouraging people from acting 'oute of measure', and holding them firmly within the bounds of sociability.[92]

Castiglione concludes that 'the kinde of jesting that is somewhat grounded upon scoffing seemeth verie meete for great men', who can use it to shame and humiliate those who 'go beyond bounds' and need to be disciplined.[93] Thomas Wilson likewise emphasises the controlling power enjoyed by those who, 'when time serveth, can geve a mery answere, or use a nippyng taunte'. Confronted with some socially unacceptable form of behaviour, such people have the ability to 'abash' the person who has failed in civility and 'make hym at his wittes ende, through the sodein quip & unloked frumpe geven.' Wilson relates that 'I have knowen some so hit of the thumbes' by the rebuking power of laughter that they have been unsure 'whether it were beste to fighte, chide, or to go their waie.' Nor is their discomfiture surprising, for 'wher the jest is aptly applied, the hearers laugh immediatly, & who would gladly be laughed to scorne?'[94]

It is true that some writers on civil conversation express certain scruples at this stage in the argument. If, as Guazzo puts it, we find a companion on the brink of 'committing some absurditie either in wordes or in matter', we might think it more magnanimous to attempt 'discreetely to prevent him'. We ought perhaps to 'take holde of him' and 'staye him up: not staying till hee fall, to make the companie fall a laughing, and him selfe to bee ashamed.'[95] Yet more emphatically, Giovanni della Casa wholly rejects the idea of using laughter to impose civility. His *Galateo* is an attempt, very much in the spirit of Castiglione's *Courtier*, to explain how best to conduct ourselves in our 'familiar conversation, and behaviour

---

[91] Cleland 1607, p. 175.   [92] Castiglione 1994, p. 163.   [93] Castiglione 1994, p. 179.
[94] Wilson 1553, sig. T, 2r.   [95] Guazzo 1581, Bk 2, fo. 28v.

with men.'[96] As a papal Nuncio, however, and a man of firm religious faith, della Casa writes in a style of much greater earnestness.[97] He advises that under no circumstances should we allow 'that a man should scorne or scoffe at any man, what so ever he be: no not his very enimy, what displeasure so ever he beare him'.[98] Anyone who has 'a sporte and a pleasure to make a man blush' is guilty of 'spitefull behaviours' that make him 'unworthy to beare the name of an honest gentleman'. If we wish to follow 'good maner & honesty', we must make sure that we 'scorne no man in any case'.[99]

Norbert Elias in his classic study of *The Civilising Process* singles out della Casa as the archetypal instance of a Renaissance writer on the values of *civilité* and how they should be enforced. This leads Elias to conclude that a 'polite, extremely gentle' approach to the enforcement of civility was taken to be 'much more compelling as a means of social control' than 'insults, mockery, or any threat of physical violence.'[100] For most writers on civil conversation, however, this was virtually the opposite of what they believed. Generally they were not merely willing but eager to provide anecdotes and examples to illustrate how we can and ought to use insults and mockery to keep the vices of incivility at bay.

First they argue that we need to know how to achieve this result in the case of those whom della Casa had characterised as the froward and the obstinate.[101] The count in Book I of *The Courtier* gives an example of how this was successfully managed in an encounter between a gentlewoman and a froward military man:

A worthie Gentlewoman in a noble assembly spake pleasauntly unto one, that shall be namelesse for this tyme, whome she to shewe hym a good countenance, desired to daunce with her, and he refusing both that, and to heare musick and many other entertainmentes offred him, alwaies affirming suche trifles not to be his profession, at last the Gentlewoman demaundyng him, What is then your profession? He aunswered with a frowning looke: To fight.

Then saide the Gentlewoman: Seing you are not nowe at the warre nor in place to fight, I woulde thinke it beste for you to bee well besmered and set up in an armorie with other implementes of warre till time wer that you should be occupied, least you waxe more rustier then you are.[102]

The lady's mockery produced exactly the desired effect. Her response gave rise to 'muche laughinge of the standers by', thereby reducing the froward warrior to an object of contempt.[103]

---

[96] Casa 1576, p. 4. [97] As noted in Burke 1993, pp. 98–102. [98] Casa 1576, p. 62.
[99] Casa 1576, p. 63. [100] Elias 1994, p. 65.
[101] Casa 1576, p. 25; cf. Guazzo 1581, Bk 1, fo. 39v. [102] Castiglione 1994, p. 43.
[103] Castiglione 1994, p. 43. On the increasing perception of the warrior as a dangerous anachronism see Thomas 2009, pp. 67–76.

We also need to know how to produce the same result in the case of the prideful and the haughty. Thomas Wilson illustrates how to do so by telling the story of a young man 'of great landes & small witte' who unwisely assumed that his wealth automatically entitled him to respect. He 'talked largely at a supper, and spake wordes scant worth the hearyng'. One of his hearers, 'muche greeved with his foolie, saied to hym: Sir I have taken you for a plaine meanyng gentleman, but I know nowe, there is not a more deceiptfull bodie in al Englande'. When another guest remonstrated, he retorted that 'I must nedes say he is deceiptful, for I toke hym heretofore for a sober wittie young man, but now I perceive, he is a foolish bablyng felowe, & therfore I am sure he hath deceived me like a false craftie child'. The power of this kind of ridicule to impose control is explicitly pointed out. 'They al laughed, and the gentleman was muche abashed'.[104]

Most of all, the writers on civil conversation are keen to illustrate how derisive laughter can be used to discipline the boastful and the vainglorious. Guazzo is particularly irritated by the vanity of those who are self-assured but ignorant. He gives the example of the visit paid by Alexander the Great to the house of the celebrated painter Apelles. Alexander began 'reasoning of painting' to his host and proceeded to speak in a manner 'impertinent and contrarie to that art'. Whereupon 'the wise Painter whispered him in the eare, that hee shoulde speake no more of that matter, or els that he shoulde speake softly, for that his prentices laught him to scorne'.[105] A second and, as Guazzo puts it, a more odious example is provided by the 'poore feeble Sophist' who came before King Cleomenes and 'reasoned in his presence of valour and force'. The king immediately 'fell a laughing', and replied that, if an eagle were to speak to him of strength he would listen, but if a swallow were to do so 'I shoulde not forebeare laughing' at such absurdity.[106]

Speaking of vanity and self-regard, Castiglione and Guazzo express a special distaste for ageing courtiers who continue to practise 'the trickes that in yonge men be galauntnesse, courtesie and precisenesse so acceptable to women'.[107] Gaspare warns that, faced with an old man behaving with such vanity, the young will rightly 'mocke him behinde his backe', while women will 'have none other delite in him but to make him a jestinge stocke'.[108] The figure of Annibale in Guazzo's dialogue speaks in similar terms. The old will be well-advised 'to suffer their minde to waxe olde together with their bodie, and not to behave themselves

---

[104] Wilson 1553, sig. Aa, 4v.
[105] Guazzo 1581, Bk 2, fo. 22r. For a different version see Brathwaite 1630, p. 276.
[106] Guazzo 1581, Bk 2, fo. 23v.   [107] Castiglione 1994, p. 339.
[108] Castiglione 1994, p. 339.

youthfully in their age.' If they attempt to do so they will find themselves
'had in contempt and derision' and will justly be humiliated.[109]

Of all those who are mocked for vaingloriousness, the most laughable
character is agreed to be the one originally satirised by Plautus as the *miles
gloriosus*, the soldier who seeks to disguise his cowardice by boasting of his
military prowess. The count in Book I of *The Courtier* lays it down that 'a
gentilman that is a man at armes' should be 'modest, of few wordes, and
no bragger', and must take care that he never 'craketh of himself', or 'with
a bravery seemeth to threaten the worlde.'[110] Anthony Munday introduces us to just such a *miles gloriosus* in his *Fountaine of Fame* of 1580. The
hero presents himself as a 'comely Champion', but when he is unexpect-
edly confronted by a female warrior he becomes full of 'craking curage',
loses any 'Courtly civilitie' and instantly challenges the lady to single
combat.[111] He is swiftly and humiliatingly vanquished, upon which the
lady subjects him to merciless mockery. 'Where is now thy braverie?
Where is thy vaine vaunting?'[112] Munday is at pains to underline the
reforming effect of the lady's ridicule. The luckless champion is forced to
admit that 'I can crave no forgivenesse, and my deede so desperatly
doone, that it deserveth due discipline'.[113]

The most notorious *miles gloriosus* in Renaissance literature is Parolles
in Shakespeare's *All's Well That Ends Well*. Although he begins by boasting of his daring martial exploits in Italy, his name alerts us to the fact that
he amounts to nothing but words. When he is tricked by the Lord
Dumaine into believing he has been captured by the enemy, he instantly
betrays his army's secrets in the hope of saving his skin. He is thus
unmasked, in Dumaine's words, as 'a most notable Coward'.[114]
Dumaine admits that he instigated the trick 'for the love of laughter',[115]
and the disgraced Parolles is made to acknowledge the disciplining effect
of Dumaine's ridicule:

> who knowes himself a braggart
> Let him feare this; for it will come to passe,
> That every braggart shall be found an Asse.[116]

Parolles indomitably ends by promising himself a new life, but he is forced
to admit that his old one has been laughed into oblivion.

---

[109] Guazzo 1581, Bk 2, fo. 35r.   [110] Castiglione 1994, p. 55.
[111] Munday 1580, p. 43.   [112] Munday 1580, pp. 44–5.   [113] Munday 1580, p. 45.
[114] Shakespeare 1986, *All's Well That Ends Well* (hereafter *A.W.*), TLN 1604, p. 985 (3. 6.
7–8).
[115] Shakespeare 1986, *A.W.*, TLN 1629, p. 985 (3. 6. 26).
[116] Shakespeare 1986, *A.W.*, TLN 2275–7, p. 992 (4. 3. 281–3).

The social functions of laughter have been much discussed by cultural historians of the Renaissance, who have generally accepted Mikhaïl Bakhtin's classic analysis of how the saturnalian power of laughter was used to disrupt and undermine the culture of the elite.[117] There is no doubt that laughter frequently played such a subversive role. As the writers on civil conversation illustrate, however, this is only half the story. Laughter was also deployed as a means of enforcing the values of the courtly and governing class. It was used not merely to uphold an ideal of civil behaviour, but at the same time to police its boundaries and to discipline anyone attempting to step out of line.

IV

Hobbes's political theory has rarely been considered in relation to the genre of *la civil conversazione*, and we have even been urged to see in *Leviathan* an impulse to transcend any preoccupation with what Hobbes describes as 'Decency of behaviour' and 'other points of the *Small Moralls*'.[118] But in fact Hobbes was well acquainted with, and much preoccupied by, Renaissance traditions of writing on precisely these themes. While serving as tutor to the second earl of Devonshire in the 1620s he compiled a catalogue of the library in the earl's residence at Hardwick Hall, and there he recorded copies of Peacham's *Compleat Gentleman* and Cleland's *Institution of a young noble man*[119] as well as Castiglione's *Courtier* in English, French, Italian and Latin,[120] della Casa's *Galateo* in Latin[121] and Guazzo's *Civile Conversation* in English, Italian and Latin.[122] Hobbes and the young earl studied Castiglione's *Courtier* together, and Hobbes even required his pupil to produce a Latin translation of the opening book.[123]

It is clear, moreover, that Hobbes was much indebted to these writers in formulating his own account of sociable and civilised life. It is true that, in his discussion of ingratitude, he introduces a theme of almost no interest to the Italian writers on civil conversation. But otherwise he closely follows their anatomy of incivility, focusing as they had done on the

---

[117] See Bakhtin 1970, Verberckmoes 1999 and for a similar approach see Jones 2011.
[118] Hobbes 2012, vol. 2, ch. 11, p. 150. Cf. Farneti 2000, pp. 489, 498. For an important exception see Thomas 1965, esp. pp. 205–7.
[119] Hobbes MSS (Chatsworth), MS E. 1. A, pp. 70, 105.
[120] Hobbes MSS (Chatsworth), MS E. 1. A, pp. 69, 70, 126.
[121] Hobbes MSS (Chatsworth), MS E. 1. A, p. 84. The work is listed as 'Galataeus de moribus'.
[122] Hobbes MSS (Chatsworth), MS E. 1. A, pp. 83, 84, 128. Cf. Santi 2013, pp. 95–6.
[123] Malcolm 2007, p. 4. See Hardwick MSS (Chatsworth) MS 64. The MS includes corrections and additions, some in Hobbes's hand.

froward, the vainglorious, the prideful and the arrogant. More generally, he is in basic agreement with the principles of civil conversation as laid down by Castiglione, Guazzo and their English followers. First and most basically, he fully corroborates their broad understanding of the concept of conversation itself.[124] When he summarises the laws of nature in *The Elements of Law*, he explains that they are specifically described as moral laws 'because they concern men's manners and conversation one towards another.'[125] When he comments in *De cive* on those who fail to keep their promises, he objects that this form of injustice is inimical to our *conversatio* or dealings with our fellow-citizens.[126] And when he speaks in *Leviathan* about the importance of good judgment 'in matter of conversation and businesse', he translates this phrase in the Latin version of his text as 'in conversatione civili'.[127] Finally, when he offers his summary of the laws of nature at the end of chapter 15 of *Leviathan*, he goes so far as to proclaim that 'Morall Philosophy is nothing else but the Science of what is *Good*, and *Evill*, in the conversation, and Society of man-kind.'[128] Hobbes's aim is not merely to show us how to live in obedient subjection to the laws of the state; it is also to show us how to follow the virtues that bring a 'peaceable, sociable, and comfortable' way of life.[129]

When Hobbes goes on to consider how such a code of civility might be imposed, he draws on a number of classical arguments already invoked by the writers on civil conversation. These intellectual allegiances are most clearly revealed in his analysis of laughter and the range of emotions it may be said to express.[130] It is true that, in his first and fullest analysis in chapter 9 of *The Elements*, he begins with a noisy proclamation of his own originality:

There is a passion which hath no name, but the sign of it is that distortion of the countenance we call LAUGHTER, which is always joy; but what joy, what we think, and wherein we triumph when we laugh, hath not hitherto been declared by any.[131]

After this self-congratulating flourish, however, Hobbes gives an analysis very similar to the one already developed by Castiglione on the basis of his classical authorities.[132] Hobbes agrees that what generally provokes us to laugh is a sense of our own superiority over other people's incapacities or absurdities. As he phrases it in his formal definition, 'the passion of

---

[124] For a full discussion see Santi 2013, pp. 98–102.   [125] Hobbes 1969, 18. 1, p. 95.
[126] Hobbes 1983, III. III, p. 109.   [127] Hobbes 2012, vol. 2, ch. 8, pp. 104, 105.
[128] Hobbes 2012, vol. 2, ch. 15, p. 242.   [129] Hobbes 2012, vol. 2, ch. 15, p. 242.
[130] For a full discussion see Heyd 1982.   [131] Hobbes 1969, 9. 13, p. 41.
[132] This is perhaps surprising, for in the intervening period this way of thinking about laughter had been extensively criticised. See Skinner 2004, pp. 149–53.

laughter is nothing else but a sudden glory arising from sudden concep-tion of some eminency in ourselves, by comparison with the infirmities of others, or with our own formerly.'[133] He also agrees that the laughter in which we express our joy at this 'sudden imagination of our own odds and eminence'[134] cannot fail to embody an element of condescension or contempt. 'Men laugh at the infirmities of others, by comparison of which their own abilities are set off and illustrated', and at jests in which 'the wit whereof always consisteth in the elegant discovering and conveying to our minds some absurdity or another.'[135] To laugh is to glory over others, and is thus to dishonour them.[136] 'To be laughed at' is conse-quently to be 'derided, that is, triumphed over' and viewed with scorn.[137]

For Hobbes, accordingly, laughter can hardly fail to be seriously offen-sive, and in *The Elements* he suggests that there is only one way of indul-ging in it 'without offence'.[138] This is when we laugh together in company at the follies of the world. When this happens, we pour scorn upon 'absurdities and infirmities abstracted from persons' and 'all the company may laugh together.'[139] But in all other instances our laughter takes the form of 'recommending ourselves to our own good opinion, by compar-ison with another man's infirmities or absurdity'.[140] The possibility that we might sometimes laugh at our own absurdity is explicitly ruled out. 'When a jest is broken upon ourselves ... we never laugh thereat'.[141] So it is hardly surprising, Hobbes concludes, 'that men take it heinously to be laughed at', for in fact they are being treated as worthy only of contempt.[142]

A still harsher analysis is developed in chapter 6 of *Leviathan*. The idea that there might be a victimless form of laughter is now suppressed, and Hobbes strongly reaffirms that laughter is almost invariably an expression of superiority and a means of glorying over others:

Sudden Glory, is the passion which maketh those *Grimaces* called LAUGHTER; and is caused either by some sudden act of their own, that pleaseth them; or by the apprehension of some deformed thing in another, by comparison whereof they suddenly applaud themselves.[143]

---

[133] Hobbes 1969, 9. 13, p. 42. See also Hobbes 1983, I. II, p. 90, where he adds in still more classical vein that we laugh at *turpitudo* as well as *infirmitas*.
[134] Hobbes 1969, 9. 13, p. 41.   [135] Hobbes 1969, 9. 13, pp. 41–2.
[136] Hobbes 1969, 9. 13, p. 42.
[137] Hobbes 1969, 9. 13, p. 42; Hobbes 2012, vol. 2, ch. 6, p. 88.
[138] Hobbes 1969, 9. 13, p. 42.   [139] Hobbes 1969, 9. 13, p. 42.
[140] Hobbes 1969, 9. 13, p. 42.   [141] Hobbes 1969, 9. 13, p. 42.
[142] Hobbes 1969, 9. 13, p. 42. For laughter as a means of expressing and soliciting contempt see Hobbes 1983, I. VII, p. 94.
[143] Hobbes 2012, vol. 2, ch. 6, p. 88.

Hobbes had spoken in *The Elements* about the infirmities of others as a cause of laughter, but here he echoes still more strongly the classical and Renaissance view that deformity is likewise an appropriate object of mirth. As he intimates, however, he is chiefly interested in moral rather than physical deformity, and this emphasis is brought out still more clearly in his final attempt to supply a definition of laughter, which he puts forward in his *De homine* of 1658. Here he rounds off his observations by aligning himself yet more closely with the writers on civil conversation, claiming that 'invariably, the passion of laughter is a sudden commendation of oneself prompted by the *indecorousness* of someone else'.[144]

V

Hobbes endorses so many of the arguments originally deployed by the writers on civil conversation that, when it comes to the question of how to impose civility, one might expect him once more to follow their lead. But at this stage he suddenly takes a very different tack. Not only does he part company with their line of argument, but it would scarcely be an exaggeration to say that much of what he goes on to suggest is framed as a direct response to, and repudiation of, what they had proposed.

First of all, Hobbes is horrified by the idea of enforcing civility by means of private revenge.[145] He acknowledges that, in the society of his time, 'all signes of hatred, or contempt, provoke to fight; insomuch as most men choose rather to hazard their life, than not to be revenged'.[146] He also admits that 'private Duels are, and always will be Honourable, though unlawfull, till such time as there shall be Honour ordained for them that refuse.'[147] But he speaks out with intense vehemence against the prevalent tendency to regard '*avoir tué son homme*' as an honourable exercise of power.[148] He refuses even to permit the state to consider vengeance a possible justification for punishment. 'The aym of Punishment', he roundly declares, 'is not a revenge'.[149] As for avenging incivilities by duelling to the death, he denounces this so-called code of honour as nothing better than an upstart and vainglorious custom 'not many years since begun, amongst young and vain men'.[150] The alleged hurts assuaged by duels are 'not Corporeall, but Phantasticall', and are therefore not worth the attention

---

[144] Hobbes 1839b, XII. 7, p. 108: 'universaliter passio ridentium, est sui sibi ex indecoro alieno subita commendatio.' Italics added. For Hobbes on decorum see Malcolm 2015, pp. 80–4.

[145] For Hobbes on duelling see Thomas 1965, pp. 194–6.

[146] Hobbes 2012, vol. 2, ch. 15, p. 234.   [147] Hobbes 2012, vol. 2, ch. 10, p. 142.

[148] Hobbes 1969, 8. 5, p. 35.   [149] Hobbes 2012, vol. 2, ch. 28, p. 486.

[150] Hobbes 2012, vol. 2, ch. 27, p. 466.

of anyone 'assured of his own courage'.[151] He expresses bewilderment that men are prepared to use lethal violence merely to uphold their sense of self-worth, and are consequently ready to fight 'for trifles, as a word, a smile, a different opinion, and any other signe of undervalue'.[152] He praises 'the Lawes of the Greeks, Romans, and other both antient, and moderne Common-wealths' for refusing to acknowledge 'the offence men take, from contumely, in words, or gesture, when they produce no other harme, than the present griefe of him that is reproached'.[153] Most dismissively of all, he maintains that the real reason why vainglorious young men are prone to murderous acts of vengeance is that, paradoxically, they lack courage and magnanimity. As wise legislators recognise, 'the true cause of such griefe' consists 'not in the contumely, (which takes no hold upon men conscious of their own vertue,) but in the Pusillanimity of him that is offended by it.'[154]

Hobbes is no less vehemently opposed to the suggestion that incivility should be controlled by derision and ridicule. He first announces his dissent in *The Elements*, declaring it to be one of the laws of nature '*That no man reproach, revile, deride, or any otherwise declare his hatred, contempt, or disesteem of any other.*'[155] He returns to the argument in *De cive*, insisting that laughter amounts to just such an expression of disesteem. 'It is prescribed *by the law of nature that no one should exhibit hatred or contempt of other people by what they do, or by what they say, or by how they look at them, or by laughing at them.*'[156] He reiterates the point in *Leviathan*, treating it once again as a precept of the law of nature '*That no man by deed, word, countenance, or gesture, declare Hatred, or Contempt of another.*'[157]

Here Hobbes directly opposes the view generally taken by the writers on civil conversation about how to control the vices of incivility. But at the same time he closely aligns himself with earlier critics, notably Giovanni della Casa, who had already voiced similar doubts. It is true that Hobbes's reasons for forbidding scornful laughter were at first rather different from those of della Casa. As we have seen, della Casa's objection had been that such mockery is an instance of dishonourable incivility itself. By contrast, Hobbes's initial argument is at least as much prudential as moral in character. As he explains in *The Elements*, his reason for outlawing laughter is that 'all signs which we shew to one another of hatred and contempt, provoke in the highest degree to quarrel and battle' and

---

[151] Hobbes 2012, vol. 2, ch. 27, p. 466.   [152] Hobbes 2012, vol. 2, ch. 13, p. 192.
[153] Hobbes 2012, vol. 2, ch. 27, p. 480.   [154] Hobbes 2012, vol. 2, ch. 27, p. 480.
[155] Hobbes 1969, 16. 11, p. 86.
[156] Hobbes 1983, III. XII, p. 113: '*lege naturali* praescriptum esse, *nequis vel factis, vel verbis, vel vultu, vel risu, alteri ostendat se illum vel odisse, vel contemnere.*'
[157] Hobbes 2012 vol. 2, ch. 15, p. 234.

consequently undermine civil peace.[158] The same argument reappears in *De cive*, in which Hobbes explains that 'because all pleasure and exaltation of the mind consists in being able to think highly of oneself by comparison with others, it is impossible for people to avoid exhibiting some mutual contempt, whether they express it by laughter, or by words, or by some gesture or other sign'.[159] As he warns, however, 'nothing gives greater offence to the mind than such behaviour, and nothing is more likely to give rise to a desire to hurt' and a consequent relapse into the condition of war.[160]

If we turn, however, to Hobbes's final remarks about laughter in *Leviathan*, we encounter a wholly different argument. He now aligns himself with the most eirenic writers on civil conversation and denounces scornful laughter in the same moralistic style. He already speaks with disapproval in *The Elements*, declaring that 'it is vain glory, and an argument of little worth, to think the infirmities of another sufficient matter for his triumph.'[161] But in *Leviathan* he goes much further, arguing that scornful laughter is a sign of cowardice, and therefore dishonourable. Hobbes is often held up as the leading exponent of the view that laughter is an expression of superiority.[162] But this is almost the opposite of what he argues in *Leviathan*, in which he claims that laughter is 'incident most to them, that are conscious of the fewest abilities in themselves; who are forced to keep themselves in their own favour, by observing the imperfections of other men.'[163] Echoing Guazzo, he adds that such laughter also reflects a failure of magnanimity. 'For of great minds, one of the proper workes is, to help and free others from scorn; and compare themselves onely with the most able.'[164] Hobbes's final reason for rejecting scornful laughter is thus the same as his reason for condemning duels. Both appear to reflect high confidence, but both are in truth expressions of cowardice.

With this conclusion, however, Hobbes simply returns us to the question from which we started out. He forbids us to control the uncivil and the unsociable by means of any form of physical or even verbal violence. But he agrees that the ungrateful, the froward, the vainglorious, the prideful and the arrogant are continually prone to act in violation of

---

[158] Hobbes 1969, 16. 11, p. 86.
[159] Hobbes 1983, I. V, p. 94: 'Cumque omnis animi voluptas omnisque alacritas in eo sita sit, quod quis habeat, quibuscum conferens se, possit magnifice sentire de se ipso, impossibile est quin odium & contemptum mutuum ostendant aliquando, vel risu, vel verbis, vel gestu, vel aliquo signo'.
[160] Hobbes 1983, I. V, p. 94: 'qua quidem nulla maior animi est molestia, neque ex qua laedendi libido maior oriri solet.' See also Hobbes 2012, vol. 2, ch. 15, p. 234.
[161] Hobbes 1969, 9. 13, p. 42; cf. Hobbes 1983, I. II, p. 90.
[162] See, for example, Morreall 1983, pp. 4–14.   [163] Hobbes 2012, vol. 2, ch. 6, p. 88.
[164] Hobbes 2012, vol. 2, ch. 6, p. 88.

the laws of nature, and are liable in consequence to generate conflict and war. If there is to be any prospect of living together in peace, they will somehow have to be coped with or controlled. But how?

When Hobbes squarely addresses this question, as he does in chapter 15 of *Leviathan*, one of the social vices on which he concentrates is frowardness. A froward person is defined as someone who refuses '*to accommodate himselfe to the rest*' and consequently acts in contravention of the fifth law of nature, which prescribes accommodation or 'compleasance'.[165] Hobbes displays an increasing anxiety about this vice in successive recensions of his civil science. In *The Elements* he confines himself to observing that we ought not to be reluctant to accommodate ourselves to one another.[166] In *De cive* he adds that those who refuse accommodation are like irregular stones which cannot easily be fitted into a building.[167] But in *Leviathan* he goes on to propose an extraordinarily radical solution to the problems raised by those who exhibit this kind of irregularity. He begins by reiterating that 'there is in mens aptnesse to Society, a diversity of Nature, rising from their diversity of Affections, not unlike to that we see in stones brought together for building of an Aedifice.'[168] When a builder comes upon a stone that, 'by the asperity, and irregularity of Figure, takes more room from others, than it selfe fills; and for the hardnesse, cannot be easily made plain, and thereby hindereth the building', what he does is to ensure that it is 'cast away as unprofitable, and troublesome'.[169] Hobbes now proposes that the same fate should be meted out to men who are '*Stubborn, Insociable, Froward, Intractable*'.[170] 'So also', he concludes, 'a man that by asperity of Nature, will strive to retain those things which to himselfe are superfluous, and to others necessary' is 'to be left, or cast out of Society, as combersome thereunto.'[171]

This proposal, however, does little to resolve the dilemma that Hobbes has identified. He never explains how we can hope to prevent froward persons from helping to institute a state, and he never offers any account of how they might later be expelled. Nor does he ever suggest that the same solution might be adopted in the case of the other vices of incivility. The dilemma accordingly remains. Even if we can somehow manage to rid ourselves of the froward, we shall still be left with the ungrateful, the vainglorious, the prideful and the arrogant. But the behaviour of these people will remain a standing threat to peace, and will consequently have to be disciplined and controlled. But how?

---

[165] Hobbes 2012, vol. 2, ch. 15, p. 232. On compleasance see Rhodes 2009 and Bejan 2017, esp. pp. 98–101.
[166] Hobbes 1969, 16. 8, p. 85.   [167] Hobbes 1983, III. IX, p. 112.
[168] Hobbes 2012, vol. 2, ch. 15, p. 232.   [169] Hobbes 2012, vol. 2, ch. 15, p. 232.
[170] Hobbes 2012, vol. 2, ch. 15, p. 232.   [171] Hobbes 2012, vol. 2, ch. 15, p. 232.

VI

To raise this question is to uncover a rare element of hesitancy and incompleteness in Hobbes's analysis of civil association. He never proposes a systematic solution to the problem of how to contain the social vices. The most he offers are two tentative suggestions, the first of which is that the answer may lie in cultivating our individual capacity for self-discipline and self-control.[172] Specifically, we may be able to use the powers of natural reason to limit the destructive effects of incivility. This is not to say that reason can ever motivate us to give up our proclivity for behaving ungratefully, vaingloriously, proudly or arrogantly. As Hobbes explains in chapter 6, reason can never serve as such a motivating force; all our actions originate in our passions, and specifically in our changing aversions and appetites.[173] Given, however, that there are certain ends we desire, reason can show us which actions may be conducive to the attainment of those ends, and which actions may be liable to defeat our purposes.[174]

This line of argument is first applied to the vice of ingratitude. To act ungratefully is to requite a man for a benefit in such a way that he has '*reasonable cause to repent him of his good will*'. But if this is how we behave, we shall find ourselves bereft of any prospect of 'mutuall help' or 'reconciliation of one man to another'. This is because our actions will be in breach of 'the first and Fundamentall Law of Nature', and hence in breach of the basic dictate of reason about the means to ensure a peaceable life.[175] The same argument is next applied to the sin of pride. To act pridefully is to refuse to '*acknowledge other for his Equall by Nature*'.[176] But men 'will not enter into conditions of Peace, but upon Equall termes'.[177] To refuse to recognise other people as equals will consequently bring about conflict and war. This outcome, however, will obviously be against our interests, because it will bring in its train the prospect of imminent death. Reason may therefore be said to show us that, even if nature has not made men equal, 'yet because men that think themselves equall, will not enter into conditions of Peace, but upon Equall termes, such equalitie must be admitted.'[178] Finally, the same argument is applied to the vice of arrogance. The arrogant man is someone who attempts '*to reserve to himselfe any Right, which he is not content should be reserved to every one of the rest.*' But this is again to refuse any 'acknowledgement of naturall

---

[172] This is the theme explored in Cooper 2010.
[173] For a full discussion see James 1997, pp. 126–36, 269–84.
[174] Hobbes 2012, vol. 2, ch. 13, p. 196.   [175] Hobbes 2012, vol. 2, ch. 15, p. 230.
[176] Hobbes 2012, vol. 2, ch. 15, p. 234.   [177] Hobbes 2012, vol. 2, ch. 15, p. 234.
[178] Hobbes 2012, vol. 2, ch. 15, p. 234. See Hoekstra 2013a on the need to acknowledge human equality (whether or not it is a fact) in the name of upholding peace.

equalitie', and is consequently liable to lead to conflict and war.[179] This outcome, however, is so obviously against our interests that reason may be said to show that everyone needs to control their 'desire of more than their share'.[180]

Hobbes writes with considerable confidence about our capacity to deploy natural reason to control our passionate natures, and this confidence has been traced to the influence on his thinking of neo-stoic discussions about the techniques of self-mastery and self-discipline.[181] It is not clear, however, how deeply affected Hobbes was by this strand of thought, for at other times he seems much less confident about our ability to achieve this kind of self-control.[182] He already admits in *The Elements* that all men are liable to be 'carried away by the violence of their passion', and that those who 'call for right reason to decide' are usually asking for nothing more than their own reason to determine the case.[183] He writes still more pessimistically in *De cive*, in which he warns that, 'because of their iniquitous appetite for their own immediate advantage', men 'are minimally inclined to follow' what reason requires, with the result that the laws of nature are minimally observed.[184] Still darker is the pessimism of *Leviathan*. Hobbes now speaks of such passions as ambition and covetousness as 'perpetually incumbent, and pressing; whereas Reason is not perpetually present, to resist them'.[185] He complains that 'Potent men, digest hardly any thing that setteth up a Power to bridle their affections; and Learned men, any thing that discovereth their errours, and thereby lesseneth their Authority'.[186] He now admits that 'there be very few, perhaps none, that in some cases are not blinded by self love, or some other passion', with the result that the laws of nature are 'of all Laws the most obscure'.[187]

It is at this moment, however, that Hobbes offers his second and more extended answer to the difficulty he has raised. Although natural reason may not be capable of controlling the vices of incivility, it may be possible to constrain men 'by Education, and Discipline' into acting with the 'constant Civill Amity' that peace and security require.[188] There are said to be two different ways in which the right kind of education may be capable of producing this effect. One is by directly inculcating a

---

[179] Hobbes 2012, vol. 2, ch. 15, pp. 234–6.   [180] Hobbes 2012, vol. 2, ch. 15, pp. 236.
[181] See Burchell 1999, esp. pp. 518–24.
[182] For Hobbes on the limits of reason see Skinner 1996, pp. 87–93, 347–51, 427–35.
[183] Hobbes 1969, 15. 1, p. 75 and 29. 8, p. 188.
[184] Hobbes 1983, III. XXVII, p. 118: 'prae iniquo praesentis commodi appetitu ... observare minime apti sunt'.
[185] Hobbes 2012, vol. 2, ch. 27, p. 462.   [186] Hobbes 2012, vol. 2, ch. 30, p. 524.
[187] Hobbes 2012, vol. 2, ch. 26, p. 430.
[188] Hobbes 2012, vol. 3, A Review, and Conclusion, p. 1132.

disposition to obedience.[189] Hobbes first presents this argument in chapter 18 of *Leviathan*, in which he lays down that the sovereign must be 'Judge of what Opinions and Doctrines are averse, and what conducing to Peace', and must be ready to enforce these judgments on their subjects.[190] The holders of sovereign power must remember that 'the Actions of men proceed from their Opinions; and in the wel governing of Opinions, consisteth the well governing of mens Actions, in order to their Peace, and Concord'.[191] The sovereign must therefore be prepared to outlaw opinions dangerous to peace, while instructing the people 'that Subjects owe to Soveraigns, simple Obedience, in all things, wherein their obedience is not repugnant to the Lawes of God'.[192]

Among opinions dangerous to peace, Hobbes is particularly anxious about the popularity of classical ideas about freedom and self-government.[193] 'By reading of these Greek, and Latine Authors, men from their childhood have gotten a habit (under a false shew of Liberty,) of favouring tumults, and of licentious controlling the actions of their Soveraigns', which has resulted in 'the effusion of so much blood; as I think I may truly say, there was never any thing so deerly bought, as these Western parts have bought the learning of the Greek and Latine tongues.'[194] He expresses particular hostility to Aristotle's claim that '*in democracy*, Liberty *is to be supposed: for 'tis commonly held, that no man is Free in any other Government*'.[195] He responds with a denunciation of Aristotle's influence, ending with the declaration that the universities cannot properly be said to teach philosophy at all, but only Aristotelity.[196]

As so often with Hobbes's assaults on the universities, these complaints are somewhat out of date.[197] As I showed in chapter 1, the syllabus in philosophy at the University of Oxford when he was a student there was not only far more broadly based than he implies, but included the requirement to study Plato's critique of democracy in *The Republic* as well as Aristotle's defence in his *Nicomachean Ethics*. As for the University of Cambridge, we have already seen in chapter 6 that among the set texts in moral philosophy during the decades preceding the civil war were Giovanni della Casa's *Galateo* and Henry Peacham's *Compleat Gentleman*, two works in which the obligation to live in obedience to the law as well as the rules of civility had been strongly emphasised.[198]

---

[189] This aspect of Hobbes's educational programme is assessed in Lloyd 1997.
[190] Hobbes 2012, vol. 2, ch. 18, p. 272.   [191] Hobbes 2012, vol. 2, ch. 18, p. 272.
[192] Hobbes 2012, vol. 2, ch. 31, p. 554.   [193] As noted in Bejan 2010, pp. 612–13.
[194] Hobbes 2012, vol. 2, ch. 21, p. 334.   [195] Hobbes 2012, vol. 2, ch. 21, p. 334.
[196] Hobbes 2012, vol. 3, ch. 46, p. 1074.
[197] On Hobbes's hostility to the universities see Ross 1997; Serjeantson 2006, pp. 122–30, 134–7.
[198] See Casa 1576, pp. 45–6; Peacham 1622, p. 18.

Hobbes always insists, however, that what he calls 'the poyson of seditious doctrines' is a never-ending threat to peace.[199] He suggests that one way of countering the danger is to make sure that no seditious books can 'be publikely read, without present applying such correctives of discreet Masters, as are fit to take away their Venime'.[200] But he also puts forward a positive programme designed to prevent any rebellious upheavals from breaking out. One of his proposals is that the state should appoint teachers to ensure proper instruction of the people 'in the Essential Rights (which are the Naturall, and Fundamentall Lawes) of Soveraignty'.[201] They must be prepared to set aside 'some certain times, in which they may attend those that are appointed to instruct them'.[202] He envisages a series of public meetings 'wherein they may assemble together' and 'hear those their Duties told them, and the Positive Lawes, such as generally concern them all, read and expounded'.[203] But his main proposal stems from his belief that 'the Instruction of the people, dependeth wholly, on the right teaching of Youth in the Universities'.[204] The universities must educate the people in their fundamental duty to obey the powers that be, and the state must prevent the universities from infecting their students with 'the Venime of Heathen Politicians' such as Aristotle with his rebellious hostility to monarchy.[205]

According to Hobbes, the imposition of this educational programme would directly serve the cause of peace. If holders of sovereignty were to instruct their subjects in the need for submission to absolute power, one result would be to improve their own security.[206] And if the universities were obliged to promote the same doctrine of obedience, 'by that means the most men, knowing their Duties', would be 'less subject to serve the Ambition of a few discontented persons, in their purposes against the State'.[207] Summarising in chapter 23, Hobbes reaffirms that, if the state were to supply the means 'to teach the people their duty to the Soveraign Power, and instruct them in the knowledge of what is just, and unjust', the outcome would be 'to render them more apt to live in godlinesse, and in peace amongst themselves'.[208]

Of greater importance for my present discussion is Hobbes's second claim about the role of education in the promotion of civic amity. He

---

[199] Hobbes 2012, vol. 2, ch. 29, p. 502.   [200] Hobbes 2012, vol. 2, ch. 29, p. 508.
[201] Hobbes 2012, vol. 2, ch. 30, p. 524. For a discussion see Bejan 2010, pp. 617–18.
[202] Hobbes 2012, vol. 2, ch. 30, p. 528.   [203] Hobbes 2012, vol. 2, ch. 30, p. 528.
[204] Hobbes 2012, vol. 2, ch. 30, p. 532. For Hobbes on the Universities and civic duty see Serjeantson 2006, pp. 116–18.
[205] Hobbes 2012, vol. 3, A Review, and Conclusion, p. 1140.
[206] Hobbes 2012, vol. 2, ch. 30, p. 524.
[207] Hobbes 2012, vol. 3, A Review, and Conclusion, p. 1141.
[208] Hobbes 2012, vol. 2, ch. 23, p. 378.

believes that 'instruction and discipline' can also be used to instil good social attitudes, thereby fashioning a type of character well-suited to leading a peaceful way of life.[209] The writers on civil conversation had already emphasised the power of education to discipline the passions in this way. Guazzo had argued in *The Civile Conversation* that 'the minde in infantes is like a payre of tables, wherein nothing is written, and like a tender twig which may be bowed every way', so that 'vertue or vice may easily be planted in it.'[210] Hobbes closely echoes this argument, observing that 'the Common-peoples minds, unlesse they be tainted with depen-dance on the Potent, or scribbled over with the opinions of their Doctors, are like clean paper, fit to receive whatsoever by Publique Authority shall be imprinted in them.'[211] Peacham in his *Compleat Gentleman* had simi-larly maintained that 'our affections are perswaded, and our ill manners mollified' by 'the knowledge of good learning'.[212] Hobbes likewise lays it down in *De cive* that 'man is made fit for social life by discipline, not by nature',[213] and in *Leviathan* he confirms that the passions 'are different, not onely from the difference of mens complexions; but also from their difference of customes, and education.'[214] By good discipline and instruction, the passions that tend to make us unfit for social life can be moderated, and perhaps even corrected and transformed.

Chapter 30 of *Leviathan* explains how this transformation can be effected, and one of Hobbes's claims is that some of the vices of incivility can by this means be held in check.[215] He believes that, in the case of ingratitude, this can best be achieved by the kind of discipline and instruction that children receive within the family.[216] Children should not only be obedient to their parents, but should also 'acknowledge the benefit of their education, by externall signes of honour' in later life, 'as gratitude requireth'.[217] When Hobbes turns to the other vices of incivility, he suggests by contrast that the required discipline and instruction should

---

[209] Hobbes 2012, vol. 2, ch. 3, p. 44–6 and ch. 30, p. 532. There has been little discussion of this aspect of Hobbes's theory of civil conversation. Vaughan 2002 concentrates on Hobbes's views about political education, concluding that his aim was to show how much fear it is rational for subjects to experience. A major exception is Dietz 1990, who provides a detailed examination of what she calls (p. 92) 'the dispositions necessary to citizenship'. There are also pertinent remarks in Tuck 1998, pp. 154–5 and McClure 2013, pp. 117–19.

[210] Guazzo 1581, Bk 3, fo. 27r.   [211] Hobbes 2012, vol. 2, ch. 30, p. 524.

[212] Peacham 1622, sig. A, 4r.

[213] Hobbes 1983, I. II. *Annotatio*, p. 92: '*Ad Societatem ergo homo aptus, non natura sed disciplina factus est.*'

[214] Hobbes 2012, vol. 2, ch. 8, p. 110.

[215] See Dietz 1990, p. 107 on Hobbes's aspiration to 'reconstitute' subjects as citizens.

[216] For Hobbes on the role of the family in education see Bejan 2010, pp. 619–20.

[217] Hobbes 2012, vol. 2, ch. 30, p. 528.

be provided by the state. But he follows only rather approximately the typology he had laid down in chapter 15, and has disappointingly little to add to it. He merely speaks of the need for the people to be instructed never to speak contemptuously of those in authority,[218] and never to engage in the kind of violence that vainglorious men are prone to inflict in pursuit of private revenge.[219]

If we reflect on the two main strands in Hobbes's educational thinking, it is not difficult to see how the first component in his programme – the inculcation of obedience – might be made to work. Hobbes always makes it clear that any act of disobedience involving a violation of the positive laws will be punished by the sovereign representative. As he summarises in chapter 31, 'he onely is properly said to Raigne, that governs his Subjects, by his Word, and by promise of Rewards to those that obey it, and by threatning them with Punishment that obey it not.'[220] To train people to recognise their fundamental duty of submission, it will only be necessary to ensure that the positive laws are 'read and expounded', and that the penalties annexed to acts of disobedience are spelled out.[221]

It is less easy to see how the other half of Hobbes's educational programme is supposed to work. What specific kind of instruction does he think will prevent the arrogant from behaving contemptuously, or persuade the vainglorious to offer charity instead of revenge? The only clue he offers is when he speaks about the influence of unsuitable books. The reading of romances, he suggests in *The Elements*, can give rise to an almost insane 'height of vain glory',[222] while the reading of classical philosophy, he adds in *Leviathan*, can encourage arrogance and disobedience.[223] But if this is so, it might seem to follow that, by insisting on the reading of more suitable books, it might be possible to bring these vices of incivility under control.

But which books? The only answer Hobbes offers in chapter 30 of *Leviathan* directs us to the teachings of the Bible. He makes little effort, however, to explain how this advice relates to his general argument. He confines himself, in a somewhat unconvincing passage, to suggesting that we might be prompted to avoid the vices of incivility by reflecting on their parallels with the violation of the Ten Commandments.[224] His only other specific recommendation is that *Leviathan* itself might 'be profitably

---

[218] Hobbes 2012, vol. 2, ch. 30, p. 526. See also Hobbes 2012, vol. 3, ch. 32, p. 580, where such 'selfe conceit' is explicitly equated with 'foolish arrogance'.
[219] Hobbes 2012, vol. 2, ch. 30, p. 530.   [220] Hobbes 2012, vol. 2, ch. 31, p. 554.
[221] Hobbes 2012, vol. 2, ch. 30, p. 528.   [222] Hobbes 1969, 10. 9, p. 52.
[223] Hobbes 2012, vol. 2, ch. 29, pp. 506–8.
[224] Hobbes 2012, vol. 2, ch. 30, pp. 526–30.

printed, and more profitably taught in the Universities'.[225] If we shift our attention to his later discussion of the universities in *Behemoth*, we find that his only additional proposal is that the state should make it compulsory for students to be taught not only to obey the king but to 'injure no man' and to 'live soberly and free from scandall.'[226] If we turn for further enlightenment to Hobbes's own pedagogical practice as tutor to the young earls of Devonshire, the only additional clue we find is that he thought it worthwhile to make a close study of Castiglione's *Courtier*. I have been arguing that *The Courtier* and *Leviathan* are indeed among the most important discussions of the vices of incivility in the tradition of thinking about civil conversation. But they hardly amount to a syllabus, and it might well be thought that Hobbes owes his readers more information about what he takes to be the appropriate content of civic education than he ever deigns to provide.

Despite this large lacuna, Hobbes feels able, in the Review and Conclusion of *Leviathan*, to bring his analysis to a close on a cautiously optimistic note. He concedes that, due to 'the contrariety of mens Opinions, and Manners in generall', there will always be 'great difficulties' about maintaining 'a constant Civill Amity with all those, with whom the Businesse of the world constrains us to converse'. But he urges us to recognise that, while 'these are indeed great difficulties', they are 'not Impossibilities'. By means of the right kind of education they 'may bee, and are sometimes reconciled'.[227] Although Hobbes has little to say about the contents of the right kind of education, he seems confident that the reconciliation of which he speaks can be brought about, and thus that a peaceful way of life is within our grasp.

---

[225] Hobbes 2012, vol. 3, A Review, and Conclusion, p. 1140.
[226] Hobbes 2010, p. 183.
[227] Hobbes 2012, vol. 3, A Review, and Conclusion, p. 1132.

I

To write about Hobbes's theory of representative government is inescapably a polemical task, so it may be best to start by identifying the principal targets at which my analysis is aimed. Hanna Pitkin in her classic work, *The Concept of Representation*, argues that Hobbes provides us with 'the first extended and systematic discussion of representation in English'.[1] It is in Hobbes's *Leviathan*, she has since claimed, that we encounter 'the first examination of the idea of representation in political theory'.[2] Lucien Jaume in his more recent book on representative government speaks in similar terms. He too begins with *Leviathan*, and he too sees Hobbes as 'the first philosopher to define a concept of representation' and place it at the heart of a theory of government.[3]

These judgments seem to me to offer a doubly misleading impression of Hobbes's achievement. They overlook the fact that, by the time Hobbes published *Leviathan* in 1651, a number of English political writers had already developed a fully fledged theory of representative government. Furthermore, they had put their theory to revolutionary use in the course of the 1640s to challenge the government of Charles I and eventually to legitimise the conversion of England into a republic or 'free state' in 1649. My other criticism is that the judgments I have quoted give a distorted view of Hobbes's own project in *Leviathan*. Far from enunciating a theory of political representation for the first time, what Hobbes is doing in *Leviathan* is presenting a critical commentary on a range of existing theories, especially those put forward by the parliamentarian opponents of the Stuart monarchy at the beginning of the English civil wars.[4]

This contention brings me to my other main target, Philippe Crignon's study of Hobbes entitled *De l'incarnation à la représentation*. According

This chapter is a revised and much extended version of Skinner 2005b. For permission to draw on this earlier work I am indebted to John Wiley and Sons. For commenting on drafts I am deeply grateful to Kinch Hoekstra, Susan James and Philip Pettit.
[1] Pitkin 1967, p. 14.   [2] Pitkin 1989, p. 140.   [3] Jaume 1986, p. 7.
[4] A suggestion pursued in Baumgold 1988.

to Crignon, any attempt to relate Hobbes's analysis to the ideological debates of the English revolution is doomed to yield 'a completely misleading as well as insufficient' genealogy of his theory of representative government.[5] It is Crignon's thesis that Hobbes's way of understanding the concept of representation announced 'an historical rupture' so complete that he stands apart from all these arguments. Hobbes's achievement was to produce 'a total refoundation of the concept', separating him off from everything that went before.[6]

I shall attempt to show, by contrast, that we cannot hope to understand Hobbes's view of political representation unless we are prepared to examine it in relation not merely to the theories prevailing in his time, but also in relation to the long-standing traditions of thinking out of which these theories arose. To try to make good this claim, I shall need to begin by speaking at some length about a number of political writers who are scarcely household names. This being so, I perhaps need to emphasise that I do not take myself, in the opening sections of this chapter, to be providing mere 'background' to the understanding of Hobbes's thought. Rather I am trying to question any strong distinction – of the kind Crignon wishes to reinstate – between the background of partisan political tracts on the one hand and Hobbes's civil science on the other. One way of summarising my argument would be to say that I am trying to illustrate the extent to which Hobbes's *Leviathan* is itself a partisan political tract, albeit a large and ambitious one.

II

I take as my starting-point the period in which the vocabulary of legal and political representation first began to be widely deployed in the English language, a development that can roughly be traced to the opening decades of the sixteenth century. For a sense of how the concept was initially – and enduringly – understood, we can hardly do better than consult the two earliest Latin-English dictionaries, Sir Thomas Elyot's *Dictionary* of 1538 and Thomas Cooper's *Thesaurus* of 1565. As I showed in chapter 2, the verb *repraesentare* had principally been used in classical Latin to refer to the act of creating a resemblance of the external appearance of someone or something. If we turn to Elyot and Cooper, we find this meaning fully preserved. Cooper defines *praesentare* as 'to represent: to resemble',[7] while Elyot defines *repraesentare* as 'to bryng in presence, . . . to lay before one'.[8] I also showed, however, that in early Christian culture

---

[5] Crignon 2012, p. 328.   [6] Crignon 2012, pp. 337–43.   [7] Cooper 1565, sig. 5F, 2r.
[8] Elyot 1538, sig. X, 4r.

the verb *repraesentare* began to be used in contexts where one might have expected such phrases as *gerere personam* or *suscipere personam* to be invoked. It began to be used, in other words, to express the very different idea of taking on someone's role and playing their part. This is not to deny that, if we revert to Elyot's and Cooper's dictionaries, we find them continuing to translate some of these formulae in classical style. When, for example, Elyot comes to the phrase *induere personam alterius*, his suggested translation is 'to speake in the name or stede of a nother man', while Cooper renders Cicero's phrase *servire personam* as 'to behave him selfe accordyng to the parte that he playeth.'[9] Sometimes, however, they prefer the word 'represent' in these contexts instead. When Elyot translates *induere personam iudicis*, he does not speak of sustaining the person of a judge; rather he renders the phrase as 'to represent a judge'.[10] Similarly, Cooper translates Quintilian's phrase *suscipere personam* as 'to represent one'[11] and Cicero's phrase *gerere personam civitatis* as 'to represent the state and person of a whole citie'.[12] From the outset – and with consequences dangerous to clarity of understanding – we find the single word *represent* employed to refer both to *standing for* and *acting for* someone or something else.[13]

Among early Anglophone discussions about representation, some of the most prominent were primarily concerned with theological issues. These were largely grounded on the rhetorical assumption that representatives are essentially actors who, in Elyot's phrase, may be said 'to speake in the name or stede of a nother man'.[14] This is the assumption underpinning the lengthy discussion among puritan divines about the standing of Christ as a 'common person' representative of us all.[15] The pioneering exponent of this line of thought was William Perkins in the massive sequence of tracts he published in 1600 as *A golden Chaine*, and his arguments were subsequently taken up by Paul Baynes, Richard Sibbes, Thomas Goodwin and others. According to Perkins, Christ 'is to be considered as a publike man sustaining the person of all the elect.'[16] When we speak of Christ as sustaining our person, Perkins later explains, we are saying that he acted 'as a publike person representing all men that are to come to life eternall'.[17] Just as 'the burgesse of a towne in the parliament house beareth the person of the whole towne', so Christ 'stood

---

[9] Elyot 1538, sig. 2L, 3r; Cooper 1565, sig. 4Z, 3v.   [10] Elyot 1538, sig. 2L, 3r.
[11] Cooper 1565, sig. 4Z, 3v.   [12] Cooper 1565, sig. 3H, 4r.
[13] As noted in Brito Vieira and Runciman 2008, p. x.   [14] Elyot 1538, sig. 2L, 3r.
[15] For the possible influence of these writers on Hobbes see Hill 1986, pp. 318–19; Martinich 1992, pp. 147–50.
[16] [Perkins] 1600, p. 116.   [17] [Perkins] 1600, p. 378; cf. also p. 254.

in our place, and bare our person'.[18] Baynes subsequently repeats the argument, claiming that Christ acted 'in all our names', and in doing so behaved in the same manner as an elected representative, of whom it can be said that 'what he doth or speaketh, it is in the name of the Corporation, who doth it in him.'[19]

The fullest development of this line of thought can be found in Thomas Goodwin's tract *Christ Set Forth*, first published in 1642. Here Christ is characterised as a representative person who shares our attributes and may be said to typify us.[20] He was '*All men*, by way of representation', and was consequently able to act representatively.[21] The sense in which he sanctifies us is that we are 'representatively sanctified in him'; the sense in which he takes possession of heaven for us is that he does so 'representatively' for all who have been saved.[22] We can therefore think of him as 'a *Common person* representing us'.[23] By a common person, Goodwin explains, he means 'one who represents, personates, and acts the part of another' and is 'reckoned to doe' whatever is done in his name.[24] Christ behaved as 'a *Common person* bearing our persons' in just this sense, thereby acting not merely 'in our names' but 'in our right'.[25]

Of still greater significance for the entrenchment of the same vocabulary was an earlier theological dispute related to the Elizabethan ecclesiastical settlement. One question at issue was St Augustine's understanding of the primitive church. As I showed in chapter 2, Augustine had alluded in his *De agone christiano* to Cicero's contention that magistrates may be said to bear the person of the *civitas*, and had argued that it can similarly be said of St Peter that he bore or carried the *persona Ecclesiae catholicae*, the person of the Catholic Church.[26] This line of thought was taken up by a number of English Catholic opponents of the Elizabethan settlement. As early as 1567 we find Nicholas Sander, the pioneering historian of the Anglican schism, arguing in his *Rocke of the Churche* that St Peter 'did beare the person of the Churche' in virtue of being its 'chiefe officer' and 'the head and Rocke of the whole.'[27] Thomas Fitzherbert, the head of a prominent English Catholic family, who later became a Jesuit priest, reiterated the argument in his *Adjoynder* of 1613. Fitzherbert agrees 'that *S. Peter* bare the person of the Church',[28] and explains why Peter 'rather than others of the Apostles' is thereby 'said to represent the

---

[18] [Perkins] 1600, p. 395.   [19] Baynes 1634, p. 103.
[20] Goodwin (Thomas) 1642, p. 59.   [21] Goodwin (Thomas) 1642, p. 73.
[22] Goodwin (Thomas) 1642, pp. 73, 193.
[23] Goodwin (Thomas) 1642, pp. 49, 65, 66, 71, 74, 107.
[24] Goodwin (Thomas) 1642, p. 47.   [25] Goodwin (Thomas) 1642, pp. 72, 104, 106.
[26] Augustine 1791, ch. XXX, p. 141: 'Ecclesiae catholicae personam sustinet Petrus'.
[27] Sander 1567, pp. 164–5.   [28] [Fitzherbert] 1613, pp. 6, 136.

whole Church'.[29] He was 'Head or supreme Governor thereof', and had special 'Pastorall authority' to guide and rule over it.[30] A year later, William Bishop, an English Catholic priest teaching at the Sorbonne, returned to the argument in *A Disproofe*, declaring once again that 'S. Peter bare the person of the church', and that this 'argueth him to bee the chief governor of the church'.[31]

Among the Anglican apologists who confronted these arguments, some cast doubt on St Peter's alleged supremacy by questioning the underlying assumption about the supposed rights of representatives. Francis White, one of James I's chaplains, objected that when someone 'receives any thing in the person of another', the right must lie not with the receiver but rather with 'him whose person hee sustains, while he receives it'. St Peter is consequently seen as a mere delegate of the Church and subject to its rule. The majority of Anglican writers, however, remained so respectful of St Augustine that they were largely content to ratify his account of St Peter's role, provided that his headship was not taken to have descended by apostolic succession to the Pope. William Fulke in his reply to Nicholas Sander accepts that St Peter 'in respect of his primacy represented the whole Church', although he rejects the claim that he did so in virtue of being its 'soveraigne ruler and generall officer'.[32] Samuel Collins, another of James I's chaplains, who published a lengthy response to Thomas Fitzherbert, agrees that 'S. Peter bare the person of the Church' just as a magistrate 'beareth the person of the citie'.[33] Collins accepts that St Peter was thereby able 'to represent the Churches person',[34] although he too questions whether it follows that St Peter was 'indued with Supreame authoritie over the Church'.[35]

This debate was important for the development of an Anglophone vocabulary of legal and political representation in a yet further way. A number of Catholic controversialists chose to highlight the implications of their ecclesiological arguments for the theory of the state. The first to do so was Sander in a remarkable passage from his *Rocke of the Churche* on how 'S. Augustine affirmeth in many places, that S. Peter did represent the whole Churche'.[36] By this we are to understand that Peter was 'the head and Rocke of the whole', just as that 'everie prince doth beare the figure and as it were the generall person of his subjectes, and of them who are committed to his Charge', because 'they all are, as it were, gathered

[29] [Fitzherbert] 1613, p. 5.
[30] [Fitzherbert] 1613, pp. 5, 136, 151. See also the summary in Fitzherbert 1621, pp. 4–5 and the restatement of the case in [Anderton] 1634, pp. 188–92, in which we are again told (p. 189) that 'Peter may be said to beare the person of the Church'.
[31] [Bishop] 1614, p. 140.   [32] Fulke 1580, p. 219.   [33] Collins 1617, p. 3.
[34] Collins 1617, p. 70.   [35] Collins 1617, p. 3.   [36] Sander 1567, p. 163.

togeather and united in him alone'.[37] We may therefore say of the law that
it 'interpreteth and expoundeth the chiefe officer of a common weal, to
bear the person of the self common weal.'[38] To be a sovereign, in short, is
to represent the commonweal or state.

Still more remarkable is Fitzherbert's contention in his *Adjoynder* that
St Peter may be said 'to represent the whole Church' in the same way
that it can be said of any 'chiefe or supreme Magistrate' that he '*beareth
the person of the Citty.*'[39] This observation of Cicero's had already been
echoed by a number of English writers of political advice-books. For
example, Anthony Rush in his *President for a Prince* of 1566 had declared
that a good ruler must not only 'care for the whole common wealth'
but recognise that 'he beareth and susteyneth the person of the whole
Realme'.[40] Pursuing the parallel with the Church, Fitzherbert argues that
'whatsoever is given to the King, as King, and Head of the Common-
wealth, the same is given to the Common-wealth, wherof he beareth and
representeth the person: and so in like manner what was given to *S. Peter*
as Head of the Church, the same was given to the Church which he
representeth'.[41] William Bishop speaks in similar terms in his *Disproofe*
of 1614. Just as we gather from the words of Saint Augustine 'that S. Peter
sometimes did represent the whole church, because he was head and chief
pastor therof', so in the same manner 'a king doth in some cases represent
a kingdome'.[42]

Fitzherbert later returned to the issue in his counterblast to Samuel
Collins in 1621, reiterating that St Peter 'did beare heere two persons, the
one true, and proper, which was his owne naturall person, and the other
figurative, which was the person of the Church.'[43] If we focus on the
second of these *personae*, we find that St Peter must have been endowed
with the same powers as rulers of commonwealths. Fitzherbert then
proceeds to lay out the nature and extent of these powers:

He who doth beare the person, & figure of the commonwealth doth also represent
the majesty of it; for he that representeth the whole commonwealth representeth al
that is in it, and properly belongeth unto it, be it majesty, authority, jurisdiction,
prerogatives, priviledges, or what els soever is properly the commonwealthes, the
same being al virtually in the Governour, and derived from him, to every member
of the commonwealth, according to their severall functions, and offices.[44]

The conclusion at which these writers arrive is thus that a commonwealth
or state should be considered as a legal or 'figurative' *persona* of which the

[37] Sander 1567, p. 164.   [38] Sander 1567, p. 165.   [39] [Fitzherbert] 1613, p. 5.
[40] Rush 1566, sig. D, 2v.   [41] [Fitzherbert] 1613, p. 5.   [42] [Bishop] 1614, p. 141.
[43] Fitzherbert 1621, p. 25.   [44] Fitzherbert 1621, p. 13.

sovereign should be regarded, as in the case of St Peter's headship of the Church, as having the standing of an authorised representative.

III

The theological debates I have been sketching were of far greater significance for the development of English theories of legal and political representation than has generally been recognised. As many commentators have rightly noted, however, the principal and strongly contrasting context in which these concepts were initially discussed in the English language was in connection with the standing of Parliament.[45] Here, moreover, the vocabulary of 'bearing the person' and playing the part of someone else was never invoked. The earliest writers on Parliament as a representative assembly instead foreshadow what later became known as the theory of virtual representation. The claim they advance is that Parliament is not merely an agent of the people with authority to speak and act in their name, but owes its authority to being at the same time a representation – a recognisable image or likeness – of the people as a whole.

One of the earliest adumbrations of this doctrine can be found in Christopher Saint German's *Dialogue* between a doctor of divinity and a student of the common laws, first published in Latin in 1528 and translated into English with additions in 1532. The lawyer affirms that 'there is no statute made in this realme but by the assent of ye lordes spirituall & temporall & of all the comons'. By 'all the comons', he explains, he means 'the knightes of the shyre Cytizens & Burgeses that be chosen by assente of the comons whiche in the parliament represente the estate of the hoole commons'. As a result of this act of representation, 'every statute there made is of as strong effecte in the lawe as if all the comons were there present personallie', and may therefore be regarded as 'made by theyr authoritie'.[46]

A generation later, this view about the place of the two Houses in the mixed constitution was summarised by John Vowel in the account he published in 1575 of 'the dignitie, power and authoritie of the Parlement', an account based, he tells us, on his experience of sitting in the House of Commons in 1571.[47] Vowel notes that 'every Baron in Parlement doth represent but his owne person, & speaketh in the behalf of him self alone'. By contrast, 'in the Knights, Citizens, and Burgesses: are represented the Commons of the whole Realme, and every of these giveth not consent onely for him self: but for those also for whom he is sent'. It is because the

---

[45] See, for example, Brito Vieira and Runciman 2008, pp. 15–19.
[46] Saint German 1532, fo. 115v.   [47] Vowel 1575, fos. 20r, 31r.

House of Commons constitutes an image or representation of the whole body of the people that 'the King with the consent of his Commons: had ever a sufficient and ful authoritie to make, ordain & establish good & wholesome Laws for the common welth of his Realme'.[48]

The best known of these early descriptions of Parliament as a representative assembly appears in Sir Thomas Smith's *De republica Anglorum*, written while he was ambassador to France in the early 1560s and first published in 1583. Smith's chapter 'Of the Parliament and the authority thereof' begins by affirming that 'the most high and absolute power of the realme of Englande, is in the Parliament.' The upper House consults and acts 'for the nobilitie and lordes', while the House of Commons does so 'for the lower part of the common wealth'.[49] Whatever they decide 'is the Princes and the whole realmes deede: whereupon justlie no man can complaine, but must accommodate himselfe to finde it good and obey it.' This is because Parliament 'representeth and hath the power of the whole realme both the head and the bodie.' When Parliament acts, it is as if the whole people act, 'for everie Englishman is entended to bee there present, either in person or by procuration and attornies'. It is due to being an image or representation of the people that Parliament has the power to pursue policies in their name, 'and the consent of the Parliament is taken to be everie mans consent.'[50]

These claims continued to be voiced under the reigns of James I and Charles I in the early seventeenth century, but they also underwent a dramatic development in the years immediately following Charles I's recall of Parliament in 1640 after his failed attempt at personal rule. A hostile group of parliamentarian writers restated the idea of the mixed constitution in the form of a radical theory of representation grounded on the sovereignty of the people. A number of lawyers began to write in this almost republican vein in the second half of 1642, notably Henry Parker and William Prynne, as did a wide circle of divines, including John Goodwin, Charles Herle, Philip Hunton and William Bridge. To this roll-call must be added an extensive group of propagandists who have remained anonymous, among them the authors of such anti-monarchist tracts as *Maximes Unfolded* and *A Soveraigne Salve*, both of which were published in the early months of 1643.

I shall mainly focus on the most original and penetrating of these theorists, Henry Parker, and his most widely influential treatise, his

---

[48] Vowel 1575, fo. 31v.
[49] On Smith's 'commonwealth' view of the state see Dauber 2016, pp. 81–113.
[50] Smith 1982, pp. 78–9.

Observations of July 1642.[51] Like the clerical writers who followed his lead, Parker saw himself as needing to confront and deal with a recrudescence among his royalist opponents of the theory of the divine right of kings. According to this vision of politics, the existing social and political fabric is directly ordained by God. To question any part of it is consequently tantamount to challenging the divine will. As Charles I himself was to affirm at the outset of his *Answer* to Parliament in June 1642, 'Our Regall authority' is a form of power 'which God hath entrusted us with for the good of Our People', and the responsibility for the exercise of this power is ultimately owed to God alone.[52]

The parliamentarian propagandists begin by offering a contrasting account of the condition in which we are placed in the world by God. The analysis they put forward can be expressed in negative as well as positive terms. Stated negatively, their claim is that there is no reason to treat our existing system of law and government as a special gift of God's providence. As Parker insists at the outset of his *Observations*, although 'the King attributeth the originall of his royalty to God', the truth is that 'God is no more the author of Regall, then of Aristocraticall power, nor of supreame, then of subordinate command.'[53] John Goodwin agrees that 'it is no ordinance or appointment of God that any particular Nation or society of men, should have either this or that speciall forme of government', so that our present 'Kingly Government' can be 'no ordinance of God in this sense.'[54]

Stated positively, the parliamentarian argument is that what exists in nature is not states and governments but simply free communities endowed with all the necessary means to regulate their own affairs. Political power, Parker explains, 'is nothing else but that might and vigour which such or such a societie of men contains in it selfe.'[55] Philip Hunton repeats that, before the members of any such society 'yeeld up themselves to a Person, to be commanded by his will', they constitute 'a free and not pre-engaged People' who 'at first had power over themselves.'[56] Applying the argument to the people of England, William Prynne confirms that, like any other free people, they must originally have been in possession of 'Nationall authority, power, and priviledges', and hence the fullest 'authority, power, and liberty'.[57]

One reason why these writers emphasise the natural freedom of the people is that this enables them to portray the establishment of civil

---

[51] On Parker see Zaller 1991; Mendle 1995; Sabbadini 2016, pp. 166–75; for a contrasting approach see Cromartie 2016. On royalist versus parliamentarian views of the body politic see Harris 2007.

[52] [Charles I] 1642, pp. 1–2.   [53] [Parker] 1642, p. 1.   [54] Goodwin (John) 1642, p. 8.

[55] [Parker] 1642, p. 1.   [56] [Hunton] 1643, pp. 13, 23.   [57] Prynne 1643, I. p. 91.

associations entirely as an outcome of human decision and choice. If what exists in nature is not government but merely the capacity to institute it, then the whole body of the people must count as the authors of whatever authority is subsequently placed over them. In Parker's words, it is not God but man who acts as 'the free and voluntary Author' of whatever powers are 'derived' into the hand of kings and magistrates. The people are always 'the Authors, or ends of all power' and hence 'the finall cause of Regall Authoritie'.[58] Charles Herle, Parker's closest follower, agrees that man is always 'the cause and author' of government,[59] while the writer of *Maximes Unfolded* assures us that 'God is not so exact in the choice of Magistrates as to be their Authours', preferring to leave it to the people to decide by whom they wish to be governed. As he concludes – in an arrestingly Hobbesian turn of phrase – they always act as 'the Authors, Instruments, matter, forme and end of Government.'[60]

Several of these writers emphasise a further terminological point. If lawful government can be instituted only when the people as the authors of all power make a grant of their original authority, we can equally well say that the people must *authorise* their kings and magistrates, and thus that governments are legitimate if and only if they are duly authorised. William Bridge explains that the legal act which takes place when 'Secular or Civill power' is 'given to one, or more, by the people' is that 'some are authorized to exercise jurisdiction in Common-wealths over others.'[61] Philip Hunton, perhaps the most sophisticated constitutional thinker among the writers I am considering, points to the strictness of the boundaries imposed by such agreements on the jurisdictions of kings. When the people authorise a ruler, 'then is his Authority limited', and 'neither are the instruments of his will exceeding those lawes, authorized'. Should he subsequently violate this 'definement of Authority', his resulting acts 'are not *Legall* and binding, that is, are *non-Authoritative*.'[62]

These grants of authority, Parker goes on, must always be expressed in the form of an explicit act of 'common consent and agreement'.[63] Hunton agrees that every government 'drawes its force and right from the consent and choice of that Community over which it swayeth', so that 'every Monarch hath his power from the consent of the whole body' of the populace.[64] These acts of consent are expressed in the form of contracts

---

[58] [Parker] 1642, pp. 1, 2, 3.
[59] [Herle] 1642, p. 23. Herle and Parker are considered together in Judson 1988, pp. 409–33.
[60] *Maximes Unfolded* 1643, p. 14.   [61] Bridge 1643b, p. 3.
[62] [Hunton] 1644, pp. 27, 31. On Hunton's constitutionalism see Judson 1988, pp. 397–409.
[63] [Parker] 1642, pp. 1, 13.   [64] [Hunton] 1643, pp. 15, 19.

or covenants by which the people signal their acceptance of a king or other supreme magistrate. It is only through 'the Pactions and agreements of such and such politique corporations', in Parker's words, that lawful governments can ever be set up.[65] Hunton makes clear the polemical direction of the argument when he adds that 'Kings have not divine words and binding Lawes to constitute them in their Soveraignty'. They can be instituted only by 'the consent and fundamentall contract of a Nation of men, which consent puts them in their power, which can be no more nor other then is conveyed to them by such contract of subjection' as the people may find acceptable.[66]

One might well ask how an entire populace can perform such a unitary legal act as contracting and hence consenting to government. Acknowledging the difficulty, the parliamentarian writers answer that the people must never be regarded as a mere multitude; they must always be recognised at the same time as a unified and corporate group. As Parker puts it, it is always possible to view them not merely *divisim*, as single subjects, but also *conjunctim*, as a *universitas* or 'politique corporation'.[67] Bridge similarly argues that we can think of the people either *divisivè* or *unitivè*.[68] The significance of the distinction is that if we think of the people 'conjunctively' we can say that the agent consenting and contracting is 'the Commonalty' or 'the Common-weale' itself.[69] The author of *Maximes Unfolded* repeats that, when the people act by 'the common consent of all', they may be said to act by 'their united power', and hence in the manner of a single person with one will and voice.[70]

These writers have a second and connected reason for insisting on the natural freedom of the people. If we are all born free, it cannot be imagined that we would ever submit to an arbitrary or absolute form of rule. To see why this is self-evident, it is only necessary to reflect that, if you live under arbitrary power, you will be dependent on the will of your ruler for the preservation of your life, liberty and estates. But this is to say that, even though you may have *de facto* enjoyment of your rights, you will nevertheless be in the predicament of a slave. As I showed in chapter 7, Goodwin provides a particularly heartfelt statement of this case. If your relationship with your ruler obliges you 'to be at their arbittterments and wills in all things, to doe and to suffer, to have and to possesse as they shall appoint and thinke meet for you', then you are living in an intolerable condition of 'bondage and slavery'.[71] This explains why, as Prynne declares, it is 'not once to be imagined of any people' that they would

[65] [Parker] 1642, p. 1.   [66] [Hunton] 1643, p. 12. Cf. also [Hunton] 1644, p. 21.
[67] [Parker] 1642, p. 18.   [68] Bridge 1643a, p. 1.   [69] Bridge 1643a, pp. 2–3.
[70] *Maximes Unfolded* 1643, p. 26.   [71] Goodwin (John) 1642, p. 39.

grant their rulers 'an absolute, irrevocable uncontroulable Supremacy over them'. To do so would simply be to make 'themselves and their Posterity absolute slaves and vassals for ever'.[72]

If free peoples would never voluntarily subject themselves to absolute power, what form of government would they set up? By way of answer, the parliamentarian writers like to sketch a history of how lawful governments assumed their present shape. Parker provides the most detailed of these narratives, beginning with the concession that men would admittedly have found it necessary from an early stage to subject themselves to rulers and magistrates. 'Man being depraved by the fall of *Adam* grew so untame and uncivill a creature, that the Law of God written in his brest was not sufficient to restrayne him from mischiefe, or to make him sociable'.[73] It soon became obvious that 'without society men could not live, and without lawes men could not be sociable, and without authority somewhere invested, to judge according to Law, and execute according to judgement, Law was a vaine and void thing.'[74] These were the circumstances in which communities resolved to authorise some virtuous and trusted leader to create and administer a system of laws to uphold the peace.

As Parker adds, however, we must never forget that the people who authorised these leaders were, at the time of doing so, in full possession of the power to govern themselves. All lawful kings must therefore be lesser in standing than the body of the people from whom their authority is acquired. Here Parker invokes the formula that, as I noted in chapter 2, had originally been introduced into the debate about *summa potestas* by the jurist Azo Portius in commenting on the *Lex regia*. 'We see that power is but secondary and derivative in Princes', and that 'the fountaine and efficient cause is the people.' 'From hence', Parker concludes, 'the inference is just, the King, though he be *singulis Maior*, yet he is *universis minor*', lesser in standing than the *universitas* or 'politique corporation' of the people from whom his rights and powers are derived.[75]

This designation of kings as *maior singulis sed minor universis* was widely repeated in the ensuing constitutional debate. Prynne inserts into the Appendix to his *Soveraigne Power of Parliaments* a translation of the passages in which the author of the *Vindiciae, contra tyrannos* had affirmed that 'all the people are Superior to the king', although 'every one of them apart be inferior'.[76] Picking up the argument, the author of *Maximes Unfolded* reverts to the original Latin, reiterating that any king 'is *Maior singulis, universis minor*' and explaining that 'Comparatively the

[72] Prynne 1643, I. p. 91.   [73] [Parker] 1642, p. 13.   [74] [Parker] 1642, p. 13.
[75] [Parker] 1642, pp. 1, 2.   [76] Prynne 1643, Appendix, p. 143.

King is the greatest', but that he is 'no King till he be made, neither are the Subjects so to be counted till they have made themselves such.'[77]

From this maxim the parliamentarian writers derive one further inference. If the people are greater than their kings, it must be within their power to grant authority on strictly limited terms. The body of the people, in Parker's words, 'may ordaine what conditions, and prefix what bounds it pleases', thereby placing their ruler under an obligation to govern according to the terms of a 'conditionate' trust.[78] Herle agrees that the *universitas* of the people is always 'greater, and more powerfull then the King', and thus that kings are always 'created upon certaine lawes and conditions' by the people.[79] Prynne goes further, concluding that the people, 'if we take them collectively', are not only 'above the king' but are able in consequence 'to restrain and question his actions, his Mal-Administrations, if there be just cause.'[80]

Does this imply that, if a king should fail to meet the terms of his trust, he can rightfully be resisted and removed by the people who originally trusted him? Writing before the outbreak of the civil war, Parker is careful to avoid any such inflammatory inference. A few months later, however, we find such writers as Herle and Prynne vehemently proclaiming the right of the people to defend their interests by taking up arms, as Parliament had by that time done. Any free people, Prynne insists, must always 'reserve the supremest power and jurisdiction to themselves, to direct, limit, restrain their Princes supremacy & the exorbitant abuses of it, when they should see just cause.' Should their rulers act without their consent and against their interests, they can and ought to call them to account and forcibly resist 'by necessary defensive Armes'.[81]

If we return to Parker, we next find him postulating that the opening chapter in his history of mankind would undoubtedly have ended badly. 'Man is by nature of restlesse ambition', and those invested with power are always corrupted by it.[82] We can therefore be confident that, although the people initially authorised their kings to rule only according to the terms of their pactions or contracts, they would soon have found themselves 'subject to unnaturall destruction, by the Tyranny of intrusted magistrates, a mischiefe almost as fatall as to be without all magistracie.'[83] A period of anarchy would then have ensued. Finding themselves betrayed, and lacking any constitutional means to redress their grievances, 'the body of the people was ever constrained to rise, and by the force of a Major party to put an end to all intestine strifes.' But 'many

---

[77] *Maximes Unfolded* 1643, p. 26.   [78] [Parker] 1642, pp. 2, 4.   [79] [Herle] 1643a, p. 18.
[80] Prynne 1643, I. p. 104.   [81] Prynne 1643, I. p. 91.   [82] [Parker] 1642, pp. 39–40.
[83] [Parker] 1642, p. 13.

times calamities grew to a strange height', so that 'after much spoile and effution of bloud, sometimes onely one Tyranny was exchanged for another.'[84]

With this imagined crisis Parker reaches the second chapter in his history of mankind, the chapter in which a happy ending is reached. The solution at which 'most Countries' eventually arrived was that of authorising representative assemblies to govern in co-operation with their kings, balancing their power and if necessary holding them in check.[85] This contention brings Parker to the heart of his argument, and he has two connected claims to make. The first is that, having been granted authority by the people to serve as their representatives, such assemblies are not only 'vested with a right both to counsell and consent' but to 'appear in the right of the whole Kingdome.'[86] His other claim is that what invests these assemblies with their sovereign right is that they constitute a representation – an image or likeness – of those who have authorised them.[87] The English Parliament owes its authority to its character as a 'representation' on a smaller scale of the 'reall body of the people', so that when Parliament makes a decision 'the whole body of the State' may be said to act.[88]

Parker takes the visual implications of his metaphor very seriously. He goes so far as to appraise the English Parliament as a work of art,[89] commending its 'purity of composition', its 'Art and order', and its 'admirably composed' features.[90] He makes it clear that he has two visual ideas in mind, both of which carry powerful political resonances. The first arises because the 'reall body of the people' is too cumbersome and irregular in its movements to be capable of acting for itself.[91] It follows that an effective representation will need to take the form of a portrait on a considerably smaller scale. As Parker later explains in his *Ius populi* of 1644, one reason why the English Parliament offers such a good 'representation' of the people is that the process of election enables 'the rude bulk of the universality' to be 'reduced' in just such an 'artificial' or artful way to a more manageable size.[92]

Parker's second suggestion is that an artful representation of the people, like any satisfactory portrait, must be a likeness in which no features are exhibited out of scale. He expresses confidence that, in the case of the English Parliament, this proportionality has duly been achieved. Not only are the members of the House of Commons drawn 'out of all parts' of the country, but they come together in a body 'equally, and geometrically

---

[84] [Parker] 1642, p. 14.   [85] [Parker] 1642, pp. 14–15.   [86] [Parker] 1642, pp. 9–10.
[87] See Sabbadini 2016, pp. 169–70.   [88] [Parker] 1642, pp. 15, 45.
[89] [Parker] 1642, p. 15.   [90] [Parker] 1642, pp. 15, 23.   [91] [Parker] 1642, pp. 14–15.
[92] [Parker] 1644, p. 18.

proportionable.' The people in their different states or estates 'doe so orderly contribute their due parts' that, in the resulting representation of the people, 'no one can be of any extreame predominance.'[93] The outcome, he adds in *Ius populi*, is as 'full and neer representation' as can be given of the 'real' body itself.[94]

These claims were met with instant ridicule by Parker's royalist opponents. The most scathing response came from Sir John Spelman, whose counterblast to Parker's *Observations* was published in January 1643.[95] How, Spelman asks, can we treat the House of Commons as an accurate picture or representation of the people when 'at least nine parts of the Kingdome, neither doe nor may Vote in their election'? The clergy are not permitted to vote; and nor are women; and nor are 'the most substantiall Coppy-holders, Farmours nor Lessees for yeers'. How, in addition, can the representation of the people be regarded as proportionable when 'halfe the Kingdome in which there are but few Burroughes, be equalled and overborne in Voting by two Counties', and when '*Old Sarum* shal have as many Votes in Parliament, as the Citty of *London*, or County of Wiltes'.[96]

These objections leave Parker unmoved. For him the question of the franchise is of no relevance, and he never discusses it. The whole weight of his argument rests on the claim that, when the members of the House of Commons are elected in equal numbers from the different part of the body politic, this has the effect of constituting a proportionate image of the people as a whole. When this elected body acts, it cannot fail to act as the real body would have acted. The reason, in other words, why Parliament cannot fail to serve the interests of the people is that Parliament simply *is* the people in the sense of being a representative sample. It is 'vertually the whole kingdom it selfe;'[97] it can therefore be regarded as 'the voyce of the whole Kingdom' and its decisions as those of 'the whole body of the State'.[98]

As Spelman observes, Parker appears to be telling us that, by means of representation, 'the vertue and power of the whole Realme' comes to be embodied in Parliament, and seemingly 'in the Commons alone'.[99] Restating his argument in his *Ius populi*, Parker is happy to confirm that the authority of Parliament does indeed stem from its being 'nothing else, but the very people it self artificially congregated'. Parliament 'differs many wayes from the rude bulk of the universality', but 'in power, in honour, in majestie, in commission, it ought not at all to be divided, or

---

[93] [Parker] 1642, pp. 11, 23.   [94] [Parker] 1644, p. 19.
[95] [Spelman] 1643; date (26 January 1643) from BL (Thomason) copy.
[96] [Spelman] 1643, sig. D, 2r.   [97] [Parker] 1642, p. 28.
[98] [Parker] 1642, pp. 37, 39, 45.   [99] [Spelman] 1643, sig. D, 2r.

accounted different as to any legall purpose'.[100] Parker's basic claim is thus that, by the miracle of representation, Parliament is rendered 'virtually' – that is, in respect of its virtues or powers – identical with the body of the people, and consequently in possession of their ultimate sovereignty.

Parker's theory of virtual representation was widely taken up.[101] Goodwin in his *Anti-Cavalierisme* repeats that Parliament 'in a representative and legall consideration, is the whole body of the Nation, and of all the persons in it'. As an image of the nation, it possesses 'the same power and authority by Law, and in conscience too, to do every whit as much in every respect, as the whole Nation, and all the particular persons therein could have, if they were met together.'[102] The author of *A Soveraigne Salve* agrees that Parliament serves as a 'representation' of 'the whole kingdome', so that when sovereign power is held by Parliament it may be said to remain 'in the peoples owne hands', as a result of which the decisions of Parliament enjoy a 'politique infallibilitie'.[103] Hunton similarly speaks of the House of Commons as an image or 'representation' of the people,[104] while Herle adds the promise that no dangers can arise from entrusting the fullest sovereignty to Parliament, because 'their representations are of us, and interests the same with us.'[105] Everyone agrees that the two Houses offer an image or picture of the people so exact and lifelike that we can think of Parliament and people as effectively one and the same.

The parliamentarian writers like to claim that the upshot of their argument is a reassuringly familiar one. England, they conclude, is a mixed monarchy, and mixed monarchy is the best and most stable form of government. Parker ends his *Observations* by insisting that 'I speak not this in favour of any alteration in *England*'. He concedes that 'in some things I know tis dangerous to circumscribe Princes', merely adding that 'in others there may be great danger in leaving them to their pleasure'.[106] Herle more forthrightly begins his *Fuller Answer* by proclaiming that England 'is a Coordinative, and mixt Monarchy' and that in this mixture lies 'the very supremacy of power itselfe'.[107] Hunton makes it the central argument of his *Treatise of Monarchie* that 'the Authority of this Land is of a compounded and mixed nature in the very root and constitution

---

[100] [Parker] 1644, pp. 18–19.
[101] It is sometimes said that the virtual theory was first developed during the imperial crisis in eighteenth-century England. See, for example, Greene 2010, pp. 69–71. But as Nelson 2014, pp. 66–107 shows, what happened was simply that the parliamentarian theory of the 1640s was revived and reapplied.
[102] Goodwin (John) 1642, p. 28.   [103] *A Soveraigne Salve* 1643, pp. 4, 8, 17, 22.
[104] [Hunton] 1643, p. 47.   [105] [Herle] 1643b, p. 12.   [106] [Parker] 1642, p. 41.
[107] [Herle] 1642, p. 3.

thereof'.[108] The doctrine is summarised by the anonymous author of *The Maximes of Mixt Monarchy*, in which we are told that in the English constitution 'Politique power is in three estates', and that 'they all challenge a right in the policy of the Kingdome'.[109]

These contentions, however, are doubly misleading as an account of the constitutional position that Parker and his followers had by this stage reached. It is true that Hunton, shocked by the outbreak of war, cleaves to the traditional view – put forward by Charles I himself in his *Answer to the Nineteen Propositions*[110] – that every element in the mixed constitution possesses its own unquestionable standing and powers. He is thus led to conclude that the only means of settling the crisis will be for the king voluntarily to cede some of his undoubted constitutional rights.[111] But most of the parliamentarian writers repudiate this view of the mixed constitution in favour of an interpretation in which ultimate supremacy is granted to the two Houses of Parliament. Herle is particularly insistent that, if we acknowledge the 'coordinative' nature of the constitution, we are bound to accept that, when the two Houses agree, they can lawfully override the king simply by outvoting him. He accordingly concludes that 'the final and casting result of the States judgement' must lie with Parliament alone.[112] The same position is summarised in *The Maximes of Mixt Monarchy*, in which we are bluntly told that the three estates are 'Co-ordinate'; that 'Co-ordination is in Parliament'; that 'Parliament is above all Persons'; and that 'All persons are bound to obey it'.[113]

Even this conclusion, however, understates the revolutionary implications of the parliamentarian case. Parker had affirmed at the outset of his *Observations* that 'power is originally inherent in the people, and is nothing else but that might and vigour which such or such a societie of men containes in it selfe'.[114] The people may decide as a matter of convenience to bestow the use of their sovereignty upon a representative body to exercise in their name, but 'the proper Subject' or owner of sovereign power can only be 'the whole universality' of the people.[115] Parker's position is underpinned, in short, by a theory of popular sovereignty, and after civil war broke out in August 1642 the protagonists of the parliamentary cause began to articulate this commitment much more forcefully. The author of *A Soveraigne Salve*, first published in February 1643, declares that 'the radicall, primary supreme power' lies with the

---

[108] [Hunton] 1643, p. 39.   [109] *The Maximes of Mixt Monarchy* 1643, sig. A, 2v.
[110] [Charles I] 1642, pp. 17–22.
[111] [Hunton] 1643, p. 79. On Hunton's continued defence of the mixed constitution see Sabbadini 2016, pp. 172–4.
[112] [Herle] 1642, p. 2.   [113] *The Maximes of Mixt Monarchy* 1643, title-page.
[114] [Parker] 1642, p. 1.   [115] [Parker] 1642, p. 44.

people, 'who made Kings, not Kings people'. The body of the people reserves sovereignty 'ever in its owne hands', ready to 'draw backe to the fountaine the derivate power' granted to kings and magistrates if the alternative proves to be a life of servitude.[116] Bridge similarly maintains in his *Truth of the Times* of July 1643 that 'the first subject, seat and receptacle of ruling civil power' lies in 'the whole people or body politicke'.[117] Although 'the authority of ruling in a Commonwealth be given by the people to him that ruleth', this grant is always made on the understanding that there will be a 'reflux of authority' back to the people if the powers they cede are not justly exercised.[118] Nor is it ever an act of usurpation if the people 'look to themselves' in this way, for their resistance will never be anything other than 'a stirring up, acting and exercising of that power which alwayes was left in themselves'.[119]

IV

The parliamentarian theory of popular sovereignty instantly came under violent attack. The clerical defenders of divine right surged forward to repudiate every premise of the parliamentarian case. Gryffith Williams, bishop of Ossory, was one of the first in the field with his *Vindiciae Regum*, a counterblast to Parker and Goodwin published in February 1643. No power, Williams replies, can ever arise from the body of the people. God is 'the immediate Author of the Regall power', so that 'the power and authority of Kings is originally and primarily (as S. Paul saith) the ordinance of God'.[120] Furthermore, this ordination grants absolute authority to the present king, so that no one can ever resist him 'without apparent sacriledge against God.'[121] If we ask about the relationship between the king and Parliament in this scheme of things, Williams is careful to allow that Parliament is of course 'the representative body of all his Kingdom.'[122] But because it is merely a body of subjects, it can never be anything more than a consultative assembly, and cannot exercise any binding powers. 'As the King hath a power to call, so he hath a power to dissolve all Parliaments; and having a power of dissolving it when he will, he must needs have a power of denying what he pleaseth.'[123]

Soon afterwards the Levellers launched a strongly contrasting but scarcely less withering attack. Richard Overton in his *Appeale* of July 1647 treats it as the merest hypocrisy to suggest that the existing Parliament constitutes anything like a recognisable image or representation of the

---

[116] *A Soveraigne Salve*, 1643, p. 18.   [117] Bridge 1643b, p. 4.
[118] Bridge 1643b, pp. 5, 8.   [119] Bridge 1643b, p. 15.   [120] Williams 1643, pp. 48–9.
[121] Williams 1643, p. 52.   [122] Williams 1643, pp. 63, 67.   [123] Williams 1643, p. 67.

body and hence the will of the people. The fundamental will and desire of the people is that their security and liberty should be preserved. But the two Houses have transformed themselves into 'so many traytors to the safety and weale of the people.'[124] They 'cannot be the Representers of the Free-men of England', for 'such as are the representers of Free-men, must be substantial and reall Actors for freedome and liberty.'[125] It follows that the current conduct of Parliament lacks any legitimacy. The two Houses have 'devested and degraded themselves from their betrusted authority of the people, and become no longer their representory Deputies, or Trustees, except tyranny and oppression be the very substance and end of their Trust.'[126]

Among the opponents of the parliamentarian writers, no one engaged with their arguments more tenaciously, nor reacted to them with more implacable hostility, than Hobbes in *Leviathan*. Before considering his response, however, it is important to note that it was not until *Leviathan* that he concerned himself with the propagandists whom he was later to stigmatise in *Behemoth* as the 'Democraticall Gentlemen'.[127] Almost all their works were published after Hobbes circulated *The Elements of Law* in 1640, and even after the appearance of *De Cive* at the beginning of 1642. By contrast, it would scarcely be an exaggeration to say that Hobbes's entire theory of representative government in *Leviathan* takes the form of a critical commentary on the parliamentarian arguments I have so far anatomised.

This is not to say that Hobbes contradicts the democratical gentlemen at every turn. On the contrary, he goes out of his way to emphasise how much he agrees with the basic premises of their argument. He endorses their rejection of divine right, accepting that our natural condition is one of equal freedom, and thus that no specific form of government is directly imposed by God.[128] He likewise agrees about the extent of our freedom in the state of nature. 'The absolute Libertie of Nature' consists in 'an exemption from Lawes', and is thus equivalent to 'the Liberty which the Law of Nature gave us.'[129] He is also in agreement about the means by which our natural liberty can lawfully be replaced by subjection to government. The only legitimate mechanism is that 'all the *Rights*, and *Facultyes* of him, or them, on whom the Soveraigne Power is conferred' must be assigned 'by the consent of the People assembled'.[130] The

---

[124] [Overton] 1647, p. 9 (*recte* p. 13).   [125] [Overton] 1647, p. 12.
[126] [Overton] 1647, p. 12.   [127] Hobbes 2010, p. 158; cf. pp. 133, 141, 373.
[128] Hobbes 2012, vol. 2, ch. 13, pp. 190–2.
[129] Hobbes 2012, vol. 2, ch. 21, pp. 328, 344; ch. 26, p. 450.
[130] Hobbes 2012, vol. 2, ch. 18, p. 264.

chapter on civil law later confirms that sovereigns in every kind of commonwealth must be 'Constituted by the consent of every one'.[131]

So far these arguments would have been familiar to any reader of *The Elements* or *De Cive*. Hobbes had already maintained in both these texts that the state of nature is one of complete 'natural liberty',[132] and that the only means by which this liberty can lawfully be curtailed is by the explicit consent of those who agree to submit to government.[133] When, however, Hobbes speaks in these earlier texts about this act of curtailment, he describes it as a simple relinquishment of rights.[134] As he summarises in *The Elements*, 'when a man covenanteth', he 'giveth up, and relinquisheth to another, or others, the right of protecting and defending himself'.[135] The effect is to enable the will of everyone to be 'included and involved' in the will of the sovereign,[136] so that we may say, as *De cive* adds, that the king now 'is' the people.[137]

By contrast, when Hobbes outlines the same process in *Leviathan*, he makes a striking alteration to his argument. He now invokes and endorses the precise political vocabulary articulated by the parliamentarian writers in the 1640s.[138] He begins by echoing the account they had given of the people as the authors of all lawful power. He willingly grants that, when we covenant to institute a commonwealth, we become 'by this Institution Author of all the Actions, and Judgments of the Soveraigne Instituted'.[139] Unless we are the authors of the powers to which we submit, the resulting powers will not be legitimate. The reason is that 'no man is obliged by a Covenant, whereof he is not Author; nor consequently by a Covenant made against, or beside the Authority he gave'.[140]

Hobbes also agrees about the specific nature of the act of authorisation performed by those who assign political authority to others.[141] When I covenant, the affirmation I make is that '*I Authorise and give up my Right of Governing my selfe, to this Man, or to this Assembly of men, on this*

---

[131] Hobbes 2012, vol. 2, ch. 26, p. 426; cf also ch. 28, p. 492.
[132] Hobbes 1969, 14. 11, p. 73; Hobbes 1983, I. VII, p. 94.
[133] Hobbes 1969, 19. 4, p. 101; Hobbes 1983, V. V, p. 133.
[134] Hobbes 1969, 19. 10, p. 104 and 20. 5, p. 110; Hobbes 1983, II. III, p. 100.
[135] Hobbes 1969, 19. 7 and 10, pp. 103–4 and 20. 5, p. 110. Cf. Hobbes 1983, II. III, p. 100 where Hobbes uses the verbs *transfere* and *reliquere*.
[136] Hobbes 1969, 21. 11, p. 124.
[137] Hobbes 1983, XII. VIII, p. 190: '*Rex* est *populus*'.
[138] Hobbes fully works out this analysis only in the case of what he calls a 'Common-wealth by *Institution*', not in the case of a 'Common-wealth by *Acquisition*'. See Hobbes 2012, vol. 2, ch. 17, p. 262. I therefore confine myself in what follows to commenting on the former case.
[139] Hobbes 2012, vol. 2, ch. 18, p. 270.   [140] Hobbes 2012, vol. 2, ch. 16, p. 246.
[141] For Hobbes on authorisation see Gauthier 1969, pp. 120–77; Baumgold 1988, pp. 36–55.

condition, that thou give up thy Right to him, and Authorise all his Actions in like manner.'[142] Hobbes admittedly continues to refer in this initial formulation to the relinquishment of rights.[143] As he develops his argument, however, he focuses exclusively on the claim that we authorise someone to exercise them in our stead. He already speaks in these terms in chapter 18, in which he states that a commonwealth is instituted when a representative is selected, at which stage 'every one, as well he that *Voted for it* as he that *Voted against it*, shall *Authorise* all the Actions and Judgements, of that Man, or Assembly of men'.[144] He confirms this analysis in chapter 21, in which he lays it down that 'the Consent of a Subject to Soveraign Power, is contained in these words, *I Authorise, or take upon me, all his actions*; in which there is no restriction at all, of his own former naturall Liberty'.[145]

Hobbes continues to follow the parliamentarian writers when he asks what it means to authorise someone. As we have seen, he agrees that we need in the first place to count as an 'author', that is, someone capable of 'owning' their actions and accepting responsibility for their consequences. When, as an author, we then perform an act of authorisation, what we do is to grant someone authority to speak or act in our name. As Hobbes puts it, 'he that owneth his words and actions, is the AUTHOR' and when he authorises someone to act for him, then 'the Actor acteth by Authority'. As a result, 'by Authority, is always understood a Right of doing any act: and *done by Authority*, done by Commission, or Licence' from the author who possesses the right to perform the act of authorisation involved.[146]

These arguments constitute a major revision of Hobbes's earlier analysis in *The Elements* and *De Cive*, in which he had made no mention of authors or authorisation, nor of representation or representatives.[147] Commentators who have noted the change have generally argued that Hobbes must have identified some weaknesses or even contradictions in the initial statement of his case, and must have decided to recast it in an effort to cope with them.[148] By contrast with these somewhat speculative hypotheses, my principal aim in what follows will be to suggest a different kind of explanation for the extensive modifications Hobbes introduced. What seems to me crucial is the extensive use he makes in the revised version of his theory of the distinctive political vocabulary articulated by his parliamentarian adversaries. What he is doing, I shall next attempt to

---

[142] Hobbes 2012, vol. 2, ch. 17, p. 260.   [143] As noted in Martinich 2016, pp. 316–23.
[144] Hobbes 2012, vol. 2, ch. 18, p. 264.   [145] Hobbes 2012, vol. 2, ch. 21, p. 338.
[146] Hobbes 2012, vol. 2, ch. 16, p. 244.
[147] But Tuck 2015, pp. 105–6 argues that Hobbes might be thought to be groping for this vocabulary in these earlier texts.
[148] See, for example, Gauthier 1969, pp. 99, 120, 126; Zarka 1999, pp. 325, 333.

show, is seeking to discredit them by demonstrating that it is possible to accept the basic structure of their theory without endorsing any of the radical implications they had drawn from it.

V

To see how Hobbes pursues this rhetorical strategy, we need to begin by focusing on the moment when he parts company with the democratical gentlemen. They had assumed that civil associations must initially have arisen out of free and natural communities in which the *universitas* or body of the people possessed sovereign power. This, according to Hobbes, is an egregious error, and one of his main purposes in presenting his melodramatic description of the state of nature is to lay the error bare. There is simply no such thing, he retorts, as the body of the people. 'The Multitude naturally is not *One*, but *Many*'.[149] If we look beyond the bounds of civil association, what we find is not a corporate body but merely a throng or multitude of 'particular men'.[150] Furthermore, it is a multitude in which, due to the similarity of everyone's desires and powers, we are all 'dissociate' from one another and 'every man is Enemy to every man'.[151] As a result, the natural condition of mankind is not merely a state of men 'in Solitude', a state in which there is 'no Society' and 'neither *Propriety*, nor *Community*'; it is also 'a condition of warre one against another', a perpetual war 'of every man, against every man.'[152]

By failing to recognise the frightening truth about our natural condition, the democratical gentlemen betray themselves into offering a misleading account of the political covenant, and hence the character of lawful rule. They argue that the unified body of the people, acting in the manner of one person, contracts with a designated ruler and consents to submit to him on agreed terms. Hobbes is now able to dismiss this part of their analysis out of hand. It makes no sense to talk in this way about 'the *Unity* of the Represented'.[153] Before becoming subject to sovereign power the people 'are not one Person'; they are nothing more than the separate and mutually hostile members of 'a disunited Multitude'.[154] The parliamentarian vision of 'the whole multitude, as one party to the Covenant' is simply impossible.[155]

It might seem, however, that this all-out assault on the corporatist assumptions of the democratical gentlemen overreaches itself. If there is

[149] Hobbes 2012, vol. 2, ch. 16, p. 250.   [150] Hobbes 2012, vol. 2, ch. 13, p. 196.
[151] Hobbes 2012, vol. 2, ch. 13, pp. 192, 194.
[152] Hobbes 2012, vol. 2, ch. 13, pp. 192, 196, 388.
[153] Hobbes 2012, vol. 2, ch. 16, p. 248.   [154] Hobbes 2012, vol. 2, ch. 18, pp. 264, 266.
[155] Hobbes 2012, vol. 2, ch. 18, p. 266.

no such thing as a body of people in need of representation, how can we make sense of the idea of representative government? By way of answer Hobbes starts by laying out a general analysis of the concept of representation, his topic in chapter 16 of *Leviathan*. His basic claim is that to represent someone is simply to put on their mask, to speak their lines, and thereby perform some role or function in their name. Here he draws on the Ciceronian vocabulary I examined in chapter 2, in which the term *persona* had been used to refer to the mask worn by actors in the Roman theatre to make clear what characters they were playing. Hobbes agrees that 'a *Person*, is the same that an *Actor* is, both on the Stage and in common Conversation', so that 'to *Personate*, is to *Act*, or *Represent* himselfe, or an other'.[156] This originally theatrical usage, he adds, has now come to encompass 'any Representer of speech and action, as well in Tribunalls, as Theaters', so that anyone representing someone else is now 'said to beare his Person, or act in his name'.[157]

Hobbes also emphasises the convention that, when someone plays a part in the theatre, the actions they perform 'in character' are not taken to be their own, but are attributed to the character they are playing. According to Hobbes this is true in all instances of representing others, as he observes when putting forward his intertwined definitions of personhood and representation at the beginning of chapter 16:

A PERSON, is he, *whose words or actions are considered, either as his own, or as representing the words or actions of an other man, or of any other thing to whom they are attributed, whether Truly or by Fiction.*

When they are considered as his owne, then is he called a *Naturall Person*: And when they are considered as representing the words and actions of an other, then is he a *Feigned* or *Artificiall person*.[158]

Here Hobbes defines a representative as someone who takes upon himself the 'artificial' role of speaking or acting in the name of another man (or another *thing*) in such a way that the words or actions of the representative can be attributed to the person being represented. He adds that this relationship remains in place even when the words and actions cannot 'truly' be attributed to the person being represented, but only by a fiction of law. At the same time he defines a person as anyone (or any thing) capable of being represented, that is, of having speech and action attributed to them. As he later confirms in summarising this passage, a person is simply 'he that is Represented'.[159]

---

[156] Hobbes 2012, vol. 2, ch. 16, p. 244. For Hobbes on the language of personation see Pettit 2008, pp. 55–69.
[157] Hobbes 2012, vol. 2, ch. 16, p. 244.   [158] Hobbes 2012, vol. 2, ch. 16, p. 244.
[159] Hobbes 2012, vol. 3, ch. 42, p. 776.

One implication of this all-encompassing view of personhood is that 'there are few things, that are uncapable of being represented by Fiction', since almost anything is susceptible of having words and actions attributed to it if someone is able to show that he is speaking or acting in its name.[160] As we saw in chapter 2, Hobbes gives the examples of 'a Church, an Hospital, a Bridge', all of which 'may be personated by a Rector, Master, or Overseer', with authority to act in their affairs.[161] He adds, yet more inclusively, that even 'an Idol, or meer Figment of the brain' can be successfully represented, as happened with 'the Gods of the Heathen' in ancient Rome.[162] These alleged deities did not even exist, but in consequence of being represented by priests they were able to hold possessions and exercise legal rights. It is of course true that, as Hobbes concedes, it is only 'by Fiction' that any of these entities can be said to possess agency. They are capable of having words and actions attributed to them if and only if they are represented. But because there is no difficulty about representing them, there is equally no difficulty about holding them responsible for actions attributed to them in virtue of being performed in their name.

As we have seen, this Ciceronian understanding of personhood initially entered Anglophone political discourse in the theologico-political disputes of the English Reformation. Hobbes refers to Cicero's own formulation, quoting the passage in which he had described how 'I beare three Persons; my own, my Adversaries, and the Judges'.[163] He also echoes with striking closeness Thomas Goodwin's definition of a representative as someone who 'personates, and acts the part of another'[164] and Thomas Fitzherbert's repeated claim that what it means to serve as a representative is to 'bear the person' of someone else.[165] Hobbes was clearly aware of all these writers, and it is from these sources that he derives his fundamental insight that the act of representation is a matter not of producing images or likenesses but simply of speaking and acting in the name of others.

Armed with this general analysis, Hobbes next proceeds to explicate the idea of representing a multitude. Here he lays out a theory in which two distinct but related features can be distinguished. One takes the form of the claim that a relationship of representation must be understood to obtain between any sovereign and each of his individual subjects. Commentators have sometimes denied that Hobbes makes any use of the language of representation to describe this relationship.[166] But he

---

[160] Hobbes 2012, vol. 2, ch. 16, p. 246.   [161] Hobbes 2012, vol. 2, ch. 16, p. 246.
[162] Hobbes 2012, vol. 2, ch. 16, p. 248.   [163] Hobbes 2012, vol. 2, ch. 16, p. 244.
[164] Goodwin (Thomas) 1642, pp. 47, 72.   [165] [Fitzherbert] 1613, pp. 5, 6, 13, 136.
[166] See, for example, Runciman 2009, p. 19.

does so in a number of passages in which he closely echoes one of the distinctive claims put forward by such covenanting theologians as Perkins and Goodwin. As we have seen, they had argued that, in consequence of sharing our individual qualities, Christ was able to behave representatively, to bear the person of each one of us and act in the name of us all. Hobbes likewise refers to the sovereign as 'one Representative Person'[167] who can be regarded as 'the Person representative of all and every one of the Multitude'.[168] He further claims that, in consequence of possessing this vital quality of representativeness, any sovereign can similarly speak and act as a 'common Represener' or 'common Representative' of us all.[169] A sovereign is someone who, in virtue of agreeing 'to represent them every one', is enabled to serve as the 'Representative of all his own Subjects'.[170]

It might seem that, as some commentators have concluded, Hobbes is arguing that the sovereign only 'represents or is the agent for the citizens *taken as individuals*' and that this is 'the fundamental Hobbesian thought'.[171] It is true that, because 'the Multitude naturally is not *One*, but *Many*', the only form that the political covenant can take is a 'Covenant of every man with every man'. Everyone must agree, each with each, 'to conferre all their power and strength upon one Man, or upon one Assembly of men'.[172] It is crucial for Hobbes, however, that this act of mutual covenanting gives rise to two further political consequences. First it has the effect of converting the individual members of the multitude into a single person. When they covenant to confer their power, they consent to 'reduce all their Wills, by plurality of voices, unto one Will'.[173] But to affirm that they are now able to act with a single will is to say that they are no longer a mere multitude. The effect of their mutual agreement is to produce 'a reall Unitie of them all', so that they are now 'united in one Person'.[174] The other consequence is that the sovereign becomes the representative of the person they conjure into existence by the act of agreeing to be represented. When they covenant, this is 'as much as to say' that they 'appoint one Man, or Assembly of men, to beare their Person; and every one to owne, and acknowledge himselfe to be Author of whatsoever he that so beareth their Person, shall Act, or cause to be Acted, in those things which concerne the Common Peace and

---

[167] Hobbes 2012, vol. 2, ch. 29, p. 512; cf. Hobbes 2012, vol. 2, ch. 25, p. 404.
[168] Hobbes 2012, vol. 2, ch. 19, p. 284.
[169] Hobbes 2012, vol. 2, ch. 16, p. 250; ch. 22, p. 348; ch. 26, p. 418.
[170] Hobbes 2012, vol. 2, ch. 19, p. 286 and Hobbes 2012, vol. 3, ch. 35, p. 646.
[171] Tuck 2015, pp. 105, 137.   [172] Hobbes 2012, vol. 2, ch. 16, p. 250; ch. 17, p. 260.
[173] Hobbes 2012, vol. 2, ch. 17, p. 260.   [174] Hobbes 2012, vol. 2, ch. 17, p. 260.

Safetie'.[175] The sovereign becomes the 'representer' of the union of the people as a whole.[176] As Hobbes summarises, 'it is the Representer that beareth the Person, and but one Person: And *Unity*, cannot otherwise be understood in Multitude.'[177]

The sovereign continues to receive his authorisation from each and every one of his subjects. 'Because the Multitude naturally is not *One*, but *Many*; they cannot be understood for one; but many Authors, of every thing their Representative saith, or doth in their name'.[178] But in authorising a sovereign they grant him 'the *Right* to *Present* the Person of them all',[179] so that his basic duty becomes that of acting as 'their common Representer'.[180] With the sovereign thus installed, Hobbes at last feels able to speak not of the mere multitude but rather of the people. As he concludes, any sovereign may now be described as 'the absolute Representative of the people' and may be said to govern 'by the consent of the People'.[181]

Hobbes next turns his fire on his parliamentarian adversaries, deploying this analysis to question and undermine the radical inferences they had drawn from their rival account of what it means for the people to be represented. They had first argued that, because the people were originally possessed of sovereign power, it follows that, when they covenant with a king, the *universitas* of the people must remain *maior* or greater in standing than the king himself. Hobbes had offered no comment on this argument in *The Elements* or *De Cive*, but in *Leviathan* he deploys his analysis of representation to wave it aside. 'There is little ground', he scornfully replies, 'for the opinion of them, that say of Soveraign Kings, though they be *singulis maiores*, of greater Power than every one of their Subjects, yet they be *Universis minores*, of lesse power than them all together'.[182] The reason is that, because there is no such thing as the *universitas* or corporate body of the people, we can only make sense of the statement in one of two equally unsatisfactory ways. One is to suppose that, when the parliamentarian writers talk about 'all together' in contrast with 'every one', they are referring not to the person into which the multitude transforms itself when it authorises a sovereign representative, but simply to the multitude itself. But if this is so, then their argument can readily be dismissed. 'For if by *all together*, they mean not the collective

---

[175] Hobbes 2012, vol. 2, ch. 17, p. 260.
[176] Hobbes 2012, vol. 2, ch. 16, pp. 246, 248 and ch. 22, p. 354.
[177] Hobbes 2012, vol. 2, ch. 16, p. 248.   [178] Hobbes 2012, vol. 2, ch. 16, p. 250.
[179] Hobbes 2012, vol. 2, ch. 18, p. 264.   [180] Hobbes 2012, vol. 2, ch. 16, p. 250.
[181] Hobbes 2012, vol. 2, ch. 18, p. 264 and ch. 19, p. 286. On Hobbes's distinction between the multitude and the people see Astorga 2011.
[182] Hobbes 2012, vol. 2, ch. 18, p. 280.

body as one person, then *all together*, and *every one*, signifie the same; and the speech is absurd.' The only alternative is to suppose that, when they say 'all together', they *are* referring to the person into which the multitude transforms itself by authorising a sovereign representative. But if this is so, then their argument can be no less readily dismissed. For 'if by *all together*, they understand them as one Person (which person the Soveraign bears,) then the power of all together, is the same with the Soveraigns power; and so again the speech is absurd'.[183]

The parliamentarian writers had next argued that, when the people authorise a sovereign, it is open to them to negotiate the terms of his rule and, as Hobbes puts it, to impose conditions on him 'before-hand'.[184] Hobbes responds that this contention is even more obviously entangled in absurdity. Suppose the members of the multitude make a covenant with a designated ruler who, after his institution, instigates 'a breach of the Covenant' to which he initially agreed. By this stage the ruler will have entered upon his sovereign rights, in consequence of which his subjects will be obliged to 'own' whatever actions he may choose to perform in their names, because he will be performing them 'in the Person, and by the Right of every one of them in particular'. But this means that, whatever limitations on his actions he may have accepted beforehand, these agreements will now be null and void, because 'what act soever can be pretended by any one of them for breach thereof, is the act both of himselfe, and of all the rest'.[185] Any subject who now complains about his sovereign's behaviour will be lodging a complaint, ludicrously enough, against himself. As Hobbes confirms in his chapter on the liberty of subjects, 'nothing the Soveraign Representative can doe to a Subject, on what pretence soever, can properly be called Injustice, or Injury; because every Subject is Author of every act the Soveraign doth; so that he never wanteth Right to any thing.'[186]

A further implication drawn by the parliamentarian writers had been that, if a king should fail to honour the terms and conditions of his rule, he can be resisted by his own subjects and if necessary removed from power. Hobbes returns once more to his rival analysis of authorisation to show that this is the greatest absurdity of all. He considers the argument both in relation to 'casting off' an incumbent monarch and in relation to punishing or putting him to death. It is self-contradictory, he first responds, for a people to suppose they can 'transferre their Person from him that beareth it, to another Man, or other Assembly of men'. They have already bound themselves 'every man to every man, to Own, and be reputed Author

[183] Hobbes 2012, vol. 2, ch. 18, p. 280.   [184] Hobbes 2012, vol. 2, ch.18, p. 266.
[185] Hobbes 2012, vol. 2, ch. 18, p. 266.   [186] Hobbes 2012, vol. 2, ch. 21, p. 330.

of all, that he that already is their Soveraigne, shall do, and judge fit to be done'.[187] To cast him off will thus be to fall into the confusion of authorising and repudiating his actions at one and the same time. It is equally self-contradictory for the people to think of punishing an incumbent monarch or putting him to death. Given that 'every Subject is Author of the actions of his Soveraigne', this simply leads to the same confusion as before. Any subject who seeks to punish his sovereign will be condemning him for 'actions committed by himselfe.'[188]

The upshot of the theory of virtual representation developed by the parliamentarian writers had been that no political representation can be legitimate unless it takes the form of a recognisable image or likeness of the people as a whole. By the end of the 1640s this assumption had become so deeply entrenched that we find the protagonists of Parliament referring – in a now obsolete usage – to any body of people with the right to act in the name of a larger body as 'A Representative'.[189] This is obviously a commitment lethal to monarchy, and Hobbes fiercely rejects it. Given that there is nothing to be represented except the individual bodies 'of all and every one of the Multitude', there is no reason why this act of representation should not be performed equally well – and perhaps much better – by an individual body as by a body of people.[190] Hobbes draws this contrasting inference with heavy emphasis when considering the different forms of lawful government:

It is manifest, that men who are in absolute liberty, may, if they please, give Authority to One man, to represent them every one; as well as give such Authority to any Assembly of men whatsoever; and consequently may subject themselves, if they think good, to a Monarch, as absolutely, as to any other Representative.[191]

Hobbes speaks here of giving authority to a man, but he is careful to add that a woman can equally well stand as the person representative of us all.[192] He even suggests that, because women are sometimes more prudent than men, and because prudence is self-evidently a desirable virtue in a representative, women may in some cases be better suited than men to exercise dominion over others.[193] With this emphatic and inclusive vindication of monarchy, the parliamentarian contention that a satisfactory representation of the body of the people must itself be a body of people is summarily dismissed.

[187] Hobbes 2012, vol. 2, ch. 18, p. 264.   [188] Hobbes 2012, vol. 2, ch. 18, p. 270.
[189] See, for example, Gardiner (ed.) 2006, pp. 386, 387.
[190] Hobbes 2012, vol. 2, ch. 19, p. 284.   [191] Hobbes 2012, vol. 2, ch. 19, p. 286.
[192] Hobbes 2012, vol. 2, ch. 20, p. 310 refers to sovereign Queens, while Hobbes 2012 vol. 3, ch. 47, p. 1114 specifically mentions Queen Elizabeth of England.
[193] Hobbes 2012, vol. 2, ch. 20, p. 308.

The parliamentarian writers had sought to present the outcome of their argument in carefully reassuring terms. Somewhat disingenuously, they had maintained that they were merely defending a version of the familiar theory of mixed monarchy. The people of England, they suggested, were eventually able to establish just such a constitution, one in which the people were able to institute a representative assembly to check and balance the power of their kings. Turning to this final argument, Hobbes abandons his normally objective style of writing and reacts in tones of outrage. What this narrative completely fails to acknowledge is that the act of instituting the monarchy of which king Charles I was the eventual inheritor was *already* the act of authorising a representative. 'I know not', Hobbes replies, 'how this so manifest a truth, should of late be so little observed; that in a Monarchy, he that had the Soveraignty from a descent of 600 years, was alone called Soveraign, had the title of Majesty from every one of his Subjects, and was unquestionably taken by them for their King, was notwithstanding never considered as their Representative'.[194]

Once we recognise that Charles I was indeed the authorised representative of all his subjects, we can readily see according to Hobbes that the theories of mixed monarchy propounded by the democratical gentlemen are dangerously confused. He begins by referring to the standard version of the theory, according to which 'the Power of making Lawes' is made to depend (as he scornfully puts it) on 'the accidentall consent' of one man with two separate representative Assemblies. This system requires that 'the King bear the person of the People' while 'the generall Assembly bear also the person of the People' and 'another Assembly bear the person of a Part of the people'. But this arrangement cannot be described as a viable form of 'mixt Monarchy', because it is not a viable system of government at all. The effect is to institute 'not one Person, nor one Soveraign, but three Persons, and three Soveraigns', thereby creating 'not one independent Common-wealth, but three independent Factions', a perfect recipe for chaos and civil war.[195]

Hobbes admits, however, that this is not the understanding of mixed monarchy most favoured by the democratical gentlemen. They usually maintain that there are two basic elements in the mixture, king and Parliament, and that Parliament as the representative assembly of the sovereign people must predominate over the king. Hobbes replies that this is simply to repeat the same mistake. When the people of England instituted their monarchy, they granted to their kings 'the *Right* to *Present* the Person of them all'.[196] But 'where there is already erected a Soveraign

---

[194] Hobbes 2012, vol. 2, ch. 19, p. 286.   [195] Hobbes 2012, vol. 2, ch. 29, p. 512.
[196] Hobbes 2012, vol. 2, ch. 18, p. 264.

Power, there can be no other Representative of the same people, but onely to certain particular ends, by the Soveraign limited'.[197] The reason, Hobbes reminds us, is that otherwise the effect will be 'to erect two Soveraigns; and every man to have his person represented by two Actors'.[198] The only possible outcome will again be war, an outcome 'contrary to the end for which all Soveraignty is instituted.'[199]

The remaining question for Hobbes is thus about the true status of Parliaments under hereditary monarchies. Addressing this issue in chapter 22, he underscores the absurdity of supposing that they can ever be representative assemblies in the sense of having an independent right to speak and act in the name of the people. The reason, he repeats, is that the monarch will already be 'the absolute Representative of all the subjects', from which it follows that 'no other, can be Representative of any part of them, but so far forth, as he shall give leave'.[200] Hobbes's answer is thus that Parliaments can never amount to anything more than purely consultative bodies which monarchs may choose to summon from time to time if they happen to want some information or advice.

This is an astonishingly reactionary response. Despite everything that had happened in the meantime, Hobbes is simply reverting to the position taken up by the most high-flying defenders of divine right at the start of the civil war. There can be little doubt, however, that he fully intended to adopt as deflating a tone as possible when confronting the theories of parliamentary and popular sovereignty that had triumphed in the intervening years. He is willing, of course, to allow that any sovereign monarch, should he happen to think fit, may choose 'to give command to the towns, and other severall parts of their territory, to send to him their Deputies, to enforme him of the condition, and necessities of the Subjects, or to advise with him for the making of good Lawes, or for any other cause'.[201] He is even willing to concede that we can think of such deputies as representatives of the people, so that when summoned and brought together they may be said to constitute 'a Body Politique, representing every Subject'.[202] But he is unrepentant in concluding that we cannot possibly think of them as having an independent right at any stage to speak and act in the name of the populace as a whole. As he never tires of reminding us, to grant them this status would be to institute 'two Soveraigns, over the same people; which cannot consist with their Peace'.[203]

---

[197] Hobbes 2012, vol. 2, ch. 19, p. 286.   [198] Hobbes 2012, vol. 2, ch. 19, p. 286.
[199] Hobbes 2012, vol. 2, ch. 19, p. 286.   [200] Hobbes 2012, vol. 2, ch. 22, p. 350.
[201] Hobbes 2012, vol. 2, ch. 22, p. 366.   [202] Hobbes 2012, vol. 2, ch. 22, p. 366.
[203] Hobbes 2012, vol. 2, ch. 22, p. 368.

VI

Hobbes's theory of representative government might appear to leave him with an awkward difficulty. Of whom, on his account, is sovereignty to be predicated? To put the question the other way round – as Henry Parker had done – who is 'the proper Subject' of sovereign power?[204] The defenders of divine right had replied that sovereignty is the defining attribute of kings. But according to Hobbes no king enjoys a status any higher than that of an authorised representative. The democratical gentlemen had argued that the body of the people is the original and natural subject of sovereignty. But according to Hobbes there is no such thing as the body of the people. If, however, sovereignty is the property neither of kings nor of peoples, who can lay claim to it?

One of my aims in my concluding chapter will be to explain how Hobbes arrives at the distinctive answer he gives to this conundrum. Here, as a preview to that discussion, I simply wish to note his answer itself. As we have seen, he maintains that, when the members of a multitude agree 'every man with every man' to authorise an individual or an assembly to represent them, the effect is to convert them into one person. What we need to know, therefore, is the name of the person engendered by the multitude out of their agreement to authorise a representative. For this will be to know the true subject of the sovereignty that the sovereign representer merely holds the right to exercise.

As I noted at the end of chapter 2, Hobbes answers by way of reintroducing the classical argument later developed by a number of legal Commentators: that the name of the person who possesses sovereignty over a *civitas* or state must be the *persona civitatis* itself, the person of the state. Hobbes first tells us that 'a COMMON-WEALTH, or STATE, (in latine CIVITAS)'[205] can be defined as '*One Person, of whose Acts a great Multitude, by mutuall Covenants one with another, have made themselves every one the Author*'.[206] He then adds that the name of the person who 'bears' or 'carries' this person is the sovereign, who serves as 'the Representant of the Common-wealth'.[207] Here, as before, Hobbes closely echoes the Ciceronian terminology first introduced into Anglophone political discourse in the course of the English Reformation. As we have seen, Thomas Fitzherbert had already concluded that the sovereign of any state 'doth beare the person, & figure of the commonwealth'.[208] Hobbes likewise concludes that any sovereign representer 'beareth the

[204] [Parker] 1642, p. 44.
[205] For this formula see Hobbes 2012, vol. 2, The Introduction, p. 16.
[206] Hobbes 2012, vol. 2, ch. 17, p. 260.   [207] Hobbes 2012, vol. 3, ch. 42, p. 920.
[208] Fitzherbert 1621, p. 13.

Person' of the commonwealth or state,[209] so that 'the name of the person Commanding' is always '*Persona Civitatis*, the Person of the Commonwealth.'[210]

Hobbes tells us in the Epistle Dedicatory to *Leviathan* that 'I speak not of the men, but (in the Abstract) of the Seat of Power'.[211] He concludes by insisting that this seat is occupied not by any natural person or body of persons, but rather by the disembodied *persona fictione* or person 'by Fiction' of the state. However, he is conventional enough to believe that, like the offspring of any lawful union, the person 'generated' by the union of the multitude deserves its own name. Following out his metaphor of marriage and procreation, he accordingly goes on to perform the appropriate act of baptism. He gravely announces that 'this is the Generation of that great LEVIATHAN, or rather (to speake more reverently) of that *Mortall God*, to which wee owe under the *Immortall God*, our peace and defence'.[212]

Hobbes's allusion is to the sea monster described in chapter 41 of the Book of Job, which he treats as an image of terrifying strength. The claim that we need to submit to such an absolute form of power had been denounced by the newly sovereign House of Commons as recently as its *Declaration* of March 1649. 'Such an unaccountable Officer', Parliament had warned, would be 'a strange Monster to be permitted by mankinde.'[213] Hobbes unhesitatingly hurls back the taunt. The main burden of his theory of representation is that we have no option but to permit our sovereign to personate just such a monster if we are to have any prospect of living together in security and peace.

---

[209] Hobbes 2012, vol. 2, ch. 16, p. 248. See also Hobbes 2012, vol. 2 ch. 17, p. 262 and ch. 18, p. 264, on how the sovereign 'carryeth' and has 'the *Right* to *Present*' the Person of the state.

[210] Hobbes 2012, vol. 2, ch. 26, pp. 414, 416.

[211] Hobbes 2012, vol. 2, sig. A, 2r, p. [4].   [212] Hobbes 2012, vol. 2, ch. 17, p. 260.

[213] *A Declaration* 1649, p. 14.

10   Hobbes and the Humanist Frontispiece

I

Although Hobbes's intellectual interests shifted towards the physical sciences in his middle years, I have been arguing that his later writings continue to bear many traces of his earlier engagement with the humanistic disciplines. The present chapter is concerned with the most visible of these traces: his enduring interest in the visual representation of his political ideas, and his consequent inclusion of emblematic frontispieces in his works of civil science as well as in his translations of classical texts.

To explain this commitment, we first need to return to the rhetorical tradition in which Hobbes was nurtured as a student at the University of Oxford in the opening years of the seventeenth century. As I showed in chapter 1, the avowed aim of the classical rhetoricians was to offer instructions on how to write and speak in the most 'winning' style. One of the most potent means of persuading an audience to adopt your point of view will always be to add *pathos* to *logos*, to arouse the emotions of your hearers in such a way as to shift them round to your side. The figure of Antonius puts the point with characteristic frankness in Cicero's *De oratore*, arguing that 'you must try to move them so that they become ruled not by deliberation and judgment but rather by sheer impetus and perturbation of mind.'[1]

This chapter is largely a new piece of work, but its origins lie in Skinner 2008a, pp. 182–98 and Skinner 2009b. For permission to draw on Skinner 2008a I am indebted to the Cambridge University Press; for permission to make use of material from Skinner 2009b my thanks are due to Konstantinos Peslis and Cambridge Scholars Publishing. For commenting on these earlier texts I remain extremely grateful to Annabel Brett, Dominique Colas, Susan James, Oleg Kharkhordin, Noel Malcolm, Eric Nelson and James Tully, while to Rowan Dorin I owe special thanks for invaluable research assistance. Most of all I want to thank Kinch Hoekstra for a lecture he delivered at the European University Institute in 2005 on Hobbes's political iconography, to which my article of 2009 was much indebted. The present chapter has additionally benefited from discussions with Susanna Berger, Horst Bredekamp, Carlo Ginsburg, Susan James, Thomas Maissen, Eric Nelson, Raffaella Santi and Wolfgang Schmale.
[1] Cicero 1942, II. XLII. 178, vol. 1, p. 324: 'ipse sic moveatur, ut impetu quodam animi et perturbatione, magis quam iudicio aut consilio regatur.' For a fuller discussion see Skinner 1996, pp. 120–7.

As to how this can be done, the rhetoricians have a number of practical suggestions to make. One of the most important is that you must learn to present your case with so much vividness and immediacy that your audience comes to 'see' what you are trying to describe. This is the quality described by Quintilian as *enargeia*, the capacity we display 'when we not only say what is true but in a certain sense reveal it to the sight'.[2] If we can learn to speak with this degree of vividness, we can present our hearers with 'an image of an entire scene that is somehow painted in words'.[3] The orator's power to persuade is thus held to depend in large part on the ability to appeal, in Quintilian's phrase, 'to the eyes of the mind.'[4]

This belief in the persuasive force of *enargeia* was strongly reinforced by the rhetoricians of the English Renaissance. Abraham Fraunce refers in his treatise on poetics to Horace's dictum *ut pictura poesis*, describing poetry as 'a speaking picture, and paynting, a dumbe poetry'.[5] Fraunce goes on to argue that 'the picturing, fashioning, figuring or, as it were, personall representing of things in verse after this manner, is most effectuall and avayleable, to move mens mindes'.[6] Henry Peacham similarly argues in *The Garden of Eloquence* that one of the most compelling means of winning round an audience is to 'expresse and set forth a thing so plainly and lively, that it seemeth rather painted in tables, then declared with words.'[7] Richard Sherry adds in his *Treatise of Schemes and Tropes* that the best means of painting such verbal pictures is by an apt use of metaphors. No other trope 'perswadeth more effecteouslye, none sheweth the thyng before our eyes more evidently', and in consequence 'none moveth more mightily the affections'.[8]

A number of humanists soon began to develop a further and closely related argument. If, they proposed, these emotional effects can be produced by the creation of verbal images, then an even more effective means of producing the same effects will be to supply our auditors with *actual* images to accompany the statement of our case. This is the commitment underlying the rise to overwhelming popularity in the middle decades of the sixteenth century of the new genre of *emblemata* or emblem-books.[9] As Henry Estienne was later to explain in his *Art of Making Devises*, it came to be recognised that the most compelling means of presenting weighty moral and religious arguments is to put words and pictures

[2] Quintilian 2001. 4. 2. 64, vol. 2, p. 250: 'veri non dicendum est sed quodammodo etiam ostendum est'. Quintilian repeats the point at 6. 2. 32, vol. 3, p. 60.
[3] Quintilian 2001, 8. 3. 63, vol. 3, p. 376: 'tota rerum imago quodammodo verbis depingitur'.
[4] See Quintilian 2001, 8. 3. 62, vol. 3, p. 376 on 'oculis mentis'.
[5] Fraunce 1592, fo. 3v. Cf. Horace 1926, p. 480, l. 361.   [6] Fraunce 1592, fo. 4r.
[7] Peacham 1593, pp. 134–5.   [8] Sherry 1550, sig. C, 4v.
[9] See Clements 1960; Watson 1993; Bath 1994.

together. The emblemists realised that, 'by subjecting the figure to our view, and the sense to our understanding', they could hope to convey moral messages in a style more 'pleasant and significative' than by words alone.[10]

The earliest writer to put this insight into practice was the humanist jurist Andrea Alciato, whose collection of *Emblemata* was first published at Augsburg in 1531.[11] Alciato's text was frequently reprinted, and the definitive Latin version was issued at Lyon in 1550, the year of his death.[12] Alciato's technique of juxtaposing edifying pictures with explanatory verses was initially taken up with particular enthusiasm in France, where the pioneers were Barthélemy Aneau and Guillaume de la Perrière.[13] Aneau directly refers to Horace's dictum about poetry as picturing, entitling his collection of emblems *Picta poesis*.[14] Meanwhile the Italian tradition of emblem-books remained vital to the evolution of the genre as a vehicle for moral and political reflection in the latter part of the century. Achille Bocchi's *Symbolicarum Quaestionum* was published in 1555 and again in 1574,[15] and in 1593 there appeared at Rome one of the most influential of all these works, Cesare Ripa's *Iconologia*, which went through seven further Italian printings in the first half of the seventeenth century.[16] The genre may be said to have arrived in England in 1586, the year in which Geffrey Whitney, drawing heavily on Alciato, produced his *Choice of Emblemes*,[17] after which similar texts were published by Henry Peacham, George Wither and Francis Quarles in the opening decades of the new century.[18]

A further development in the use of *emblemata* arose in France and the Netherlands in the latter part of the sixteenth century. From using illustrative verses to explain puzzling pictures, a number of printers took the more ambitious step of producing moral and religious works in which an attempt was made to encapsulate the entire argument of the book in a prefatory image. The aim was not merely to embellish the text, but to introduce and summarise its contents in a memorable and persuasive style.[19] By the early seventeenth century, these images were already being described by English writers as frontispieces. Richard Brathwaite notes in his *Schollers Medley* of 1614 that a growing number of works are being published 'with faire and beautifull frontispices' to suggest that

---

[10] Estienne 1646, pp. 7–8.
[11] The information in this paragraph is taken from Skinner 2008a, pp. 7–9.
[12] Alciato 1550.   [13] Perrière 1553.   [14] Aneau 1552.
[15] On Bocchi see Watson 1993.   [16] The edition I use is Ripa 1611.
[17] Whitney 1586. Manning 1988 discusses Whitney's debt to Alciato, from whom he took more than eighty images.
[18] Bath 1994, pp. 90–129, 199–232.
[19] This is the principal change outlined in Corbett and Lightbown 1979, pp. 14–34.

'rare buildings of Art and Nature' stand behind these 'comely portalles' and deserve to be further explored.[20] By this stage the emblematic frontispiece had become a fact of English publishing life.

II

So far I have been examining the assumptions about the power of images that would have been familiar to anyone who – like Hobbes – had been nurtured in the rhetorical culture of Renaissance humanism. I now wish to consider the impact of these assumptions on the production of treatises in the *studia humanitatis* in early-modern England. We first need to note that the emergence of the emblematic frontispiece as a distinct artistic genre brought with it several alterations to the appearance of printed books. To create a simple decorative frontispiece it had been sufficient to make use of woodcuts. But emblematic frontispieces called for greater detail and more complex illusionist effects, thereby making the use of engravings virtually indispensable. The resulting images either took the form of etchings, in which an incised plate was exposed to acid, or else of dry-chisel engravings, in which the plate was directly incised. For the rendering of the finest detail the latter method was normally preferred, but both techniques soon began to be widely used in the production of illustrated books.

We also need to note some changes to the way in which book-titles were displayed. With woodcut frontispieces the typical arrangement had been to insert the title into the centre of the ornamental border in movable type so that the design could be reused.[21] But with the advent of emblematic frontispieces several new styles came into vogue. Sometimes the frontispiece contained no reference to the title, so that a separate title-page was required. Sometimes the design incorporated the title, but the book was nevertheless given a separate title-page – as in the case of Hobbes's *Leviathan*. But the most usual arrangement was for the frontispiece to serve as the sole title-page – as in Hobbes's translation of Thucydides.[22] The title, in other words, was engraved rather than set in type, generally giving rise to a more elegant effect.

Although these developments were introduced over a long period, the names of two notable pioneers stand out. One was Christopher Plantin (*c*.1520–89), a native of Touraine who established a printing-house in

[20] Brathwaite 1614, p. 21.   [21] Corbett and Lightbown 1979, pp. 5–6.
[22] For other examples see Homer 1611, Seneca 1620, Ovid 1626, Virgil 1632. Bearing this in mind, we ought not to distinguish too sharply between 'frontispieces' and 'engraved title-pages' as some commentators have done. See, for example, Prokhovnik 1991, p. 147, n. 1.

Antwerp in 1555, rapidly transforming it into a major business in which large numbers of printers and engravers were trained. He became celebrated as a publisher of emblem-books, and produced the first edition of the earliest English contribution to the genre, Geffrey Whitney's *Choice of Emblemes* of 1586. Plantin's most important project was the creation of the Antwerp Polyglot Bible, which he issued in eight volumes between 1568 and 1573, with copious illustrations and five fully engraved emblematic frontispieces.[23]

A second leading innovator was Jacques Callot (c.1592–1635), who began by training as an etcher in Rome and Florence before returning to his native France in 1621.[24] He invented several new techniques, one of which enabled etchers to achieve the detailed effects previously obtainable only by dry-chisel engraving. These innovations were subsequently publicised by his pupil Abraham Bosse (c.1602–74), who worked with Callot in Paris between 1628 and 1630[25] and became one of the most prolific engravers of the next generation in France.[26] Bosse included an account of Callot's discoveries in his treatise on the art of engraving in 1645, prefacing it with a fine encomium in which he declared that Callot 'has so extremely perfected this art that one can say he has brought it to the highest point one can make it reach'.[27]

There had been no English tradition of engraving in the sixteenth century, but with the growing popularity of emblematic frontispieces there was suddenly a rising demand for the skill. A prominent role in meeting the requirements of the new market was played by a Dutch family named van de Passe. Crispijn van de Passe (c.1564–1637) began by making prints for Christopher Plantin and other publishers in Antwerp,[28] but went on to establish his own printing business in Cologne and later in Utrecht.[29] One of his apprentices in Cologne appears to have been Renold Elstrack (1570–c.1625),[30] one of the earliest English engravers to establish himself in London, who later became well-known for his frontispiece to James I's *Workes*.[31] Crispijn van de Passe's eldest son Simon (1595–1647) emigrated to London in 1616, where he worked until 1622.[32] He seems in turn to

---

[23] Bowen and Imhof 2008, pp. 84–102, 205–7.   [24] Sadoul 1969, pp. 381–2.

[25] Goldstein 2012, p. 5. On Callot in Paris see Sadoul 1969, pp. 391–2.

[26] Goldstein 2012, p. 6 estimates that Bosse produced over 1,500 prints.

[27] Bosse 1645, p. 2: Callot 'a extremement perfectionné cét art, & de telle sorte qu'on peut dire qu'il la mis au plus haut poinct qu'on le puisse faire aller'.

[28] Veldman 2001, pp. 29–31; Bowen and Imhof 2008, pp. 44, 347.

[29] Veldman 2001, pp. 43, 173.

[30] According to DNB Elstrack was 'in all probability a pupil' of de Passe. But this claim is not repeated in ODNB.

[31] The frontispiece is signed 'Renold Elstrack sculpsit'. For a reproduction see Hind 1952–64, vol. 2, Plate 112(a); for a discussion see Corbett and Lightbown 1979, pp. 136–42.

[32] Veldman 2001, pp. 243, 251.

have trained – and undoubtedly influenced – two other English engravers of this pioneering period, Thomas Cecill (fl.1625–40) and John Payne (1607–47).[33]

I now turn to consider how these developments affected the production of English books in the *studia humanitatis*. As I noted in chapter 1, there were three main elements in 'humanistic' learning: poetry, moral philosophy and ancient history. If we turn first to moral philosophy we find that, when the earliest English version of Aristotle's *Nicomachean Ethics* was published in 1547, its title-page was elaborately adorned (Figure 10.1).[34] So too was the title-page of Cicero's *De officiis* in the bilingual edition first published in 1568, and so too was the title-page of Thomas Lodge's translation of Seneca's moral works in 1620 (Figures 10.2 and 10.3).[35]

With Lodge's edition, however, we pass far beyond the limitations of the earlier frontispieces. The woodcuts prefacing the Aristotle and Cicero translations consist of little more than crude caryatidic figures on either side of the title with escutcheons above. By contrast, Lodge's translation is prefaced by a folio-sized engraving that introduces the reader to many details about Seneca's life and thought. The artist was Renold Elstrack, who may have received his original training, as we have seen, in the workshop of Crispin van de Passe.[36] To the left of the title Elstrack displays the crowned Nero carrying the lyre on which he fiddled while Rome burned, while below him is a scene of the kind of lasciviousness with which tyranny was associated. To the right, and opposing Nero, stands a representation of Seneca's stoicism in the form of Temperance, a female figure seen in the act of diluting wine with water, while below her is a scene of studious contemplation. Above the title appear the stoic philosophers from whom Seneca learned about the virtues; underneath is an illustration of the constancy that their teachings promoted in his life. Beneath the title we see the suicide of Seneca, who has opened his veins in his bath. Stoic constancy is shown to triumph over tyranny only through a willingness to embrace death.

A similar narrative can be traced in the publishing of classical poetry. When Virgil's *Aeneid* was first printed in English in 1553, the title-page was embellished with a woodcut showing a classical wreath surrounding the title with two *putti* kneeling below (Figure 10.4).[37]

When Arthur Golding produced the earliest English version of Ovid's *Metamorphoses* in 1565, the title-page was surmounted by an escutcheon and similarly embellished with classical details, including four musicians

---

[33] Hind 1952–64, vol. 3, pp. 6, 31; Veldman 2001, p. 245.
[34] Aristotle 1547, a translation by John Wilkinson of Brunetto Latini's abridgement of Aristotle's text.
[35] Cicero 1568; Seneca 1620.   [36] The frontispiece is signed 'R. E. sc:'.
[37] Virgil 1553.

Figure 10.1 Aristotle (1547). *The Ethiques of Aristotle*, trans. John Wilkinson, London, Frontispiece.

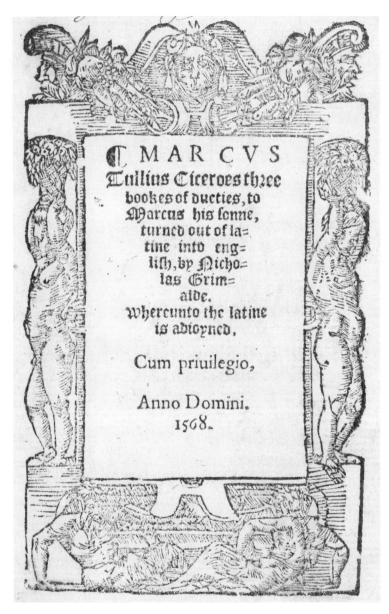

Figure 10.2 Cicero (1568). *Marcus Tullius Ciceroes three bookes of dueties*, trans. Nicholas Grimalde, London, Frontispiece.

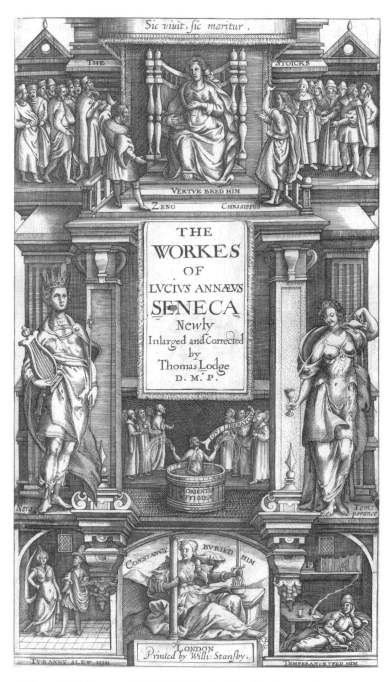

Figure 10.3 Seneca (1620). *The Workes of Lucius Annaeus Seneca*, trans. Thomas Lodge, 2nd edn, London, Frontispiece by Renold Elstrack.

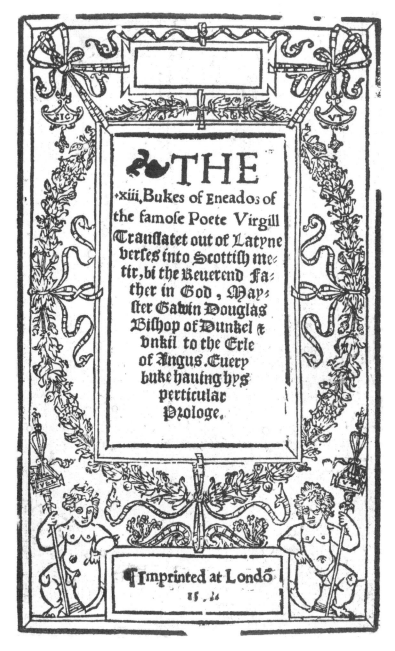

Figure 10.4 Virgil (1553). *The XIII Bukes of Eneados*, trans. Gawin Douglas, London, Frontispiece.

whose presence gestures at the parallels between music and lyric poetry (Figure 10.5).[38]

When Arthur Hall's pioneering translation of Homer appeared in 1581, this too was prefaced with a mainly decorative frontispiece surmounted by an escutcheon, although in this case the figures of Fame and Victory were also introduced (Figure 10.6).[39]

If we now turn, however, to English translations of the same texts published a generation later, we find these simple woodcuts superseded by complex emblematic frontispieces in which an attempt is made to introduce and summarise the leading themes of the work. When George Chapman published his translation of Homer's *Iliad* in 1611, he prefaced it with an engraved title-page in which he provided his readers with much information about the poem (Figure 10.7).[40] The artist with whom Chapman worked was William Hole, best-known for creating the frontispiece to the London edition of the Geneva Bible in 1607.[41] From Hole's design for the *Iliad* we learn that Homer's narrative centres on a confrontation between Achilles and Hector, and thus between Greece and Troy. Both heroes are portrayed in full armour, and both stand on plinths on which their names are inscribed. Above Hector reposes Apollo with his lyre; an accompanying cartouche informs us that 'Apollo stood for Troy'. Opposite him reclines Vulcan, holding a Greek helmet in his right hand and a hammer in his left, an allusion to his forging of the armour of Achilles; his cartouche informs us that 'Vulcan was against Troy'.[42] Between them the blind Homer is crowned by a winged cherub with laurel wreaths.[43]

When George Sandys published his new translation of Ovid's *Metamorphoses* in 1626, this was likewise prefaced by an elaborate engraved title-page. The artist was Thomas Cecill, by this time one of the leading dry-chisel engravers of his time.[44] Sandys took the opportunity to press on his readers a general interpretation of the mythical transformations that Ovid loves to describe (Figure 10.8).[45] The most celebrated of these – Circe changing Ulysses's men into pigs – is duly illustrated.[46] But the main argument of the frontispiece is that, as

---

[38] Ovid 1565.

[39] Homer 1581. On either side of the escutcheon we see Fame with her trumpet and a winged Victory with her palm of glory and laurel wreath.

[40] Homer 1611.   [41] The frontispiece is signed 'Will: Hole sculp:'.

[42] The cartouches together make a quotation from Ovid's *Tristia*: 'Mulciber in Troiam, pro Troia stabat Apollo.' See Ovid 1924, I. II. 5, p. 12.

[43] For further discussion see Corbett and Lightbown 1979, pp. 112–18.

[44] The frontispiece is signed 'T. Cecill sculq. Lon'.   [45] Ovid 1626.

[46] Ovid 1977–84, XIV. 273–85, 299–305, vol. 2, pp. 318–20. The roundel surrounding the image quotes Horace's *Satires*: 'Affigit humo divinae particulam aurae' – '[the body] fastens to earth a fragment of the divine spirit.' See Horace 1926, II. II. 79, p. 142.

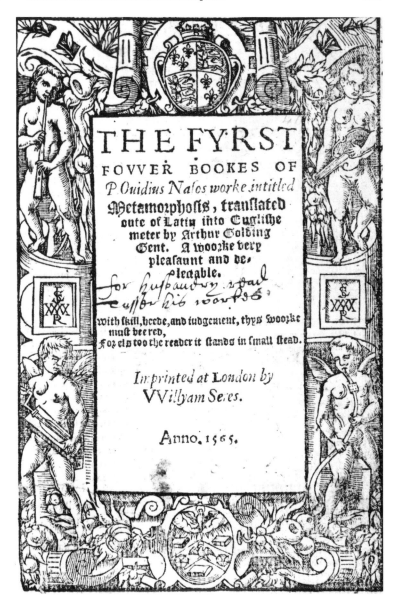

Figure 10.5 Ovid (1565). *The Fyrst Fower Bookes of P. Ovidius Nasos worke intitled Metamorphosis*, London, Frontispiece.

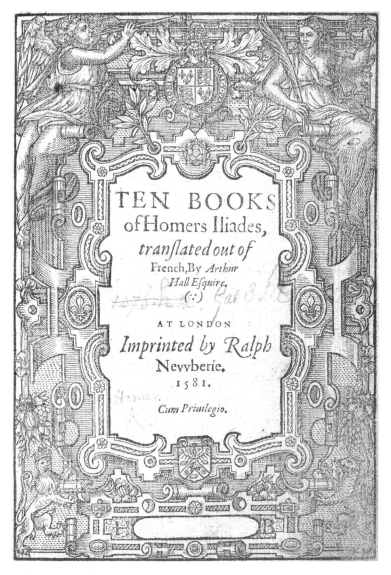

Figure 10.6 Homer (1581). *Ten Books of Homers Iliades*, trans. Arthur Hall, London, Frontispiece.

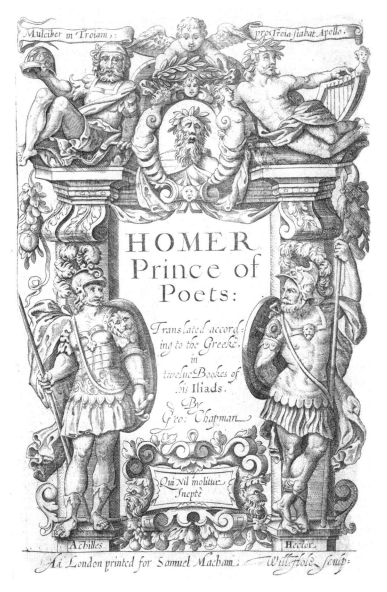

Figure 10.7 Homer (1611). *Homer Prince of Poets*, trans. George Chapman, London, Frontispiece by William Hole.

Figure 10.8 Ovid (1626). *Ovid's Metamorphosis Englished by G[eorge] S[andys]*, London, Frontispiece by Thomas Cecill.

it states, Ovid 'taught us what is formed by reason and by love.'[47] More specifically, Ovid is claimed to have argued that the power of love must be subdued by wisdom if we are to attain our highest goals. Although Venus is portrayed in the company of Cupid, and strikes an alluring pose, Minerva stands opposed to her in battle array, wielding a lance and holding a shield to ward off Cupid's darts.[48] We are also given a strong hint that Apollo, who reclines above them with his lyre, must have a prominent role in the narrative. Ovid does indeed hold his lustfulness up to scorn, especially in Book I, in which he falls in love with Daphne at first sight. She escapes by persuading her father to transform her into a laurel, thereby leaving Apollo to make absurd protestations of love to a tree.[49] The motto above Apollo's head admonishes us to avoid such excesses, proclaiming that 'it is virtue that brings us heavenwards'.[50] The entire design offers us an introduction to the *Metamorphoses* in which Ovid's amorous tales are reassuringly moralised.

When John Vicars's new translation of Virgil's *Aeneid* appeared in 1632, this too was prefaced by an engraved title-page containing extensive information about the poem (Figure 10.9).[51] The artist was John Payne, who was probably trained, as we have seen, by Simon van de Passe.[52] From the posture of the two dominating warriors in Payne's design we are able to infer that the poem must treat of a conflict between Aeneas and Turnus. Each stands on a plinth inscribed with his name, and each confronts the other ferociously and fully armed. There is also a strong hint that two women must have played a prominent role in the narrative. Above Aeneas's head Dido sits in the company of Cupid, an indication that she will be smitten with love for Aeneas. Above Turnus's head we see Juno in the company of her peacocks, conveying by her proximity to Turnus her enmity towards the Trojans, and above all to Aeneas. Below the antagonists Aeneas is shown carrying his father and leading his son away from burning Troy, while above them sails a galleon symbolizing the voyage that led Aeneas to Italy and the founding of Rome.

If we look finally at the third humanist discipline, that of ancient history, a similar narrative can again be traced. The earliest English version of a major work of classical history was Anthony Cope's translation of Livy's narrative of the Punic wars, first published in 1544 (Figure 10.10).[53]

[47] Figure 10.8: 'Docuit quae amore et sapientia formantur.'
[48] We also see the four elements, and are told that 'ex his oriuntur cuncta' – 'from these everything arises'. The quotation is from Lucretius 1975, I. 714–15, p. 58. Earth is shown with her fruits, water is symbolised by Neptune, fire by Jupiter with a salamander (which flourishes in flames) and air by Juno, consort of Jupiter and queen of the air.
[49] Ovid 1977–84, I. 473–567, vol. 1, pp. 34–42.   [50] Figure 10.8: 'Ad aethera virtus.'
[51] Virgil 1632.   [52] The frontispiece is signed 'I.P'.   [53] Livy 1544.

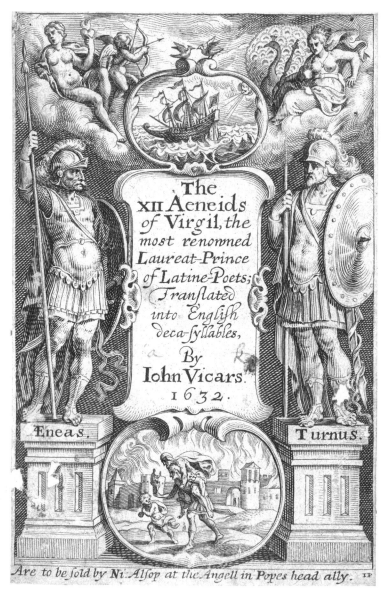

Figure 10.9 Virgil (1632). *The XII Aeneids of Virgil*, trans. John Vicars, London, Frontispiece by John Payne.

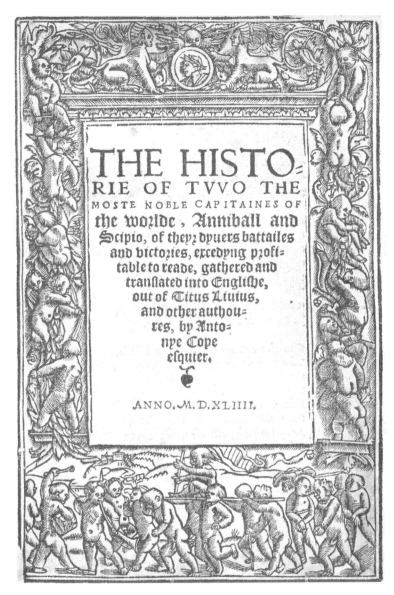

Figure 10.10 Livy (1544). *The Historie of Two the Moste Noble Captaines of the worlde, Anniball and Scipio*, trans. Anthony Cope, London, Frontispiece.

Cope's translation was followed by Thomas Nicolls's version of Thucydides, which appeared in 1550 (Figure 10.11).[54] Next came Nicholas Smyth's translation of Poliziano's Latin version of Herodian in 1556 (Figure 10.12), and in the following year appeared Thomas Paynell's and Alexander Barclay's translation of the two surviving histories of Sallust (Figure 10.13).[55] The final work in this early group was Arthur Golding's rendering of Caesar's account of 'his martiall exploytes in the Realme of Gallia', first published in 1565 (Figure 10.14).[56]

Opening any of these books, we come upon a title-page adorned with a woodcut. As before, the decorative conventions are severely limited. We typically see an escutcheon at the top, with *putti* and other classical elements surrounding the titles. In the case of Herodian (Figure 10.12), the woodcut showing two *putti* kneeling beneath a classical wreath simply reuses the one we have already seen in the 1553 translation of the *Aeneid* (Figure 10.4). The only instance in which these conventions are not followed is in the Sallust title-page, which shows two caryatidic figures supporting the title (Figure 10.13). But here too the image is conventional, and we have already encountered it in the translation of Aristotle's *Ethics* in 1547 and Cicero's *De officiis* in 1568 (Figures 10.1 and 10.2).

If, however, we shift our attention to the translations of the same works published in the next generation, we come upon some remarkable developments.[57] Consider first Anthony Cope's translation of Livy, which was reissued in 1590. As before there is a frontispiece, but in place of the decorative *putti* of 1544 we find a rhetorical reading of the alleged moral to be drawn from Livy's account of how Scipio defeated Hannibal (Figure 10.15).[58] At the top Victory is shown reclining with her palm of glory and laurel wreath. On either side of the title stand two statues, both on pedestals under canopies, who are likewise in classical garb. To the left stands Justice with her sword; to the right Prudence with her snake, a reminder of St Matthew's injunction (10:16) to be wise as serpents and innocent as doves. The edifying argument conveyed by the frontispiece is that Scipio achieved his victory over Hannibal solely by means of virtue.

A no less complex emblem adorns the title-page of Philemon Holland's translation of the complete extant books of Livy's history, which was first published in 1600 (Figure 10.16).[59] We see at the top of this image the walled city of Rome, with the *persona civitatis* fully armed for protection and conquest, while a motto surrounding the central roundel informs

---

[54] Thucydides 1550.   [55] Herodian 1556 and Sallust 1557.   [56] Caesar 1565.

[57] This is not to say we always find a shift from decorative to emblematic frontispieces. When Golding's translation of Caesar was reissued in 1590, and when Heywood's new version of Sallust was published in 1608, neither included a frontispiece at all.

[58] Livy 1590.   [59] Livy 1600.

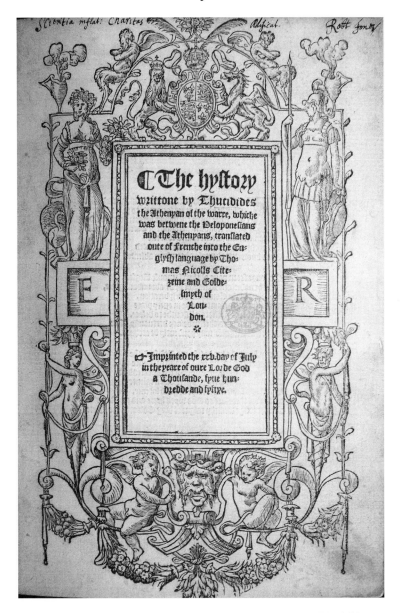

Figure 10.11 Thucydides (1550). *The hystory writtone by Thucidides*, trans. Thomas Nicolls, London, Frontispiece.

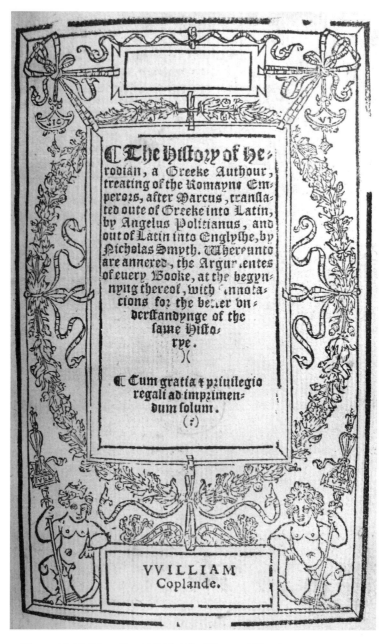

¶ The History of Herodian, a Greeke Authour, treating of the Romayne Emperors, after Marcus, translated oute of Greeke into Latin, by Angelus Politianus, and out of Latin into Englyshe, by Nicholas Smyth. Whereunto are annexed, the Argumentes of euery Booke, at the begynnyng thereof, with Annotacions for the better vnderstandynge of the same Histo-rye.
)(

¶ Cum gratia & priuilegio regali ad impzimen-dum solum.
(·)

VVILLIAM
Coplande.

Figure 10.12 Herodian (1556). *The History of Herodian*, trans. Nicholas Smyth, London, Frontispiece.

Figure 10.13 Sallust (1557). *The Conspiracie of Catiline ... with the historye of Jugurth,* trans. Alexander Barclay, London, Frontispiece.

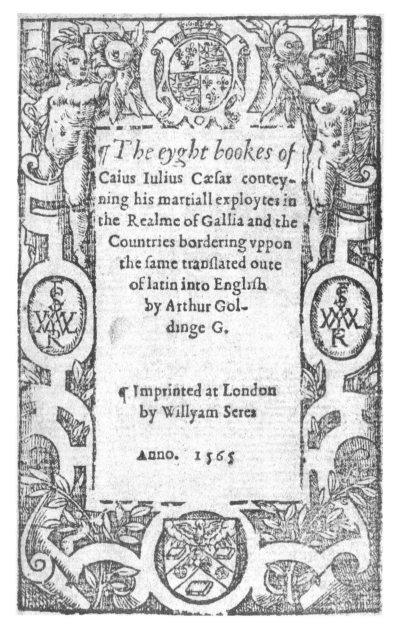

Figure 10.14 Caesar (1565). *The eyght bookes of Caius Julius Caesar conteyning his martiall exploytes in the Realme of Gallia*, trans. Arthur Golding, London, Frontispiece.

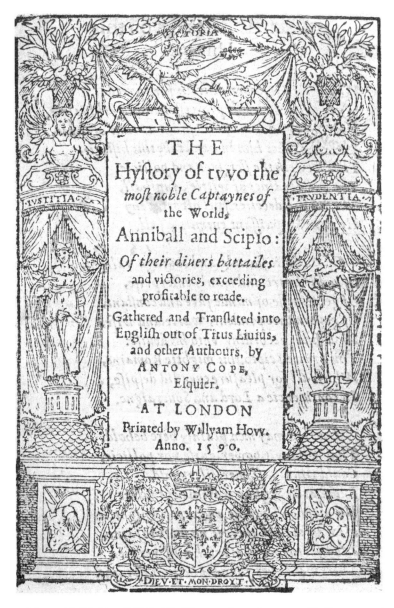

Figure 10.15 Livy (1590). *The Hystory of two the moste noble Captaynes of the World, Anniball and Scipio*, trans. Anthony Cope, London, Frontispiece.

Figure 10.16 Livy (1600). *The Romane Historie Written by T. Livius of Padua*, trans. Philemon Holland, London, Frontispiece.

us of 'the means by which the republic was conserved'. The indispensable means is said to have been the maintenance of justice, whose scales are shown in equipoise, together with a cornucopia to assure us that one of the fruits of justice is prosperity. The message conveyed is that, by means of these qualities, the republic was not only preserved but rose to fame and glory. On the left is Fame with her trumpet, while on the right we again see Victory with her palm of glory and laurel wreath. The frontispiece powerfully adumbrates a central commitment of Livy's history, his unrepentant preference for the republic over the principate.

Consider next Herodian's history of Imperial Rome. When James Maxwell published his new translation in 1635, the text was again prefaced with a frontispiece. But in place of the classical *putti* and wreathes of the 1556 edition we find a melodramatic image, the meaning of which is spelled out in some accompanying verses promising the reader a varied and lurid set of tales (Figure 10.17).[60] The central tree represents the imperial state of Rome, the branches of which are being shaken by Fate. The emperors, who are falling like leaves, are being collected into two urns at the base of the picture. The bearded man on the left – a portrait of Herodian himself – weighs their actions in the scales of justice, after which he delivers his verdict to Fame on the right, who trumpets their resulting glory or shame.

I turn finally to Thucydides's history of the Peloponnesian war. As we have seen, this was initially translated into English by Thomas Nicolls in 1550. But this version was wholly reliant on Claude de Seyssel's French translation, which had been taken not from the original Greek but from the Latin translation made by Lorenzo Valla in the 1460s. For English students of the humanities, one outstanding challenge accordingly remained that of producing a translation of Thucydides's notoriously difficult text directly from the Greek. The scholar who successfully met this challenge was Thomas Hobbes. Basing himself on Emilio Porta's edition, Hobbes issued his version in 1629 as *Eight Bookes of the Peloponnesian Warre*.[61] This was Hobbes's first published work, and revealed him at a stroke as a philologist of exceptional accomplishment. It also showed him to be a follower of humanist literary practices in a more eye-catching way. The title-page of Nicolls's translation of 1550 had been adorned with a conventional woodcut showing two *putti* beneath the title and an escutcheon above (Figure 10.11). By contrast, Hobbes underlines his humanist credentials by prefacing his work with a spectacular engraved title-page in which he not only introduces his readers to some of Thucydides's leading arguments, but seeks to highlight what he evidently takes to be the central moral of Thucydides's work (Figure 10.18).[62]

The artist of the title-page was Thomas Cecill, whom we have already encountered as the designer of the frontispiece to Sandys's translation of Ovid in 1626.[63] Hobbes must undoubtedly have authorised Cecill's design, which contains so much information about Thucydides's narrative as to suggest that Hobbes must also have had a hand in creating it. We learn from the three panels at the top that the war mentioned in

---

[60] Herodian 1635.
[61] Hobbes 1629. For his use of Porta's edition see Hobbes 1843, vol. 8, p. ix.
[62] Hobbes 1629.   [63] The frontispiece is signed 'T Cecill sculp.'

Figure 10.17 Herodian (1635). *Herodian of Alexandria His Historie*, trans. J[ames] M[axwell], London, Frontispiece.

Figure 10.18 Thucydides (1629). *Eight Bookes of the Peloponnesian Warre*, trans. Thomas Hobbes, London, Frontispiece by Thomas Cecill.

Thucydides's title took place in Greece, and that it was fought between Athens and Sparta. The broad panel running across the base shows that there was fighting at sea as well as on land, while the two larger panels below the pictures of the rival cities show that the leaders of the conflict were Archidamus and Pericles, who confront one another in full armour and warlike stance.

We are also given a strong sense of the relative capacity of Sparta and Athens to wage the war. Pericles, as the *titulus* on the panel below his portrait reveals, was associated with the *hoi polloi*, the many-headed multitude. Rather than deliberating, the members of the Athenian democracy are shown passively listening (or in some cases not listening) to a harangue, which is being delivered by a demagogue gesturing with the open palm of rhetoric, thereby suggesting that he is merely playing on the emotions of the crowd. The moral we are clearly expected to draw is one that Hobbes was later to emphasise in *The Elements of Law*. Under democracy 'there is no means any ways to deliberate and give counsel what to do', so that 'a democracy, in effect, is no more than an aristocracy of orators, interrupted sometimes with the temporary monarchy of one orator.'[64]

In sharp contrast, Archidamus is associated with a body of *Aristoi*, an aristocratic council pictured in the panel below his portrait. The man seated at the left-hand end of the table appears to be Archidamus himself. He has a forked beard, and he wears a spiked crown, just as he does in his portrait above. He is carrying a sceptre, the only member of the group to bear an insignium of political authority, and he appears to be presiding over the meeting. The man on his left turns his open hand towards the king, thereby conveying (according to Quintilian's analysis of gesture) that he is putting a question.[65] The king and four of his seven counsellors respond by raising an index-finger, this being the standard sign (Quintilian tells us) for indicating a commitment.[66] The two other counsellors do not react; one is lost in thought, while the other learnedly consults a book. Nevertheless, and even without the vote of the king, a majority opinion has clearly been reached on whatever question was raised, and has evidently been arrived at by serious deliberation and debate.

As an explication of the constitution of Sparta, however, this portrayal is unrecognisable. Ever since the publication of North's translation of Plutarch's *Lives* in 1579, it had been widely known that, from an early date, Sparta had been ruled by two hereditary kings, never a single king.[67]

---

[64] Hobbes 1969, 21. 5, pp. 120–1. On the anti-democratic bias of the frontispiece see also Iori 2015, pp. 217–20.
[65] Quintilian 2001, 11. 3. 101, vol. 5, p. 136.
[66] Quintilian 2001, 11. 3. 94, vol. 5, p. 132.   [67] Plutarch 1579, pp. 47–8.

Furthermore, political power had lain not with a council of seven *Aristoi*, as Hobbes's frontispiece suggests, but with a group of five annually elected *Ephori*, whose authority was so extensive that – as Thucydides notes – it included the right to imprison the kings.[68] It is of course possible that Hobbes was unaware of these historical facts. Although Thucydides speaks of the power of the *Ephori*, he never says how many there were, and at no point does he discuss the Spartan aristocracy. Nor does he ever tell us that Sparta had two kings. When Archidamus delivers his oration to the Athenians before the outbreak of war, Thucydides gives the impression that he is speaking as their sole ruler,[69] and Hobbes correctly translates him as referring to 'Archidamus their king'.[70] But it is equally possible that Hobbes is taking advantage of these silences on Thucydides's part to give the impression that the government of Sparta resembled the kind of absolute monarchy he himself preferred.[71] With the contrast he contrives between rational deliberation under a single king, and the mere exercise of demagoguery under democracy, he may even be hinting that this helps to explain why Sparta won the war.

Besides using his frontispiece to supply a vivid and partisan summary of Thucydides's argument, Hobbes follows a number of visual conventions that had by this time become strongly entrenched in the production of engraved frontispieces. These conventions were largely drawn from the rules of classical architecture.[72] The word frontispiece had originally been a technical term used to describe the front elevation of a building, and this remained its standard application in architectural writing throughout the seventeenth century. We still find this usage, for example, in John Raymond's account of his visit to Italy in the 1640s. When he describes the temple of Castor and Pollux in Naples he speaks of 'the Frontispiece, or Porch of ancient Pillars, with a Greek Inscription over it', and when he expresses his admiration for St Mark's Cathedral in Venice he notes that 'the whole facade, or Frontispiece, is beset with Pillars, of Serpentine and Porphyre'.[73]

To apply the term frontispiece to a book was thus to speak metaphorically. The metaphor imagines the book as a building and the frontispiece as its entrance. This explains why so many engraved title-pages take the form of intricate portals, with square piers or fluted columns on either side

---

[68] Thucydides 2013, I. 131. 2, p. 77.   [69] Thucydides 2013, I. 79, p. 48.
[70] Hobbes 1843, vol. 8, p. 85.
[71] Nelson 2008, pp. lxi–lxix and Catanzaro 2015, pp. 97–194 point to numerous passages in which, in his translations of Homer, Hobbes similarly attempts to represent Agamemnon in the *Iliad*, and Alcinous in the *Odyssey*, as more absolute monarchs than they appear in the poems.
[72] As noted in Corbett and Lightbown 1979, pp. 4–6.   [73] Raymond 1648, pp. 140, 191.

of the title, with classical figures standing on plinths next to the columns, with decorated capitals (usually Corinthian) crowning the columns, and with heavy entablatures and broken pediments surmounting the design. The general effect is to portray the title-page as a gateway into a building of obvious importance. We already encounter these conventions in embryonic form in Figures 10.1 and 10.13, while in Figures 10.7, 10.28, 10.33 and 10.34 the idea of a massive baroque portal is spectacularly realised.

These architectural features gave rise to a further series of visual metaphors. One treats the columns and classical figures as supporters and protectors of the book. These were initially portrayed as caryatidic in style, as in the Aristotle translation of 1547 (Figure 10.1), the Sallust translation of 1557 (Figure 10.13) and the Cicero translation of 1568 (Figure 10.2). This convention was much elaborated in the next generation, in which we frequently encounter heroic characters standing by the titles of books. Here it is important to note that *standing by* already carried the connotation of offering help and support. We come upon repeated reassurances in sermons of the period that God 'hath promised to stand by us to helpe us', that He will 'stand by us, and guard us' and that He is 'ever readie to help us and stand by us'.[74] The frontispiece to Chapman's translation of the *Iliad* duly shows Achilles and Hector standing by the title of the book and protectively shielding it, while at the same time standing next to columns to indicate their role as pillars of strength (Figure 10.7). A similar arrangement appears in the frontispiece of Vicars's translation of the *Aeneid*, in which Aeneas and Turnus are shown on plinths next to the title, once again standing by the book as if to shield it from attack (Figure 10.9). Hobbes's translation of the *Iliad* and *Odyssey*,[75] the last of his works to be published with an engraved frontispiece, likewise shows two soldiers in armour. Each of them is carrying a pike, and both of them are standing by the title of the book in the posture of armed guards (Figure 10.19).

These juxtapositions are also used to illustrate the rhetorical contention that, in matters of moral and political debate, there will always be two sides to the question, so that it will always be possible to argue *in utramque partem*. Achilles and Hector, as well as Aeneas and Turnus, not only stand by the books in which their exploits are celebrated; they also stand in postures of hostile confrontation with one another. They are all in armour, they are all helmeted and they all carry staves and shields. The same conventions remain in place when the conflict is between abstractions

---

[74] Webster 1613, p. 118; Norden 1620, p. 127; Bachiler 1625, p. 37.
[75] See Hobbes 1677.

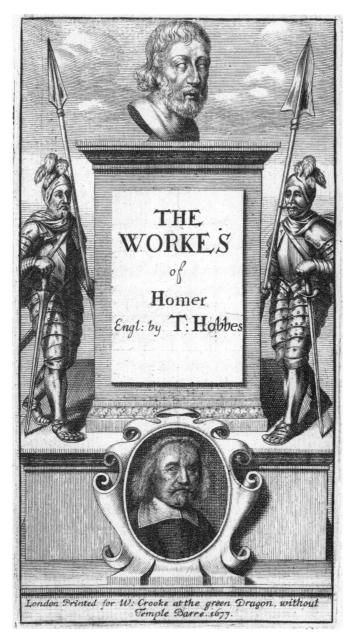

Figure 10.19 Homer (1677). *The Workes of Homer*, trans. Thomas Hobbes, London, Frontispiece.

rather than individuals, as in the opposition between Tyranny and Temperance in the Seneca frontispiece of 1620 (Figure 10.3), or between Love and Wisdom in the Ovid frontispiece of 1626 (Figure 10.8). The principal aim is to dramatise a collision between two irreconcilable forces, whether martial or psychological in character.

According to a further and related metaphor, a frontispiece can also be viewed as a threshold we are being invited to cross.[76] Some early frontispieces already display the title of the book superimposed on the open space of a gateway, as in the Aristotle translation of 1547 (Figure 10.1), the Sallust translation of 1557 (Figure 10.13) and the Homer translation of 1611 (Figure 10.7). By the time we come to the complex engravings of the 1620s, the convention of treating frontispieces as if they are means of drawing readers into the contents of the book had become fully established. The perspective of the Seneca frontispiece of 1620 carries the eye beyond the title of the book towards one of the most challenging topics it handles, the potentially liberating value of suicide (Figure 10.3). The perspective of the Ovid frontispiece of 1626 likewise draws the eye beyond the title, as if plunging the reader into contents of the book, while the vanishing lines converge on the initials of George Sandys, the translator of the work (Figure 10.8).

The frontispiece of Hobbes's translation of Thucydides reiterates the full range of these visual arguments. The overall design, with its three vertical and horizontal divisions, hints at two columns and an entablature framing the title of the book. The title itself, which appears above a portrait of Thucydides, is flanked by two military leaders. Both are standing by the title, fully armed, while at the same time standing in front of columns as pillars of strength. Meanwhile the scroll held by Thucydides assures us that his book is indeed an object worthy of protection, for it quotes him describing it as a possession for all time. The stance adopted by Archidamus and Pericles also reminds us that, in the quarrel between Athens and Sparta, there were two sides to the question, and consequently two leaders opposed to one another. Both are shown in full armour and in the posture of enemies, with Archidamus raising his sword against Pericles while Pericles stands ready to defend himself with his shield and staff. Finally, and by way of accentuating the significance of their hostility, the perspective of the image draws the eye beyond the title of the book and into the space occupied by the two leaders, thereby drawing us into the conflict that forms the subject of Thucydides's narrative.

---

[76] On frontispieces as 'antechambers' of books see Saenger 2006, pp. 35–94.

III

Soon after publishing his translation of Thucydides, Hobbes turned away from his humanist studies to cultivate pastures new. While serving as tutor to the third earl of Devonshire in the early 1630s he began to take part in the scientific experiments being conducted by the earl's cousins, Sir Charles Cavendish and the earl of Newcastle.[77] Hobbes's fascination with the natural sciences deepened between 1634 and 1636 when he accompanied the young earl on his Grand Tour of France and Italy. It was during this period that he met the aged Galileo in Florence and first became acquainted with Marin Mersenne and his circle of *savants* in Paris.[78] He also embarked on the investigations eventually published as *De corpore* in 1655 and *De homine* in 1658. Most significantly, these were the years in which he began to apply his scientific principles to the study of political life, giving rise to the publication of *De cive* in 1642 and *Leviathan* in 1651.[79]

There are several ways, however, in which Hobbes remained faithful to his earlier humanist commitments, and perhaps the most obvious is that he never gave up his interest in the visual representation of his political ideas. Summing up his theory of rights and obligations at the end of *Leviathan*, he still speaks of attempting 'to set before mens eyes' the specific conclusions he wants us to accept.[80] He often equates the process of understanding with seeing, and he compares our misperceptions with being dazzled and blinded.[81] His principal task, he likes to imply, is to lighten our darkness and help us to see things perspicuously. One of the means by which he tries throughout *Leviathan* to make his readers visually grasp his argument is through an inventive and often satirical use of the figures and tropes of speech.[82] But the most dramatic way in which he attempts to convert his readers into spectators – in *De cive* no less than in *Leviathan* – is by the inclusion of emblematic frontispieces, and no account of his civil science can afford to neglect this evidence about how he wanted to be understood.

The frontispiece of *De cive*, as it appeared in the original Paris edition of 1642, was the work of the engraver Jean Matheus, who also served as the printer of the book (Figure 10.20).[83]

---

[77] Tuck 1989, pp. 11–13; Malcolm 1994b, pp. 802–3, 813–14.
[78] Skinner 1996, pp. 252–4.   [79] Skinner 1996, pp. 250–6.
[80] Hobbes 2012, vol. 3, A Review, and Conclusion, p. 1141.
[81] See, for example, Hobbes 2012, vol. 2, ch. 19, p. 288; vol. 3, ch. 44, pp. 958, 960; vol. 3, ch. 46, p. 1076.
[82] Skinner 1996, pp. 376–425.
[83] The title-page is signed 'Math. f.', i.e. Matheus fecit (or faciebat).

Figure 10.20 Hobbes, Thomas (1642). *Elementorum Philosophiae Sectio Tertia De Cive*, Paris, Frontispiece by Jean Matheus.

If, however, we look at the manuscript copy that Hobbes presented to the earl of Devonshire in 1641, some months in advance of its printing, we already find an almost identical frontispiece (Figure 10.21).[84]

---

[84] Hobbes MSS (Chatsworth) MS A. 3. For reproductions see Warrender 1983, opp. title-page; Bredekamp 2003, p. 159.

Figure 10.21 Hobbes, Thomas (1641). *Elementorum Philosophiae Sectio
Tertia De Cive*, Chatsworth, Hobbes MS A. 3, sketch of Frontispiece.

It would appear that Matheus must have worked from this earlier
sketch, for which Hobbes himself may partly have been responsible, and
the iconography of which he must undoubtedly have approved.

As in the case of his Thucydides translation, Hobbes uses the frontispiece of *De cive* to introduce us to his leading themes.[85] We are confronted

---

[85] The account that follows draws on Skinner 2008a, pp. 99–103.

with an image divided horizontally by an entablature on which the word *Religio* is inscribed. From the entablature hangs the title of the book, and on either side stand two female figures, each on a plinth, the one on the left marked *Imperium*, the one on the right *Libertas*. If we consult the table of contents, we duly discover that *De cive* is organised into three corresponding sections, beginning with four chapters on *Libertas*, continuing with ten on *Imperium* and concluding with four on *Religio*.[86]

Turning back to the frontispiece, we find that the relationship between these concepts is explicated by means of a powerful visual metaphor combining the spatial and normative senses of standing *above* or *under* other persons or things. All human life, Hobbes's image suggests, whether lived in a condition of *libertas* or in subjection to *imperium*, takes place under religion, and we need to remember that we shall eventually be judged by those who stand above. The message is heavily underscored by the emphatic way in which the word *Religio* divides and organises the frontispiece as a whole.

Hobbes appears to have two ideas in mind, one of which is conveyed in written rather than pictorial terms. Above the date and place of publication ('Paris 1642') is a quotation from the Book of Proverbs in which the voice of God proclaims that 'By me kings reign, and princes decree justice'.[87] Above this quotation appears the title of the book, *De cive*. We are being told that the *civis* or citizen will be Hobbes's main concern, and that one of the duties of citizens is to recognise that, in obeying their kings, they will at the same time be obeying God.

If we return to the text of *De cive*, we find that God's relationship with human government is indeed one of Hobbes's chief preoccupations in his section on *Religio*, the opening chapter of which is entitled 'On the kingdom of God by nature'.[88] Here we learn that one of the means – and the only reliable means – by which God's will is made known is through what Hobbes describes as God's rational word.[89] 'Due to the rational nature common to everyone',[90] he explains, we are able to understand God's commands as 'the dictates of right reason' and are consequently able to put them into practice.[91] It follows that all kings – and indeed all

---

[86] Hobbes 1983, *Index capitum*, pp. 87–8.
[87] This is the rendering of Proverbs 8: 15 in the Authorised version. The Vulgate version, quoted on the Frontispiece, reads 'Per me Reges regnant et legum conditores iusta decernunt'. A more literal translation would read 'Through me Kings reign and the givers of laws discern what is just'.
[88] Hobbes 1983, ch. XV, p. 219: '*De Regno Dei per naturam*'.
[89] On the 'Verbum rationale Dei' see Hobbes 1983, XV. III, p. 220.
[90] Hobbes 1983, XV. IV, p. 221: 'propter naturam rationalem omnibus communem'.
[91] Hobbes 1983, XV. IV, p. 221: 'dictamina rectae Rationis'.

sovereigns, whether monarchs or assemblies[92] – have the capacity to understand God's laws, and hence to institute his will as the law of the state. '*By right reasoning*', Hobbes summarises, 'we are said to hear God'.[93] As a result, it is unquestionably true that, as the Book of Proverbs states, it is through God that kings reign and institute the laws that bring justice and peace.

The other lesson we learn from the frontispiece about living under religion is that there will be a Day of Judgment. Above the entablature we see Christ with his cross appearing in clouds of heavenly glory in the company of angels and cherubim. To his right a gathering of men and women stand under the guidance of two angels, one of whom points heavenwards, while a third follows a group of the blessed into the heavenly clouds. To his left a contrasting group of men and women are separated from the blessed by an avenging angel carrying a flaming sword, and are forced by winged demons to descend into a fiery and smoking pit.

Turning back to Hobbes's text, we find that the day of final judgment, *dies iudicii ultimi*,[94] is one of his chief concerns in the third chapter of his section on *Religio*, which is entitled 'The Kingdom of God by the new Covenant'.[95] Hobbes makes no attempt to render in visual terms the other two leading themes in his chapters on *Religio* – the discussion in chapter XVI of God's relationship with his chosen people and in chapter XVIII of the beliefs necessary for salvation. But if we focus on his discussion of the new Covenant, we find his argument fully anticipated by the frontispiece. Hobbes tells us that the world will end 'when Christ appears in majesty in the company of angels' to establish his heavenly kingdom.[96] He also tells us that this will involve a day of judgment 'in which God will separate the sheep from the goats',[97] a process later equated with the moment when the good congregate together 'and are separated from the reprobate' with the final inauguration of the kingdom of Christ.[98]

The only prominent element in the upper part of the frontispiece not echoed in Hobbes's text is the portrayal of the reprobate being forced

---

[92] Hobbes 1983, XV. XVII, p. 231.

[93] Hobbes 1983, XV. III, p. 220: 'audire Deum dicimur, *Ratiocinatio recta*'.

[94] On the *dies iudicii ultimi* see Hobbes 1983, XVII. V, p. 254.

[95] Hobbes 1983, ch. XVII, p 249: '*De Regno Dei* per *Pactum novum*'.

[96] Hobbes 1983, XVII. V, p. 253: 'cum [Christus] venturus est in maiestate comitantibus Angelis'. Here Hobbes also quotes Matthew 25. 31: 'the Son of man shall come in his glory, and all the holy angels with him'.

[97] Hobbes 1983, XVII. V, p. 254: 'in quo Deus oves ab haedis separabit'. Here Hobbes quotes Matthew 25. 32: 'he shall separate them . . . as a shepherd divideth his sheep from the goats'.

[98] Hobbes 1983, XVII. XXII, p. 268: 'quam a reprobis quidem segregentur'. On Christ's kingdom as heavenly see Hobbes 1983, XVII. VI, p. 254.

down into a fiery and smoking pit. Here the frontispiece instead draws directly on a set of iconographical conventions first established in the early years of the German Reformation. The entrenchment of this visual tradition was largely due to the diffusion of some celebrated woodcuts and engravings of the Last Judgment by such artists as Albrecht Dürer, Lucas Cranach the Elder and Breugel the Elder. Admittedly – and some-what ironically – Hobbes's frontispiece fails to represent perhaps the most memorable feature of the moment of judgment as imagined by these artists. They all show the reprobate being herded into the mouth of a devouring sea-monster. Apart from this detail, however, the *De cive* frontispiece closely follows the northern Renaissance tradition, especially as articulated by Dürer in his woodcut *On the Last Judgment of the World* (Figure 10.22).[99]

This image was first published in Dürer's *Passio Christi* of 1511, a sequence of thirty-seven woodcuts illustrating the life of Christ, with accom-panying verses by Benedikt Schwalbe, a humanist from Nuremberg.[100] The Dürer woodcut and the *De cive* frontispiece both show angels amid the congregation of the blessed; both show a long-haired naked woman promi-nent among those who have been saved; both show the congregation being shepherded towards a beam of sunlight; and both show Christ enthroned above in heavenly clouds.

If we shift our gaze from the upper to the lower half of the *De cive* image, we can hardly fail to be struck by the extent to which it reproduces the most widely established conventions of Renaissance humanist frontis-pieces. The figures of *Imperium* and *Libertas*, both standing on plinths, are at the same time standing by the title of the book. They are armed and opposed to one another, indicating that there is a question to be debated *in utramque partem*. Should we subject ourselves to supreme power, or should we cleave to a life of natural liberty?[101] We are not only invited to ponder the question, but to think of the frontispiece as drawing us past its threshold and into the debate. The vanishing lines established by the two plinths have the effect of carrying the eye beyond the title and, as it were, into the centre of the book, and hence into the heart of the argument.

The frontispiece also introduces us to the answer given in the body of the text. What if we choose submission to supreme power? We are shown that, if we accept this form of subjection, we can hope for a life based on justice. The figure of *Imperium*, a sovereign wearing a closed imperial crown, holds aloft the sword of penal justice in her left hand while carrying

---

[99] See 'De ultimo mundi iudicio' in Dürer 1511, sig. E, 4v–5r.
[100] Schwalbe latinised his name as Benedictus Cheliodonius. See Dürer 1511.
[101] On the portrayal of this choice see Brett 2011, pp. 4–6.

Figure 10.22 Dürer, Albrecht (1511). 'De ultimo mundi iudicio' in *Passio Christi*, Nuremberg, sig. E, 4v–5r.

the scales of distributive justice in her right. We also learn that, if we are willing to assign the *ius gladii* or right of the sword to such a ruler, we can gain security and prosperity, the kind of life illustrated in the landscape within which *Imperium* is placed. In the background we see a sunlit city on a hill, while in the foreground men with scythes peacefully harvest the fruitful fields. To underline her virtuous character, *Imperium* stands below the right hand of Christ, and the gesture with which she points upwards with her sword suggests a connection between the pursuit of justice on earth and the attainment of salvation when we come to be judged.

If we return to Hobbes's text, we find him closely echoing these arguments. The opening chapter of the section on *Imperium* lays it down that 'we can never gain the security we need for the practice of *natural justice* without establishing some common power to govern every individual by fear of punishment.'[102] He adds that the name of this common power is 'SUMMUM IMPERIUM or DOMINIUM',[103] and that the essence of *Imperium* consists in having the right to wield the *gladium iustitiae* or sword of justice.[104] Hobbes also describes the outcome of imposing *Imperium* upon ourselves. 'When everyone is protected against the violence of others sufficiently to live in security, we shall have instituted what is necessary for peace'.[105] Once peace and security have been assured, we shall be able to enjoy a *vita beata* in which 'everyone is able to live as pleasantly as the condition of human life will permit'.[106]

What if we instead choose *Libertas*? If we turn with this question in mind to the Renaissance emblem-books, we find the condition of freedom celebrated as the best way of life. Achille Bocchi in his *Symbolicarum quaestionum* presents us with a particularly rousing image of civic liberty as the ruling principle of his native Bologna (Figure 10.23). Surrounding the figure of *Libertas*, who stands helmeted and in classical garb, we see the beneficial results of living a free way of life. The arms and armour on the right tell us that one result will be military prowess; the legal texts on the left remind us that, as one of them states, 'this is what Bologna teaches', thereby promoting liberty under law. The accompanying verses confirm that 'the virtue of *libertas* binds together four things: property, laws, security and territory'.[107]

Cesare Ripa in his *Iconologia* presents us with a more domesticated version of the same values (Figure 10.24).[108] Here a smiling *Libertà* is shown in the company of a cat. (Cats like to go their own way, as the accompanying commentary reminds us.) As before, liberty is represented

---

[102] Hobbes 1983, V. V, p. 133: 'sine potestate aliqua communi, per quam metu poenae singuli regantur, non sufficit ad securitatem quae requiritur ad exercitium *iustitiae naturalis.*'

[103] Hobbes 1983, V. XI, p. 134.   [104] Hobbes 1983, VI. V and VI, p. 138.

[105] Hobbes 1983, VI. III, p. 138 argues that we shall have instituted what is '*paci necessarium*' when 'unusquisque in tantum protegatur contra coeterorum violentiam, ut possit secure vivere'.

[106] See Hobbes 1983, XIII. IV, p. 196 on the 'vita beata' and on managing 'ut possent, quantum conditio fert humana, iucundissime vivere.'

[107] Bocchi 1574, p. 243: 'Libertas, census, leges, custodia, fines / Quattuor hos virtus continet'.

[108] Ripa 1611, p. 313.

Figure 10.23 Bocchi, Achille (1574). 'Libertas Populi Bononiensis' in
Symbolicarum quaestionum, Bologna, Symb. CXV, p. 242.

in classical garb, holding a sceptre to show that freedom reigns, together
with her *pilleus* or cap of liberty to signify her independence from servitude. The moral we are expected to draw, as Mathias Holtzwart had
already proclaimed in his *Emblematum Tyrocinia* of 1581, is that 'he who
lives in liberty lives in the best way' (Figure 10.25).

Figure 10.24 Ripa, Cesare (1611). 'Libertà' in *Iconologia*, Padua, p. 313.

By contrast with these admiring images, the frontispiece of *De cive* offers us an iconographically unprecedented view of liberty as an unwanted and burdensome state. We are warned that, if we choose not to submit to a sovereign who can offer us protection, we shall have to stand ready to protect ourselves. The hunched figure of *Libertas* is shown in a posture of self-defence, a longbow in her left hand and an arrow in her right. Gone is any sense of liberty as a triumphant ruling force. To live in liberty, the image additionally warns us, is to commit ourselves to a savage and dangerous way of life. By contrast with *Imperium*'s serene expression, the face of *Libertas* is riven with anxiety; and by contrast with the sumptuous robes worn by *Imperium*, the body of *Libertas* is displayed in a state of primitive undress. Gone is any suggestion that the fruits of liberty are security and social betterment.

Figure 10.25 Holtzwart, Mathias (1581). 'Qui liber vivit, optimè vivit' in *Emblematum Tyrocinia*, Strasbourg, Emblem XXVIII, sig. E, 4r.

Hobbes informs us in the text of *De cive* that 'the peoples of America provide us with an example of this way of life even at the present time'.[109] More eloquently, his frontispiece draws on a number of visual as well as literary traditions in which the allegedly primitive life of the native peoples of North America had already been portrayed.[110] One possible source is the emblem entitled 'America' from Cesare Ripa's *Iconologia* (Figure 10.26).[111] Both Ripa' image above and the *De cive* frontispiece display a skirted woman

[109] Hobbes 1983, I. XIII, p. 96: 'Exemplum huius rei saeculum praesens Americanos exhibet'.
[110] Corbett and Lightbown 1979, pp. 224–5.   [111] Ripa 1611, p. 360.

A M E R I C A.

Figure 10.26 Ripa, Cesare (1611). 'America' in *Iconologia*, Padua,
p. 360.

in semi-undress; both show her holding a bow in her left hand and an arrow
in her right; and both convey the ominous implication that, in a condition of
mere nature, you will need to equip yourself with your own means of
defence.

Still more relevant is the work of two earlier artists, John White and
Theodore de Bry. John White, at the behest of Walter Raleigh, had
produced a number of watercolours of Virginia in the 1580s, including
the earliest European images of native Americans.[112] White's paintings
were copied and engraved by de Bry, who used them to illustrate Thomas
Hariot's *Briefe and true report of the new found land of Virginia* in 1590.[113]

---

[112] For reproductions of White's paintings see Sloan 2007.
[113] Hariot 1590, sig. D, 3r states that White's drawings were commissioned by Raleigh in
1585 and 'first published by Theodore de Bry'.

Figure 10.27 Bry, Theodore de (1590). 'A weroan or great Lorde of Virginia' in *A briefe and true report of the new found land of Virginia*, Frankfurt, Figure III, sig. A, 1r.

One of White's portraits had shown a North Carolina Algonquian chief,[114] an image that de Bry made famous while at the same time radically altering it (Figure 10.27).[115] As we see above, de Bry not only gave the chief a more swaggering stance, but added a back view of the same figure and arranged them in a fanciful landscape in which a hunt is shown to be taking place.

A similar image appears on the title-page of Hariot's book (Figure 10.28). The chief is now shown standing on a plinth in front of a fluted column in the customary martial pose. With his bow and arrow at the ready, he is also shown standing by the title of the book. The vanishing lines established by the pedestals converge on the name RALEIGH, the first authorised governor of Virginia, drawing the eye towards the centre of the title and the presiding spirit of the book.

The frontispiece of *De cive* reproduces several features of de Bry's fanciful landscape, but at the same time transforms it into something

---

[114] Sloan 2007, p. 121. The area described in the 1580s as 'Virginia' includes what is now North Carolina.
[115] Hariot 1590, Figure III, 'A weroan or great Lorde of Virginia'.

Figure 10.28 Hariot, Thomas (1590). *A briefe and true report of the new found land of Virginia*, Frankfurt, Frontispiece by Theodore de Bry.

much more sinister. The hunt pictured by de Bry shows four braves with bows and arrows shooting at a stag. Hobbes's frontispiece shows three near-naked men, two of whom are similarly armed, shooting at two fellow human beings who are running for their lives, while a fourth stands ready to strike them down with a club. A second disquieting alteration is that, whereas de Bry's engraving had merely sketched a woodland behind the stag, Hobbes's frontispiece shows a clearing in which two men squat next to a trestle on which a dismembered limb appears to be hung.

Some further consequences of choosing the life of liberty are no less grimly sketched. By contrast with the fertile fields behind *Imperium* there lies an uncultivated landscape; by contrast with the peaceful city on the hill we see a group of primitive huts surrounded by a defensive palisade. Here too there is a strong echo of de Bry, whose illustration of Virginian settlements had shown similar encampments of huts with semi-circular roofs surrounded by the same type of palisade.[116] A final contrast recalls how *Imperium* points her sword heavenwards, gesturing at a connection between justice and salvation. We see *Libertas*, standing on the left side of Christ – the sinister side – holding her arrow pointing downwards, hinting at an analogous connection between the life of natural liberty and the fate of the damned.

These features of Hobbes's frontispiece vividly anticipate the pivotal argument of his book. His opening chapter, in which he examines 'the state of men outside civil society', immediately asks what it would be like to lead a life of natural liberty.[117] He answers in a celebrated passage that 'man is not born fit for society.'[118] We suffer from 'mutual fear, the cause of which arises partly from our willingness to harm one another'.[119] Due to this universal hostility, 'we cannot expect to gain any security from others, nor can we find sufficient means to maintain security for ourselves'.[120] The condition of natural liberty would lack any law or justice, and would be 'devoid of any of the comforts and adornments of life'.[121] Worst of all, it would lack any peace. As Hobbes summarises, 'it is impossible to deny that the natural state of men before they joined together in society was one of War; and not simply of war, but a war of everyone against everyone else.'[122] As in the

---

[116] Hariot 1590, Figure XIX, 'The Towne of Pomeiooc'.

[117] Hobbes 1983, I. I, p. 89: '*De statu Hominum extra Societatem civilem*'.

[118] Hobbes 1983, I. II, *Annotatio*, p. 92: 'Hominem ad Societatem aptum natum non esse.'

[119] Hobbes 1983, I. III, p. 93: 'Causa metus mutui consistit ... partim in mutua laedendi voluntate'.

[120] Hobbes 1983, I. III, p. 93: 'neque ab aliis expectare, neque nobismetipsis securitatem praestare valeamus'.

[121] Hobbes 1983, I. XIII, p. 96: 'vitae solatio atque ornatu carentes'.

[122] Hobbes 1983, I. XII, p. 96: 'negari non potest quin status hominum naturalis antequam in societatem coiretur Bellum fuerit; neque hoc simpliciter, sed bellum omnium in omnes.'

frontispiece, so in the text, the moral we are asked to draw is that *imperium* must be chosen over *libertas* if there is to be any prospect of living a happy life.

IV

After completing *De cive* Hobbes reverted to his scientific pursuits, devoting most of the 1640s to the work he eventually published as *De corpore* in 1655. He interrupted these studies, however, after receiving the shocking news of the execution of king Charles I in 1649. As he tells us in his autobiography, he could not bear 'to tolerate so many crimes'.[123] He at once decided to answer his enemies by writing *Leviathan*, 'a work that now fights on behalf of all kings and all who, under whatever name, hold regal rights'.[124]

Hobbes assures us in *Leviathan* that the scientific investigation of the laws of nature 'is the true and onely Moral Philosophy', and he undoubtedly regarded his treatise as a work of science.[125] By this stage, however, he had lost his earlier confidence in the power of unaided reason to persuade. He now warns us that 'the Sciences, are small Power', and that we need to find some means of moving people to accept the truths that reason finds out.[126] Furthermore, he had come to accept the rhetoricians' contention that the surest means of writing movingly is to 'adorn' the truth. As he explains in the Review and Conclusion, 'Reason, and Eloquence, (though not perhaps in the Naturall Sciences, yet in the Morall) may stand very well together. For wheresoever there is place for adorning and preferring of Errour, there is much more place for adorning and preferring of Truth'.[127]

Hobbes accordingly displays a strong interest in *Leviathan* in adding persuasion to proof by means of adding *ornamenta* to his arguments. The resulting adornments are mainly verbal, and chiefly take the form of satirical figures and tropes designed to show that his intellectual adversaries are worthy of nothing but contempt.[128] But by far the most memorable *ornamentum* is the emblematic frontispiece standing opposite the title-page (Figure 10.30), and it is this image that I next want to discuss.

---

[123] Hobbes 1839a, p. xcii, lines 189–90: 'pati tot tantaque foeda / . . . nolo'.

[124] Hobbes 1839a, p. xcii, lines 200–2: 'Militat ille liber nunc regibus omnibus, et qui / Nomine sub quovis regia iura tenent.'

[125] Hobbes 2012, vol. 2, ch. 15, p. 242.   [126] Hobbes 2012, vol. 2, ch. 10, p. 134.

[127] Hobbes 2012, vol. 3, A Review, and Conclusion, p. 1133.

[128] Skinner 1996, pp. 376–425.

As in the case of *De cive*, there can be no doubt that Hobbes approved the iconographical scheme that his frontispiece lays out.[129] Before publishing *Leviathan*, he commissioned a magnificent manuscript version of the text for presentation to Charles I's son and heir, the future Charles II. This unique copy (now in the British Library)[130] contains a frontispiece in the form of an ink drawing on vellum which is virtually identical with the frontispiece in the published version of the text (Figure 10.29).[131] It seems inconceivable that Hobbes would have included in his presentation copy an image to which he had not given his approval, so this earlier version may be assumed to carry his imprimatur. Furthermore, so exact is the summary it offers of the central argument in *Leviathan* about the character of the state that Hobbes must not only have approved the drawing and the subsequent etching, but must have been closely involved in the design of both.[132]

Horst Bredekamp has established beyond reasonable doubt that the artist with whom Hobbes collaborated was Abraham Bosse, whom we have already encountered as a pupil of Jacques Callot and one of the most successful French etchers of the seventeenth century.[133] Bosse was born in Tours, but began his apprenticeship in Paris in 1620 and remained there for the rest of his life.[134] Hobbes too lived in Paris during his exile between 1640 and 1652,[135] where he lodged on the pont Saint-Michel, only a few minutes' walk from Bosse's workshop in the rue Harlay.[136] Hobbes would undoubtedly have known of Bosse as a designer of frontispieces – of which he produced more than a hundred[137] – and may additionally have been attracted to work with him in consequence

---

[129] By contrast, this was clearly not the case with the frontispiece to the unauthorised *De cive* translation of 1650, which is why I do not consider it.

[130] BL Egerton MS 1910. For a discussion see Malcolm 2012, pp. 128–35.

[131] The only significant differences are that, in the drawing, the quotation from the Book of Job at the top of the printed version is missing, and the figures who make up the body of the colossus are differently displayed.

[132] The closeness of their collaboration is noted in Brown 1978, pp. 26, 30; Bredekamp 2003, pp. 46–7; Malcolm 2012, pp. 133–4.

[133] Bredekamp 2003, pp. 34–47. Corbett and Lightbown 1979, pp. 221–2 had already argued that the frontispiece was probably the fruit of a collaboration between Bosse and Hobbes. Bredekamp additionally suggests that Bosse made the ink drawing in the manuscript of *Leviathan*, and argues that it postdates the published frontispiece. But as Brown 1978, p. 29 and Malcolm 2012, p. 132 observe, it seems more probable that the drawing predates the etching. Malcolm agrees that both images are the work of Bosse, but Brown 1978, pp. 24–8 argues that the drawing was made by Wenceslas Hollar, while the frontispiece is the work of an unknown English engraver (whom Brown sternly criticises).

[134] Préaud 2004, p. 11.   [135] Skinner 2002b, pp. 9, 23.   [136] Malcolm 2012, p. 134.

[137] Goldstein 2012, p. 6.

Figure 10.29 British Library Egerton MS 1910: Thomas Hobbes, *Leviathan*, Frontispiece by Abraham Bosse.

of Bosse's interest in the geometry of perspective drawing, on which he published a treatise in 1653.[138]

The etched frontispiece of *Leviathan* (Figure 10.30) has become a celebrated image, and of late it has been the subject of much valuable research. It remains arguable, however, that the nature of its originality has not been fully appreciated. This is partly because its connections with the iconographical traditions I have been sketching have not been sufficiently investigated, and these are the connections I next wish to explore.

Consider first the relationship between the frontispieces of *Leviathan* and *De cive*. If, as I have argued, Hobbes saw them both as visual summaries of his principal arguments, it is notable how far he seems to have changed his mind about which elements in his political theory most needed to be singled out. This is not to deny the obvious and important continuity between the two images. Both prominently display a representation of the concept of *Imperium* or *Suprema potestas*. It is true that the representations are differently gendered. But this merely reflects the fact that, although the majority of abstract nouns in Latin are feminine in gender, the word *imperium* is neuter, so that the concept expressed by the term can equally well be represented by a male or female form. The frontispiece of *De cive* chooses to show *Imperium* as a woman, no doubt to maintain symmetry with *Libertas* standing opposite her. By contrast, the bearded and heavily moustachioed colossus who dominates the frontispiece of *Leviathan* is unquestionably male. But he is no less obviously intended to represent a bearer of *Imperium* or *Suprema potestas*. Like the figure of *Imperium* he wears a closed imperial crown, while above his head a verse from the Book of Job confirms that 'there is no *potestas* over the earth that can be compared with him'.[139]

Even here, however, the variations in iconography between *De cive* and *Leviathan* are remarkable. One would have expected *Imperium* or *Suprema potestas* to be represented by a figure in classical pose and garb. If we look, for example, at the illustration of *Potestà* in Cesare Ripa's *Iconologia* (Figure 10.31),[140] we find the concept symbolised by an enthroned woman in flowing classical robes.

This convention is closely followed in the frontispiece of *De cive*, but it is wholly absent from the frontispiece of *Leviathan*. The colossus who faces us is not in classical garb, and nor is he wearing armour in the manner of the ancient heroes whom we have encountered in so

---

[138] Bosse 1653.

[139] The motto reads: 'Non est potestas Super Terram quae Comparetur ei. Job. 41. 24.' Hobbes is giving the Vulgate reference; in the Authorised Version the reference is Job 41: 33.

[140] Ripa 1611, p. 40.

Figure 10.30 Hobbes, Thomas (1651). *Leviathan*, London, Frontispiece by Abraham Bosse.

A V T T O R I T A`, O P O T E S T A`.

Figure 10.31 Ripa, Cesare (1611). 'Auttorità, o Potestà' in *Iconologia*, Padua, p. 40.

many earlier frontispieces. In fact he is not garbed at all, since his body is not that of a natural person, but takes the form of a body politic made up of his own subjects. Yet more striking is the alteration in the symbols associated with supreme political authority. The figure of *Imperium* in the *De cive* frontispiece holds the sword and scales symbolising penal and distributive justice, thereby suggesting a purely secular form of power. But the colossus in the *Leviathan* frontispiece brandishes a bishop's crozier in addition to the sword of justice, thereby indicating that supreme jurisdiction in the state must include the right to wield ecclesiastical as well as civil power.

If we now compare the other main elements in the two images, what is most striking is the extent to which the *Leviathan* frontispiece challenges and repudiates the political messages as well as the iconographical traditions embodied in the frontispiece to *De cive*. The earlier image continues to endorse the humanist convention of picturing an argument *in utramque partem*. We are shown that, under religion, we are faced with a choice: we can either submit to *imperium* or cleave to a life of natural *libertas*. But in the *Leviathan* frontispiece there is no hint of any such alternative. We might even say that the image illustrates a later phase in Hobbes's narrative about the formation of the state. We are shown a time when the choice between *libertas* and *imperium* has already been made. No longer are there two sides to the question; there is only a single dominating force. The life of *libertas* is literally out of the picture.

A still more striking alteration relates to the place in Hobbes's narrative of the Day of Judgment. While the *dies ultimi iudicii* is prominently and conventionally pictured in the frontispiece of *De cive*, it makes no appearance in the frontispiece of *Leviathan* at all. In part this omission no doubt reflects the fact that, in the years between the publication of the two works, Hobbes had examined the biblical texts on the kingdom of Christ with much closer attention, and had arrived at a number of conclusions that undermined his earlier account.[141] As we have seen, the *De cive* frontispiece had shown Christ appearing in majesty in the company of his angels, several of whom are shepherding the blessed as they begin their ascent to join him on his heavenly throne. The text of *De cive* duly confirms that this is how our present way of life on earth will end.[142] But if we turn to chapter 38 of *Leviathan* we find Hobbes at pains to point out that 'I have not found any text that can probably be drawn, to prove' that anyone will ascend 'into any *Coelum Empyreum*, or other aetheriall Region' at the Last Judgment.[143] Still less, he now insists, is there any scriptural warrant for the supposition that the blessed can expect to join Christ on his heavenly throne. As he somewhat piously adds, the suggestion 'seemeth not sutable to the dignity of a King, nor can I find any evident text for it in holy Scripture.'[144]

The frontispiece of *De cive* had additionally shown a division on the Day of Judgment between the blessed and the damned. Hobbes had quoted St Matthew's claim about the separation of the sheep from the goats,[145] and the frontispiece had pictured the reprobate being goaded by demons into a fiery pit. But if we go back to chapter 38 of *Leviathan* we find Hobbes nothing less than scornful of the belief that, 'after the day of Judgment, the wicked are all Eternally to be punished' in the fires of

[141] On the Last Judgment in *Leviathan* see Hackenbracht 2014, pp. 104–10.
[142] Hobbes 1983, XVII. V, pp. 253–4.
[143] Hobbes 2012, vol. 3, ch. 38, p. 726; cf. ch. 38, p. 704.
[144] Hobbes 2012, vol. 3, ch. 38, p. 726.
[145] Matthew 25: 32; Hobbes 1983, XVII. V, p. 253.

Hell.[146] He dismissively (and somewhat optimistically) observes that nowadays 'there is none, that so interprets the Scripture', and concludes that everything said in the Bible about hell fire, fiery lakes and so forth amounts to nothing more than a tissue of metaphors.[147]

A further and still more dramatic contrast arises from the strong emphasis in the *De cive* frontispiece on the visual metaphor according to which all human life is lived *under* religion, the power of which is shown to stand *over* everyone, whether they are living a life of *libertas* or submission to *imperium*. This idea is not merely missing from the frontispiece of *Leviathan* but appears to be explicitly repudiated. As we have seen, the later image is surmounted by a quotation from the Book of Job, a quotation so closely associated with the colossus that his crown interrupts the line of the verse. This alludes to the idea of power over us, but insists with reference to the colossus that there is no power *super terram* – no power over the earth – that can be compared with him. Nothing stands above him,[148] and his head reaches into the clouds. By contrast with the frontispiece of *De cive*, Hobbes's vision of supreme political power is now presented in wholly secular terms.

V

I now turn to examine the broader visual context of the *Leviathan* title-page that the humanist genre of emblematic frontispieces may be said to provide. As we have seen, one convention that quickly became established was that of constructing the linear perspective so as to draw the viewer into the book. Given the prominence of this convention, it is noteworthy that in *Leviathan* Hobbes appears deliberately to eschew this visual effect. The lower half of the frontispiece presents us with two sequences of emblems in which the use of perspective is of minimal significance. Meanwhile the colossus who dominates the upper half, far from welcoming us into the book, stands at a great distance behind the title and confronts us with a less than encouraging stare.

A further well-established convention was that of showing the titles of books as worthy of protection and support. While these supporters had initially been portrayed as caryatidic in style, it later became customary to represent them as martial figures, often placed next to classical columns, who are shown standing by the title of the book. There is a sense in which, in the *Leviathan* frontispiece, this convention is retained. Although there are no supporting figures, the lower half of the picture shows two parallel

---

[146] Hobbes 2012, vol. 3, ch. 38, p. 714.   [147] Hobbes 2012, vol. 3, ch. 38, pp. 712, 714.
[148] Except, as Strong 1993, p. 131 rightly notes, this one line of Scripture.

columns on either side of a fringed and embroidered cloth of honour on which the title of the book is displayed.[149] However, the symbolic significance usually associated with such pairs of columns is violently reversed. We are not looking at a body of supporters prepared to stand by the Commonwealth Ecclesiasticall and Civil. Rather we are looking at the commonwealth's deadliest enemies, who are shown stacked against it and pressing upon it from both sides.

The enemies in question are portrayed in two sets of pictures framed in the style typical of emblem-books, and we are clearly expected to read down the columns as well as across.[150] Commentators have often suggested that, if we do so, what we come to appreciate is the extent and reach of sovereign power.[151] But this seems to me a misreading of Hobbes's visual argument. If we read across, we find ourselves confronting two comparable sources of faction that threaten the stability of all commonwealths. If we read downwards, we learn about the capacity of both these forces to bring about – in three comparable steps – the disasters of civil division and war.

We are first introduced to the threat posed by over-mighty subjects. At the top of the left-hand column we see a castle with a cannon firing from its ramparts, and below it a marquis's coronet to symbolise the power of the aristocracy.[152] The rounded shape of the coronet echoes the rounded towers of the castle, strongly suggesting that it is not 'a royal seat', as has sometimes been proposed,[153] but the fortified dwelling of a member of the nobility. Discussing the dissolution of commonwealths in chapter 29, Hobbes confirms that 'the Popularity of a potent Subject', especially if he finds means to raise an army, will always run the danger of drawing people 'away from their obedience to the Lawes', and consequently amounts to 'plain Rebellion' against the state.[154]

---

[149] Bosse's presentation of the title on a cloth of honour follows a well-established convention. For other examples see Hind 1952–64, vol. 3, Plates 18(c), 35(b), 72(b), 75(a).

[150] As noted in Bredekamp 2003, p. 8. Brown 1978, p. 30 instead proposes we read upwards, a possibility also raised in Berger 2017, p. 206. But this would be highly unconventional, and would also suggest that the images are designed to convey (as Brown contends) a gradual increase of 'authority, and command'. Prokhovnik 1991, pp. 142–3, Schmitt 2008, p. 18, Champion 2010, p. 260 and Di Bello 2010, p. 153 argue in similar terms. But what is illustrated, I am claiming, is not a widening sphere of authority but the process by which states come to be dissolved.

[151] See, for example, Corbett and Lightbown 1979, p. 225; Bredekamp 2003, p. 8.

[152] The representation is of a coronet, not a royal crown as is often said. (See, for example, Lloyd 1992, p. 226; Champion 2010, p. 259; Di Bello 2010, p. 153; Kristiansson and Tralau 2014, p. 205.) The presence specifically of a marquis's coronet might appear to suggest some allusion to Hobbes's patron William Cavendish, who had been created marquis of Newcastle in 1643. But it seems inconceivable that Hobbes would have wished to associate him with the cause of rebellion.

[153] See, for example, Corbett and Lightbown 1979, p. 225.

[154] Hobbes 2012, vol. 2, ch. 29, p. 516.

At the top of the right-hand column we see a church, a no less potentially dangerous site of discord, and below it a bishop's mitre to symbolise the analogous threat posed by over-mighty ecclesiastical subjects. The two halves of the mitre echo the twin towers of the church above. Here the warning Hobbes conveys is that, as he confirms in chapter 29, 'when the spirituall power, moveth the Members of a Common-wealth', this 'must needs thereby Distract the people, and either Overwelm the Commonwealth with Oppression, or cast it into the Fire of a Civill warre.'[155]

Below these images, two pairs of panels reveal in a visual metaphor how the claims of the church and aristocracy are *upheld*. Half-way down the left-hand column a massive cannon points directly at the Commonwealth Ecclesiasticall and Civil. The larger panel underneath shows a classical 'trophy', including banners, swords, cannons and crossed muskets as well as numerous pikes with their sharpenend ends much accentuated. There is also a drum to give the call to arms, a motif strongly connecting the display of weaponry with the misuse of aristocratic power: the circle of the drum echoes the wheel of the cannon above, the wheel echoes the circle of the marquis's coronet, the coronet echoes the castle's circular towers.[156] The trophy also displays the *fasces*, the symbol of consular authority in ancient Rome. This might seem a merely conventional addition,[157] but if we return to chapter 29 of *Leviathan* we find that the factious use of military force to overthrow the Roman republic is one of the examples that Hobbes specifically has in mind. 'By this means it was', he explains, that Julius Caesar, 'having won to himselfe the affections of his Army, made himselfe Master, both of Senate and People' and thereby established his dictatorship.[158]

Half-way down the column on the right we see a conventional representation of a *fulmen* or thunderbolt, with one set of arrows likewise pointing directly against the Commonwealth Ecclesiasticall and Civil. Hobbes explains the allusion in a scornful passage in his discussion of ecclesiastical power in chapter 42. There he speaks of '*the Thunderbolt of Excommunication*', the use of which 'proceeded from an imagination of the bishop of Rome, which first used it, that he was King of Kings'.[159] The larger panel underneath parallels the 'trophy' on the left, and shows the no less lethally sharpened weapons that the doctors of the Church like to wield.[160] The left-hand fork is marked 'Syllogisme', while the one on the right is marked 'Real/Intentional', a reference to the scholastic distinction

---

[155] Hobbes 2012, vol. 2, ch. 29, p. 512.
[156] As noted in Brown 1978, p. 30 and Malcolm 2012, p. 130.
[157] As argued in Corbett and Lightbown 1979, p. 226.
[158] Hobbes 2012, vol. 2, ch. 29, p. 516.   [159] Hobbes 2012, vol. 3, ch. 42, p. 806.
[160] On verbal combat and military action see Berger 2017, p. 195.

between real things and the intentional objects of our passions and thoughts. The distinction is one Hobbes views with particular contempt, as he makes clear when speaking about '*Intentionality*, *Quiddity*, and other insignificant words of the School.'[161] The two forks in the middle are marked 'Spiritual/Temporal' and 'Directe/Indirecte'. Hobbes gives a deeply hostile analysis of the forms of power to which these terms refer. The Pope, he explains, seeks to claim 'the Supreme *Temporall Power* INDIRECTLY', by which he means 'that such Temporall Jurisdiction belongeth to him of Right', so that 'to the Pastorall Power (which he calls Spirituall) the Supreme Power Civill is necessarily annexed'.[162] The overarching danger is that, when the Church is able to challenge the legislative authority of the state by enforcing ecclesiastical laws 'there must needs be two Commonwealths, of one & the same Subjects; which is a Kingdome divided in it selfe, and cannot stand.'[163]

With the two large panels at the base of each column we reach the third and final step in the argument. A number of royalist propagandists at the start of the civil war had cautioned that, in the words of Thomas Morton, any such internecine conflict 'must needs bring a Land to the lowest depth'.[164] Hobbes's panels duly illustrate, in a further visual metaphor, *the lowest depth* to which a commonwealth can sink. On the right we see an ecclesiastical court in session, with the members wearing the tall birettas that mark them out as Catholic priests.[165] Whether they are asserting an indirect or a direct control over the state, they are undoubtedly usurping the jurisdictional power that ought to be wielded exclusively by the bearer of *Imperium*. On the left is a field of battle with cavalry shooting at each other and pikemen ready to collide in mass slaughter. The challenge of aristocratic faction to the unity of the state is shown to culminate in the carnage and horror of civil war.

We need to know how to respond to such dangerous enemies. The answer generally given by the political writers of the age was that, in a much-used phrase, they must at all costs be *kept under*. Jean Bodin in his chapter on the rise and fall of states in his *Six Bookes of a Commonweale* speaks in exactly these terms about the duke of Athens, who seized control of Florence in the mid-fourteenth century. He not only 'commaunded the citizens to lay down armes', but recognised the need 'to keepe under the seditious and rebellious' in order to secure his rule.[166] The duc de Rohan writes in similar terms in his *Treatise of the Interest of the Princes* about Henry III of France. The king 'had noe children of

---

[161] Hobbes 2012, vol. 2, ch. 4, p. 48.   [162] Hobbes 2012, vol. 3, ch. 42, p. 908.
[163] Hobbes 2012, vol. 2, ch. 29, p. 510.   [164] Morton 1642, p. 4.
[165] As noted in Corbett and Lightbown 1979, p. 229.   [166] Bodin 1962, IV. I, p. 425.

his owne', and consequently had to expend much energy 'in keeping under those which lifted up themselves to the prejudice of his *Royall authoritie*'.[167] Robert Ward in his *Animadversions of Warre* of 1639 informs us that the most effective means of preventing such disturbances is to muster an army 'to guard the heart of the Land, and to keepe under dis-affected persons' whenever any 'times of danger' threaten the state.[168]

The frontispiece of *Leviathan* develops the same argument about the need to ensure that the state's enemies are *kept under* if peace is to be preserved. As in the case of *De cive*, the frontispiece is divided by a strong horizontal line, giving rise to an image in two halves. The pullulating forces of disorder are shown under the line, while above it the colossus protects and almost enfolds the quiet city and its sunlit countryside, beyond which a calm sea stretches to the horizon and a clear sky above.

The contrast between the dangerous forces being kept under and the peaceful scene above seems strongly marked. Nevertheless, it has recently been argued that war is being waged above the line as well as below. We are told that, in the sea behind the left hand of the colossus, there are 'four ships approaching land'.[169] They are 'part of hostile military forces' which are 'attacking from the sea' and are being attacked in turn by 'artillery fired from a fortress towards the ship closest to the shoreline'.[170] But this reading seems wholly misconceived. We see no artillery represented, and there is nothing to distinguish the building in question as a fortress. Nor is there anything to identify the ships as armed vessels, and it is a mistake to say that they are approaching the shore. It is possible to see only the two closest in sufficient detail, but both are clearly shown sailing away towards the horizon with their sterns towards us.

There are in any case many other signs that we should think of the land laid out before the colossus as living in peace. The only mystery is that the scene is so eerily quiet. Apart from the soldiers manning the citadel, and two men standing near the west door of the church, the streets of the city are completely deserted.[171] (I shall return to this mystery in section VI.) But this feature only adds to the general air of calm and serenity. The city gates stand open and unguarded; the settlements in the countryside are unfortified; the sun shining from the east bathes the city in bright morning light.[172] The invocation of light in *Leviathan* always symbolises the power of reason to guarantee peace, specifically by enabling us to follow the

---

[167] Rohan 1640, p. 48.   [168] Ward 1639, p. 42.
[169] Kristiansson and Tralau 2014, p. 304.
[170] Kristiansson and Tralau 2014, pp. 304, 306, 315.   [171] Bredekamp 2003, p. 105.
[172] We can assume that the Church is orientated east and west. The shadows cast by the soldiers in the citadel fall on the left, so the light must be coming from the east, and thus from a morning sun.

dictates of the laws of nature. Although the church in the frontispiece is shown occupying a dominant position, the light pervading the city reassures us that, as Hobbes observes in chapter 29, the civil Authority, by 'standing in the cleerer light of naturall reason' can hope to maintain peace and prevent 'the darknesse of Schoole distinctions' from troubling and undermining the state.[173]

When in chapter 29 of *Leviathan* Hobbes lists the causes of the dissolution of commonwealths, he enumerates no less than nine principal diseases of the body politic capable of bringing about its death. Among these, the danger of ceding or dividing any element of sovereign power is assigned a prominent place, just as it is in the frontispiece. But the other danger we see illustrated – the power of over-mighty subjects – is described as 'not so great', although 'not unfit to be observed'.[174] Why, then, is the need to control the aristocracy given equal prominence in the frontispiece with the need to keep sovereignty undivided in the face of the jurisdictional pretentions of the Church?

It may be relevant that *Leviathan* was composed in Paris at the time when the *Fronde des nobles* was devastating much of France. Hobbes began writing in the summer of 1649, only a few months after several leading aristocrats had joined the Parlement of Paris in its protests against the government of Cardinal Mazarin, prompting a blockade of the city that lasted for several months.[175] Hobbes continued writing throughout 1650, a period of aristocratic revolt in many parts of France. After Mazarin arrested the prince de Condé and duc de Longueville in January 1650 their supporters began a series of uprisings in Normandy and Burgundy, while in August 1650 a Spanish army led by the Vicomte de Turenne invaded from the north.[176] Early in 1651, just as Hobbes was sending *Leviathan* to be printed, there was renewed aristocratic unrest in Paris, and Mazarin was forced to flee.[177] It would not have been surprising if, at the moment when the frontispiece to *Leviathan* was being designed, the threat of over-mighty subjects to the stability of states seemed to Hobbes no less a danger than the usurping aspirations of the Catholic Church.

VI

I now wish to concentrate on the colossus who looms over the upper half of the frontispiece and ask about his identity. The frontispiece itself offers a partial answer with its quotation from chapter 41 of the Book of Job. The chapter opens by asking 'Canst thou draw out leviathan with an

---

[173] Hobbes 2012, vol. 2, ch. 29, pp. 510, 512.   [174] Hobbes 2012, vol. 2, ch. 29, p. 514.
[175] Ranum 1993, pp. 197–212.   [176] Collins 2009, pp. 91–4.   [177] Collins 2009, p. 94.

hook'. There follows a long description of Leviathan as a fire-breathing sea monster with terrifying teeth and with scales 'so near to another that no air can come between them.' We are told that 'none is so fierce that dare stir him up'; that 'when he raiseth up himself, the mighty are afraid'; and that 'he is a king over all the children of pride'.[178]

This description supplies Hobbes with more meaning than he needs.[179] Although his frontispiece shows the colossus rising out of the sea, Hobbes has no further use for the idea of a sea monster.[180] He might even be thought to have had a reason for regretting his choice, given that so many of his adversaries ridiculed his apparent admission that he had described a monstrous state.[181] What he basically wants to depict is an image of *Imperium* or *Suprema potestas*. Challenging the Protestant injunction that biblical interpretation should strive to be literal rather than allegorical,[182] he explains that the point of his comparison with the description of Leviathan in 'the one and fortieth of *Job*' is to emphasise the prideful nature of man and 'the great power of his Governour', who is needed to curb '*all the children of pride*' and fill them with awe.[183]

A recent attempt has admittedly been made to establish that the body of the colossus is nevertheless that of a sea monster.[184] The only reason given, however, is that 'his torso is covered with scales just like those of a fish',[185] and specifically 'just like the Leviathan in the Old Testament text'.[186] But the torso of the colossus is not covered with scales; it is covered with several hundred men and women, and Bosse has made no attempt to make them resemble the scales of a fish. Certainly they are very far from resembling the scales of Leviathan as described in the Old Testament. As we have seen, these are said to be 'so near to another that no air can come between them'. But while the figures on the frontispiece are closely congregated, there are spaces between all of them, and on the right arm of the colossus they are quite widely separated.

The colossus has often been identified as a sovereign or king.[187] But in Hobbes's political theory sovereigns are natural persons, whereas what we see is not a natural person but a large number of individuals united as a

---

[178] Job 41: 10, 16, 25, 34.
[179] Unless, as Malcolm 2012, p. 115 suggests, Hobbes thought of the description as an allegory for the state.
[180] This is not to say there is no iconographical tradition associating sovereigns with sea-monsters. See Bredekamp 2016, Plates 4 and 6, pp. 23, 25 for medieval images of figures holding sceptres and 'sitting above Leviathan' (*sedens super Leviathan*).
[181] As noted in Farneti 2001.   [182] As noted in Springborg 1995.
[183] Hobbes 2012, vol. 2, ch. 28, p. 496.   [184] Kristiansson and Tralau 2014, p. 299.
[185] Kristiansson and Tralau 2014, p. 312.   [186] Kristiansson and Tralau 2014, p. 303.
[187] Dietz 1990, p. 91; Lloyd 1992, p. 224; Gamboni 2005, p. 164; Kristiansson and Tralau 2014, pp. 299, 303.

body politic under a single crowned head. I have already considered in chapter 9 the process by which, according to Hobbes, it is possible for a multitude to form such a union. As we saw, he argues that it is in consequence of authorising a sovereign to act as their representative that the individual members of a multitude become united. The outcome of their agreeing, each with each, on who should be their sovereign representative is that they acquire a single will and voice, that of their sovereign, to whom they assign the right to speak and act in the name of them all. But to say that they now possess one will and voice is to say that they have ceased to be a mere multitude and have become one person. 'A Multitude of men, are made *One* Person, when they are by one man, or one Person, Represented'.[188] We also learn the name of the person brought into existence by the members of the multitude as a result of agreeing on a sovereign to represent them. 'The Multitude so united in one Person, is called a COMMON-WEALTH, in latine CIVITAS' or the state.[189]

It is this conception of the sovereign state that the frontispiece illustrates. What we see, we can now state more precisely, is a multitude of individuals united as one person in consequence of having agreed on a sovereign representative, and what the text of *Leviathan* adds is that the name of the multitude united under a sovereign is the state. So it is now possible to give a name to the colossus who stands behind and dominates the town and countryside: his name is Leviathan, the proper name that Hobbes assigns to the state. The frontispiece also provides a written summary when it informs us that the title of the work is *Leviathan*, while adding that to speak of Leviathan is to refer to 'The Matter, Forme, and Power of a Common-wealth Ecclesiasticall and Civil.' The matter is provided by the members of the multitude; the power is that of their sovereign representative; and the agreement of the multitude to institute a sovereign is what gives form to the commonwealth or state.[190]

Hobbes adds a hint that what he has illustrated may be something even more specific: not merely the *persona fictione* or person 'by Fiction' of the state,[191] but the moment of its being instituted.[192] Hobbes began writing *Leviathan* at the time when the monarchy had just been abolished in England and the polity officially established as 'a Commonwealth and Free State'.[193] He notes in his Review and Conclusion that he has been

---

[188] Hobbes 2012, vol. 2, ch. 16, p. 248.

[189] Hobbes 2012, vol. 2, The Introduction, p. 16; see also ch. 17, p. 260.

[190] On these formulae, and their Aristotelian antecedents, see Brett 2010.

[191] For *personae fictione* see Quintilian 2001, 9. 3. 89, vol. 3, p. 154. For Hobbes on persons 'by Fiction' see Hobbes 2012, vol. 2, ch. 16, pp. 244, 246.

[192] As suggested in Corbett and Lightbown 1979, p. 224; Prokhovnik 1991, p. 142; Berger 2017, pp. 200–3, 206.

[193] Gardiner (ed.) 1906, p. 388.

composing his treatise during 'the revolution of States', and he adds that, at such a time, when 'the dissolvers of an old Government' have triumphed, we cannot hope to see anything more than 'the backs of them that erect a new'.[194] The backs of many people are what we see in the frontispiece, which suggests that they may be at the moment of erecting a new state. Perhaps this explains why the city depicted in the frontispiece is almost bereft of inhabitants. They have left the citadel guarded, but otherwise they have departed – men, women and children alike – to make their obeisance to a new head of state, the act we see them perform.[195]

Although the ruler to whom the people are submitting appears to be in possession of undivided power, it has recently been argued that this assumption embodies a misunderstanding of the frontispiece. Rather, we are told, the image portrays 'the obvious link between the body of Leviathan and the parliamentary representation of political rule'. The frontispiece should be read 'in terms of the structure of medieval society, with its clergy, its nobility pledged to military service and its city-dwelling burghers'. The overall design is said to recall 'the seating plan of the estates Parliament', in which 'the king as head of the body politic [is] flanked on his right and left by the clergy and nobility'. The representation of Leviathan should accordingly be understood 'as an embodiment of parliament'.[196]

The price of accepting this interpretation seems extravagantly high. One problem is that, in any portrayal of a parliament of estates, one would expect to find the representatives of the third estate prominently displayed. But in the *Leviathan* frontispiece they are nowhere to be seen. A further problem is that this reading has the effect of turning Hobbes's frontispiece into a contradiction rather than an illustration of his theory of government. Hobbes expresses a strong dislike in every recension of his civil science for theories of mixed rule in which power is divided between kings, lords and commons. He objects that, 'although few perceive, that such government, is not government, but division of the Common-wealth into three Factions, and call it mixt Monarchy; yet the truth is, that it is not one independent Common-wealth, but three independent Factions', which can only spell ruin for the state.[197] The reason is that, 'where there is already erected a Soveraign Power, there can be no other

---

[194] Hobbes 2012, vol. 3, A Review, and Conclusion, p. 1141. On this passage see Bredekamp 2003, p. 106 and n.
[195] But perhaps the city is plague-ridden, as suggested in Falk 2011, who argues that the two figures standing near the west door of the church are wearing the beaked masks of plague doctors. But are they? The image is too indistinct to allow a definite answer, but the one on the left appears merely to be wearing a broad-brimmed hat.
[196] Manow 2010, p. 29.   [197] Hobbes 2012, vol. 2, ch. 29, p. 512.

Representative of the same people, but onely to certain particular ends, by the Soveraign limited. For that were to erect two Soveraigns; and every man to have his person represented by two Actors', which cannot fail to produce conflict and war.[198] Hobbes concludes that, 'if there had not first been an opinion received of the greatest part of *England*, that these Powers were divided between the King, and the Lords, and the House of Commons, the people had never been divided, and fallen into this Civill Warre'.[199]

It is, in short, as far as possible from Hobbes's purposes to illustrate a parliamentary system of representation or a theory of government by the three estates. Hobbes even suggests that monarchs should try to avoid summoning the estates so far as possible. Given that all monarchs are already absolute representatives, they should 'take heed how they admit of any other generall Representation upon any occasion whatsoever'.[200] They not only need to remember that 'the Rights, which make the Essence of Soveraignty' are 'incommunicable, and inseparable';[201] they also need to remember that they alone possess the right to represent the person of the state.

That Hobbes's image is intended as a representation of undivided sovereignty is confirmed by the fact that the head of state carries a bishop's crozier in his left hand (not a sceptre, as is sometimes said)[202] in addition to the sword of justice in his right. The crozier is tilted forwards across the landscape and downwards towards the other emblems of ecclesiastical authority, all of which the civil sovereign is thus shown to dominate. At the same time the shadows cast by the sword and crozier underline the pervasive presence of the colossus in the country over which he holds sway.[203] This need for ecclesiastical as well as civil authority to be held in the sovereign's hands is strongly confirmed in the text of *Leviathan*, from which we learn in chapter 42 that all pretensions to ecclesiastical power are groundless as well as dangerously divisive. 'It is the Civill Soveraign' who 'hath the Supreme Power in all causes, as well Ecclesiasticall as Civill', and 'these Rights are incident to all Soveraigns, whether Monarchs, or Assemblies'.[204] Dismissing Bellarmine's claims about the independent powers of the Church, Hobbes adds that, in the name of preserving civil unity and peace, all pastors must be treated as nothing more than ministers of civil sovereigns 'in the same manner as the Magistrates of Towns, Judges

[198] Hobbes 2012, vol. 2, ch. 19, p. 286.   [199] Hobbes 2012, vol. 2, ch. 18, p. 278.
[200] Hobbes 2012, vol. 2, ch. 19, p. 286.   [201] Hobbes 2012, vol. 2, ch. 18, p. 278.
[202] See, for example, Springborg 1995, p. 363.
[203] The effect is even more clearly visible in the drawn version of the frontispiece. See Figure 10.29.
[204] Hobbes 2012, vol. 3, ch. 42, p. 866.

in Courts of Justice, and Commanders of Armies, are all but Ministers of him that is the Magistrate of the whole Common-wealth'.[205]

The gesture with which the head of state brandishes his crozier appears to be straightforwardly affirmative. But if we turn to the sword of justice in his right hand, we come upon a more complex message about the character of sovereign power. He is not shown flourishing the sword aloft, as the figure of *Imperium* does in the frontispiece of *De cive*. Nor is the sword poised or pointed as if ready to strike. Rather it is tilted backwards from the landscape towards the sea and the sky beyond. The head of state is shown, in other words, *holding back* the sword of justice, 'staying his hand' in a gesture of mercy that Hobbes's readers would have recognised from the story twice told in the Old Testament about the wrath of God incurred by David when he numbered the people of Israel. The Lord sent a pestilence, after which an angel stretched out his hand to destroy Jerusalem. But at that moment 'the Lord repented him of the evil, and said to the angel that destroyed the people, It is enough: stay now thine hand'.[206]

This is not to deny that the rulers of Hobbes's age were counselled to exercise great caution in staying the hand of justice. Preaching an Assize sermon in 1619, William Pemberton had advised the judges that, 'after the cause is discerningly *heard* with the eare of justice, and the *sentence* equally pronounced with the mouth of justice, then must *execution* be exactly done by the hand of justice', for 'unlesse this exact *execution* do follow, the former processe is altogether fruitlesse, and tends to no profit or good effect.'[207] Nor does Hobbes disagree that, if peace is to be kept, the laws must be enforced by the sword. The people need to recognise that 'the Lawes are of no power to protect them, without a Sword in the hands of a man, or men, to cause those laws to be put in execution.'[208] The sovereign must stand ready 'to prescribe the Rules of Right and Wrong; that is, to make Laws; and with the Sword of Justice to compel men to obey his Decisions'.[209] Furthermore, this lawmaking power must be 'Absolute and Arbitrary', for without it 'the Civill Soveraign is fain to handle the Sword of Justice unconstantly, and as if it were too hot for him to hold', a frequent cause of the dissolution of states.[210]

Everyone agreed, however, that one distinctive duty of sovereigns is a readiness to stay the hand of justice and offer mercy in its place. Even so inflexible an absolutist as Gryffith Williams, whom we have already encountered as an implacable defender of the divine right of kings, notes

---

[205] Hobbes 2012, vol. 3, ch. 42, p. 852.   [206] II. Samuel 24: 16; cf I. Chronicles 21: 15.
[207] Pemberton 1619, p. 51.   [208] Hobbes 2012, vol. 2, ch. 21, p. 328.
[209] Hobbes 2012, vol. 3, ch. 42, p. 900.
[210] Hobbes 2012, vol. 3, A Review, and Conclusion, p. 1135.

how often it happens in the Bible that 'when the Sword is drawne, and the hand ready to strike, yet mercy steppes in', so that 'mercy stayes the hand of Justice'.[211] The value of compassion continued to be strongly emphasised even at the height of the English civil wars. Preaching to the House of Commons in 1645, George Walker exhorted its members to distinguish true malignants from those who have merely been deceived. Speaking of the latter, he called on Parliament to 'have compassion on them, and put a difference, pulling them out of the fire, by the hand of justice tempered with mercy'.[212]

As Hobbes makes clear in the text of *Leviathan*, and even more vividly in the frontispiece, he strongly endorses the view that sovereigns should be prepared to stay the hand of justice. The principal duty of the sovereign is to procure '*the safety of the people*; to which he is obliged by the Law of Nature', a law to which every sovereign 'is as much subject, as any of the meanest of his People'.[213] But one precept of the law of nature is to show clemency whenever possible. Hobbes lists nineteen separate laws of nature in chapter 15 of *Leviathan*, but he also likes to single out the most salient, and when he does so he always includes the requirement of mercy among them.[214] As he concludes, 'there is place many times for Lenity, without prejudice to the Common-wealth; and Lenity when there is such place for it, is required by the Law of Nature.'[215] All sovereigns have a positive duty to hold back the sword when this can be done without danger to the state.

Although Hobbes asks for the sword of justice to be wielded with moderation, he does not consider any head of state to be bound by a contractual obligation to exercise his authority in any particular way. Here his view of the rights of those who exercise supreme power stands in sharp contrast with the long-standing constitutional tradition according to which kings and chief magistrates are held to be legally tied or bound to act in accordance with the requirements of justice. As I noted in chapter 2, the earliest written constitutions enacted in the city-republics of the *Regnum Italicum* had called for civic officials to be 'bound' by statute to the performance of their duties and 'tied' to their particular brief.[216] We see this view of public power illustrated in Ambrogio Lorenzetti's portrayal of the holder of *Suprema potestas* as someone who also bears the *persona* of the *civitas* (Figure 2.3). The right hand of this dominating figure, in which he clasps his sceptre, is knotted to a cord that

---

[211] Williams 1624, p. 195.   [212] Walker 1645, p. 19.
[213] Hobbes 2012, vol. 2, ch. 30, pp. 520, 534.
[214] Hobbes 2012, vol. 2, ch. 15, p. 242; ch. 17, p. 254; ch. 31, p. 560.
[215] Hobbes 2012, vol. 2, ch. 30, p. 544.
[216] Banchi (ed.) 1866, p. 7: 'alligatur Statuto ... suo Breve speciali ligetur'.

ties and binds him – through the mediation of the body of citizens – to enact the dictates of justice.

More immediately, Hobbes's hostility to this line of thought strongly contrasts with the outlook of the parliamentarian propagandists whose attacks on the Crown at the outbreak of the civil war I discussed in chapter 9. Henry Parker had declared in his *Observations* of 1642 that the king not only has an obligation to 'defend and uphold all our lawes', but is also 'bound to consent to new Lawes if they be necesssary'.[217] Philip Hunton in his *Treatise of Monarchy* of 1643 had agreed that 'the very Being of our Common and Statute Lawes, and our Kings acknowledging themselves bound to governe by them' prove that the English constitution is mixed and limited.[218] These commitments were weightily reinforced when the greatest of the 'monarchomach' tracts, the *Vindiciae, contra tyrannos*, was translated into English in 1648. From the *Vindiciae* we learn that no king can lawfully be handed 'the Scepter and rod of Justice' until he has agreed with his subjects that 'he is bound to confirme their priviledges' and is 'tied to the performance'.[219]

Hobbes is consequently rejecting a long-standing political as well as iconographical tradition when he shows the right hand of the head of state as *untied*, so that he is never *bound* to act except according to his will. That this is a visual message Hobbes wants to convey is strongly confirmed in the text of *Leviathan*. Chapter 18 contains a vehement denunciation of 'the opinion that any Monarch receiveth his Power by Covenant, that is to say on Condition'.[220] This erroneous belief arises 'from want of understanding this easie truth, that Covenants being but words, and breath, have no force to oblige, contain, constrain, or protect any man, but what it has from the publique Sword; that is, from the untyed hands of that Man, or Assembly of men that hath the Soveraignty'.[221] The hand holding the public sword must never be tied. As Hobbes confirms in chapter 21, a true sovereign 'never wanteth Right to any thing'.[222] To be able to act with untied hands is the very definition of sovereignty.

VII

With his portrayal of the sovereign state Hobbes may be said to provide an illustration of the central element in his civil science. But this by no means brings him to the end of his visual argument. The upper half of his frontispiece contains a number of further details that not only confirm but

---

[217] [Parker] 1642, pp. 4–5.   [218] [Hunton] 1643, p. 32.   [219] *Vindiciae* 1648, p. 100.
[220] Hobbes 2012, vol. 2, ch. 18, p. 268.   [221] Hobbes 2012, vol. 2, ch. 18, p. 268.
[222] Hobbes 2012, vol. 2, ch. 21, p. 330.

greatly add to his depiction of the character of the state. One becomes clear as soon as we reflect on the orientation of the church dominating the cityscape. We can assume that it faces east and west, and thus that we are looking at it from the south. But if this is so, then the figure of Leviathan must be looming up out of the north. Here Hobbes may be alluding to the discussion initiated by Jean Bodin with his analysis in Book V of his *Six Bookes of a Commonweale* of the impact of climate on the rise and fall of states. Bodin had noted that, while the subtlest philosophies have always come out of the south, 'great armies and mighty powers have come out of the North'.[223] The image of Leviathan arising out of a northern sea may additionally have been suggested by a further passage from the Book of Job, in which we are told (in a verse already echoed by Bodin) that 'terrible majesty' as well as fair weather 'cometh out of the north'.[224]

A further and still more arresting effect we can hardly fail to register – although it has scarcely been discussed[225] – is that Leviathan is holding his sword and crozier in such a way as to create two strongly marked diagonal lines. The impression they convey is that a further geometrical shape is hovering over the rectangular form of the frontispiece as a whole. Suppose we follow this hint, drawing the diagonals in both directions and thereby creating the shape towards which they gesture. We find that we have constructed a triangle encompassing not merely the figure of Leviathan but the entirety of the frontispiece (Figure 10.32).

The triangle we see here is not isosceles;[226] Leviathan holds his sword further away from his body than he does his crozier, so that the left side of the triangle is longer than the right. For an exact classification of the resulting geometrical shape, Hobbes would have been able to consult Thomas Urquhart's *Trissotetras*, first published in 1645. From Urquhart's table showing 'the whole Doctrine of Triangles' we learn that what has been incorporated into the *Leviathan* frontispiece is a xemenoro, one of the six types of oblique triangle.[227]

For Hobbes's original readers, this superimposition would have carried some powerful symbolic resonances. They would have been accustomed in the first place to hearing Britain described as a triangle. This image had initially been popularised by John Lyly in his *Euphues* of 1580, in which he refers to the island 'called now England, heretofore named Britaine',

---

[223] Bodin 1962, V. I, p. 550. Bodin's discussion was much taken up. For an early example see Du Bartas 1598, p. 72.

[224] Job 37: 22.

[225] The important exception is Brandt 1987 (reprinted in Manow and Simon 2012, pp. 13–41). See also Olsson 2007, pp. 233–4.

[226] Still less is it equilateral, as claimed in Olsson 2007, p. 233.

[227] Urquhart 1645, sig. a, 1v–2r.

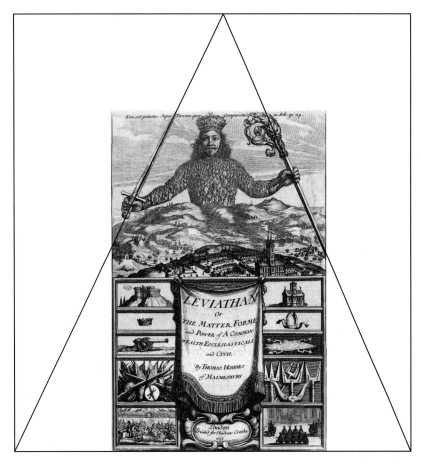

Figure 10.32 Hobbes, Thomas (1651). *Leviathan*, London,
Frontispiece by Abraham Bosse with superimposed triangle.

which is 'in forme lyke unto a Triangle, being broadest in the South part,
and gathering narrower & narrower till it come to the farthest point of
Cathnesse'.[228] A generation later, this way of picturing Britain was taken
up in the increasingly popular genre of gazeteers in which the various
countries of the world were surveyed and described. These compilations
generally begin by offering an explication of the name of each country
followed by an account of its size and shape. Of all the countries described
as triangular, Britain is usually taken to be the most obvious case. John

[228] Lyly 1580, fo. 109r–v.

Norden in his *Speculum Britanniae* notes that 'the forme of this land is Trianguler, much like Cicilia';[229] William Camden begins his *Britain* by observing that the country 'lieth against Germanie and France trianglewise',[230] and Mercator in his *Historia Mundi* agrees that 'the figure of it is Triangular, or three cornerd, and it runneth forth into three severall Angles.'[231]

With the union of the crowns of Scotland and England in 1603 this shape took on a further symbolic significance, as the court preachers were fond of pointing out. When in March 1603 Lancelot Andrewes delivered a sermon at Whitehall in the presence of James I to mark the inauguration of the new reign, he rejoiced that the king had now become 'head, not of One Angle, as You were before', but 'Caput Trianguli, Head now of three, even of a whole Triangle.'[232] The same imagery can be found in the sermon preached by John Pyne at the accession of Charles I in 1625. Pyne concludes by expressing the fervent hope that 'the same Almightie hand of the ever-living God who hath placed and planted our Soveraigne as the Heart in the bodie of this Triangled Iland' will 'reserve ever to it selfe only, that little Triangle of his heart'.[233]

The extent of these allusions suggests that the hovering triangle may in part be there to indicate that the sea-girt land dominated by the figure of Leviathan is the British isles.[234] This possibility is reinforced by the frequency with which Hobbes assures us in *Leviathan* that he is primarily addressing his fellow countrymen. He speaks of 'our most wise King, King *James*' and his attempted union of his two realms.[235] He gives it as one of his main reasons for writing his treatise 'that the Civill warres have not yet sufficiently taught' the people of England about the relations between protection and obedience.[236] And he ends by noting that he is writing at a time when 'the dissolvers of an old Government' in England are trying to construct a new regime.[237]

To many of Hobbes's original readers, however, the hovering triangle would have carried a further message of far deeper significance. With their three sides and three angles, triangles were widely recognised as symbols

---

[229] Norden 1593, p. 8.
[230] Camden 1610, p. 1. This was the earliest translation of Camden's work, which was originally published in Latin in 1586.
[231] Mercator 1635, p. 40.   [232] Andrewes 1611, p. 31.   [233] Pyne 1628, p. 21.
[234] It has been suggested that Hobbes may have had an even more specific recollection of his native land in mind. A view of Malmesbury painted in 1646 contains details sometimes said to resemble those on the frontispiece of *Leviathan*. But the differences seem to me more striking than the similarities.
[235] Hobbes 2012, vol. 2, ch. 19, p. 304.
[236] Hobbes 2012, vol. 3, A Review, and Conclusion, p. 1133.
[237] Hobbes 2012, vol. 3, A Review, and Conclusion, p. 1141.

of the Holy Trinity, and were thus a standard means of alluding to the nature and powers of God. This line of thought may originally have been popularised in England by John Foxe in his so-called book of martyrs. Foxe relates how one of his heroes, Hierome of Prague, was forced to correct a misunderstanding due to his having described the Trinity as 'a certayne triangle' and as 'the shield of fayth', thereby appearing to exclude the powers of the Church. We are told that, while denying the implication, Hierome strongly reasserted his description of the Holy Trinity as a triangle, in which 'one divine essence consisted in three subjects or persons in themselves distinct'.[238]

This way of explicating the Trinity was widely popularised by late Elizabethan and Jacobean divines. Thomas Playfere, Lady Margaret Professor of Divinity at Cambridge, spoke in a sermon of 1593 about 'a triangle, made according to the image of the Trinity'.[239] John Boys in his *Exposition* of the liturgy in 1610 similarly referred to 'a triangle, representing the sacred Trinitie',[240] while William Loe, one of James I's chaplains, argued in a sermon of 1619 that God 'is one in nature and three in persons', just as 'in a triangle are three angles, yet one figure'.[241] The comparison quickly passed into general currency. By 1630 Richard Brathwaite in *The English Gentleman* was able to treat it as self-evident that to describe something as 'triangle-wise' is to say it resembles 'the image of the blessed *Trinitie*'.[242]

The same generation saw the emergence of a widespread iconographical convention of portraying the Holy Trinity as a triangle. The use of this symbol appears to have been rare in medieval England, except for a brief period in the thirteenth century.[243] But with the need to counter the growing threat of Socinianism in the early seventeenth century, the image began to be enthusiastically deployed as a means of reaffirming orthodox Trinitarian doctrine in a clear and memorable style.[244] William Hole's frontispiece to the 1607 printing of the Geneva Bible is dominated by a triangle enclosing the tetragrammaton (YHWH), the standard version of God's name in Hebrew (Figure 10.33).[245]

---

[238] Foxe 1583, p. 634, the fourth edition, the last published in Foxe's lifetime.
[239] Playfere 1603, sig. D, 1r.   [240] Boys 1610, p. 116.   [241] Loe 1619, p. 46.
[242] Brathwaite 1630, p. 442.
[243] Corbett and Lightbown 1979, pp. 40, 100. For thirteenth-century examples see Evans 1982, pp. 22–5 and Plates 5(a) and (b). The contrast with Italy is marked. McGinn 2006, pp. 192–4 (and illustration at p. 194) notes that, as early as the twelfth century, Joachim of Fiore in his *Liber Figurarum* pictured the Trinity as a triangle, and the iconography remained popular in the Renaissance. To take only the most celebrated example, Kemp 1990 p. 48 observes that the geometry of Leonardo's Last Supper is wholly organised around two triangles converging on the right eye of Christ.
[244] On Socinus's anti-trinitarianism see Mortimer 2010, pp. 33–8; on the growth of anti-Trinitarianism in England see Mortimer 2010, pp. 40–2; Lim 2012, pp. 16–68.
[245] *The Bible* 1607. The frontispiece is signed 'Guillelmus Hole fecit'.

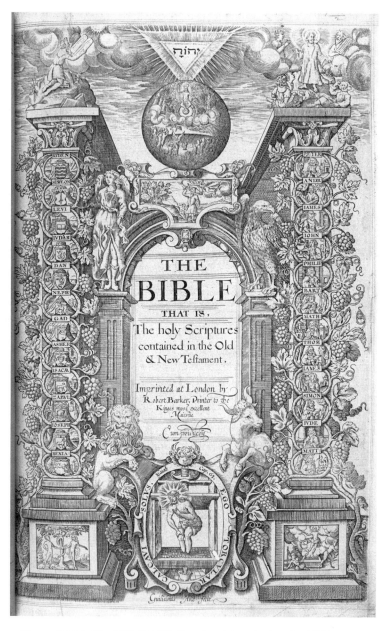

Figure 10.33 *The Bible* (1607). London, Frontispiece by William Hole.

The anonymous frontispiece in the 1618 Book of Common Prayer is the first of many that similarly display a triangle surrounded by clouds and enclosing the tetragrammaton (Figure 10.34).[246]

Thomas Cecill's frontispiece for Thomas Heywood's treatise on angels of 1635 shows a triangle within a circle surrounded by clouds and cherubim, across the centre of which appears the tetragrammaton, while the words *Sanctae Triunitatis* are written on the upright lines of the triangle (Figure 10.35).[247]

The frontispiece of the 1637 Scottish printing of the Authorised Version of the Bible again shows a triangle within a circle, together with an attempted explication of the doctrine of the Trinity. Written across the triangle is the declaration that the Father 'is not' the Son, that the son 'is not' the Holy Spirit and that the Spirit 'is not' God. But we are also told that each of them 'is' God, who is represented by the tetragrammaton at the centre of the triangle (Figure 10.36).[248]

Perhaps most significantly for my present argument, the same image of a heavenly triangle was also employed by Abraham Bosse, who included it in his frontispiece for Charles Drelincourt's *Consolations de l'âme* in 1651 (Figure 10.37).[249] Surrounding the triangle Bosse also shows circles of cherubim, who stare out at us in much the same way as do the faces that form the torso of Leviathan in Bosse's drawing of the *Leviathan* frontispiece (Figure 10.29).

During the late Elizabethan period, this image of the triangular Trinity began in turn to be associated with a specific argument about the relationship between man and God. The starting-point was the observation that the human heart is triangular in shape. All the divines I have cited make the point, speaking of 'the heart of man, which is a triangle'[250] or noting that 'the heart of man is made like a triangle' or 'of the forme of a triangle'.[251] They then argue that, because the triangular heart is obliged to live in a circular world, it can never truly be at home. As Thomas Playfere puts it in his sermon of 1603 on *Hearts delight*, 'as a circle can never fill a triangle' so 'the round world, which is a circle, can never fill the heart of man, which is a triangle'.[252] Our only salvation lies in 'the

---

[246] *The Booke of Common Prayer* 1618.

[247] Heywood 1635. The frontispiece is signed 'T. Cecill sculp:'.

[248] *The Holy Bible* 1637. Triangles enclosing tetragrammatons can also be found in the frontispieces of many non-religious works from the same period. See, for example, Hind 1952–64, vol. 2, Plate 117 (d) (a frontispiece by Renold Elstrack) and vol. 3, Plate 11 (a frontispiece by John Payne). See also Quarles 1635, p. 176.

[249] Drelincourt 1651.   [250] Playfere 1603, sig. D, 1r.

[251] Boys 1610, p. 116; Chaloner 1623, p. 273. For later examples see Stoughton 1640, p. 76; Loe 1645, p. 10.

[252] Playfere 1603, sig. D, 1r.

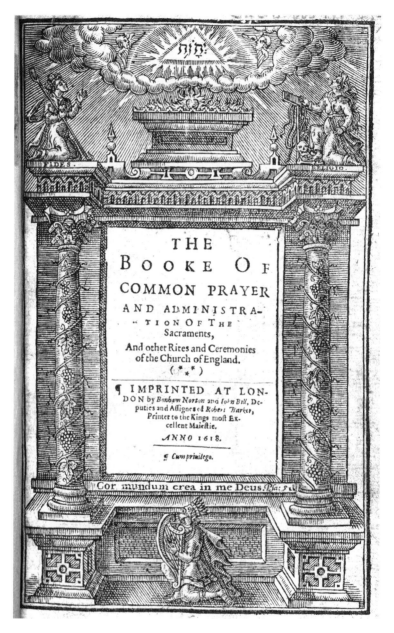

Figure 10.34 *The Booke of Common Prayer* (1618). London,
Frontispiece.

Figure 10.35 Heywood, Thomas (1635). *The Hierarchie of the blessed Angells*, London, Frontispiece by Thomas Cecill.

Figure 10.36 *The Holy Bible* (1637). Edinburgh, Frontispiece.

Figure 10.37 Drelincourt, Charles (1651). *Les Consolations de l'âme fidele*, Paris, Frontispiece by Abraham Bosse.

glorious trinitie', which is also triangular, and consequently 'filleth the triangle of the heart'.[253] Martin Fotherby, bishop of Salisbury, reiterates the argument in his *Atheomastix* of 1622. 'The world is of a circular forme: but the heart of man is of a triangular'. We must recognise that 'the onely object that is able to fill this three cornered heart' is 'the Holy and undivided Trinitie', which is likewise triangular and is thus 'an all-filling object' that enables us to be fulfilled.[254]

I now turn to the connection between God's triangular nature and the hovering triangle in the *Leviathan* frontispiece. Hobbes's fundamental contention is that, just as the Holy and undivided Trinity is made up of *tres personae*, so the state is likewise a unity made up of three persons. In chapter 16 he tells us the names of the persons involved. First there is the natural person or body of persons whom the members of the multitude choose to represent them. If they choose a single natural person, then he or she will of course have a proper name (such as, in the case of Britain, Charles Stuart). Next there is the artificial person of the representative whom the multitude thereby authorise. The name of this person is the sovereign, who may be a single natural person (as in a Monarchy) or an Assembly of natural persons (as in an Aristocracy or Democracy).[255] Finally, there is the *persona fictione*, the person 'by Fiction' brought into being by the multitude when they agree to submit to a sovereign representative and thereby acquire a single will and voice. The name of this person – the person whom the sovereign represents – is Leviathan, the commonwealth or state.

Why is it so important to Hobbes to show that, like the triune God, the state is made up of three persons? Because Hobbes wants us to think of the state as a kind of God. Just as the Anglican theologians of his time maintain that we can only hope for religious fulfilment if we accommodate ourselves to the triune nature of the immortal God, so Hobbes analogously argues that we can only attain fulfilment in civil life if we accommodate ourselves to the will of the triune state. Admittedly the state is nothing more than a 'Mortall God' whom we conjure into existence ourselves.[256] But it is nevertheless the God to whom 'wee owe under

---

[253] Playfere 1603, sig. D, 1v.
[254] Fotherby 1622, p. 209. See also Chaloner 1623, pp. 273–4; Stoughton 1640, pp. 76–7.
[255] This point is clarified in Hobbes 2012, vol. 2, ch. 19, p. 284. Strictly speaking, this means that Hobbes's frontispiece illustrates one of two possible conceptions of the state. According to Hobbes's theory, the person of the sovereign could equally well have taken the form of an Assembly. But this idea would have been hard to render in visual terms, and Hobbes prefers to show the head of a single natural person in the role of head of state.
[256] On Hobbes's mortal God, and the possible sources of this image in the *Corpus Hermeticum*, see Paganini 2010a.

the *Immortall God*, our peace and defence'.[257] It is this almost blasphe-mous image of state power that the hovering triangle is there to signal and underline.

It might seem, however, that there is an obvious difference between the *tres personae* of the Holy Trinity and the three persons who constitute the state. According to the orthodox doctrine of the Trinity, the relationship between the *tres personae* is one of identity; most crucially, God the son is also God. But the relationship between the persons who make up the state is one of representation; the artificial person of the sovereign represents the person of the multitude, thereby creating the person 'by Fiction' of the state. For Hobbes, however, there is no difference here, because he thinks of the *tres personae* of the Holy Trinity not as different manifesta-tions of the same substance, but rather as God's authorised representa-tives, just as he thinks of lawful heads of state as authorised by the multitude to act as their sovereign representative.[258]

Hobbes lays out his startling analysis of the nature (and, even more startlingly, the specific persons) of the Holy Trinity at the outset of his discussion of ecclesiastical power in chapter 42 of *Leviathan*. He begins by reminding us that 'the proper signification' of the word person is 'that which is Represented by another'.[259] This being so, we can see that 'God the Father, as Represented by Moses, is one Person; and as Represented by his Sonne, another Person; and as Represented by the Apostles, and by the Doctors that taught by authority from them derived, is a third Person; and yet every Person here, is the Person of one and the same God.'[260] The only relevant difference between the immortal God and the mortal God of the state is that the former authorises his own representation, whereas the representation of the state by the sovereign needs to be authorised by its own subjects.

By way of rounding off, it is worth considering one doubt sometimes raised about the adequacy of Hobbes's attempted representation of the state. When, in the Introduction to *Leviathan*, Hobbes anatomises the properties of his 'Artificiall Man' by comparing them with the properties of a natural man, he writes that 'the *Soveraignty* is an Artificiall *Soul*, as giving life and motion to the whole body'.[261] The Latin version helpfully clarifies the ambiguity by indicating that, in speaking of 'the *Soveraignty*', he means '*the man who holds supreme Power*'.[262] The objec-tion sometimes raised is that Hobbes's iconographical scheme is not equal

---

[257] Hobbes 2012, vol. 2, ch. 17, p. 260.
[258] See Matheron 1990; for a full discussion see Brito Vieira 2009, pp. 209–33.
[259] Hobbes 2012, vol. 3, ch. 42, p. 776.   [260] Hobbes 2012, vol. 3, ch. 42, p. 776.
[261] Hobbes 2012, vol. 2, The Introduction, p. 16.
[262] Hobbes 2012, vol. 2, [Introduction], p. 17: '*Is qui summam habet Potestatem*'.

to portraying this conception of the sovereign as the soul of the state, and is consequently obliged to fall back on a more traditional representation of the sovereign as head of state.[263]

For Hobbes, however, the soul is simply the name of an animating force. It is not the name of a separate and non-corporeal substance, and it makes no sense to ask where it is located. As Hobbes observes, 'The *Soule* in Scripture, signifieth alwaies, either the Life, or the Living Creature; and the Body and Soule jointly, the *Body alive*.'[264] He accordingly sees no contradiction in referring to the sovereign both as the soul and head of the state. In chapter 29 he declares that 'the Soveraign, is the publique Soule, giving Life and Motion to the Commonwealth,' but in chapter 42 he says that 'the Civill Soveraign in every Common-wealth, is the *Head* . . . from which all Jurisdiction is derived.'[265] Hobbes's portrayal of the sovereign as head of state is simply his attempt to capture the idea of an animating force in iconographically familiar terms.

There is one respect, however, in which the frontispiece of *Leviathan* is undoubtedly more conventional than the text: it shows the head of state as a man and not a woman. Hobbes concedes that 'for the most part Commonwealths have been erected by the Fathers, not by the Mothers of families.'[266] As his phrasing makes clear, however, he rejects any suggestion that dominion must necessarily be held by men. He argues that, in the state of nature, dominion over children 'is in the Mother' rather than the father.[267] He adds in his *Considerations* of 1662 that anyone who supposes that the artificial person of a sovereign can be borne only by the natural person of a man is forgetting that, 'though *man* may be *male* and *female*, *authority* is not'.[268] Hobbes was fully accustomed to the idea that women can possess supreme authority not merely in households but in states. He was born in 1588, and consequently lived for the first fifteen years of his life as the subject of a queen regnant. He entered the employment of the Devonshire family in 1608, but when the second earl died in 1628 he was dismissed by the new head of the family, the earl's young widow.[269] Hobbes would have had no theoretical objection to the portrayal of the head of state in the frontispiece of *Leviathan* as a woman. The decision to illustrate the head of a man is – to cite his own phrase – no more than an acknowledgement of what 'for the most part' happens in the world.

Before leaving the figure of Leviathan, it is worth observing that many attempts have been made to establish that Bosse's image of the crowned

---

[263] I mistakenly raised this objection in Skinner 2008a, p. 190.
[264] Hobbes 2012, vol. 3, ch. 44, p. 974.
[265] Hobbes 2012, vol. 2, ch. 29, p. 518; vol. 3, ch. 42, p. 904.
[266] Hobbes 2012, vol. 2, ch. 20, p. 308.   [267] Hobbes 2012, vol. 2, ch. 20, p. 310.
[268] Hobbes 1840b, p. 434.   [269] Skinner 1996, p. 220.

head of state must have been intended as a representation of some identifiable historical character. Some have taken it to be a portrait of Oliver Cromwell, who in 1651 was the head of the English Council of State. Others have argued that it must be a portrait of the future Charles II, who was restored as head of state in 1660. Still others have suggested that Hobbes must have requested – presumably in a moment of mega-lomania – that the head should be a portrait of himself.[270]

It is arguable, however, that these suggestions are based on a misunder-standing of the iconographical conventions at work. Hobbes is not so much interested in sovereigns as in the concept of sovereignty. What he needed from Bosse was a generalised image of a head of state. Bosse was required on more than one occasion to execute this task, and in doing so he liked to create a picture of a long-haired, straight-nosed, short-bearded and moustachioed man wearing a closed imperial crown. This is how he depicts the head of the monarch in the frontispiece he designed for Charles Drelincourt's *Consolations de l'âme* in 1651 (Figure 10.37) and this is how – in the same year – he depicts the head of the sovereign in the frontispiece of Hobbes's *Leviathan*.

There is no reason to suppose that in either instance he intended any-thing other than a standard emblematic portrait with generic attributes. The only significant difference between his two etchings of 1651 is that, in the case of the *Leviathan* frontispiece, Bosse takes some pains to produce an image in which the expression is appropriate to a head of state. Not only does the sovereign gaze out at us with serenity and a certain severity, but he also looks us straight in the eye. Although his role may only be that of acting as a representative of the state, we are left with a final reminder that it is nevertheless through the will of the sovereign that the power of the state is able to take effect.

VIII

I have interpreted Hobbes's colossus as a portrait of the multitude united as one person through the act of authorising a sovereign, and thus as a representation of Hobbes's idea of the state. It remains to ask what Hobbes's frontispiece has to tell us about the proper relations between such sovereigns and their subjects. When heads of state are depicted in Renaissance emblem books they are generally shown carrying a sceptre, seated on a throne or judgment-seat and surrounded by a group of

---

[270] Brown 1978, pp. 32–4; Corbett and Lightbown 1979, pp. 221–2; Goldsmith 1990, pp. 654 and 671–3; Martinich 1992, pp. 362–3; Strong 1993, pp.130–1, 159; Gamboni 2005, p. 165.

counsellors, a set of images designed to suggest their primary concern with the dispensing of justice. This, for example, is how the *bonus rex* or good king is portrayed by Alciato in his *Emblemata*, by Aneau in his *Picta poesis*, by Perrière in his *Morosophie* and later by Frideric in his *Emblemes nouveaux*.[271]

According to an alternative visual narrative, however, we should think of our rulers less in judicial terms and more as a protective force. Bredekamp invokes the tradition of the sheltering *Madonna della misericordia*, a prominent motif in Italian religious art from as early as the *trecento*.[272] As Bredekamp also notes, this guarding and enfolding figure was sometimes represented as a bearer of sovereign power with arms outstretched in a defending pose.[273] This too is how we see the power of the Senate and people of Rome displayed in the frontispiece of Holland's translation of Livy in 1600 (Figure 10.16), and something similar can be seen in Henry Peacham's image of 'Roiall dignitie' in his *Minerva Britanna* of 1612 as well as in Abraham Bosse's allegorical portrait of Louis XIII as Hercules of 1635.[274]

It is this latter iconographical tradition that Hobbes and Bosse recall in the frontispiece of *Leviathan*. Hobbes's head of state is shown standing rather than seated, wielding a sword rather than a sceptre, and at the same time dominating and almost enfolding the city and countryside lying before him. The implication that everyone has a paramount need to be protected is strongly confirmed in the body of the text. Man cannot flourish outside the state, 'for whose protection and defence it was intended'.[275] Without the state's absolute power, the multitude can expect 'no defence, nor protection, neither against a Common enemy, nor against the injuries of one another'.[276] Provided, however, that they agree to subject themselves to an untrammelled form of sovereignty, they can hope 'to live peaceably amongst themselves, and be protected against other men'.[277] We must never forget that it is wholly due to the power of the state that we are able to enjoy 'our peace and defence'.[278]

---

[271] Alciato 1550, p. 157; Aneau 1552, p. 70 (without counsellors); Perrière 1553, sig. K, 3v; Frideric 1617, p. 76.

[272] Bredekamp 2003, pp. 77–8. On the tradition in Italy see van Asperen 2013. It can also be found in Poland at an early stage. The Madonna della misericordia in St James's Church in Toruń has been dated to *c*.1350.

[273] Bredekamp 2003, p. 78.

[274] Peacham 1612, p. 107 (a crowned lion with arms outstretched, a sword in its right hand); Lothe 2008, Plate 135, p. 238 (the king in armour brandishing a club in his right hand).

[275] Hobbes 2012, vol. 2, The Introduction, p. 16.

[276] Hobbes 2012, vol. 2, ch. 17, p. 256.   [277] Hobbes 2012, vol. 2, ch. 18, p. 264.

[278] Hobbes 2012, vol. 2, ch. 17, p. 260.

The attitude we ought therefore to adopt towards the mortal God of the state should be – as with the immortal God – not merely one of fear but of reverence. When Hobbes enumerates the laws of nature he first lays it down that there must always be 'feare of some coërcive Power' if peace is to be kept.[279] But when he explains the political covenant he adds that this fear must always be accompanied by a sense of awe, and he instructs us never to speak of sovereign power except with reverence.[280] It is right that subjects should be made to experience awe in the face of the state,[281] just as it is right that successful sovereigns should be 'reverenced and beloved'.[282]

Hobbes's frontispiece introduces a similar argument. The united members of the multitude are shown looking up to their head of state, and some of them are kneeling at the same time.[283] The idiom that speaks of *looking up to* someone – harbouring feelings of veneration or respect – was already in widespread use in Hobbes's time, and was much invoked by theological writers to suggest the feelings we must be sure to register when we contemplate what we owe to God. Henry Church in his *Miscellanea Philo-theologica* of 1637 tells us to 'looke-up, that GOD may looke downe', and to make sure that 'we looke-up with Reverence, and subjection'.[284] The London preacher John Gore similarly counsels us in *The God of Heaven*, a sermon of 1638, that in hard times we should 'with feare and reverence looke up to God'.[285] John Jackson in his 1649 abridgement of the Old Testament repeats that, because it is beyond our powers to comprehend God's mercy, we should simply 'with admiration looke up to heaven', thereby expressing our gratitude.[286]

Some commentators have treated the reverence displayed by the body of the people in the *Leviathan* frontispiece as the depiction of a similarly religious response.[287] But the subjects who are looking up to their head of state are acknowledging their subjection not to God but merely to a mortal God whom they have created for their own purposes, and the reverence they exhibit is purely civil in character. (No one, for example, has felt obliged to remove his hat.) They are simply displaying an appropriate feeling of thankfulness for the protection they receive. It is sometimes said that only men are pictured performing this act of obeisance, but on closer inspection we find that women are also present (many wearing

---

[279] Hobbes 2012, vol. 2, ch. 14, p. 210.   [280] Hobbes 2012, vol. 2, ch. 30, p. 526.

[281] On the need for subjects to be kept in awe see Hobbes 2012, vol. 2, ch. 13, p. 192; ch. 15, p. 224; ch. 17, pp. 256, 260. On awe in Hobbes's frontispiece see Ginsburg 2015, pp. 71–6.

[282] Hobbes 2012, vol. 2, ch. 30, p. 550.

[283] This is true of a number of the figures pictured on Leviathan's right arm.

[284] Church 1637, p. 68.   [285] Gore 1638, p. 17.   [286] Jackson 1649, p. 70.

[287] See, for example, Bredekamp 2003, p. 106.

bonnets and shawls) and young children too.[288] The state is shown accepting under its protection not merely the adult males who have covenanted, but the entire body of the people, all of whom in turn express their gratitude and respect.

There is, however, one conspicuous difference between this image and the earlier version of the frontispiece in the manuscript of *Leviathan* presented by Hobbes to the future king Charles II. If we compare this version with the published one, we find that a number of changes have been introduced. These are chiefly matters of detail: some trees in the left foreground have been removed, while the towers of the church within the city have been shortened by two storeys.[289] The one significant modification is that the individuals who make up the body of Leviathan are represented very differently. In the published version they stand sideways or with their backs to us, and in many instances we see them at full-length. But in the manuscript version we are shown only their faces, some looking sideways or downwards while others directly return our gaze.[290]

This alteration might seem to imply that the visual metaphor of looking up to the sovereign may have occurred to Hobbes and Bosse only at a late stage. But as Hoekstra has observed, we need only reflect on the audiences for whom the two different versions of the frontispiece were intended to see that the same point is being made in each case.[291] The manuscript version, in which the faces of the sovereign's subjects stare out at the viewer, was intended only for the sovereign himself. Scrutinising this image, the future Charles II would have found himself confronted with the spectacle of a number of subjects not only gazing back but looking up to him. By contrast, to scrutinise the published version of the frontispiece is to find oneself in the same position as the members of the body politic, all of whom are looking up to their head of state.

Hobbes's final message might thus appear to be that the proper relationship of subject to sovereign is one of complete subordination to unsurpassable power, and this is how the frontispiece has generally been interpreted. But we could equally well think of it as a warning about the

---

[288] This is even more clearly the case in Abraham Bosse's frontispiece for the French translation of Hobbes's *De corpore politico* of 1652. See Bredekamp 2003, pp. 12–13, 107–8.

[289] For further details see Brown 1978, pp. 31–2; Bredekamp 2003, pp. 32–3.

[290] As Bredekamp 2003 pp. 45–6 shows, Bosse had already produced an image of a man whose cloak is decorated with faces gazing on the viewer. This is one of Bredekamp's reasons for attributing the design of the *Leviathan* frontispiece to Bosse. See also Join-Lambert and Préaud 2004, Plate 94, p. 138; Berger 2017, pp. 196, 198. For another resemblance see Frideric 1617, p. 2, an image of the world composed of the many faces of its inhabitants.

[291] Hoekstra 2015, pp. 241–2. See also Ginsburg 2015, p. 70.

limitations and fragility of the state. Hobbes is always emphatic that, although Leviathan is a 'great power', it is also 'mortall, and subject to decay, as all other Earthly creatures are'.[292] 'Though Soveraignty, in the intention of them that make it, be immortall; yet is it in its own nature, not only subject to violent death, by forreign war; but also through the ignorance, and passions of men, it hath in it, from the very institution, many seeds of a naturall mortality'.[293] These inherent weaknesses provide Hobbes with his theme in chapter 29, in which he itemises what he describes as the 'internall diseases' of the body politic and its constant exposure to disorders and death.[294]

The disorders Hobbes goes on to list are those which inspire subjects to rebel,[295] and hence to be 'drawn away from their obedience' to their head of state.[296] When he specifically refers to the danger of being drawn away, he has two particular threats in mind. One arises from 'the Popularity of a potent Subject', which can easily have the effect of encouraging the people 'to follow a man, of whose vertues, and designes they have no knowledge.'[297] But the most dangerous threat arises when the people come to believe in the independent jurisdictional powers of the Church. Once the capacity of the civil power to 'draw to it' the body of the people is successfully challenged by the ecclesiastical authorities, the commonwealth will be 'divided in it selfe, and cannot stand'.[298] Rather it will be in imminent danger, as Hobbes likes to put it, of being dissolved, that is, of disintegrating into its constituent elements, and thus into a disunited multitude.[299] Hobbes likens this disease to 'the Epilepsie, or Falling-sicknesse', in which the sufferer is agitated by 'an unnaturall spirit', experiences 'violent, and irregular motions', cannot manage to stand and 'falleth down sometimes into the water, and sometimes into the fire.'[300]

This figuring of rebellion as an act of *falling* or *falling away* from obedience was frequently invoked by royalist opponents of the parliamentary cause. Henry Burton in his sermon *For God, and the King* of 1636 solemnly warns against those who 'change and breake the Commandement of God, and of their Princes, and fall away from the feare of God, and the King in their rebellious life.'[301] Gryffith Williams in his *Vindiciae regum* of 1643 similarly turns to the experience of civil war for 'a fearfull example, to see

---

[292] Hobbes 2012, vol. 2, ch. 28, p. 496.   [293] Hobbes 2012, vol. 2, ch. 21, p. 344.
[294] Hobbes 2012, vol. 2, ch. 29, p. 498.   [295] Hobbes 2012, vol. 2, ch. 29, pp. 498, 506.
[296] Hobbes 2012, vol. 2, ch. 29, p. 516.   [297] Hobbes 2012, vol. 2, ch. 29, p. 516.
[298] Hobbes 2012, vol. 2, ch. 29, p. 510.
[299] On 'dissolution' see Hobbes 2012, vol. 2, ch. 29, pp. 498, 502, 504, 506, 510, 518.
[300] Hobbes 2012, vol. 2, ch. 29, p. 512.   [301] Burton 1636, p. 7.

how suddenly men do fall away from God, and from their true Religion, after they have rebelled against their lawfull King'.[302]

Hobbes's frontispiece introduces his readers to the same line of argument. Although the people are shown as united, the manner in which they make up the arms and body of Leviathan leaves them in obvious danger of falling away. It is of course true that, should any of them fall, the outcome will be disastrous for themselves. Like the sufferer from epilepsy, they will tumble into the water, or more precisely into the sea out of which Leviathan has arisen, and will undoubtedly meet their deaths. But the outcome of any such fall will be no less disastrous for the state. As the frontispiece shows, it is only due to the artificial unity of the people that the sovereign is supported and sustained. If only a few subjects fall away, the head of state will topple. Furthermore, it is only through the power of the people that the sovereign is armed. If they fall away, he will lose his arms and with them any capacity to impose the sword of justice or wield the crozier to control the insubordination of the Church.

Meanwhile, in an especially potent visual metaphor, the sword carried by the sovereign is shown as double-edged. As Thomas Vicars had observed in his sermon of 1627 entitled *The Sword-Bearer*, the significance of the image is that such a sword can be wielded either to produce 'health and salvation' or else to engender 'death and destruction'.[303] If the people fall away, the power of the sword to produce health and salvation will be lost. The sword will fall to the ground, and the commonwealth will be dissolved. By contrast with the frontispiece of *De cive*, in which power is shown as coming from above, Hobbes's final word in the frontispiece of *Leviathan* is that all power comes from below. Unless it is accompanied by a willing submission, the commonwealth 'is but a word, without substance, and cannot stand'.[304]

IX

Hobbes's portrayal of the sovereign state yields an emblem of arresting originality. But his basic contention that states are instituted when the many are converted into one was not without precedent, and I should like to end by focusing on a number of sources – all of which Hobbes seems to have known – in which the idea of transforming a multitude into 'a reall Unitie of them all'[305] had already been discussed and illustrated. I begin with one remarkably close verbal rather than visual antecedent. This can be found in the address 'To the Reader' in Edward Forset's *Comparative*

[302] Williams 1643, p. 57.   [303] Vicars 1627, p. 17.
[304] Hobbes 2012, vol. 2, ch. 31, p. 554.   [305] Hobbes 2012, vol. 2, ch. 17, p. 260.

Discourse of the Bodies Natural and Politique of 1606.[306] Hobbes undoubt-edly knew this book, which he lists in his catalogue of the Hardwick Library.[307] Forset begins by observing that commonwealths can be 'set forth by sundry fit resemblances', but 'by none more properly than eyther by the universall masse of the whole world', in which 'all the severall subsistances' are 'compact and united', or else 'by the body of man', which can be viewed in a similar way. Not only does Forset refer here to the uniting of disparate elements, but he goes on to draw some-thing like a verbal picture of the colossus in the *Leviathan* frontispiece. The resemblances between 'the body of man' and the body politic, he notes, 'have beene both sweetly and soundly conceaved by that thrice renowmed Philosopher *Trismegistus*, when he imagined an huge and mightie Gyant, whose head was above the firmament, his necke, shoulders, and upper parts in the heavens, his armes and hands reaching to East and West' and 'his legges and feet within the earth.'[308]

Nor is this image of the state lacking in visual as well as literary precedents. One example is provided by Alciato's emblem of *Concordia insuperabilis*, which George Wither reproduced in his *Collection of Emblemes* in 1635. Alciato had shown a crowned and six-armed colossus in armour, carrying a sword of justice together with a lance and sceptre in his three right arms, while holding a shield in his three left hands.[309] Wither repeats the image of sword and sceptre, and the style in which the colossus wields his sword is remarkably reminiscent of the *Leviathan* frontispiece (Figure 10.38).

It cannot be said, however, that Wither's image anticipates Hobbes's fundamental claim about the many and the one. Although Wither is already concerned with 'many-Forces joyned', he lacks Hobbes's sense that the nature of the bond must be 'more than Consent, or Concord' and must involve 'a reall unitie of them all'.[310]

There are, however, two precise visual analogies with this basic claim, and I should like to end by examining them. One has already been discussed by Horst Bredekamp and Noel Malcolm: the way in which the many can be transformed into one by the technique of dioptric anamorphosis.[311] These exercises in 'curious perspective' required an artist to begin by creating a group of separate pictures on a panel.

---

[306] As noted in Prior 2004.

[307] Hobbes MSS (Chatsworth), MS E. 1. A, p. 80: 'Forsett. of ye Body Naturall and Politique'.

[308] Forset 1606, sig. §, 3r–v.   [309] Alciato 1550, p. 47.

[310] Hobbes 2012, vol. 2, ch. 17, p. 260.

[311] As argued in Malcolm 1998. See also Bredekamp 2003, pp. 83–90; Malcolm 2012, pp. 135–41. On anamorphosis see also Baltrušaitis 1955; Greenblatt 1980, pp. 17–21, 260–1.

Where many-Forces *joyned are*,
Vnconquerable-pow'r, *is there*

Figure 10.38 Wither, George (1635). 'Concordia Insuperabilis' in *A Collection of Emblemes, Ancient and Moderne*, London, p. 179.

A cylinder containing a special lens was then set up in front of the image. The skill lay in placing each separate picture on a segment that, when viewed through the cylinder, was picked up by the correcting lens to form a new and supervening image. The viewer begins by seeing many different pictures, but on applying the eye to the cylinder a hidden image is disclosed and the many become one.

Hobbes was well-acquainted with a celebrated example of this type of anamorphosis, which had been painted by Jean François Niceron and was kept in the library of the Minim convent on the Place Royale in Paris.[312] It was there that Marin Mersenne convened regular meetings of *savants* at which Hobbes was often present. Hobbes may also have known about the painting from Niceron's illustration of it in the treatise he published on *La perspective curieuse* in 1638. Hobbes was clearly much impressed by Niceron's ingenuity, which he mentions in the *Answer* he wrote in 1650 to Sir William Davenant's *Preface to Gondibert*:

I beleeve (Sir) you have seene a curious kind of perspective, where, he that lookes through a short hollow pipe, upon a picture conteyning diverse figures, sees none of those that are there paynted, but some one person made up of their partes, conveighed to the eye by the artificiall cutting of a glasse.[313]

Hobbes's purpose in recalling Niceron's *perspective curieuse* is to bestow a compliment on Davenant, in whose epic poem, he declares, 'the vertues you distribute there amongst so many noble Persons, represent (in the reading) the image but of one mans vertue to my fancy, which is your owne'.[314] But at the same time, by referring to the technique of transforming 'diverse figures' into 'one person', Hobbes alludes to the central element in his theory of the state.

The parallel with the *Leviathan* frontispiece is not of course exact.[315] When we look at the frontispiece, we are able to see the composite colossus and the members of the multitude simultaneously. But when we look at a dioptric anamorphosis we must focus either on the individual figures or else apply our eye to the cylinder for the composite image to be disclosed. Nevertheless, there is a sense in which Niceron's anamorphosis offers a strong analogy to Hobbes's conception of the state.[316] The state according to Hobbes has no existence apart from the individual members of the multitude who covenant to submit to it. If they fall away, the state becomes 'but a word, without substance, and cannot stand'.[317] So too with the anamorphosis. Although the picture revealed by the use of the correcting lens is the master image, it likewise lacks any substance apart from the individual segments out of which it is composed. As in the case of the *persona fictione* of the state, the many are transformed into one, but the one is merely a construction out of the many, and has no independent reality.

I end by examining a further genre in which the many are shown united as one. Although it has never, so far as I know, been discussed in relation to Hobbes's frontispiece, in some ways it provides the closest visual

---

[312] Malcolm 2012, p. 139.
[313] Hobbes 1971, p. 55. For a discussion see Skinner 1996, pp. 387–9.
[314] Hobbes 1971, p. 55.   [315] As noted in Malcolm 2012, pp. 140–1.
[316] Malcolm 2012, p. 140.   [317] Hobbes 2012, vol. 2, ch. 31, p. 554.

forerunner. The genre in question is that of anthropomorphic maps in which the different countries of Europe are imagined as parts of one person. The pioneer in this form of cartography was the Swiss humanist Johannes Putch (1516–42), who produced a woodcut map for a Paris printer in 1537 in which Europe was portrayed *ad formam virginis*, in the form of a virgin queen.[318] Putch's design was subsequently adapted by the German Protestant pastor Heinrich Bünting (*c*.1545–1606), whose *Itinerarium Sacrae Scripturae*, a survey of the journeys described in the Bible, was first published in 1581.[319] When Bünting reissued his work in 1587 he included a woodcut map entitled 'Europe, the principal part of the world, in the form of a virgin',[320] an illustration subsequently reused in the editions of 1597, 1598 and 1606.[321] (The 1597 version is reproduced as Figure 10.39.)[322]

A year after Bünting's map was first published, a different version appeared in a new edition of the *Cosmographia* by Sebastian Munster (1488–1552). Munster's celebrated work had first been printed in 1544,[323] but the Basel edition of 1588 was the first to contain the anthropomorphic map, which took the form of an engraving thereafter reused in every edition up to 1628.[324] (The 1588 version is reproduced as Figure 10.40.)[325]

There are many similarities between the two maps. Both display a female monarch in a full-length garment covering almost the whole of her body. She bears the insignia of *imperium*, wearing a closed imperial crown and carrying an orb in her right hand and a sceptre in her left. A multitude of different countries – from Spain to Bulgaria, from Denmark to Sicily – make up the parts of her body, with Spain shown as her head, while Germany and Bohemia appear as her heart. The underlying political message appears to be that the Habsburg monarchy of Spain, together with the Habsburg succession in the Holy Roman Empire, furnish Europe with its animating and unifying strength.

---

[318] For an illustration of the map see Meurer 1991, Plate 56. On Putch see Meurer 2008, pp. 358–62.

[319] Meurer 2008, p. 362. The 1581 edition was reissued in Magdeburg in 1585, but again without the map.

[320] 'Europa Prima Pars Terrae In Forma Virginis'. On this edition, published in Wittenberg, see Meurer 2008, pp. 362–4.

[321] Information from BL copies. Several English translations appeared between 1619 and 1636, but none with the map.

[322] See Bünting 1597, pp. 29–31. The heading (p. 29) reads: 'Subiicio Nunc Europae, primae partis orbis terrarum picturam, sub Effigie Virginis'. The map itself (which instead reads 'forma virginis') follows at pp. 30–1.

[323] The date is often given as 1545 (see for example Meurer 2008, p. 364) but there is a copy in the library of New College Oxford dated 1544.

[324] Information from BL copies. Cf. Meurer 2008, p. 264.

[325] Munster 1588, Das erste Buch, p. xli.

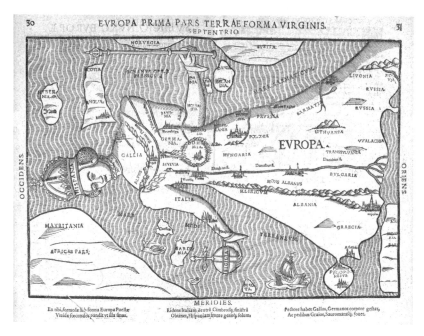

Figure 10.39 Bünting, Heinrich (1597). 'Europa' in *Itinerarium et Chronicon Ecclesiasticum Totius Sacrae Scripturae*, Magdeburg, pp. 30–1.

Of the two images, however, Munster's is the more consciously emblematic one. Bünting presents the figure of Europe in conventional geographical orientation, with Spain at the west and the lettering running west to east. Munster orientates the map to present an upright figure, thereby placing more emphasis on the idea of Europe as a single *persona*. Bünting remains more concerned with geographical detail, and marks a number of islands – Corsica, Malta, Sardinia and the British Isles – that remain unincorporated into the *persona* of Europe. Munster once again gives more prominence to the idea of the many becoming one. The British Isles appear as nothing more than a pennant on Europe's sceptre, while Corsica, Malta and Sardinia are simply eliminated.

The outcome in the case of Munster's map is an image serving at once to recall the *Leviathan* frontispiece and at the same time to raise it, so to speak, to a higher political plane. Whereas Hobbes shows a multitude of individuals uniting to form the *persona* of a state, Munster shows a multitude of countries uniting to form the *persona* of a continent. More specifically, whereas Hobbes shows individual subjects providing the state with its arms and enabling the sovereign to carry the insignia of supreme

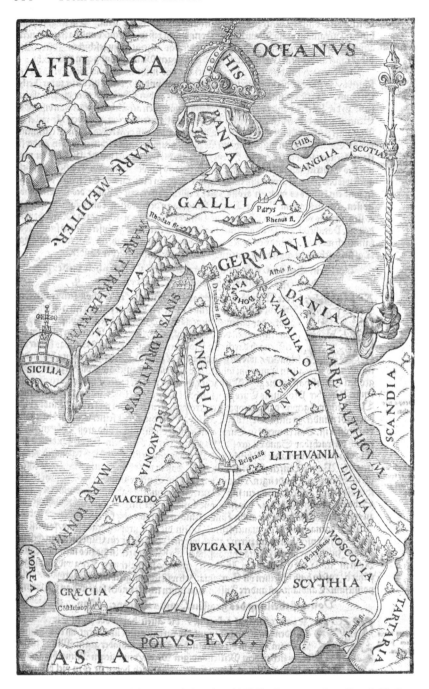

Figure 10.40 Munster, Sebastian (1588). *Cosmographey*, Basel, Bk I, p. xli.

power, Munster shows individual countries performing the same function, with Denmark enabling Europe to uphold her sceptre while Sicily
provides her with her orb.

Hobbes was always keenly interested in cartography, and there is some
evidence that he may have known of Munster's map. Aubrey records that,
when Hobbes was a student at Oxford, he 'took great delight there to go to
the book-binders' shops, and lye gaping on Mappes'.[326] Later Hobbes
mentions with evident pride in the introduction to his translation of
Thucydides that, on finding it impossible to locate a map of Greece
with place-names marked on it, 'I was constrained to draw one as well
as I could myself.'[327] Still more suggestively, Munster's name appears in
Hobbes's catalogue of the Hardwick Library, in which the relevant
entry reads 'Munster. Historia Universalis. fol.'[328] Munster wrote no
such work, but a number of Hobbes's entries are somewhat approximate,
and this could well be a reference to Munster's cosmography. When it was
first printed at Basel in 1544 it was simply entitled *Cosmographia*, but
in subsequent Basel printings it was sometimes called *Cosmographiae
Universalis* (1554, 1572) or *La Cosmographie Universelle* (1552).[329]
Hobbes may well have written *Historia Universalis* when he meant
Cosmographiae Universalis.

Munster's portrayal of Europe and Hobbes's portrayal of Leviathan are
both images of a political union in which the many come together as one.
But Hobbes's image proved to be the more prescient one. Munster's
emphasis on Habsburg Spain and Germany, together with his elimination
of the sea-powers of the Netherlands and Great Britain, presents an image
of Europe under the domination of a single dynasty. This ideal of universal empire admittedly died hard. The Habsburgs may have been on the
verge of losing their hegemonic standing in Hobbes's own time, but a new
contender for the role soon arose in France. The battle to unify Europe
was eventually lost, however, not by the conquest of one hegemon by
another, but by the emergence of individual nation-states. This is the
development of which Hobbes was the pioneering theorist, and this is
what has helped to give the frontispiece of *Leviathan* its lasting resonance.

---

[326] Aubrey 1898, vol. 1, p. 329.
[327] Hobbes 1843, vol. 1, p. x. On the maps in Hobbes's translation of Thucydides see Iori
2015, pp. 194–214.
[328] Hobbes MSS (Chatsworth) MS E. 1. A, p. 96; cf. also p. 86.
[329] For these details see BL catalogue.

11   Hobbes on Hereditary Right

I

Hobbes is always reluctant to criticise monarchy. When he first compares the different forms of government in *The Elements of Law*, he insists that all the inconveniences to which subjects are inevitably exposed are least troublesome under this type of state.[1] He also assures us that 'all the ancients have preferred monarchy before other governments', failing even to mention the clear preference for republican rule expressed by Cicero, Livy and other ancient authorities.[2] Returning to the same comparison in *De cive*, he speaks in yet more forthright terms. He argues, as before, that there are only three possible forms of government,[3] but he now adds the unequivocal declaration that 'among these types of *civitas* – the *Democratic*, the *Aristocratic* and the *Monarchical* – the best is *Monarchy*'.[4] When he later discusses the relative 'commodities' of these different constitutions at greater length in *Leviathan* he specifically argues that monarchy is the one in which we find the most effective counselling, the least inconstancy in decision-making and the greatest likelihood that the public good will be served.[5]

Hobbes feels obliged to admit, however, that there is one weakness in his account of why monarchy should always be preferred. He likes to

This chapter is a revised and extended version of Skinner 2005c. For permission to draw on this earlier work I am indebted to the Oxford University Press. I remain beholden to the late T. S. Wragg, who as Librarian of Chatsworth first showed me Hobbes's manuscript on hereditary right and photographed it for me. My principal thanks are due to the Duke of Devonshire and the Trustees of the Chatsworth Settlement for permission to examine and publish the manuscript. For reading drafts, and for many helpful comments, I am deeply grateful to Alan Cromartie, Mark Goldie, Kinch Hoekstra, Susan James, Noel Malcolm, John Morrill, Eric Nelson, David Sacks and Keith Thomas. I also owe special thanks to Noel Malcolm for indispensable technical help.

[1] Hobbes 1969, 24. 3–8, pp. 140–3.   [2] Hobbes 1969, 24. 3, p. 141.
[3] Hobbes 1983, VII. I, p. 149; cf. Hobbes 1969, 21. 1, p. 118.
[4] Hobbes 1983, X. III, p. 172: 'specierum civitatis, *Democratiae*, & *Aristocratiae* & *Monarchiae*, optima sit *Monarchia*'. See also Hobbes 1983, X. XVII, p. 180, where he repeats the claim, and Hobbes 1983, XI. IV, p. 182, where he adds that it is confirmed by Scripture.
[5] Hobbes 2012, vol. 2, ch. 19, pp. 288, 290.

claim that, as he puts it at the end of Book II of *Leviathan*, he has succeeded in establishing a 'Science of Naturall Justice' in which he has furnished proofs of 'the Theoremes of Morall doctrine' that place them beyond dispute.[6] But when he reflects on his preference for monarchy he recognises that, in this instance, he has fallen short of his goal. As he had already acknowledged in the Preface he added to *De cive* when it was reissued in 1647, 'I have presented various arguments in chapter 10 to try to persuade people that Monarchy is more advantageous than other types of state',[7] but 'I must confess that this is the one doctrine in this book which is not demonstrated but is merely put forward as a matter of probability.'[8]

Faced with this sore point in his argument, Hobbes takes considerable pains to cover it up. He does so in part by calling attention to his lack of proof as little as possible. He makes no reference to it in *The Elements*, nor in the body of the text of *De cive*. In *Leviathan* he not only remains silent about his earlier concession, but strikes a triumphalist note. He now assures us that, by drawing on 'the Principles of Naturall Reason', he has been able to arrive at the 'Truth of Speculation' about politics, and is hoping for its conversion into 'the Utility of Practice'.[9]

Hobbes further minimises his concession with repeated assurances that any doubts we may entertain about the inconveniences of monarchy apply with even greater force to other forms of government. In *The Elements* he compares monarchy only with aristocracy, and in *De cive* only with democracy, but in *Leviathan* he argues that even the two major weaknesses held to be characteristic of monarchical regimes are more serious under both these other forms of government. One alleged weakness is that monarchs often have extravagant and dangerous favourites. Hobbes replies that the favourites of assemblies are usually far more numerous and have much greater power to do harm.[10] The other objection is that under monarchy the government may descend upon a child, or upon someone who 'cannot discerne between Good and Evill'.[11] Here Hobbes retorts that, just as a child 'wants the judgement to dissent from counsell given him', so 'an Assembly wanteth the liberty, to dissent from the counsell of the major part, be it good, or bad.'[12] The paradoxical truth, Hobbes concludes, is that 'as to consultations of Peace, and Warre, and

[6] Hobbes 2012, vol. 2, ch. 31, p. 574.
[7] Hobbes 1983, Praefatio 22, p. 83: 'Licet enim Monarchiam caeteris civitatis speciebus capite decimo commodiorem esse argumentis aliquot suadere conatus sim'.
[8] Hobbes 1983, Praefatio 22, p. 83: 'quam rem unam in hoc libro non demonstratam sed probabiliter positam esse confiteor.'
[9] Hobbes 2012, vol. 2, ch. 31, p. 574.   [10] Hobbes 2012, vol. 2, ch. 19, p. 290.
[11] Hobbes 2012, vol. 2, ch. 19, p. 292.   [12] Hobbes 2012, vol. 2, ch. 19, p. 294.

making of Lawes', all sovereign assemblies are 'in the same condition, as if the Government were in a Child.'[13] The supposed incommodities of monarchical government are generally attributable 'not to the Monarchy, but to the Ambition, and Injustice of the Subjects'.[14]

As Hobbes recognises, however, even this line of defence leaves one criticism of monarchy that he cannot hope to evade. The remaining problem is that of succession. Hobbes barely addresses the issue in *The Elements*,[15] but in *De cive* he squarely faces it. 'Whereas *a whole people*, or *an aristocratic assembly*, cannot die out, if in a *Monarchy* no successor at all appears, then all the subjects are liberated from their obligations'.[16] The dire implications are subsequently spelled out in chapter 19 of *Leviathan*. 'For the death of him that hath the Soveraign power in propriety, leaves the Multitude without any Soveraign at all; that is, without any Representative in whom they should be united, and be capable of doing any one action at all'. But this is to leave the people 'incapable of Election of any new Monarch', because everyone now has 'equall right to submit himselfe to such as he thinks best able to protect him; or if he can, protect himselfe by his owne sword'. To allow this to happen, however, is to return 'to Confusion, and to the condition of a War of every man against every man', which is exactly the predicament that everyone wanted to avoid.[17]

How to solve this problem was one of the questions most vociferously debated by the protagonists of absolute monarchy and popular sovereignty in the decades preceding the outbreak of the English civil war in 1642. Consider, for example, the *Reply* produced by Sir John Hayward in 1603 to the Jesuit Robert Persons, the principal author of the 'monarchomach' tract published in 1594 under the almost treasonous title *A conference about the next succession to the crowne of Ingland*.[18] Persons begins by laying it down that 'succession to goverment by neernes of bloode is not by Law of nature, or divine, but only by humane & positive Lawes of every particuler common wealth, and consequently, may uppon just causes be altered by the same.'[19] He proceeds to itemise these 'just causes' and to

[13] Hobbes 2012, vol. 2, ch. 19, p. 294.   [14] Hobbes 2012, vol. 2, ch. 19, p. 292.
[15] Hobbes 1969, 23. 11, p. 135 notes the special problem of succession in monarchies, but not the specific danger to which this gives rise.
[16] Hobbes 1983, VII. XVIII, p. 159: 'in *Monarchia* (nam Δῆμος & *Curia optimatum* deficere non possunt) si successor nullus omnino appareat, omnes cives obligationibus suis liberantur.'
[17] Hobbes 2012, vol. 2, ch. 19. p. 300.
[18] See [Persons] 1594. The actual date of publication was 1595. See Houliston 2007, p. 72n. Houliston 2007, p. 72 notes that, while Persons wished the *Conference* to be seen as a co-operative work, it was he who wrote the final version.
[19] [Persons] 1594, p. 1. For Persons on hereditary right see Holmes 1982, pp. 149–54.

explain how they affect the basic rule that succession should be by propin-
quity of blood. To this rule we need to add 'election, consent and approbation of the realme' to provide a remedy for 'the inconveniences of bare
succession alone, which inconveniences are principaly, that some un-apt
impotent or evel prince may be offered some times to enter by priority of
blood'. Should such a crisis occur, 'the realme may deliver it selfe, by this
other meanes of not admitting him', a course of action not merely permitted but commended by 'the wisdome and high policie left by God and
nature, to every common wealth, for ther owne conservation and
maintenance'.[20]

Hayward retorts in horrified tones that hereditary monarchy is directly
ordained by God, who 'hath given us a naturall law, to preferre the first
borne' under all circumstances.[21] The eldest son of a monarch not only
has a 'natural interest to succeed' but a 'right of succession inherent in
him by birth'.[22] So strong is this right that 'the sonne of a king, may be
called King during the life of his father, as wanting nothing but
administration'.[23] Hayward adds that 'this naturall precedence both in
honour and in favour, seemeth to be expressely ratified by God', who
'forbiddeth the father to disinherit the first sonne of his double portion;
because by right of birth it is his due'.[24] The inescapable rule of succession
must therefore be that 'if the first borne die before succession fall; or if
being possessed of the kingdom, he die without issue; his right of birth
devolveth unto the next in bloud: and if he dieth in like maner, then unto
the third, and so likewise to the rest in order.'[25] Hayward also regards it as
indisputable that anyone who is 'once invested in right of succession,
cannot be deprived therof'.[26] He admits it is 'inconvenient' to be 'governed by a king, who is defective in body or in minde'.[27] But he insists that
'the eldest son of a king or other governor, although he be borne either
furious, or a foole, or otherwise defective, cannot therfore be excluded
from his succession'.[28] The natural right of the nearest in blood to
succeed cannot be gainsaid by anyone, and cannot under any circumstances be taken away.

Hobbes rejects this absolutist argument almost as firmly as he rejects
the monarchomach case. Although he agrees with Hayward that the
subjects of a monarch can never have a right to remove him from office,[29]
he repudiates any suggestion that the nearest heir of a ruling monarch has

[20] [Persons] 1594, p. 130. For a discussion see Holmes 1982, pp. 193–8.
[21] Hayward 1603, sig. N, 4v.   [22] Hayward 1603, sig. E, 1v.
[23] Hayward 1603, sig. O, 2v.   [24] Hayward 1603, sig. D, 2r.
[25] Hayward 1603, sig. D, 2r.   [26] Hayward 1603, sig. A, 1v.
[27] Hayward 1603, sig. A, 3r.   [28] Hayward 1603, sig. A, 1v.
[29] For Hobbes's strongest statement see Hobbes 2012, vol. 2, ch. 19, p. 270.

a natural or God-given right to succeed to the throne. To allow such a right would limit the powers of the reigning sovereign, and for Hobbes the idea of limited sovereignty is a contradiction in terms. It follows that there can be no such thing as a right of succession; to speak of the heir to an established monarchy can only be to identify the person whom the existing monarch has chosen to designate as his or her heir.

Hobbes holds unswervingly to this commitment. He already announces in *The Elements* that in 'an absolute monarchy' the king 'is at liberty, to dispose as well of the succession, as of the possession' of the realm.[30] He repeats in *De cive* that 'when sovereign power is transferred without qualification to a *Monarch*, he becomes able to exercise not merely *a right of possession*, but also of *succession*, because he is able to declare who shall be his successor according to his own will.'[31] He reiterates the argument at greater length in *Leviathan*, in which he concludes that the right of disposition must either lie with the person of the sovereign or with no specific person at all. If, however, the right 'be in no particular man, but left to a new choyse; then is the Common-wealth dissolved; and the Right is in him that can get it'. To allow this outcome, however, would be 'contrary to the intention of them that did institute the Common-wealth, for their perpetuall, and not temporary security.' The inference he draws is thus that 'there is no perfect forme of Government, where the disposing of the Succession is not in the present Soveraign.'[32]

What of the absolutist objection that this arrangement cheats every first-born son of a monarch of a fundamental right? Hobbes offers no explicit answer in *The Elements* or *De cive*, in which he has nothing to say about the status of heirs. But in *Leviathan* he endorses the position that, as he notes, was originally adopted by the early Roman emperors, who simply announced 'who should be their Heires'.[33] He reminds us that 'the word Heire does not of it selfe imply the Children, or nearest Kindred of a man; but whomsoever a man shall any way declare, he would have to succeed him in his Estate.' He concludes that 'if therefore a Monarch declare expresly, that such a man shall be his Heire, either by Word or Writing, then is that man immediatly after the decease of his Predecessor, Invested in the right of being Monarch'.[34] As before, what the theory of

---

[30] Hobbes 1969, 21. 9, p. 122; cf. also 21.10, p. 123.
[31] Hobbes 1983, VII. XV, p. 156: 'ut *Monarchae* cui simpliciter traditum est imperium, competat *ius* non modo *possessionis*, sed etiam *successionis*, ut possit suo arbitrio declarare successorem suum.' See also Hobbes 1983, IX. XII, p. 168.
[32] Hobbes 2012, vol. 2, ch. 19, p. 298.   [33] Hobbes 2012, vol. 2, ch. 19, p. 302.
[34] Hobbes 2012, vol. 2, ch. 19, p. 302.

sovereignty is said to dictate is that 'by the Institution of Monarchy, the disposing of the Successor, is alwaies left to the Judgment and Will of the present Possessor.'[35]

Hobbes reiterates these commitments yet again in a manuscript he dictated on the issue of hereditary right in the closing year of his life.[36] The text takes the form of a response to a question privately put to him about the right of succession. The question to which he replies is as follows:

If you allow that a king does not hold his title by divine Institution, as indeed 'tis absurd to say he does, then I suppose you will admitt that his title to Governe arises from his protecting those that are govern'd. My next Question therefore is this, If a Successour to a Crown, be for some reason or other which is notorious, incapable to protect the people, if the Government should devolve upon him, is not the Prince in possession oblig'd to putt him by, upon the request of his subiects?

Hobbes's answer, composed only a few months before his death in December 1679, contains his last reflections on the nature and range of sovereign power. The rest of this chapter will offer an analysis of the manuscript and an appraisal of Hobbes's response.

II

The question I have quoted was put to Hobbes by William Cavendish, the eldest son of the third earl of Devonshire.[37] The third earl – also called William Cavendish – had been tutored by Hobbes in the 1630s. His son and heir was born in 1640, and devoted himself from an early age to a political career. He was elected to the House of Commons as member for Derby in 1661, and served throughout the life of the so-called Cavalier Parliament until Charles II finally dissolved it in January 1679.[38] By this stage the so-called Exclusion crisis was beginning to convulse English politics, and it was in connection with this crisis that Cavendish contacted Hobbes to ask his advice about the question of hereditary right.

For some time before the dissolution of Parliament there had been growing anxieties about Charles II's high-handed attitude towards his prerogative, and about his specific use of prerogative powers to win toleration for his Catholic subjects. By the end of 1678, with the discovery of an alleged Popish Plot, these anxieties had increasingly

[35] Hobbes 2012, vol. 2, ch. 19, p. 300.
[36] Hobbes MSS (Chatsworth) MS Hobbes D. 5: 'Questions relative to Hereditary Right. Mr Hobbes'. See also Hobbes 2005.
[37] The evidence in favour of this attribution is given in the Appendix to this chapter.
[38] Smith 1999, p. 237.

come to focus on the king's younger brother, James duke of York, a known Catholic and a man of suspected absolutist sympathies.[39] Shortly after the new Parliament assembled in March 1679, the earl of Shaftesbury delivered an impassioned speech in the House of Lords on the state of the nation, warning that 'Popery and slavery, like two sisters, go hand in hand.'[40] The Scots, he declared, have already seen 'their lives, liberties, and estates subjected to the arbitrary will and pleasure of those that govern.' These developments remind us of the dangers of popery in England, including the risk that many members of the Court remain imbued with the slavish principles of the Catholic faith. 'We must still be upon our guard', recognising that 'these men are still in place and authority, who have that influence upon the mind of our excellent prince, that he is not, nor cannot be that to us, that his own nature and goodness incline him to.'[41]

Shaftesbury's supporters in the House of Commons were meanwhile professing similar concerns about the king's safety and state of mind, and on 11 May 1679 they resolved to examine 'the best ways and means of preserving the Life of his sacred majesty, and of securing the Protestant Religion, both in the reign of his majesty and his successors.'[42] After a long debate,[43] in which William Cavendish spoke immediately after Richard Hampden had moved to exclude the duke of York from the succession, the House resolved 'That a Bill be brought in to disable the Duke of York to inherit the Imperial Crown of this Realm'.[44] The Exclusion Bill duly received its first reading on 15 May 1679 and its second less than a week later.[45]

Faced with this almost treasonous challenge, Charles II reacted by proroguing Parliament on 27 May and dissolving it shortly afterwards, thereby creating a breathing-space in which everyone was able to consider where they stood in relation to these astonishing developments.[46] It was at this juncture that John Locke, who had been living in France for almost four years, returned to the household of the earl of Shaftesbury in London, which he had originally joined in the early 1670s.[47] He and Shaftesbury appear to have renewed their political discussions almost as soon as Charles II announced his abrupt dismissal of Parliament, and it seems to have been at around this time that Locke, with Shaftesbury's

---

[39] Knights 1994, pp. 29–31.
[40] Haley 1968, p. 510. Haley adds that the speech was printed in London and Norwich.
[41] Cobbett and Hansard (eds.) 1807b, cols. 1116–17.
[42] Cobbett and Hansard (eds.) 1807b, col. 1131.
[43] Jones 1961, pp. 65–6; Knights 1994, pp. 49–53.   [44] *Journals* (n. d.). vol. 9, p. 620.
[45] *Journals* (n. d.). vol. 9, pp. 623, 626.   [46] Jones 1961, p. 73; Knights 1994, p. 56.
[47] Milton 2011, p. 162.

encouragement, began to draft his account of the nature and limits of lawful rule, which he eventually published as *Two treatises of government* ten years later.[48]

While Shaftesbury was consulting Locke, William Cavendish was consulting Hobbes. Cavendish could not have failed to see that, as soon as a new Parliament was summoned, the issue of Exclusion would again be at the top of the Commons' agenda.[49] But his own views about Exclusion were far from settled, as his speech in the debate of 11 May had revealed. He had neither opposed nor supported the move to 'disable' the duke of York, but had merely spoken in a tentative fashion about the possibility of a compromise. He had suggested that 'what is proposed in the king's and chancellor's Speech' might possibly 'go a great way in what you aim at', and had ended by appealing to the House to 'consider therefore the safest ways' before doing anything desperate.[50] Cavendish was clearly in a mood of anxiety and confusion in the early summer of 1679, and all the evidence suggests that this was the moment at which he decided to bring Hobbes up to date about the Exclusion crisis and ask his opinion about it. Not only was he in need of advice, but he may have felt it almost an act of family piety to raise the matter with Hobbes. Besides being celebrated for his views about the theory of sovereignty, Hobbes had served as secretary as well as tutor to Cavendish's father for many years, and was still living at Chatsworth, the third earl's principal residence, in his final retirement.

One piece of evidence pointing in this direction is that a copy of Shaftesbury's speech in the House of Lords was evidently made for Hobbes's use at around this time. Among the items in Hobbes's papers docketed under the year 1679 is a fairly accurate (if somewhat ill-spelled) transcription endorsed 'The Right hon.[ble] the Earl of Shaftsbury's speech in the House of Lords March 25. 1679'.[51] A second piece of evidence is that Hobbes appears to have been supplied with a copy of the Exclusion Bill itself. A further item docketed in his papers under the same year is an eight-page manuscript, with an endorsement in the hand of his amanuensis, James Wheldon, which reads 'A Copy of the Bill concerning the D: of York'.[52] But the strongest evidence that Cavendish's question must date

---

[48] See Haley 1968, p. 585 on Shaftesbury and Locke; and for 1679 as the date when Locke began writing his *Second Treatise* see Laslett 1988, p. 59.

[49] This duly happened. The new Parliament finally met on 21 October 1680, and by 11 November the House of Commons had already given a third reading to its Exclusion Bill.

[50] Cobbett and Hansard (eds.) 1807b, col. 1133.

[51] Hobbes MSS (Chatsworth), MS G. 2, two conjugate leaves, making four folio pages. The speech covers the first three pages; the final page, except for the endorsement, is blank.

[52] Hobbes MSS (Chatsworth), Hobbes MS G. 3, four conjugate leaves, making eight folio pages. The Bill covers the first seven pages; the final page, except for the endorsement, is blank.

from the early summer of 1679 is that it closely follows the phraseology of the Commons debate of 11 May and the Exclusion Bill itself. Cavendish begins by asking what should be done if a problem arises with 'a Successour to a Crown'. This echoes the preamble to the Exclusion Bill, which had likewise asked what should be done if the duke of York 'should succeed to the imperial crown'.[53] Cavendish goes on to enquire about the best course of action to follow if a successor is known to be suffering from a 'notorious' incapacity. Here too he echoes the Exclusion Bill, which had opened by declaring that the duke of York 'is notoriously known' to be incapable.[54] The specific weakness Cavendish mentions is being 'incapable to protect the people'. This recalls one of the principal concerns expressed in the Commons debate of 11 May, in which several members had spoken of their fears that there would be 'no safety' and 'no probability of security' for the people under the duke of York.[55] Cavendish next asks what should be done 'if the Government should devolve' upon such a prince. Here again he draws upon the language of the Exclusion Bill, which had proposed that in such a case the government should 'devolve to the person next in Succession'.[56] Finally, Cavendish enquires whether, in the case of an incapable successor, the prince in possession is not 'oblig'd to putt him by'. This too recalls the Commons debate of 11 May, in which Edward Boscawen had defended the possibility of 'pretermitting' or putting by a 'succeeding prince' in the name of securing the government.[57]

III

I now turn to consider Hobbes's answer to Cavendish, which reads as follows:

Here agen you mistake me. I deny not but a King holds his Title by Divine right. But I deny that any Heir apparent does so. Nor did I mention the word *Institution*; nor do I know what you mean. But I will shew you what I mean by Example. If a Constable lay hands upon me for misdemeanor, I aske him by what right he meddles with me more then I with him. He will answer me, *Iure Regio* (i) by the right of the King. He needs not say, because you are a Theefe. For perhaps I might truly say as much of him. Therefore that which is said to be done *Iure Devino* in a King is said to be done by Warrant or comission from God; but that I had no commission. Law and Right differ. Law is a command. But Right is a Liberty or priviledge from a Law to some certaine person though it oblige others. Institution

---

[53] Browning (ed.) 1966, p. 113.   [54] Browning (ed.) 1966, p. 113.
[55] Cobbett and Hansard (eds.) 1807b, cols. 1132, 1135.
[56] Cobbett and Hansard (eds.) 1807b, col. 1136.
[57] Cobbett and Hansard (eds.) 1807b, col. 1135.

is no more but Enthroneing, Proclameing, Anointing, Crowning etc. Which of all humane, and done *Iure Regio*. But tis not so of Heirs apparent. For God [*word deleted and* 'is' *added in different hand*] no Heir [*three words deleted*] to any King. Nor has any inheritance to give away.

You say the Right of a King depends upon his protecting of the people. I confesse that as the King ought to protect [*two words deleted*] his people so the people ought to obey the King. For it is impossible for the best King in the world to protect his people, except his Subjects furnish him with so much money as he shall judge sufficient to doe it.

To your next question, whether the King in Possession [*one word deleted*] be not obliged to put by his next Heir in case of notorious incapacity to protect them. I answer that if the incapacity proceed from want of money, I see no reason, though he can, why he should do it. But if it proceed from want of naturall reason the King in possession may do it, but is not obliged thereunto. Therefore I will speake of that subject no more till we have such a weak King. But in case the King in possession may lawfully disinherit his diseased Heir and will not; you have not yet answered me to the question, Who shall force him for I suppose the sound King living cannot be lawfully deposed by any person or persons that are his Subjects; because the King dying is *ipso facto* dissolved; and then the people is a Multitude of lawlesse men relapsed into a condition of warr of every man against every man. Which by making a King [*word deleted and* 'they' *added in different hand*] intended to avoid.

Before discussing the details of Hobbes's argument, two general observations need to be made. One is that the text includes several indications that it originally formed part of a longer correspondence with Cavendish. The most obvious is that the number '9', an evident mark of pagination, appears at the top right corner of the first page, and '10' at the top left corner of the second. There are also several hints in the text itself that it constitutes only one section of a more extended dialogue. One is contained in Cavendish's opening words: 'If you allow that a king does not hold his title by divine Institution … ' This seems to refer to a previous argument, in the course of which Hobbes and Cavendish had evidently reached some measure of agreement. Further indications can be found in Hobbes's answer. One appears in his opening words – 'Here agen you mistake me' – which plainly alludes to an earlier dispute. A second appears when Hobbes immediately adds 'Nor did I mention the word *Institution*', and a third when he reminds Cavendish in his final paragraph that 'you have not yet answered me to the question, Who shall force him'.

Given that the surviving manuscript originally formed part of a longer disputation, it is worth asking how many questions Cavendish may already have put to Hobbes. The appearance of the manuscript suggests that Cavendish's procedure was to take a sheet of foolscap, fold it across the middle to make four quarto pages, write his question at the top of the first page and leave the rest for Hobbes to reply. If he adopted the same procedure in the case of the questions he had already asked, then it follows that the surviving section of the discussion – with '9' at the top of the first page – must contain the third of his questions to Hobbes.

My other general observation is prompted by the second half of Cavendish's opening sentence. Cavendish writes: 'If you allow that a king does not hold his title by divine Institution, as indeed 'tis absurd to say he does, then I suppose you will admitt that his title to Governe arises from his protecting those that are govern'd.' There are several reasons for finding this a somewhat peculiar remark. For one thing, it embodies a *non sequitur*, and it is perhaps surprising that Hobbes does not pick it up.[58] It is still more surprising that Cavendish asks Hobbes if he 'will admitt' that there is a mutual relation between protection and obedience, as if the acceptance of such a doctrine would represent a concession on Hobbes's part. But the proposition that protection gives a title to obedience, while any failure of protection brings the duty of obedience to an end, are among the most emphatic political arguments in *Leviathan*. 'The Obligation of Subjects to the Soveraign', as Hobbes insists, 'is understood to last as long, and no longer, than the power lasteth, by which he is able to protect them.'[59] Hobbes even avows in his Review and Conclusion that he wrote *Leviathan* 'without other designe, than to set before mens eyes the mutuall Relation between Protection and Obedience'.[60] Cavendish's question reveals a remarkable ignorance about one of the central tenets of Hobbes's theory of the state. Perhaps this helps to account for the some-what irritable tone in which Hobbes's answer is couched.

There is a further reason for wishing to stress that, according to Hobbes, we are politically obliged if and only if we are protected. Hobbes's reply to Cavendish has been interpreted as an attempt to show 'that his theory could be used as a basis for Royalism' and in particular 'that it was not incompatible with ideas of indefeasible hereditary right'.[61] As I have intimated, however, Hobbes's theory of political obligation is blankly at odds with any such ideas. Although the right of an hereditary king to rule can never be annulled by his own subjects, his right to be obeyed can never be indefeasible, simply because his subjects owe obedience if and only if he protects them. Not only is this Hobbes's consistent doctrine in *Leviathan*; it is also what he says in his answer to Cavendish. When Cavendish suggests that a king's title to

---

[58] It hardly follows, that is, from the claim that kings do not owe their titles to divine institution that they must owe them to their protective powers.

[59] Hobbes 2012, vol. 2, ch. 21, p. 344.

[60] Hobbes 2012, vol. 3, A Review, and Conclusion, p. 1141.

[61] Burgess 1990, p. 701. For a critique of the claim that Hobbes can be regarded as a royalist see Hoekstra 2003.

govern 'arises from his protecting those that are govern'd', Hobbes agrees that 'I confesse that as the King ought to protect his people so the people ought to obey the King'.

I now turn to the details of Hobbes's argument. The text is of exceptional interest not merely because it enlarges on Hobbes's earlier discussions about hereditary monarchy, but also because it constitutes his last word on politics. His reasoning is admittedly elliptical and confused in places, but there can be little doubt that he was still in full possession of his faculties when he composed the text in the early summer of 1679. A few months later, however, he was 'suddainly striken with a dead Palsie which stupified his right side from head to foote, and tooke away his speech, in truth I think his reason and sense too.' These are the words of Justinian Morse, the fourth earl of Devonshire's secretary, who adds that Hobbes died within a week of this attack.[62] His death occurred at Hardwick Hall on 4 December 1679, probably less than six months after he dictated his answer to Cavendish to his ever-faithful amanuensis, James Wheldon.[63]

The most interesting part of Hobbes's answer is arguably its final paragraph, in which he returns to the problem of succession under monarchy. But the opening two paragraphs raise several other issues about the nature and limits of sovereign power, and it will be best to examine them first of all. Hobbes begins: 'I deny not but a King holds his Title by Divine right.' This is a startling claim, and was no doubt intended to provoke. Hobbes was a sworn enemy of traditional theories of divine right, according to which kings owe their legitimacy not to the consent of those who become their subjects, but rather to the will and providence of God alone. He argues in chapter 18 of *Leviathan* that 'all the *Rights*, and *Facultyes*' of sovereigns are 'conferred by the consent of the People assembled.'[64] He returns to the argument in chapter 28, confirming that 'all Soveraign Power, is originally given by the consent of every one of the Subjects, to the end they should as long as they are obedient, be protected thereby.'[65]

To make sense of Hobbes's opening contention, we need to bear in mind the distinctive way in which he handles the concept of divine right in *Leviathan*. Hobbes uses the actual phrase 'by Divine Right' only once in the entire work, where he equates this form of rule with government 'by Authority immediate from God.'[66] As he makes clear, however, when he

---

[62] Pritchard 1980, pp. 182, 183–4.

[63] Aubrey 1898, vol. 1, pp. 382–3 contains James Wheldon's own account of Hobbes's final days.

[64] Hobbes 2012, vol. 2, ch. 18, p. 264.   [65] Hobbes 2012, vol. 2, ch. 28, p. 492.

[66] Hobbes 2012, vol. 3, ch. 40, p. 748.

speaks of holding authority '*immediately under God*' he simply means that the authority in question is held without intermediaries.[67] 'Christian Kings have their Civill Power from God immediately; and the Magistrates under him exercise their severall charges in vertue of his Commission'. We may therefore say that 'All lawfull Power is of God, immediately in the Supreme Governour, and mediately in those that have Authority under him'.[68] Kings, like everyone else, are subject to God; but the defining characteristic of kings is that, within their own territories, they are subject to no one else.

Hobbes's response to Cavendish goes on to contrast kings with heirs apparent, arguing that the latter never hold their titles by divine right. This seems a somewhat strange remark. Cavendish's question had made no mention of heirs apparent, but had merely spoken of 'a Successour to a Crown'. Furthermore, as Cavendish and Hobbes were both well aware, the urgent question of the moment was not about heirs apparent but heirs presumptive. The Exclusion crisis had arisen in part because an heir apparent was precisely what Charles II lacked. It is curious, then, to find Hobbes singling out heirs apparent in this way. It may be, however, that in doing so he was alluding once more to an earlier part of his disputation with Cavendish, in which the status of heirs apparent may already have been discussed.

After these preliminaries, Hobbes devotes the rest of his opening paragraph to laying out his views about the rights of kings. He begins by explaining what he means by 'institution', a technical term employed in *Leviathan* to refer to one method of lawfully acquiring a public office, including the office of a king. According to *Leviathan*, an official is 'instituted' when he becomes the authorised representative of someone else.[69] He becomes an authorised representative when he receives a commission or licence to exercise the rights of another person and to act in their name.[70] He is then said to act by their right or authority, for 'by Authority, is always understood a Right of doing any act: and *done by Authority*, done by Commission, or Licence from him whose right it is.'[71] Hobbes is chiefly interested in how sovereigns come to be instituted as representatives of commonwealths or states, but in chapter 42 of

---

[67] Hobbes 2012, vol. 3, ch. 33, p. 606. Although Hobbes uses the phrase 'by divine right' only once in *Leviathan*, he frequently uses the equivalent Latin phrase *de iure divino*. Whenever he does so, however, he likewise makes it clear that he is merely speaking of holding an office 'by immediate Authority from God, that is to say, *in Gods Right*'. For this remark see Hobbes 2012, vol. 3, ch. 42, p. 854. For other instances see Hobbes 2012, vol. 3 ch. 42, pp. 866, 898, 908; ch. 44, p. 964.

[68] Hobbes 2012, vol. 3, ch. 42, p. 900.   [69] Hobbes 2012, vol. 2, ch. 18, p. 264.

[70] Hobbes 2012, vol. 2, ch. 16, p. 244.   [71] Hobbes 2012, vol. 2, ch. 16, p. 244.

Leviathan he also mentions the case of instituting a constable, the example to which he returns in his answer to Cavendish.[72]

Hobbes has almost nothing to say in *Leviathan* about the kinds of ceremonies that might attend the act of instituting an official with a public role. He contents himself with observing that it is a matter of granting the official a licence, a commission or a warrant to play the part of a representative.[73] It is thus of particular interest that, in answering Cavendish, Hobbes mentions a number of such ceremonies. He now adds that, in the case of a king, the act of institution involves 'Enthroneing, Proclameing, Anointing, Crowning etc.' by way of showing that he has duly been commissioned to represent the commonwealth or state. Here Hobbes makes a modest but revealing addition to his theory of authorisation as outlined in chapter 17 of *Leviathan*.

Cavendish had spoken of those who argue (absurdly, in his view) that kings hold their titles 'by divine Institution'. Hobbes retorts that he has never mentioned the word 'institution' in the course of their discussion, to which he adds 'nor do I know what you mean'. His slightly fretful tone may reflect some suspicion of Cavendish's phraseology. Hobbes is at pains to deny that there is anything divine about the act of instituting even a sovereign king. When he speaks about enthroning, proclaiming and so on, he goes on to comment 'Which of all humane, and done *Iure Regio*.' This phrase admittedly makes little sense as it stands, but if we assume that the word 'of' should read 'are', then the meaning becomes clear enough. What Hobbes is telling us is that there is nothing *iure divino* about any of these ceremonies; they 'are all humane' and nothing more.

It is exactly this analysis of 'institution', drawn in the main from *Leviathan*, that Hobbes deploys when he next proceeds to contrast the case of the constable who acts 'by royal right' with the king who acts 'by divine right'. Hobbes articulates the distinction in Latin, speaking of the constable acting *Iure Regio* and the king acting *Iure Devino* (although the latter phrase should read *Iure Divino*, a slip by James Wheldon – who knew no Latin[74] – which Hobbes fails to correct). The distinction is used to explain how it comes about that a constable has the right 'to lay hands upon me' for theft, whereas I have no comparable right to lay hands on him. The reason is not that I am a thief. ('He needs not say, because you are a Theefe. For perhaps I might truly say as much of him.') The reason

---

[72] Hobbes 2012, vol. 3, ch. 42, p. 900.
[73] Hobbes 2012, vol. 2, ch. 16, p. 244 and vol. 2, ch. 30, p. 540.
[74] This is made clear in Hobbes 1994, letter 179, vol. 2, p. 693.

is that the constable is the holder of a recognised public office. He can therefore claim to be acting not merely in his own name – as I would be if I were to lay hands on him – but by licence or commission from the king and hence as his authorised representative. As Hobbes puts it, he can claim to be acting '*Iure Regio* (i.e.)'[75] by the right of the King'. If he arrests me, he will be doing so not in his own name but (as we still say) in the name of the law.

The significance of this analysis, it next emerges, is that it casts further light on what Hobbes means by saying that kings not only hold their titles by divine right, but are sometimes capable of acting *iure divino* as well. To say a king has acted by divine right can only mean that he has received a special licence or commission to represent God in some particular way. As Hobbes summarises – closely echoing the language of *Leviathan* – 'that which is said to be done *Iure Devino* in a King is said to be done by Warrant or comission from God; but that I had no commission.'

Hobbes next says something more about the concept of a right underlying his claim that the constable and the king can both be said to possess certain rights of action not possessed by others. He begins with two direct citations from *Leviathan*. First he declares that 'Law and Right differ', a quotation from the start of his discussion of the laws of nature.[76] He then proceeds to explicate the first half of the distinction, adding in a further quotation – this time from his discussion of civil law – that 'Law is a Command'.[77] It is the second half of the distinction in which he is principally interested, and it is striking that, in giving the required definition of a right, he provides an analysis very different from the one he had offered in *Leviathan*. There he had informed us in chapter 14 that 'RIGHT, consisteth in liberty to do, or to forbeare; whereas LAW, determineth, and bindeth to one of them'.[78] But we now find him saying instead that 'Right is a Liberty or priviledge from a Law to some certaine person though it oblige others.'

The reason for the difference, it might seem, is that in chapter 14 of *Leviathan* Hobbes is discussing the concept of a natural right, whereas here he is talking about rights or liberties within civil associations. This is partly correct, but if we turn to his account of civil rights in *Leviathan* we find that here too his analysis differs from the one he gives in answer to Cavendish. In *Leviathan* Hobbes draws a sharp distinction between two types of civil rights. He speaks about the rights or liberties rooted in 'the Silence of the Law', but also about what he calls 'the true Liberty of a

---

[75] The manuscript simply reads '(i)', but this was a standard seventeenth-century contraction for 'i.e.'.
[76] Hobbes 2012, vol. 2, ch. 14, p. 198.   [77] Hobbes 2012, vol. 2, ch. 26, p. 422.
[78] Hobbes 2012, vol. 2, ch. 14, p. 198.

Subject'.[79] The latter form of liberty is said to arise because there are various things that, 'though commanded by the Soveraign', a subject 'may nevertheless, without Injustice, refuse to do'.[80] The key to understanding the range of these rights lies in recognising that 'every Subject has Liberty in all those things, the right whereof cannot by Covenant be transferred', including the right under all circumstances to defend his own life.[81] In his answer to Cavendish, by contrast, Hobbes maintains that all civil rights are simply freedoms or exemptions from the law allowed 'to some certaine person' while others remain obliged. The implication appears to be that, although we have rights under the law, and may in addition have exemptions from the law, we have no rights against the law. The category of 'the true liberty of a subject' seems to have been dropped.

Perhaps this omission was inadvertent, or perhaps it seemed to Hobbes unnecessary to introduce this extra complication into a brief response. But it is worth asking if his apparent revision may have been deliberate. A number of critics had taken exception to his claim in *Leviathan* that, as Sir Robert Filmer had expressed it, 'right of defending life and means of living can never be abandoned'.[82] Filmer had retorted in his *Observations* that such a doctrine is 'destructive to all government whatsoever, and even to the *Leviathan* itself.'[83] It is possible that Hobbes had come to agree with him.

The first paragraph of Hobbes's answer ends with the assertion that, although kings hold their titles by divine right, and are sometimes capable of acting by warrant or commission from God, ''tis not so of Heirs apparent'. Why not? If we glance forward to Hobbes's final paragraph, we learn that the 'next Heir' of a king will always owe his title to the king himself, who has the right to decide who shall succeed him. But in the present passage Hobbes instead offers an elliptical explanation based on comparing the position of an heir apparent with that of God. One difference is said to be that 'God is no Heir to any King'. A further difference is said to be that, by contrast with human sovereigns, God does not have 'any inheritance to give away'.

Hobbes's line of reasoning appears to falter at this point. His first observation ('God is no Heir to any King') is not what Wheldon initially wrote. Hobbes cancelled his original words to render them illegible, and then rewrote them without any clear sense. Perhaps the most plausible reading of the passage is that Hobbes is already gesturing towards his

---

[79] Hobbes 2012, vol. 2, ch. 21, pp. 336, 340.
[80] Hobbes 2012, vol. 2, ch. 21, p. 336. For a discussion of these rights see Sreedhar 2010.
[81] Hobbes 2012, vol. 2, ch. 21, p. 336.   [82] Filmer 1991, p. 195.
[83] Filmer 1991, p. 195.

basic doctrine that it is entirely for kings in possession to decide who shall be their heirs. No title to succeed can ever be acquired *iure divino*, since the right of succession will always be determined *iure regio*. The reference to God is evidently intended to reinforce this argument. Unlike kings, God does not acquire His title from anyone, nor does He pass it on to anyone else. The inheritance of titles has nothing to do with God.

I turn to Hobbes's second paragraph, in which he presents another elliptical argument. He seems to be saying that people ought to obey their kings, just as kings ought to protect their people, because it is impossible for kings to offer protection unless they are given as much money as they judge necessary for the task. Perhaps the missing line of thought here is that people ought to obey their kings *when their kings ask for money to protect them*. This would certainly have been a topical observation, since the House of Commons in the Exclusion crisis sought to withhold supply to the Crown until it received assurances about the succession. My suggestion is purely speculative, but it seems the only way to make sense of the paragraph, especially as Cavendish had said nothing about taxation when asking about the rights of subjects.

It is worth noting the emphasis that Hobbes places on the impossibility of a king protecting his subjects unless they furnish him 'with so much money as he shall judge sufficient to doe it.' As I argued in chapter 7, one of the principal aims of the parliamentary opposition in the opening decades of the seventeenth century had been to establish that no taxes or impositions can lawfully be levied without the consent of both Houses of Parliament. They had sought to establish, in other words, that it is for Parliament to exercise final judgment on how much money is sufficient for the king to protect his subjects. Discussing the things 'that Weaken, or tend to the DISSOLUTION of a Common-wealth' in chapter 29 of *Leviathan*, Hobbes had replied that it is 'plainly, and directly against the essence of a Common-wealth' to suppose '*That the Soveraign Power may be divided*' or that a popular assembly can lawfully control a sovereign representative.[84] He goes so far as to say that 'if there had not first been an opinion received of the greatest part of *England*, that these Powers were divided between the King, and the Lords, and the House of Commons, the people had never been divided, and fallen into this Civill Warre'.[85] When Hobbes refers in the hereditary right manuscript to the right of sovereigns to judge how much money they require, he is restating one of the cardinal features of his theory of sovereignty.

I turn finally to Hobbes's concluding paragraph, in which he addresses Cavendish's question about whether 'the King in Possession be not obliged

---

[84] Hobbes 2012, vol. 2, ch. 29, p. 506.   [85] Hobbes 2012, vol. 2, ch. 18, p. 278.

to put by his next Heir in case of notorious incapacity'.[86] Although Hobbes had asked himself in every recension of his civil science how the problem of succession can best be managed under monarchy, he had never considered the case in which Cavendish is interested, the case of a ruler with an 'incapable' heir upon whom the rights of sovereignty may perhaps descend. Hobbes had previously limited himself to examining the situation in which a sovereign's authority has in fact descended upon a child or someone who 'cannot discerne between Good and Evill'.[87] Part of the interest of Cavendish's question is thus that it calls on Hobbes to say something more about this aspect of his theory of kingship.

Hobbes responds by exploring two different possibilities. If, he begins, the incapacity 'proceed from want of money', there are no grounds for the heir to be set aside. This is because, as Hobbes has already made clear, such a shortage can only result from a failure on the part of the king's subjects to observe the terms of their covenant. The implication appears to be that it is for them to reappraise their attitude, not for the king to penalise his heir. Hobbes next considers the case in which the incapacity arises not from lack of funds but 'from want of naturall reason'. Here he appears to allude to the usual absolutist solution to the problem – the one we encountered in Hayward's *Reply* – in order to set it aside. He refuses to accept that 'a Successour to a Crown' (in Cavendish's phrase) has any divine or natural right to succeed. Rather he restates his unwavering belief that the question must be entirely for the monarch in possession to decide. As in the case of the constable, whose right to arrest me is 'the right of the King', in whose name he has been authorised to act, so in the case of the successor to a crown, the decision is 'all humane, and done *Iure Regio*'.

Hobbes strongly reaffirms, in other words, that a king in possession must undoubtedly have the right 'to put by his next Heir' should he wish to do so. Cavendish's question, however, is about whether such a king is *obliged* 'to putt him by, upon the request of his subiects'. Cavendish's phrasing here – 'is not the Prince in possession oblig'd' – seems to imply that he agrees with the view we encountered in Persons's *Conference*: that such a monarch is indeed obliged (in the words of Persons) to follow the 'consent and approbation of the realme' and 'remedy the inconveniences of bare succession alone'. For Hobbes, however, the king in possession always has the right to arrange the succession as he chooses, so there can be no question of his having a duty to act in any particular way. As he writes, 'the King in possession may do it, but is not obliged thereunto.'

---

[86] In fact Cavendish had written 'the Prince in possession'.
[87] Hobbes 2012, vol. 2, ch. 19, p. 292.

Hobbes offers no reason for this conclusion, but his reference to the extent of what can be done *iure regio* carries us back to his claim in chapter 19 of *Leviathan* to the effect that 'There is no perfect forme of Government, where the disposing of the Succession is not in the present Soveraign'.[88] As we have seen, the reason he had given was simply that any other arrangement would involve a dangerous and indeed a self-contradictory encroachment upon the extent of the powers that sovereigns need to possess if peace is to be assured.

Having delivered himself of this judgment, Hobbes adds 'Therefore I will speake of that subject no more till we have such a weak King.' This refusal to engage further with the issue strikes a characteristically cautious note, but it may also embody a humorous allusion – of a kind Hobbes liked to make[89] – to his own extreme old age. To say (at the age of ninety-one) that he will not speak about the subject until a weak king comes to power is perhaps a rueful way of saying that he never expects to speak about it at all.

Hobbes has not finished, however, for he next considers the imagined case in which, as he phrases it, 'the King in possession may lawfully disinherit his diseased Heir and will not'. He begins by complaining – in a reference to a missing part of his discussion with Cavendish – that 'you have not yet answered me to the question, Who shall force him'. Hobbes clearly believes no king in possession can lawfully be forced to 'put by' his heir, but the reason he gives for his conclusion is hard to follow. 'I suppose', he writes, 'the sound King living cannot be lawfully deposed by any person or persons that are his Subjects; because the King dying is *ipso facto* dissolved; and then the people is a Multitude of lawlesse men relapsed into a condition of warr'.

This passage forcibly suggests that Hobbes's procedure in composing his answer must have been to dictate a draft to Wheldon, who then worked it up into the fair copy that survives, but without always managing to reproduce Hobbes's somewhat telegraphic thought-processes. Certainly Hobbes's argument at this point is so condensed as to be barely intelligible, and it offers no clue about the nature of the connection – or distinction – between the death and the dissolution of a king. We can perhaps clarify the passage, however, if we return to chapter 19 of *Leviathan*. There Hobbes had remarked that, if a ruler has 'no Power to elect his Successor', and if no one else has that power, then our predicament will be such that, when the king dies, 'the Common-wealth dieth, and dissolveth with him', thereby reducing us to a state of war.[90]

---

[88] Hobbes 2012, vol. 2, ch. 19, p. 298.
[89] See, for example, Hobbes 2012, vol. 3, A Review, and Conclusion, p. 1140.
[90] Hobbes 2012, vol. 2, ch. 19, p. 296.

In his reply to Cavendish Hobbes appears to be drawing on this line of thought, and his argument can perhaps be reconstructed as follows. If a sound king is living, then his heir cannot lawfully be deposed by any person or persons that are subjects of the sound king. The reason is that, if this is done and the sound king then dies, the Commonwealth will *ipso facto* be dissolved, at which point the people will revert to being a multitude of lawless men relapsed into a condition of war. To express the point more simply, when Wheldon wrote 'the King dying is *ipso facto* dissolved', what Hobbes must surely have meant was 'the King dying the Commonwealth is *ipso facto* dissolved', a close echo of his claim in chapter 19 of *Leviathan* that in these circumstances 'the Commonwealth dieth, and dissolveth with him'.[91]

After reflecting on these possibilities, Hobbes stops short, thereby making his answer to Cavendish a deeply evasive one. He was well aware that the great question of the hour was whether an heir whose religion differs from that of his prospective subjects can be said to be suffering from an incapacity sufficiently serious to justify his exclusion from the throne. But on this central issue he says nothing at all.

The tenor of Hobbes's argument, however, leaves little doubt as to what he would have said if pressed. He is clear that, even if an heir is so diseased as to be lacking in any natural reason, he still cannot be excluded. Such an act will always carry with it the danger of dissolving the Commonwealth, and to dissolve a Commonwealth is the most self-destructive political act that can possibly be performed. This is one of the leading themes of chapter 19 of *Leviathan*. If the succession 'be in no particular man, but left to a new choyce; then is the Common-wealth dissolved; and the Right is in him that can get it'.[92] But this dissolution will bring 'a returne to Confusion, and to the condition of a War of every man against every man', and hence an outcome 'contrary to the intention of them that did Institute the Common-wealth'.[93] Hobbes may even have had this passage open in front of him when dictating the closing words of his answer, for he ends by repeating much of what he had earlier said: 'and then the people is a Multitude of lawlesse men relapsed into a condition of warr of every man against every man. Which by making a King they intended to avoid.'

[91] Hobbes 2012, vol. 2, ch. 19, p. 296.   [92] Hobbes 2012, vol. 2, ch. 19, p. 298.
[93] Hobbes 2012, vol. 2, ch. 19, pp. 298, 300.

IV

When the new Parliament assembled on 7 October 1679, Charles II instantly prorogued it, and it did not meet again until 21 October 1680.[94] The king's prevarications were of no avail, however, for the House of Commons immediately reintroduced its Exclusion Bill, which it sent up on 15 November to the House of Lords.[95] The Lords unceremoniously threw it out, but the Commons refused to be put off. They resolved after a long debate on 15 December to bring in a further Bill 'for preventing the Duke of Yorke, or any Papist, from succeeding to the Crown'.[96] When the king refused even to entertain such a proposition, the Commons engaged in a further debate on 7 January and concluded once more that the only way to settle the succession would be by 'disabling' the duke.[97]

Cavendish contributed to both these debates, and his speeches show that he had shifted from his uncertain position of March 1679. But he had moved in a direction that Hobbes would not at all have liked. Cavendish now announced that, as he put it in his speech of 15 December, 'there can be no other way to secure the Protestant Religion' than by a Bill to exclude the duke of York.[98] His speech of 7 January underscored his commitment. 'I am fully persuaded, that we cannot be secure, neither of our religion nor peace and quietness, without this Bill' and that 'neither the king's person, nor Protestant religion can be secured any other way.'[99]

The debate of January 1681 provoked an instant dissolution, and a new Parliament was summoned to meet on 21 March in the traditionally royalist setting of Oxford. Cavendish was again elected as member for Derby, and spoke briefly on a minor matter on 25 March.[100] But he remained silent throughout the long discussion of Exclusion to which the Commons almost immediately returned, a discussion that prompted Charles II to dissolve Parliament at once and never to summon it again.[101]

This is not to say, however, that Cavendish made no contribution to this final act in the Exclusion drama, for he seems to have been the author

---

[94] *Journals* (n. d.). vol. 9, pp. 635–6; cf. Smith 1999, p. 237.

[95] Cobbett and Hansard (eds.) 1807b, col. 1215.   [96] *Journals* (n. d.). vol. 9, p. 680.

[97] Cobbett and Hansard (eds.) 1807b, col. 1293.

[98] Cobbett and Hansard (eds.) 1807b, col. 1235. Knights 1994, p. 124 states that, according to the French ambassador (who paid MPs for his information) Cavendish had become 'converted' to the cause of Exclusion by the summer of 1680.

[99] Cobbett and Hansard (eds.) 1807b, col. 1282.

[100] Cobbett and Hansard (eds.) 1807b, col. 1317.

[101] For the preliminary discussion of Exclusion see Cobbett and Hansard 1807b, cols. 1317–32. Parliament was hurriedly dissolved on 28 March. See Cobbett and Hansard (eds.) 1807b, col. 1337 and cf. Smith 1999, p. 237.

of the anonymous tract entitled *Reasons for His Majesties Passing the Bill of Exclusion*,[102] first published shortly before the opening of the Oxford Parliament.[103] Here he again announces himself unambiguously in favour of the Exclusion Bill, but expresses his disapproval of the factious way in which the Crown's critics have been attempting to impose it. He proposes that in the new Parliament an attempt should instead be made to persuade the king that his acceptance of such a Bill would not only be just but in his own best interests.

By way of supporting the justice of the Bill, Cavendish begins by reverting to one of the conclusions on which he and Hobbes had agreed nearly two years before. 'It seems to me to be an undeniable Position, that Government is intended for the safety and protection of those that are Govern'd'.[104] He then goes on to invoke the authority of Hobbes himself:

For admit, according to Mr. *Hobbes*, that Monarchical Government is form'd by an Agreement of a Society of Men, to devolve all their power and interest upon one Man, and to make him Judge of all Differences that shall arise among them; 'tis plain, that this can be for no other end, than the Security and protection of those that enter into such a Contract.[105]

Here, as before, Cavendish reveals a far from perfect understanding of Hobbes's theory of sovereignty. Hobbes had never argued that monarchies are instituted 'by an Agreement of a Society of Men, to devolve all their power and interest upon one Man'. As I emphasised in chapter 9, it makes no sense according to Hobbes to speak of a society or community of men agreeing in the manner of a single person to devolve their powers upon a sovereign of their choice. It is only through the act of instituting such a sovereign that the members of a multitude become converted into a single society or body politic capable of acting as a single person. 'A Multitude of men', as Hobbes had summarised, only become '*One* Person' when 'they are by one man, or one Person, Represented'.[106]

Even worse, Cavendish goes on to draw from his allegedly Hobbesian premises an inference which, it is safe to say, would have horrified Hobbes. What kind of people, Cavendish rhetorically asks, 'can be suppos'd to have been so void of sense, and so servilely inclin'd, as to give up their Lives and Liberties to the unbounded disposal of one man, without

---

[102] For this attribution to Cavendish see Wing 1945–51, vol. 1, p. 444.

[103] [Cavendish] 1681, p. 2 speaks of 'the Parliament which is to meet at *Oxford*', while the title-page of his tract gives its date of publication as 1681. The Parliament of 1680–1 was dissolved on 18 January 1681 and the Oxford Parliament met on 21 March 1681. See Smith 1999, p. 237. Cavendish's tract must therefore have been published between late January and early March 1681.

[104] [Cavendish] 1681, p. 2.   [105] [Cavendish] 1681, p. 2.

[106] Hobbes 2012, vol. 2, ch. 16, p. 248.

imposing the least condition upon him?' To make such a decision would be so improbable that 'Tis hard therefore to conceive, that Absolute Monarchy could ever have been constituted by consent of any Society of Men'.[107]

Cavendish's conclusion is diametrically opposed to that of Hobbes in *Leviathan*. Hobbes maintains that the political covenant arises out of our recognition that we have no alternative but to make just such an unconditional conferment of all our power and strength upon one man or Assembly of men.[108] He accordingly treats it as wholly rational to consent to the establishment of an absolute monarchy in the name of promoting our security and peace.[109] Cavendish's argument not only shows that by this time he had become a whig (albeit a cautious one) but was quixotic enough to believe that Hobbes's authority could be recruited in support of the whig cause. If Hobbes had not died a year earlier, this would surely have been enough to kill him off.

There was one moment in the Exclusion crisis, however, at which Cavendish's reflections on his own position led him to a conclusion that Hobbes would not only have endorsed, but had actually put forward in his answer to Cavendish's questions about hereditary right. When Cavendish delivered his two speeches in the Parliament of 1680–1, he acknowledged on both occasions that the king cannot be forced. Working with this assumption, his final recommendation to the Commons was therefore that any attempt to pass an Exclusion Bill ought to be given up.

Cavendish's failure to win the Commons round to this viewpoint may help to account for his silence in the Oxford Parliament, but in earlier debates he had firmly expressed this commitment. He admitted in his speech of 15 December 1680 that, because 'according to the course of parliaments, we are not like to bring this to a trial for a long time, I am of opinion, we had best try something else.'[110] Returning to the issue in the momentous debate of 7 January 1681, he reiterated his previous argument. Although an Exclusion Bill is undoubtedly necessary, 'we are not like to have it at this time'. We should therefore abandon the struggle and concentrate instead on 'those other bills that are afoot, that we may try if we can get them.'[111] With these sentiments, at least, Hobbes would surely have agreed.

---

[107] [Cavendish] 1681, p. 2.   [108] Hobbes 2012, vol. 2, ch. 17, p. 260.
[109] Hobbes 2012, vol. 2, ch. 19, p. 286.
[110] Cobbett and Hansard (eds.) 1807b, col. 1236.
[111] Cobbett and Hansard (eds.) 1807b, col. 1282.

Appendix: the manuscript of 'Questions relative to Hereditary Right'

The manuscript discussed in this chapter is Chatsworth MS Hobbes D. 5, which consists of two conjugate quarto leaves formed from a single sheet 22 x 35 cm folded in two, making four pages. An endorsement on the fourth page reads: 'Questions relative to Hereditary Right. Mr. Hobbes'. The watermark shows a curved hunting-horn within a shield surmounted by a coronet with three fleur-de-lys; below the shield is an elongated '4' with the monogram 'WR' at its base.[112] Unfortunately this design is of no help in determining the date of the manuscript, as it was common in Holland as well as England throughout the latter part of the seventeenth century.[113] As I have argued in this chapter, however, the manuscript can be confidently dated to the early summer of 1679.

The manuscript amounts to only forty-nine lines, but it seems to have formed part of a longer disputation that has since been lost. The first page is marked '9' at the top right-hand corner, the second '10' at the top left. (Except for the endorsement, the other two pages are blank.) These marks of pagination are in the same hand and ink as Hobbes's response to the question put to him.

Hobbes's questioner has previously been identified as William Cavendish, third earl of Devonshire.[114] But the handwriting is that of his eldest son, who succeeded as fourth earl in 1684 and became the first duke of Devonshire ten years later. A comparison of the hereditary right manuscript with letters written and signed by the fourth earl at around the time of his succession places this attribution beyond doubt.[115]

Hobbes's answer is in the handwriting of his amanuensis, James Wheldon, but it includes some small corrections in a further hand. These alterations are entered in a manner closely resembling Hobbes's way of correcting Wheldon's fair copy of *Behemoth*,[116] and this leads me

---

[112] Heawood 1930, pp. 284–5 suggests that the letters WR may imply that the monogram was first used by the successors of the sixteenth-century Strasbourg printer Wendelin Riehel.

[113] Heawood 1950, pp. 123–4 and Plates 344–9 illustrates twelve marks from the period between 1655 and 1705 in which all these elements appear, three from Amsterdam, three from Leiden, three from England and three of unknown provenance.

[114] Rogow 1986, p. 253; Beal 1987, p. 583.

[115] See, for example, the letters under the prefix 18 in the *Index of Letters at Chatsworth: First Series, to 1839*. Letter 18–01 and Letter 18. 2 are both in the hand of (and are signed by) the fourth earl of Devonshire. Letter 18–01 is addressed to Lord Middleton and dated 1684; Letter 18. 2 is addressed to Lady Russell and dated 1688.

[116] See St John's College Oxford MS 13: *Behemoth or the Long Parliament. By Thomas Hobbes of Malmsbury*. A presentation copy in the hand of James Wheldon, with additions and excisions by Hobbes.

to conclude that the corrections to the hereditary right manuscript must also have been made by Hobbes himself.

James Wheldon had been regularly acting as Hobbes's amanuensis from as early as the mid-1650s.[117] The first evidence that Hobbes was finding it necessary to dictate his letters dates from October 1656, when we find François du Verdus anxiously exclaiming that Hobbes's latest communication is in the hand of a scribe.[118] If one compares the letters written by Wheldon for Hobbes in the late 1670s with the handwriting of the hereditary right manuscript, it becomes clear that the latter is also in Wheldon's hand.[119]

The fact that the Hereditary Right manuscript was produced by Wheldon is a reason not for doubting but for accepting that it should be regarded as authentically Hobbes's work. As early as 1650 Hobbes had begun to suffer from what John Aubrey described as a shaking palsy,[120] and no extended piece of his handwriting survives from any period later than 1654.[121] Hobbes's correspondents were used to accepting letters in Wheldon's hand as proof that they came from Hobbes. For example, we find François du Prat informing Hobbes in 1663 that 'in Mr Sorbiere's absence, I take upon me to answer a Letter w.^{ch}, being att his house, I knew to be one of y.^{rs}, by y^e. superscription wch. is in Jame's hand.'[122] We may thus be said to have at least as good a reason for treating the hereditary right manuscript as Hobbes's own work.

My transcription of the manuscript in this chapter preserves original orthography and punctuation, but not lineation. All words underlined in the manuscript have been rendered in italics. The manuscript was first printed in Skinner 1965, pp. 217–18 and subsequently in Rogow 1986, Appendix II, pp. 253–4. My transcription differs from Rogow's at dozens of points, but I have not troubled to record them.

---

[117] Malcolm 1994a, p. xxiii. See also Hardwick MSS (Chatsworth) MS 19, James Wheldon's account book 1661–1708. The earliest surviving entries, dated January 1661, show Wheldon already being paid by Hobbes. The payments continued uninterruptedly up to the half-year ending Christmas 1679. During the 1670s Hobbes usually paid Wheldon £10 per year, a sum that doubled Wheldon's basic wage.

[118] Hobbes 1994, letter 94, vol. 1, p. 320.

[119] I have compared the Hereditary Right manuscript with letters written for Hobbes by Wheldon in 1675, 1677, 1678 and 1679. For the letters in question see Hobbes 1994, letter 198, vol. 2, pp. 751–2; letter 200, vol. 2, pp. 756–7; letter 202, vol. 2, pp. 766–7; letter 204, vol. 2, p. 769.

[120] Aubrey 1898, vol. 1, p. 352.   [121] Malcolm 1994a, p. xxiii.

[122] Hobbes 1994, letter 155, vol. 2, p. 558.

12 Hobbes and the Concept of the State

I

My aim in this concluding chapter is to situate Hobbes's theory of the state within a broader historical framework. As I argued in chapter 9, Hobbes's theory of political representation issues in the conclusion that to speak of a sovereign is to refer to a natural person (or body of persons) authorised to discharge the role of representing the person 'by Fiction' of the state. I now wish to extend my historical gaze and consider the origins and subsequent fortunes of this way of thinking about the state in Anglophone political thought.[1]

I take as my point of departure the moment when, in the opening decades of the seventeenth century, we first begin to encounter widespread references to states, statecraft and the power of states.[2] During this seminal period, the term *state* was generally used to describe the community or body politic over which rulers hold sway. This way of thinking was already implicit in the doctrine of the king's two bodies, the doctrine examined by Ernst Kantorowicz in his classic book of that name. Kantorowicz begins by quoting a verdict delivered by the English judges early in the reign of Elizabeth I. The case concerned the disposition of some royal lands, and the judges vindicated the rights of the Crown by referring to the doctrine that 'the King has in him two Bodies'. One is his

I have made several attempts to construct a genealogy of the state. While this chapter draws on each of them, it is basically a revised and extended version of Skinner 2009a. For permission to make use of this earlier work I am indebted to the British Academy. I owe particular thanks to Bernhard Jussen, who invited me to deliver the Kantorowicz Lecture at the University of Frankfurt in 2011, thereby prompting me to reconsider and expand my previous articles. For discussions and correspondence about subsequent drafts I am deeply grateful to Duncan Bell, Greg Claeys, John Dunn, Raymond Geuss, Peter Hall, Susan James, Hent Kalmo, William Klein, Janet McLean, Pete Stacey, Bo Sträth and James Tully. To Hans Baade, Ben Holland, Philip Pettit and David Runciman I owe a special debt for helping me to improve my understanding of moral and fictional personhood.

[1] My focus will thus be on the acquisition of – and debates about – the concept of the state, not on the early-modern development of the institutions of the English state. On this process see Corrigan and Sayer 1985; Braddick 2000; Hindle 2000.
[2] My chronology follows Maitland 2003, p. 38.

'Body natural', which is subject 'to all Infirmities that come by Nature or Accident', and is thus no different from 'the natural Bodies of other People'. But the other is described as his 'Body politic', which 'cannot be seen or handled', and is 'constituted for the Direction of the People, and the Management of the public weal'.[3]

From as early as the thirteenth century, according to Kantorowicz,[4] the political bodies of kings were in turn held to constitute them as heads of the *corpus politicum* of their subjects, thereby producing what Kantorowicz describes as a fiction within a fiction.[5] This further body politic was described in a variety of ways. Robert Mulcaster, translating Sir John Fortescue's mid-fifteenth-century treatise on the laws of England in 1567, makes Fortescue speak about the body of the realm.[6] Edmund Plowden, writing a century after Fortescue in his *Commentaries*, refers instead to the body of the people.[7] Sir Thomas Smith in his *De Republica Anglorum*, first published in 1583, returns to speaking of the body of the realm,[8] although he also displays a marked predeliction for writing in more humanist vein about the concept of the *res publica*,[9] and consequently describes the kings and queens of England as heads or governors of the body of the commonwealth.[10]

Kantorowicz carried his examination of the English sources no further than this point, but it is perhaps surprising that he stopped short in the late sixteenth century, especially in view of his declared ambition of contributing to an understanding of the origins and mythology of the modern secular state.[11] Had he pushed his investigations forward one further generation, he would have come upon an epoch-making moment in Anglophone discussions about the relationship between the political bodies of rulers and the *corpus politicum* of their subjects. He would have reached the stage at which, for the first time, the body over which monarchs were said to rule began to be widely described as the state.

This development was connected with the growing realisation that the organisation of political power along unified and national lines carried with it a number of advantages over the institutional arrangements characteristic of late-medieval Europe.[12] If we concentrate on the semantic shift that mirrored and helped to promote this change in the case of the English polity, we find it can chiefly be traced to the growing availability of French treatises on sovereignty[13] and Italian handbooks on 'politics' and

---

[3] Kantorowicz 1957, p. 7.   [4] Kantorowicz 1957, p. 210.   [5] Kantorowicz 1957, p. 5.
[6] See Kantorowicz 1957, pp. 223, 231 and cf. Fortescue 1567, pp. 40, 83, 112.
[7] As noted in Kantorowicz 1957, p. 7.   [8] Smith 1982, pp. 79, 88.
[9] Smith 1982, pp. 57, 62, 64.   [10] Smith 1982, pp. 77, 88.
[11] Kantorowicz 1957, pp. x–xi.   [12] See Spruyt 1996; Morris 1998, pp. 33–6.
[13] Skinner 1978, vol. 2, pp. 254–75; Thuau 2000.

reason of state.[14] With the confluence of these strands of thought, the term *state* began to be used with increasing confidence to refer to the union or civil association of those living subject to the authority of a recognised monarch or ruling group.

Both the humanists and the constitutionalist writers had their own reasons for finding the term *state* a natural one to invoke. One question addressed in the Renaissance genre of advice-books for princes had always been how a ruler should act to maintain his state, that is, to uphold his status or standing as a prince. Machiavelli was only the most famous of numerous political writers who had emphasised the importance of being able *mantenere lo stato*, and when Edward Dacres published his translation of *The Prince* in 1640 he duly made Machiavelli speak of how a prince must act 'for the maintenance of his State', and how he must 'take the surest course he can to maintain his life and State'.[15]

According to the writers of these handbooks, however, there is something of more impersonal significance that rulers must also preserve if they wish to avoid a *coup d'état*, a strike against their standing or state. They must at all costs preserve the welfare of the body politic, and they are cautioned that they cannot expect to uphold their own status unless they do everything necessary to maintain this body in security and good health. We accordingly find these writers speaking of the need for rulers not merely to maintain their own state, but to establish and preserve what they begin to describe as *lo stato*, the body of the state. As Machiavelli puts it, in Dacres's translation, a prince needs to follow whatever courses of action may be 'necessary for the founding of a State' and may also be well-adapted 'to preserve a State which is already established and setled'.[16]

The kinds of reasons that princes can adduce when justifying what needs to be done to maintain a state thus came to be described as reasons of state. Francesco Guicciardini was one of the earliest to use the phrase, and English readers became familiar with it after Robert Dallington published his collection of *Aphorismes Civill and Militarie* derived from Guicciardini's *History* in 1613. The first Aphorism in Book IV lays it down that 'Among States that have entercourse of traffick', it is essential that, 'upon the death of any Prince, in whose State appeares a new face of all things', they must chiefly consider 'what may be advantageous to them.'[17] Commenting on this judgment, Dallington observes, with specific reference to Louis XII of France, that 'it was likely in all reason of

---

[14] On this genre see Mattei 1979; Borrelli 1993; Tuck 1993, pp. 31–64; Baldwin 2004; Malcolm 2007, esp. pp. 30–73.
[15] Machiavelli 1640, pp. 139, 141; cf. also pp. 117, 169.
[16] Machiavelli 1640, pp. 168, 198. On Machiavelli as a theorist of the state see Stacey 2013.
[17] Dallington 1613, IV. I, p. 223.

State, that he would not sodainely wrap himselfe into warres beyond the Alpes, in the beginning of his reigne, before his State were well settled at home.'[18]

Machiavelli never uses the phrase *ragione di stato*. As I showed in chapter 3, however, he forcefully argues that rulers must be prepared to do anything – whether virtuous or otherwise – necessary for the preservation of the state. He repeatedly insists in *The Prince* that (as Dacres translates) 'when a Prince would maintaine the State, hee is often forced not to be good', and must stand ready to lay aside honesty 'as need shall require'.[19] It was chiefly among the enemies of this view of political necessity that it came to be characterised as reason of state. One of the most vehement of these critics was Traiano Boccalini in his *Ragguagli di Parnasso*, which was translated as *The new-found politicke* in 1626. Boccalini repeatedly denounces those who, by allowing dishonest policies to be pursued in the name of preserving the state, promote 'the diabolicall impiety of the moderne *reason of State*'.[20]

Of still greater importance in accounting for the increasing use of the terms *state* and *statecraft* may have been the contribution made by a number of legal commentators on the nature of Parliament. Over the course of the sixteenth century, these writers increasingly came to think of the English constitution as a mixed monarchy in which King, Lords and Commons represented the people in an assembly usually described as a meeting of the three estates. As Sir Thomas Smith explains in *De Republica Anglorum*, 'The people I do call that which the word *populus* doth signifie, the whole body and the three estates of the common wealth'.[21] Towards the end of the sixteenth century, these different elements in the constitution began to be widely described as the states. Robert Mulcaster already translates Fortescue in 1567 as saying that any alterations in English law require 'the assent of the commens and states of the realme'.[22] Henry Barrow invokes the same terminology in his petition of 1591 on the condition of the Church, in which he maintains that 'The bodie politike of the Realme, is, All the people in the common wealth, contracted and distinguished into the Three states of the Parliament.'[23] The same usage recurs in Sir John Hayward's *Answer* of 1603 to the treatise on popular sovereignty published by Robert Persons in 1594.[24] One of Hayward's constitutional commitments is that the origins of the English Parliament can be traced no further back than the

---

[18] Dallington 1613, IV. I, p. 224.   [19] Machiavelli 1640, pp. 118, 157.
[20] Boccalini 1626, p. 151.   [21] Smith 1982, p. 54.   [22] Fortescue 1567, p. 40.
[23] Barrow 1591, p. 17.
[24] On Hayward see Levack 1988; Sommerville 1999, pp. 51–2, 68. On Roman law in England during this period see Levack 1981.

moment when Henry I exercised his supremacy of power and 'called a councell of all the states of his realme'.[25]

It proved a short step from the assertion that monarchs are supreme over the two states in Parliament to the conclusion that they must be heads of the entire state, and this step was duly taken by a number of legal and constitutional writers in the reign of James I. The claim was put forward in the first place by numerous exponents of the so-called divine right of kings.[26] George Hakewill, one of James I's court preachers, refers in his *Answer* of 1616 to governors 'of the whole State',[27] while Samuel Collins, another court preacher, describes the king in his *Defence* of 1617 as head of the body of the state.[28] James I himself liked to speak in similar terms, especially when haranguing his Parliaments about the extent of his divinely ordained powers.[29] He refers to those who live subject to sovereign power as 'the body of the whole State'[30] and he describes the two Houses of Parliament as 'the representative body of the State'.[31] Later he adds that, because all rulers are heads of state, 'if the King want, the State wants, and therefore the strengthening of the King is the preservation and the standing of the State'.[32]

The same vocabulary was employed by a number of English writers on the theory of sovereignty who acknowledged the influence of Jean Bodin's *Six livres de la république*, which first appeared in English as *The Six Bookes of a Commonweale* in 1606.[33] At the outset of Book I Bodin supplies a definition of what his translator, Richard Knollys, calls 'the Citie or state'.[34] Bodin asserts that 'it is neither the wals, neither the persons, that maketh the citie, but the union of the people under the same soveraigntie of government'.[35] He concedes that sovereignty can be held by the people themselves, but he expresses a strong preference for kingship over all other forms of government. To institute a monarchy, he later explains, is to create a type of public authority in which 'all the people in generall, and (as it were) in one bodie' swear allegiance to a single sovereign whose duty is to devote himself to 'the health & welfare of the whole state'.[36]

---

[25] Hayward 1603, sig. F, 1v.
[26] On divine right theory in this period see Judson 1988, pp. 171–217; Sommerville 1999, pp. 9–54.
[27] Hakewill 1616, p. 66.   [28] Collins 1617, p. 75.
[29] On James I as an absolutist see Sommerville 1991a, pp. 347–53, Sommerville 1991b and Sommerville 1999, pp. 107–10, 227–30.
[30] James VI and I 1994, pp. 143, 145.   [31] James VI and I 1994, pp. 147, 149.
[32] James VI and I 1994, p. 195.
[33] See Bodin 1962. For Bodin on the state see Franklin 1973; Franklin 1991; Skinner 1978, vol. 2, pp. 284–301, 355–6.
[34] Bodin 1962, I. II, p. 10.   [35] Bodin 1962, I. II, p. 10.   [36] Bodin 1962, I. VIII, p. 97.

The English legal writer of the Jacobean period who speaks with the greatest assurance in this idiom is Sir John Hayward in his *Answer* of 1603. After an apparently concessive opening, Hayward declares that all authority arises not from the people but from God, so that even heathen rulers count as the Lord's anointed.[37] The underlying body politic cannot have been the original possessor of sovereignty, for it amounts to nothing more than 'a heedless and headless multitude' without direction or government.[38] Drawing on Bodin, Hayward concludes that it will always be more natural 'that one state, bee it great or small, should rather bee commaunded by one person'.[39] Just as 'all the members of one bodye receive both sence and motion from one heade', so 'it seemeth no lesse naturall, that one state should be governed by one commaunder' as head of state.[40]

These arguments were picked up by a number of polemicists whose primary concern was to vindicate the right of temporal sovereigns to wield absolute control over ecclesiastical no less than civil affairs. Hayward also contributed to this debate, and is one of the earliest writers to describe this Erastian commitment as an argument about the proper relations between church and state. His *Report* of 1607 on religious policy begins by reminding his readers, with a quotation from Bodin, that 'the rights of Soveraignty' consist in 'an absolute and perpetuall power, to exercise the highest actions and affaires in some certaine state'.[41] He then argues that 'there is nothing in a Common-wealth of so high nature' as the care of religion,[42] in consequence of which it is indispensable to commit 'the government for matters of Religion, to the Soveraigne power and authoritie in the State'.[43] A more systematic contribution to the same debate was made by the civil lawyer Calybute Downing,[44] whose *Discourse of the State Ecclesiasticall* first appeared in 1632.[45] Downing agrees that the king of England is 'the supreme Soveraigne' exercising 'chiefty of power over the whole body of the Common-wealth'.[46] He must therefore be recognised as 'supreme Civil head' over the ecclesiastical no less than the civil state.[47] As in all absolute monarchies, there must be one person with unquestionable authority to govern all the 'distinct and setled societies of that State.'[48]

---

[37] Hayward 1603, sig. G, 3r.   [38] Hayward 1603, sig. B, 3v; sig. H, 3r; sig. K, 2v.
[39] Hayward 1603, sig. B, 3v; Bodin is cited to this effect at sig. D, 3r.
[40] Hayward 1603, sig. B, 4r.   [41] Hayward 1607, p. 6.   [42] Hayward 1607, p. 8.
[43] Hayward 1607, p. 14.
[44] On Downing see Levack 1973, pp. 115–17, 187–8; Sommerville 1999, pp. 40–1.
[45] I quote from the extended version of 1634.   [46] Downing 1634, p. 49, 57, 69.
[47] Downing 1634, pp. 58, 68.   [48] Downing 1634, p. 46.

II

When Kantorowicz speaks of kings as the heads of bodies politic, he takes himself to be excavating the origins of the modern idea of the secular state.[49] He appears to assume, in other words, that the metaphor in which the idea of the state is best captured is that of a head presiding over a body living in subjection to its rule. This is undoubtedly one way of thinking about the state, and it was this absolutist theory (as I shall call it) that the term *state* was first employed to express. No sooner, however, did this vocabulary become entrenched in English political discourse in the opening decades of the seventeenth century than it began to be powerfully attacked. Critics largely agreed that, when we talk about the state, we are referring to a type of civic union, a body or society of people united under government. But they repudiate the image according to which, as Fortescue had expressed it, 'a people beynge headless is not worthye to be called a bodie', because 'in thinges politique a cominalte without a head is in no wise corporate'.[50] They begin to suggest it is equally possible for supreme authority to be possessed by the union or corporate body of the people themselves. We accordingly find these writers using the term *state* to refer not to a passive and obedient community living under a sovereign head, but rather to the body of the people viewed as the owners of sovereignty themselves.

It is possible to distinguish two distinct challenges mounted along these lines. One stemmed from a group of writers who are perhaps best described as political anatomists, and whose principal interest lay in comparing the various forms of government to be found in different parts of the world. As they liked to observe, there are many communities in Europe in which the people are not ruled by kings but govern themselves. Focusing on the special characteristics of these polities, they begin to label them as popular states or simply as states to distinguish them from monarchies and principalities.

If we ask why this specific terminology was used, the answer again appears to be connected with the tendency to describe representative assemblies as meetings of different estates or states. Where these assemblies were recognised as the governing bodies of their communities, it proved a short step to speaking of the government of the state. We can watch this slippage at work in Richard Knollys's translation of Bodin's *Six Bookes*. Bodin is no friend to popular states, and reviles them as 'an enemy unto wisedome and good councell'.[51] Nevertheless, in Book II of his *Six*

---

[49] Kantorowicz 1957, pp. x–xi, 208–10.   [50] Fortescue 1567, p. 30.
[51] Bodin 1962, I. VIII, p. 99.

Bookes, in which he lays out his classification of constitutions, he includes a lengthy chapter on 'popular estates', in which 'everie citisen is in a manner partaker of the maiestie of the state'.[52] This analysis leads him to introduce a categorical distinction between 'monarchies' and 'states', a distinction that subsequently echoes throughout his text.[53] We are told that 'in a popular estate nothing can bee greater than the whole body of the people', whereas 'in a monarchie it is otherwise', for 'all the people in generall' swear allegiance to a single head of state.[54]

The political anatomists argue in similar terms. An early example can be found in Edwin Sandys's *Relation* of 1605, a survey of the religious and constitutional arrangements prevailing in different parts of Europe.[55] Sandys consistently distinguishes between monarchies and states, reserving the latter term for those polities, especially in Italy, in which the people govern themselves.[56] The same is true of Giovanni Botero's *Le Relationi Universali*, which was first translated in 1601 as *Relations of the most famous kingdomes and common-wealths*, and thereafter appeared in many English versions in the opening decades of the seventeenth century.[57] When Botero speaks of Switzerland, he describes it as 'a state popular, and subject to no one Prince',[58] and when he examines the constitution of the United Provinces he likewise calls it a state.[59] Botero's appraisal is echoed by Pierre d'Avity in his chapter on the United Provinces in his *Estates, Empires & Principallities of the World*, first published in English in 1615. By contrast with neighbouring monarchies, d'Avity observes, the people of the Netherlands govern themselves in assemblies of the Estates, in which they 'treat, dispose, and determine of all matters concerning the State'.[60]

It was widely agreed that the most important contemporary example of such a state was Venice. Botero refers to 'the State of Venice',[61] and mounts a comparison between its constitution and that of France.[62] Lewes Lewkenor in his 1599 translation of Gasparo Contarini's *De magistratibus et republica Venetorum* likewise speaks of 'the state of Venice',[63] adding that it is possible for foreigners to become naturalised 'if they have done the state some notable service'.[64] Othello quotes this observation when drawing attention to his own employment by the

---

[52] Bodin 1962, II. VIII, pp. 244–52; cf. I. VI, p. 60.
[53] Bodin 1962, I. VIII, p. 101; II. I, p. 196; VI. II, pp. 653–4.
[54] Bodin 1962, I. VIII, p. 99.   [55] On Sandys's *Relation* see Rabb 1998, pp. 21–46.
[56] Sandys 1605, sig. N, 3r; sig. P, 2v; sig. S, 3r.
[57] On Botero's *Relazioni* see De Luca 1946, pp. 73–89; Mattei 1979. I quote from the final and most extensive version, translated by Robert Johnson and published in 1630.
[58] Botero 1630, p. 310.   [59] Botero 1630, pp. 200, 206.   [60] d'Avity 1615, p. 330.
[61] Botero 1630, pp. 339–61.   [62] Botero 1630, p. 597.
[63] Contarini 1599, pp. 9, 18, 126, 138, 146.   [64] Contarini 1599, p. 18.

republic, proudly remarking that 'I have done the State some service'.[65] Pierre d'Avity also describes Venice as a state,[66] and brings his analysis of the Venetian system of government to a close by avowing that the Senators 'have no other desseigne but to preserve the State in peace and libertie'.[67]

Many of these writers are happy to shift from describing republican constitutions to celebrating the superiority of such self-governing regimes. This preference was generally grounded on a view about how we can manage to retain our natural liberty while submitting to government. To live under a monarchy, it was urged, is to subject yourself to the prerogative rights of a king, and thus to live to some degree in dependence upon his will. But as I emphasised in chapter 7, Justinian's *Digest* had laid it down that to depend on the will of another is what it means to live in slavery.[68] If you wish to preserve your freedom under government, you must ensure that you institute a political order in which no prerogative or discretionary power is allowed. If and only if the laws rule, and if you personally give consent to the laws, can you remain free from servitude. The inflammatory conclusion towards which these writers are drawn is thus that, if you wish to live 'in a free state', you must be sure to live in a self-governing republic. As a result, they begin to describe such polities not merely as states by contrast with monarchies, but more specifically and more invidiously as free states by contrast with the dependence and slavery allegedly imposed by absolutist forms of kingly rule.

The chief inspiration for this line of thought can be traced to the Roman historians and their accounts of Rome's transition from monarchical to consular government.[69] It was a moment of great significance when Philemon Holland, in publishing the first complete English translation of Livy's history in 1600, chose to describe the expulsion of Rome's kings as a shift from tyranny to 'a free state'.[70] Holland went on to narrate how, when Lars Porsenna attempted to negotiate the return of the Tarquins, he was reminded 'that the people of Rome were not under the regiment of a king, but were a free state' and intended 'to be free still and at their owne libertie'.[71]

Livy's analysis was much reinforced when Thomas Heywood published his translation of Sallust in 1608. Sallust had prefaced his narrative of Catiline's conspiracy with a history of early Rome in which he had given an extraordinarily influential explanation of the city's rise to greatness. He had described 'how our Auncestors managed the state' so that it

[65] Shakespeare 1986, *Othello*, TLN 3245, p. 965 (5. 2. 348).
[66] d'Avity 1615, pp. 527, 528, 530.   [67] d'Avity 1615, p. 530.
[68] *The Digest* 1985, 1. 6. 4, vol. 1, p. 18.   [69] Skinner 2002a, pp. 308–43.
[70] Livy 1600, p. 44.   [71] Livy 1600, p. 54.

'increased and prospered' while remaining 'most just and excellent'.[72] The early Romans were able to achieve these results only after they repudiated the 'sole Soveraignty' of their kings and established a republic, thereby creating a 'forme of Liberty in Government'.[73] As soon as they instituted a regime in which 'the wisest and most sufficientest spirits, were most imployed in the affaires of the state', they rose at once to riches and power, so that 'by valor and Justice the state florished'.[74]

These doubts about monarchy were rendered fully explicit for English readers when several leading texts of Italian republicanism were translated in the early decades of the seventeenth century. Boccalini in his *Ragguagli di Parnasso* not only satirises the monarchies of Europe and their preoccupation with *ragione di stato*, but ends with a series of orations in which a group of learned spokesmen vie with one another to speak in praise of Venice.[75] Everyone agrees that the city's success has been largely due to her standing as a free state. For centuries her citizens have preserved the same republican constitution, which has provided 'the true solid foundation, wheron their Greatnesse consisted most firmly built, & withall the eternitie of their Libertie'.[76] Still more forthrightly, Edward Dacres's translation of Machiavelli's *Discorsi*, first published in 1636, affirms that 'it is an easy thing to guesse, whereupon it is that people take such an affection to their liberty: because we see by experience, that cities have never bin much amplified neither in dominion nor riches unless onely during their liberty'.[77]

During the early decades of the seventeenth century we begin to encounter a second and still more challenging line of attack on the absolutist theory of the state. Among the protagonists of free states, few had gone so far as to stigmatise monarchy as an inherently illegitimate form of rule. Even Machiavelli explicitly if confusingly concedes in his *Discorsi* that it is possible for a people (in the words of Dacres's translation) to have 'the raines of their owne government in their owne hands, either as a Commonwealth, or as a Principality'.[78] By this time, however, a number of legal and scholastic writers had constructed a theory of *summa potestas* more directly hostile to the idea of kings as absolute heads of state.[79] As I showed in chapter 2, most legal commentators on the *Lex regia* argued that, even if we think of the body of the people as naturally and originally free, we need to recognise that, in the act of submitting themselves to government, they transfer and thereby alienate their rights. But an influential minority countered that, to cite the formula

[72] Sallust 1608, sig. B, 3r–v; sig. B, 4r; sig. C, 1v.   [73] Sallust 1608, sig. B, 4r.
[74] Sallust 1608, sig. B, 4v; sig. C, 1r.   [75] On Boccalini see Tuck 1993, pp. 101–3.
[76] Boccalini 1626, p. 197.   [77] Machiavelli 1636, 2. 2, p. 260.
[78] Machiavelli 1636, 1.2, p. 8.   [79] See Brett 2006.

used by Azo in contesting the orthodoxy, 'the people never transferred this power except in such a way that they were at the same time able to retain it.'[80] As a result, it can be said even of the emperor that, 'although he possesses greater power than any individual member of the people, he does not possess greater power than the people as a whole'.[81]

As England lurched towards civil war in 1642, a number of parliamentarian propagandists began to restate these claims as a means of questioning the king's standing as head of state. As I argued in chapter 9, the chief architect of this challenge was Henry Parker, whose *Observations* of 1642 presented a theory of popular sovereignty subsequently enlarged in his *Ius populi* of 1644.[82] According to Parker the right of supreme command 'is originally inherent in the people' and is naturally the possession of 'politique corporations', taking the form of 'that might and vigour which such or such a societie of men containes in it selfe'. Parker sometimes speaks of this union as the nation,[83] and sometimes as the kingdom,[84] but he also refers to the *universitas* of the people as the body of the state, and in his *Observations* he equates 'our nationall union' with 'the whole State of England'.[85]

The central question for Parker is accordingly how political authority can justly be disposed between Crown and state. Parker's negative answer is that sovereign power can never lie with kings as heads of state. While it may be true in natural bodies that the head dominates the body, 'it is otherwise with the Head Politicall, for that receives more subsistence from the body than it gives, and being subservient to that, it has no being when that is dissolved'.[86] Parker's positive answer is thus that the true subject or bearer of sovereignty must be 'the whole universality' of the people or state.[87] 'The King is a servant to the State, and though far greater, and superiour then all particulars' is at all times 'subject to the whole State'.[88]

Parker concedes that the body of the state can never act on its own behalf. We are speaking of a body so vast and cumbersome that its powers need to be exercised on its behalf,[89] and in England these powers are normally entrusted to the king in Parliament, and in the last resort to Parliament itself. As I showed in chapter 9, however, Parker sees no inconsistency in claiming that sovereign authority lies with Parliament

[80] Azo 1966b, I. XIV. 11, p. 44: 'dic quod [populus] non transtulit ita quin sibi retineret.'
[81] Azo 1966b, VIII. LIII. 2, p. 671: 'unde non est maior potestatis imperator quam totus populus, sed quam quilibet de populo'.
[82] See Mendle 1995, pp. 32–50; Sabbadini 2016.
[83] [Parker] 1642, pp. 3, 8–9, 11, 17, etc.   [84] [Parker] 1642, pp. 3, 5, 7, 9–11, 16, etc.
[85] [Parker] 1642, p. 29.   [86] [Parker] 1642, p. 19.   [87] [Parker] 1642, p. 44.
[88] [Parker] 1644, p. 26.   [89] [Parker] 1642, pp. 14–15.

as well as with the state.[90] This is because he thinks of Parliament not merely as the representative assembly of the people, but also as a representation – an image or likeness – of the body politic so exactly proportionate that Parliament can be 'accounted by the vertue of representation, as the whole body of the State.'[91] The upshot of his argument is thus that 'Parliament is neither one nor few, it is indeed the State it self'.[92] For Parker, to say that sovereignty is held by Parliament is no different from saying that it is held by the body of the people or state.

This populist theory of the state (as I shall call it) had a visible impact on many other protagonists of the parliamentarian cause at the outset of the English civil war.[93] One early restatement can be found in *The unlimited prerogative of kings* of November 1642. Like Parker, the anonymous author begins by speaking of 'the whole body of the people' as a unity that can be 'considered together'.[94] This community was originally possessed of sovereign power, so that 'the people are the originall of the power that is in Kings'.[95] Turning to the defenders of royal supremacy, the author fastens on their contention that, if you cut off the king as 'head of the State', then 'you destroy the whole State together with Him'. This metaphor, he objects, 'doth not hold good'. We need to distinguish between 'a naturall head' and 'the civill Head of the State'. It is not true that 'if the head of the State be cut off, the State dies', for 'the whole power of all the body of the people' remains, and this sovereign body can readily choose for itself another head of state.[96]

Among the parliamentarian writers who thought in these terms, the most prominent was William Bridge, who received a commission from the House of Commons to restate its case after the outbreak of the war, and duly obliged with *The Truth of the Times* in July 1643.[97] Specifically invoking the authority of the *Vindiciae, contra tyrannos*,[98] Bridge reiterates that 'ruling power' was originally possessed by 'the whole people or body politicke'.[99] When speaking of this underlying community, Bridge usually refers to it as the commonwealth, but he also describes it as the state.[100] He adds that 'if the State be wronged and oppressed' by its ruler, it can always take back the power it mistakenly assigned to him.[101] For Bridge, as for Parker, 'the State' is at once the name of 'the whole body' of the people and the seat of sovereignty.[102]

---

[90] On these two aspects of Parker's argument see Zaller 1991.
[91] [Parker] 1642, pp. 23, 28, 45.   [92] [Parker] 1642, p. 34; cf. [Parker] 1644, p. 46.
[93] Coffey 2006, pp. 76–96.   [94] *The unlimited prerogative* 1642, sig. A, 2v.
[95] *The unlimited prerogative* 1642, sig. A, 2v.
[96] *The unlimited prerogative* 1642, sig. A, 3r.   [97] On Bridge see Nuttall 1957, pp. 11–14.
[98] Bridge 1643b, pp. 3, 5.   [99] Bridge 1643b, pp. 4–5.
[100] See, for example, Bridge 1643b, p. 14.   [101] Bridge 1643b, pp. 15, 19.
[102] Bridge 1643b, p. 8.

After the execution of King Charles I in January 1649, this line of thought was restated as a means of vindicating the newly established Commonwealth. John Goodwin, one of the first to defend the right of Parliament to take up arms in 1642,[103] explicitly claims in his *Hybristodikai* of May 1649 that the authority of the people can be equated with that of the state.[104] Any king, 'bears the Relation of a politicall Servant, or vassal, to that State, Kingdom, and people, over which he is set to Govern'.[105] The kings of England have always been placed in office by 'the people or State', in whom the rights of sovereignty reside at all times.[106] We may thus conclude that 'Kings are but vassals to the State', that is, to the sovereign body of the people.[107]

Goodwin is still prepared to think of the House of Commons as a representative body exercising power in the name of the people or state. If we turn, however, to John Milton's *Tenure of Kings and Magistrates*, we find no comparable acknowledgement of the status of Parliament. For Milton, the rights of sovereignty are lodged with the people themselves, 'in whom the power yet remaines fundamentally, and cannot be tak'n from them, without a violation of thir natural birthright'.[108] He accordingly concludes that Charles I was put on trial by his own people as 'a rebell to Law, and enemie to the State'.[109] For Milton, to speak of the powers of the state is simply a means of referring to the inalienable sovereignty of the people.

III

No sooner was the populist theory of the state put into circulation than it was vehemently repudiated by royalists and absolutists of every stamp. Some of Charles I's defenders reverted to the claim put forward by his father, James I, in support of his divine right. These writers rarely speak of the state, preferring to describe the king as immediately ordained by God to rule over his kingdom or commonwealth.[110] But some adopt the language of their adversaries and instead describe the king as head of state. Henry Ferne, the most prominent defender of the royalist cause at the start of the civil war, argues that 'seeing some must be trusted in every State, 'tis reason the highest and final trust should be in the higher or supreme Power with whom God next to himself hath entrusted the whole Kingdom'.[111] The anonymous author of *Obedience Active and Passive*

---

[103] See Coffey 2006, pp. 85–91.   [104] The BL (Thomason) copy is dated 30 May 1649.
[105] Goodwin 1649, p. 11. See Coffey 2006, pp. 180–4.   [106] Goodwin 1649, p. 12.
[107] Goodwin 1649, pp. 32, 72.   [108] Milton 1991, p. 10.   [109] Milton 1991, p. 28.
[110] See, for example, Ball 1642, pp. 5, 8.   [111] Ferne 1642, p. 18 (*recte* p. 20).

similarly speaks of kings not only as the Lord's anointed but as sovereigns endowed with 'Supreame power in a State'.[112]

The execution of Charles I and the founding of the Commonwealth in 1649 called forth a spate of similar attacks. Edward Boughen, a staunch clerical defender of episcopacy and divine right, was one of many who focused on the parliamentarian contention that kings are *minor universis*, of lesser standing than the body of the state. The king of England, Boughen retorts, is both the head of the body politic and the source of all laws upholding 'the right and peaceable administration of the State'.[113] Edmund Hall, a leading Presbyterian opponent of the new regime, similarly argued in his *Lingua testium* of 1651 that in England 'the office of State in the Head hath been unquestionable in all ages'. The kings of England have at all times 'kept the supremacy of Church and State affairs in their own hands', exercising a plenitude of authority deriving from their standing as sole and divinely ordained heads of state.[114]

By contrast with these intransigent reactions, a number of critics attempted to meet the protagonists of the populist theory on their own ground. The anonymous author of an attack on Parker entitled *Animadversions* begins by announcing himself willing to concede 'that the Parliament represents the body of the State', and even that sovereign power may originally have been possessed by 'the whole body of the people'. But he then counters that, even if the consent of the people 'did at first give power to Kings', this grant can only have been in the form of an irrevocable alienation of right.[115] John Bramhall, as I noted in chapter 2, presents a similar argument in his *Serpent Salve* of 1643. He concedes that 'Power is originally inherent in the People', and thus that it can be lawfully held only by their 'grant and consent'.[116] But he then restates the juristic orthodoxy that, when the people submit to government, they 'divest' themselves of their primitive sovereignty, granting absolute authority to their king as head of 'the whole Body' of the state.[117] As a result, there cannot be 'any State in England without the king'.[118]

While the opponents of the populist theory explore a number of different arguments, they generally agree that lawful kings must be recognised as sovereign heads of state. There were other defenders of absolute sovereignty, however, who responded by laying out a strongly contrasting theory of the state in which the relationship between subjects and sovereigns was conceptualised in unprecedented terms. The earliest Anglophone work in which we encounter this development is Hobbes's *Elements of Law*, which

---

[112] *Obedience Active and Passive* 1643, p. 17.   [113] Boughen 1650, p. 72; cf. also p. 137.
[114] Hall 1651, p. 45.
[115] *Animadversions* 1642, p. 7; see also *An examination* 1642, pp. 6–8.
[116] Bramhall 1643, pp. 6, 14.   [117] Bramhall 1643, p. 21.   [118] Bramhall 1643, p. 171.

he completed and circulated in manuscript in the spring of 1640. Among those who closely studied Hobbes's text was Dudley Digges,[119] who made extensive use of it in his *Unlawfulnesse of Subjects taking up Armes* in 1644.[120] Digges explicitly denounces Parker, Bridge and other parliamentarian propagandists,[121] to whom he replies with a strikingly Hobbesian account of how a multitude in a warlike state of nature can institute 'the essence and being of a State'.[122] For the definitive presentation of this argument, however, we must turn to Hobbes's *Leviathan* of 1651, in which he informs us at the outset that, in putting forward his theory of public power, he will be speaking 'not of the men' but 'in the Abstract' about the nature of the 'COMMON-WEALTH, or STATE'.[123]

Hobbes begins with a scathing denunciation of the populist belief that sovereign power must originally have been possessed by the body of the people. As I showed in chapter 9, one of his underlying purposes in depicting man's life in the state of nature as nasty, brutish and short is to establish that the image of the people as a united body makes no sense. The condition in which nature has placed us is one in which we live entirely 'dissociate' from everyone else, subsisting as a mere multitude in a state of solitude in which 'every man is Enemy to every man'.[124] There is therefore 'little ground for the opinion of them, that say of Soveraign Kings, though they be *singulis maiores*, of greater Power than every one of their Subjects, yet they be *Universis minores*', of less power than the body of the people. Since there is no such thing as the body of the people, we can only conclude that 'the speech is absurd'.[125]

Hobbes is no happier, however, with the absolutists and their rival contention that the proper relationship between the people and their rulers is that of a body living in subjection to a God-given head of state. He fully endorses the parliamentarian claim that the only mechanism by which lawful regimes can be brought into being is 'by the consent of every one of the Subjects', each one of whom must give authority 'from himselfe in particular' to the holders of sovereign power.[126] He likewise agrees that, even after the members of a multitude have subjected themselves to a designated sovereign, they remain the 'Authors' of whatever actions may subsequently be performed by those to whom sovereignty has been assigned.[127]

---

[119] On Digges see Tuck 1993, pp. 274–8; Smith 1994, pp. 223–6.
[120] Date (15 January 1644) from BL (Thomason) copy. For quotations from *The Elements* in *The Unlawfulnesse* see Digges 1644, pp. 3, 4, 7, 31–4.
[121] See, for example, Digges 1644, pp. 62, 64, 85, 121, 129.
[122] Digges 1644, pp. 14, 32, 64–5.
[123] Hobbes 2012, vol. 2, Epistle Dedicatory, p. [4]; The Introduction, p. 16.
[124] Hobbes 2012, vol. 2, ch. 13, p. 192.   [125] Hobbes 2012, vol. 2, ch. 18, p. 280.
[126] Hobbes 2012, vol. 2, ch. 16, p. 250; ch. 28, p. 492.
[127] Hobbes 2012, vol. 2, ch. 16, p. 250.

Due to these commitments, Hobbes rarely talks in the manner typical of absolutist theorists about the reverence due to kings as the Lord's anointed or God's vicegerents on earth. He always maintains that even the most absolute monarchs are nothing more than authorised representatives, and in chapter 30 he gives an exacting account of the duties attached to their role. They must maintain peace and uphold 'the safety of the People'; they must ensure 'that Justice be equally administered to all degrees'; and they must provide help to those who are 'unable to maintain themselves'.[128] Hobbes concedes that, because all sovereigns are by definition absolute, they cannot be punished or removed from office if they fail to discharge these obligations and instead behave iniquitously.[129] If they do fail, however, they will be in clear dereliction of their duty, which requires them 'to procure the common interest' of the people by conducting their government in a manner 'agreeable to Equity, and the Common Good'.[130]

Turning to explicate his own view of sovereigns as authorised representatives, Hobbes takes his first task to be that of analysing the concept of representation in general terms. As we saw in chapter 9, his resulting elucidation centres on the theatrical idea that to represent someone is to take on their *persona*, to wear their mask, to speak their lines and act in their name. Hobbes also emphasises the theatrical convention that, when someone plays such a role, the actions they perform 'in character' are not taken to be their own, but are instead treated as those of the character they are playing and are attributed to them. He concludes by emphasising that, if representation amounts to nothing more than this kind of role-playing, then almost anyone or anything can be successfully represented.

With this analysis Hobbes repudiates the account of virtual representation developed by Henry Parker and other populist theorists of the state in the early 1640s. As I showed in chapter 9, they had argued that the appropriate imagery for thinking about acts of representation comes from the visual arts. To represent someone is to picture or portray them, to offer a recognisable image or likeness. But according to Hobbes the appropriate imagery comes from the stage. 'A *Person*, is the same that an *Actor* is, both on the Stage and in common Conversation; and to *Personate*, is to *Act*, or *Represent* himselfe, or an other; and he that acteth another, is said to beare his Person, or act in his name'.[131]

---

[128] Hobbes 2012, vol. 2, ch. 30, pp. 520, 534, 538.
[129] Hobbes 2012, vol. 2, ch. 18, p. 270.
[130] Hobbes 2012, vol. 2, ch. 19, p. 288; ch. 24, p. 388.
[131] Hobbes 2012, vol. 2, ch. 16, p. 244. See List and Pettit 2011, pp. 171–6 on this 'performative' view of personhood.

Hobbes next proceeds to apply this general understanding of *personae* to the representation of the state. As I argued in chapter 2, the ground-work for this development had been laid as early as the fourteenth century with the revival of the classical idea that a *civitas* can be regarded as a single *persona*, and that this *persona* can in turn be represented by a single person or group, provided they have been suitably mandated or authorised. As I also noted, this way of thinking had already been revived earlier in the seventeenth century, most conspicuously by Grotius with his claim that the *civitas* or state is the 'common subject' of the sovereignty that the figure of the sovereign is granted authority to exercise.[132] We also saw in chapter 9 how a similar argument arose in Anglophone political discourse in the same period. A number of Catholic apologists, anxious to insist that St Peter had been the sover-eign representative of the person of the Church, presented their argu-ment in the form of a parallel with the theory of the state. Nicholas Sander contended that the subjects of a sovereign should be regarded as one 'general person' whom the sovereign is authorised to represent, and that the name of this general person is the commonwealth. Thomas Fitzherbert similarly argued that states or commonwealths are persons possessed of full authority and jurisdiction, while sovereigns who 'beare the person, & figure of the commonwealth' are granted the right to represent the state and exercise the powers belonging to it.

While Hobbes appears to draw on all these sources,[133] there can be no doubt that his elaboration of these arguments in *Leviathan* issued in a classic statement of the claim that the state is the name of a person 'by Fiction' distinct from both rulers and ruled. As I showed in chapter 9, Hobbes arrives at this conclusion by way of explicating the political covenant, which he considers from two contrasting perspectives. On the one hand, he denies that any such agreement can ever be made between the body of the people and a designated sovereign in the manner pre-sumed by the populist theorists of the state, simply because there is no such thing as the body of the people. A political covenant can only take the form of an agreement between each and every individual member of the multitude, all of whom must 'conferre all their power and strength upon one Man, or upon one Assembly of men' whom they agree to institute as their authorised sovereign representative.[134] On the other hand, Hobbes emphasises that this act of covenanting has the effect of giving the

<hr>

[132] Grotius 1625, I. III. VII, p. 67: 'summae potestati subiectum commune est civitas'.
[133] The catalogue of the Hardwick library drawn up by Hobbes contains works by Sander and Fitzherbert as well as Grotius. See Hobbes MSS (Chatsworth), MS E. 1. A, p. 17 (Fitzherbert), p. 43 (Sander) and p. 84 (Grotius).
[134] Hobbes 2012, vol. 2, ch. 17, p. 260.

individual members of the multitude a single will and voice, that of their
sovereign representative, whose words and actions now count as those of
them all. But to affirm that they are now able to act with one will and voice
is to say that they are no longer a mere multitude. The effect of their
mutual agreement is to produce 'a reall Unitie of them all', so that they are
now 'united in one Person'.[135]

The act of covenanting may thus be said to engender two persons who
lacked any existence in the state of nature. One is the 'artificial' person of
the representative to whom the members of the multitude give authority
to speak and act in the name of them all. The name of this person, we
already know, is the sovereign. The other is the person 'by Fiction' whom
the members of the multitude bring into being when they acquire a single
will and voice by way of authorising a man or assembly to serve as their
sovereign representative.[136] The name of this further person is now
declared to be the state.[137] 'The Multitude so united in one Person, is
called a COMMON-WEALTH',[138] and another name for a commonwealth is a
CIVITAS or STATE.[139] Hobbes accordingly concludes that a commonwealth
or state can be defined as '*One Person, of whose Acts a great Multitude, by
mutuall Covenants one with another, have made themselves every one the
Author*', while the sovereign is the name of the man or assembly that
represents or 'carries' the person of the state.[140]

Hobbes assigns the person of the state a name of its own, announcing
that what he has been describing is 'the Generation of that great
LEVIATHAN'.[141] He subsequently explains how the state can live a secure
and healthy life free from 'intestine disorder',[142] and he devotes a chapter
to examining its diseases and the dangers attendant on its death.[143] He
categorically distinguishes the state not merely from the sovereign but
also from the unity of the multitude over which the sovereign rules at any
one time. While sovereigns come and go, and while the unity of the
multitude continually alters as its members are born and die, the
person of the state endures, incurring obligations and enforcing rights

---

[135] Hobbes 2012, vol. 2, ch. 17, p. 260.

[136] On 'artificial' persons and persons 'by Fiction' see Hobbes 2012, vol. 2, ch. 16, p. 244.

[137] On the state as a person 'by Fiction' see Runciman 2000, correcting my formulation in
Skinner 1999. See also Runciman 1997, pp. 6–33 and Runciman 2003, two studies to
which I am much indebted. For further discussions see Brito Vieira 2009, pp. 153–207;
List and Pettit 2011, pp. 171–5; Abizadeh 2013; Douglas 2014. See also Tukiainen
1994 and Chwaszcza 2012, although I disagree with their claim that the state is an
artificial person. According to Hobbes artificial persons are representatives, whereas the
state is a represented person.

[138] Hobbes 2012, vol. 2, ch. 17, p. 260.

[139] Hobbes 2012, vol. 2, The Introduction, p. 16 and ch. 17, p. 260.

[140] Hobbes 2012, vol. 2, ch. 17, pp. 260, 262.   [141] Hobbes 2012, vol. 2, ch. 17, p. 260.

[142] Hobbes 2012, vol. 2, ch. 29, p. 498.   [143] Hobbes 2012, vol. 2, ch. 29, pp. 498–518.

far beyond the lifetime of any of its subjects. Hobbes concedes that no state can be immortal,[144] and he takes himself to have witnessed the death of the English state in his own time.[145] But he insists that the fundamental aim of those who institute a state will always be to make it live 'as long as Man-kind', thereby establishing a system of 'perpetuall, and not temporary security' which they can hope to bequeath to their remote posterity.[146] The aspiration is to create an institution with 'an Artificiall Eternity of life'.[147]

It is true, Hobbes concedes, that the state in the absence of a sovereign is 'but a word, without substance, and cannot stand'.[148] So it is never 'truly' the case that the person of the state performs actions and takes responsibility for them.[149] The only person who ever truly acts in such circumstances is the artificial person of the sovereign, whose role is to wear the mask or *persona* of the state. Hobbes may thus appear to be endorsing what has been called an 'eliminativist' view about the reality of group persons such as corporations or states.[150] But Hobbes does not accept the eliminativist belief that the only agents capable of action are individual human beings, and that no new agents are brought into existence when such individuals co-operate with one another. For Hobbes the state is the name of an agent with its own attitudes, which are expressed by whatever person or group has been granted authority to speak and act in its name. It is also the name of a person with distinctive obligations, since the authorised character of its actions make it responsible to those who have authorised it. The point is most clearly brought out in the Latin version of *Leviathan*, in which Hobbes rewrites his earlier claim that 'there are few things, that are uncapable of being represented by Fiction' in order to say that 'there are few things that are not capable of being Persons'.[151] To be 'represented by Fiction' is one way of being a person, and thus of bearing rights and responsibilities.

It would thus be a serious mistake, according to Hobbes, to infer from the fictional character of the state that it cannot act as an agent in the real world. Some commentators have admittedly concluded that 'Hobbes's theory is not about state sovereignty but – depending on the form – of royal, aristocratic, or popular sovereignty.'[152] But this is to forget what we saw in chapter 9 to be one of Hobbes's most fundamental contentions

---

[144] Hobbes 2012, vol. 2, ch. 29, p. 498.   [145] Hobbes 2012, vol. 2, ch. 29, p. 518.
[146] Hobbes 2012, vol. 2, ch. 19, p. 298; ch. 28, p. 498.
[147] Hobbes 2012, vol. 2, ch. 19, p. 298. On civil immortality in Hobbes see Attie 2008.
[148] Hobbes 2012, vol. 2, ch. 31, p. 554.   [149] Hobbes 2012, vol. 2, ch. 16, p. 244.
[150] See List and Pettit 2011, pp. 2–7, 73–4.
[151] See Hobbes 2012, vol. 2, ch. 16, p. 246, and cf. Hobbes 2012, vol. 2, ch. 16, p. 247: 'Paucae res sunt, quarum non possunt esse Personae'.
[152] See, for example, Abizadeh 2016, p. 410.

about representation: that when a representative speaks or acts in the name of someone or something else, the words and actions of the representative are attributed to the person or thing being represented.[153] So when a sovereign speaks and acts in his role as representative of the state, the actions he performs are attributable to the state, and are actions of the state. Once we grasp the concept of an attributed action, it is easy according to Hobbes to see how the person of the state, in spite of its fictional character, is the true bearer of sovereignty, so that 'the name of the person Commanding' is always '*Persona Civitatis*, the Person of the Common-wealth'.[154]

Hobbes admittedly retains a preference – as in this passage – for speaking of commonwealths rather than states.[155] But it is a striking fact about the composition of *Leviathan* that, as the argument unfolds, he increasingly speaks of the possessor of sovereignty as the state. When he discusses 'the Laws and Authority of the Civill State' in Part III, he informs us that sovereignty is 'Power in the State' and is expressed in 'the Civill Laws of the State'.[156] When he considers the alleged powers of churches, he lays it down that every sovereign must be recognised as 'the Governour both of the State, and of the Religion' established in it.[157] All priests and pastors 'are subject to the State' and possess no power 'distinct from that of the Civill State'.[158]

As with the earlier theories of the state I have sketched, Hobbes's theory is basically intended to furnish a means of judging the legitimacy of the actions undertaken by governments. According to the absolutist theory, such actions are legitimate if and only if they are performed by a God-given sovereign as head of state. According to the populist theory, such actions are legitimate if and only if they are performed by the will (or at least the represented will) of the sovereign body of the people. But according to what I shall call the Hobbesian theory, the actions of governments have 'a right application', in Hobbes's phrase, if and only if two related conditions are satisfied.[159] One is that they must be undertaken by a sovereign – whether a man or assembly – duly authorised by the members of the multitude to speak and act in the name of the person of the state. The other is that they must basically aim to preserve the life and health of that person, and hence 'the Common

[153] Hobbes 2012, vol. 2, ch. 16, p. 244.   [154] Hobbes 2012, vol. 2, ch. 26, p. 414.
[155] On 'the Person of the Common-wealth' see Hobbes 2012, vol. 2, ch. 15, p. 228; ch. 17, pp. 260, 262; ch. 31, p. 570.
[156] Hobbes 2012, vol. 3, ch. 42, pp. 788, 826, 868.
[157] Hobbes 2012, vol. 3, ch. 39, p. 734; ch. 47, p. 1118.
[158] Hobbes 2012, vol. 3, ch. 46, p. 1102; ch. 27, p. 1124.
[159] Hobbes 2012, vol. 2, ch. 24, p. 388; ch. 30, p. 542.

Benefit', 'the publique interest' and 'the Common Good' of its subjects not merely at the time of acting but in perpetuity.[160]

IV

Hobbes's theory of state personality had little immediate impact on English political debate.[161] During the constitutional crisis of 1679–81, when the Whigs attempted (as we saw in chapter 11) to exclude the Catholic heir presumptive from the throne, the Tories chiefly grounded their successful defence of the future James II on Sir Robert Filmer's patriarchalism,[162] and more broadly on the absolutist contention that the king must be recognised as the God-given head of state.[163] The Whigs generally responded by appealing to what I have been calling the populist theory of the state, although they preferred to speak of commonwealths rather than states, the latter term having perhaps become too closely associated with the defence of absolute sovereignty. Some revived the populist theory in its Machiavellian form, arguing that 'free states' are the only forms of government capable of upholding individual liberty. Algernon Sidney in his *Discourses Concerning Government*, written at the time of the Exclusion crisis and first published in 1698, reaffirmed this commitment, although he combined it with the language of natural rights.[164] But most defenders of Exclusion preferred to restate and develop the theory of popular sovereignty as articulated by the protagonists of the parliamentary cause at the start of the civil wars. This was John Locke's approach in his *Two treatises of government*, likewise drafted at the time of the Exclusion crisis and first published in 1689.[165] Locke endorses the republican view of liberty as absence of arbitrary power,[166] but his defence of the right of resistance to tyranny rests on a view of the body of the people as the ultimate holders of sovereignty, and hence as the ultimate judges of whether those entrusted with government are properly discharging their trust.[167]

---

[160] Hobbes 2012, vol. 2, ch. 17, p. 260; ch. 19, p. 288; ch. 24, p. 388.

[161] Parkin 2007, pp. 334–44, 361–77 reports a largely hostile reception, with no specific discussions of Hobbes's theory of the state.

[162] Laslett 1988, pp. 51–2, 57–9, 67–71; Houston 1991, pp. 89–98. For Filmer on the state see Filmer 1991, pp. 26, 30, 31–2.

[163] Houston 1991, pp. 69–98.

[164] On Sidney's combination of the two vocabularies see Hamel 2011, pp. 421–59. See Sidney 1990, pp. 211–12, 248–9 on monarchies and republics or 'states' – which he also describes as 'popular states' and 'free states', pp. 262, 270, 391. See Houston 1991, pp. 101–45, and on the distinctive freedom of free states see Hamel 2011, pp. 406–19.

[165] On Locke's *Two treatises* as an exclusion tract see Laslett 1988, pp. 35–66. For Locke on popular sovereignty see Dunn 1969, pp. 177–86.

[166] Locke 1988, IV. 22, pp. 283–4. For a discussion see Halldenius 2002.

[167] Locke 1988, XIX. 240, pp. 426–7.

During the same period, however, Hobbes's account of state personality began to capture the attention of Continental European commentators on the *ius gentium* and the law of nature. Here we need to distinguish two different channels through which his analysis began to flow into the mainstream of European legal and political thought. Some focused on the earlier version of his theory as articulated in *De cive*. There he had argued that, 'when a number of people come together to erect a *civitas*, it is to be understood that, because they voluntarily congregated, they are obliged by whatever is decided by the consent of the majority.'[168] As Hobbes underlines, this is to acknowledge that those who have come together have already made an important political decision – in favour of majoritarianism – and must therefore have been a civil association as opposed to a mere multitude at the time of making it. We may therefore say, he concludes, that 'almost by the mere fact of coming together, they are a *Democracy*.'[169]

Richard Tuck has recently claimed that Hobbes's argument in this passage brings us to 'the heart of his political theory'.[170] Tuck also maintains that in Continental Europe *De cive* 'was always the text of choice' for students of Hobbes.[171] These considerations have led him to conclude that Hobbes's civil science was chiefly attractive in Enlightenment Europe to theorists of popular sovereignty. As Tuck shows, this was undoubtedly one way in which Hobbes was read. But many European political theorists were at least as much interested in *Leviathan*, and among these readers some of the most influential were particularly drawn to Hobbes's discussion of the authorisation of sovereigns and the representation of the state. This vocabulary makes no appearance in *De cive*, but it furnishes Hobbes with the entire framework for his theory of lawful government in *Leviathan*. Rewriting his earlier account, he eliminates any reference to the founding role of democracy, substituting his new analysis of the covenant as the act by which the members of a multitude agree – not as a corporate body but each with each – to authorise one man or assembly to represent the state.[172] Hobbes later reaffirms this analysis in the Latin version of *Leviathan*, in which he speaks of the *civitas* as a *persona* of whose actions every subject is the *author*, with everyone granting *auctoritas* to a

---

[168] Hobbes 1983, VII. V, p. 152: 'Qui coierunt ad civitatem erigendam, ... ex eo quod volentes convenerunt, intelliguntur obligati ad id quod consensu maioris partis decernetur.'
[169] Hobbes 1983, VII. V, p. 152: 'pene eo ipso quod coierunt, *Democratia* sunt.'
[170] Tuck 2015, p. 86.   [171] Tuck 2015, p. 109.
[172] As noted in Sommerville 2016, pp. 385–6.

sovereign of whom it can be said in Ciceronian terms that *Civitatis Personam gerit*, he represents or 'bears the person' of the state.[173]

Tuck argues that this move on Hobbes's part 'was not often recognised by contemporaries'.[174] But it was this version of Hobbes's theory that caught the eye of Samuel Pufendorf, after which similar discussions appeared in such works as Johann Becmann's *Meditationes politicae* of 1674[175] and Ulric Huber's *De iure civitatis* of 1684.[176] When Becmann lists the leading writers on civil philosophy he singles out three 'incomparable men', Grotius, Hobbes and Pufendorf.[177] Subsequently he refers to Hobbes as well as Pufendorf in the course of arguing that the 'subject' of sovereignty is the *persona* of the state,[178] and that the *princeps* 'represents the universality of the people or state'.[179] Huber, who cites both *De cive* and *Leviathan*,[180] provides a similar but more exact analysis of how the state comes to be the subject of sovereignty. Necessity dictates 'that the will of every individual should become one will', as a result of which 'the multitude is said to achieve unity as a State' in which 'this single will is nothing other than the sovereignty of the State'.[181]

Pufendorf's adaptation of Hobbes's theory also became widely known in France, largely through the work of his translator and editor, Jean Barbeyrac, whose annotated version of Pufendorf's *De iure naturae et gentium* appeared as *Le droit de la nature et des gens* in 1706.[182] Although Barbeyrac criticises both Hobbes and Pufendorf, his translation gave further currency to the Hobbesian view of the state as the name of a multitude united as one person by their authorisation of a sovereign representative.[183] The same conception was taken up by

[173] Hobbes 2012, vol. 2, ch. 17, pp. 261, 263. On Hobbes's translation of *Leviathan* see Malcolm 2002, pp. 459–60. It was commissioned by Johan Blaeu, who first published it in 1668 in his collection of Hobbes's *Opera Philosophica*, subsequently reissuing it as a separate volume in 1670.

[174] Tuck 2015, p. 108.

[175] On Becmann see Malcolm 2002, pp. 525–7. I cite from the revised third edition (1679), on which see Malcolm 2002, p. 525n.

[176] Huber first published his treatise in 1673. In the revised edition of 1684, from which I quote, he shows a greater willingness to acknowledge his debt to Hobbes, as noted in Malcolm 2002, pp. 525–7.

[177] See Becmann 1679, 1. 6, p. 7 on these 'Incomparabiles Viri'.

[178] Becmann 1679, 12. 7, p. 172: '*Subiectum* Maiestatis est tum Respublica seu persona Moralis'. Becmann focuses on Hobbes's *Leviathan* at 6. 8, pp. 85–6.

[179] Becmann 1679, 12. 7, p. 174: 'Princeps universos seu Rempublicam repraesentat'.

[180] See Huber 1684, I. 3, p. 14 on 'tract. de cive & Leviathan vernaculo'.

[181] Huber 1684, I. 7, p. 39: 'Necessaria fuit ... omnium voluntas una fieret ... Et multitudo hoc modo unita *Civitas* dicitur ... Voluntas autem una ista nihil aliud quam *Imperium* Civitatis.'

[182] On Barbeyrac's translation see Othmer 1970, pp. 124–34.

[183] Pufendorf 1706, p. 206: 'cette union & cette soûmission de volontez, qui acheve de former l'Etat, & en fait un Corps, qu'on regarde comme une seule Personne'.

such jurists as François Richer d'Aube in his *Essais* of 1743[184] and
Martin Hubner in his *Essai sur l'histoire du droit naturel*, which first
appeared in London in 1757.[185] Of all these restatements, however,
the most influential was Emer de Vattel's in *Le droit des Gens* of 1758.
Although Vattel criticises what he calls Hobbes's paradoxes, he
acknowledges that in Hobbes 'one recognises an expert hand',[186] and
he develops an essentially Hobbesian account of state personality
which in turn played a major role in the assimilation of the idea into
Anglophone political thought.[187]

This process of assimilation may be said to have begun with the publication of Basil Kennet's translation of Barbeyrac's edition of Pufendorf
in 1717.[188] Pufendorf explicitly notes that (as Kennet's version puts it)
'Mr *Hobbes* hath given us a very ingenious Draught of a Civil State,
conceiv'd as an *Artificial Man*'.[189] Pufendorf is frequently critical of
Hobbes, but at the same time he owes a deep and obvious debt to
Hobbes's theory of state personality in *Leviathan*, as well as offering
some expansions and clarifications of Hobbes's account.[190]

Pufendorf begins by offering a fuller characterisation of the two different worlds we simultaneously inhabit. One is the world of natural
entities, the other is the world of entities we 'impose' on nature 'for the
procuring of a decent Regularity in the Method of Life'.[191] The most
important of these entities are moral persons, which constitute the
substance of the moral world. They are 'conceiv'd with analogy' to
physical persons, who are said to form (following Boethius and
Aquinas) the individual substance of rational nature.[192] Despite this
emphasis on substantiality, however, Pufendorf argues that in speaking
of such moral persons we are basically referring to the different *personae*
or roles we adopt or acquire in social life. 'One and the same Man' may
'sustain several *Persons* together', acting at the same time as 'a

---

[184] On Richer d'Aube see Glaziou 1993, pp. 62–3.

[185] On Hubner see Glaziou 1993, pp. 65–7.

[186] Vattel 1758, Preface, sig. *, 3r–v: 'on reconnoît une main habile, malgré ses paradoxes'.

[187] Jouannet 1998; Beaulac 2003, esp. pp. 254–60. But for a critique see Hunter 2010.

[188] Or perhaps, as argued in Saunders and Hunter 2003, with the publication of Andrew
Tooke's translation of Pufendorf's abridgement of *De iure naturae* in 1691.

[189] Pufendorf 1717, VII. II. XIII, p. 475, col. 2. Pufendorf's topic in VII. II is 'the Inward
Structure and Constitution of Civil States', in which he discusses the covenant as well as
the person of the state. The former discussion draws from *De cive* as well as *Leviathan*;
the latter focuses on *Leviathan*.

[190] In particular, as Elden 2013, pp. 309–21 notes, by examining the relations between
sovereignty and territoriality.

[191] Pufendorf 1717, I. I. III, p. 3, col. 1.

[192] Pufendorf 1717, I. I. XVI, p. 10, col. 2. Cf. Boethius 1571, III. fo. 12r: 'Est enim
persona, (ut dictum est) naturae rationabilis individua subsistentia' – the definition
accepted in Aquinas 1950, vol. 1, pp. 155–6.

Householder, a Senator in Parliament, an Advocate in the Halls of Justice, and a Counsellor at Court'.[193]

It might seem that Pufendorf is reiterating Hobbes's claim that the right model for thinking about such *personae* is theatrical in provenance. Pufendorf agrees that 'the term of *Person* hath been peculiarly challeng'd by the Stage', but he objects that the comparison is defective, because 'whatever such a fictitious Actor says or does, leaves no *Moral Effect* behind it.'[194] The *personae* we adopt 'ought always to presuppose such Qualities as may contribute to the solid Use and real Benefit of Human Life'.[195] Pufendorf concedes that such moral persons 'have no Self-subsistence', and are incapable of acting in the absence of natural persons who can deploy their will and intellect in discharging their roles.[196] But they nevertheless resemble natural persons in that moral properties inhere in them, which is why '*Moral Entities*, fram'd with Analogy to Substances' amount to something far more than 'idle Fictions'.[197]

When Pufendorf turns to the concept of the state, he agrees with Hobbes that it is the name given to the multitude when it is 'conceiv'd to exist like *one Person*'.[198] Referring to *Leviathan* as well as *De cive*, he maintains that states are formed when a number of natural persons 'are so united together, that what they *will* or *act* by virtue of that Union, is esteem'd a single Will, and a single Act', adding that this happens 'when the particular Members submit their Wills to the Will of one Man, or of one Council', in such a manner as to acknowledge their act as 'the common Act and Determination of them all.'[199] He further agrees that, when we constitute a state, we should aim to bring into existence a person with an artificial eternity of life and the consequent power to confer 'lasting and perpetual Advantages' not merely on ourselves but our remote posterity.'[200]

Pufendorf thus appears at first sight to be a disciple of Hobbes, and this is how he has tended to be portrayed in recent scholarship.[201] But Pufendorf disagrees in two connected ways with Hobbes's analysis of personhood in *Leviathan*, and hence with his account of the person of

---

[193] Pufendorf 1717, I. I. XIV, p. 9, col 1. For a discussion see Hunter 2001, pp. 163–8.
[194] Pufendorf 1717, I. I. XIV, p. 9, col. 2.   [195] Pufendorf 1717, I. I. XV, p. 10, col. 1.
[196] Pufendorf 1717, I. I. III, p. 3, col. 1.
[197] Pufendorf 1717, I. I. XII, p. 7, col. 2; I. I. II, p. 1, col. 2.
[198] Pufendorf 1717, VII. II. XIII, p. 475, col. 1.
[199] Pufendorf 1717, I. I. XIII, p. 8, col 2.
[200] Pufendorf 1717, VIII. II. XX, p. 481, col. 1.
[201] See, for example, Palladini 1990, Beaulac 2004. I formerly subscribed to this view myself. See Skinner 2009a, pp. 350–2. For helping me to reconsider I am much indebted to correspondence with Hans Baade and Benjamin Holland, and especially to Holland 2012.

the state. First he rejects Hobbes's general claim that a person is simply the name of anything susceptible of being represented. 'Mr *Hobbes* is mistaken, when he will have it frequently to happen in Communities, *that a Man shall bear the Person of an inanimate Thing*' such as a church, a hospital or a bridge.[202] Pufendorf acknowledges that these are all examples of substances. But they are not examples of rational substances possessed of intellect and will, which for Pufendorf is the definition of a natural person, and accordingly what moral persons must resemble and reflect. As he dismissively summarises, 'though *Men* are conceiv'd as different *Persons*, upon account of their different State or Office, yet *Things* do not raise such distinct Notions in us.'[203] For Hobbes, to be a person is simply to be capable of having words and actions attributed to oneself, but for Pufendorf persons are always distinguished by their intrinsic and especially their rational natures.[204]

More specifically, Pufendorf rejects Hobbes's central contention that the state is an example of a person 'by Fiction' created by a mere union of wills, and hence Hobbes's view that civil law reflect nothing more than 'the Will and Appetite of the State'.[205] According to Pufendorf, the state is compounded out of the moral *personae* of all the natural persons who institute it as well as the sovereign who represents it. 'A Civil State', as he explains, 'is conceiv'd to exist like *one Person*, endued with Understanding and Will, and performing other particular Acts, distinct from those of the private Members', as a result of which the state 'hath peculiar Rights and separate Properties' of a moral as well as a coercive kind.[206] It is only when a union of this moral character is completed that 'at last ariseth what we call a Common wealth, or Civil State, the strongest of all *Moral Persons*, or *Societies*.'[207] Pufendorf appears to be the first philosopher to conceive of the state in these terms, and it leads him to conclude that 'the most proper definition of a Civil State' is that it forms a *persona moralis composita*, 'a compound Moral Person, whose will, united and tied together by those Covenants, which before pass'd among the Multitude, is deem'd the Will of all'.[208]

---

[202] Pufendorf 1717, I. I. XII, p. 8. col. 1.   [203] Pufendorf 1717, I. I. XVI, p. 10, col. 1.

[204] On these rival traditions see List and Pettit 2011, pp. 170–3; Esposito 2012, pp. 74–6, 83–7.

[205] Hobbes 2012, vol. 2, ch. 16, p. 246 and vol 3, ch. 46, p. 1090.

[206] Pufendorf 1717, VII. II. XIII, p. 475, col. 1. For a discussion see Boucher 1998, pp. 236–8.

[207] Pufendorf 1717, VII. II. V, p. 468, col. 2. Beaulac 2004, pp. 138–40 treats Pufendorf as a straightforward follower of Hobbes, claiming that Hobbes formulated a 'theory of moral personality' which Pufendorf 'further developed'. But Hobbes never speaks of the state as a moral person.

[208] Pufendorf 1717, VII. II. XII, p. 475, col. 2.

This understanding in turn governs Pufendorf's account of the most suitable constitutional form in which the powers of the state should be embodied and exercised. To Hobbes, focusing on the idea of the state essentially as a coercive will, it seems preferable that the authority to exercise this will should be lodged with a single natural person acting as a sovereign representative. But to Pufendorf, giving equal weight to the place of the understanding, it seems prudent that the representation of this faculty should be assigned to different natural persons or assemblies whose relationship to the sovereign is to 'bear him Company in the adjusting of Affairs'.[209]

Nevertheless, Pufendorf is in basic agreement with Hobbes about the will of the state and its proper embodiment. He agrees that it is by a 'Submission and Union of Wills' that 'we conceive a State to be but *one Person*'.[210] He agrees that the sovereign 'bears' or represents this person, and he explicitly speaks of 'the publick Will of the Monarch, representing the Will of the State'.[211] He consequently agrees with Hobbes's fundamental contention that the person of the state is the true seat of sovereignty. 'The State in exerting and exercising its Will, makes use either of a single Person, or of a Council', but the actions of that person or council count as those of the sovereign state.[212]

Pufendorf also endorses, and further elaborates, Hobbes's account of why it is essential to a satisfactory analysis of public power to think of the state not merely as a person distinct from rulers and ruled, but also as endowed with an artificial eternity of life. One reason is that we need to ensure some continuity of public order beyond the lifetime of any particular regime. Pufendorf takes the example of public debt, arguing that it is 'Just, and for the peace of the State' to recognise that, even if such debts may have been incurred under a defunct government, 'yet the *Debts* it has contracted are still due'.[213] But his principal reason for marking a categorical distinction between states and governments is that this yields a means of testing the legitimacy of any actions that governments undertake. He is adamant that, because the state is the name of the united will and understanding of an entire body of people, the special obligation of those who hold the reins of power must be to act for the good of the body as a whole. This is not to concede that subjects may lawfully resist a

---

[209] Pufendorf 1717, VII. VI. IX, p. 527, col. 2. On this aspect of Pufendorf's argument see Holland 2012.

[210] Pufendorf 1717, VII. II. VIII, p. 470, col. 1.

[211] Pufendorf 1717, VII. II. XIV, p. 476, col. 1.

[212] Pufendorf 1717, VII. II. XIV, p. 476, col. 1. On this distinction between states and governments see Tully 1991, pp. xxxiii–xxxv; Hunter 2001, pp. 186–91.

[213] Pufendorf 1717, VIII. XII. II, p. 128, col. 1 (second pagination).

sovereign who fails to act for the good of the state.[214] But it is emphatically to affirm that – as Hobbes had already insisted – any such sovereign will be in dereliction of his basic duty towards his subjects. 'The general Rule which Sovereigns are to proceed by' is '*Let the Safety of the People be the Supreme Law*'.[215]

We next need to take note of two moments of still greater significance in the reception of the Hobbesian theory of the state into the mainstream of Anglophone political thought. The first was the publication of John Morrice's English translation of Jean Barbeyrac's French edition of Grotius's *De iure belli ac pacis* in 1738.[216] Grotius had offered in Book I chapter 3 what Morrice translates as 'An Explication of the supreme Power', in which Grotius had asked about the 'subject' of sovereign power.[217] He had answered that 'the proper Subject' is 'one or more Persons, according to the Laws and Customs of each Nation'.[218] As we saw in chapter 2, however, he had added that, just as 'the Body is the common Subject of Sight, the Eye the proper', so 'the common Subject of Supreme Power is the State'.[219] The state is the underlying authority in whose name sovereignty is exercised.

Soon afterwards this view received an even more influential endorsement when an English version of Emer de Vattel's treatise on the law of nations was published in London in 1760. Vattel defines the *ius gentium* as the law governing the relations between independent sovereign states, and accordingly begins by examining the concept of the state itself. His analysis is partly critical of Pufendorf as well as Hobbes. He follows Pufendorf in rejecting Hobbes's claim that states are represented simply by the will of the sovereign, accepting Pufendorf's contention that states are compounded out of the understanding as well as the will of each individual subject. The state, as Vattel puts it, is consequently 'a moral person, having an understanding and a will peculiar to itself'.[220] But he rejects Pufendorf's proposal that the will and understanding of the state should be separately represented, preferring Hobbes's solution that a single sovereign should be 'cloathed

---

[214] Pufendorf 1717, VII. II. XIV, p. 476, col. 1.

[215] Pufendorf 1717, VII. IX. III, p. 569, col. 1.

[216] On Morrice's translation see Tuck 2005, pp. xxxv–xxxvi.

[217] Grotius 2005, I. III. VII, p. 259. Cf. Grotius 1625, I. III. VII, p. 67: 'Haec ergo summa potestas, quod subiectum habeat videamus.'

[218] Grotius 2005, I. III. VII, p. 260. Cf. Grotius 1625, I. III. VII, p. 67: 'Subiectum proprium est persona una pluresve pro cuiusque gentis legibus ac moribus'.

[219] Grotius 2005, I. III. VII, p. 259. Cf. Grotius 1625, I. III. VII, p. 67: 'ut visus subiectum commune est corpus, proprium oculus; ita summae potestati subiectum commune est civitas'.

[220] Vattel 1760, Preliminaries, para. 2, p. 1; cf. I. IV. 40, p. 20.

with the public authority' and 'with every thing that constitutes the moral personality' of the underlying nation and state.[221]

Vattel's ensuing discussion is fundamentally Hobbesian in character. He agrees with Hobbes that states are able to act if and only if they are personated by sovereigns authorised to act in their name, and he consequently emphasises what he describes as 'the representative character attributed to the sovereign', who 'unites in his own person all the majesty that belongs to the entire body' of the nation and state.[222] He also agrees that, when sovereign representatives speak or act, their words or actions must be attributed to the state, which is the true seat of sovereignty. 'The sovereign, or conductor of the state' is 'the subject, in which reside the obligations and rights relative to government', but those obligations and rights belong to the moral person of the state itself.[223] Most importantly, he agrees that 'a wise conductor of society, ought to have his mind impressed with this great truth, that the sovereign power is solely intrusted with him for the safety of the state', and that all his efforts must be directed 'to the great advantage of the state and people who have submitted to him'.[224]

Vattel continues to speak in Hobbesian vein when he examines the relations between states. He begins by singling Hobbes out as the first writer properly to understand the theory of international relations, quoting him as saying that 'states in a certain sense acquire personal properties', so that 'the same Law that we call Natural when speaking about the Duties of Individuals is named the Law of Nations when applied to the whole Body of a State'.[225] Vattel draws the inference that relations between governments can never be properly regulated in the absence of a theory of state personality. 'Every nation that governs itself, under what form soever', is 'a *sovereign state*', and all such states must be recognised as 'moral persons who live together in a natural society'.[226] They must therefore be 'considered by foreign states, as making only one whole, one single person',[227] and the theory of international affairs must take as its subject-matter the proper behaviour of such persons in relation to one another.[228]

---

[221] Vattel 1760, I. IV. 41, p. 21.   [222] Vattel 1760, I. IV. 40, p. 21.
[223] Vattel 1760, I. IV. 40, pp. 20–1.   [224] Vattel 1760, I. IV. 39, p. 20.
[225] Here I quote from Vattel 1758, which gives a clearer sense of what Vattel takes from Hobbes than does the translation of 1760. See Vattel 1758, sig. *, 3v, translating Hobbes 1983, XIV. IV, p. 208: 'comme les Etats acquièrent en quelques manière des proprietétés personnelles; la même Loi qui se nomme Naturelle, lorsq'on parle des Devoirs des Particuliers, s'appelle Droit de Gens, lorsq'on l'applique au Corps entire d'un Etat'.
[226] Vattel 1760, I. I. 4, p. 10.   [227] Vattel 1760, II. VII. 81, p. 147.
[228] Vattel 1760, Preliminaries, paras. 7–9, pp. 2–3.

The implications of this argument are pursued most fully in Vattel's chapter on treaties, the establishment of which he takes to be the most important transaction between states. Any 'real treaty' must be capable of outlasting changes of government and even variations in the constitution of the state. But these requirements can only be met if we acknowledge that the signatories of such treaties cannot be governments; they can only be states.[229] Any 'real alliance', as Vattel puts it, 'is affixed to the body of the state, and subsists as long as the state'.[230] Like Hobbes and Pufendorf, Vattel ends by offering a vision of the state not merely as a guarantor of the legitimacy of governmental action, but as an agent capable of incurring obligations and exercising rights over indefinitely long periods of time.

By this stage the Hobbesian theory had begun to catch the attention of English legal and political writers, a process no doubt fostered by the appearance in 1750 of the first collection of Hobbes's political works issued in England since the publication of *Leviathan* a century before.[231] One of the principal ways in which the concept of state personality began to assume a new importance was as a means of thinking about how to legitimise closer and less fractious ties between Britain and her north American colonies. One of the leading contributors to this debate was Thomas Pownall, who served as governor of Massachusetts in the 1750s and published his treatise on *The Administration of the Colonies* in 1764. Pownall pleads for the creation not merely of a single imperial Parliament, but for what he calls 'a grand marine dominion of our possessions in the Atlantic and in America united into a one Empire, in a one center'.[232]

Pownall had already laid the theoretical foundations for this project in his *Principles of Polity*, first published in 1752. According to Book I, in which Pownall denounces every prevailing account of the contractual origins of government, we need to think of the state in Aristotelian terms as a natural community, a single body politic, and hence as 'an Union of several Individuals under one common Interest and Empire'.[233] Pursuing the implications in Book III, Pownall argues that we need to conceive of 'the whole Body politic, as a one Person', on the analogy of a private person possessed of reason and will.[234] The name of this person is the state, so that 'States, in their Actions and Reasonings towards each other' must 'be consider'd as distinct *Persons* and independent' of one another.[235] We can even say that, because 'the Community is not only a one Whole, but a one Individual', the person of the state possesses 'a distinct Interest, distinct from the several respective Interests of the

[229] Vattel 1760, II. XII. 184, pp. 182–3.   [230] Vattel 1760, II. XII. 183, p. 182.
[231] Hobbes 1750.   [232] Pownall 1765, pp. 9–10.   [233] Pownall 1752, p. 5.
[234] Pownall 1752, p. 117.   [235] Pownall 1752, p. 116.

Constituents'.[236] The essence of this interest is the preservation of the state itself, which must be recognised as the fundamental goal of government.

Among English legal and political writers drawn to this Hobbesian view of the state in the middle decades of the eighteenth century, none enjoyed a higher reputation than Sir William Blackstone, who incorporated its basic tenets into his introductory essay 'Of the Nature of Laws in general' in the first volume of his *Commentaries on the Laws of England* in 1765.[237] Blackstone opens in Hobbesian style by insisting that it makes no sense to treat the body of the people as a natural collectivity. 'The only true and natural foundations of society are the wants and the fears of individuals'.[238] The problem thus raised, however, is that 'inasmuch as political communities are made up of many natural persons, each of whom has his particular will and inclination, these several wills cannot by any *natural* union be joined together' to produce 'one uniform will of the whole'.[239] The only solution is to institute what Blackstone calls a '*political* union' of the multitude. As he explains – in a virtual quotation from *Leviathan* – everyone must agree 'to submit their own private wills to the will of one man, or of one or more assemblies of men, to whom the supreme authority is entrusted', thereby enabling them to act as a single person or (as Blackstone prefers to put it) as if they are 'one man' with 'one uniform will'.[240] The name of this political union is said to be the state.[241] 'For a state is a collective body, composed of a multitude of individuals, united for their safety and convenience and intending to act together as one man'.[242] The distinguishing mark of sovereignty – authority to legislate – may equally well 'reside' in different forms of government. But the authority itself is always part of 'the natural, inherent right that belongs to the sovereignty of a state',[243] while the members of the political union 'are bound to conform themselves to the will of the state'.[244]

V

By the mid-eighteenth century, the Hobbesian theory of the state was beginning to be widely accepted not merely by Continental European writers on natural jurisprudence, but also by English writers on common

---

[236] Pownall 1752, p. 113.
[237] For Blackstone on law and the English state see Cairns 1984; Lieberman 1989, pp. 31–67.
[238] Blackstone 1765, p. 47.   [239] Blackstone 1765, p. 52.   [240] Blackstone 1765, p. 52.
[241] Although Blackstone appears silently to quote from Hobbes, there are more complex filiations to be traced, as noted in Barker 1957, p. xliii.
[242] Blackstone 1765, p. 52.   [243] Blackstone 1765, p. 49.
[244] Blackstone 1765, pp. 52–3.

law. This is by no means to say, however, that this way of thinking about public power ceased to be contested in Anglophone political thought. Even after the revolution of 1688 the absolutist theory remained a powerful weapon in the hands of such unyielding defenders of divine right as Henry Sacheverell and Charles Leslie.[245] Leslie in particular repeatedly challenged the Whigs with an account of the English constitution grounded on the belief that the 'Original Institution' of government is invariably the work of God alone. One sign of God's providence, Leslie unrepentantly maintains, is that he grants supreme and unquestionable power immediately to kings as absolute heads of state.[246] The image of the king's two bodies died a very slow death.

During the next generation, we also encounter a widespread reassertion of what I have been calling the populist theory of the state. According to such leading supporters of the American Revolution as Tom Paine and Richard Price, the only type of civil association in which it is possible to live freely is a self-governing community in which sovereignty is possessed by the people as a whole. This commitment leads Price to reason that, as he puts it at the outset of his *Observations on the Nature of Civil Liberty* in 1776, when we speak of a lawful state we can only be referring to the sovereign power of 'the collective body of the people'.[247] 'The will of the state', he repeats in *Additional Observations*, is equivalent to the general will of the community, 'the will of the whole'.[248] Judged by this criterion, the American colonists are living in slavish dependence on the British Crown, in consequence of which they have a natural right to liberate themselves from their unnatural condition of servitude and establish their own free state.

Nevertheless, the Hobbesian theory eventually achieved the status almost of an orthodoxy in the political thinking of the Enlightenment. Perhaps the clearest reflection of this development can be seen in the attempt by Louis de Jaucourt to summarise conventional wisdom in his article entitled *L'etat* in the *Encyclopédie* of 1756.[249] 'The state can be defined as a civil society through which a multitude of men are united together by their dependence upon a sovereign'.[250] The state 'can thus be considered as a moral person, of which the sovereign is the head and all individuals are the members.'[251] Once again the state is seen as the true

---

[245] Schochet 1975, pp. 192–224.   [246] Leslie 1709, pp. 56–7, 74.
[247] Price 1991, p. 22.   [248] Price 1991, p. 76.
[249] See further Skinner 2002a, pp. 408–9.
[250] Jaucourt 1756, p. 19: 'on peut définir *l'état*, une société civile, par laquelle une multitude d'hommes sont unis ensemble sous le dépendance d'un souverain'.
[251] Jaucourt 1756, p. 19: 'On peut considérer *l'etat* comme une personne morale, dont le souverain est la tête, & les particuliers les membres'.

bearer of sovereignty, the possessor of 'certain rights which are distinct from those of each individual citizen, and which no individual or group of citizens can arrogate to themselves'.[252]

Towards the end of the eighteenth century, however, the English branch of the genealogy I have been tracing began to ramify in a strongly contrasting direction,[253] and there emerged a way of thinking about public power in which the concept of the state as an independent legal entity began to slip from sight. To understand this further development, we first need to note that some doubts had always been expressed – not surprisingly in a strongly Protestant country – about the idea of state personality. To think in such terms is to assume that, by a mere act of covenanting, it is possible for a multitude of individuals to transform themselves into a single person without that person coming to occupy any identifiable space. But this was to echo with disturbing exactitude the assertions made by the Catholic Church about the sacrament of the Eucharist, in which the transubstantiation of the bread and wine was taken to make present the person of Christ, although without any change in outward appearances.

This belief had been fiercely repudiated by the Protestant Churches in the course of the Reformation, and the need to confute the Tridentine restatement of the doctrine remained a central preoccupation of Anglican apologists throughout the seventeenth century. William Attersoll in his *Treatise of the Sacraments* of 1610 denounced transubstantiation as 'the most misshapen monster that ever lived or was devised'.[254] Thomas Morton in his *Defence of the Church of England* of 1619 dismissed as idolatrous the belief that 'the Element of bread' can possibly be 'the very person of Christ',[255] while Henry More in his *Modest Enquiry* of 1664 similarly objected that to speak of being able 'to transform a piece of Bread into the real Person of Christ' is a monstrous doctrine and the mother of idolatry.[256]

Of great importance to all these writers is the claim that the doctrine of transubstantiation embodies a misunderstanding of what it means to be a person. How is it possible, Attersoll wants to know, for a person to fail to occupy a discernible space? 'Take away space of place from a body, and it remaineth no longer a true body, but the essence of it is abolished'.[257]

---

[252] Jaucourt 1756, p. 19: 'certains droits distincts de ceux de chaque citoyen, & que chaque citoyen, ni plusieurs, ne sauroient s'arroger'.

[253] For this contrast see Dyson 1980. The idea of the state as a non-corporeal body can still be found in the late eighteenth century. See Ihalainen 2009, esp. pp. 34–5. On the subsequent loss of the concept see Dow 2008.

[254] Attersoll 1606, p. 388.   [255] Morton 1619, p. 293.   [256] More 1664, p. 53.

[257] Attersoll 1606, p. 388.

Henry More similarly asks how the person of Christ can possibly be at once in heaven and at the same time present at the celebration of the Mass. Surely 'there is not a more certain and infallible sign of two bodily Persons being *two* bodily Persons, and not the *same* Person, than distance of place?'[258] How in any case can we speak of persons appearing in our presence when nothing seems 'to any of our Senses any thing altered from what it was before'?[259]

During the eighteenth century, these ontological doubts began to receive powerful support from within the domain of English legal and political thought. With the rise of classical utilitarianism, and especially with the reforming jurisprudence of Jeremy Bentham, the invocation of legal fictions was suddenly subjected to an almost lethal attack. Bentham's earliest published work, his *Fragment on Government* of 1776, takes the form of a scornful and vituperative critique of precisely those sections of Blackstone's *Commentaries* to which I have referred.[260] Launching his tirade, Bentham announces that 'the season of *Fiction* is now over'.[261] The time has come to ground legal arguments on observable facts about real individuals, and especially on their capacity for experiencing, in relation to political power, the pain of restraint and the pleasure of liberty.[262] Bentham's response to Blackstone's description of the state of nature, the union of the multitude and the creation of the state is accordingly to pronounce these passages completely *unmeaning*, a mere sequence of fictions of just the kind that legal theory must learn to eschew.[263]

Bentham's purported demystification leaves him with nothing to say about the state except that, if the term has any meaning, it can only refer to some actual body of persons in charge of some identifiable apparatus of government. This is what he finally tells us towards the end of his *Introduction to the Principles of Morals and Legislation* of 1789 when he considers 'offences against the state'. He lays it down that what it means to have a state is simply to have 'particular persons invested with powers to be exercised for the benefit of the rest'. If there were no such persons equipped with such powers 'there would be no such thing as a *state*'.[264]

---

[258] More 1686, p. 22.   [259] More 1664, p. 54.
[260] For Bentham on Blackstone see Burns 1989; Schofield 2006, pp. 51–7; McLean 2012, pp. 19–20.
[261] Bentham 1988, p. 53.   [262] Schofield 2006, pp. 32–44.
[263] Bentham 1988, p. 113. For Bentham on fictions see Schofield 2006, pp. 14–27, 74–7.
[264] Bentham 1996, 17. 1. 18, p. 292. Cf. Bentham's definition of the state in his 'Preparatory Principles' (Bentham MSS, University College London, UC69.89): 'A State is a number of persons [in succession] agreed, or accustomed, to obey the commands, concerning any matter whatsoever, or to conduct themselves, in all things, according as a person, or persons, of a certain description have commanded.' I owe this reference to Douglas Long.

This is because, as his opening chapter had already explained, when we speak about the interests or actions of a group, the only meaning we can attribute to statements about any such 'fictitious *body*' is that we are talking about 'the sum of the interests of the several members who compose it.'[265]

Bentham's repudiation of legal fictions exercised an overwhelming influence on the subsequent direction of utilitarian political thought. We look in vain among other early utilitarians – William Paley, William Godwin, James Mill – for any sustained discussion of the idea of the state, and insofar as we encounter such discussions in later utilitarian theory they generally echo Bentham's reductionist account. A classic instance is provided by John Austin's lectures on *The Province of Jurisprudence Determined* of 1832.[266] When we speak of the state, according to Austin, we simply denote 'the individual person, or the body of individual persons, which bears the supreme powers in an independent political society.'[267] To say of the state, or indeed of any group, that it is capable of acting is merely to employ a 'figment' or metaphor 'for the sake of brevity in discourse'.[268] Later we find the same view summarised – along with so much else in the utilitarian creed – by Henry Sidgwick in his *Elements of Politics* of 1891. Sidgwick explicitly denies that the bond of union underlying the state can be anything other than an agreement by a number of individuals to obey the same laws, and accordingly describes the state as nothing more than an apparatus of government empowered to command the exclusive allegiance of those living under it.[269]

It is true that by this time a reaction had set in against what I am calling this reductionist view of the state. During the closing decades of the nineteenth century a determined effort was made to reintroduce into English legal and political theory the idea of the state as the name of a distinct person. One aspect of this development took the form of an attempt to classify the state as part of a more broadly based theory of corporations. The legal theorist who did most to reanimate this argument was F. W. Maitland, who had been a pupil of Sidgwick's at the University of Cambridge. Drawing on Gierke's magisterial treatise on the history of group personality (parts of which he translated) Maitland went on to publish a series of classic articles in which he bewailed the gaps and inconsistencies introduced into English law as a consequence of its failure to create an adequate theory of fictitious persons, among which he listed the *persona ficta* of the state as the most triumphant fiction of all.[270]

---

[265] Bentham 1996, 1. 4, p. 12.
[266] On Austin and Bentham see Lobban 2007, pp. 173–87.
[267] Austin 1869, vol. 1, p. 249n.   [268] Austin 1869, vol. 1, p. 358.
[269] Sidgwick 1897, p. 221.
[270] Maitland 2003, p. 71. On Gierke and Maitland see Runciman 1997, pp. 89–123.

Still more contentiously, an influential group of English moral philosophers of the same generation turned to Rousseau and Hegel for help in articulating the claim that the state is the name not merely of a fictional person but of a person with a real will of its own.[271] T. H. Green edged towards this position in his *Lectures on the Principles of Political Obligation*, posthumously published in 1886, in which he argued that the state is an institution with a duty to maintain the rights and serve the common good of its citizens,[272] and that 'it is not a state unless it does so'.[273] Green's argument was subsequently elaborated with greater boldness (or perhaps merely with less nuance) by Bernard Bosanquet in his *Philosophical Theory of the State* in 1899.[274] Although Bosanquet praises Hobbes for recognising the state to be the name of a distinct person,[275] his own theory embodies a denial of the assumption, vital to Hobbes, that it is a legal fiction to describe the state as having a will and being able to act. Bosanquet responds in Hegelian style that the person of the state is far from being 'an empty fiction'.[276] The state possesses its own substantial will, the contents of which are equivalent to what we would ourselves will if we were acting with full rationality. Bosanquet is thus led to propose what he calls 'the identification of the State with the Real Will of the Individual in which he wills his own nature as a rational being'.[277] The moral freedom of citizens resides in their ability to conform to the requirements of their real or rational wills, and thereby conform to the will of the moral person of the state.

For a short while this way of thinking enjoyed a considerable vogue, but it soon provoked a vociferous restatement of the reductionist view originally put forward by the Benthamites.[278] One of the most irascible of these critiques can be found in L. T. Hobhouse's polemic, *The Metaphysical Theory of the State*, which first appeared in 1918. Confronted with Bosanquet's definition of the state as the person who wills the real will of the people, Hobhouse's instinct is to respond in self-consciously commonsensical style by asking what we ordinarily mean by the word *state*. 'By the state', he declares, 'we ordinarily mean either the government or, perhaps a little more accurately, the organisation which is at the back of law and government'.[279] The state is merely the

---

[271] On the connections between Maitland and this group see McLean 2012, pp. 71–7.
[272] Green 1986, section G, pp. 89–106. For a discussion see Nicholson 1990, pp. 157–65, 186–97.
[273] Green 1986, p. 103.
[274] See Nicholson 1990, pp. 198–230; Boucher and Vincent 2000, pp. 87–126.
[275] Bosanquet 1910, pp. 93–4, 105.   [276] Bosanquet 1910, p. 94.
[277] Bosanquet 1910, p. 154.   [278] See Nicholson 1990, pp. 189–90.
[279] Hobhouse 1918, p. 75.

name of a 'governmental organisation', and in speaking of the powers of the state we are simply referring to acts of government.[280]

A year later, Harold Laski launched a similar attack in *Authority in the Modern State*. Laski begins by criticising Rousseau and his disciples for committing the dangerous error of supposing the state to be the name of a distinct person. This analysis fails to meet the obvious objection that 'our obedience, in reality, goes to a government'.[281] 'A realistic analysis of the modern state thus suggests', he goes on, 'that what we term state-action is, in actual fact, action by government'. Bosanquet and Green are castigated for introducing further confusion by arguing that the state is the name of a 'collective moral person'.[282] The 'sober fact', Laski repeats, is that when we talk about the state we are merely referring to a prevailing system of legal and executive power, together with an associated apparatus of bureaucracy and coercive force.[283]

It is almost a century since Hobhouse and Laski published their treatises, but it would scarcely be an exaggeration to say that their basic view has remained the orthodoxy in Anglophone political theory ever since. As many recent commentators have observed, the state has come to be seen as nothing more than 'an apparatus of rule, an apparatus distinguished pre-eminently by the fact that it involves a monopoly of coercion' over some specific territory.[284] One might go even further and say that, in common parlance, *state* and *government* have by now become synonymous terms, a development widely reflected in textbook discussions of the state, in which the two words are now regularly used interchangeably.[285]

As political theorists have increasingly worked with this reductionist view of the state, they have begun to voice an even more radical doubt. Should we be centring our accounts of public power on the concept of the state at all? According to a growing body of commentators, recent economic and political changes have undermined and discredited the very idea of the state. Perhaps the most obvious of these developments has been the rise of multinational corporations and other economic institutions of international reach. With their capacity to control investment and employment, they are visibly able to coerce individual states into accommodating their demands even when these may conflict with the social and

---

[280] Hobhouse 1918, pp. 75–6. For a discussion see Panagakou 2005.

[281] Laski 1919, p. 30.   [282] Laski 1919, pp. 26, 66.   [283] Laski 1919, pp. 29, 37.

[284] Forsyth 1991, p. 504. See also Green 1988, p. 64 on the Anglophone 'tradition of scepticism' about the concept of the state and Taggart 2003 on the absence of the concept in British legal thought.

[285] See, for example, Held 1984, which begins by speaking (p. 29) of 'the state – or apparatus of "government"'.

economic priorities of the states concerned.[286] At the same time, the past generation has witnessed the continuing evolution of international organisations with authority to overturn the local jurisdictions of individual states, a process much reinforced by the widening acceptance of an overarching ideal of universal human rights. The European Court of Human Rights, originally instituted in 1959, was permanently re-established in 1998 not merely with authority to point out violations of the Convention on Human Rights promulgated in 1950, but with further authority to require its jurisprudence to be taken into account by individual member states. More recently, some international legal theorists have taken the further step of arguing that, in the name of securing such rights, it may be permissible to interfere, by military force if necessary, in the internal arrangements of purportedly sovereign states.[287] Confronted with these developments, commentators have increasingly begun to insist that to speak of states and statehood 'is becoming increasingly inappropriate in face of the forces at work in the contemporary world'.[288]

Some powerful currents of recent political thinking have further contributed to this questioning of state power with a series of moral denunciations of the deficiencies of states. Among conservative writers in the period after World War II, the increasing levels of control assumed by welfare states were viewed with hostility and even alarm, and we were forcefully warned (by Hayek and others) that even democratic states can readily become totalitarian in their behaviour. Among Marxist critics, the objection continues to be raised that states amount to little more than the executive arms of their ruling classes, an objection that has gained much ground of late in the face of an increased willingness to tolerate extremes of social and economic inequality. Meanwhile no one doubts that even purportedly democratic states have been, and remain, agents of extensive suffering and injustice.

Of late, a growing neo-liberal consensus has caused these anxieties about the state to be replaced by contempt. We are now invited to think of democratic states less as sources of oppression than as agents of bureaucratic inefficiency and waste. Rather than relying on the power of governments to shape our societies, we are urged, we should cultivate systems of 'governance'. The revival of this piece of medieval terminology – with its implications of wise guidance as opposed to mere command – appears to have originated with the rhetoric of the World Bank in the 1980s and its desire to impress upon the peoples of the developing world the desirability

---

[286] For examples see Strange 1996, pp. 91–109, 122–79; Hertz 2001, pp. 40–61, 170–84.
[287] Tesón 1997; Wheeler 2000; Caney 2005, esp. pp. 231–46; for a survey see Weiss 2007.
[288] Beetham 1984, p. 221.

of making themselves more open to decentralisation and market forces. 'Government' was seen as bad, the monopolistic enemy of competition and enterprise. 'Governance' was seen as good, the enabling friend of innovation and initiative.[289] To the relatively neutral observations of international relations theorists about the erosion of state sovereignty have thus been added some frankly normative claims about the decline and fall of the state as a consummation devoutly to be wished.

These and other transformations have convinced a number of commentators that, in power as well as in reputation, the state is now in terminal decline. The institutions of the state, we are told, are shrinking, retreating, 'fading into the shadows'.[290] As a result, the concept of the state itself is said to be losing any theoretical significance.[291] Foucault drew the moral that it is time 'to cut off the King's head' in political theory, liberating ourselves from the illusion that it still makes any sense to talk about sovereign states.[292] Frank Ankersmit has recently gone so far as to conclude that 'now for the first time in more than half a millennium the State is on the way out'.[293] My genealogy comes to an end not with a bang but a whimper.

VI

When we trace the genealogy of a concept, we not only uncover the various ways — the often unfamiliar and surprising ways — in which it was used in earlier times. We also equip ourselves with a means of reflecting critically on how the concept is currently understood.[294] To express the point in more grandiose terms, to write a genealogy is always a normative act, an act of commendation or critique.[295] I want finally to ask how this consideration applies to the genealogy I have attempted to sketch.

As I have shown, the concept of the state has been a subject of continuous contestation and debate in Anglophone political theory ever since the opening decades of the seventeenth century. Of late, however, we have chosen to confront this complex intellectual heritage in such a way as to leave ourselves astonishingly little to say about it. We have largely been content to reiterate the two propositions underlying the latest version of what I have been calling the reductionist view of the state: that the term is

---

[289] Williams and Young 1994.   [290] Strange 1996, pp. 82–7; Creveld 1999, pp. 420–1.
[291] For discussion and criticism of this claim see Trainor 1998; Creveld 1999; Hertz 2001, esp. pp. 18–37; Bartelson 2001, pp. 148–91; Ryan 2008; Krasner 2010; Delwaide 2011.
[292] Foucault 1980, p. 121.   [293] Ankersmit 2007, p. 36.
[294] See Geuss 1999; Geuss 2005; Bevir 2008; Krupp 2008.
[295] Not necessarily an act of critique, as Nietzscheans assume.

best understood simply as a way of referring to an established apparatus of government; and that such governments are of discredited standing and diminishing significance in our market-oriented and increasingly globalised world.

This response strikes me as deeply unsatisfactory, and is rightly beginning to be called in doubt. It remains undeniable that states have lately forfeited some of the traditional attributes of sovereignty, and that the concept of sovereignty itself has become at least partly disjoined from its earlier associations with the rights of individual states.[296] But to say that states are no longer sovereign is (*pace* Foucault) by no means to deconstruct the concept of the state.[297] There are growing populist demands for the interests of individual states to be placed above those of supranational elites. So vociferously are these demands being pressed that there is even some doubt as to how far such 'post-sovereignty' projects as the European Union can manage to survive. We may be witnessing the nemesis of the neo-liberal hope that the power of globalised markets may eventually supersede the power of the state. Meanwhile it is obvious that the world's leading nation-states remain the principal actors on the international stage, and by far the most significant political agents within their own territories.[298] Of late they have become much more aggressive, patrolling their borders with increasing vigilance, closing them against alleged undesirables, and maintaining an unparalleled level of surveillance over their own citizens. They have also become more interventionist, and in the face of their collapsing banking systems they have even proved willing to step forward as lenders of last resort.[299] They continue to print money, to impose taxes, to enforce contracts, to penalise errant citizens, to subsidise cultural life, to provide health and welfare services, to facilitate the operation of markets[300] and to legislate with an unprecedented degree of complexity. To speak in these circumstances of the state 'fading into the shadows' seems one-sided to the point of inattentiveness.

Despite the aspiration of neo-liberalism to will away the state, it remains obvious that most of us are living in nation-states, that this is likely to remain the case for some considerable time, and that statelessness remains an appalling prospect for anyone to confront. But even if it is agreed that we need to start thinking again about the idea of the state, it remains to ask whether it is sufficient to operate with what I have been calling the reductionist view that *state* and *government* are effectively

---

[296] Bellamy 2003; Prokhovnik 2007, pp. 183–246; McCormick 2010; Lipping 2010. On the 'post-sovereign' state see Praet 2010.
[297] As noted in Grimm 2015, pp. 101–28.   [298] As noted in Morris 1998; Troper 2010.
[299] On the implications for the contention that states are 'on their way out' see Altman 2009.
[300] For examples see Mazzucato 2011.

synonymous terms. What, if anything, has been lost as a result of the widespread abandonment of the view that states must be categorically distinguished from governments?

Among recent political theorists who have addressed this question, two contrasting answers have been given. According to one strand of thought, what has been lost is the insight that states should be 'distinguished from "government" as the whole is distinguished from the part'. The state, we are told, is 'a larger notion that refers, essentially, to the entirety of political society', and is 'roughly synonymous with "civil society"'.[301] If, however, we return to the philosophical tradition I have mainly discussed, we find ourselves confronting the very different claim that what most of all needs to be recovered is the insight that states are distinct persons, and hence distinct agents in our political world.

It is this latter perspective that seems to me particularly worth re-examining. If we are to undertake this task, however, we first need to recall that, within the genealogy I have been tracing, states have been conceived as persons in two contrasting ways. According to one view, the state is not merely the name of a political actor; it is also the name of a real person, as Bosanquet would say, whose intentions and purposes are independent even of those who represent it. It is this understanding of the state, according to Alexander Wendt and other recent theorists of international relations,[302] that needs to be re-embraced if we are not to fall back into the 'realist' position of dismissing the state as a non-existent entity and concluding that, when we speak about the state, this is merely another way of referring to an apparatus of government.[303]

One implication of the genealogy I have traced is that this is a false dichotomy.[304] As we have seen, there is at least one further possibility, that of viewing the state not as a real but a fictional or moral person which is nevertheless capable of acting because it is capable of being represented by real agents whose actions count as those of the state. This avoids the ontological strangeness of speaking about real persons who manage to outlive the human span. We need only speak about common purposes that undoubtedly outlive us all, and of the continuous representation of these purposes by real (but therefore changing) human agents.[305] To speak in these terms, however, is not merely to argue that it is 'as if' actions are performed by states.[306] It is to claim that states are genuine actors, because actions can validly be attributed to them.

---

[301] Steinberger 2004, pp. 9–10.
[302] See Wendt 2004, and on group ownership giving rise to real entities see Getzler 2008.
[303] See for example Gilpin 1986.   [304] As noted in Jackson 2004, esp. pp. 286–7.
[305] Barker 1957, pp. lvii–lxxxvii.   [306] For this contrast see Wendt 2004, p. 289.

But are there any good reasons for thinking about the state in these Hobbesian terms? A growing number of legal and political theorists have begun to answer in the affirmative.[307] By way of supporting their case, I should like to end by recalling the two main reasons given by the original protagonists of the Hobbesian theory for insisting on a categorical distinction between governments and states. First of all, we need to be able to make sense of the assertion that some governmental actions may have the intended effect of binding not merely the body of the people but their remote posterity. One obvious example, as noted by Pufendorf and many later legal theorists, would be the decision to take on a large burden of public debt.[308] We need to ask who becomes the debtor. We can hardly answer that the debt must be owed by the government. Even if the government changes or falls, the debt will remain to be paid. The only way to make sense of the situation, Pufendorf concluded, is to recognise that the debtor must be a person with an artificial eternity of life, and must therefore be the state.[309] The same considerations apply to what Vattel calls real treaties. The aspiration lying behind such alliances is that they should remain binding on all parties for an unlimited time.[310] But if this is to be possible, then the signatories will again have to be persons with an artificial span of life, and will therefore have to be states.

According to the Hobbesian theory, there is a further and far more important reason for wishing to make a categorical distinction between states and governments. The fundamental duty of government – to repeat Hobbes's words – is to pursue 'the publique interest' and 'the Common Benefit'.[311] Acting in the name of the state, the basic duty of government is to procure 'the safety of the people', to ensure 'that Justice be equally administered' and to look after those 'unable to maintain themselves'.[312] The fundamental reason for wishing to distinguish between states and governments is thus to provide a standing test of the legitimacy of governmental action, and hence a sense of the limits as well as the grounds of our obligation to obey the state.

It is sometimes objected that this way of thinking about states reveals them to be distinctly sinister entities. But this anxiety reflects

---

[307] Runciman 1997, 2000, 2003; Morris 1998; Trainor 1998, 2001, 2005; Bartelson 2001, esp. pp. 149–81; McLean 2003, 2005, 2012; Jackson 2004. For related views see Rabkin 2005; Song 2012.

[308] The issue was much debated in the French revolution, with Sieyès insisting that the Nation must be the debtor. For an important later English discussion see Maitland 2003, pp. 39–45, 70–1.

[309] For further discussion see McLean 2003, pp. 175–6, 178–83.

[310] Vattel 1760, II. XII. 183, p. 182.

[311] Hobbes 2012, vol. 2, ch. 17, p. 260; ch. 19, p. 288; ch. 24, p. 388.

[312] Hobbes 2012, vol. 2, ch. 30, pp. 520, 534, 538.

a misunderstanding of the Hobbesian theory I have been laying out. According to the Hobbesian view, to speak of the state as a distinct person with characteristic obligations and rights is merely a way of referring to the body of the people united as equal citizens under an authorised system of rule. When we speak about the interests of the state we are merely referring to the common good or public interest of the people as a whole. To a Nietzschean this will seem a Panglossian response, a mere refusal to recognise that states are cold monsters mendaciously posing as the people. It is of course true that, if governments are to promote the vision of the common good underlying the Hobbesian view of the state, they will need to be assigned so much power that the outcome could easily be destructive of the very interests they are instituted to promote. But we have now reached a stage at which neo-liberal aspirations to replace states by markets have begun to wreck the lives of millions. Perhaps this is a good moment to think anew about those theories of the state which are grounded on the assumption that we can meaningfully speak about a substantial ideal of the common good that governments have a duty to promote.

Bibliography

Manuscript Sources

Cambridge

Cambridge University Library:
Mm. v. 46: *The names of the Benefactors* [to the Fellows' Building, Christ's College] ... *written by Dr Michael Honywood*, fos. 181r–188v.

Christ's College Muniments Room:
T. 11. 1: Joseph Mede [*Account-book, volume 1*].
T. 11. 3: Joseph Mede [*Account-book, volume 3*].
Shelf 85: *A catalogue of the names of ye Benefactors for the new Building, 1639.*

Chatsworth, Derbyshire

Chatsworth MSS: *Index of Letters at Chatsworth: First Series, to 1839.*
Hardwick MS 19: [James Wheldon's account book 1661–1708].
Hardwick MS 64: Untitled. [Bound MS volume, 84pp. Heading on opening page: 'The first booke of the Courtier'].
Hobbes MS A. 3: *Elementorum Philosophiae Sectio Tertia De Cive.*
Hobbes MS D. 1: *Latin Exercises* [Bound MS volume, including *Ex Aristot: Rhet.*, pp. 1–143].
Hobbes MS D. 5: 'Questions relative to Hereditary Right. Mr Hobbes'.
Hobbes MS E. 1. A: Untitled. [Bound MS volume, 143pp.; *Old Catalogue* on spine. Catalogue of the Hardwick Library].
Hobbes MS G. 2: 'The Right hon.^ble the Earl of Shaftsbury's speech in the House of Lords March 25. 1679'.
Hobbes MS G. 3: 'A Copy of the Bill concerning the D: of York'.

London

British Library:
Egerton MS 1910: Thomas Hobbes, *Leviathan Or the Matter, Forme, and Power of A Common-wealth Ecclesiastical and Civil.*

Harleian MS 4235: Thomas Hobbes, *The Elements of Law, Naturall and Politique.*
Lansdowne MS 119: [1550 'Laws' for Bury St Edmunds Grammar School].

University College London:
Bentham MS UC69.89: Jeremy Bentham, 'Preparatory Principles'.

Oxford

St John's College:
MS 13: *Behemoth or the Long Parliament. By Thomas Hobbes of Malmsbury.*

Printed Primary Sources

Abbot, George (1636). *A Briefe Description of the Whole World*, London.
Alberico de Rosate (1586). *In Secundam Infortiati Partem Commentarii*, Venice.
Alberto de Gandino (1891). *Quaestiones Statutorum*, ed. Enrico Solmio in *Bibliotheca iuridica medii aevi*, ed. Augusto Gaudenzi, 3 vols., Bologna, vol. 3, pp. 155–214.
Alciato, Andrea (1550). *Emblemata*, Lyon.
Almain, Jacques (1706). 'Tractatus de autoritate ecclesiae' in Jean Gerson, *Opera Omnia*, ed. Louis Ellies du Pin, 5 vols., Antwerp, vol. 2, cols. 976–1012.
Althusius, Johannes (1932). *Politica Methodice Digesta*, ed. Carl J. Friedrich, Cambridge, MA.
Ambrose (1845). 'Epistola XV' in *Patrologiae Cursus Completus*, ed. J.-P. Migne, 221 vols., Paris, vol. 16, cols. 955–9.
[Anderton, Lawrence] (1634). *The Triple Cord or A Treatise Proving the Truth of the Roman Religion*, Saint-Omer.
Andrewes, Lancelot (1611). *A Sermon Preached Before His Majestie at White-Hall*, London.
Aneau, Barthélemy (1552). *Picta poesis*, Lyon.
Animadversions upon those Notes which the Late Observator hath Published (1642). London.
Anselm (1854). 'Ennarationes in Evangelium Matthaei' in *Patrologiae Cursus Completus*, ed. J.-P. Migne, 221 vols., Paris, vol. 162, cols. 1227–500.
Aquinas, Thomas (1950). *Summa Theologiae*, ed. Piero Caramello, Rome.
Arber, Edward (1875–94). *A Transcript of the Registers of the Company of Stationers of London; 1554–1640 AD*, London.
Aristotle (1547). *The Ethiques of Aristotle*, trans. John Wilkinson, London.
Aristotle (1926). *The 'Art' of Rhetoric*, ed. and trans. J. H. Freese, London.
Aristotle (1985). *Nicomachean Ethics*, trans. Terence Irwin, Indianapolis, IN.
Aristotle (1986). 'A Briefe of the Art of Rhetorique', trans. Thomas Hobbes in *The Rhetorics of Thomas Hobbes and Bernard Lamy*, ed. John T. Harwood, Carbondale and Edwardsville, IL, pp. 33–128.
Aristotle (1995). *Poetics*, ed. and trans. Stephen Halliwell, London.
Attersoll, William (1606). *The Badges of Christianity. Or, A Treatise of the Sacraments*, London.

Aubrey, John (1898). *'Brief Lives', chiefly of Contemporaries, set down by John Aubrey, between the years 1669 & 1696*, ed. Andrew Clark, 2 vols., Oxford.

Augustine (1791). 'De agone christiano' in *Veterum Patrum Theologia Universa: Pars Tertia: Philosophia Moralis*, ed. Angelus Cigheri, Florence, pp. 127–43.

Austin, John (1869). *Lectures on Jurisprudence or The Philosophy of Positive Law*, ed. Robert Campbell, 2 vols., London.

Avity, Pierre d' (1615). *The Estates, Empires & Principallities of the World*, trans. Edward Grimestone, London.

Azo Portius (1966a). *Summa super codicem*, ed. Mario E. Viora, Turin.

Azo Portius (1966b). *Lectura super codicem*, ed. Mario E. Viora, Turin.

Bachiler, Samuel (1625). *Miles Christianus, or The Campe Royal*, Amsterdam.

Baldwin, William (1579). *A Treatice of Morall Philosophy*, London.

Ball, William (1642). *A Caveat for Subjects, Moderating the Observator*, London.

Banchi, Luciano (ed.) (1866). 'Breve degli officiali', *Archivio storico italiano* 4, pp. 7–104.

Bandello, Matteo (1567). *Certaine tragicall discourses*, trans. Geffraie Fenton, London.

Barbaro, Ermolao (1559). *De Arte Dicendi Libri III*, Paris.

Barckley, Richard (1598). *A Discourse of the Felicitie of Man*, London.

Barclay, William (1600). *De regno et regali potestate adversus Buchananum, Brutum, Boucherium & reliquos Monarchomachos*, Paris.

Barrow, Henry (1591). *A petition directed to Her Most Excellent Majestie*, London.

Bartas, Guillaume du (1598). *The Colonies of Bartas*, London.

Bartolus of Sassoferrato (1588a). 'In Primam Digesti Veteris Partem Commentaria' in *Opera*, 11 vols., Basel, vol. 1, pp. 1–644.

Bartolus of Sassoferrato (1588b). 'In Primam Digesti Novi Partem Commentaria' in *Opera*, 11 vols., Basel, vol. 5, pp. 1–528.

Bartolus of Sassoferrato (1588c). 'In Secundam Digesti Novi Partem Commentaria' in *Opera*, 11 vols., Basel, vol. 6, pp. 1–710.

Bartolus of Sassoferrato (1588d). 'Tractatus de regimine civitatis' in *Opera*, 11 vols., Basel, vol. 10, pp. 417–21.

Baynes, Paul (1634). *A Commentarie Upon the First and Second Chapters of Saint Paul to the Colossians*, London.

Becmann, Johann (1679). *Meditationes Politicae*, Frankfurt a.d. Oder.

Bentham, Jeremy (1988). *A Fragment on Government*, ed. J. H. Burns and H. L. A. Hart, Introduction by Ross Harrison, Cambridge.

Bentham, Jeremy (1996). *An Introduction to the Principles of Morals and Legislation*, ed. J. H. Burns and H. L. A. Hart, Introduction by F. Rosen, Oxford.

Bentley, Thomas (1582). *The Monument of Matrones conteining seven severall Lamps of Virginitie, or distinct treatises*, London.

The Bible, That Is, The holy Scriptures contained in the Old & New Testament (1607). London.

[Bishop, William] (1614). *A Disproofe of D. Abbots Counterproofe*, Paris.

Blackstone, William (1765). 'Of the Nature of Law in General' in *Commentaries on the Laws of England*, vol. 1: *Of the Rights of Persons*, Oxford, pp. 38–62.

Boccalini, Traiano (1626). *The new-found politicke*, trans. William Vaughan, London.

Bocchi, Achille (1574). *Symbolicarum quaestionum*, Bologna.

[Bodenham, John] (1600). *Bel-vedére Or The Garden of the Muses*, London.

Bodin, Jean (1962). *The Six Bookes of a Commonweale*, ed. Kenneth D. McRae, Cambridge, MA.

Boethius (1571). 'De duabus naturis et una persona Christi' in *Scripta Veterum Latina, de una persona et duabus naturis Domini*, Basel, fos. 10v–15r.

The Booke of Common Prayer and Administration of the Sacraments, And other Rites and Ceremonies of the Church of England (1618). London.

Bosanquet, Bernard (1910). *The Philosophical Theory of the State*, 2nd edn, London.

Bosse, Abraham (1645). *Traite des manieres de graver en taille douce sur l'airin*, Paris.

Bosse, Abraham (1653). *Moyen universel de pratiquer la perspective*, Paris.

Botero, Giovanni (1630). *Relations of the most famous kingdomes and commonwealths thorowout the world*, trans. Robert Johnson, London.

Boughen, Edward (1650). *Master Geree's Case of Conscience Sifted*, London.

Boys, John (1610). *An Exposition of the Dominical Epistles and Gospels*, London.

Bracton, Henry de (1640). *De Legibus et Consuetudinibus Angliae, Libri Quinque*, London.

Bramhall, John (1643). *The Serpent Salve*, n. p.

Brathwaite, Richard (1614). *The Schollers Medley, Or, An Intermixt Discourse upon Historicall and Poeticall Relations*, London.

Brathwaite, Richard (1630). *The English Gentleman*, London.

Bridge, William (1643a). *The Wounded Conscience Cured, the Weak One strengthened, and the doubting satisfied*, London.

Bridge, William (1643b). *The Truth of the Times Vindicated*, London.

Browning, Andrew (ed.) (1966). *English Historical Documents 1660–1714*, London.

Bruni, Leonardo (1987). 'On the Study of Literature' in *The Humanism of Leonardo Bruni: Selected Texts*, trans. Gordon Griffiths, James Hankins and David Thompson, Binghampton, NY, pp. 240–51.

Bryskett, Lodowick (1606). *A discourse of civill life containing the ethike part of morall philosophie*, London.

Bünting, Heinrich (1592). *Itinerarium Sacrae Scripturae*, trans. Dannele Adama, Prague.

Bünting, Heinrich (1597). *Itinerarium et Chronicon Ecclesiasticum Totius Sacrae Scripturae*, Magdeburg.

Burgersdicius, Franciscus (1631). *Idea Philosophiae tum Naturalis, tum Moralis*, Oxford.

Burton, Henry (1636). *For God, and the King*, London.

Butler, Charles (1629). *Rhetoricae Libri Duo*, London.

Caesar (1565). *The eyght bookes of Caius Julius Caesar conteyning his martiall exploytes in the Realme of Gallia*, trans. Arthur Golding, London.

Camden, William (1610). *Britain*, trans. Philemon Holland, London.

Casa, Giovanni della (1576). *Galateo ... A treatise of the maners and behaviours, it behoveth a man to use and eschewe, in his familiar conversation*, trans. Robert Peterson, London.

Casa, Giovanni della (1619). *Galateus, seu de morum honestate, et elegantia*, trans. Nathan Chytraeus, Hanover.

Castiglione, Baldassare (1561). *The courtyer of Count Baldessar Castilio . . . done into English by Thomas Hoby*, London.

Castiglione, Baldassare (1994). *The Book of the Courtier*, trans. Thomas Hoby, ed. Virginia Cox, London.

[Cavendish, William] (1681). *Reasons for His Majesties Passing the Bill of Exclusion. In a Letter To a Friend*, London.

Chaloner, Edward (1623). *Sixe Sermons*, London.

[Charles I] (1642). *His Majesties Answer to the XIX. Propositions of Both Houses of Parliament*, London.

Charles I (1643). 'His Majesties Answer to a Printed Book' in Edward Husbands (ed). *An Exact Collection Of all Remonstrances, Declarations, Votes, Orders, Ordinances, Proclamations, Petitions, Messages, Answers*, London, pp. 282–99.

[Charles I] (1649). *King Charls His Speech Made upon the Scaffold*, London.

Christ's College Magazine No. 8 (1888). Cambridge.

Church, Henry (1637). *Miscellanea Philo-theologica*, London.

Cicero (1534). *The thre bookes of Tullyes offices both in latyne tonge & in englysshe lately translated by Roberte Whytinton*, London.

Cicero (1568). *Marcus Tullius Ciceroes three bookes of dueties*, trans. Nicholas Grimalde, London.

Cicero (1579). *Rhetoricorum ad C. Herennium Libri Quattuor. M. T. Ciceronis De Inventione Libri Duo*, London.

Cicero (1913). *De officiis*, ed. and trans. Walter Miller, London.

Cicero (1928). *De legibus*, ed. and trans. Clinton Walker Keyes, London.

Cicero (1942). *De oratore*, ed. and trans. E. W. Sutton and H. Rackham, 2 vols., London.

Cicero (1949). *De inventione*, ed. and trans. H. M. Hubbell, London.

Cicero (1999). *Letters to Atticus*, ed. and trans. D. R. Shackleton Bailey, 4 vols., London.

Cino da Pistoia (1493). *Lectura super Codicis*, Venice.

Cleland, James (1607). *Hero-paideia, or the institution of a young noble man*, Oxford.

Cobbett, William and T. C. Hansard (eds.) (1807a). *The Parliamentary History of England, from the Earliest Period to the Year 1803. . . .*, vol. 2: AD *1625–1642*, London.

Cobbett, William and T. C. Hansard (eds.) (1807b). *The Parliamentary History of England, from the Earliest Period to the Year 1803. . . .*, vol. 4: AD *1660–1668* [*recte 1688*], London.

Cogan, Thomas (1577). *The Well of Wisedome, conteining chiefe and chosen sayinges . . . bestowed in usuall common places in order of A.B.C.*, London.

Collections of Statutes for the University and the Colleges of Cambridge (1840). London.

Collins, Samuel (1617). *Epphata to F. T., or, The Defence of . . . the Lord Bishop of Elie*, Cambridge.

Conches, Guillaume de (1929). *Moralium Dogma Philosophorum*, ed. John Holmberg, Uppsala.

Considerations for the Commons, in This Age of Distractions (1642). N. p.

Contarini, Gasparo (1599). *The Common-wealth and Government of Venice*, trans. Lewes Lewkenor, London.

Cooper, Thomas (1565). *Thesaurus Linguae Romanae & Britannicae*, London.

Cope, Esther S. and Willson H. Coates (eds.) (1977). *Proceedings of the Short Parliament of 1640*, London.

Cotgrave, Randle (1611). *A Dictionarie of the French and English Tongues*, London.

Dallington, Robert (1613). *Aphorismes Civill and Militarie*, London.

Day, Angel (1592). *A Declaration of all such Tropes, Figures or Schemes, as . . . are specially used in this Methode*, London.

A Declaration of the Parliament of England (1649). London.

De figuris vel schematibus (1993). Ed. Marisa Squillante, Rome.

Despauterius, Johannes (1555). *De Figuris Liber*, Antwerp.

The Digest of Justinian (1985). Ed. Theodor Mommsen and Paul Krueger, translation ed. Alan Watson, 4 vols., Philadelphia, PA.

[Digges, Dudley] (1642). *An Answer to a Printed Book*, Oxford.

[Digges, Dudley] (1643). *A Review of the Observations*, Oxford.

[Digges, Dudley] (1644). *The Unlawfulnesse of Subjects taking up Armes against their Soveraigne, in what case soever*, Oxford.

Downing, Calybute (1634). *A Discourse of the State Ecclesiasticall of this Kingdome, in relation to the Civill*, 2nd edn, Oxford.

Drelincourt, Charles (1651). *Les Consolations de l'âme fidele*, Paris.

Dürer, Albrecht, with Benedictus Chelidonius (1511). 'De ultimo mundi iudicio' in *Passio Christi ab Alberto Durer*, Nuremberg, sig. E, 4v–5r.

Eliot, George (1996). *Romola*, ed. Dorothea Barrett, Penguin Classics edition, London.

Elyot, Thomas (1531). *The boke named the Governour*, London.

Elyot, Thomas (1538). *The Dictionary of syr Thomas Eliot knyght*, London.

Elyot, Thomas (1559). *Bibliotheca Eliotae . . . by Thomas Cooper the third tyme corrected*, London.

Erasmus, Desiderius (1542). *Apophthegmes*, trans. Nicolas Udall, London.

Estienne, Henry (1646). *The Art Of making Devises*, trans. Thomas Blount, London.

Ferne, Henry (1642). *The Resolving of Conscience*, London.

Filmer, Robert (1991). 'Observations Concerning the Original of Government' in *Patriarcha and Other Writings*, ed. Johann Sommerville, Cambridge, pp. 184–234.

[Fitzherbert, Thomas] (1613). *An Adjoynder*, Saint-Omer.

Fitzherbert, Thomas (1621). *The Obmutesce of F. T. to the Apphata of D. Collins*, Saint-Omer.

Fletcher, R. (1651). *Radius Heliconicus: Or, The Resolution of a Free State*, London.

Florus (1619). *The Roman Histories*, trans. Edmund Bolton, London.

Forset, Edward (1606). *A Comparative Discourse of the Bodies Natural and Politique*, London.

Fortescue, John (1567). *A learned commendation of the politique lawes of Englande*, trans. Robert Mulcaster, London.

Foster, Elizabeth Read (ed.) (1966). *Proceedings in Parliament 1610*, 2 vols., New Haven, CT.

Fotherby, Martin (1622). *Atheomastix*, London.

Foxe, John (1583). *Actes and Monuments of matters most special and memorable, happenyng in the Church . . . newly revised*, London.

Fraunce, Abraham (1588). *The Arcadian Rhetorike*, London.

Fraunce, Abraham (1592). *The third part of the Countesse of Pembrokes Yuychurch Entituled Amintas Dale*, London.

Frideric, André (1617). *Emblemes nouveaux*, Frankfurt.

Fulbecke, William (1587). *A Booke of Christian Ethicks or Moral Philosophie*, London.

Fulke, William (1580). *A Retentive, To Stay Good Christians, . . . Also A Discoverie of the Daungerous Rocke of the Popish Church*, London.

Gardiner, S. R. (ed.) (1906). *The Constitutional Documents of the Puritan Revolution, 1625–1660*, 3rd edn, Oxford.

George of Trebizond (1523). 'In Tres Rhetoricorum Aristotelis Libros' in *Rhetoricorum libri quinque*, Venice, fos. 109–35.

Gibson, Strickland (ed.) (1931). *Statuta Antiqua Universitatis Oxoniensis*, Oxford.

Giovanni da Viterbo (1901). 'Liber de regimine civitatum', ed. Caietano Salvemini in *Bibliotheca iuridica medii aevi*, ed. Augusto Gaudenzi, 3 vols., Bologna, vol. 3, pp. 215–80.

Goodwin, John (1642). *Anti-Cavalierisme*, London.

Goodwin, John (1649). *Hybristodikai. The obstructours of justice*, London.

Goodwin, Thomas (1642). *Christ Set Forth*, London.

Gore, John (1638). *The God of Heaven*, London.

Green, T. H. (1986). *Lectures on the Principles of Political Obligation and Other Writings*, ed. Paul Harris and John Morrow, Cambridge.

Gregory I (1887–99). 'Epistola I, 1' in *Registrum Epistolarum*, ed. P. Edwald and L. M. Hartmann, 2 vols., Berlin, vol. 1, pp. 1–2.

Grotius, Hugo (1625). *De iure belli ac pacis libri tres*, Paris.

Grotius, Hugo (2005). *The Rights of War and Peace*, ed. Richard Tuck, 3 vols., Indianapolis, IN.

Guazzo, Stefano (1581). *The Civile Conversation*, trans. George Pettie, London.

Habermann, Johann (1579). *The enimie of securitie or A dailie exercise of godly meditations drawne out of the pure fountaines of the holie Scriptures*, trans. Thomas Rogers, London.

Hakewill, George (1616). *An Answere to a treatise written by Dr. Carier, by way of a letter to his Majestie*, London.

[Hall, Edmund] (1651). *Lingua testium*, London.

Hariot, Thomas (1590). *A briefe and true report of the new found land of Virginia*, Frankfurt.

Harrington, James (1992). 'A System of Politics' in *The Commonwealth of Oceana and a System of Politics*, ed. J. G. A. Pocock, Cambridge, pp. 267–93.

Hayward, John (1603). *An Answer to the First Part of a Certaine Conference, Concerning Succession*, London.

Hayward, John (1607). *A Report of a Discourse Concerning Supreme Power in Affaires of Religion*, London.

[Herle, Charles] (1642). *A Fuller Answer to A Treatise Written by Doctor Ferne*, London.

[Herle, Charles] (1643a). *An Answer to Mis-led Doctor Fearne*, London.

[Herle, Charles] (1643b). *An Answer to Doctor Fernes Reply, Entitled Conscience Satisfied*, London.

Herodian (1556). *The History of Herodian*, trans. Nicholas Smyth, London.

Herodian (1635). *Herodian of Alexandria His Historie*, trans. J[ames] M[axwell], London.

Heywood, Thomas (1635). *The Hierarchie of the blessed Angells*, London.

Hildebert of Tours (1854). 'Moralis philosophia de honesto et utili' in *Patrologiae Cursus Completus*, ed. J.-P. Migne, 221 vols., Paris, vol. 171, cols. 1003–56.

Hitchcock, Robert (1590). *The quintesence of wit ... Wherin is set foorth sundrye excellent and wise sentences*, London.

Hobbes, Thomas (1629). *Eight Bookes of the Peloponnesian Warre*, trans. Thomas Hobbes, London.

Hobbes, Thomas (1642). *Elementorum Philosophiae Sectio Tertia De Cive*, Paris.

Hobbes, Thomas (1677). *The Workes of Homer*, trans. Thomas Hobbes, London.

Hobbes, Thomas (1750). *The Moral and Political Works of Thomas Hobbes, of Malmesbury*, London.

Hobbes, Thomas (1839a). 'Thomae Hobbes Malmesburiensis Vita Carmine Expressa' in *Thomae Hobbes Malmesburiensis opera philosophica quae Latine scripsit omnia*, ed. William Molesworth, 5 vols., London, vol. 1, pp. lxxxi–xcix.

Hobbes, Thomas (1839b). 'Elementorum philosophiae sectio secunda de homine' in *Thomae Hobbes Malmesburiensis opera philosophica*, ed. William Molesworth, 5 vols., London, vol. 2, pp. 1–132.

Hobbes, Thomas (1839c). 'Elements of Philosophy. The First Section, Concerning Body' in *The English Works of Thomas Hobbes of Malmesbury*, ed. William Molesworth, 11 vols., London, vol. 1, pp. v–xii, 1–532.

Hobbes, Thomas (1840a). 'An Answer to a Book Published by Dr Bramhall' in *The English Works of Thomas Hobbes of Malmesbury*, ed. William Molesworth, 11 vols., London, vol. 4, pp. 279–384.

Hobbes, Thomas (1840b). 'Considerations upon the Reputation, Loyalty, Manners, and Religion, of Thomas Hobbes, of Malmesbury' in *The English Works of Thomas Hobbes of Malmesbury*, ed. William Molesworth, 11 vols., London, vol. 4, pp. 409–40.

Hobbes, Thomas (1841). 'Leviathan, sive De Materia, Forma, & Potestate Civitatis Ecclesiasticae et Civilis' in *Thomae Hobbes malmesburiensis opera philosophica*, ed. William Molesworth, 5 vols., London, vol. 3, pp. v–viii and 1–569.

Hobbes, Thomas (1843). 'The History of the Grecian War Written by Thucydides' in *The English Works of Thomas Hobbes of Malmesbury*, ed. William Molesworth, 11 vols., London, vols. VIII and IX.

Hobbes, Thomas (1969). *The Elements of Law Natural and Politic*, ed. Ferdinand Tönnies, 2nd edn, Introduction by M. M. Goldsmith, London.

Hobbes, Thomas (1971). 'The Answer of Mr Hobbes to Sir Will. D'Avenant's Preface Before Gondibert' in *Gondibert*, ed. David F. Gladish, Oxford, pp. 45–55.

Hobbes, Thomas (1983). *De Cive: The Latin Version*, ed. Howard Warrender, The Clarendon Edition of the Works of Thomas Hobbes vol. II, Oxford.

[Hobbes, Thomas] (1986). 'A Briefe of the Art of Rhetorique' in *The Rhetorics of Thomas Hobbes and Bernard Lamy*, ed. John T. Harwood, Carbondale and Edwardsville, IL, pp. 33–128.

Hobbes, Thomas (1994). *The Correspondence of Thomas Hobbes*, ed. Noel Malcolm, The Clarendon Edition of the Works of Thomas Hobbes vols. VI and VII, Oxford.

Hobbes, Thomas (2005). 'Questions relative to Hereditary Right', ed. Quentin Skinner in *Writings on Common Law and Hereditary Right*, ed. Alan Cromartie and Quentin Skinner, The Clarendon Edition of the Works of Thomas Hobbes vol. XI, Oxford, pp. 153–80.

Hobbes, Thomas (2010). *Behemoth or the Long Parliament*, ed. Paul Seaward, The Clarendon Edition of the Works of Thomas Hobbes vol. X, Oxford.

Hobbes, Thomas (2012). *Leviathan*, ed. Noel Malcolm, The Clarendon Edition of the Works of Thomas Hobbes vols. III–V, Oxford.

Hobhouse, Leonard T. (1918). *The Metaphysical Theory of the State: A Criticism*, London.

The Holy Bible Containing the Old Testament and the New (1637). Edinburgh.

Holtzwart, Mathias (1581). *Emblematum Tyrocinia*, Strasbourg.

Homer (1581). *Ten Books of Homers Iliades*, trans. Arthur Hall, London.

Homer (1611). *Homer Prince of Poets*, trans. George Chapman, London.

Horace (1914). *The Odes and Epodes*, ed. and trans. C. E. Bennett, London.

Horace (1926). 'Ars Poetica' in *Satires, Epistles and Ars Poetica*, ed. and trans. H. Rushton Fairclough, London, pp. 450–88.

Huarte, Juan (1594). *The Examination of mens Wits*, trans. Camillo Camili, London.

Huber, Ulrich (1684). *De iure civitatis libri tres*, 3rd edn, Franeker.

Hubner, Martin (1757–8). *Essai sur l'histoire du droit naturel*, 2 vols., London.

[Hunton, Philip] (1643). *A Treatise of Monarchie*, London.

[Hunton, Philip] (1644). *A Vindication of the Treatise of Monarchy*, London.

Husbands, Edward (ed.) (1643). *An Exact Collection Of all Remonstrances, Declarations, Votes, Orders, Ordinances, Proclamations, Petitions, Messages, Answers*, London.

Hyperides (1944). 'Fragment of a speech against Aristophon' in *Minor Attic Orators*, ed. and trans. K. J. Maidment and J. O. Burtt, 2 vols., London, vol. 2, p. 575.

Innocent IV (1481). *Apparatus decretalium domini Innocentii Pape quarti*, Venice.

Isidore of Seville (1983). *Etymologies Book II: Rhetoric*, ed. and trans. Peter K. Marshall, Paris.

Jackson, John (1649). *The Pedigree and Perigrination of Israel*, London.

James VI and I (1994). *Political Writings*, ed. Johann Sommerville, Cambridge.

Jaucourt, Louis de (1756). 'Etat' in *Encyclopédie, ou Dictionnaire raisonné, des Sciences, des Arts et des Métiers*, ed. Denis Diderot and Jean d'Alembert, 17 vols., Paris, vol. 6, p. 19.

Johnson, Robert C. and Maija Jansson Cole (eds.) (1977a). *Commons Debates 1628, vol. 2: 17 March–19 April 1628*, New Haven, CT.

Johnson, Robert C., Mary Frear Keeler, Maija Jansson Cole and William B. Bidwell (eds.) (1977b). *Commons Debates 1628*, vol. 3: *21 April–27 May 1628*, New Haven, CT.

Journals of the House of Commons (n. d.). vol. IX. [October 1667 to April 1687], London.

Junius, Franciscus (1638). *The Painting of the Ancients, in three Bookes*, London.

Justa Edouardo King naufrago (1638). Cambridge.

[Langbaine, Gerard] (1651). *The Foundation of the Universitie of Cambridge*, London.

Larke, John (1532). *The boke of wysdome folowynge the auctoryties of auncyent phylosophers*, London.

Larke, John (1575). *The boke of wisdome otherwise called the flower of virtue*, London.

Laski, Harold J. (1919). *Authority in the Modern State*, London.

Latini, Brunetto (1948). *Li Livres dou trésor*, ed. Francis J. Carmody, Berkeley, CA.

[Leslie, Charles] (1709). *The Constitution, Laws and Government, of England, Vindicated*, London.

Lilburne, John (1649a). *Englands New Chains Discovered*, London.

Lilburne, John (1649b). *An Impeachment of High Treason against Oliver Cromwel*, London.

Lipsius, Justus (1594). *Six Bookes of Politickes or Civil Doctrine*, trans. William Jones, London.

Lisini, Alessandro (ed.) (1903). *Il costituto del Comune di Siena volgarizzato nel 1309–1310*, 2 vols., Siena.

Livy (1544). *The Historie of Two the Moste Noble Captaines of the worlde, Anniball and Scipio*, trans. Anthony Cope, London.

Livy (1590). *The Hystory of two the moste noble Captaynes of the World, Anniball and Scipio*, trans. Anthony Cope, London.

Livy (1600). *The Romane Historie Written by T. Livius of Padua*, trans. Philemon Holland, London.

Livy (1929). *Ab urbe condita, Books XXI–XXII*, ed. and trans. B. O. Foster, London.

Locke, John (1988). *Two Treatises of Government*, ed. Peter Laslett, Student edition, Cambridge.

Loe, William (1619). *The Mysterie of Mankind*, London.

Loe, William (1645). *A Sermon Preached at Lambeth*, London.

Lucretius (1975). *De rerum natura*, ed. and trans. W. H. D. Rouse, revised Martin F. Smith, London.

Lyly, John (1868). *Euphues. The Anatomy of Wit*, ed. Edward Arber, London.

Machiavelli, Bernardo (1954). *Libro di ricordi*, ed. Cesare Olschki, Florence.

Machiavelli, Niccolò (1532a). *Il principe*, Rome.

Machiavelli, Niccolò (1532b). *Il principe*, Florence.

Machiavelli, Niccolò (1636). *Machiavels Discourses*, trans. Edward Dacres, London.

Machiavelli, Niccolò (1640). *Nicholas Machiavel's Prince*, trans. Edward Dacres, London.

Machiavelli, Niccolò (1995). *Il principe*, ed. Giorgio Inglese, Turin.

Machiavelli, Niccolò (2000). *Discorsi sopra la prima deca di Tito Livio*, ed. Corrado Vivanti, Turin.

Magirus, Johannes (1619). *Physiologiae Peripateticae Libri Sex*, London.

Maioraggio, Antonio (1591). *De Arte Rhetorica Libri Tres*, Venice.

Maitland, F. W. (2003). *State, Trust and Corporation*, ed. David Runciman and Magnus Ryan, Cambridge.

Mancinelli, Antonio (1493). *Carmen de figuris*, Venice.

Marbeck, John (1581). *A Booke Of Notes and Common places*, London.

Marlowe, Christopher (1998). 'Tamburlaine the Great Parts 1 and 2', ed. David Fuller in *The Complete Works of Christopher Marlowe*, 5 vols. (to date), Oxford, vol. 5, pp. 3–155.

Marsh, John (1642). *An Argument Or, Debate in Law*, London.

Marsilius of Padua (1928). *Defensor pacis*, ed. C. W. Previté-Orton, Cambridge.

Marsilius of Padua (2005). *The Defender of the Peace*, ed. and trans. Annabel Brett, Cambridge.

Maximes Unfolded (1643). London.

Mede, Joseph (1643). *The Key of the Revelation, searched and demonstrated*, London.

Mercator, Gerhard (1635). *Historia Mundi Or Mercators Atlas*, London.

Milton, John (1641). *The Reason of Church-governement Urg'd against Prelaty*, London.

[Milton, John] (1642). *An Apology Against a Pamphlet Call'd A Modest Confutation of the Animadversions upon the Remonstrant against Smectymnuus*, London.

[Milton, John] (1644). *Of Education*, London.

Milton, John (1991). 'The Tenure of Kings and Magistrates' in *John Milton: Political Writings*, ed. Martin Dzelzainis, Cambridge, pp. 1–48.

Milton, John (1998). *The Complete Poems*, ed. John Leonard, London.

Mirabellius, Domenicus, with Bartholomaeus Amantius and Franciscus Tortius (1600). *Polyanthea. hoc est Opus . . . sententiarum*, Lyon.

A Miracle: An Honest Broker (1643). London.

Mirandula, Octavianus (1598). *Illustrium Poetarum Flores . . . in locos communes digesti*, London.

More, Henry (1664). *A Modest Enquiry into the Mystery of Iniquity*, London.

More, Henry (1686). *A Brief Discourse of the Real Presence*, London.

Morton, Thomas (1619). *A Defence of the Innocencie of the Three Ceremonies of the Church of England*, London.

Morton, Thomas (1642). *Englands warning-piece: shewing the nature, danger, and ill effects of civill-warre*, London.

Munday, Anthony (1580). *Zelauto: The Fountaine of Fame*, London.

Munday, Anthony (1605). *The Triumphes of re-united Britania*, London.

Munster, Sebastian (1588). *Cosmographey*, Basel.

Nedham, Marchamont (1969). *The Case of the Commonwealth of England, Stated*, ed. Philip A. Knachel, Charlottesville, VA.

Norden, John (1593). *Speculum Britanniae*, n.p.

Norden, John (1620). *A Poore Mans Rest*, London.

Noue, François de la (1587). *The Politicke and Militarie Discourses*, London.

Obedience Active and Passive Due to the Supream Power (1643). Oxford.

Obsequies to the memorie of Mr Edward King (1638). Cambridge.

Oculus pastoralis (1966). Ed. Dora Franceschi in *Memorie dell'accademia delle scienze di Torino* 11, pp. 19–70.

Orfino da Lodi (1869). *De regimine et sapientia potestatis*, ed. Antonio Ceruti in *Miscellanea di storia italiana* 7, pp. 33–94.

[Osborne, Francis] (1652). *A Perswasive to A Mutuall Compliance Under The Present Government. Together with A Plea for A Free State compared with Monarchy*, Oxford.

Overton, Richard (1646). *An Arrow Against All Tyrants, And Tyrany*, n. p.

[Overton, Richard] (1647). *An Appeale From the degenerate Representative Body*, London.

Ovid (1565). *The Fyrst Fower Bookes of P. Ovidius Nasos worke intitled Metamorphosis*, London.

Ovid (1626). *Ovid's Metamorphosis Englished by G[eorge] S[andys]*, London.

Ovid (1924). 'Tristia' in *Tristia. Ex Ponto*, ed. and trans. Arthur L. Wheeler, London, pp. 2–260.

Ovid (1977–84). *Metamorphoses*, ed. and trans. Frank J. Miller, revised G. P. Gould, 2 vols., London.

[Parker, Henry] (1640). *The Case of Shipmony briefly discoursed*, London.

[Parker, Henry] (1642). *Observations upon some of his Majesties late Answers and Expresses*, London.

[Parker, Henry] (1643). *The Contra-Replicant, His Complaint To His Maiestie*, n. p.

[Parker, Henry] (1644). *Ius Populi*, London.

Peacham, Henry (1577). *The Garden of Eloquence Conteyning the Figures of Grammer and Rhetorick*, London.

Peacham, Henry (1593). *The Garden of Eloquence, … Corrected and augmented*, London.

Peacham, Henry [the younger] (1612). *Minerva Britanna or A Garden of Heroical Devises*, London.

Peacham, Henry [the younger] (1622). *The Compleat Gentleman, Fashioning him absolute in the most necessary & commendable Qualities concerning Minde or Bodie*, London.

Peile, John (1910–13). *Biographical Register of Christ's College 1505–1905*, 2 vols., Cambridge.

Pemberton, William (1619). *The Charge of God and the King To Judges and Magistrates, for execution of Justice*, London.

Perault, Guillaume (1587). *Summae Virtutum ac vitiorum*, Antwerp.

[Perkins, William] (1600). *A golden Chaine: Or, The Description of Theologie*, Cambridge.

Perrière, Guillaume de la (1553). *Morosophie*, Lyon.

[Persons, Robert] (1594). *A conference about the next succession to the crowne of Ingland*, Antwerp.

Philodemius, Eleutherius (1649). *The Armies Vindication*, London.

Plato (1484). 'De republica' in *Marsilii ficini florentini in libros Platonis ad Laurentium medicem Virum Magnanimum*, Florence, fos. 293v–376r.

Plato (1935). *The Republic, Books VI–X*, ed. and trans. Paul Shorey, London.

Playfere, Thomas (1603). *Hearts delight*, Cambridge.

Pliny (1952). *Natural History Books XXXIII–XXXV*, ed. and trans. H. Rackham, London.

Plutarch (1579). *The Lives of the Noble Grecians and Romanes, Compared*, trans. Thomas North, London.

Plutarch (1603). *The Philosophie, commonlie called The Morals*, trans. Philemon Holland, London.

[Ponet, John] (1556). *A Shorte Treatise of Politike Power*, Strasbourg.

Pownall, Thomas (1752). *Principles of Polity, Being the Grounds and Reasons of Civil Empire*, London.

Pownall, Thomas (1765). *The Administration of the Colonies*, 2nd edn, London.

Price, Richard (1991). *Political Writings*, ed. D. O. Thomas, Cambridge.

Prynne, William (1643). *The Soveraigne Power of Parliaments and Kingdomes: Divided into Foure Parts*, London.

Prynne, William (1649). *The Arraignment, Conviction and Condemnation of the Westminsterian-Juncto's Engagement*, n. p.

Pufendorf, Samuel (1672). *De iure naturae et gentium libri octo*, Lund.

Pufendorf, Samuel (1706). *Le droit de la nature et des gens*, trans. Jean Barbeyrac, Amsterdam.

Pufendorf, Samuel (1717). *Of the Law of Nature and Nations*, trans. Basil Kennet, 3rd edn, London.

[Puttenham, George] (1589). *The Arte of English Poesie*, London.

Pyne, John (1628). *The Heart of the King; and the King of the Heart*, London.

Quarles, Francis (1635). *Emblemes*, London.

Quintilian (2001). *Institutio oratoria*, ed. and trans. Donald A. Russell, 5 vols., London.

Rackham, H. (ed.) (1927). *Early Statutes of Christ's College, Cambridge*, Cambridge.

Raymond, John (1648). *An Itinerary Contayning A Voyage, Made through Italy, In the yeare 1646, and 1647*, London.

Reasons Why this Kingdome ought to adhere to the Parliament (1642). N. p.

A Remonstrance in Defence of the Lords and Commons in Parliament (1642). London.

Rhetorica ad Herennium (1954). Ed. and trans. Harry Caplan, London.

Ripa, Cesare (1611). *Iconologia*, Padua.

[Robinson, Henry] (1649). *A Short Discourse between Monarchical and Aristocratical Government*, London.

Robson, Simon (1577). *The courte of civill courtesie*, London.

Rohan, Henri, duc de (1640). *A Treatise of the Interest of the Princes and States of Christendome*, trans. H[enry] H[unt], Paris.

Rush, Anthony (1566). *A President for a Prince*, London.

Rutilius Lupus, Publius (1970). *De figuris sententiarum et elocutionis*, ed. Edward Brooks, Leiden.

Saint German, Christopher (1532). *The fyrst dialogue in Englisshe with newe additions*, London.

Salisbury, John of (1909). *Policraticus*, ed. C. C. J. Webb, 2 vols., Oxford.

Sallust (1557). *The Conspiracie of Catiline ... with the historye of Jugurth*, trans. Alexander Barclay, London.

Sallust (1608). *The two most worthy and notable histories*, trans. Thomas Heywood, London.

Sallust (1921). 'Bellum Catilinae' in *Sallust*, ed. and trans. J. C. Rolfe, London, pp. 2–128.

Sander, Nicholas (1567). *The Rocke of the Churche*, Louvain.

Sandys, Edwin (1605). *A relation of the state of religion and with what hopes and pollicies it hath beene framed, and is maintained in the severall states of these westerne parts of the world*, London.

Seneca (1620). *The Workes of Lucius Annaeus Seneca*, trans. Thomas Lodge, 2nd edn, London.

Seneca (1928). 'De clementia' in *Moral Essays*, ed. and trans. John W. Basore, 3 vols., London, vol. 1, pp. 356–446.

Seneca (1935). 'De beneficiis' in *Moral Essays*, ed. and trans. John W. Basore, 3 vols., London, vol. 3.

Shakespeare, William (1593). *Venus and Adonis*, London.

Shakespeare, William (1594). *Lucrece*, London.

Shakespeare, William (1986). *The Complete Works: Original-Spelling Edition*, gen. eds. Stanley Wells and Gary Taylor, Oxford.

Shakespeare, William (2003). *The Merchant of Venice*, ed. M. M. Mahood, Cambridge.

Sherry, Richard (1550). *A Treatise of Schemes and Tropes*, London.

Sidgwick, Henry (1897). *The Elements of Politics*, 2nd edn, London.

Sidney, Algernon (1990). *Discourses Concerning Government*, ed. Thomas G. West, Indianapolis, IN.

Sigonio, Carolo (1565). *De Arte Rhetorica Libri Tres*, Bologna.

Silvayn, Alexander (1596). *The Orator: Handling a hundred severall Discourses, in forme of Declamations*, trans. L[azarus] P[iot], London.

Sleiden, Johann (1556). *De Quatuor Summis Imperiis, Libri Tres*, n. p.

Smith, Thomas (1982). *De Republica Anglorum*, ed. Mary Dewar, Cambridge.

A Soveraigne Salve to Cure the Blind (1643). London.

[Spelman, John] (1643). *A View of a Printed Book Intituled Observations upon his Majesties Late Answers and Expresses*, Oxford.

The Statutes of Queen Elizabeth for the University of Cambridge (1838). London.

Stoughton, John (1640). *The Heavenly Conversation. And the Naturall Mans Condition*, London.

Sturm, Johannes (1538). *De Literarum Ludis Recte Aperiendis Liber*, Strasbourg.

Susenbrotus, Johannes (1562). *Epitome troporum ac schematum*, London.

Tacitus (1925). *The Histories, Books I–III*, ed. and trans. Clifford H. Moore, London.

Thomas, Thomas (1592). *Dictionarium tertio ... emendatum*, Cambridge.

Thucydides (1534). *L'Histoire de Thucydide*, trans. Claude de Seyssel, Lyon.

Thucydides (1550). *The hystory writtone by Thucidides*, trans. Thomas Nicolls, London.

Thucydides (1564). *De bello Peloponnesiaco libri octo, Iidem Latine ex interpretatione Lorenzo Valla, recognita Henricus Stephanus*, Geneva.

Thucydides (1629). *Eight Bookes of the Peloponnesian Warre*, trans. Thomas Hobbes, London.

Thucydides (2013). *The War of the Peloponnesians and the Athenians*, ed. and trans. Jeremy Mynott, Cambridge.

Touching the Fundamentall Lawes, Or Politique Constitution of this Kingdome (1643). London.

The unlimited prerogative of kings subverted (1642). London.

Urquhart, Thomas (1645). *The trissotetras: or, a most exquisite table for resolving all manner of triangles*, London.

Valerius, Cornelius (1571). *The Casket of Jewels: contaynynge a playne description of morall philosophie*, London.

Vattel, Emer de (1758). *Le Droit des Gens ou Principes de la Loi Naturelle Appliqués à la Conduite & aux Affaires des Nations & des Souverains*, London.

Vattel, Emer de (1760). *The Law of Nations; or Principles of the Law of Nature: applied to the conduct and affairs of nations and sovereigns*, London.

Venn, John (1897–1901). *Biographical History of Gonville and Caius College 1349–1897*, 3 vols., Cambridge.

Veron, John (1575). *A Dictionary in Latine and English ... newly corrected and enlarged ... By R[alph] W[addington]*, London.

Vicars, Thomas (1627). *Romphaiopheros The Sword-Bearer*, London.

Vindiciae, Contra Tyrannos (1579). Edinburgh.

Vindiciae contra Tyrannnos: A Defence of Liberty against Tyrants (1648). London.

Vindiciae, contra tyrannos (1994). Ed. and trans. George Garnett, Cambridge.

Virgil (1553). *The XIII Bukes of Eneados*, trans. Gawin Douglas, London.

Virgil (1632). *The XII Aeneids of Virgil*, trans. John Vicars, London.

Vives, Juan Luis (1913). *Vives: On Education*, trans. Foster Watson, Cambridge.

Vossius, Gerardus (1609). *Oratoriarum Institutionum Libri Sex*, 2nd edn, Dordrecht.

Vossius, Gerardus (1631). *Rhetorices Contractae, sive Partitionum Oratoriarum Libri V*, Oxford.

Vowel, John (1575). *The Order and usage of the keeping of a Parlement in England*, London.

Walker, George (1645). *A Sermon Preached before the Honourable House of Commons*, London.

[Ward, Richard] (1642). *The Vindication of the Parliament And their Proceedings*, London.

Ward, Robert (1639). *Animadversions of Warre*, London.

Webster, William (1613). *The plaine mans pilgrimage*, London.

Werdenhagen, Johann (1632). *Introductio Universalis in omnes Respublicas sive Politica Generalis*, Amsterdam.

West, William (1601). *The second part of Symboleography, newly corrected and amended*, London.

White, Francis (1624). *A Replie to Jesuit Fishers answere*, London.

Whitney, Geffrey (1586). *A Choice of Emblemes, and Other Devises*, Leiden.

Williams, Gryffith (1624). *Seven Goulden Candlestickes Houlding The Seaven Greatest Lights of Christian Religion*, London.

Williams, Gryffith (1643). *Vindiciae Regum; or, The grand rebellion*, Oxford.

Wilson, Thomas (1553). *The Arte of Rhetorique, for the use of all suche as are studious of Eloquence*, London.

Wither, George (1635). *A Collection of Emblemes, Ancient and Moderne*, London.

Woodhouse, A. S. P. (ed.) (1938). *Puritanism and Liberty: Being the Army Debates (1647–9)*, London.

Wordsworth, Christopher (1968). *Scholae Academicae: Some Account of Studies at the English Universities in the Eighteenth Century*, London.

Wyatt, Sir Thomas (1978). *The Complete Poems*, ed. R. A. Rebholz, London.

Secondary Sources

Abizadeh, Arash (2013). 'The Representation of Hobbesian Sovereignty: Leviathan as Mythology' in *Hobbes Today: Insights for the 21st Century*, ed. S. A. Lloyd, Cambridge, pp. 113–52.

Abizadeh, Arash (2016). 'Sovereign Jurisdiction, Territorial Rights, and Membership in Hobbes' in *The Oxford Handbook of Hobbes*, ed. A. P. Martinich and Kinch Hoekstra, Oxford, pp. 397–431.

Adamson, Sylvia, Gavin Alexander and Katrin Ettenhuber (eds.) (2007). *Renaissance Figures of Speech*, Cambridge.

Adelman, Janet (2008). *Blood Relations: Christian and Jew in The Merchant of Venice*, Chicago, IL.

Alexander, Gavin (2007). 'Prosopopoeia: The Speaking Figure' in *Renaissance Figures of Speech*, ed. Sylvia Adamson, Gavin Alexander and Katrin Ettenhuber, Cambridge, pp. 95–112.

Altman, R. C. (2009). 'Globalization in Retreat', *Foreign Affairs* 88, pp. 2–7.

Ankersmit, F. R. (2007). 'Political Representation and Political Experience: An Essay on Political Psychology', *Redescriptions* 11, pp. 21–4.

Artifoni, Enrico (1986). 'I podestà professionali e la fondazione retorica della politica comunale', *Quaderni storici* 63, pp. 687–719.

Artifoni, Enrico (1997). 'Sapientia Salomonis: une forme de présentation du savoir rhétorique chez les *dictatores* italiens' in *La Parole du prédicateur*, ed. Rosa Maria Dessì and Michel Lauwers, Nice, pp. 291–310.

Artifoni, Enrico (2012). 'Preistorie del bene comune' in *Il bene Comune: Forme di governo e gerarchie sociali nel basso medioevo* (Atti del XLVIII Convegno storico internazionale), Spoleto, pp. 63–87.

Asperen, Hanneke van (2013). 'The Sheltering Cloak: Images of Charity and Mercy in Fourteenth-Century Italy' in *Textile: Cloth and Culture* 11, pp. 262–81.

Astorga, Omar (2011). 'Hobbes's Concept of Multitude', *Hobbes Studies* 24, pp. 5–14.

Attie, Katherine B. (2008). 'Re-membering the Body Politic: Hobbes and the Construction of Civil Immortality', *English Literary History* 75, pp. 497–530.

Baker, Philip (2013). 'The Franchise Debate Revisited: The Levellers and the Army' in *The Nature of the English Revolution Revisited*, ed. Stephen Taylor and Grant Tapsell, Woodbridge, pp. 103–22.

Bakhtin, Mikhaïl (1970). *L'Oeuvre de François Rabelais et la culture populaire au Moyen Age et sous la Renaissance*, trans. Andrée Robel, Paris.

Baldwin, Geoffrey (2004). 'Reason of State and English Parliaments, 1610–42', *History of Political Thought* 25, pp. 620–41.

Baldwin, T. W. (1944). *William Shakspere's Small Latine & less Greeke*, 2 vols., Urbana, IL.

Baltrušaitis, Jurgis (1955). *Anamorphoses ou perspectives curieuses*, Paris.

Barber, C. L. (2012). *Shakespeare's Festive Comedy: A Study of Dramatic Form and its Relation to Social Custom*, new edn, Princeton, NJ.

Barber, Sarah (1998). *Regicide and Republicanism: Politics and Ethics in the English Revolution, 1646–1659*, Edinburgh.

Barker, Ernest (1957). 'Translator's Introduction' in Otto Gierke, *Natural Law and the Theory of Society 1500 to 1800*, trans. Ernest Barker, Boston, pp. ix–xci.

Bartelson, Jens (2001). *The Critique of the State*, Cambridge.

Barthas, Jérémie (2013). 'Un lapsus machiavélien: *Tenuto/temuto* dans le chapitre XVI du *Prince*' in *Renaissance studies in honor of Joseph Connors*, ed. M. Israëls and L. Waldman, 2 vols., Florence, vol. 2, pp. 83–90.

Bath, Michael (1994). *Speaking Pictures: English Emblem Books and Renaissance Culture*, London.

Baumgold, Deborah (1988). *Hobbes's Political Theory*, Cambridge.

Baumlin, Tita French (2001). 'Thomas Wilson' in *British Rhetoricians and Logicians 1500–1650*, First Series, ed. Edward A. Malone, Detroit, MI, pp. 282–306.

Beal, Peter (1987). *Index of English Literary Manuscripts*, vol. II: *1625–1700 Part I Behn-King*, London.

Beard, Mary (2014). *Laughter in Ancient Rome: On Joking, Tickling and Cracking Up*, Berkeley, CA.

Beaulac, Stéphanie (2003). 'Emer de Vattel and the Externalization of Sovereignty', *Journal of the History of International Law* 5, pp. 237–92.

Beaulac, Stéphanie (2004). *The Power of Language in the Making of International Law*, Leiden.

Beetham, David (1984). 'The Future of the Nation State' in *The Idea of the Modern State*, ed. Gregor McLennan, David Held and Stuart Hall, Milton Keynes, pp. 208–22.

Bejan, Teresa (2010). 'Teaching the *Leviathan*: Thomas Hobbes on Education', *The Oxford Review of Education* 36, pp. 607–26.

Bejan, Teresa (2017). *Mere Civility: Disagreement and the Limits of Toleration*, Cambridge, MA.

Bellamy, Richard (2003). 'Sovereignty, Post-Sovereignty and Pre-Sovereignty: Three Models of the State, Democracy and Rights within the EU' in *Sovereignty in Transition*, ed. Nigel Walker, Oxford, pp. 167–89.

Bello, Anna di (2010). *Sovranità e rappresentanza: la dottrina dello stato in Thomas Hobbes*, Naples.

Benner, Erica (2009). *Machiavelli's Ethics*, Princeton, NJ.

Benner, Erica (2013). *Machiavelli's Prince: A New Reading*, Oxford.

Benner, Erica (2014). 'Machiavelli's Ironies: The Language of Praise and Blame in *The Prince*', *Social Research* 81, pp. 61–84.

Benston, Alice N. (1991). 'Portia, the Law, and the Tripartite Structure of *The Merchant of Venice*' in *The Merchant of Venice: Critical Essays*, ed. Thomas Wheeler, New York, NY, pp. 163–94.

Berger, Susanna (2017). *The Art of Philosophy: Visual Thinking in Europe from the Late Renaissance to the Early Enlightenment*, Princeton, NJ.

Bevir, Mark (2008). 'What Is Genealogy', *Journal of the Philosophy of History* 2, pp. 263–75.

Billelo, Thomas C. (2007). 'Accomplished with What She Lacks: Law, Equity, and Portia's Con' in *The Law in Shakespeare*, ed. Constance Jordan and Karen Cunningham, Basingstoke, pp. 109–26.

Black, Robert (2001). *Humanism and Education in Medieval and Renaissance Italy*, Cambridge.

Blythe, James M. (1992). *Ideal Government and the Mixed Constitution in the Middle Ages*, Princeton, NJ.

Bobbitt, Philip (2013). *The Garments of Court and Palace: Machiavelli and the World That He Made*, New York, NY.

Bonomi, Patricia U. (1998). *The Lord Cornbury Scandal: The Politics of Reputation in British America*, Chapel Hill, NC.

Borrelli, Gianfranco (1993). *Ragion di stato e Leviatano*, Bologna.

Borrelli, Gianfranco (2000). *Non Far Novità: Alle radici della cultura italiana della conservazione politica*, Naples.

Borrelli, Gianfranco (2009). 'Hobbes lettore e interprete di Machiavelli: *contentment* e *contention*' in *Anglo-American Faces of Machiavelli*, ed. Alessandro Arienzo and Gianfranco Borrelli, Monza, pp. 95–148.

Boucher, David (1998). *Political Theories of International Relations*, Oxford.

Boucher, David and Andrew Vincent (2000). *British Idealism and Political Theory*, Edinburgh.

Boucheron, Patrick (2013). *Conjurer la peur. Sienne, 1338. Essai sur la force politique des images*, Paris.

Boutry, Monique (2004). 'Introduction' in Petrus Cantor, *Verbum Abbreviatum*, Turnhout, pp. vii–lxxiv.

Bowen, Karen L. and Dirk Imhof (2008). *Christopher Plantin and Engraved Book Illustrations in Sixteenth-Century Europe*, Cambridge.

Bowsky, William M. (1981). *A Medieval Italian Commune: Siena under the Nine, 1287–1355*, London.

Boyer, Marjorie Nice (1964). 'The Bridgebuilding Brotherhoods', *Speculum* 39, pp. 635–50.

Braddick, Michael J. (2000). *State Formation in Early Modern England c.1550–1700*, Cambridge.

Brandt, Reinhard (1987). 'Das Titelblatt des Leviathan', *Leviathan: Zeitschrift für Sozialwissenschaft* 15, pp. 164–86.

Bredekamp, Horst (2003). *Stratégies visuelles de Thomas Hobbes: Le Léviathan, archétype de l'État moderne: Illustrations des oeuvres et portraits*, trans. Denise Modigliani, Paris.

Bredekamp, Horst (2016). *Der Behemoth: Metamorphosen des Anti-Leviathan*, Berlin.

Brett, Annabel (1997). *Liberty, Right and Nature: Individual Rights in Later Scholastic Thought*, Cambridge.

Brett, Annabel (2002). 'Natural Right and Civil Community: The Civil Philosophy of Hugo Grotius', *The Historical Journal* 45, pp. 31–51.

Brett, Annabel (2006). 'Scholastic Political Thought and the Modern Concept of the State' in *Rethinking the Foundations of Modern Political Thought*, ed. Annabel Brett and James Tully with Holly Hamilton-Bleakley, Cambridge, pp. 130–48.

Brett, Annabel (2010). '"The matter, Forme, and Power of a Common-wealth": Thomas Hobbes and Late Renaissance Commentary on Aristotle's *Politics*', *Hobbes Studies* 23, pp. 72–102.

Brett, Annabel (2011). *Changes of State: Nature and the Limits of the City in Early Modern Natural Law*, Princeton, NJ.

Brito Vieira, Mónica (2009). *The Elements of Representation in Hobbes: Aesthetics, Theatre, Law, and Theology in the Construction of Hobbes's Theory of the State*, Leiden.

Brito Vieira, Mónica and David Runciman (2008). *Representation*, Cambridge.

Brown, John Russell (1955). 'Critical Introduction' in *The Merchant of Venice*, The Arden Shakespeare, London, pp. xxxvii–lviii.

Brown, Keith (1978). 'The Artist of the *Leviathan* Title-Page', *British Library Journal* 4, pp. 24–36.

Bullough, Geoffrey (1957–75). *Narrative and Dramatic Sources of Shakespeare*, 8 vols., London.

Burchell, David (1999). 'The Disciplined Citizen: Thomas Hobbes's Neostoicism and the Critique of Classical Citizenship', *Australian Journal of Politics and History* 45, pp. 506–24.

Burgess, Glenn (1986). 'Usurpation, Obligation and Obedience in the Thought of the Engagement Controversy', *The Historical Journal* 29, pp. 515–36.

Burgess, Glenn (1990). 'Contexts for the Writing and Publication of Hobbes's *Leviathan*', *History of Political Thought* 11, pp. 675–702.

Burke, Peter (1993). *The Art of Conversation*, Cambridge.

Burns, J. H. (1989). 'Bentham and Blackstone: A Lifetime's Dialectic', *Utilitas: A Journal of Utilitarian Studies* 1, pp. 22–40.

Cairns, John W. (1984). 'Blackstone, an English Institutionalist: Legal Literature and the Rise of the Nation State', *Oxford Journal of Legal Studies* 4, pp. 318–60.

Caney, Simon (2005). *Justice Beyond Borders: A Global Political Theory*, Oxford.

Canfora, Luciano (1997). 'Tucidide e Machiavelli', *Rinascimento* 37, pp. 29–44.

Canning, Joseph (1982). 'Ideas of the State in Thirteenth and Fourteenth-Century Commentators on the Roman Law', *Transactions of the Royal Historical Society* 5th series, 33, pp. 1–27.

Canning, Joseph (1987). *The Political Thought of Baldus de Ubaldis*, Cambridge.

Caplan, Harry (1954). 'Introduction' in *Rhetorica ad Herennium*, London, pp. vii–xl.

Carlyle, R. W. and A. J. (1932). *A History of Mediaeval Political Theory in the West*, 6 vols., London, vol. 2.

Carpi, Daniela (2005). 'Law, Discretion, Equity in *The Merchant of Venice* and *Measure for Measure*', *Cardozo Law Review* 26, pp. 2317–29.

Catanzaro, Andrea (2015). *Hobbes e Omero: Una traduzione 'politica'?*, Florence.

Chambers, Mortimer (2008). *Valla's Translation of Thucydides in Vat. Lat. 1801*, Vatican City.

Champion, Justin (2010). 'Decoding the *Leviathan*: Doing the History of Ideas through Images, 1651–1714' in *Printed Images in Early Modern Britain*, ed. Michael Hunter, Farnham, pp. 155–75.

Chernaik, Warren (2011). *The Myth of Rome in Shakespeare and his Contemporaries*, Cambridge.

Chwaszcza, Christine (2012). 'The Seat of Sovereignty: Hobbes on the Artificial Person of the Commonwealth or State', *Hobbes Studies* 25, pp. 132–42.

Clark, J. Willis and Arthur Gray (1921). *Old Plans of Cambridge 1574 to 1798*, Cambridge.

Clements, Robert J. (1960). *Picta Poesis: Literary and Humanistic Theory in Renaissance Emblem Books*, Rome.

Coffey, John (2006). *John Goodwin and the Puritan Revolution: Religion and Intellectual Change in Seventeenth-Century England*, Woodbridge.

Cohen, G. A. (1995). *Self-Ownership, Freedom and Equality*, Oxford.

Colley, John S. (1980). 'Launcelot, Jacob and Esau: Old and New Law in *The Merchant of Venice*', *Yearbook of English Studies* 10, pp. 181–9.

Collins, James B. (2009). *The State in Early Modern France*, 2nd edn, Cambridge.

Condren, Conal (1994). *The Language of Politics in Seventeenth-Century England*, London.

Connell, William J. (2015). *Machiavelli nel Rinascimento italiano*, Milan.

Connolly, Joy (2007). *The State of Speech: Rhetoric and Political Thought in Ancient Rome*, Princeton, NJ.

Connolly, Joy (2009). 'The Politics of Rhetorical Education' in *The Cambridge Companion to Ancient Rhetoric*, ed. Erik Gunderson, Cambridge, pp. 126–41.

Cooper, Julie E. (2010). 'Vainglory, Modesty and Political Agency in the Political Theory of Thomas Hobbes', *The Review of Politics* 72, pp. 241–69.

Corbett, Margery and Ronald Lightbown (1979). *The Comely Frontispiece: The Emblematic Title-Page in England 1550–1660*, London.

Corrigan, Philip and Derek Sayer (1985). *The Great Arch: English State Formation as Cultural Revolution*, Oxford.

Costa, Pietro (1999). *Civitas: storia della cittadinanza in Europa, I: Dalla civiltà comunale al settecento*, Rome-Bari.

Costello, William T. (1958). *The Scholastic Curriculum at Early Seventeenth-Century Cambridge*, Cambridge, MA.

Cox, Virginia (1989). 'Rhetoric and Politics in Tasso's *Nifo*', *Studi Secenteschi* 30, pp. 3–98.

Cox, Virginia (1997). 'Machiavelli and the *Rhetorica ad Herennium*: Deliberative Rhetoric in *The Prince*', *Sixteenth Century Journal* 28, pp. 1109–41.

Cox, Virginia (2010). 'Rhetoric and Ethics in Machiavelli' in *The Cambridge Companion to Machiavelli*, ed. John Najemy, Cambridge, pp. 173–89.

Crane, Mary Thomas (1993). *Framing Authority: Sayings, Self, and Society in Sixteenth-Century England*, Princeton, NJ.

Crawford, Patricia (2001). '"The Poorest She": Women and Citizenship in Early Modern England' in *The Putney Debates of 1647: The Army, the Levellers and the English State*, ed. Michael Mendle, Cambridge, pp. 197–218.

Cressy, David (1975). *Education in Tudor and Stuart England*, London.

Creveld, Martin van (1999). *The Rise and Decline of the State*, Cambridge.

Crignon, Philippe (2012). *De l'incarnation à la représentation: l'ontologie politique de Thomas Hobbes*, Paris.

Cromartie, Alan (1999). 'The Constitutionalist Revolution: The Transformation of Political Culture in Early Stuart England', *Past and Present* 163, pp. 76–120.

Cromartie, Alan (2016). 'Parliamentary Sovereignty, Popular Sovereignty, and Henry Parker's Adjudicative Standpoint' in *Popular Sovereignty in Historical Perspective*, ed. Richard Bourke and Quentin Skinner, Cambridge, pp. 142–63.

Cross, M. Claire (1953). 'The Free Grammar School of Leicester', *Department of English Local History Occasional Papers No. 4* [University College of Leicester], Leicester.

Cunningham, John and Stephen Slimp (2002). 'The Less into the Greater: Emblem, Analogue, and Deification in *The Merchant of Venice*' in *The Merchant of Venice: New Critical Essays*, ed. John W. Mahon and Ellen Macleod Mahon, London, pp. 225–82.

Curtis, Cathy (2002). 'Richard Pace's *De fructu* and Early Tudor Pedagogy' in *Reassessing Tudor Humanism*, ed. Jonathan Woolfson, Basingstoke, pp. 43–77.

Cust, Richard (2015). 'The Collapse of Royal Power in England, 1637–1642' in *The Oxford Handbook of the English Revolution*, ed. Michael Braddick, Oxford, pp. 60–76.

Daly, James (1971). 'John Bramhall and the Theoretical Problems of Royalist Moderation', *The Journal of British Studies* 11, pp. 26–44.

Danson, Lawrence (1978). *The Harmonies of The Merchant of Venice*, New Haven, CT.

Dauber, Noah (2016). *State and Commonwealth: The Theory of the State in Early Modern England, 1549–1640*, Princeton, NJ.

Dawson, Anthony B. and Gretchen E. Minton (2008). 'Introduction' and 'Appendix 2' in *Timon of Athens*, The Arden Shakespeare, London, pp. 1–145 and 401–7.

Delwaide, Jacobus (2011). 'The Return of the State?', *European Review* 19, pp. 69–91.

Denzer, Horst (1972). *Moralphilosophie und Naturrecht bei Samuel Pufendorf*, Munich.

Dietz, Mary G. (1990). 'Hobbes's Subject as Citizen' in *Thomas Hobbes and Political Theory*, ed. Mary G. Dietz, Lawrence, KS, pp. 91–119.

Donawerth, Jane (1984). *Shakespeare and the Sixteenth-Century Study of Language*, Chicago, IL.

Dondaine, Antoine (1948). 'Guillaume Peyraut: Vie et Oeuvres', *Archivum Fratrum Praedicatorum* 18, pp. 162–236.

Douglas, Robin (2014). 'The Body Politic "Is a Fictitious Body"', *Hobbes Studies* 27, pp. 126–47.

Dow, Douglas C. (2008). 'Decline as a Form of Conceptual Change: Some Considerations on the Loss of the Legal Person', *Contributions to the History of Concepts* 4, pp. 1–26.

Drakakis, John (2010). 'Introduction' to *The Merchant of Venice*, The Arden Shakespeare, London, pp. 1–159.

Dunn, John (1969). *The Political Thought of John Locke: An Historical Account of the Argument of the 'Two Treatises of Government'*, Cambridge.

Dyson, Kenneth H. F. (1980). *The State Tradition in Western Europe*, Oxford.

Elden, Stuart (2013). *The Birth of Territory*, Chicago, IL.

Elias, Norbert (1994). *The Civilising Process: The History of Manners and State formation and Civilisation*, trans. Edmund Jephcott, Oxford.

Eschmann, Th. (1946). 'Studies on the Notion of Society in St Thomas Aquinas', *Mediaeval Studies* 8, pp. 1–42.

Esposito, Roberto (2012). *Third Person: Politics of Life and Philosophy of the Impersonal*, Cambridge.

Evans, G. R. (1983). *Alan of Lille: The Frontiers of Theology in the Later Twelfth Century*, Cambridge.

Evans, Michael (1982). 'An Illustrated Fragment of Peraldus's *Summa* of Vice: Harleian MS 3244', *Journal of the Warburg and Courtauld Institutes* 45, pp. 14–68.

Evrigenis, Ioannis D. (2014). *Images of Anarchy: The Rhetoric and Science in Hobbes's State of Nature*, Cambridge.

Falk, Francisca (2011). 'Hobbes' *Leviathan* und die aus dem Blick gefallenen Schnabelmasken', *Leviathan* 39, pp. 247–66.

Farneti, Roberto (2000). 'Una civile conversazione. Una proposta di etica italiana', *Iride* 3, pp. 489–508.

Farneti, Roberto (2001). 'The "Mythical Foundation" of the State: *Leviathan* in Emblematic Context', *Pacific Philosophical Quarterly* 82, pp. 362–82.

Feingold, Mordechai (1997). 'The Humanities' in *The History of the University of Oxford*, vol. 4: *Seventeenth-Century Oxford*, ed. Nicholas Tyacke, Oxford, pp. 209–357.

Ferente, Serena (2013). 'The Liberty of Italian City-States' in *Freedom and the Construction of Europe, vol.* 1: *Religious and Constitutional Liberties*, ed. Quentin Skinner and Martin van Gelderen, Cambridge, pp. 157–75.

Ferente, Serena (2016). 'Popolo and Law: Late Medieval Sovereignty in Marsilius and the Jurists' in *Popular Sovereignty in Historical Perspective*, ed. Richard Bourke and Quentin Skinner, Cambridge, pp. 96–114.

Fletcher, Harris F. (1956–61). *The Intellectual Development of John Milton*, 2 vols., Urbana, IL.

Flood, John (2008). '"It droppeth as the gentle rain": Isaiah 45:8 and *The Merchant of Venice* IV. 1. 181', *Notes and Queries* 253, pp. 176–7.

Foisneau, Luc (2010). 'Elements of Fiction in Hobbes's System of Philosophy' in *Fiction and the Frontiers of Knowledge in Europe, 1500–1800*, ed. Richard Scholar and Alexis Tadié, Farnham, pp. 71–85.

Folena, Gianfranco (1959). '"Parlamenti" podestarili di Giovanni da Viterbo', *Lingua Nostra* 20, pp. 97–105.

Fontano, Benedetto (2003). 'Sallust and the Politics of Machiavelli', *History of Political Thought* 24, pp. 86–108.

Forsyth, Murray (1991). 'State', in *The Blackwell Encyclopaedia of Political Thought*, ed. David Miller, revised edn, Oxford, pp. 503–6.

Fortier, Mark (2005). *The Culture of Equity in Early Modern England*, Aldershot.

Foucault, Michel (1980). 'Truth and Power' in *Power/Knowledge: Selected Interviews and Other Writings 1972–1977*, ed. Colin Gordon, Brighton, pp. 109–33.

Foxley, Rachel (2013). *The Levellers: Radical Political Thought in the English Revolution*, Manchester.

Franceschi, Dora (1966). Introduction to *Oculus pastoralis* in *Memorie dell'accademia delle scienze di Torino* 11, pp. 19–70.

Frank, Joseph (1961). *The Beginnings of the English Newspaper 1620–1660*, Cambridge, MA.

Franklin, Julian H. (1973). *Jean Bodin and the Rise of Absolutist Theory*, Cambridge.

Franklin, Julian H. (1991). 'Sovereignty and the Mixed Constitution: Bodin and his Critics' in *The Cambridge History of Political Thought 1450–1700*, ed. J. H. Burns and Mark Goldie, Cambridge, pp. 298–328.

Freedman, Joseph S. (1997). 'The Career and Writings of Bartholomew Keckermann', *Proceedings of the American Philosophical Society* 141, pp. 305–64.

Friedeburg, Robert von (2016). *Luther's Legacy: The Thirty Years War and the Modern Notion of 'State' in the Empire, 1530s to 1790s*, Cambridge.

Fryde, E. B. (1983). *Humanism and Renaissance Historiography*, London.

Gamboni, Dario (2005). 'Composing the Body Politic: Composite Images and Political Representation, 1651–2004' in *Making Things Public: Atmospheres of Democracy*, ed. Bruno Latour and Peter Weibel, Cambridge, MA, pp. 162–95.

Garnett, George (1994). 'Editor's Introduction' in *Vindiciae, contra tyrannos*, ed. and trans. George Garnett, Cambridge, pp. xix–lxxvi.

Garver, Eugene (2003). 'After *Virtù*: Rhetoric, Prudence and Moral Pluralism in Machiavelli' in *Prudence: Classical Virtue, Postmodern Practice*, ed. Robert Hariman, University Park, PA, pp. 67–97.

Gauthier, David P. (1969). *The Logic of Leviathan: The Moral and Political Theory of Thomas Hobbes*, Oxford.

Gay, Penny (2008). *The Cambridge Introduction to Shakespeare's Comedies*, Cambridge.

Getzler, Joshua (2008). 'Plural Ownership, Funds, and the Aggregation of Wills', *Theoretical Inquiries in Law* 10, pp. 241–70.

Geuna, Marco (2006). 'Skinner, Pre-Humanist Rhetorical Culture and Machiavelli' in *Rethinking the Foundations of Modern Political Thought*, ed. Annabel Brett and James Tully with Holly Hamilton-Bleakley, Cambridge, pp. 50–73.

Geuss, Raymond (1999). 'Nietzsche and Genealogy' in *Morality, Culture, and History: Essays on German Philosophy*, Cambridge, pp. 1–28.

Geuss, Raymond (2005). 'Genealogy as Critique' in *Outside Ethics*, Princeton, NJ, pp. 153–60.

Gillet, Pierre (1927). *La Personnalité juridique en droit ecclésiastique*, Malines.

Gilpin, Robert (1986). 'The Richness of the Tradition of Political Realism' in *Neorealism and its Critics*, ed. Robert Keohane, New York, NY, pp. 301–21.

Ginsburg, Carlo (2015). *Paura reverenza terrore: Cinque saggi di iconografia politica*, Milan.

Glaziou, Yves (1993). *Hobbes en France au XVIIIe siècle*, Paris.

Glover, Samuel Dennis (1999). 'The Putney Debates: Popular versus Elitist Republicanism', *Past and Present* 164, pp. 47–80.

Goldie, Mark (2006). 'The Context of *The Foundations*' in *Rethinking the Foundations of Modern Political Thought*, ed. Annabel Brett and James Tully with Holly Hamilton-Bleakley, Cambridge, pp. 3–19.

Goldie, Mark (2011). 'Absolutism' in *The Oxford Handbook of the History of Political Philosophy*, ed. George Klosko, Oxford, pp. 282–95.

Goldsmith, M. M. (1990). 'Hobbes's Ambiguous Politics', *History of Political Thought* 11, pp. 639–73.

Goldstein, Carl (2012). *Print Culture in Early Modern France: Abraham Bosse and the Purposes of Print*, Cambridge.

Green, Ian (2009). *Humanism and Protestantism in Early Modern English Education*, Farnham.

Green, Lawrence D. and James J. Murphy (2006). *Renaissance Rhetoric Short-Title Catalogue 1460–1700*, 2nd edn, Aldershot.

Green, Leslie (1988). *The Authority of the State*, Oxford.

Greenblatt, Stephen (1980). *Renaissance Self-Fashioning: From More to Shakespeare*, Chicago, IL.

Greene, Jack P. (2010). *The Constitutional Origins of the American Revolution*, Cambridge.

Grendler, Paul F. (1989). *Schooling in Renaissance Italy*, Baltimore, MD.

Grimm, Dieter (2015). *Sovereignty*, trans. Belinda Cooper, New York, NY.

Gross, Kenneth (2006). *Shylock Is Shakespeare*, Chicago, IL.

Hackenbracht, Ryan (2014). 'Hobbes's Hebraism and the Last Judgement in *Leviathan*' in *Identities in Early Modern English Writing: Religion, Gender, Nation*, ed. Lorna Fitzsimmons, Turnhout, pp. 85–115.

Haley, K. H. D. (1968). *The First Earl of Shaftesbury*, Oxford.

Halio, Jay L. (1993). 'Portia: Shakespeare's Matlock?', *Cardozo Studies in Law and Literature* 5, pp. 57–64.

Halldenius, Lena (2002). 'Locke and the Non-Arbitrary', *European Journal of Political Theory* 2, pp. 261–79.

Hamel, Christopher (2011). *L'Esprit républicain: droits naturels et vertu civique chez Algernon Sidney*, Paris.

Hampsher-Monk, Iain (1976). 'The Political Theory of the Levellers: Putney, Property and Professor Macpherson', *Political Studies* 24, pp. 397–422.

Hankins, James (2010). 'Exclusivist Republicanism and the Non-Monarchical Republic', *Political Theory* 38, pp. 452–82.

Harmon, A. G. (2004). *Eternal Bonds, True Contracts: Law and Nature in Shakespeare's Problem Plays*, Albany, NY.

Harris, Ian (2007). '"Rien qu'un serviteur éminent de l'État": la royauté et le corps politique pendant la guerre civile anglaise' in *Monarchie et république au XVIIe siècle*, ed. Yves Charles Zarka, Paris, pp. 127–67.

Heawood, Edward (1930). 'Papers Used in England after 1600, I: The Seventeenth Century to c.1680', *The Library*, 4th Series, 11, pp. 263–99.

Heawood, Edward (1950). *Watermarks Mainly of the 17th and 18th Centuries*, Monumenta Chartae Papyraceae I, Hilversum.

Held, David (1984). 'Central Perspectives on the Modern State' in *The Idea of the Modern State*, ed. Gregor McLennan, David Held and Stuart Hall, Milton Keynes, pp. 29–79.

Herrick, Marvin J. (1964). *Comic Theory in the Sixteenth Century*, Urbana, IL.

Hertz, Noreena (2001). *The Silent Takeover: Global Capitalism and the Death of Democracy*, London.

Hexter, J. H. (ed.) (1992). *Parliament and Liberty from the Reign of Elizabeth to the English Civil War*, Princeton, NJ.

Heyd, David (1982). 'The Place of Laughter in Hobbes's Theory of the Emotions', *Journal of the History of Ideas* 43, pp. 285–95.

Heywood, James and Thomas Wright (1854). *Cambridge University Transactions during the Puritan Controversies of the 16th and 17th Centuries*, 2 vols., London.

Hill, Christopher (1986). *The Collected Essays of Christopher Hill*, vol. 3: *People and Ideas in 17th Century England*, Brighton.

Hind, Arthur M. (1952–64). *Engraving in England in the Sixteenth and Seventeenth Centuries*, 3 vols., Cambridge.

Hindle, Steve (2000). *The State and Social Change in Early Modern England, c.1550–1640*, Houndmills.

Hirschfield, Heather (2006). '"We all expect a gentle answer, Jew": *The Merchant of Venice* and the Psychotheology of Conversion', *English Literary History* 73, pp. 61–81.

Hoekstra, Kinch (2003). 'The *De Facto* Turn in Hobbes's Political Philosophy' in *Leviathan after 350 Years*, ed. Tom Sorell and Luc Foisneau, Oxford, pp. 33–73.

Hoekstra, Kinch (2006). 'A Lion in the House: Hobbes and Democracy' in *Rethinking the Foundations of Modern Political Thought*, ed. Annabel Brett and James Tully with Holly Hamilton-Bleakley, Cambridge, pp. 191–218.

Hoekstra, Kinch (2013a). 'Hobbesian Equality' in *Hobbes Today: Insights for the 21st Century*, ed. S. A. Lloyd, Cambridge, pp. 76–112.

Hoekstra, Kinch (2013b) 'Early Modern Absolutism and Constitutionalism', *Cardozo Law Review* 34, pp. 1079–98.

Hoekstra, Kinch (2015). '*Leviathan* and its Intellectual Context', *Journal of the History of Ideas* 76, pp. 237–57.

Hofmann, Hasso (1974). *Repräsentation: Studien zur Wort- und Begriffsgeschichte von der Antike bis ins 19. Jahrhundert*, Berlin.

Holderness, Graham (1993). *The Merchant of Venice*, Harmondsworth.

Holland, Ben (2012). 'Pufendorf's Theory of Facultative Sovereignty: On the Configuration of the Soul of the State', *History of Political Thought* 33, pp. 427–54.

Holloway, Carson (2007). 'Shakespeare's "Coriolanus" and Aristotle's Great-Souled Man', *Review of Politics* 69, pp. 353–74.

Holmer, Joan O. (1995). *The Merchant of Venice: Choice, Hazard and Consequence*, Basingstoke.

Holmes, Peter (1982). *Resistance and Compromise: The Political Thought of the Elizabethan Catholics*, Cambridge.

Honohan, Iseult (2002). *Civic Republicanism*, London.

Hood Phillips, Owen (1972). *Shakespeare and the Lawyers*, London.

Höpfl, Harro (2004). *Jesuit Political Thought: The Society of Jesus and the State, c.1540–1630*, Cambridge.

Houliston, Victor (2007). *Catholic Resistance in Elizabethan England: Robert Persons and Jesuit Polemic, 1580–1610*, Aldershot.

Houston, Alan Craig (1991). *Algernon Sidney and the Republican Heritage in England and America*, Princeton, NJ.

Howell, Wilbur S. (1956). *Logic and Rhetoric in England, 1500–1700*, Princeton, NJ.

Hughes, Ann (2012). *Gender in the English Revolution*, London.

Hunter, Ian (2001). *Rival Enlightenments: Civil and Metaphysical Philosophy in Early Modern Germany*, Cambridge.

Hunter, Ian (2010). 'Vattel's Law of Nations: Diplomatic Casuistry for the Protestant Nation', *Grotiana* 31, pp. 108–40.

Ihalainen, Pasi (2009). 'Towards an Immortal Political Body: The State Machine in Eighteenth–Century English Political Discourse', *Contributions to the History of Concepts* 5, pp. 4–47.

Iori, Luca (2015). *Thucydides Anglicus: gli Eight Bookes di Thomas Hobbes e la ricezione inglese delle storie di Tucicide (1450–1642)*, Rome.

Jackson, Patrick T. (2004). 'Hegel's House, or "People Are States Too"', *Review of International Studies* 30, pp. 281–7.

James, Susan (1997). *Passion and Action: The Emotions in Seventeenth-Century Philosophy*, Oxford.

Jaume, Lucien (1983). 'La Théorie de la "personne fictive" dans le *Léviathan* de Hobbes', *Revue française de science politique* 33, pp. 1009–35.

Jaume, Lucien (1986). *Hobbes et l'etat représentatif moderne*, Paris.

Javitch, Daniel (1972). 'Poetry and Court Conduct: Puttenham's *Arte of English Poesie* in the Light of Castiglione's *Cortegiano*', *Modern Language Notes* 87, pp. 865–82.

Join-Lambert, Sophie and Maxime Préaud (eds.) (2004). *Abraham Bosse savant graveur*, Paris.

Jones, Colin (2011). 'French Crossings, II: Laughing Over Boundaries', *Transactions of the Royal Historical Society* 21, pp. 1–38.

Jones, Howard (1998). *Master Tully: Cicero in Tudor England*, Nieuwkoop.

Jones, J. R. (1961). *The First Whigs: The Politics of the Exclusion Crisis 1678–1683*, Oxford.

Jones, Philip (1997). *The Italian City-State: From Commune to Signoria*, Oxford.

Jordan, Bill (1985). *The State: Authority and Autonomy*, Oxford.

Jouannet, Emmanuelle (1998). *Emer de Vattel et l'émergence doctrinale du droit international classique*, Paris.

Jowett, John (2004). 'Introduction' in *The Life of Timon of Athens*, The Oxford Shakespeare, Oxford, pp. 1–153.

Judson, Margaret A. (1988). *The Crisis of the Constitution: An Essay in Constitutional and Political Thought in England, 1603–1645*, Foreword by J. H. Hexter, New Brunswick, NJ.

Jue, Jeffrey K. (2006). *Heaven Upon Earth: Joseph Mede (1586–1638) and the Legacy of Millenarianism*, Dordrecht.

Julius, Anthony (2010). *Trials of the Diaspora: A History of Anti-Semitism in England*, Oxford.

Kahn, Coppélia (1997). *Roman Shakespeare: Warriors, Wounds, and Women*, London.

Kahn, Victoria (1985). *Rhetoric, Prudence, and Skepticism in the Renaissance*, Ithaca, NY.

Kahn, Victoria (1994). *Machiavellian Rhetoric: From the Counter-Revolution to Milton*, Princeton, NJ.

Kantorowicz, Ernst H. (1957). *The King's Two Bodies: A Study in Mediaeval Political Theology*, Princeton, NJ.

Kapust, Daniel (2007). 'Cato's Virtues and *The Prince*: Reading Sallust's *War with Catiline* with Machiavelli's *The Prince*', *History of Political Thought* 28, pp. 433–48.

Keeton, George W. (1967). *Shakespeare's Legal and Political Background*, London.

Kemp, Martin (1990). *The Science of Art*, New Haven, CT.

Klein, Karl (2001). 'Introduction' in *Timon of Athens*, The New Cambridge Shakespeare, Cambridge, pp. 1–66.

Klein, William E. (2007). 'Machiavelli, Thucydides, and the Anglo-American Tradition' in *Seeking Real Truths: Multidisciplinary Perspectives on Machiavelli*, ed. Patricia Vilches and Gerald Seaman, Boston, MA, pp. 389–420.

Knight, W. Nicholas (1974). 'Equity, *The Merchant of Venice*, and William Lambarde', *Shakespeare Survey* 27, pp. 93–104.

Knights, Mark (1994). *Politics and Opinion in Crisis, 1678–81*, Cambridge.

Kornstein, Daniel J. (1994). *Kill All the Lawyers? Shakespeare's Legal Appeal*, Princeton, NJ.

Kramer, Mathew (2003). *The Quality of Freedom*, Oxford.

Krasner, Stephen D. (2010). 'The Durability of Organised Hypocrisy' in *Sovereignty in Fragments: The Past, Present and Future of a Contested Concept*, ed. Hent Kalmo and Quentin Skinner, Cambridge, pp. 96–113.

Kristeller, Paul Oskar (1961). *Renaissance Thought: The Classic, Scholastic, and Humanist Strains*, New York, NY.

Kristiansson, Magnus and Johan Tralau (2014). 'Hobbes's Hidden Monster: A New Interpretation of the Frontispiece of *Leviathan*', *European Journal of Political Theory* 13, pp. 299–320.

Krupp, Tyler (2008). 'Genealogy as Critique?' *Journal of the Philosophy of History* 2, pp. 315–37.

Larner, John (1971). *Culture and Society in Italy, 1290–1420*, London.

Laslett, Peter (1988). Introduction to John Locke, *Two Treatises of Government*, Student edition, Cambridge, pp. 3–133.

Lee, Daniel (2016). *Popular Sovereignty in Early Modern Constitutional Thought*, Oxford.

LeFanu, W. R. (1959–64). 'Thomas Vautrollier, Printer and Bookseller', *Proceedings of the Huguenot Society of London* 20, pp. 12–25.

Leijenhorst, Cees (1998). *Hobbes and the Aristotelians: The Aristotelian Setting of Thomas Hobbes's Natural Philosophy*, Utrecht.

Leimberg, Inge (2011). '*What may words say … ?*' A Reading of The Merchant of Venice*, Lanham, MD.

Levack, Brian P. (1973). *The Civil Lawyers in England 1603–1641: A Political Study*, Oxford.

Levack, Brian P. (1981). 'The English Civilians, 1500–1750' in *Lawyers in Early Modern Europe and America*, ed. Wilfred Prest, London, pp. 108–28.

Levack, Brian P. (1988). 'Law and Ideology: The Civil Law and Theories of Absolutism in Elizabethan and Jacobean England' in *The Historical Renaissance: New Essays on Tudor and Stuart Literature and Culture*, ed. Heather Dubrow and Richard Strier, Chicago, IL, pp. 220–41.

Lewalski, Barbara K. (1962). 'Biblical Allusion and Allegory in "The Merchant of Venice"', *Shakespeare Quarterly* 13, pp. 327–43.

Lewalski, Barbara K. (2000). *The Life of John Milton: A Critical Biography*, London.

Lieberman, David (1989). *The Province of Legislation Determined: Legal Theory in Eighteenth-Century Britain*, Cambridge.

Lim, Paul C. H. (2012). *Mystery Unveiled: The Crisis of the Trinity in Early Modern England*, Oxford.

Lipping, Jüri (2010). 'Sovereignty Beyond the State' in *Sovereignty in Fragments: The Past, Present and Future of a Contested Concept*, ed. Hent Kalmo and Quentin Skinner, Cambridge, pp. 186–204.

List, Christian and Philip Pettit (2011). *Group Agency: The Possibility, Design, and Status of Corporate Agents*, Oxford.

Lloyd, S. A. (1992). *Ideals as Interests in Hobbes's Leviathan: The Power of Mind over Matter*, Cambridge.

Lloyd, S. A. (1997). 'Coercion, Ideology, and Education in Hobbes's *Leviathan*' in *Reclaiming the History of Ethics: Essays for John Rawls*, ed. Andrew Reath, Barbara Herman and Christine M. Korsgaard, Cambridge, pp. 36–65.

Lobban, Michael (2007). *A History of the Philosophy of Law in the Common Law World, 1600–1900*, Dordrecht.

Lothe, José (2004). 'Les Livres illustré par Abraham Bosse' in *Abraham Bosse savant graveur*, ed. Sophie Join-Lambert and Maxime Préaud, Paris, pp. 41–52.

Lothe, José (2008). *L'Oeuvre gravé d'Abraham Bosse: graveur parisien du XVIIe siècle*, Paris.

Loughlin, Martin (2003). *The Idea of Public Law*, Oxford.

Loxley, James (2010). '*Dramatis Personae*: Royalism, Theatre and the Political Ontology of the Person in Post-Regicide Writing' in *Royalists and Royalism during the Interregnum*, ed. Jason McElliott and David Smith, Manchester, pp. 149–70.

Luca, Luigi de (1946). *Stato e Chiesa nel pensiero politico di G. Botero*, Rome.

Lyon, John (1988). *The Merchant of Venice*, London.

McClure, Christopher (2013). 'War, Madness, and Death: The Paradox of Honor in Hobbes's *Leviathan*', *The Journal of Politics* 76, pp. 114–25.

MacCormick, Neil (2010). 'Sovereignty and After' in *Sovereignty in Fragments: The Past, Present and Future of a Contested Concept*, ed. Hent Kalmo and Quentin Skinner, Cambridge, pp. 151–68.

McDowell, Nicholas (2003). *The English Radical Imagination: Culture, Religion, and Revolution, 1630–1660*, Oxford.

McGinn, Bernard (2006). 'Theologians as Trinitarian Iconographers' in *The Mind's Eye: Art and Theological Argument in the Middle Ages*, ed. Jeffrey F. Hamburger and Anne-Marie Bouché, Princeton, NJ, pp. 186–207.

Mack, Peter (2002). *Elizabethan Rhetoric: Theory and Practice*, Cambridge.

MacKay, Maxine (1964). '*The Merchant of Venice*: A Reflection of the Early Conflict between Courts of Law and Courts of Equity', *Shakespeare Quarterly* 15, pp. 371–5.

Maclean, Ian (1999). 'Legal Fictions and Fictional Entities in Renaissance Jurisprudence', *The Journal of Legal History* 20, pp. 1–24.

McLean, Janet (2003). 'Government to State: Globalization, Regulation, and Governments as Legal Persons', *Indiana Journal of Global Legal Studies* 10, pp. 173–97.

McLean, Janet (2005). 'Divergent Legal Conceptions of the State: Implications for Global Administrative Law', *Law and Contemporary Problems* 68, pp. 167–87.

McLean, Janet (2012). *Searching for the State in British Legal Thought: Competing Conceptions of the Public Sphere*, Cambridge.

Macpherson, C. B. (1962). *The Political Theory of Possessive Individualism: Hobbes to Locke*, Oxford.

Mahood, M. M. (2003a). 'Introduction' in *The Merchant of Venice*, ed. M. M. Mahood, The New Cambridge Shakespeare, Cambridge, pp. 1–65.

Mahood, M. M. (2003b). 'Appendix: Shakespeare's use of the Bible in *The Merchant of Venice*' in *The Merchant of Venice*, ed. M. M. Mahood, The New Cambridge Shakespeare, Cambridge, pp. 196–201.

Maiolo, Francesco (2007). *Medieval Sovereignty: Marsilius of Padua and Bartolus of Saxoferrato*, Delft.

Malcolm, Noel (1994a). 'General Introduction' in *The Correspondence of Thomas Hobbes*, ed. Noel Malcolm in The Clarendon Edition of the Works of Thomas Hobbes vol. VI, pp. xxi–xli.

Malcolm, Noel (1994b). 'Biographical Register of Hobbes's Correspondents' in *The Correspondence of Thomas Hobbes*, ed. Noel Malcolm in The Clarendon Edition of the Works of Thomas Hobbes vol. VII, pp. 777–919.

Malcolm, Noel (1998). 'The Title Page of *Leviathan*, Seen in a Curious Perspective', *The Seventeenth Century* 13, pp. 124–55.

Malcolm, Noel (2002). *Aspects of Hobbes*, Oxford.

Malcolm, Noel (2007). *Reason of State, Propaganda, and the Thirty Years' War: An Unknown Translation by Thomas Hobbes*, Oxford.

Malcolm, Noel (2012). 'Editorial Introduction' in Thomas Hobbes, *Leviathan*, ed. Noel Malcolm in The Clarendon Edition of the Works of Thomas Hobbes vols. III–V, vol. III.

Malcolm, Noel (2015). 'Hobbes and Sexual Desire', *Hobbes Studies* 28, pp. 77–102.

Mandelbrote, Scott (2007). 'Le Lieutenant de Dieu et la quête de la tolérance: l'expérience de John Dury (1596–1680)' in *Monarchie et république au XVIIe siècle*, ed. Yves Charles Zarka, Paris, pp. 169–92.

Manning, John (1988). 'Geffrey Whitney's Unpublished Emblems: Further Evidence of Indebtedness to Continental Traditions' in *The English Emblem and the Continental Tradition*, ed. Peter M. Daly, New York, NY, pp. 83–107.

Manow, Philip (2010). *In The King's Shadow: The Political Anatomy of Democratic Representation*, trans. Patrick Camiller, Cambridge.

Manow, Philip, Friedbert W. Rüb and Dagmar Simon (eds.) (2012). *Die Bilder des Leviathans: Eine Deutungsgeschichte*, Baden-Baden.

Margolies, David (2012). *Shakespeare's Irrational Endings: The Problem Plays*, Basingstoke.

Martel, James R. (2007). *Subverting the Leviathan: Reading Thomas Hobbes as a Radical Democrat*, New York, NY.

Martinich, A. P. (1992). *The Two Gods of Leviathan: Thomas Hobbes on Religion and Politics*, Cambridge.

Martinich, A. P. (2016). 'Authorisation and Representation in Hobbes's *Leviathan*' in *The Oxford Handbook of Hobbes*, ed. A. P. Martinich and Kinch Hoekstra, Oxford, pp. 315–38.

Mason, H. A. (1986). *Sir Thomas Wyatt: A Literary Portrait*, Bristol.

Masson, David (1881–94). *The Life of John Milton*, revised edn, 7 vols., London.

Matheron, Alexandre (1990). 'Hobbes, la Trinité et les caprices de la représentation' in *Thomas Hobbes: philosophie première, théorie de la science et politique*, Paris, pp. 381–90.

Mattei, Rodolfo de (1979). *Il problema della 'ragion di stato' nell' età della controriforma*, Milan.

Mazzucato, Mariana (2011). *The Entrepreneurial State*, London.

Ménager, Daniel (1995). *La Renaissance et le rire*, Paris.

Mendle, Michael (1995). *Henry Parker and the English Civil War: The Political Thought of the Public's 'Privado'*, Cambridge.

Mendle, Michael (2001). 'Putney's Pronouns: Identity and Indemnity in the Great Debate' in *The Putney Debates of 1647: The Army, the Levellers and the English State*, ed. Michael Mendle, Cambridge, pp. 125–47.

Meurer, Peter (1991). *Fontes Cartographici Orteliani*, Weinheim.

Meurer, Peter (2008). 'Europa Regina: 16th Century Maps of Europe in the Form of a Queen', *Belgeo: Revue belge de géographie* 3(4), pp. 355–70.

Michaud-Quantin, Pierre (1970). *Universitas: expressions du mouvement communautaire dans le moyen-age latin*, Paris.

Migne, J.-P.(1854). 'Praefatio ad lectorem' in *Patrologiae Cursus Completus*, 221 vols., Paris, vol. 171, pp. 1003–8.

Miles, Geoffrey (1996). *Shakespeare and the Constant Romans*, Oxford.

Milton, J. R. (2011). 'The Unscholastic Statesman: Locke and the Earl of Shaftesbury' in *Anthony Ashley Cooper, First Earl of Shaftesbury, 1621–1683*, ed. John Spurr, Aldershot, pp. 153–81.

Moisan, Thomas (1987). '"Which is the merchant here? and which the Jew?": Subversion and Recuperation in *The Merchant of Venice*' in *Shakespeare Reproduced: The Text in History and Ideology*, ed. Jean E. Howard and Marion F. O'Connor, London, pp. 188–206.

Monfasani, John (1976). *George of Trebizond: A Biography and a Study of his Rhetoric and Logic*, Leiden.

Moriarty, Michael (2011). *Disguised Vices: Theories of Virtue in Early Modern French Thought*, Oxford.

Morreall, John (1983). *Taking Laughter Seriously*, Albany, NY.

Morris, Christopher W. (1998). *An Essay on the Modern State*, Cambridge.

Morris, Christopher W. (2004). 'The Modern State', in *Handbook of Political Theory* ed. Gerald F. Gaus and Chandran Kukathas, London, pp. 195–209.

Mortimer, Sarah (2010). *Reason and Religion in the English Revolution: The Challenge of Socinianism*, Cambridge.

Moss, Ann (1996). *Printed Commonplace-Books and the Structuring of Renaissance Thought*, Oxford.

Najemy, John (1994). 'Brunetto Latini's "Politica"', *Dante Studies* 112, pp. 33–51.

Najemy, John M. (1995). 'Language and *The Prince*' in *Niccolò Machiavelli's The Prince: New Interdisciplinary Essays*, ed. Martin Coyle, Manchester, pp. 89–114.

Najemy, John M. (2013). 'Machiavelli and Cesare Borgia: A Reconsideration of Chapter 7 of *The Prince*', *The Review of Politics* 75, pp. 539–56.

Nelson, Eric (2007). '"Talmudical Commonwealthsmen" and the Rise of Republican Exclusivism', *The Historical Journal* 50, pp. 809–35.

Nelson, Eric (2008). 'General Introduction' in *Thomas Hobbes: Translations of Homer*, ed. Eric Nelson in The Clarendon Edition of the Works of Thomas Hobbes, vols. XXIV and XXV, vol. XXIV, pp. xi–lxxvi.

Nelson, Eric (2014). *The Royalist Revolution: Monarchy and the American Founding*, Cambridge, MA.

Nicholl, Charles (2007). *The Lodger: Shakespeare on Silver Street*, London.

Nicholson, Peter P. (1990). *The Political Philosophy of the British Idealists: selected studies*, Cambridge.

Noble, Richard (1935). *Shakespeare's Biblical Knowledge and Use of the Book of Common Prayer*, London.

Norbrook, David (1999). *Writing the English Republic: Poetry, Rhetoric and Politics, 1627–1660*, Cambridge.

Nuttall, Geoffrey F. (1957). *Visible Saints: The Congregational Way 1640–1660*, Oxford.

O'Callaghan, Michelle (2007). *The English Wits: Literature and Sociability in Early Modern England*, Cambridge.

Olsson, Gunnar (2007). *Abysmal: A Critique of Cartographic Reason*, Chicago, IL.

Othmer, Sieglinde (1970). *Berlin und die Verbreitung des Naturrechts in Europa*, Berlin.

Owen, David (2017). 'Machiavelli's *Il Principe* and the Politics of Glory', *European Journal of Political Theory* 16, pp. 41–60.

Pade, Marianne (2006). 'Thucydides' Renaissance Readers' in *Brill's Companion to Thucydides*, ed. Antonios Rengakos and Antonis Tsakmakis, Leiden, pp. 779–810.

Paganini, Gianni (2010a). 'Hobbes's "Mortal God" and Renaissance Hermeticism', *Hobbes Studies* 23, pp. 7–28.

Paganini, Gianni (2010b). 'Thomas Hobbes e la questione dell'umanesimo' in *L'umanesimo scientifico dal Rinascimento all'Illuminismo*, ed. Lorenzo Bianchi and Gianni Paganini, Naples, pp. 135–58.

Paganini, Gianni (2016). 'Thomas Hobbes against the Aristotelian Account of the Virtues and his Renaissance Source Lorenzo Valla' in *Early Modern Philosophers and the Renaissance Legacy*, ed. Cecilia Muratori and Gianni Paganini, Cham, pp. 221–38.

Palladini, Fiammetta (1990). *Samuel Pufendorf, discepolo di Hobbes*, Bologna.

Panagakou, Stamatoula (2005). 'Defending Bosanquet's Philosophical Theory of the State: A Reassessment of the Bosanquet-Hobhouse Controversy', *The British Journal of Politics & International Relations* 7, pp. 29–47.

Panichi, Nicola (1994). *La Virtù eloquente: la 'civil conversazione' nel rinascimento*, Urbino.

Parker, William Riley (1968). *Milton: A Biography*, 2 vols., Oxford.

Parkin, Jon (2007). *Taming the Leviathan: The Reception of the Political and Religious Ideas of Thomas Hobbes in England 1640–1700*, Cambridge.

Peile, John (1900). *Christ's College*, London.

Peltonen, Markku (1995). *Classical Humanism and Republicanism in English Political Thought 1570–1640*, Cambridge.

Peltonen, Markku (2003). *The Duel in Early Modern England: Civility, Politeness and Honour*, Cambridge.

Peltonen, Markku (2007). 'Rhetoric and Citizenship in the Monarchical Republic of Queen Elizabeth I' in *The Monarchical Republic of Early Modern England*, ed. John F. McDiarmid, Aldershot, pp. 109–27.

Peltonen, Markku (2009). 'Political Rhetoric and Citizenship in *Coriolanus*' in *Shakespeare and Early Modern Political Thought*, ed. David Armitage, Conal Condren and Andrew Fitzmaurice, Cambridge, pp. 234–52.

Peltonen, Markku (2013). *Rhetoric, Politics and Popularity in Pre-Revolutionary England*, Cambridge.

Pennington, Kenneth (1993). *The Prince and the Law, 1200–1600: Sovereignty and Rights in the Western Legal Tradition*, Berkeley, CA.

Percival, W. Keith (1983). 'Grammar and Rhetoric in the Renaissance' in *Renaissance Eloquence: Studies in the Theory and Practice of Renaissance Rhetoric*, ed. James J. Murphy, Berkeley, CA, pp. 303–30.

Pettit, Philip (1997). *Republicanism: A Theory of Freedom and Government*, Oxford.

Pettit, Philip (2008). *Made with Words: Hobbes on Language, Mind, and Politics*, Princeton, NJ.

Pettit, Philip (2008). 'Republican Freedom: Three Axioms, Four Theorems' in *Republicanism and Political Theory*, ed. Cécile Laborde and John Maynor, Oxford, pp. 102–30.

Pettit, Philip (2009). 'Varieties of Public Representation' in *Political Representation*, ed. Ian Shapiro, Susan Stokes, Elizabeth Wood and Alexander Kirschner, Cambridge, pp. 61–89.

Pettit, Philip (2012). *On the People's Terms: A Republican Theory and Model of Democracy*, Cambridge.

Pitkin, Hanna Fenichel (1967). *The Concept of Representation*, Berkeley, CA.

Pitkin, Hanna Fenichel (1989). 'Representation' in *Political Innovation and Conceptual Change*, ed. Terence Ball, James Farr and R. L. Hanson, Cambridge, pp. 132–54.

Platt, Peter G. (2009). *Shakespeare and the Culture of Paradox*, Farnham.

Plett, Heinrich (2012). *Enargeia in Classical Antiquity and the Early Modern Age*, Leiden.

Poggi, Gianfranco (1978). *The Development of the Modern State: A Sociological Introduction*, London.

Porter, H. C. (1958). *Reformation and Reaction in Tudor Cambridge*, Cambridge.

Posner, Richard (2009). *Law and Literature*, 3rd edn, Cambridge MA.

Praet, Patrick (2010). 'Prolegomena to the Post-Sovereign *Rechsstaat*' in *Sovereignty in Fragments: The Past, Present and Future of a Contested Concept*, ed. Hent Kalmo and Quentin Skinner, Cambridge, pp. 169–85.

Préaud, Maxime (2004). 'Abraham Bosse et les débuts de la taille-dous à Paris' in *Abraham Bosse savant graveur*, ed. Sophie Join-Lambert and Maxime Préaud, Paris, pp. 11–15.

Prior, Charles W. A. (2004). 'Trismegistus "His Great Giant": A Source for the Title-Page of Hobbes' *Leviathan*', *Notes and Queries*, New Series 51, pp. 366–70.

Pritchard, Allan (1980). 'The Last Days of Hobbes: Evidence of the Wood Manuscripts', *The Bodleian Library Record* 10, pp. 178–87.

Prokhovnik, Raia (1991). *Rhetoric and Philosophy in Hobbes' Leviathan*, London.

Prokhovnik, Raia (2007). *Sovereignties: Contemporary theory and practice*, Basingstoke.

Rabb, Theodore K. (1998). *Jacobean Gentleman: Sir Edwin Sandys, 1561–1629*, Princeton, NJ.

Rabkin, Jeremy (2005). *Law Without Nations: Why Constitutional Government Requires Sovereign States*, Princeton, NJ.

Rackin, Phyllis (1983). 'Coriolanus: Shakespeare's Anatomy of *Virtus*', *Modern Language Studies* 13, pp. 68–79.

Ranum, Orest (1993). *The Fronde: A French Revolution 1648–1652*, New York, NY.

Reiss, Timothy J. (2003). *Mirages of the Selfe: Patterns of Personhood in Ancient and Early Modern Europe*, Stanford, CA.

Rhodes, Rosamond (2009). 'Hobbes's Fifth Law of Nature and its Implications', *Hobbes Studies* 22, pp. 144–59.

Richards, Jennifer (2003). *Rhetoric and Courtliness in Early Modern Literature*, Cambridge.

Rogow, Arnold A. (1986). *Thomas Hobbes: Radical in the Service of Reaction*, London.

Ross, George Macdonald (1997). 'Hobbes and the Authority of the Universities', *Hobbes Studies* 10, pp. 68–80.

Rumrich, John (1986). 'Mead and Milton', *Milton Quarterly* 20, pp. 136–41.

Runciman, David (1997). *Pluralism and the Personality of the State*, Cambridge.

Runciman, David (2000). 'What Kind of Person Is Hobbes's State? A Reply to Skinner', *The Journal of Political Philosophy* 8, pp. 268–78.

Runciman, David (2003). 'The Concept of the State: The Sovereignty of a Fiction' in *States and Citizens*, ed. Quentin Skinner and Bo Sträth, Cambridge, pp. 28–38.

Runciman, David (2009). 'Hobbes's Theory of Representation: Anti-Democratic or Proto-Democratic' in *Political Representation*, ed. Ian Shapiro, Susan Stokes, Elizabeth Wood and Alexander Kirschner, Cambridge, pp. 15–34.

Russell, Conrad (1979). *Parliaments and English Politics 1621–1629*, Oxford.

Ryan, Kiernan (2009). *Shakespeare's Comedies*, Basingstoke.

Ryan, Magnus (2000). 'Bartolus of Sassoferrato and Free Cities', *Transactions of the Royal Historical Society*, New series 10, pp. 65–89.

Ryan, Walter (2008). 'Reconciling Foucault and Skinner on the State: The Primacy of Politics?', *History of the Human Sciences* 21, pp. 94–114.

Sabbadini, Lorenzo (2016). 'Popular Sovereignty and Representation in the English Civil War' in *Popular Sovereignty in Historical Perspective*, ed. Richard Bourke and Quentin Skinner, Cambridge, pp. 164–86.

Sadoul, Georges (1969). *Jacques Callot miroir de son temps*, Paris.

Saenger, Michael (2006). *The Commodification of Textual Engagements in the English Renaissance*, Aldershot.

Santi, Raffaella (2012). *Ragione geometrica e legge in Thomas Hobbes*, Milan.

Santi, Raffaella (2013). 'Hobbes e Guazzo: civil conversazione e filosofia civile' in *L'antidoto di Mercurio. La "civil conversazione" tra Rinascimento ed età moderna*, ed. Nicola Panichi, Florence, pp. 95–111.

Saunders, David and Ian Hunter (2003). 'Bringing the State to England: Andrew Tooke's Translation of Samuel Pufendorf's *De offico hominis et civis*', *History of Political Thought* 24, pp. 218–34.

Saunders, W. H. (1932). *A History of the Norwich Grammar School*, Norwich.

Schaede, Stephen (2004). *Stellvertretung: Begriffsgeschichtliche Studien zur Soteriologie*, Tübingen.

Schmitt, Carl (2008). *The Leviathan in the State Theory of Thomas Hobbes*, trans. George Schwab and Erna Hilfstein, Chicago, IL.

Schmitt, Charles (gen. ed.) (1988). *The Cambridge History of Renaissance Philosophy*, Cambridge.

Schochet, Gordon (1975). *Patriarchalism in Political Thought*, Oxford.

Schofield, Philip (2006). *Utility and Democracy: The Political Thought of Jeremy Bentham*, Oxford.

Schuhmann, Karl (1983). 'Thomas Hobbes und Francesco Patrizi', *Archiv für Geschichte der Philosophie* 68, pp. 253–79.

Schuhmann, Karl (1988). 'Hobbes and Telesio', *Hobbes Studies* 1, pp. 109–33.

Schuhmann, Karl (1990). 'Hobbes and Renaissance Philosophy' in *Hobbes oggi*, ed. Andrea Napoli, Milan, pp. 331–49.

Scott, Jonathan (2004). *Commonwealth Principles: Republican Writing of the English Revolution*, Cambridge.

Serjeantson, R. W. (2006). 'Hobbes, the Universities, and the History of Philosophy' in *The Philosopher in Early Modern Europe: The Nature of a Contested Identity*, ed. Conal Condren, Stephen Gaukroger and Ian Hunter, Cambridge, pp. 113–39.

Shapiro, James (1996). *Shakespeare and the Jews*, New York, NY.

Shrank, Cathy (2004). *Writing the Nation in Reformation England 1530–1580*, Oxford.

Simonetta, Marcello (1997). 'Machiavelli lettore di Tucidide', *Esperienze Letterarie* 22, pp. 53–68.

Skinner, Quentin (1965). 'Hobbes on Sovereignty: An Unknown Discussion', *Political Studies* 13, pp. 213–18.

Skinner, Quentin (1978). *The Foundations of Modern Political Thought*, 2 vols., Cambridge.

Skinner, Quentin (1996). *Reason and Rhetoric in the Philosophy of Hobbes*, Cambridge.

Skinner, Quentin (1998). *Liberty Before Liberalism*, Cambridge.

Skinner, Quentin (1999). 'Hobbes and the Purely Artificial Person of the State', *The Journal of Political Philosophy* 7, pp. 1–29.

Skinner, Quentin (2000). *Machiavelli*, Oxford.

Skinner, Quentin (2002a). *Visions of Politics*, vol. 2: *Renaissance Virtues*, Cambridge.

Skinner, Quentin (2002b). *Visions of Politics,* vol. 3: *Hobbes and Civil Science,* Cambridge.

Skinner, Quentin (2002c). 'A Third Concept of Liberty', *Proceedings of the British Academy* 117, pp. 237–68.

Skinner, Quentin (2004). 'Hobbes and the Classical Theory of Laughter' in *Leviathan after 350 Years,* ed. Tom Sorell and Luc Foisneau, Oxford, pp. 139–66.

Skinner, Quentin (2005a). 'The Generation of John Milton' in *Christ's: A Cambridge College over Five Centuries,* ed. David Reynolds, London, pp. 41–72.

Skinner, Quentin (2005b): 'Hobbes on Representation', *European Journal of Philosophy* 13, pp. 155–84.

Skinner, Quentin (2005c). 'Historical Introduction' to Thomas Hobbes, 'Questions relative to Hereditary Right' in *Writings on Common Law and Hereditary Right,* ed. Alan Cromartie and Quentin Skinner, The Clarendon Edition of the Works of Thomas Hobbes vol. XI, Oxford, pp. 159–76.

Skinner, Quentin (2006). 'Rethinking Political Liberty in the English Revolution', *History Workshop Journal* 61, pp. 1–15.

Skinner, Quentin (2007). 'Paradiastole: Redescribing the Vices as Virtues' in *Renaissance Figures of Speech,* ed. Sylvia Adamson, Gavin Alexander and Katrin Ettenhuber, Cambridge, pp. 147–63.

Skinner, Quentin (2008a). *Hobbes and Republican Liberty,* Cambridge.

Skinner, Quentin (2008b). 'Freedom as the Absence of Arbitrary Power' in *Republicanism and Political Theory,* ed. Cécile Laborde and John Maynor, Oxford, pp. 83–101.

Skinner, Quentin (2009a). 'A Genealogy of the Modern State', *Proceedings of the British Academy* 162, pp. 325–70.

Skinner, Quentin (2009b). 'The Material Presentation of Thomas Hobbes's Theory of the Commonwealth' in *The Materiality of Res Publica: How to Do Things with Publics,* ed. Dominique Colas and Oleg Kharkhordin, Newcastle, pp. 115–57.

Skinner, Quentin (2009c). 'Shakespeare and Humanist Culture' in *Shakespeare and Early Modern Political Thought,* ed. David Armitage, Conal Condren and Andrew Fitzmaurice, Cambridge, pp. 271–81.

Skinner, Quentin (2014). *Forensic Shakespeare,* Oxford.

Skinner, Quentin (2016). 'Hobbes and the Social Control of Sociability' in *The Oxford Handbook of Hobbes,* ed. A. P. Martinich and Kinch Hoekstra, Oxford, pp. 432–50.

Skinner, Quentin (2017a). 'Machiavelli and the Misunderstanding of Princely Virtù' in *Machiavelli on Liberty and Conflict,* ed. David Johnston, Nadia Urbinati, and Camila Vergara, Chicago, IL, pp. 139–63.

Skinner, Quentin (2017b). 'Why Shylocke Loses his Case: Judicial Rhetoric in *The Merchant of Venice*' in *The Oxford Handbook of English Law and Literature, 1500–1700,* ed. Lorna Hutson, Oxford, pp. 97–117.

Sloan, Kim (2007). *A New World: England's First View of America,* London.

Slomp, Gabriella (2007). 'Hobbes on Glory and Civil Strife' in *The Cambridge Companion to Hobbes's Leviathan,* ed. Patricia Springborg, Cambridge, pp. 181–98.

Smith, David (1994). *Constitutional Royalism and the Search for Settlement c.1640–1649*, Cambridge.

Smith, David (1999). *The Stuart Parliaments 1603–1689*, London.

Smith, Emma (2013). 'Was Shylock Jewish?', *Shakespeare Quarterly* 62, pp. 188–219.

Smith, Timothy B. and Judith B. Steinhoff (eds.) (2012). *Art as Politics in Late Medieval and Renaissance Siena*, Farnham.

Sokol, B. J. and Mary Sokol (1999). 'Shakespeare and the English Equity Jurisdiction: *The Merchant of Venice* and the Two Texts of *King Lear*', *The Review of English Studies* 50, pp. 417–39.

Sommerville, Johann (1991a). 'Absolutism and Royalism' in *The Cambridge History of Political Thought 1450–1700*, ed. J. H. Burns and Mark Goldie, Cambridge, pp. 347–73.

Sommerville, Johann (1991b). 'James I and the Divine Right of Kings: English Politics and Continental Theory' in *The Mental World of the Jacobean Court*, ed. Linda Levy Peck, Cambridge, pp. 55–70, 283–9.

Sommerville, Johann (1996). 'English and European Political Ideas in the Early-Seventeenth Century: Revisionism and the Case of Absolutism', *Journal of British Studies* 35, pp. 168–94.

Sommerville, Johann (1999). *Royalists and Patriots: Politics and Ideology in England 1603–1640*, 2nd edn, Harlow.

Sommerville, Johann (2007). 'English and Roman Liberty in the Monarchical Republic of Early Stuart England' in *The Monarchical Republic of Early Modern England*, ed. John F. McDiarmid, Aldershot, pp. 201–16.

Sommerville, Johann (2016). 'Hobbes and Absolutism' in *The Oxford Handbook of Hobbes*, ed. A. P. Martinich and Kinch Hoekstra, Oxford, pp. 378–96.

Song, Sarah (2012). 'The Boundary Problem in Democratic Theory: Why the Demos Should Be Bounded by the State', *International Theory* 4, pp. 39–68.

Sorbelli, Albano (1944). 'I teorici del reggimento comunale', *Bullettino dell' Istituto storico italiano per il medio evo* 59, pp. 31–136.

Sorell, Tom (1986). *Hobbes*, London.

Southard, Edna C. (1978). 'The Frescoes in Siena's Palazzo Pubblico, 1289–1539', PhD dissertation, University of Indiana, Bloomington, IN.

Springborg, Patricia (1995). 'Hobbes's Biblical Beasts: Leviathan and Behemoth', *Political Theory* 23, pp. 353–75.

Spruyt, Hendrik (1996). *The Sovereign State and its Competitors: An Analysis of Systems Change*, Princeton, NJ.

Sreedhar, Susanne (2010). *Hobbes on Resistance: Defying the Leviathan*, Cambridge.

Stacey, Peter (2007). *Roman Monarchy and the Renaissance Prince*, Cambridge.

Stacey, Peter (2013). 'Free and Unfree States in Machiavelli's Political Philosophy' in *Freedom and the Construction of Europe, vol. 1: Religious and Constitutional Liberties*, ed. Quentin Skinner and Martin van Gelderen, Cambridge, pp. 176–94.

Stacey, Peter (2014). 'Definition, Division, and Difference in Machiavelli's Political Philosophy', *Journal of the History of Ideas* 75, pp. 189–212.

Starnes, DeWitt T. (1954). *Renaissance Dictionaries: English-Latin and Latin-English*, Austin, TX.

Steinberger, Peter J. (2004). *The Idea of the State*, Cambridge.

Stone, Lawrence (1964). 'The Educational Revolution in England, 1560–1640', *Past and Present* 28, pp. 41–80.

Strange, Susan (1996). *The Retreat of the State: The Diffusion of Power in the World Economy*, Cambridge.

Strier, Richard (2010). 'Excuses, Bepissing, and Non-Being: Shakespearean Puzzles about Agency' in *Shakespeare and Moral Agency*, ed. Michael D. Bristol, New York, NY, pp. 55–68.

Strier, Richard (2013). 'Shakespeare and Legal Systems: The Better the Worse (But Not Vice Versa)' in *Shakespeare and the Law: A Conversation among Disciplines and Professions*, ed. Bradin Cormack, Martha C. Nussbaum and Richard Strier, Chicago, IL, pp. 174–200.

Stritmatter, Roger (2000). '"Old" and "New" Law in *The Merchant of Venice*: A Note on the Source of Shylock's Morality in Deuteronomy 15', *Notes and Queries* 245, pp. 70–2.

Strong, Tracy B. (1993). 'How to Write Scripture: Words, Authority, and Politics in Thomas Hobbes', *Critical Inquiry* 20, pp. 128–59.

Taggart, M. B. (2003). 'The Nature and Functions of the State' in *The Oxford Handbook of Legal Studies*, ed. Peter Cane and Mark Tushnet, Oxford, pp. 101–18.

Tesón, Fernando R. (1997). *Humanitarian Intervention: An Inquiry into Law and Morality*, 2nd edn, New York, NY.

Thomas, Keith (1965). 'The Social Origins of Hobbes's Political Thought' in *Hobbes Studies*, ed. Keith Brown, Oxford, pp. 185–236.

Thomas, Keith (1972). 'The Levellers and the Franchise' in *The Interregnum: The Quest for Settlement 1646–1660*, ed. G. E. Aylmer, London, pp. 57–78.

Thomas, Keith (2009). *The Ends of Life: Roads to Fulfilment in Early Modern England*, Oxford.

Thompson, Christopher (1980). 'Maximilian Petty and the Putney Debate on the Franchise', *Past and Present* 88, pp. 63–9.

Thuau, Etienne (2000). *Raison d'etat et pensée politique à l'epoque de Richelieu*, Paris.

Tierney, Brian (1955). *Foundations of the Conciliarist Theory*, Cambridge.

Tiffany, Grace (2002). 'Names in *The Merchant of Venice*' in *The Merchant of Venice: New Critical Essays*, ed. John W. Mahon and Ellen Macleod Mahon, London, pp. 353–67.

Tiffany, Grace (2010). 'Law and Self-Interest in *The Merchant of Venice*' in *William Shakespeare's The Merchant of Venice*, new edn, ed. Harold Bloom, New York, NY, pp. 173–85.

Todescan, Franco (1979). *Diritto e realtà: storia e teoria della fictio iuris*, Padua.

Tovey, Barbara (1981). 'The Golden Casket: An Interpretation of *The Merchant of Venice*' in *Shakespeare as Political Thinker*, ed. John Alvis and Thomas G. West, Durham, NC, pp. 215–37.

Toyoda, Tetsuya (2009). 'La Doctrine vattelienne de l'égalité souveraine dans le context neuchâtelois', *Journal of the History of International Law* 11, pp. 103–24.

Trainor, Brian T. (1998). *Justice and the State: On Liberal Organicism and the Foundations of Emancipatory Politics*, Quebec.

Trainor, Brian T. (2001). 'Hobbes, Skinner and the Person of the State', *Hobbes Studies* 14, pp. 59–70.

Trainor, Brian T. (2005). 'Back to the Future: The Emancipatory Essence of the State', *European Journal of Political Theory* 4, pp. 413–28.

Troper, Michel (2010). 'The Survival of Sovereignty' in *Sovereignty in Fragments: The Past, Present and Future of a Contested Concept*, ed. Hent Kalmo and Quentin Skinner, Cambridge, pp. 132–50.

Tuck, Richard (1989). *Hobbes*, Oxford.

Tuck, Richard (1993). *Philosophy and Government, 1572–1651*, Cambridge.

Tuck, Richard (1996). 'Hobbes's Moral Philosophy' in *The Cambridge Companion to Hobbes*, ed. Tom Sorell, Cambridge, pp. 175–207.

Tuck, Richard (1998). 'Hobbes on Education' in *Philosophers on Education: Historical Perspectives*, ed. Amélie Oksenberg Rorty, London, pp. 148–56.

Tuck, Richard (2005). 'Introduction' in Hugo Grotius, *The Rights of War and Peace*, 3 vols., Indianapolis, IN, vol. 1, pp. ix–xxxiii.

Tuck, Richard (2015). *The Sleeping Sovereign: The Invention of Modern Democracy*, Cambridge.

Tucker, E. F. J. (1976). 'The Letter of the Law in "The Merchant of Venice"', *Shakespeare Survey* 29, pp. 93–101.

Tukiainen, Arto (1994). 'The Commonwealth as a Person in Hobbes's *Leviathan*', *Hobbes Studies* 7, pp. 44–55.

Tully, James (1991). 'Introduction' in Samuel Pufendorf, *On the Duty of Man and Citizen According to Natural Law*, ed. James Tully, Cambridge, pp. xiv–xxxvii.

Tully, James (1999). 'The Agonic Freedom of Citizens', *Economy and Society* 28, pp. 161–82.

Vallance, Edward (2001). 'Oaths, Casuistry and Equivocation: Anglican Responses to the Engagement Controversy', *The Historical Journal* 44, pp. 59–77.

Vallance, Edward (2015). 'Political Thought' in *The Oxford Handbook of the English Revolution*, ed. Michael Braddick, Oxford, pp. 430–46.

Vaughan, Geoffrey M. (2002). *Behemoth Teaches Leviathan: Thomas Hobbes on Political Education*, Lanham, MD.

Veldman, Ilja M. (2001). *Crispijn de Passe and his Progeny (1564–1670): A Century of Print Production*, trans. Michael Hoyle, Rotterdam.

Venn, John (1913). *Early Collegiate Life*, Cambridge.

Verberckmoes, Johan (1999). *Laughter, Jestbooks and Society in the Spanish Netherlands*, Basingstoke.

Vickers, Brian (2002). *Shakespeare, Co-Author: A Historical Study of Five Collaborative Plays*, Oxford.

Vincent, Andrew (1987). *Theories of the State*, Oxford.

Viroli, Maurizio (1998). *Machiavelli*, Oxford.

Waley, Daniel (1988). *The Italian City-Republics*, 3rd edn, London.

Walker, William (2006). 'Sallust and Skinner on Civil Liberty', *European Journal of Political Theory* 5, pp. 237–59.

Wallace, John (1964). 'The Engagement Controversy 1649–1652: An Annotated List of Pamphlets', *Bulletin of the New York Public Library* 68, pp. 384–405.

Ward, Ian (1999). *Shakespeare and the Legal Imagination*, London.

Warrender, Howard (1983). Introduction to Thomas Hobbes, *De Cive: The Latin Version*, ed. Howard Warrender, The Clarendon Edition of the Works of Thomas Hobbes vol. II, Oxford, pp. 1–67.

Watson, Elizabeth See (1993). *Achille Bocchi and the Emblem Book as Symbolic Form*, Cambridge.

Watt, Gary (2009). *Equity Stirring: The Story of Justice Beyond Law*, Oxford.

Weiss, Thomas (2007). *Humanitarian Intervention: Ideas in Action*, London.

Wells, Stanley and Gary Taylor, with John Jowett and William Montgomery (1987). *William Shakespeare: A Textual Companion*, Oxford.

Wendt, Alexander (2004). 'The State as Person in International Theory', *Review of International Studies* 30, pp. 289–316.

Wheeler, Nicholas J. (2000). *Saving Strangers: Humanitarian Intervention in International Society*, Oxford.

Whigham, Frank (1984). *Ambition and Privilege: The Social Tropes of Elizabethan Courtesy Theory*, Berkeley, CA.

Whitaker, Virgil (1953). *Shakespeare's Use of Learning: An Inquiry into the Growth of his Mind & Art*, San Marino, CA.

Wiggins, Martin with Catherine Richardson (2013). *British Drama 1533–1642. A Catalogue*, vol. 3: *1590–1597*, Oxford.

Wilde, Marc de (2011). '*Fides publica* in Ancient Rome and its Reception by Grotius and Locke', *The Legal History Review* 79, pp. 455–87.

Williams, David and Tom Young (1994). 'Governance, the World Bank and Liberal Theory', *Political Studies* 42, pp. 84–100.

Williams, John R. (1957). 'The Quest for the Author of the *Moralium Dogma Philosophorum*, 1931–56', *Speculum* 32, pp. 736–47.

Willis, Robert and John W. Clark (1886). *The Architectural History of the University of Cambridge*, 4 vols., Cambridge.

Willson, Michael J. (1995). 'A View of Justice in Shakespeare's *The Merchant of Venice* and *Measure for Measure*', *Notre Dame Law Review* 70, pp. 695–726.

Wing, Donald (1945–51). *Short-Title Catalogue … 1641–1700*, 3 vols., New York, NY.

Withington, Phil (2010). *Society in Early Modern England: The Vernacular Origins of Some Powerful Ideas*, Cambridge.

Withington, Phil (2011). '"Tumbled into the Dirt": Wit and Incivility in Early Modern England', *Journal of Historical Pragmatics* 12, pp. 156–77.

Wolters, Wolfgang (1976). *La scultura veneziana gotica (1300–1460)*, 2 vols., Venice.

Woolf, C. N. S. (1913). *Bartolus of Sassoferrato: His Position in the History of Medieval Political Thought*, Cambridge.

Worden, Blair (2007). *Literature and Politics in Cromwellian England: John Milton, Andrew Marvell, Marchamont Nedham*, Oxford.

Worden, Blair (2009). *The English Civil Wars 1640–1660*, London.

Yaffe, Martin D. (1997). *Shylock and the Jewish Question*, Baltimore, MD.

Zaller, Robert (1991). 'Henry Parker and the Regiment of True Government', *Proceedings of the American Philosophical Society* 135, pp. 255–85.

Zarka, Yves Charles (1999). *La Décision métaphysique de Hobbbes: conditions de la politique*, 2nd edn, Paris.

Zurcher, Andrew (2010). *Shakespeare and Law*, London.

Index

Alain de Lille 23
Alberico de Rosate 29, 38
Alberto de Gandino 29
Alciato, Andrea 224, 304, 309
Alcibiades (Shakespeare, *Timon of Athens*) 9, 108–10
Althusius, Johannes 41 and n. 208
Ambrose, St 18
anamorphosis 309–11
Andrewes, Lancelot 292
Aneau, Barthélemy 224, 304
Ankersmit, Frank 379
Anselm, St 20
anthropomorphic maps 311–15
Aquinas, St Thomas 13, 20, 364
Aristotle 38, 129, 132, 185, 186
    frontispieces 227 n. 34, 228, 240, 252, 254
    laughter 168–9
    paradiastole 94, 96–7, 100, 112
    virtue 99
    Art of rhetoric 3, 51, 55 n. 89, 94, 96–7, 100, 168 and n. 58
    Elenchi 129, 132
    Nicomachean Ethics 3, 129, 133, 185, 227 and n. 34, 240, 252
Attersoll, William 373
Aubrey, John 118, 121, 168, 315, 327 n. 63, 340
Augustine, St 20, 193, 194, 195
Austin, John 375
Avity, Pierre d' 348
Azo Portius 36–7, 38, 39, 40, 201, 351

Baker, Philip 151
Bakhtin, Mikhaïl 176
Baldus de Ubaldis 36, 40
Baldwin, William 107 and n. 122
Bandello, Matteo 74
Barbaro, Ermolao 94, 96 n. 58, 97 n. 63
Barbeyrac, Jean 363, 368

Barclay, Alexander 240, 243
Barclay, William 39
Barrow, Henry 344
Bartolus of Sassoferrato
    civitas 30–1, 42
    persona repraesentata 28, 30
    universitates 28, 30–1
Baynes, Paul 192
Becmann, Johann 363 and n. 175
Bellarmine, Robert 286
Bentham, Jeremy 374–5
Bible, the 105, 131, 188, 226, 232, 277, 288, 293 and n. 245, 294, 295 and n. 248, 298, 312
    Chronicles 287 n. 206
    Ecclesiasticus 79 n. 118
    Job 221, 271 n. 131, 273 and n. 139, 277, 282, 283, 290
    Matthew 20, 240, 259 n. 96, 276
    Micah 64
    Proverbs 78 n. 112, 258 and n. 87, 259
    Samuel 131, 287 n. 206
    Wisdom 24, 33
Bishop, William 194, 195
Blackstone, William 371, 374
Boccalini, Traiano 344, 350
Bocchi, Achille 224, 262, 263
Bodin, Jean 280, 290, 345, 346, 347
Boethius 13, 364
Book of Common Prayer 295, 296
Bosanquet, Bernard 376, 381
Boscawen, Edward 324
Bosse, Abraham 226, 271 and n. 133, 272, 274, 283, 295, 299, 302, 304, 306 and n. 288
Botero, Giovanni 348
Boughen, Edward 354
Boys, John 293
Bracton, Henry de 141–2
Bramhall, John 40, 141, 354
Brathwaite, Richard 224, 293

423